STAR WARS

OMNIBUS

X-WING ROGUE SQUADRON

STAR WARS

OMNIBUS

X-WING ROGUE SQUADRON
VOLUME 1

DARK HORSE BOOKS™

cover illustration Doug Wheatley
publisher Mike Richardson
series editors Randy Stradley, Ryder Windham, and Peet Janes
collection editor Randy Stradley
assistant editor Dave Marshall
collection designers Lia Ribacchi and Tina Alessi

Special thanks to Sue Rostoni, Leland Chee, and Amy Gary at Lucas Licensing.

The editor gratefully acknowledges the assistance of Sabrina Fried and Ian Roney.

Star Wars® Omnibus: X-Wing Rogue Squadron Volume One

This volume collects issues #1-3 of *Star Wars X-Wing Rogue Leader*; #1-4 of *Star Wars X-Wing Rogue Squadron: The Rebel Opposition*; #1-4 of *Star Wars X-Wing Rogue Squadron: The Phantom Affair*; and *Star Wars Handbook: Rogue Squadron*, all originally published by Dark Horse Comics.

Published by Dark Horse Books,
a division of Dark Horse Comics, Inc.
10956 SE Main Street
Milwaukie, OR 97222

darkhorse.com | starwars.com

To find a comics shop in your area, call the Comic Shop Locator Service toll-free at 1-888-266-4226

First edition: May 2006
ISBN 10: 1-59307-572-3
ISBN 13: 978-1-59307-572-9

10 9 8 7 6 5 4 3 2 1
Printed in China

The fighter squadrons of the Rebel Alliance were the home units of many great heroes in the battles against Palpatine's Galactic Empire, and none were more renown than the pilots of Rogue Squadron. But it was after the turning point of the Battle of Endor when the Rogues, under the leadership of Wedge Antilles, proved their true importance to the New Republic.

With an assortment of different fighter craft, and an ever-changing roster of pilots, Rogue Squadron was instrumental in keeping the Imperial remnants in check and allowing the fledgling New Republic the time it needed to solidify its political and military base.

Here are the Rogues' stories . . .

Incom Corporation T-65 X-Wing Space Superiority Fighter

The X-wing is the Rebellion's main single-pilot snub-fighter. The X-wing takes its name from its pair of double-layered wings, deployed into the familiar X formation for combat. During normal sublight space flight, the double-layered wings are closed, giving the fighter the appearance of having only two wings. It's known for its durability, with a reinforced titanium-alloy hull and high-powered Chempat shield generators. It is a forgiving fighter and normally can take minor hits without a serious loss of performance. It has a full ejection system, and Alliance pilots have fully sealed suits and helmets. X-wings are equipped with an Incom GBk-585 hyperdrive unit for travel to other systems. The X-wing is Rogue Squadron's fighter of choice.

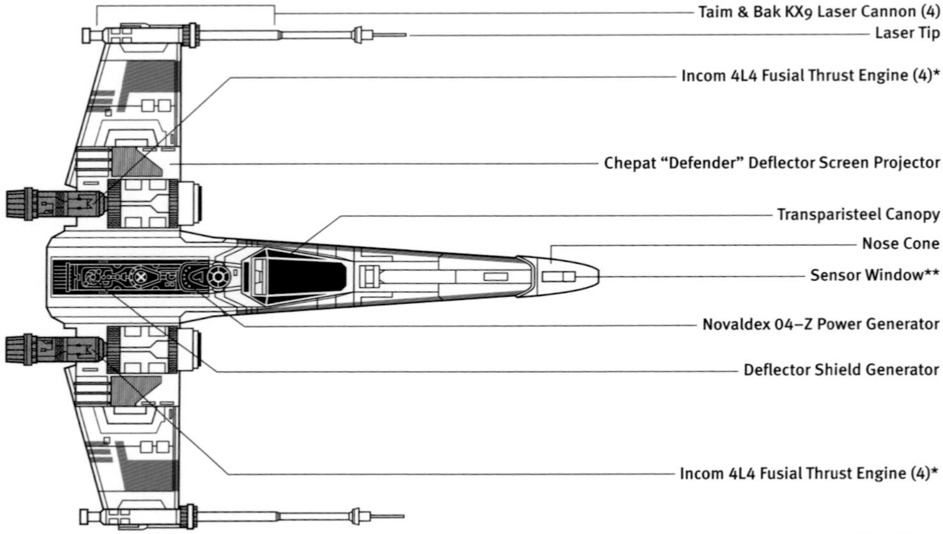
Taim & Bak KX9 Laser Cannon (4)
Laser Tip
Incom 4L4 Fusial Thrust Engine (4)*
Chepat "Defender" Deflector Screen Projector
Transparisteel Canopy
Nose Cone
Sensor Window**
Novaldex 04–Z Power Generator
Deflector Shield Generator
Incom 4L4 Fusial Thrust Engine (4)*

Top View

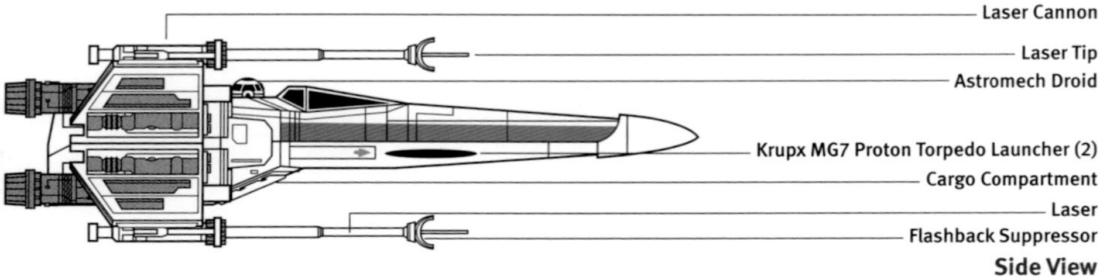
Laser Cannon
Laser Tip
Astromech Droid
Krupx MG7 Proton Torpedo Launcher (2)
Cargo Compartment
Laser
Flashback Suppressor

Side View

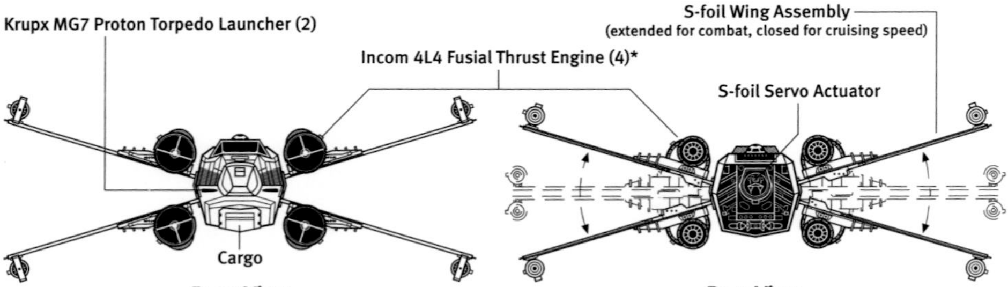
Krupx MG7 Proton Torpedo Launcher (2)
S-foil Wing Assembly
(extended for combat, closed for cruising speed)
Incom 4L4 Fusial Thrust Engine (4)*
S-foil Servo Actuator
Cargo

Front View **Rear View**

*Alternate Configurations May Use Incom 4J.4 Fusial Thrust Engines.

** Houses Carbanti Transceiver Package with Fabritech ANs-5d "Lock Track" Full-spectrum Transceiver, Melihat "Multi Imager" Dedicated Energy Receptor, Tana Ire Electro-photo Receptor and Fabritech Anq 3.6 Sensor Computer. Alternate Configuration Typically Combines Long Range Fabritech ANS-5d Units with Long Range PTSA #PA-9r Unit and Short Range PTAG #PG-7u Unit.

Schematic by Troy Vigil.

Rogue Leader | illustration by Gary Erskine

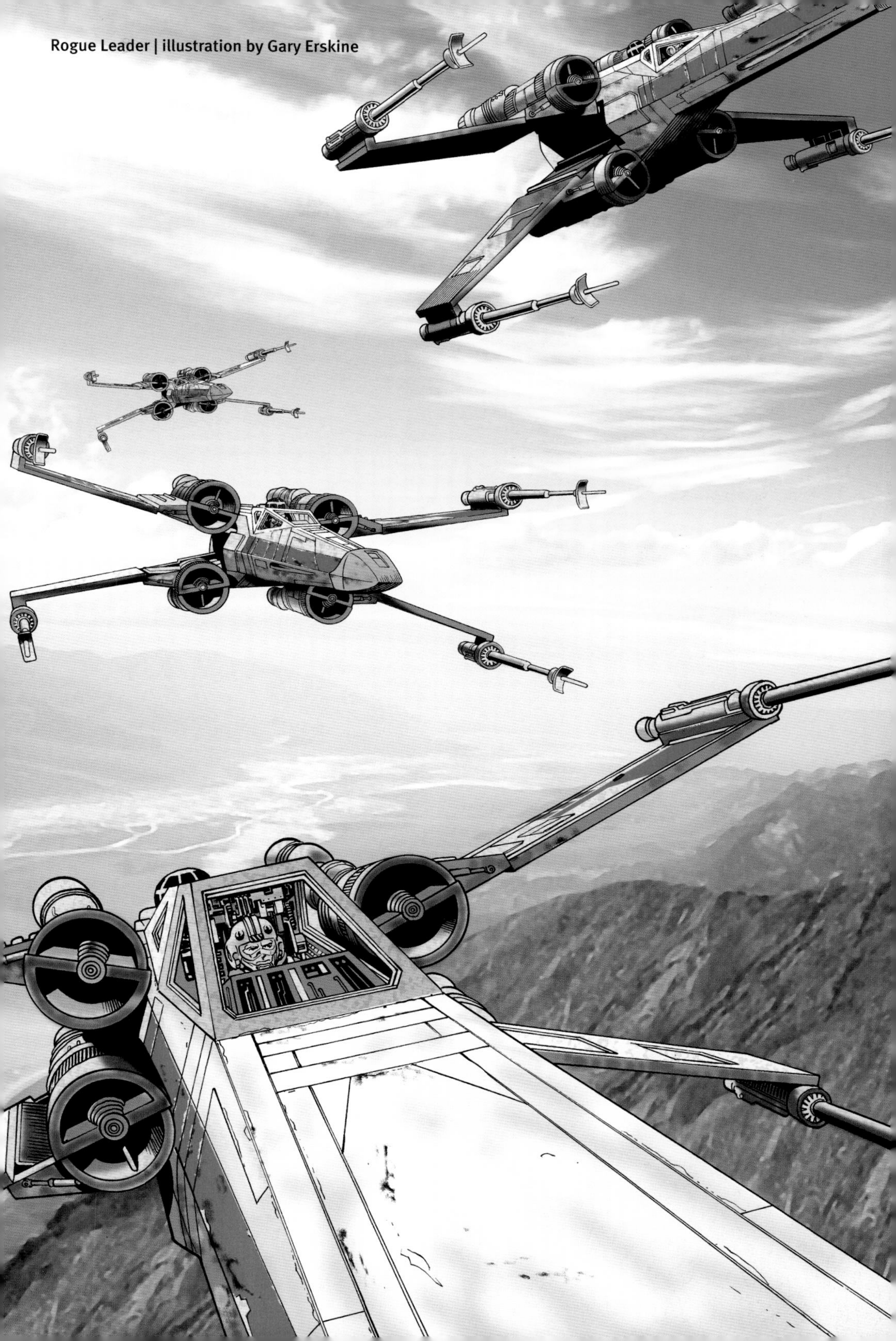

Shortly after the Battle of Endor . . .

script by Haden Blackman
art by Tomás Giorello
colors by Michael Atiyeh
letters by Michael David Thomas

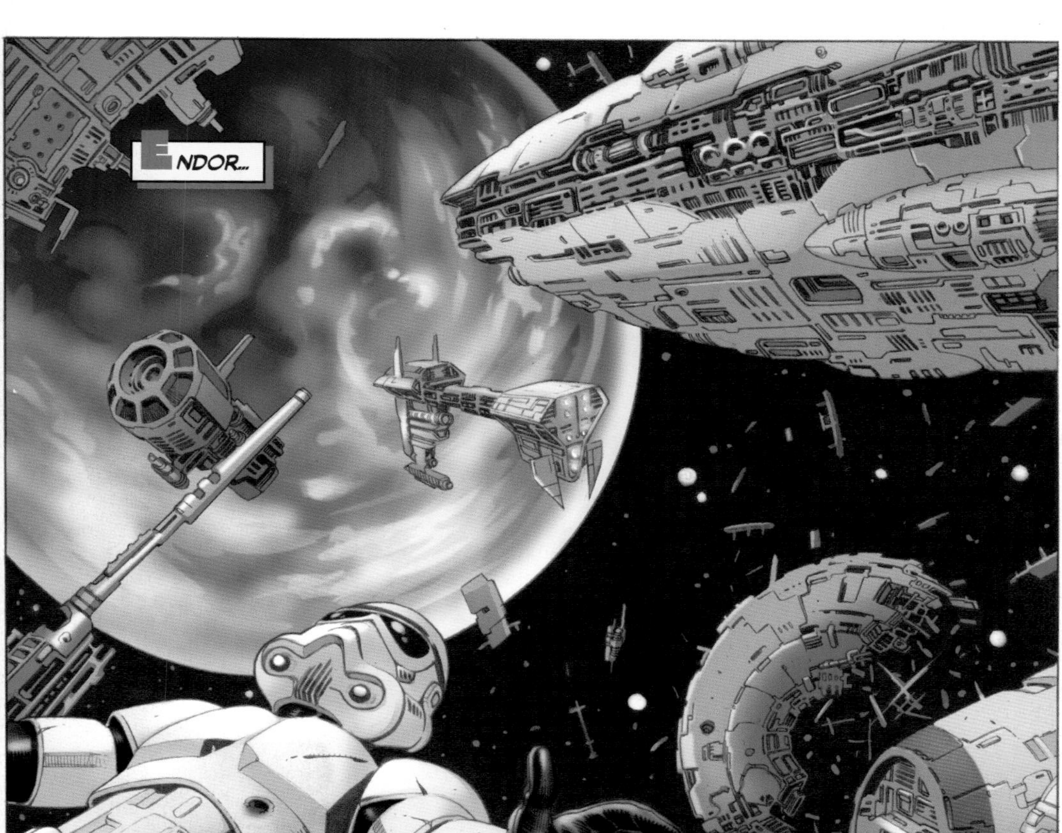
ENDOR...

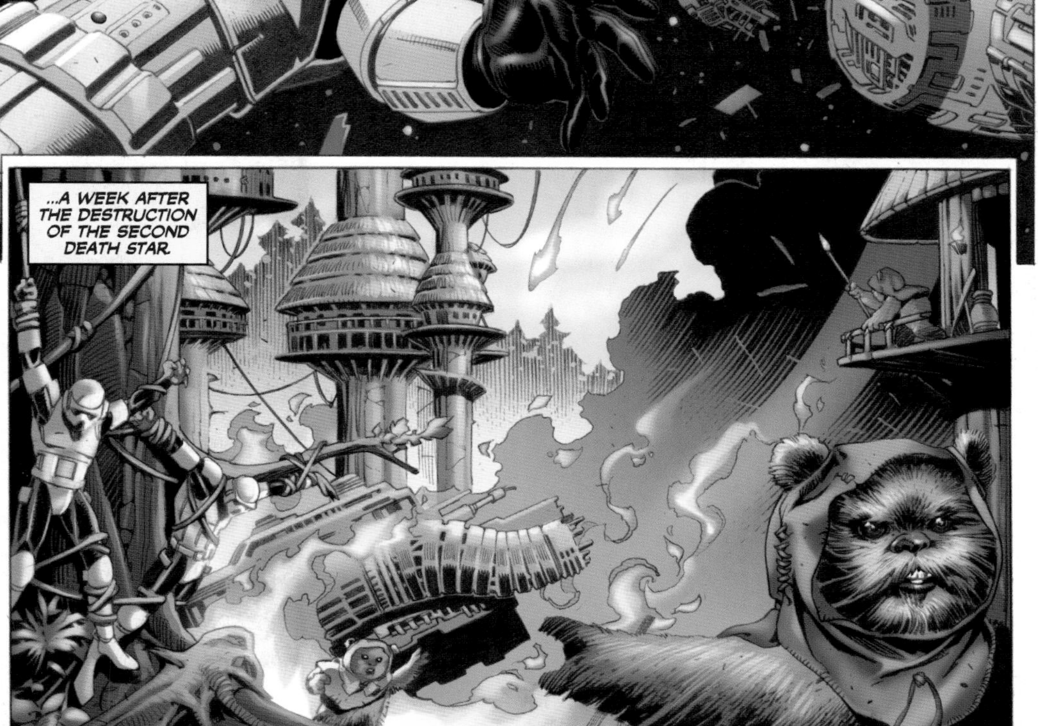
...A WEEK AFTER THE DESTRUCTION OF THE SECOND DEATH STAR.

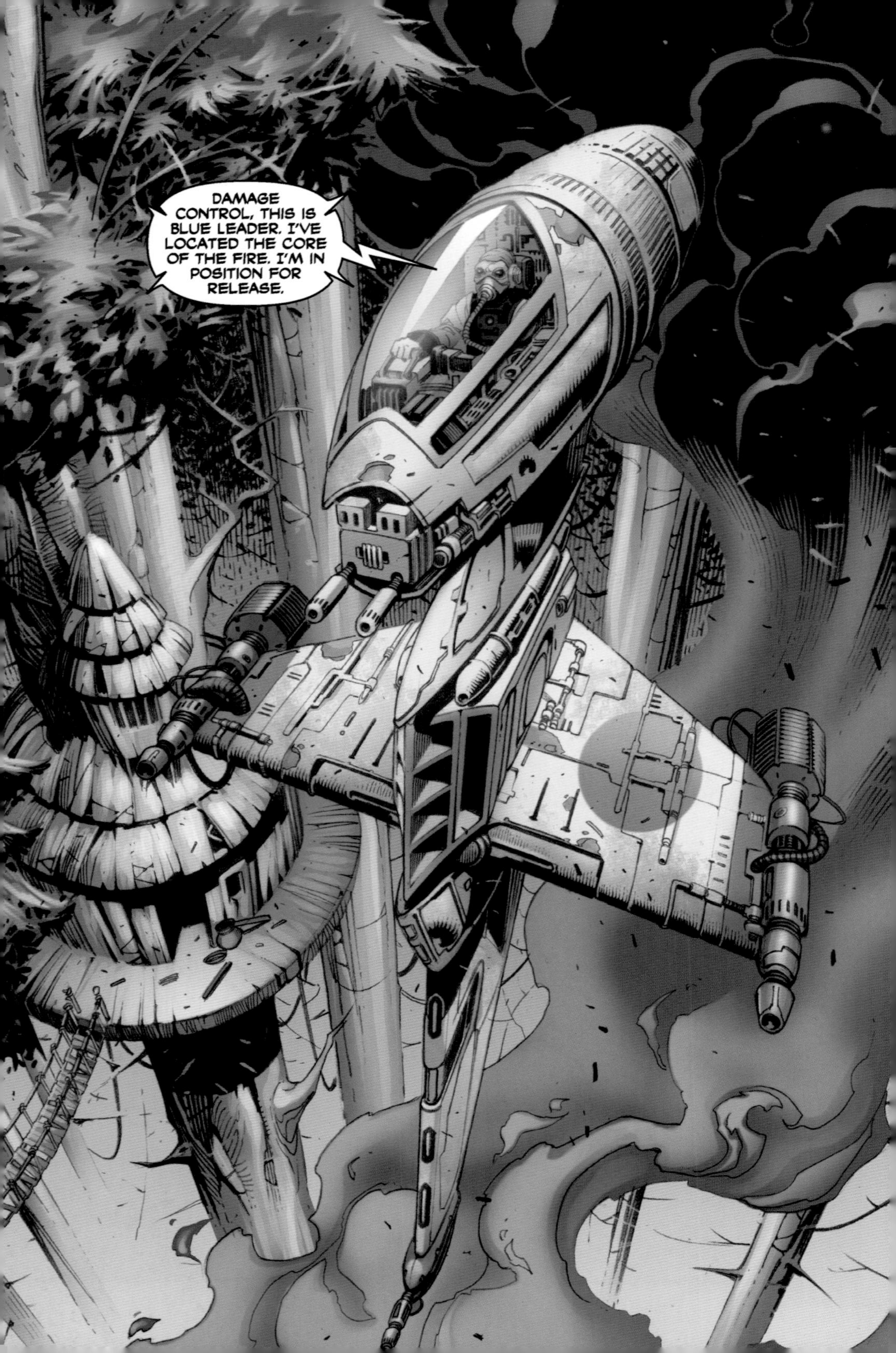
DAMAGE CONTROL, THIS IS BLUE LEADER. I'VE LOCATED THE CORE OF THE FIRE. I'M IN POSITION FOR RELEASE.

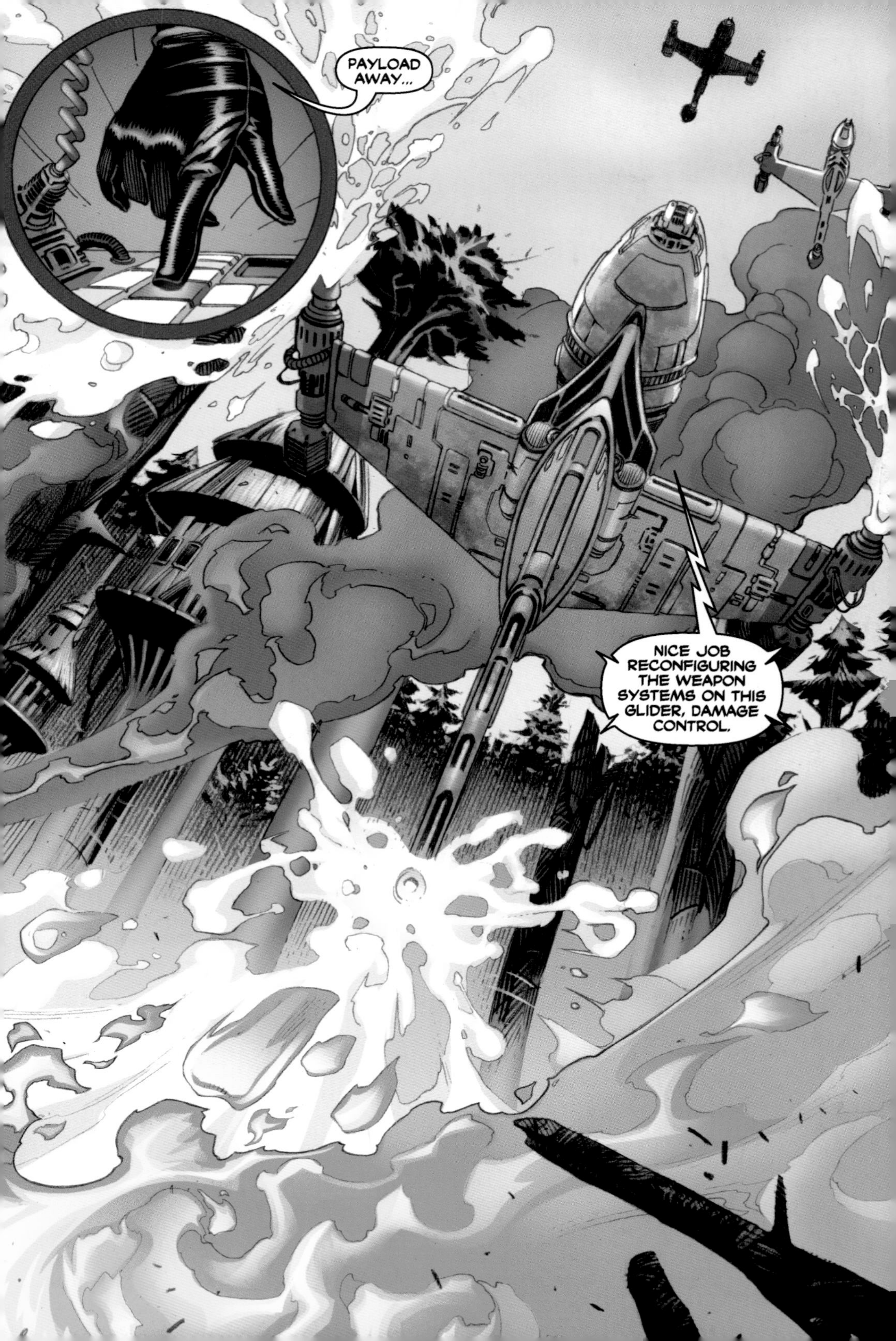
PAYLOAD AWAY...
NICE JOB RECONFIGURING THE WEAPON SYSTEMS ON THIS GLIDER, DAMAGE CONTROL.

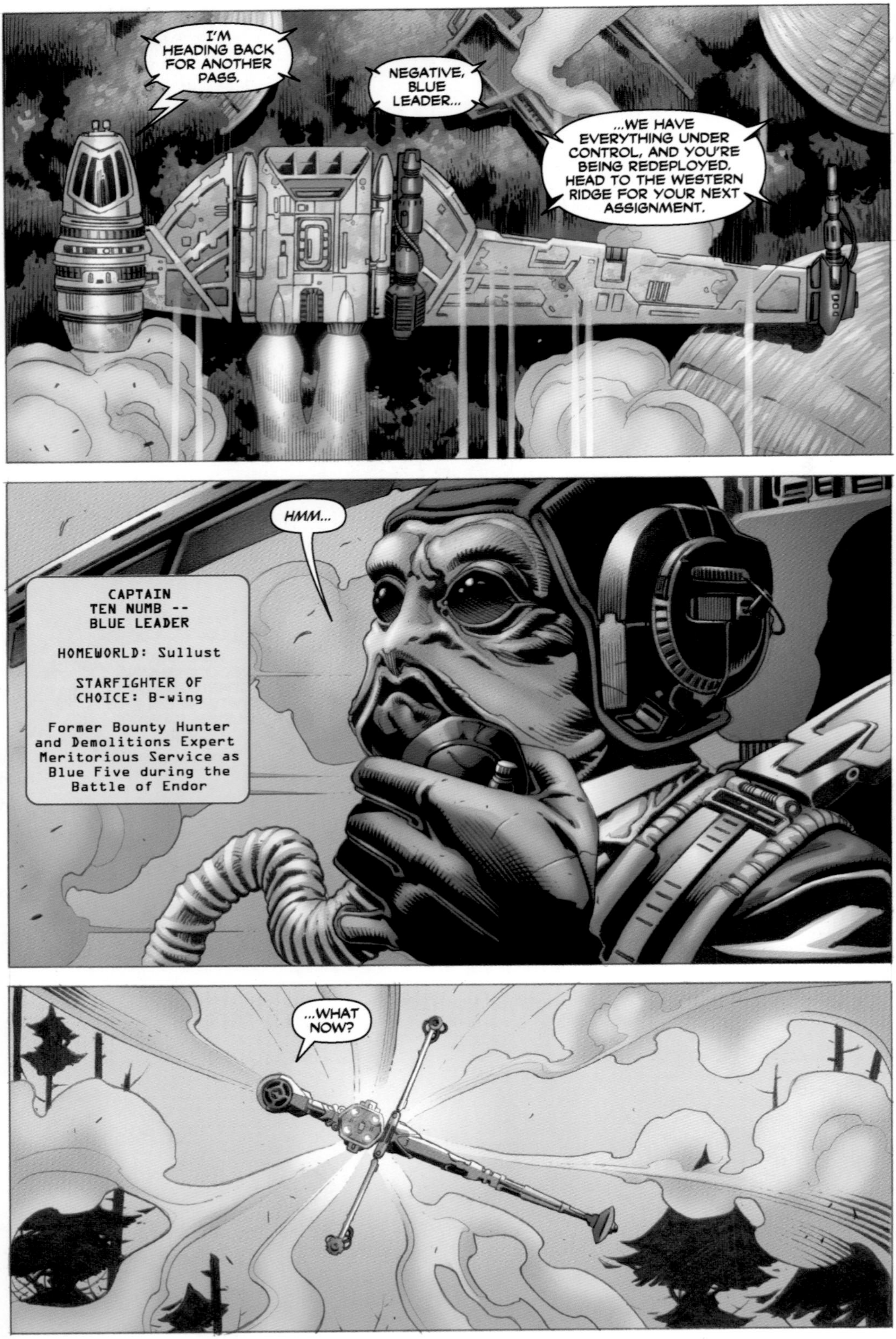
I'M HEADING BACK FOR ANOTHER PASS.
NEGATIVE, BLUE LEADER...
...WE HAVE EVERYTHING UNDER CONTROL, AND YOU'RE BEING REDEPLOYED. HEAD TO THE WESTERN RIDGE FOR YOUR NEXT ASSIGNMENT.
HMM...
CAPTAIN TEN NUMB -- BLUE LEADER
HOMEWORLD: Sullust
STARFIGHTER OF CHOICE: B-wing
Former Bounty Hunter and Demolitions Expert Meritorious Service as Blue Five during the Battle of Endor
...WHAT NOW?

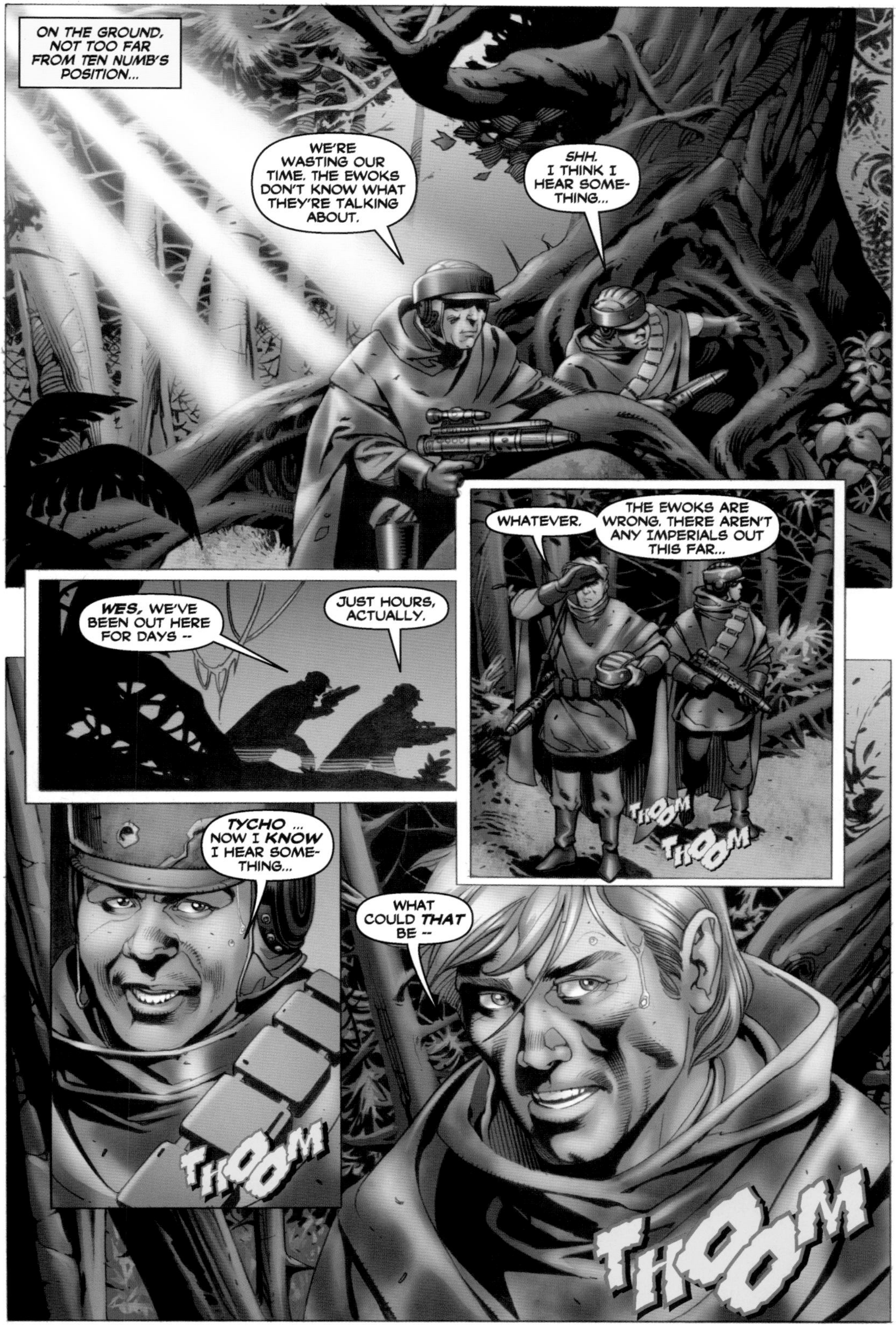
ON THE GROUND, NOT TOO FAR FROM TEN NUMB'S POSITION...
WE'RE WASTING OUR TIME. THE EWOKS DON'T KNOW WHAT THEY'RE TALKING ABOUT.
SHH. I THINK I HEAR SOME-THING...
WES, WE'VE BEEN OUT HERE FOR DAYS --
JUST HOURS, ACTUALLY.
WHATEVER.
THE EWOKS ARE WRONG. THERE AREN'T ANY IMPERIALS OUT THIS FAR...
THOOM
THOOM
TYCHO ... NOW I KNOW I HEAR SOME-THING...
THOOM
WHAT COULD THAT BE --
THOOM

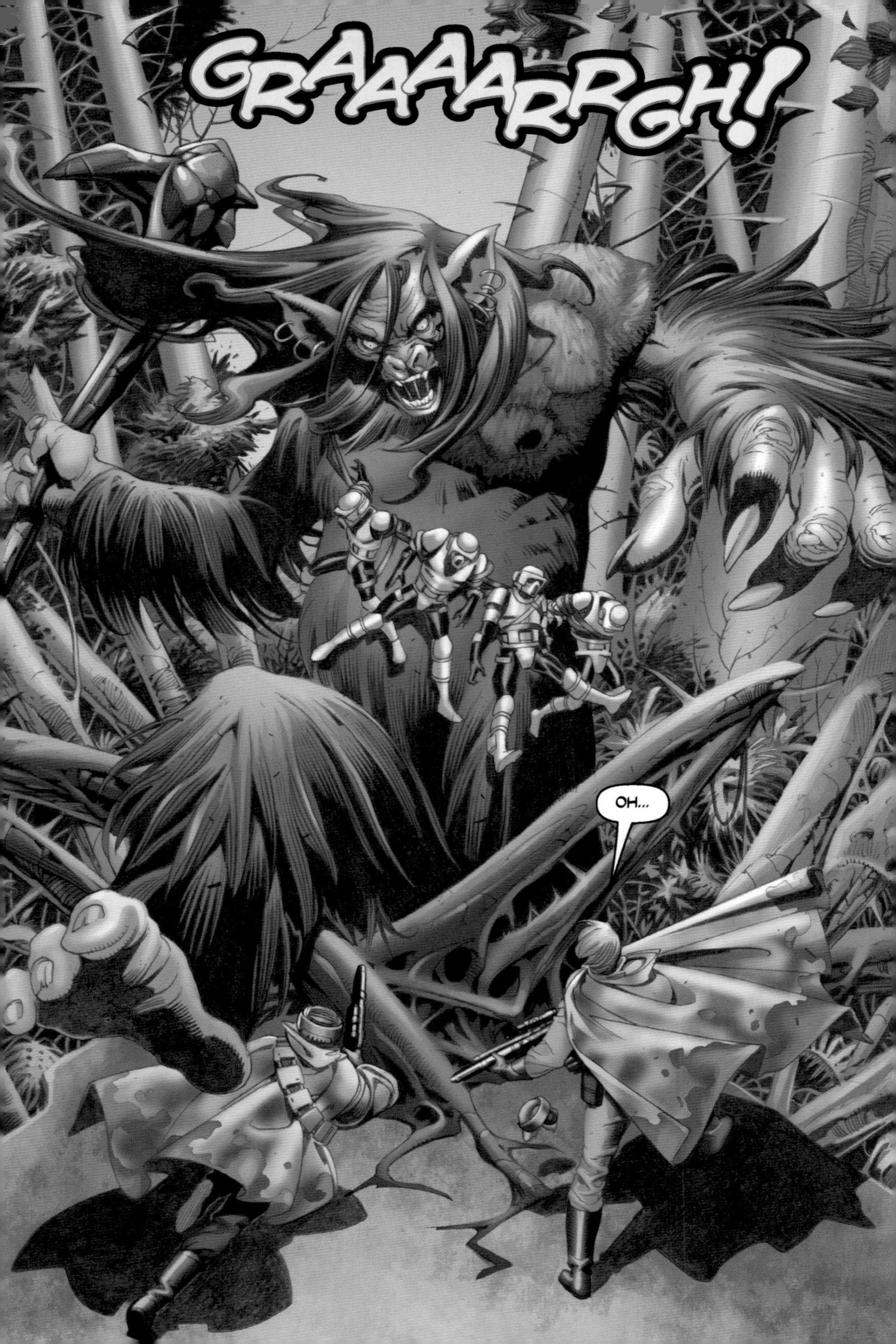
GRAAAARRGH!
OH...

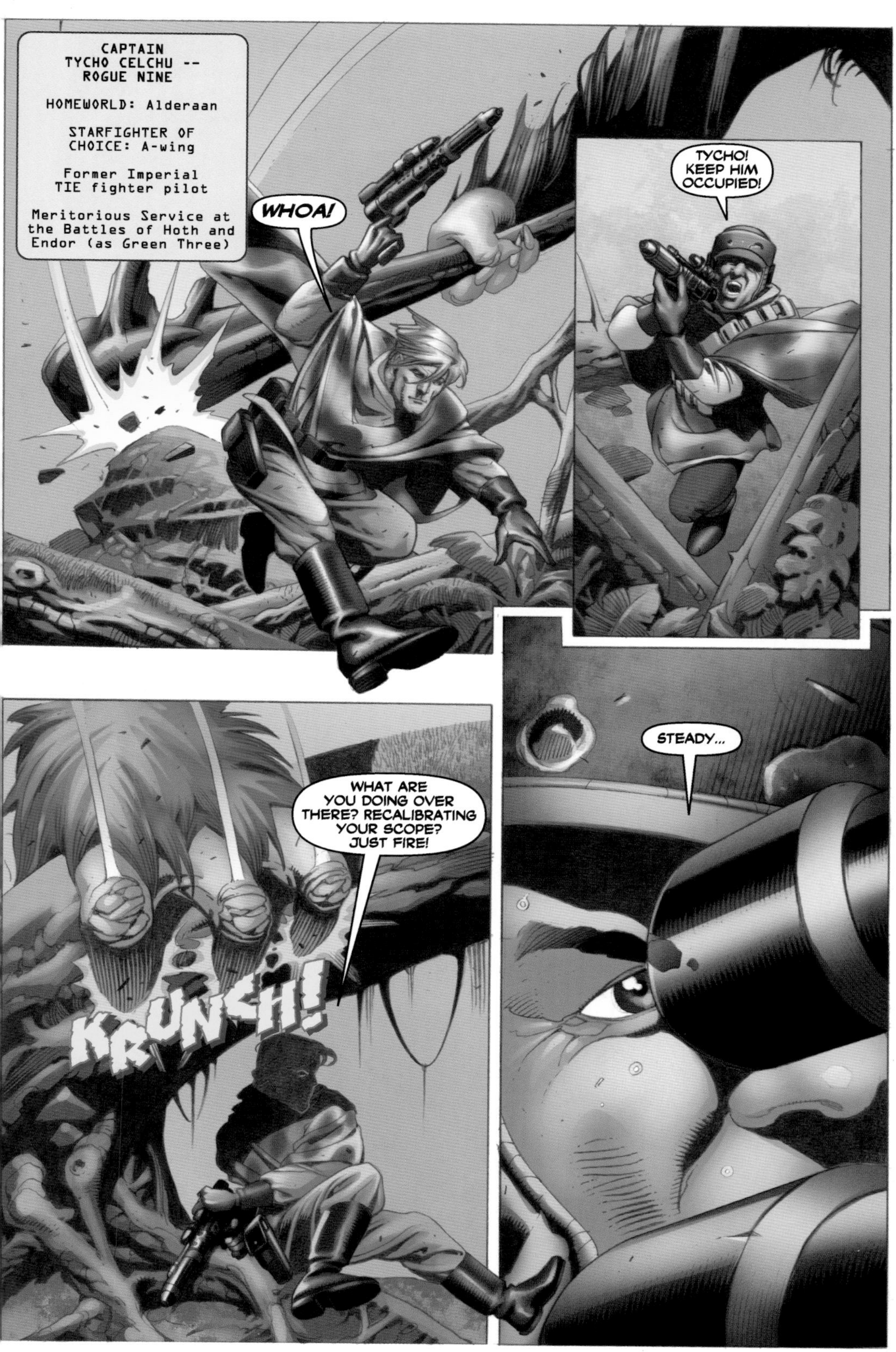

CAPTAIN
TYCHO CELCHU --
ROGUE NINE

HOMEWORLD: Alderaan

STARFIGHTER OF
CHOICE: A-wing

Former Imperial
TIE fighter pilot

Meritorious Service at
the Battles of Hoth and
Endor (as Green Three)
WHOA!
TYCHO! KEEP HIM OCCUPIED!
WHAT ARE YOU DOING OVER THERE? RECALIBRATING YOUR SCOPE? JUST FIRE!
KRUNCH!
STEADY...

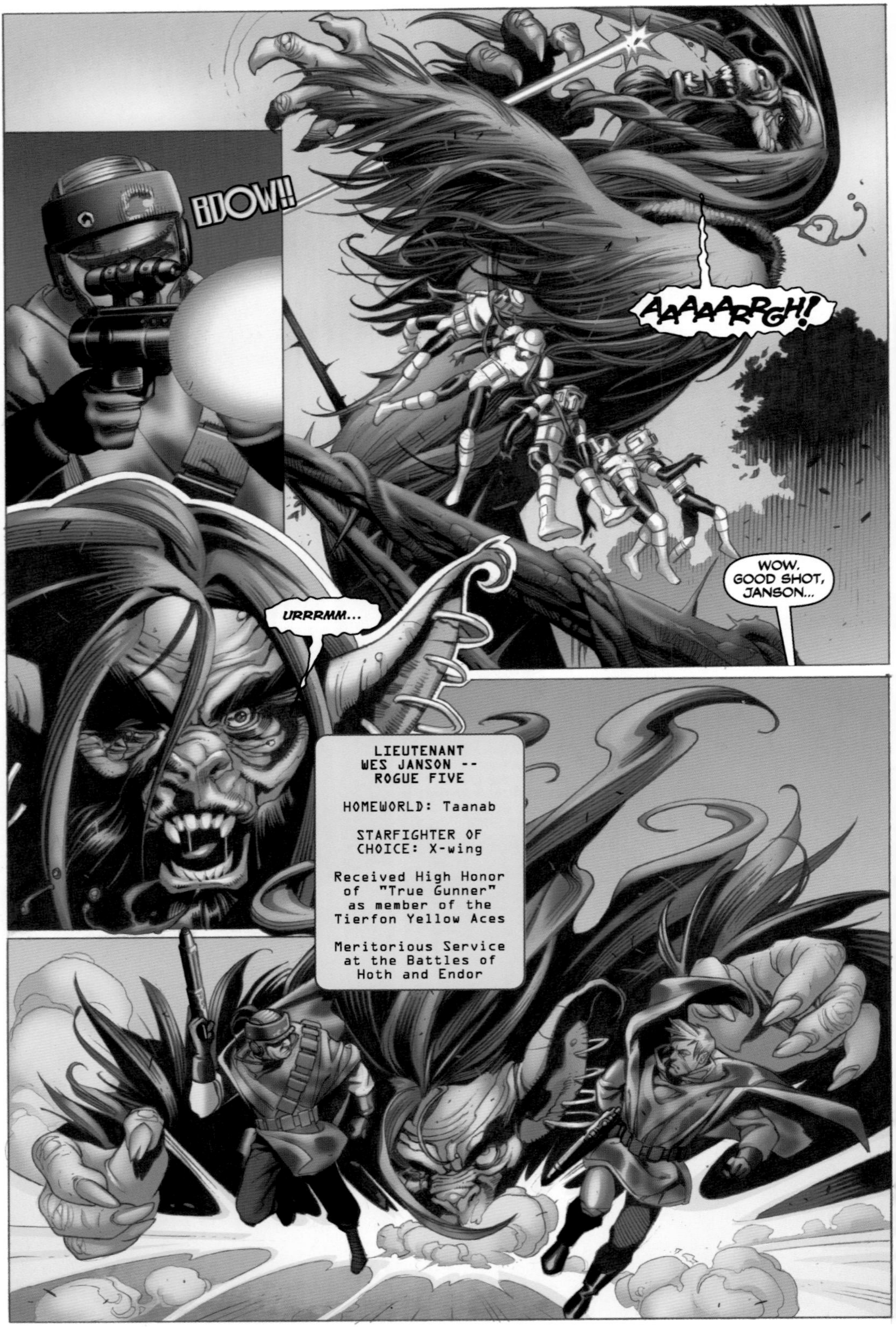
BDOW!!
AAAAARRGH!
WOW, GOOD SHOT, JANSON...
URRRMM...
LIEUTENANT WES JANSON -- ROGUE FIVE
HOMEWORLD: Taanab
STARFIGHTER OF CHOICE: X-wing
Received High Honor of "True Gunner" as member of the Tierfon Yellow Aces
Meritorious Service at the Battles of Hoth and Endor

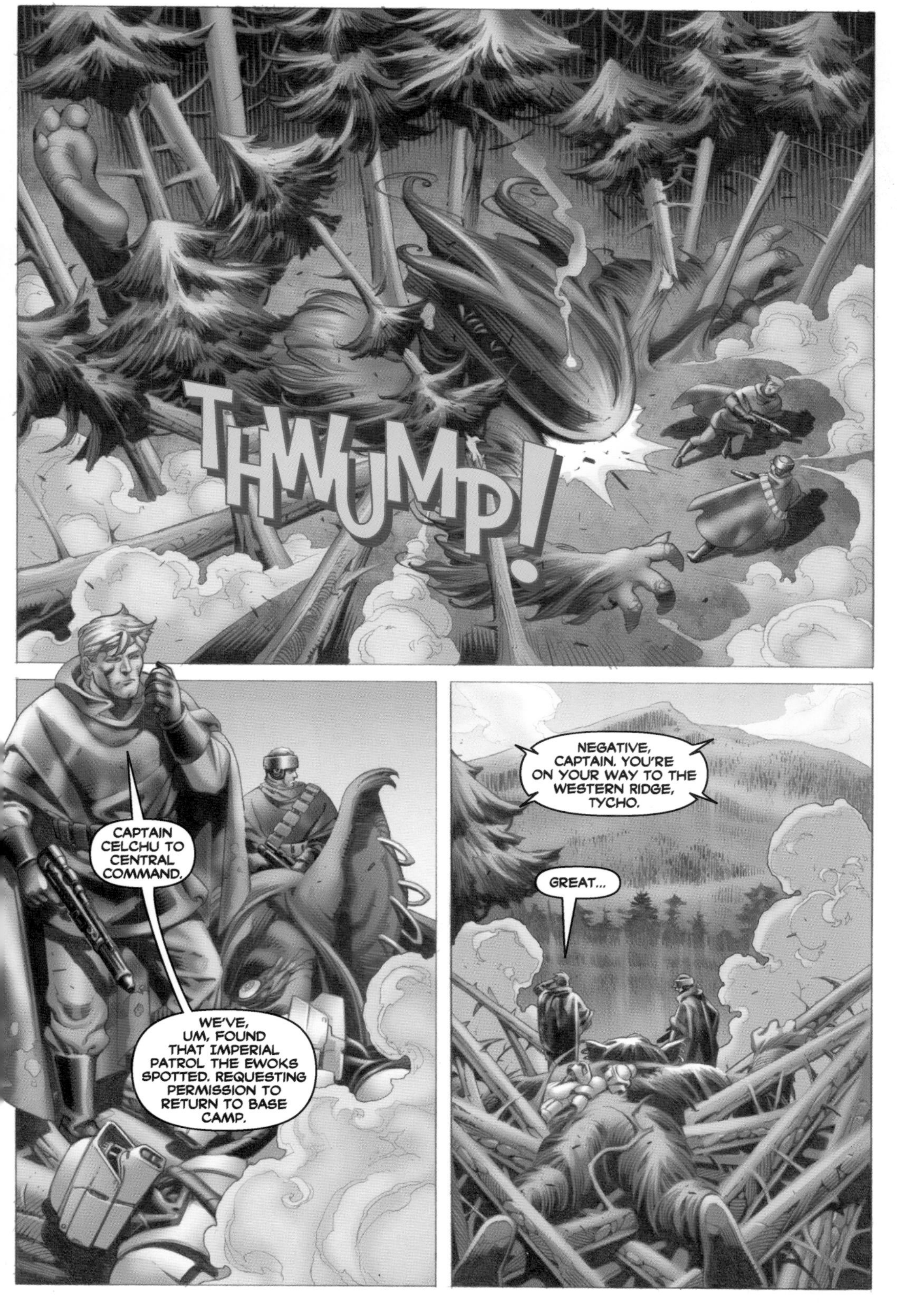
THWUMP!
CAPTAIN CELCHU TO CENTRAL COMMAND.
WE'VE, UM, FOUND THAT IMPERIAL PATROL THE EWOKS SPOTTED. REQUESTING PERMISSION TO RETURN TO BASE CAMP.
NEGATIVE, CAPTAIN. YOU'RE ON YOUR WAY TO THE WESTERN RIDGE, TYCHO.
GREAT...

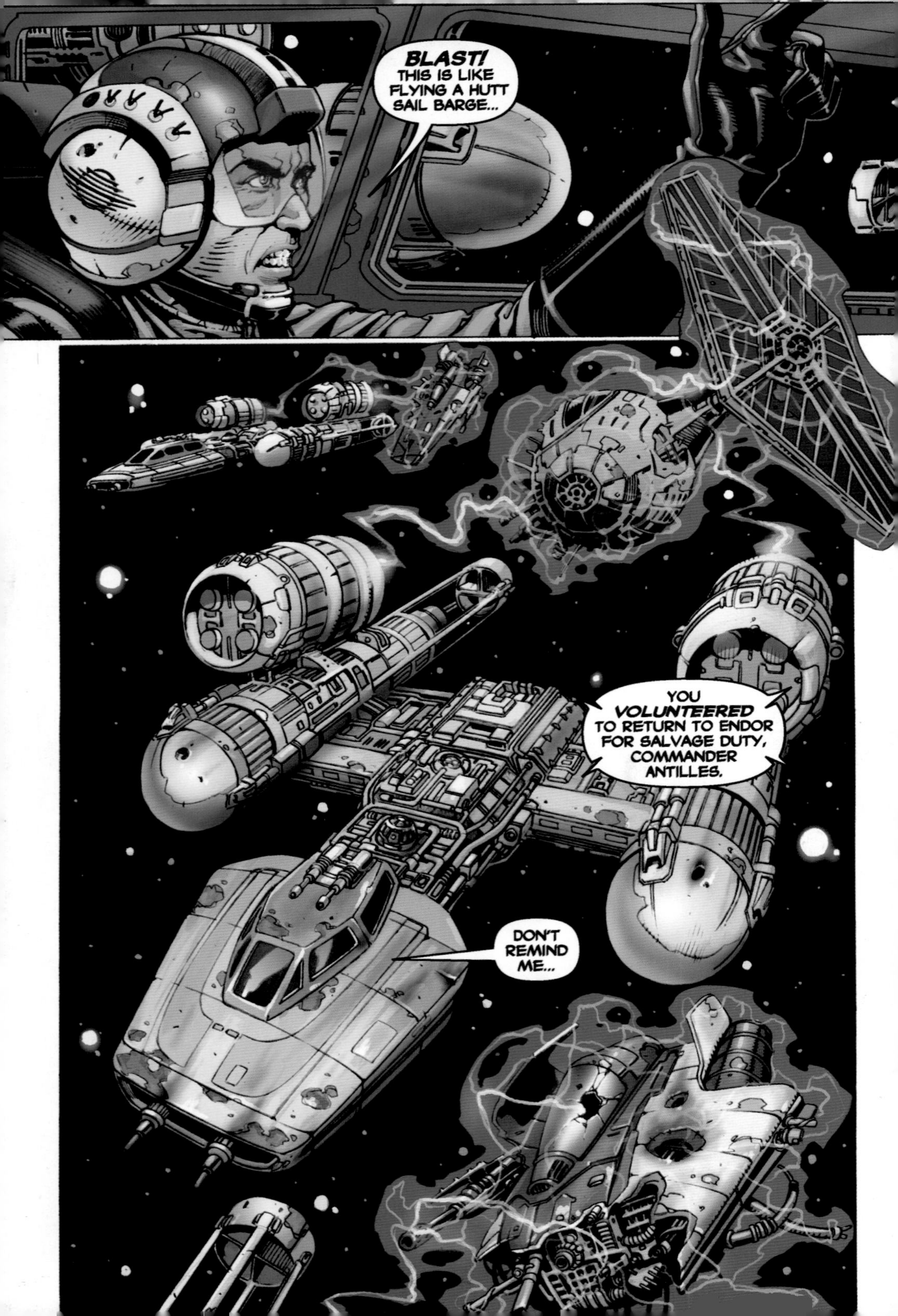
BLAST! THIS IS LIKE FLYING A HUTT SAIL BARGE...
YOU VOLUNTEERED TO RETURN TO ENDOR FOR SALVAGE DUTY, COMMANDER ANTILLES.
DON'T REMIND ME...

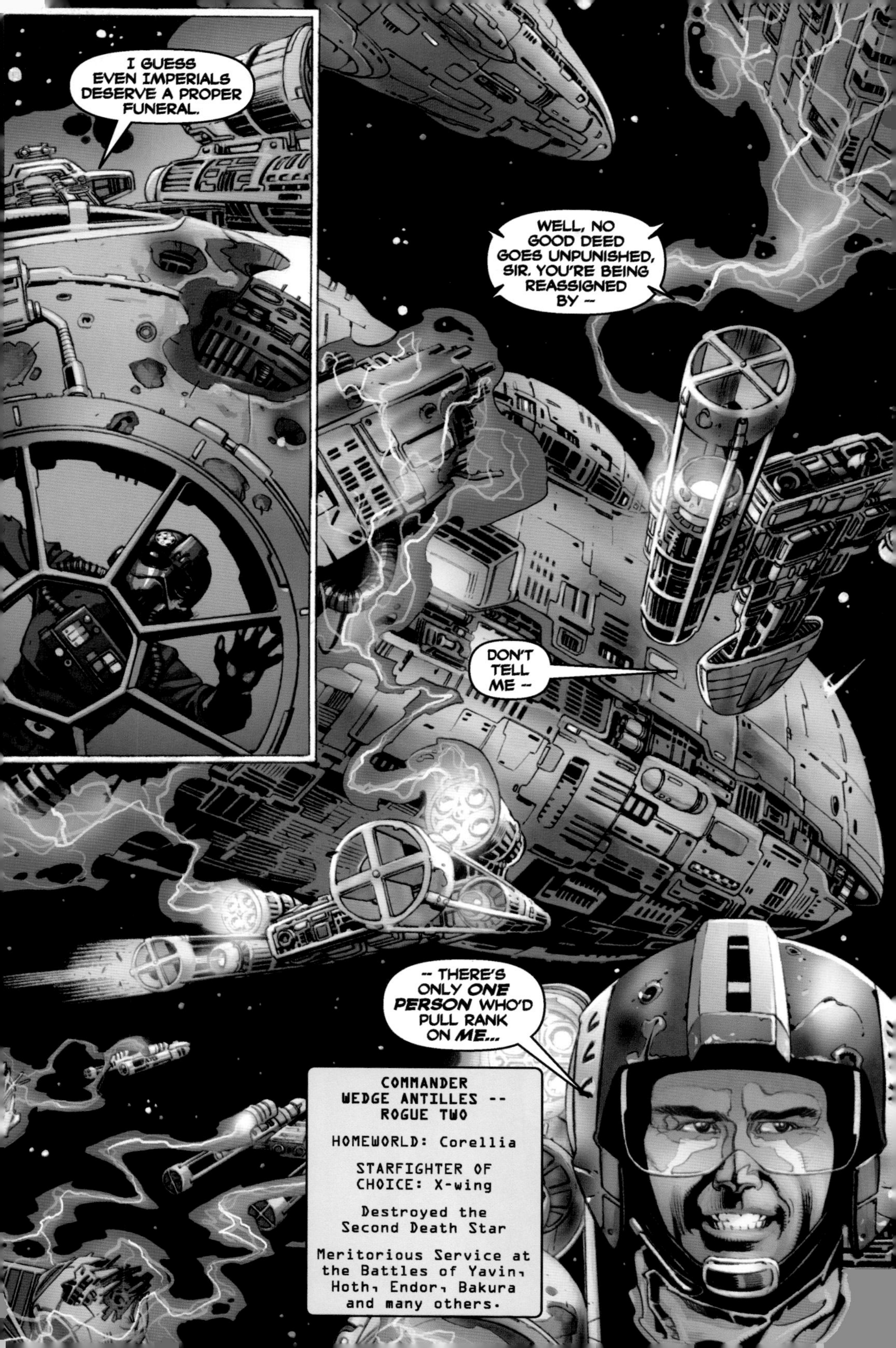
I GUESS EVEN IMPERIALS DESERVE A PROPER FUNERAL.
WELL, NO GOOD DEED GOES UNPUNISHED, SIR. YOU'RE BEING REASSIGNED BY --
DON'T TELL ME --
-- THERE'S ONLY *ONE PERSON* WHO'D PULL RANK ON *ME*...
COMMANDER WEDGE ANTILLES -- ROGUE TWO
HOMEWORLD: Corellia
STARFIGHTER OF CHOICE: X-wing
Destroyed the Second Death Star
Meritorious Service at the Battles of Yavin, Hoth, Endor, Bakura and many others.

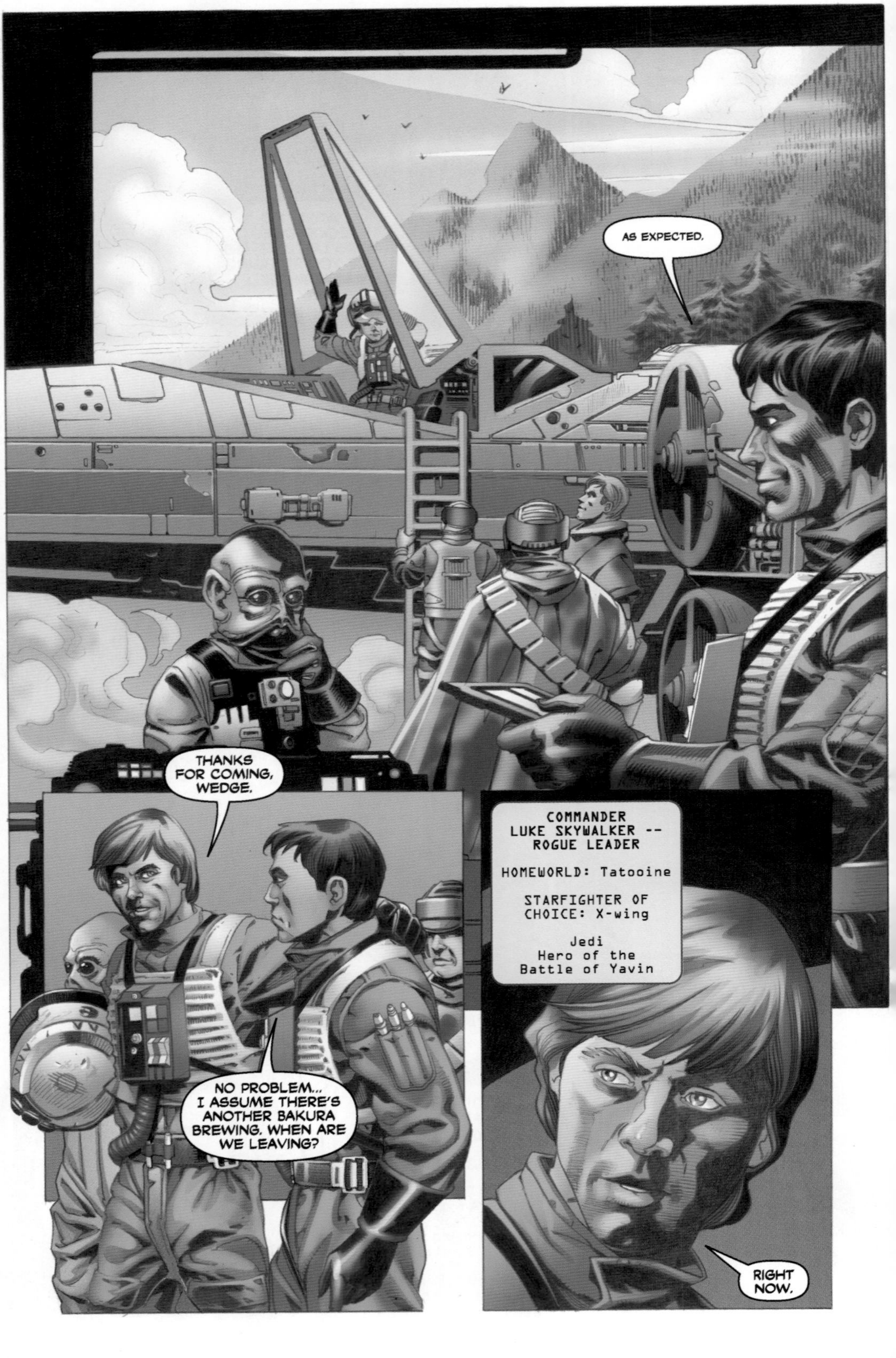
AS EXPECTED.
THANKS FOR COMING, WEDGE.
NO PROBLEM... I ASSUME THERE'S ANOTHER BAKURA BREWING. WHEN ARE WE LEAVING?
COMMANDER LUKE SKYWALKER -- ROGUE LEADER
HOMEWORLD: Tatooine
STARFIGHTER OF CHOICE: X-wing
Jedi
Hero of the Battle of Yavin
RIGHT NOW.

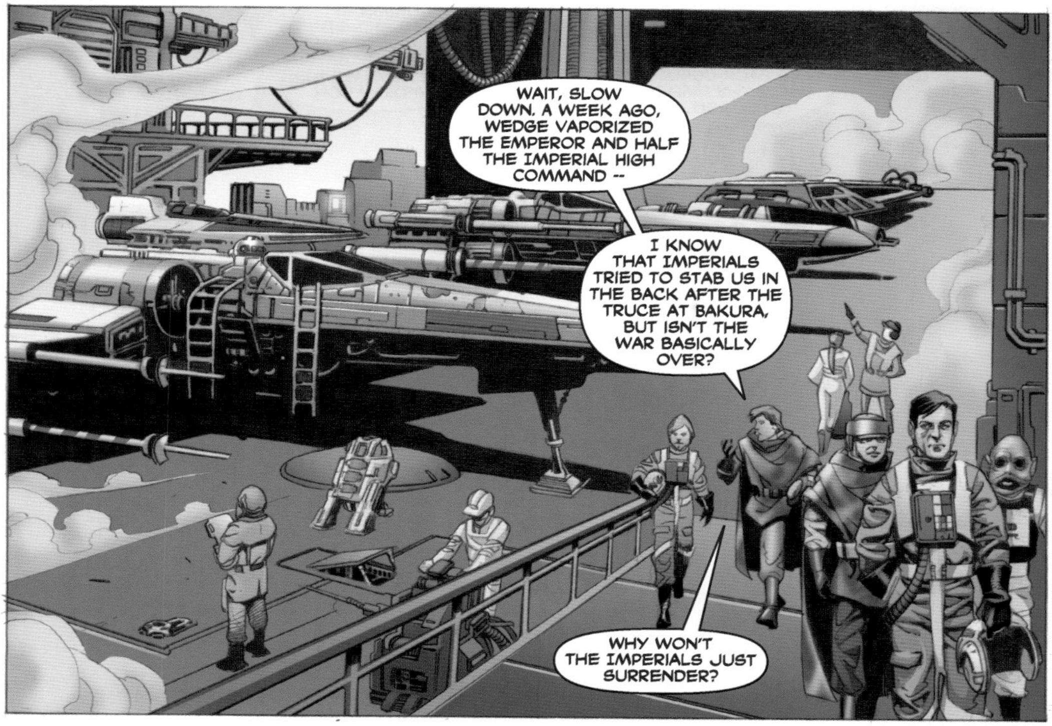
WAIT, SLOW DOWN. A WEEK AGO, WEDGE VAPORIZED THE EMPEROR AND HALF THE IMPERIAL HIGH COMMAND --
I KNOW THAT IMPERIALS TRIED TO STAB US IN THE BACK AFTER THE TRUCE AT BAKURA, BUT ISN'T THE WAR BASICALLY OVER?
WHY WON'T THE IMPERIALS JUST SURRENDER?

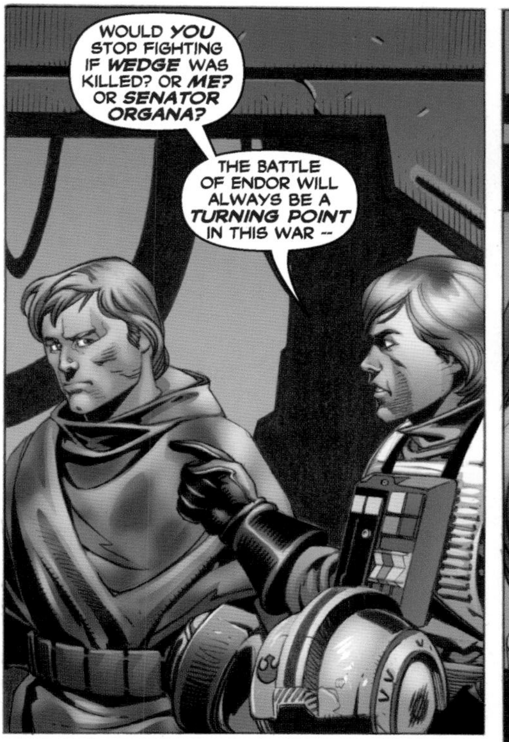
WOULD *YOU* STOP FIGHTING IF *WEDGE* WAS KILLED? OR *ME?* OR *SENATOR ORGANA?*
THE BATTLE OF ENDOR WILL ALWAYS BE A *TURNING POINT* IN THIS WAR --

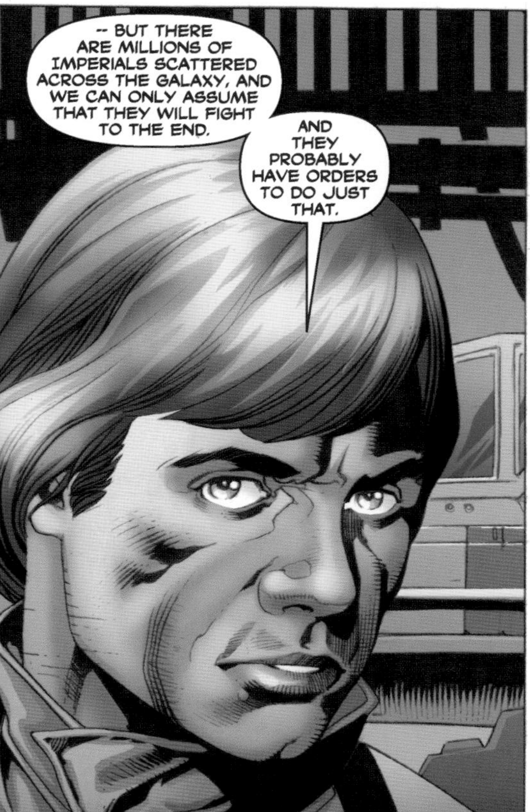
-- BUT THERE ARE MILLIONS OF IMPERIALS SCATTERED ACROSS THE GALAXY, AND WE CAN ONLY ASSUME THAT THEY WILL FIGHT TO THE END.
AND THEY PROBABLY HAVE ORDERS TO DO JUST THAT.

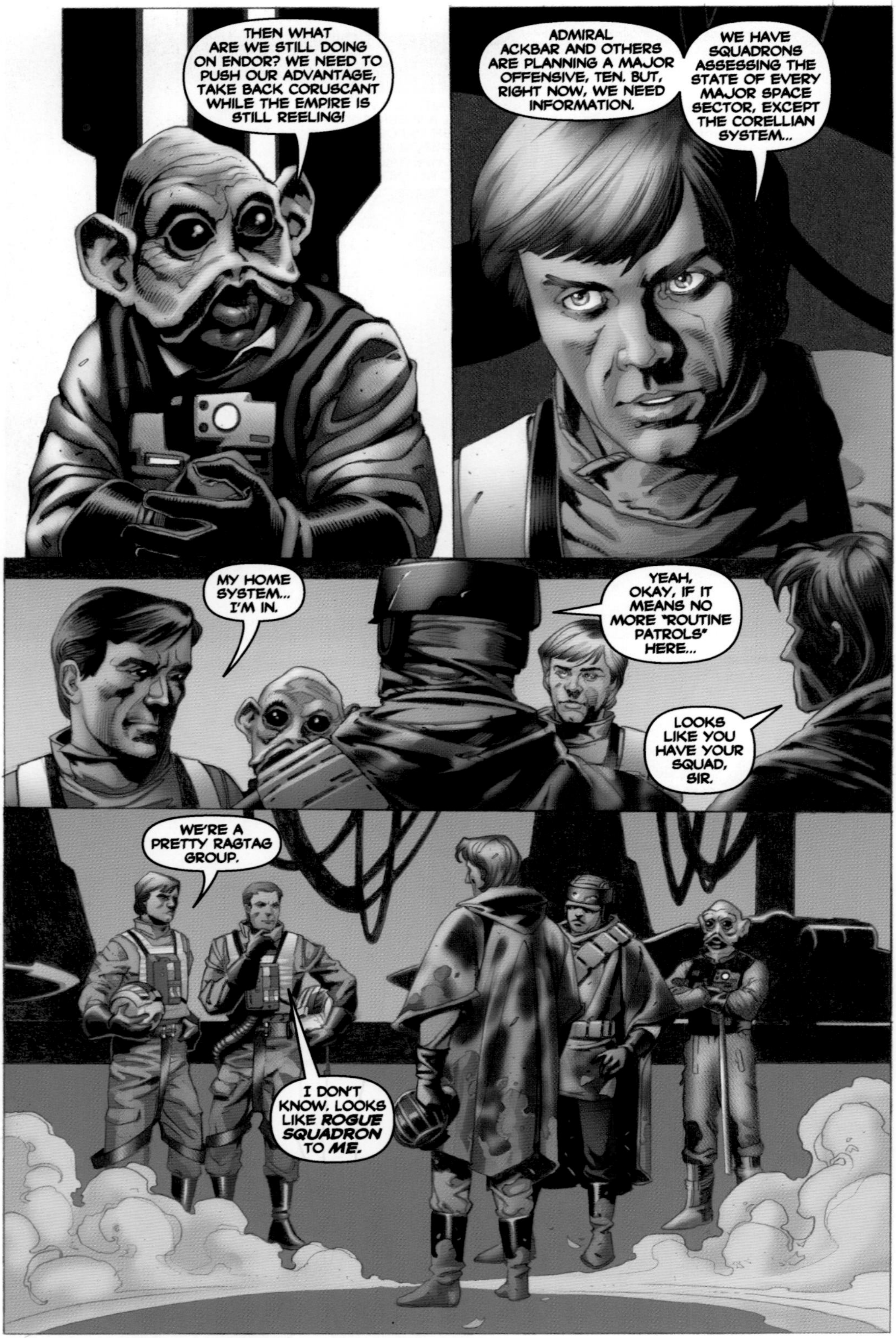
THEN WHAT ARE WE STILL DOING ON ENDOR? WE NEED TO PUSH OUR ADVANTAGE, TAKE BACK CORUSCANT WHILE THE EMPIRE IS STILL REELING!
ADMIRAL ACKBAR AND OTHERS ARE PLANNING A MAJOR OFFENSIVE, TEN. BUT, RIGHT NOW, WE NEED INFORMATION.
WE HAVE SQUADRONS ASSESSING THE STATE OF EVERY MAJOR SPACE SECTOR, EXCEPT THE CORELLIAN SYSTEM...
MY HOME SYSTEM... I'M IN.
YEAH, OKAY, IF IT MEANS NO MORE "ROUTINE PATROLS" HERE...
LOOKS LIKE YOU HAVE YOUR SQUAD, SIR.
WE'RE A PRETTY RAGTAG GROUP.
I DON'T KNOW. LOOKS LIKE *ROGUE SQUADRON* TO *ME.*

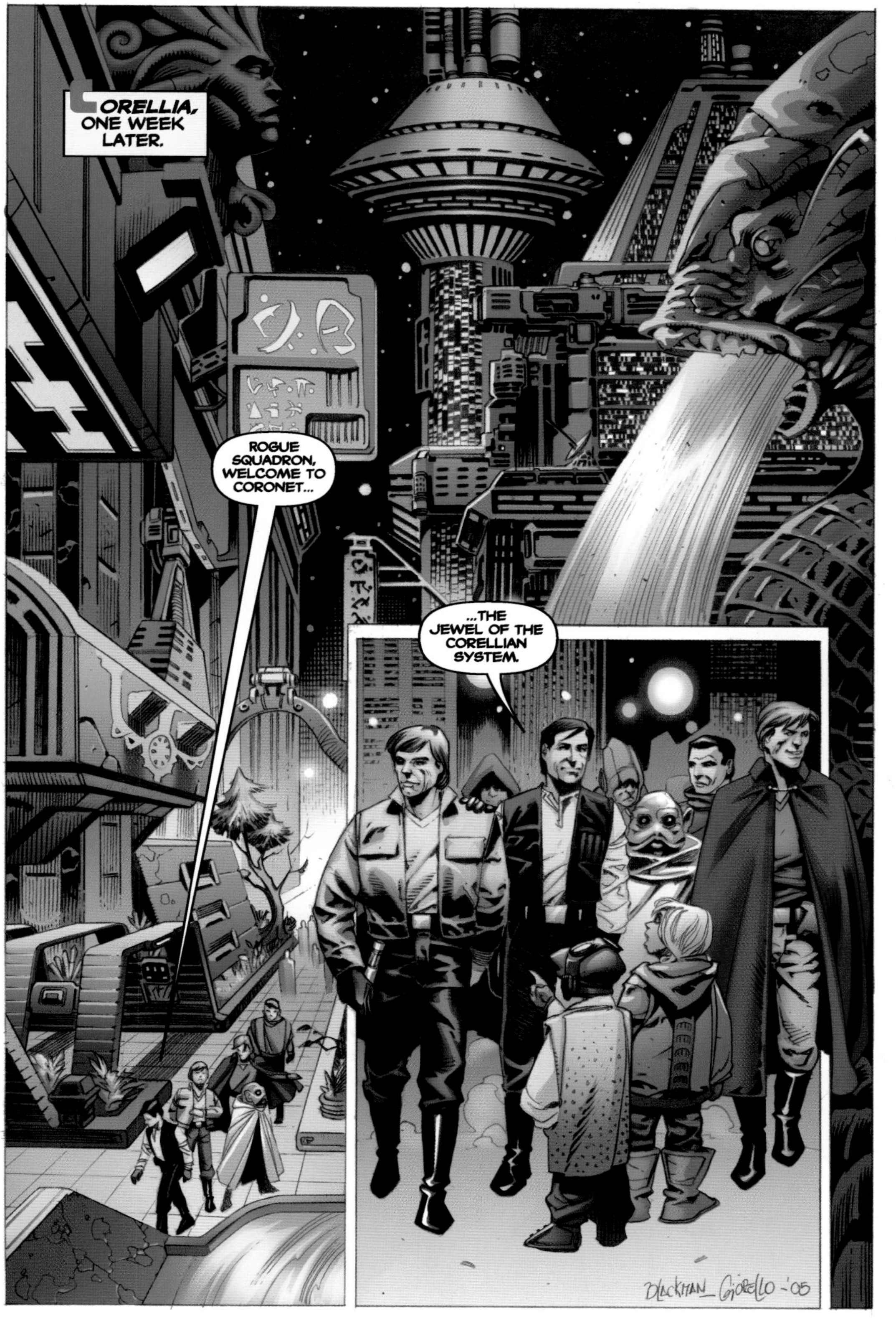
CORELLIA, ONE WEEK LATER.
ROGUE SQUADRON, WELCOME TO CORONET...
...THE JEWEL OF THE CORELLIAN SYSTEM.
BLACKMAN_GIORELLO -'05

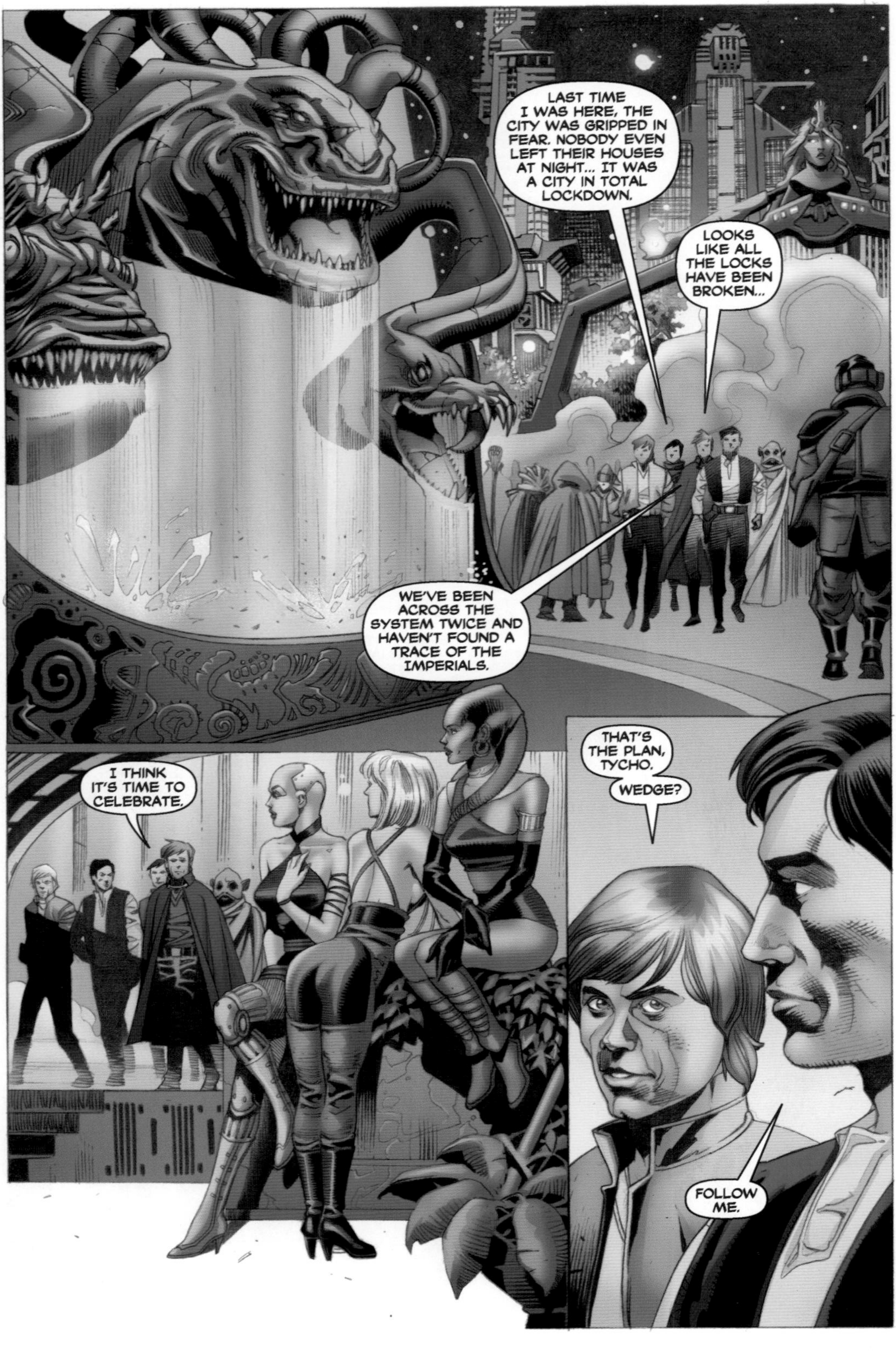
LAST TIME I WAS HERE, THE CITY WAS GRIPPED IN FEAR. NOBODY EVEN LEFT THEIR HOUSES AT NIGHT... IT WAS A CITY IN TOTAL LOCKDOWN.
LOOKS LIKE ALL THE LOCKS HAVE BEEN BROKEN...
WE'VE BEEN ACROSS THE SYSTEM TWICE AND HAVEN'T FOUND A TRACE OF THE IMPERIALS.
I THINK IT'S TIME TO CELEBRATE.
THAT'S THE PLAN, TYCHO.
WEDGE?
FOLLOW ME.

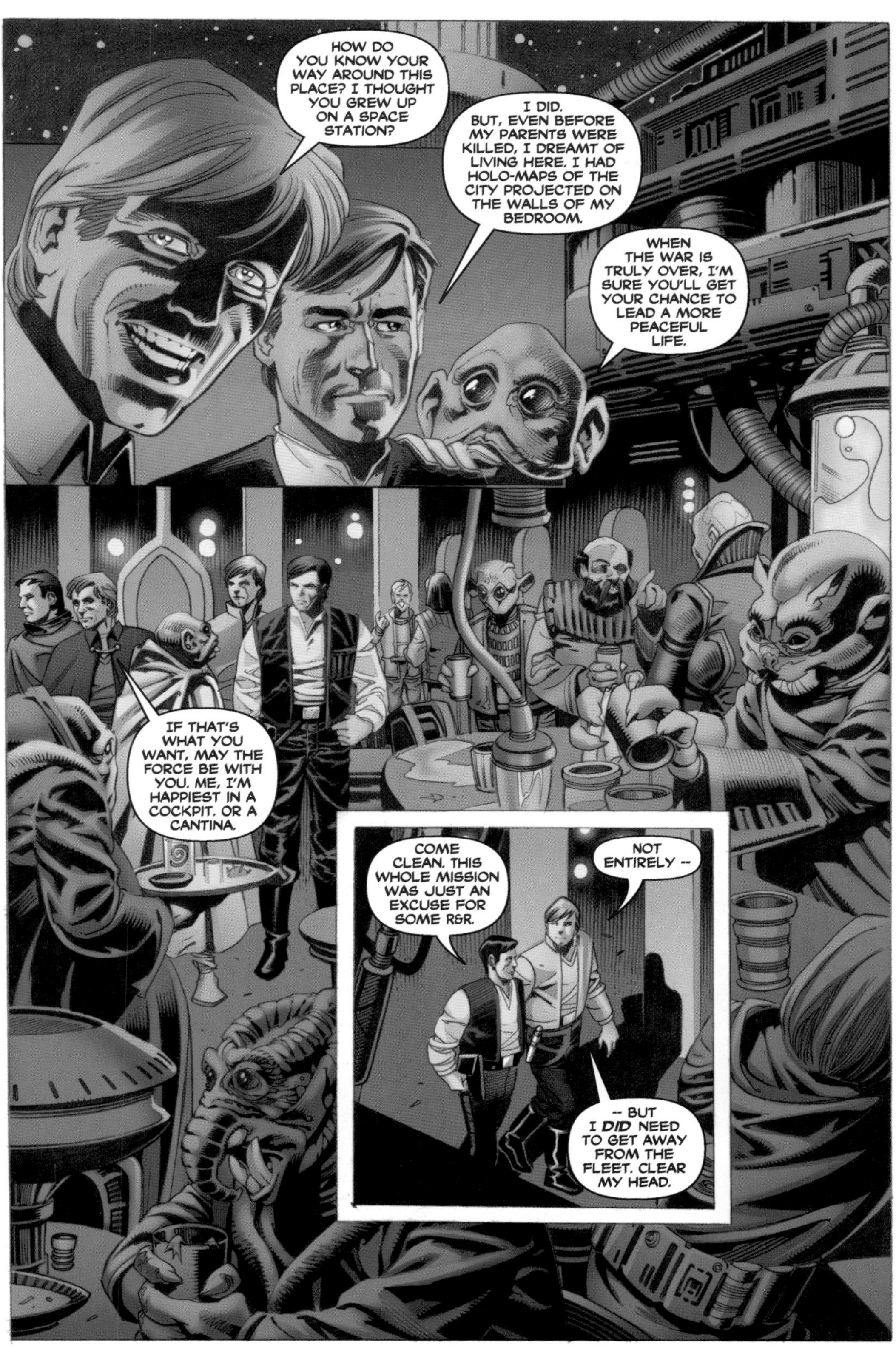

HOW DO YOU KNOW YOUR WAY AROUND THIS PLACE? I THOUGHT YOU GREW UP ON A SPACE STATION?
I DID. BUT, EVEN BEFORE MY PARENTS WERE KILLED, I DREAMT OF LIVING HERE. I HAD HOLO-MAPS OF THE CITY PROJECTED ON THE WALLS OF MY BEDROOM.
WHEN THE WAR IS TRULY OVER, I'M SURE YOU'LL GET YOUR CHANCE TO LEAD A MORE PEACEFUL LIFE.
IF THAT'S WHAT YOU WANT, MAY THE FORCE BE WITH YOU. ME, I'M HAPPIEST IN A COCKPIT. OR A CANTINA.
COME CLEAN. THIS WHOLE MISSION WAS JUST AN EXCUSE FOR SOME R&R.
NOT ENTIRELY --
-- BUT I *DID* NEED TO GET AWAY FROM THE FLEET. CLEAR MY HEAD.

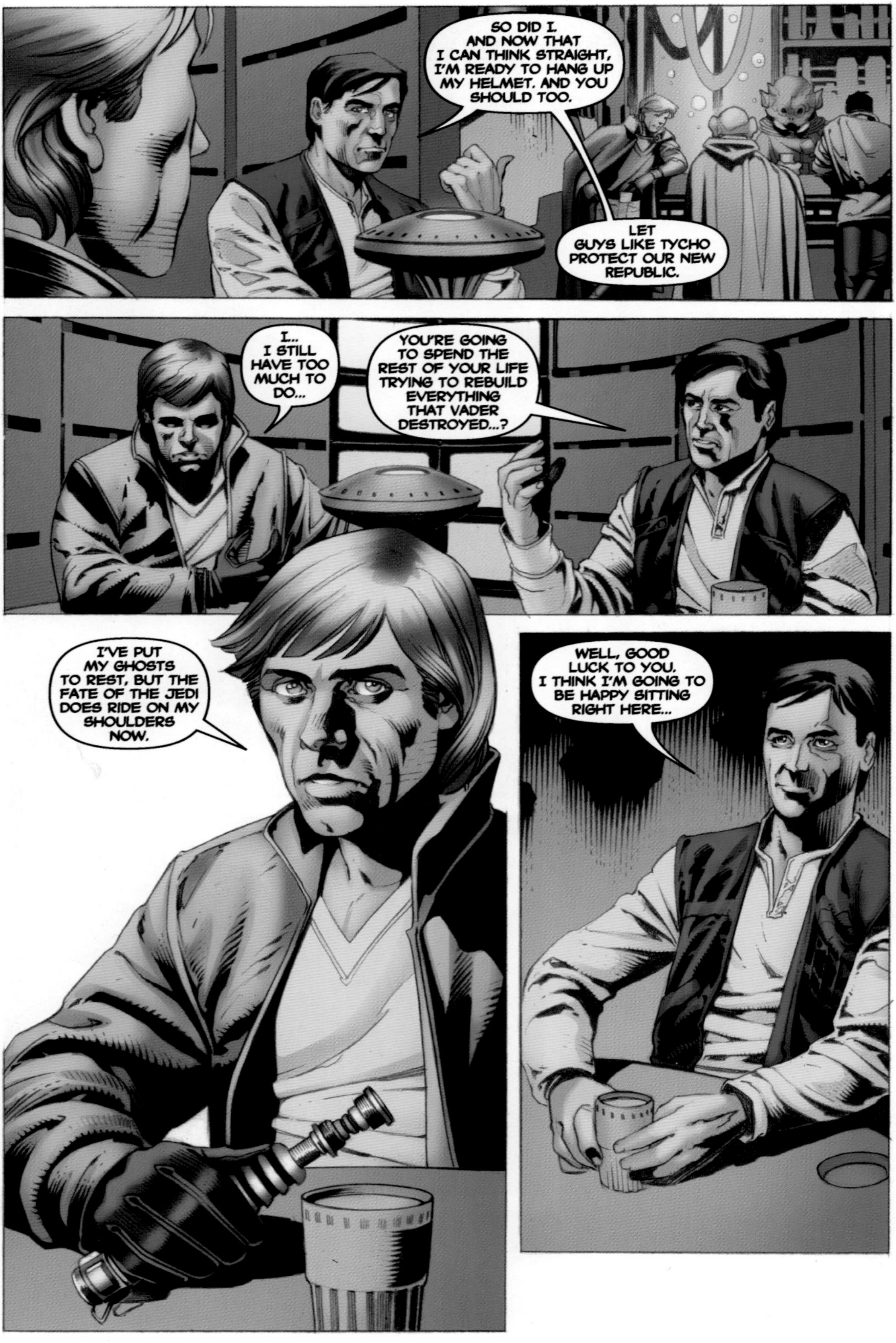
SO DID I. AND NOW THAT I CAN THINK STRAIGHT, I'M READY TO HANG UP MY HELMET. AND YOU SHOULD TOO.
LET GUYS LIKE TYCHO PROTECT OUR NEW REPUBLIC.
I... I STILL HAVE TOO MUCH TO DO...
YOU'RE GOING TO SPEND THE REST OF YOUR LIFE TRYING TO REBUILD EVERYTHING THAT VADER DESTROYED...?
I'VE PUT MY GHOSTS TO REST, BUT THE FATE OF THE JEDI DOES RIDE ON MY SHOULDERS NOW.
WELL, GOOD LUCK TO YOU. I THINK I'M GOING TO BE HAPPY SITTING RIGHT HERE...

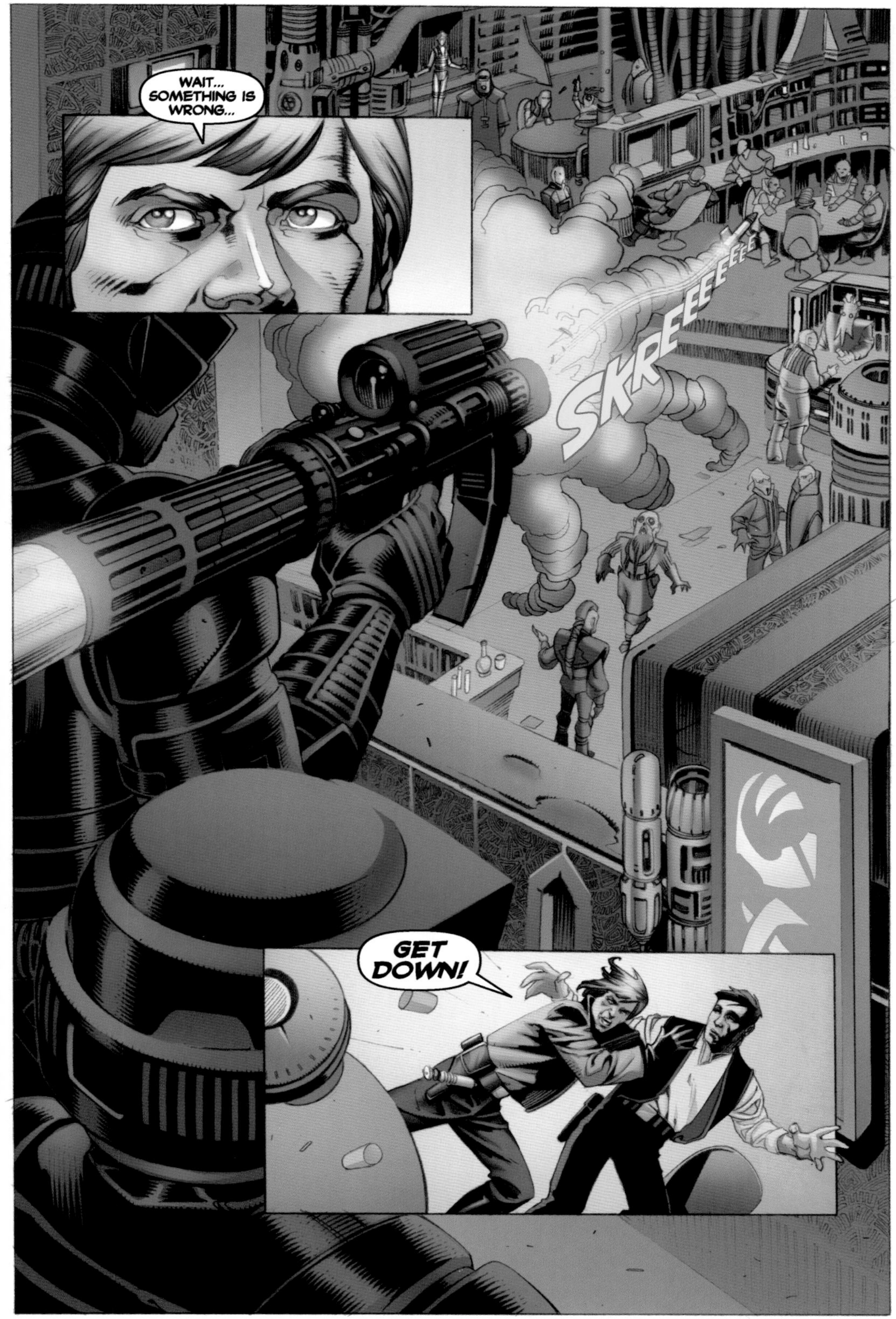
WAIT... SOMETHING IS WRONG...
SKREEEEEEE
GET DOWN!

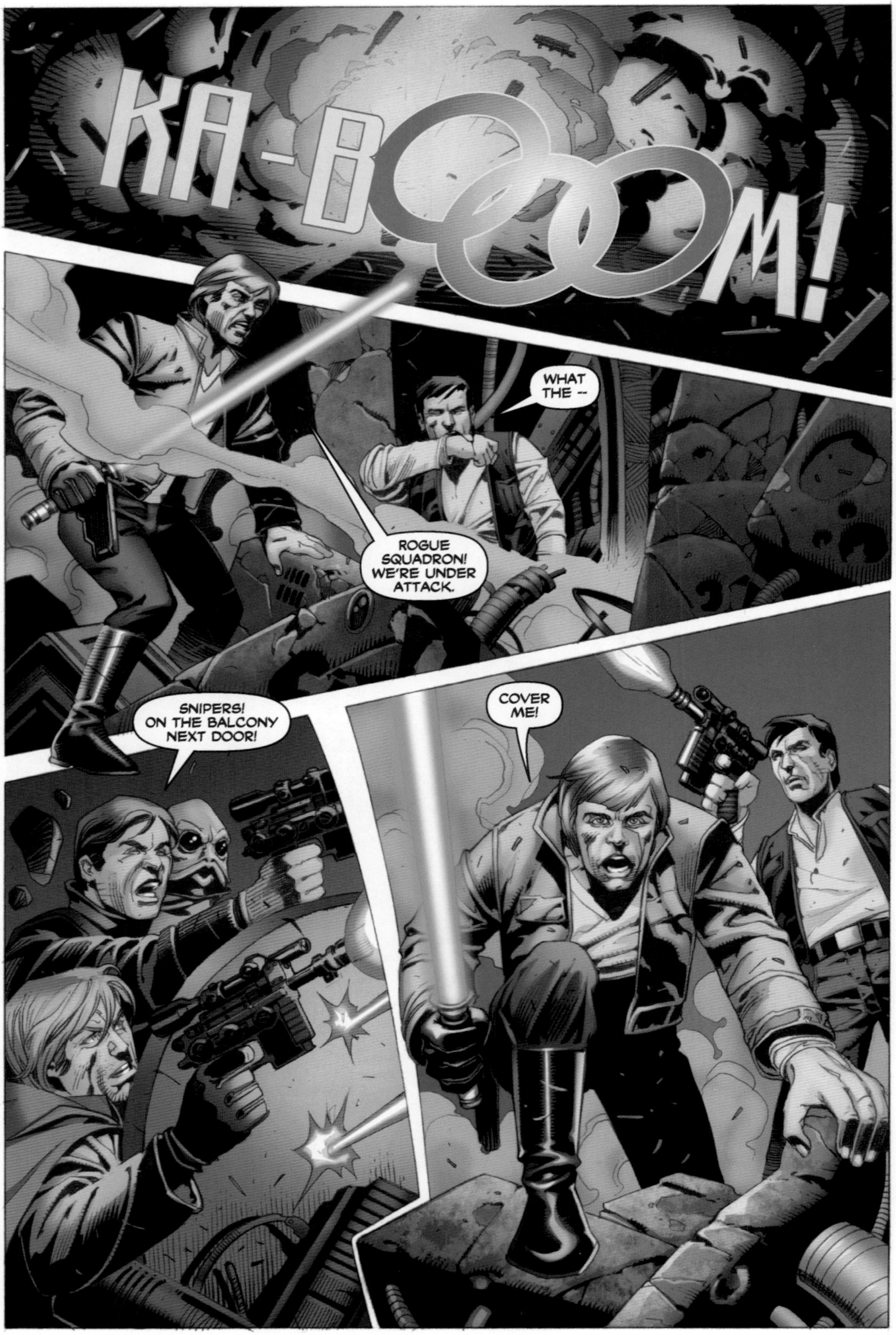
KA-BOOOM!
WHAT THE --
ROGUE SQUADRON! WE'RE UNDER ATTACK.
SNIPERS! ON THE BALCONY NEXT DOOR!
COVER ME!

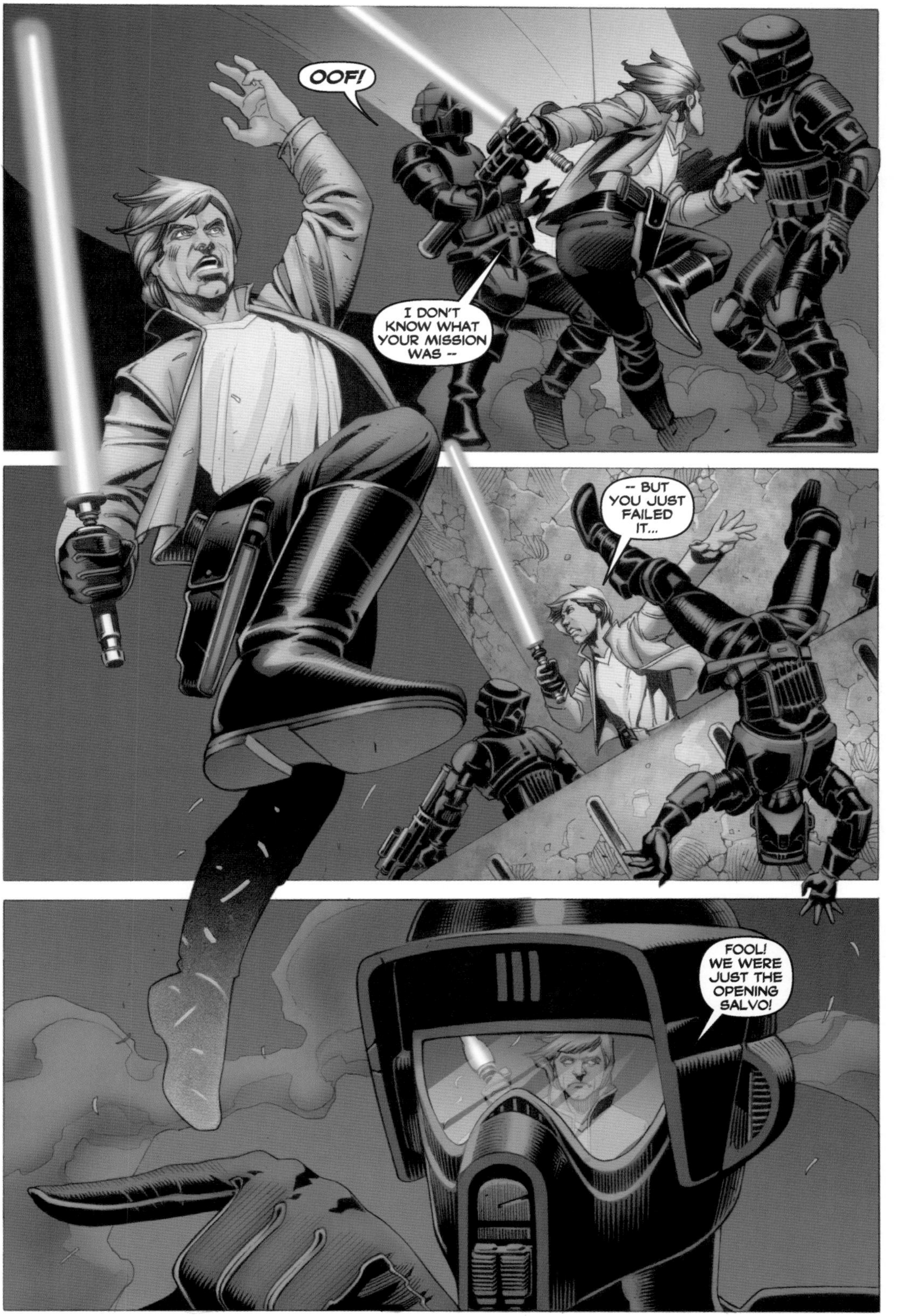
OOF!
I DON'T KNOW WHAT YOUR MISSION WAS --
-- BUT YOU JUST FAILED IT...
FOOL! WE WERE JUST THE OPENING SALVO!

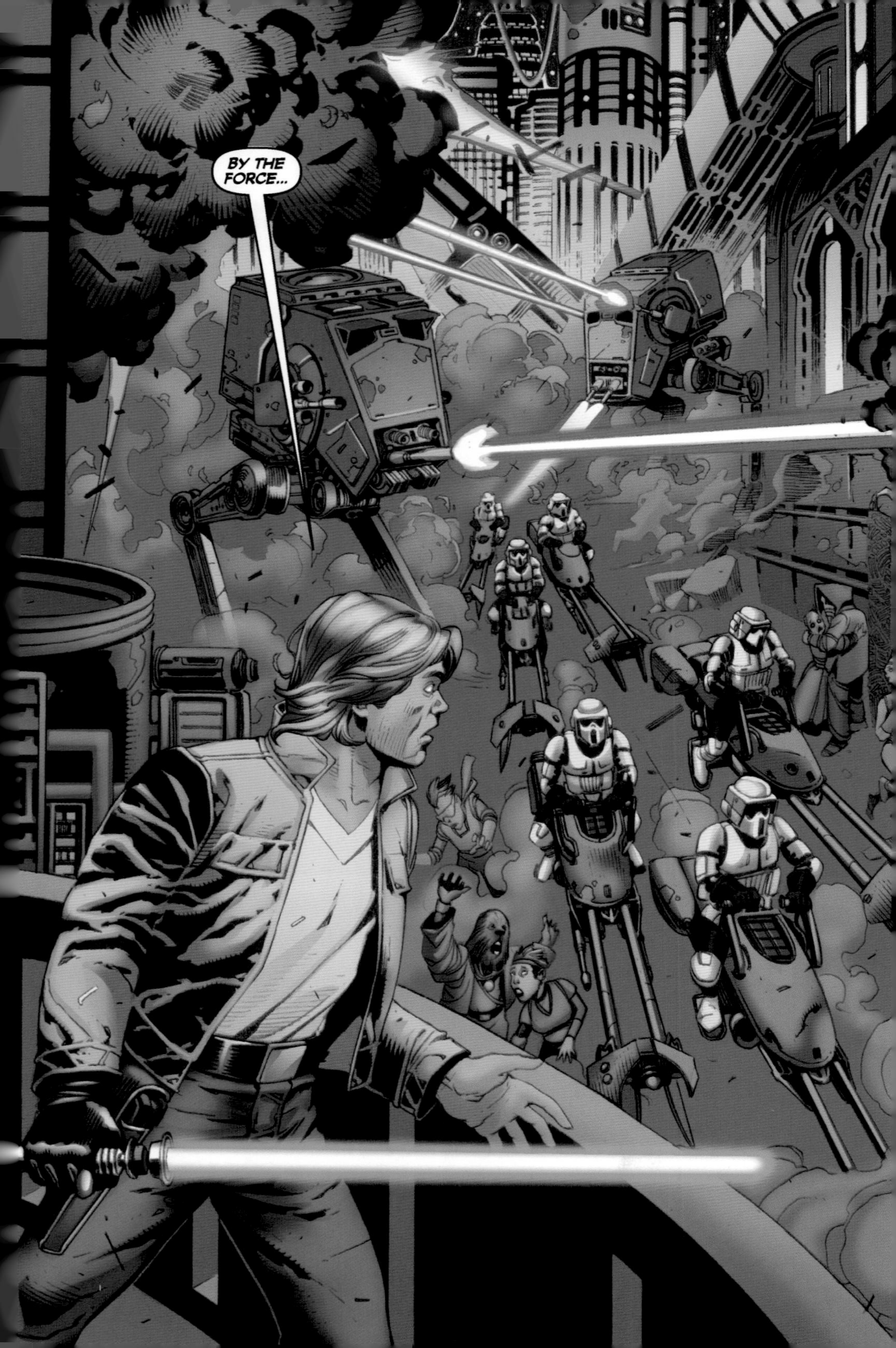
BY THE FORCE...

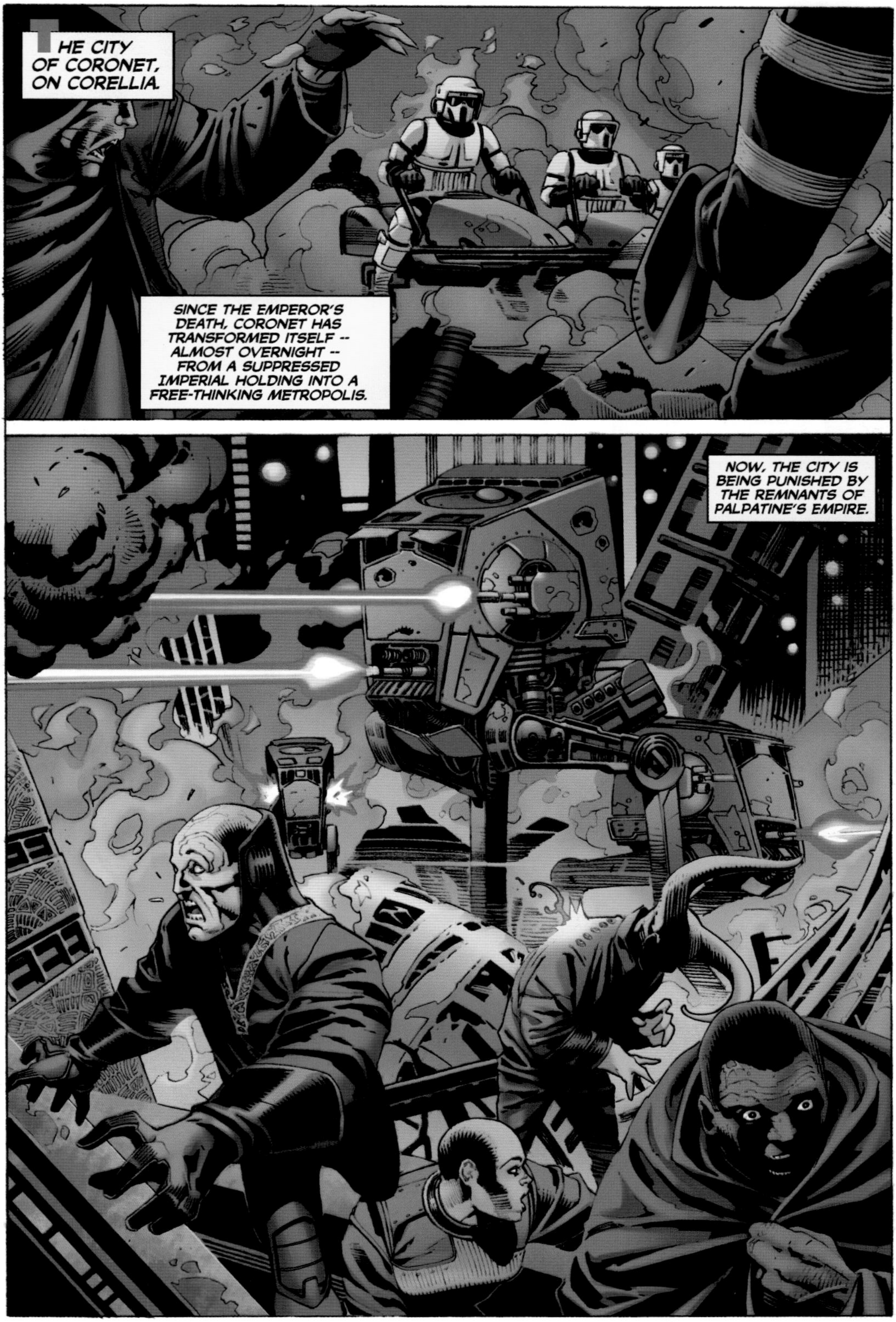
THE CITY OF CORONET, ON CORELLIA.
SINCE THE EMPEROR'S DEATH, CORONET HAS TRANSFORMED ITSELF -- ALMOST OVERNIGHT -- FROM A SUPPRESSED IMPERIAL HOLDING INTO A FREE-THINKING METROPOLIS.
NOW, THE CITY IS BEING PUNISHED BY THE REMNANTS OF PALPATINE'S EMPIRE.

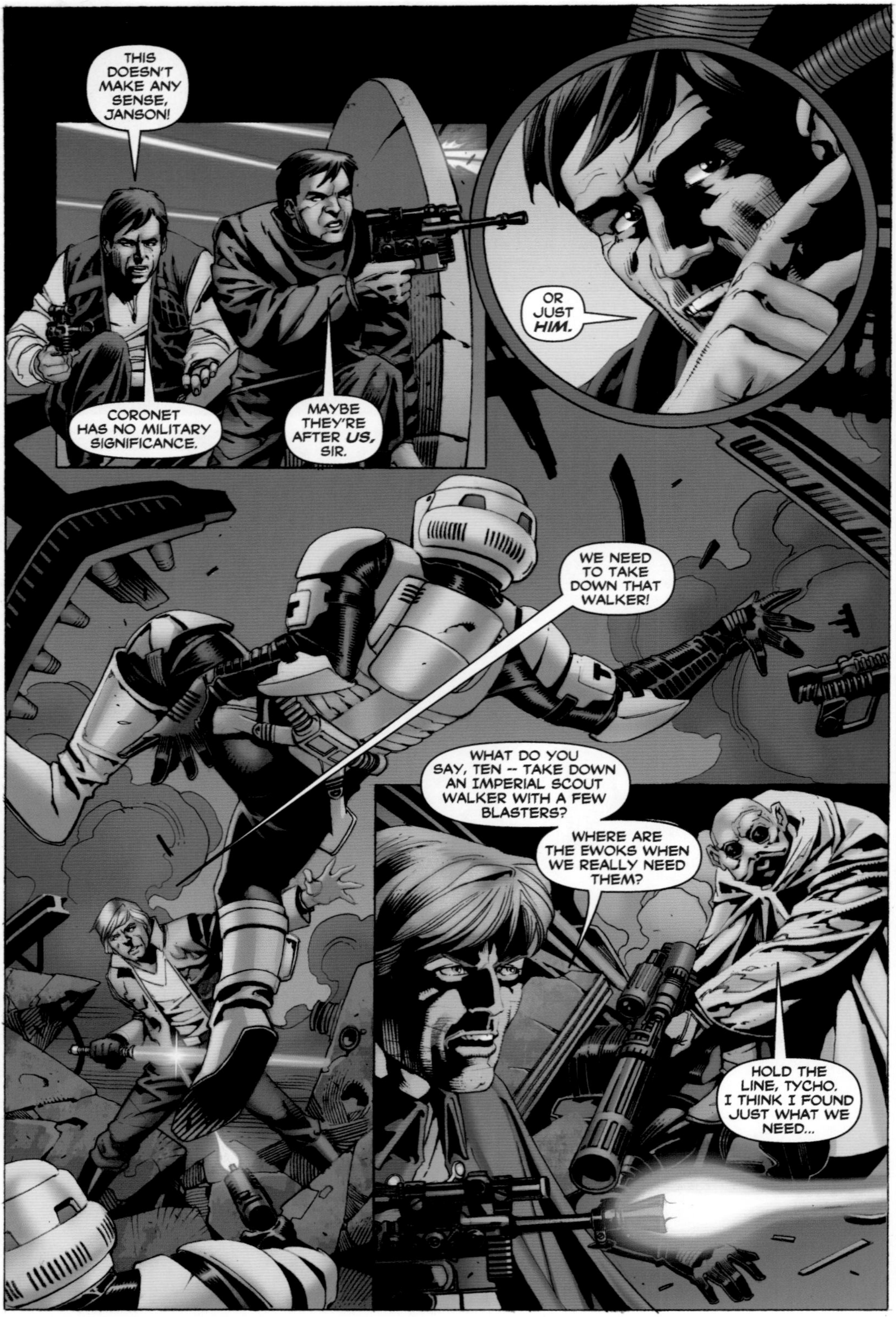
THIS DOESN'T MAKE ANY SENSE, JANSON!
CORONET HAS NO MILITARY SIGNIFICANCE.
MAYBE THEY'RE AFTER *US,* SIR.
OR JUST *HIM.*
WE NEED TO TAKE DOWN THAT WALKER!
WHAT DO YOU SAY, TEN -- TAKE DOWN AN IMPERIAL SCOUT WALKER WITH A FEW BLASTERS?
WHERE ARE THE EWOKS WHEN WE REALLY NEED THEM?
HOLD THE LINE, TYCHO. I THINK I FOUND JUST WHAT WE NEED...

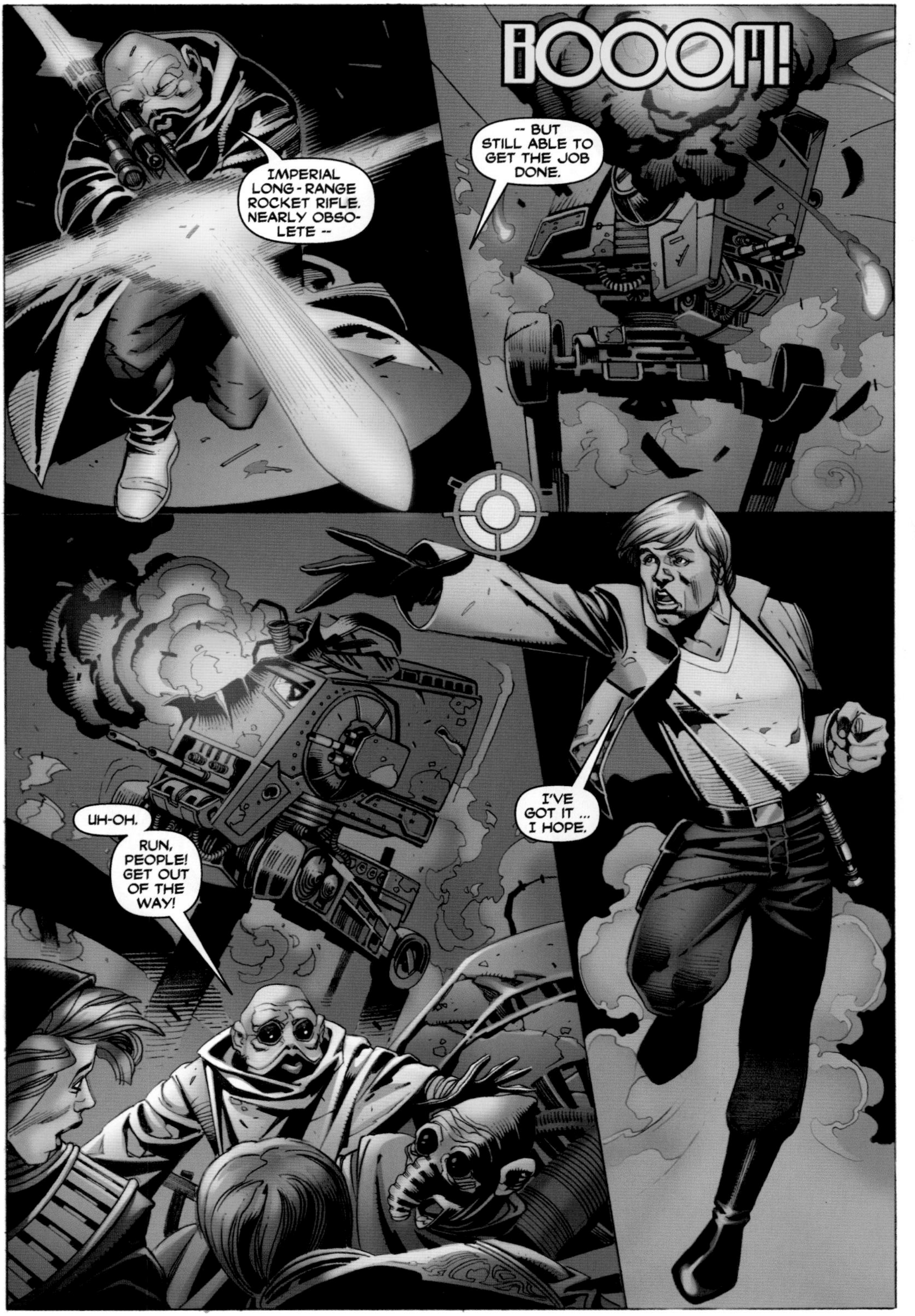

BOOOM!
IMPERIAL LONG-RANGE ROCKET RIFLE. NEARLY OBSOLETE --
-- BUT STILL ABLE TO GET THE JOB DONE.
UH-OH.
RUN, PEOPLE! GET OUT OF THE WAY!
I'VE GOT IT ... I HOPE.

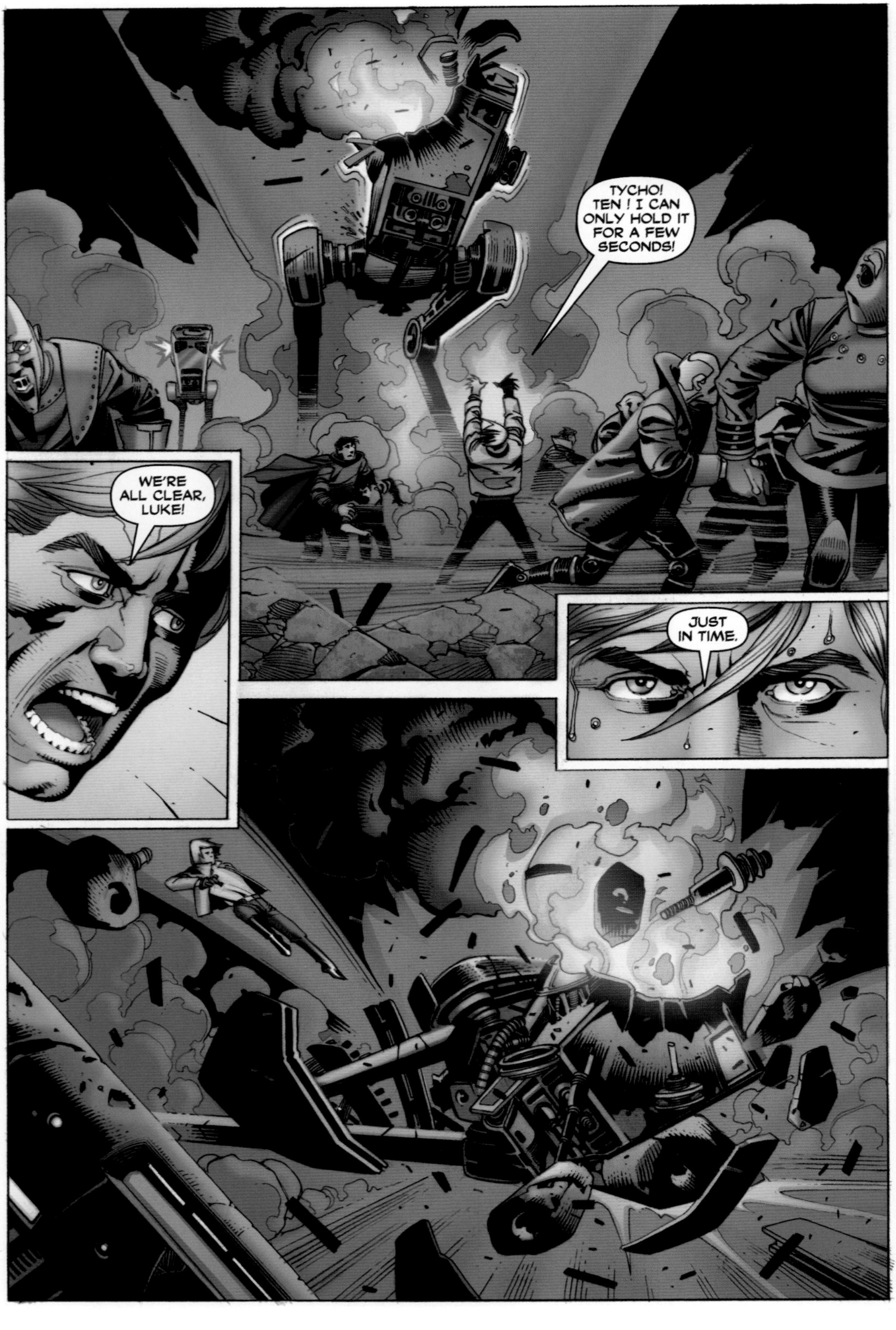
TYCHO! TEN ! I CAN ONLY HOLD IT FOR A FEW SECONDS!
WE'RE ALL CLEAR, LUKE!
JUST IN TIME.

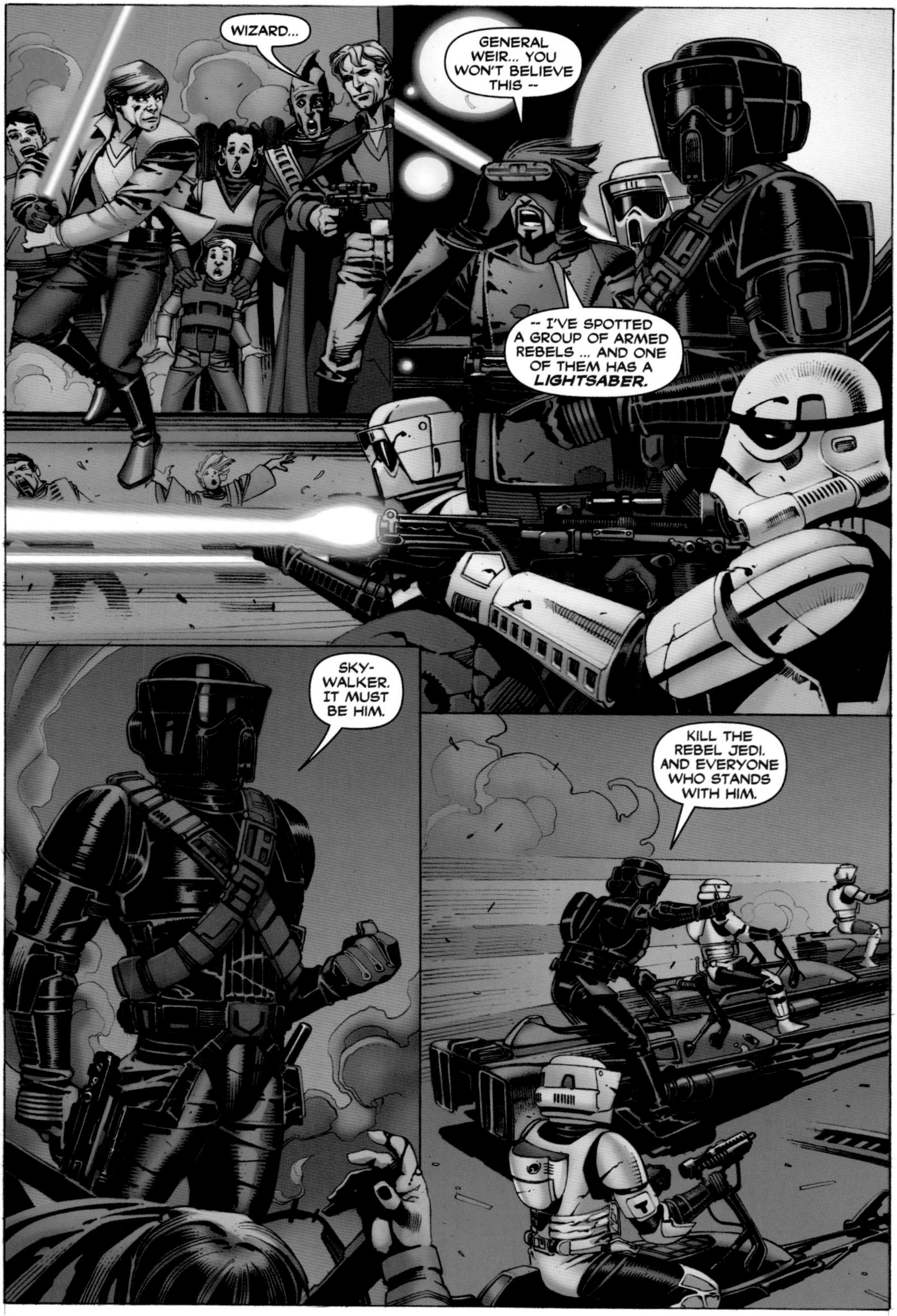
WIZARD...
GENERAL WEIR... YOU WON'T BELIEVE THIS --
-- I'VE SPOTTED A GROUP OF ARMED REBELS ... AND ONE OF THEM HAS A *LIGHTSABER.*
SKY-WALKER. IT MUST BE HIM.
KILL THE REBEL JEDI. AND EVERYONE WHO STANDS WITH HIM.

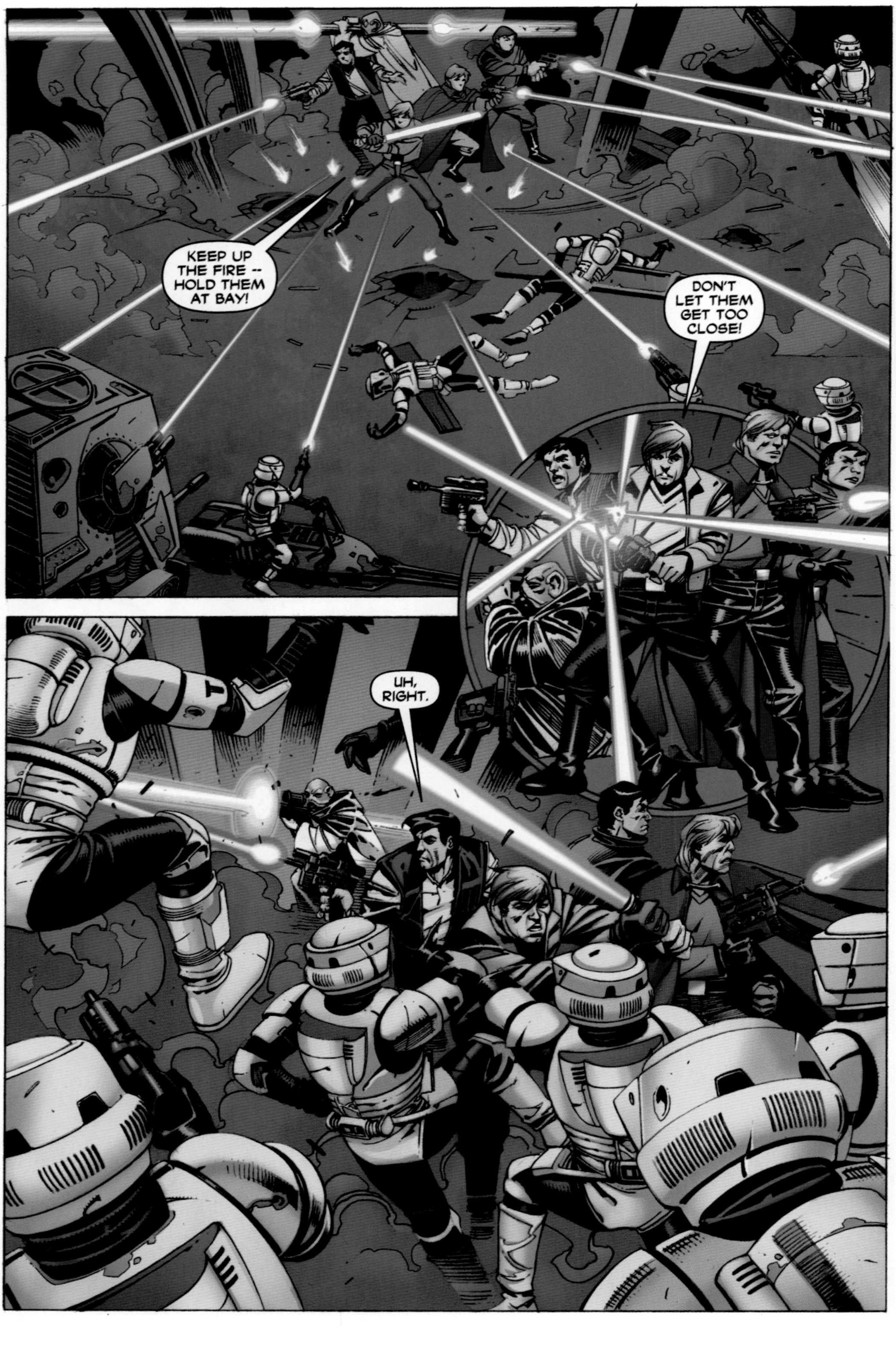

KEEP UP THE FIRE -- HOLD THEM AT BAY!
DON'T LET THEM GET TOO CLOSE!
UH, RIGHT.

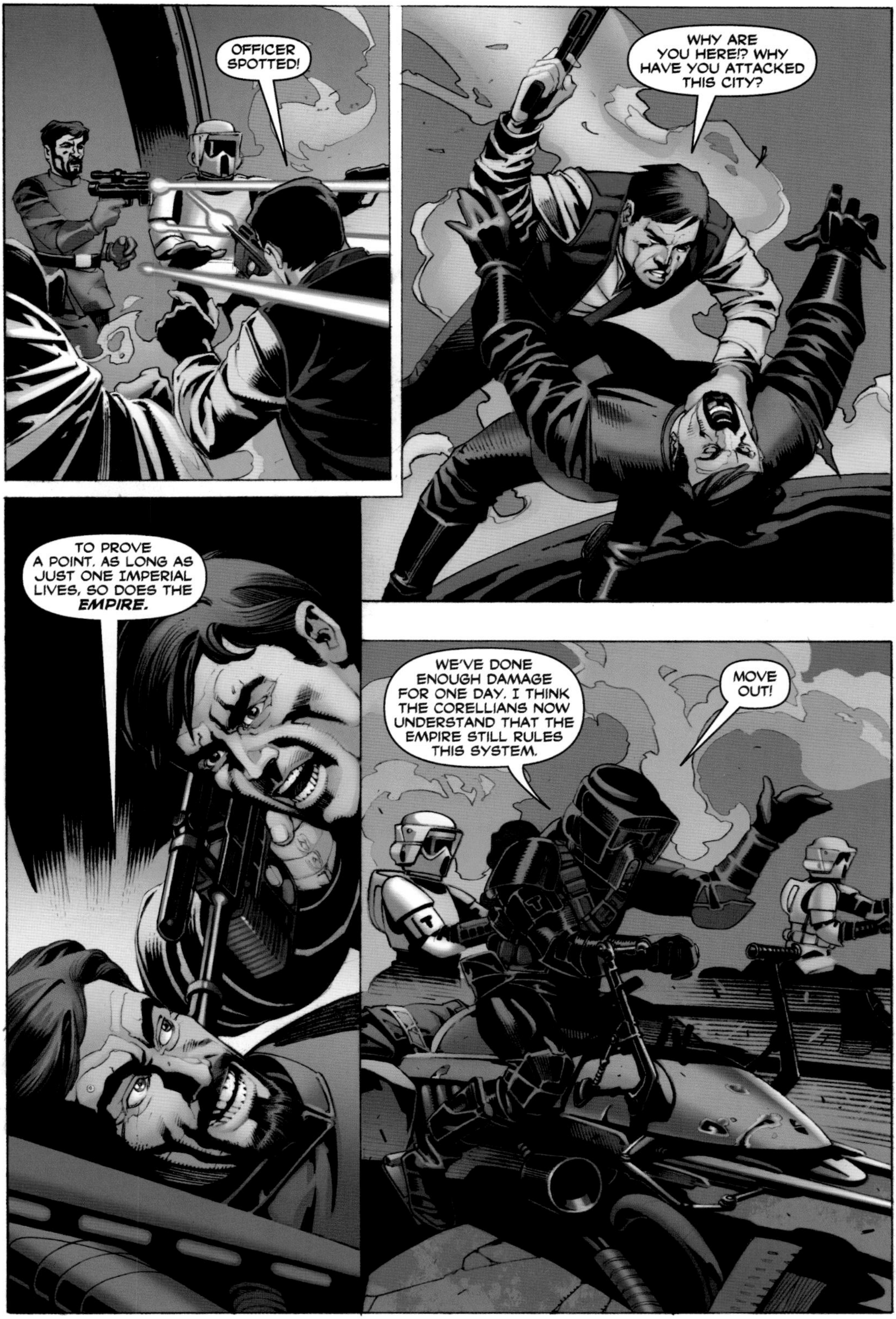

OFFICER SPOTTED!
WHY ARE YOU HERE!? WHY HAVE YOU ATTACKED THIS CITY?
TO PROVE A POINT. AS LONG AS JUST ONE IMPERIAL LIVES, SO DOES THE *EMPIRE.*
WE'VE DONE ENOUGH DAMAGE FOR ONE DAY. I THINK THE CORELLIANS NOW UNDERSTAND THAT THE EMPIRE STILL RULES THIS SYSTEM.
MOVE OUT!

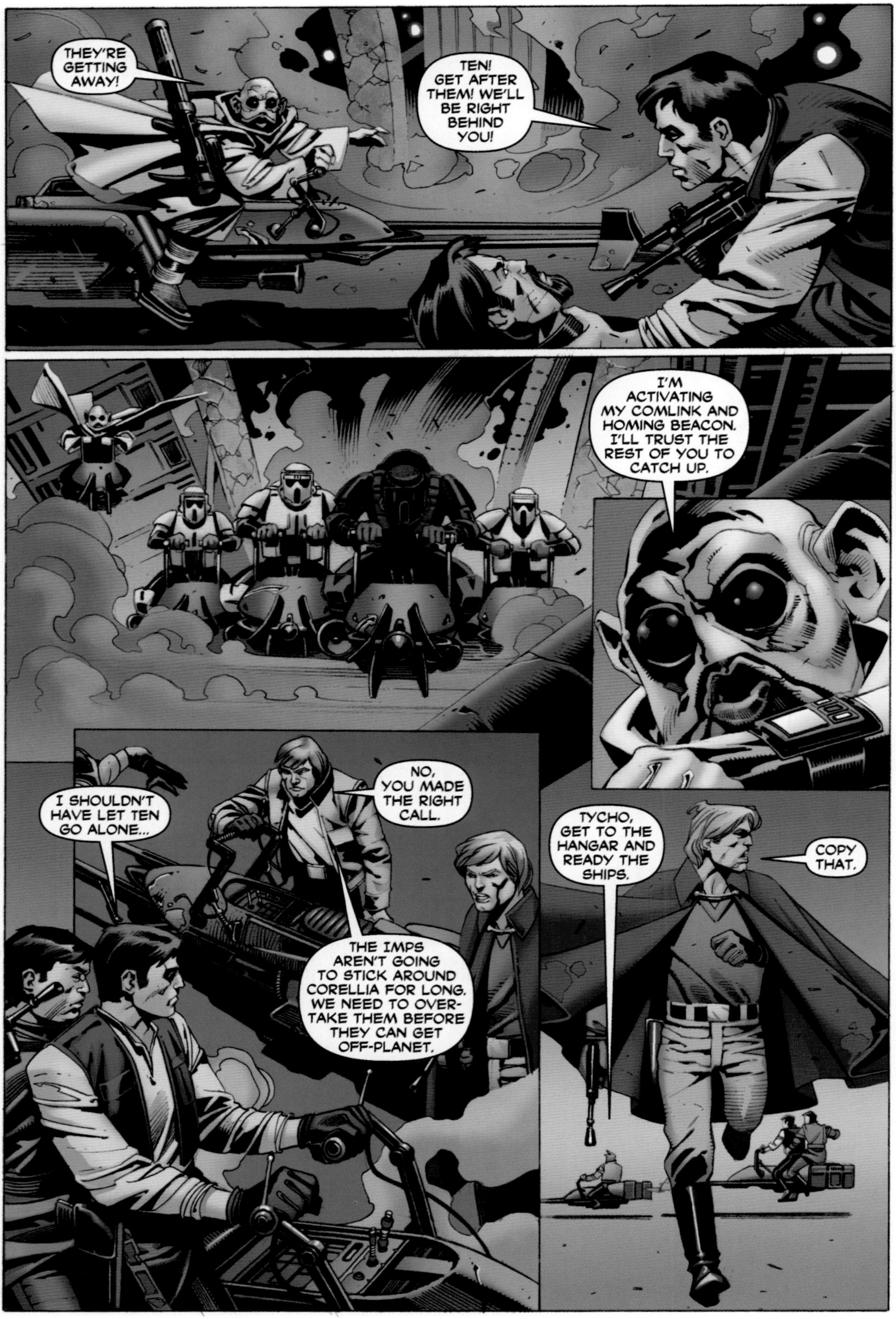
THEY'RE GETTING AWAY!
TEN! GET AFTER THEM! WE'LL BE RIGHT BEHIND YOU!
I'M ACTIVATING MY COMLINK AND HOMING BEACON. I'LL TRUST THE REST OF YOU TO CATCH UP.
I SHOULDN'T HAVE LET TEN GO ALONE...
NO, YOU MADE THE RIGHT CALL.
THE IMPS AREN'T GOING TO STICK AROUND CORELLIA FOR LONG. WE NEED TO OVER-TAKE THEM BEFORE THEY CAN GET OFF-PLANET.
TYCHO, GET TO THE HANGAR AND READY THE SHIPS.
COPY THAT.

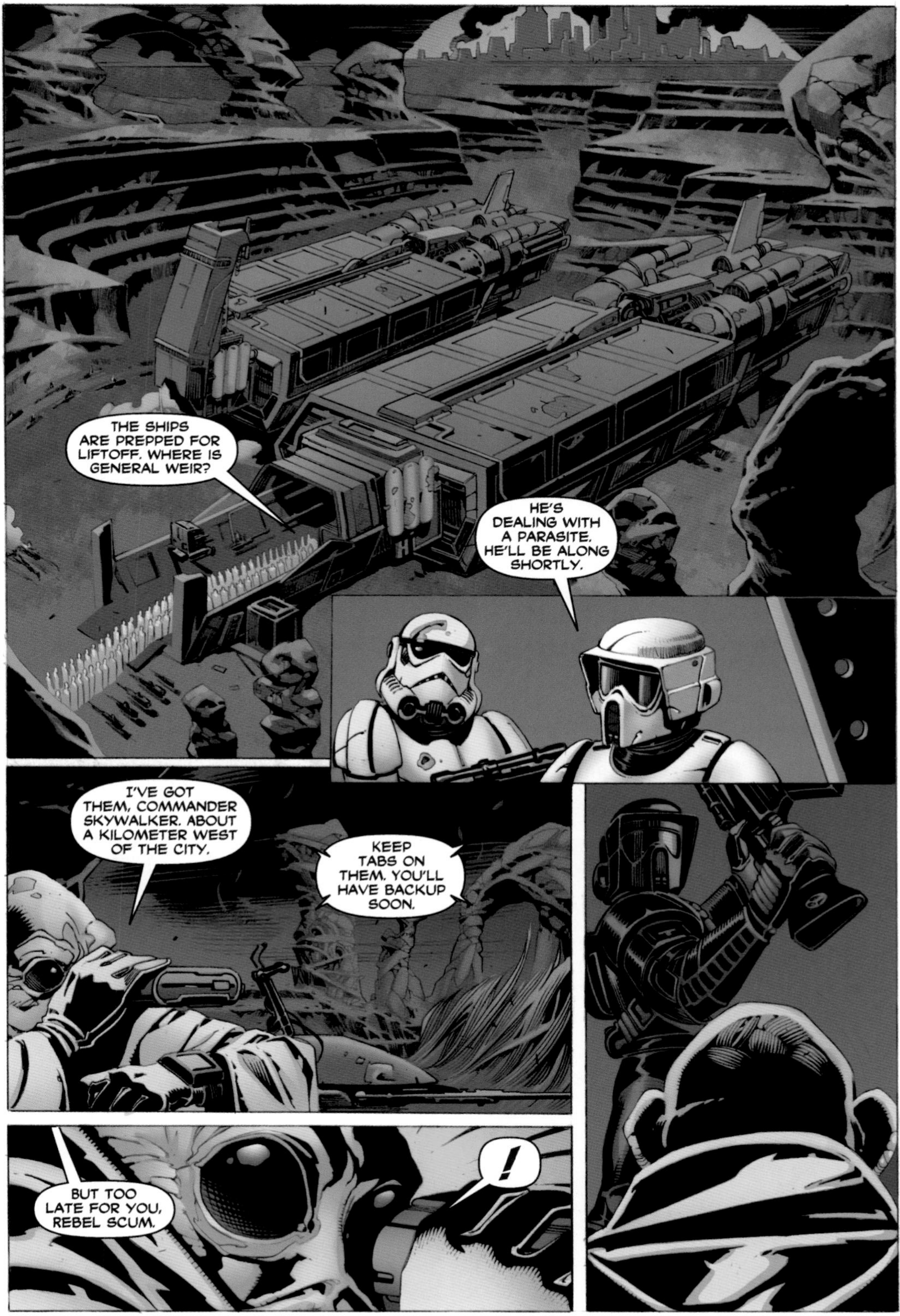
THE SHIPS ARE PREPPED FOR LIFTOFF. WHERE IS GENERAL WEIR?
HE'S DEALING WITH A PARASITE. HE'LL BE ALONG SHORTLY.
I'VE GOT THEM, COMMANDER SKYWALKER. ABOUT A KILOMETER WEST OF THE CITY.
KEEP TABS ON THEM. YOU'LL HAVE BACKUP SOON.
BUT TOO LATE FOR YOU, REBEL SCUM.
!

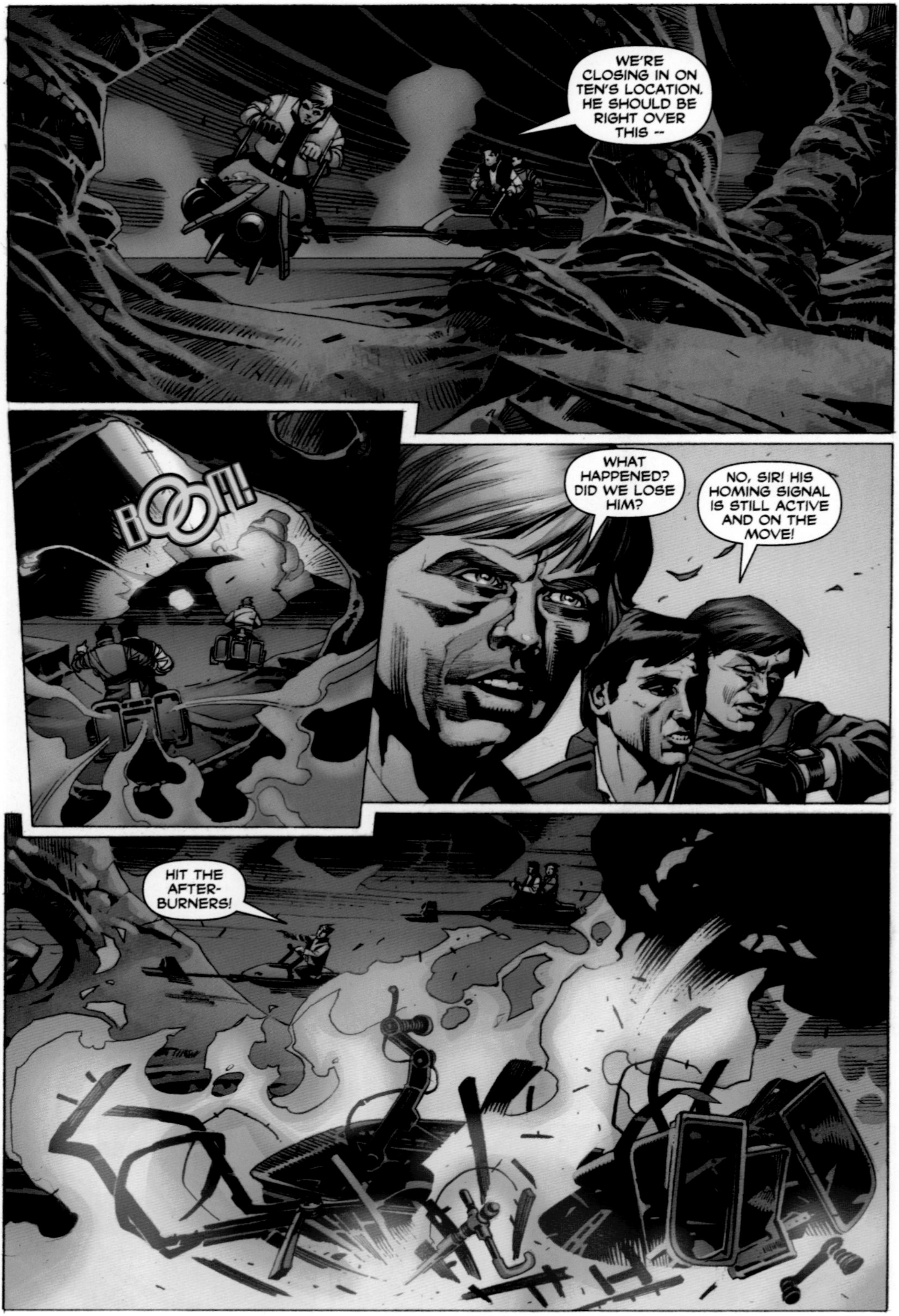
WE'RE CLOSING IN ON TEN'S LOCATION. HE SHOULD BE RIGHT OVER THIS --
BOOM!
WHAT HAPPENED? DID WE LOSE HIM?
NO, SIR! HIS HOMING SIGNAL IS STILL ACTIVE AND ON THE MOVE!
HIT THE AFTER-BURNERS!

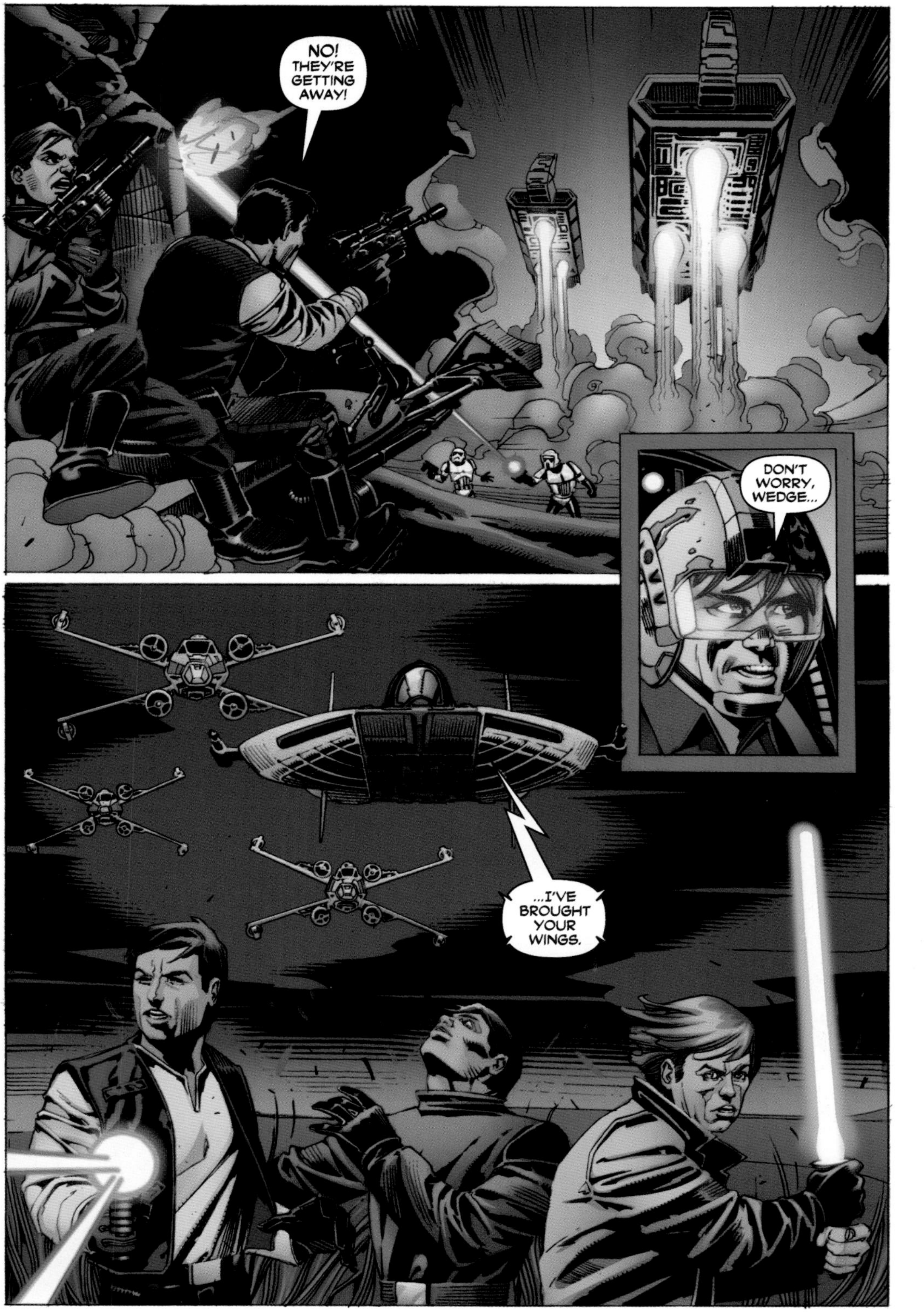
NO! THEY'RE GETTING AWAY!
DON'T WORRY, WEDGE...
...I'VE BROUGHT YOUR WINGS.

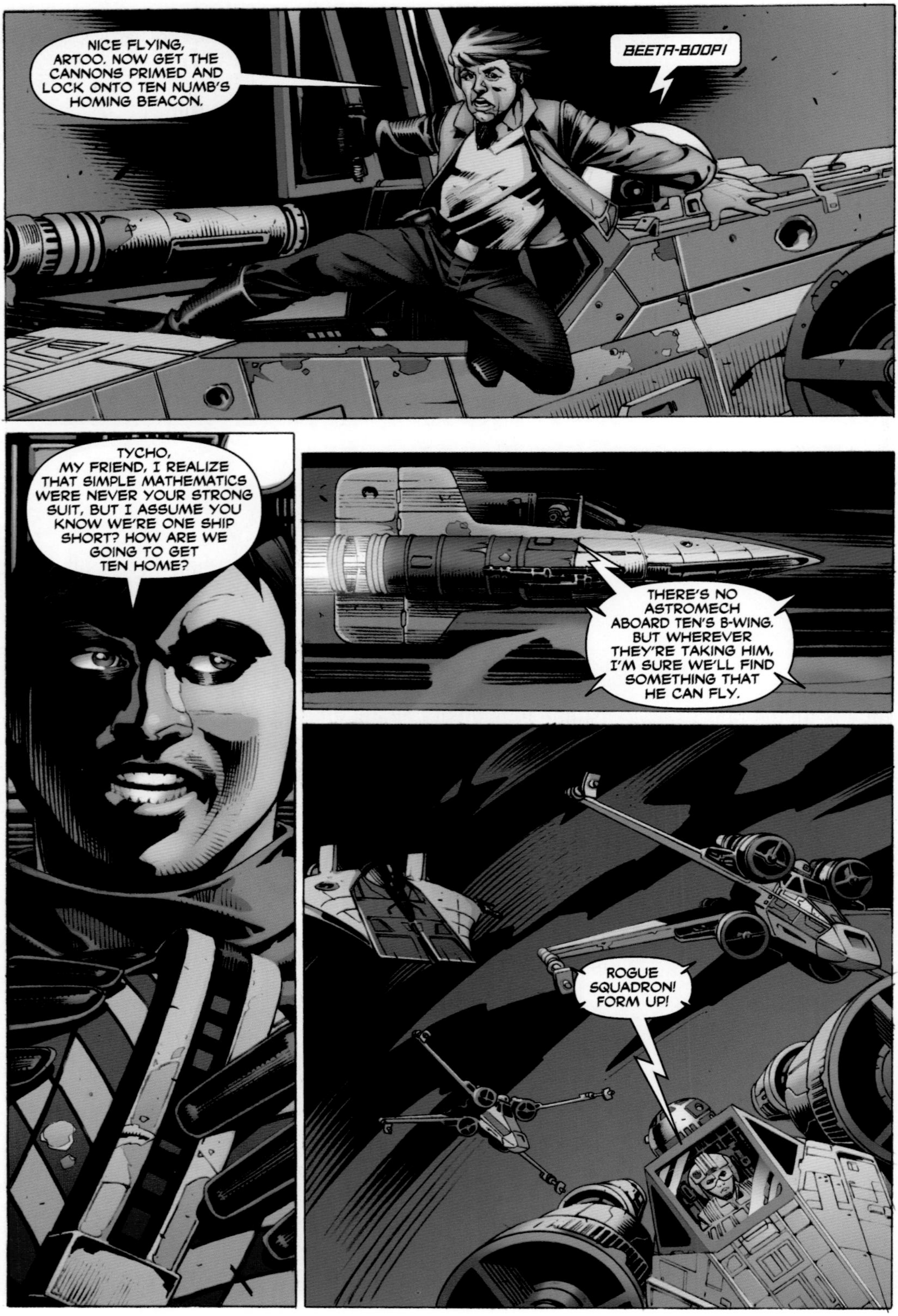
NICE FLYING, ARTOO. NOW GET THE CANNONS PRIMED AND LOCK ONTO TEN NUMB'S HOMING BEACON.
BEETA-BOOP!
TYCHO, MY FRIEND, I REALIZE THAT SIMPLE MATHEMATICS WERE NEVER YOUR STRONG SUIT, BUT I ASSUME YOU KNOW WE'RE ONE SHIP SHORT? HOW ARE WE GOING TO GET TEN HOME?
THERE'S NO ASTROMECH ABOARD TEN'S B-WING. BUT WHEREVER THEY'RE TAKING HIM, I'M SURE WE'LL FIND SOMETHING THAT HE CAN FLY.
ROGUE SQUADRON! FORM UP!

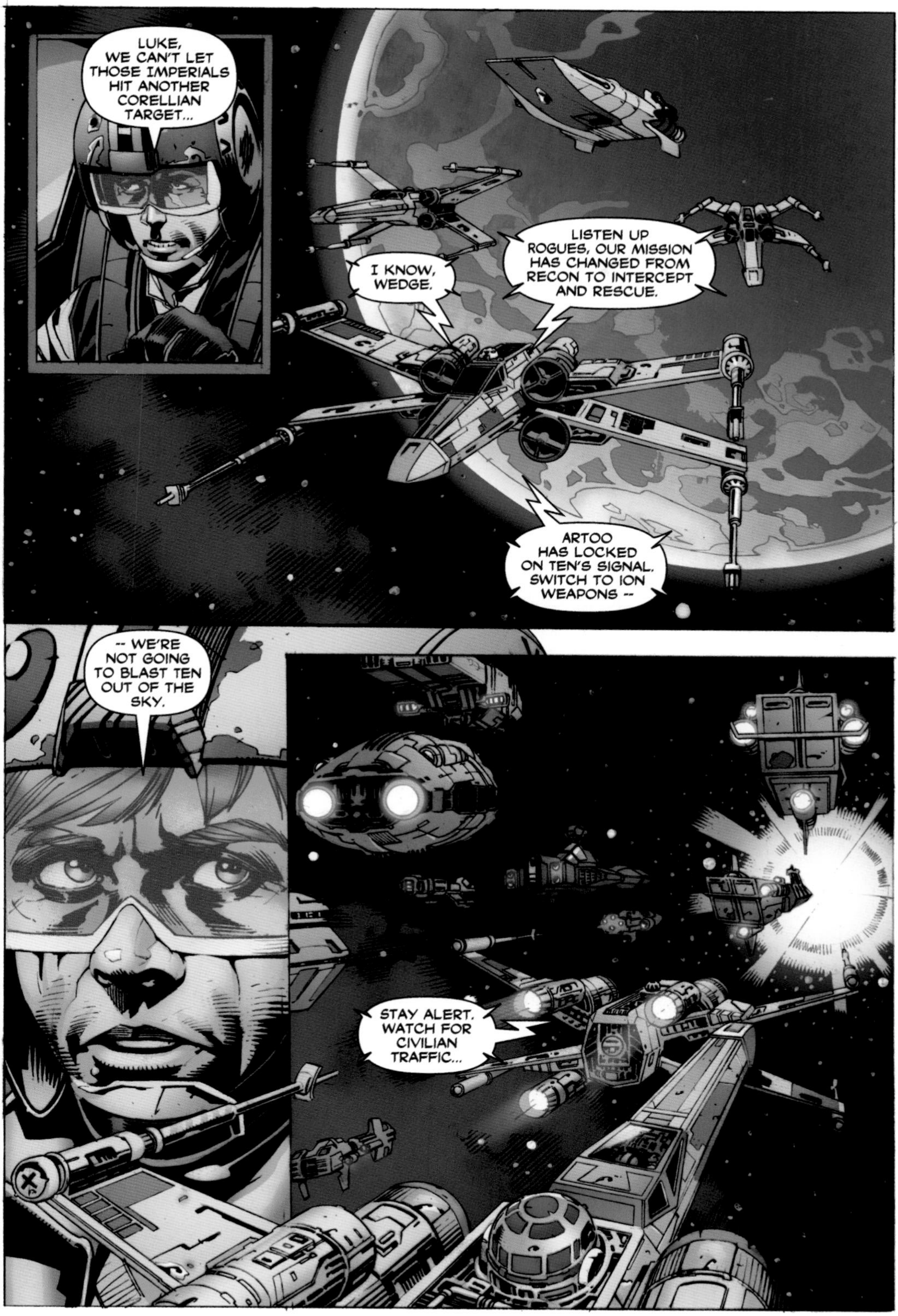
LUKE, WE CAN'T LET THOSE IMPERIALS HIT ANOTHER CORELLIAN TARGET...
I KNOW, WEDGE.
LISTEN UP ROGUES, OUR MISSION HAS CHANGED FROM RECON TO INTERCEPT AND RESCUE.
ARTOO HAS LOCKED ON TEN'S SIGNAL. SWITCH TO ION WEAPONS --
-- WE'RE NOT GOING TO BLAST TEN OUT OF THE SKY.
STAY ALERT. WATCH FOR CIVILIAN TRAFFIC...

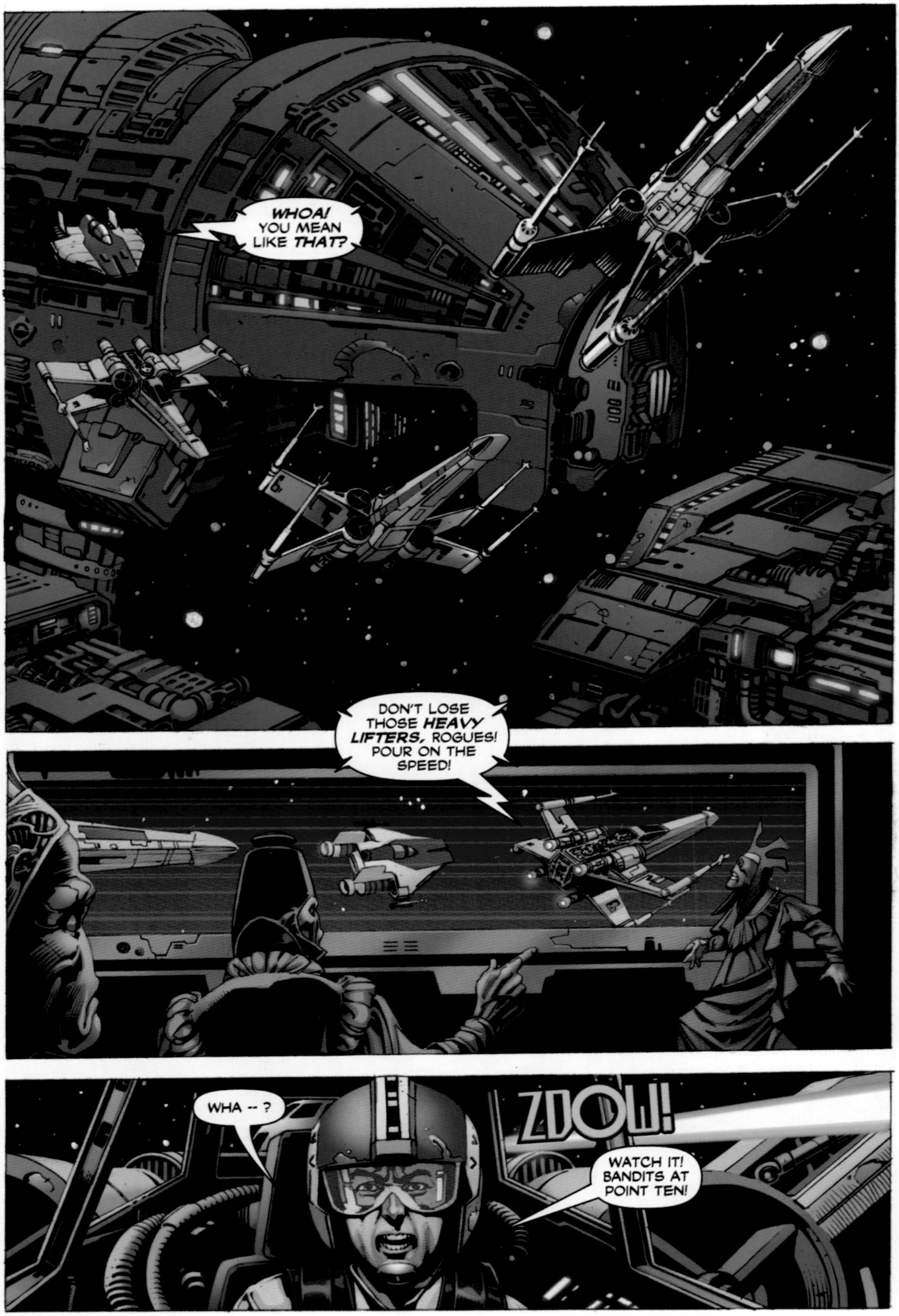
WHOA! YOU MEAN LIKE THAT?
DON'T LOSE THOSE HEAVY LIFTERS, ROGUES! POUR ON THE SPEED!
WHA -- ?
ZDOW!
WATCH IT! BANDITS AT POINT TEN!

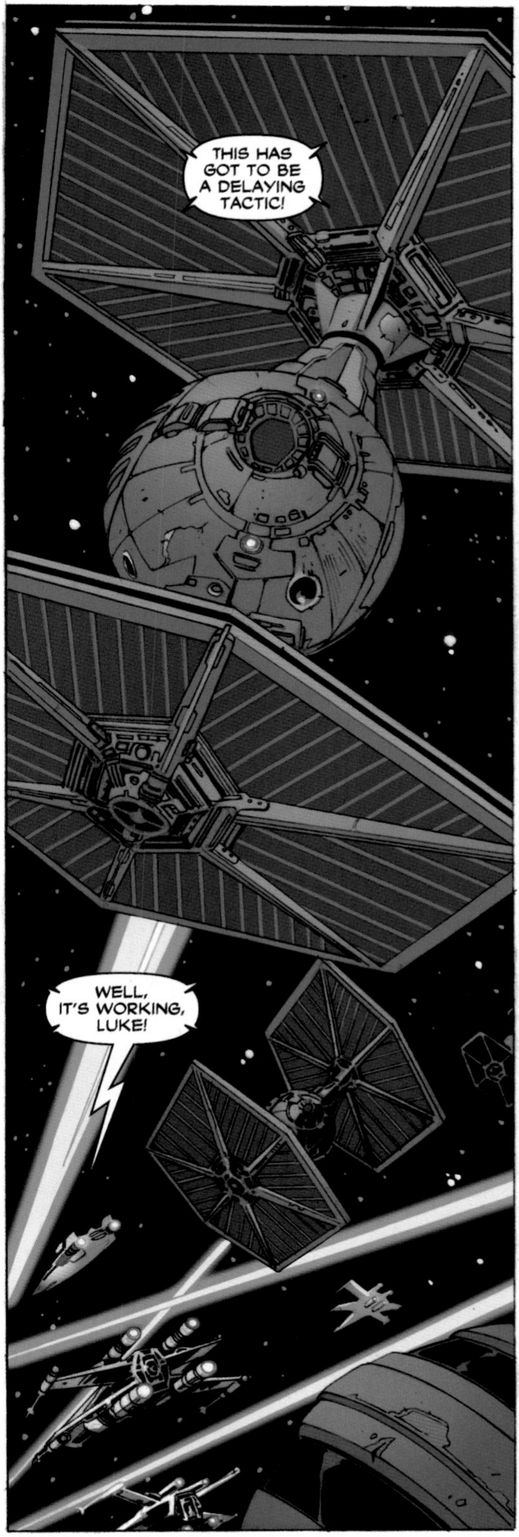
THIS HAS GOT TO BE A DELAYING TACTIC!
WELL, IT'S WORKING, LUKE!

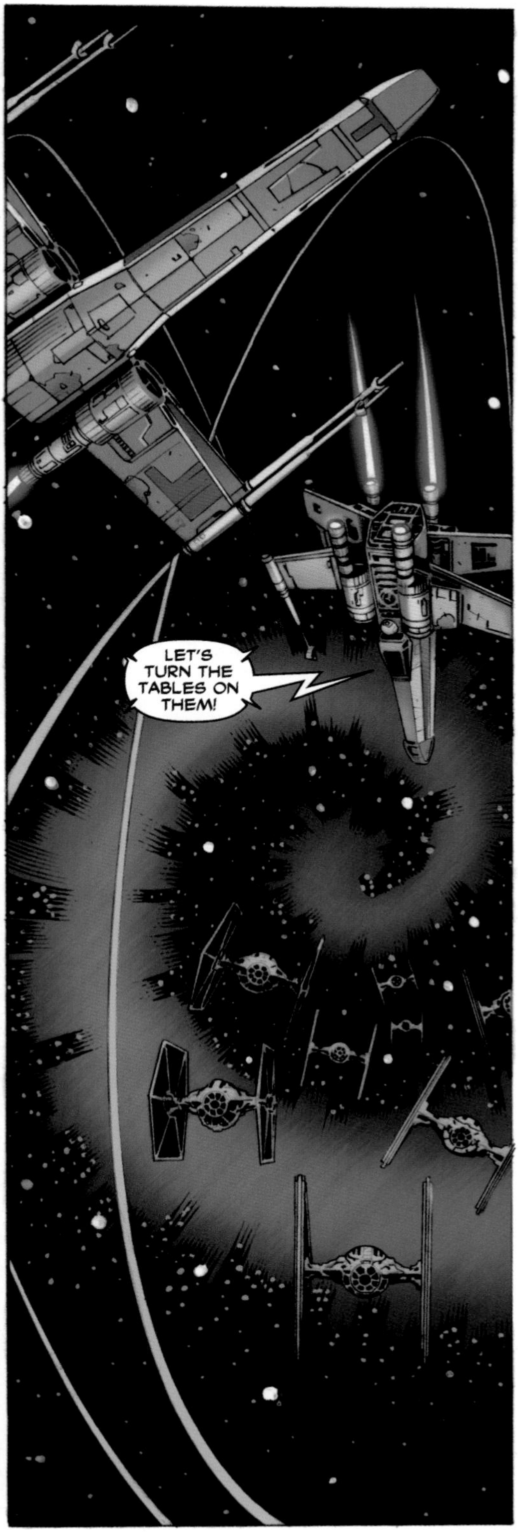
LET'S TURN THE TABLES ON THEM!

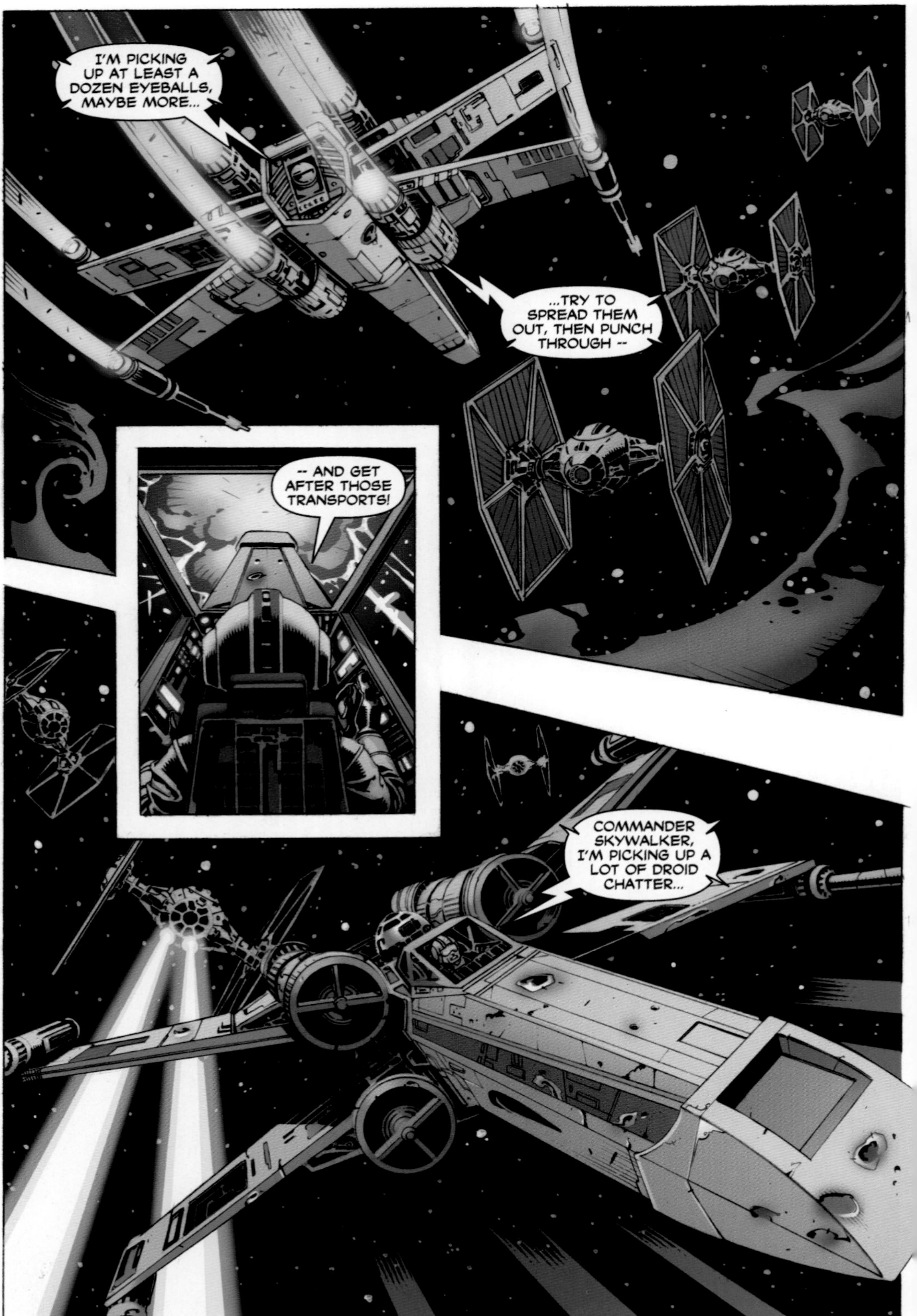

I'M PICKING UP AT LEAST A DOZEN EYEBALLS, MAYBE MORE...
...TRY TO SPREAD THEM OUT, THEN PUNCH THROUGH --
-- AND GET AFTER THOSE TRANSPORTS!
COMMANDER SKYWALKER, I'M PICKING UP A LOT OF DROID CHATTER...

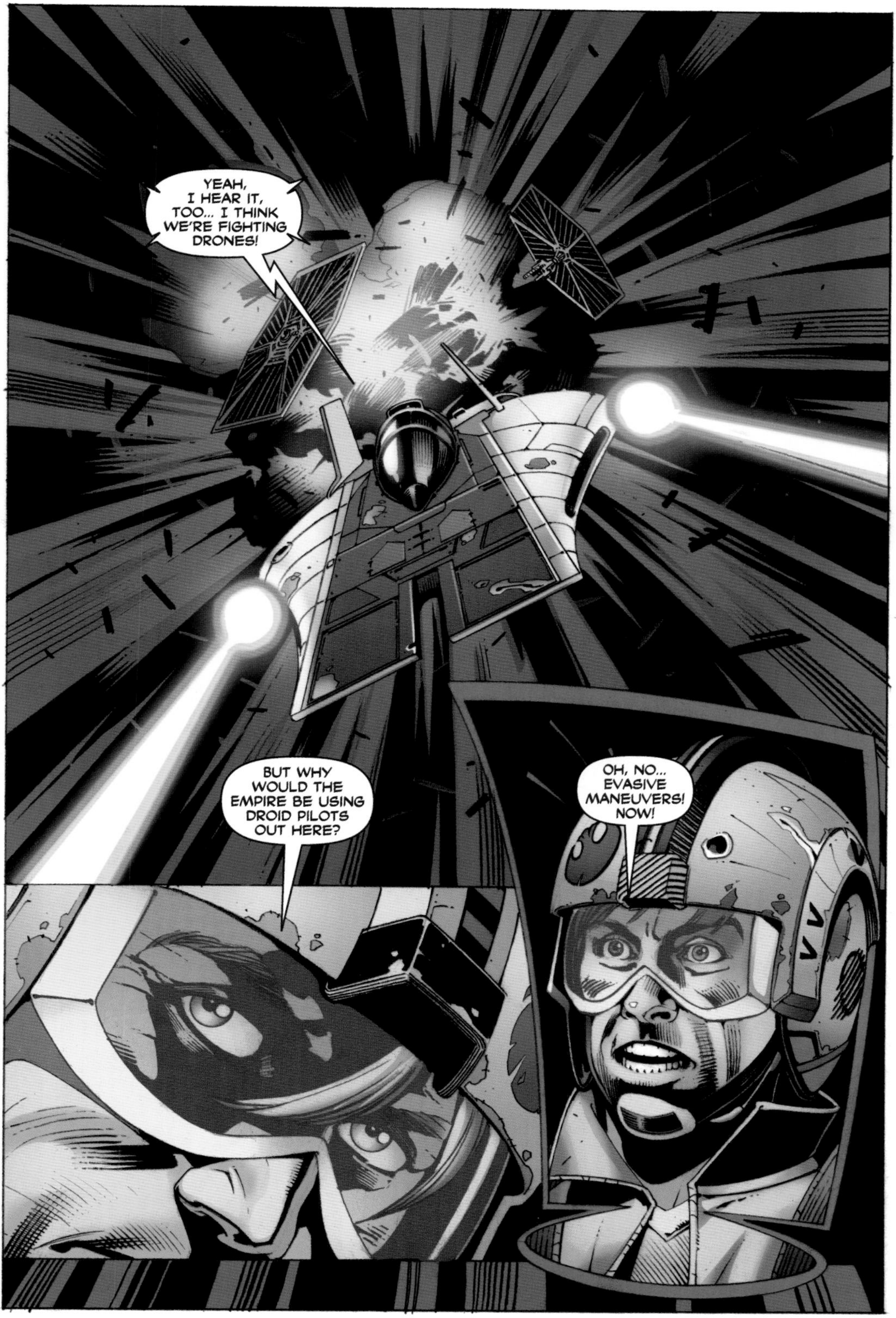
YEAH, I HEAR IT, TOO... I THINK WE'RE FIGHTING DRONES!
BUT WHY WOULD THE EMPIRE BE USING DROID PILOTS OUT HERE?
OH, NO... EVASIVE MANEUVERS! NOW!

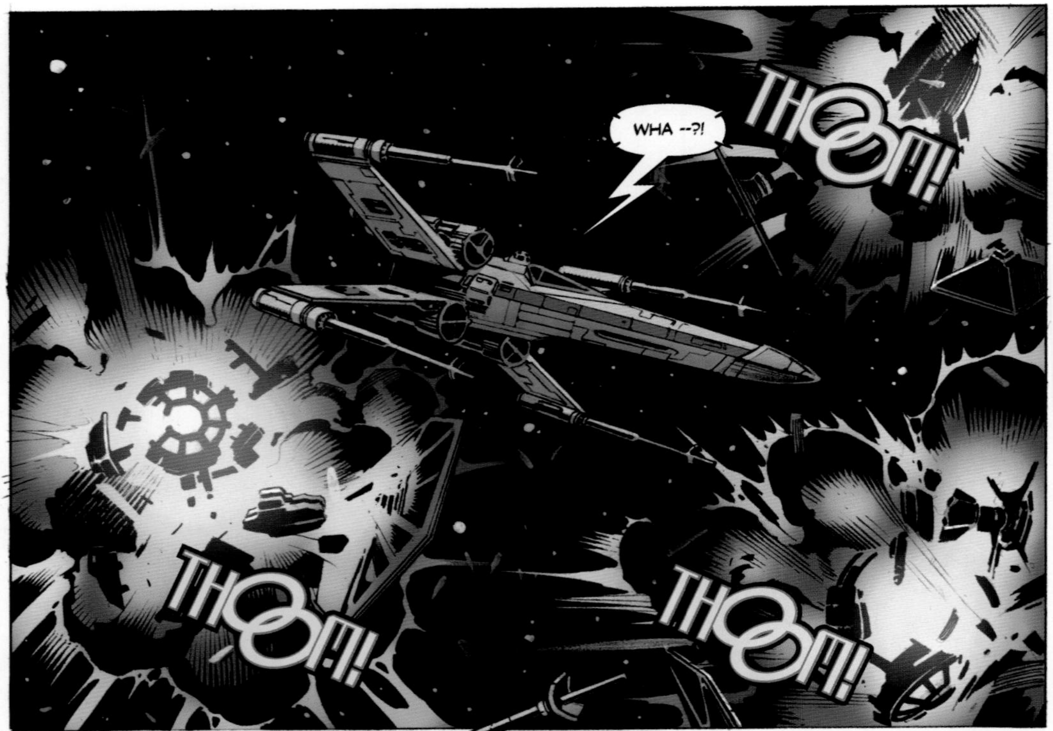
THOOM!
WHA --?!
THOOM!
THOOM!

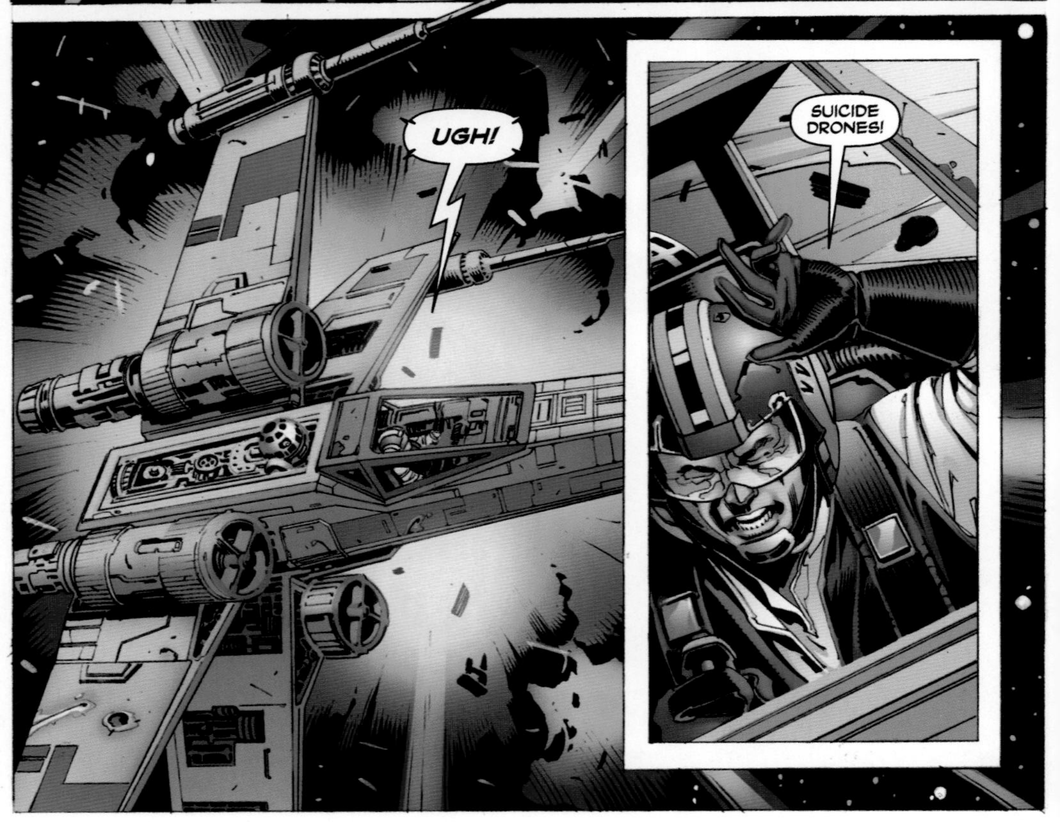
UGH!
SUICIDE DRONES!

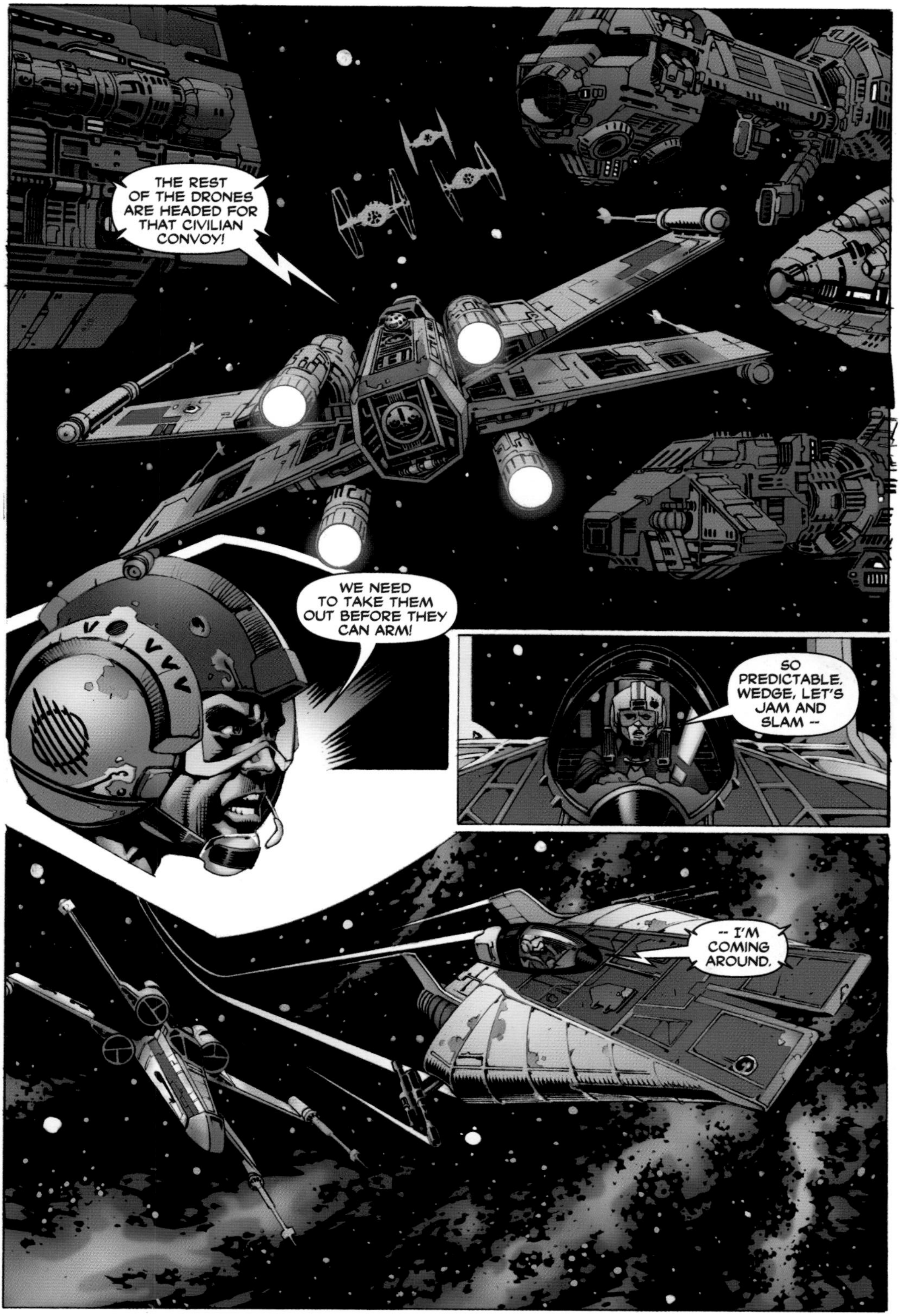
THE REST OF THE DRONES ARE HEADED FOR THAT CIVILIAN CONVOY!
WE NEED TO TAKE THEM OUT BEFORE THEY CAN ARM!
SO PREDICTABLE, WEDGE. LET'S JAM AND SLAM --
-- I'M COMING AROUND.

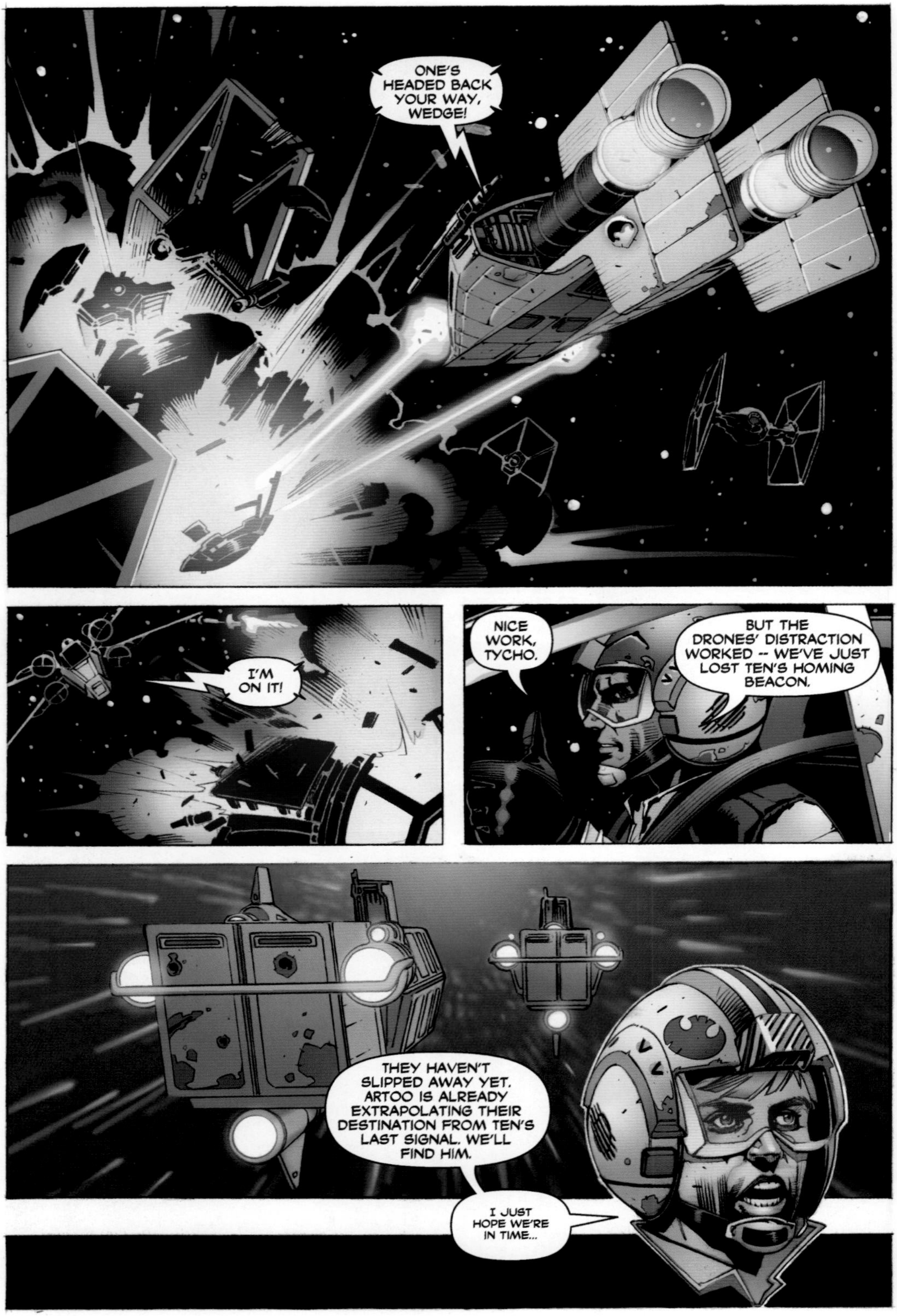
ONE'S HEADED BACK YOUR WAY, WEDGE!
I'M ON IT!
NICE WORK, TYCHO.
BUT THE DRONES' DISTRACTION WORKED -- WE'VE JUST LOST TEN'S HOMING BEACON.
THEY HAVEN'T SLIPPED AWAY YET. ARTOO IS ALREADY EXTRAPOLATING THEIR DESTINATION FROM TEN'S LAST SIGNAL. WE'LL FIND HIM.
I JUST HOPE WE'RE IN TIME...

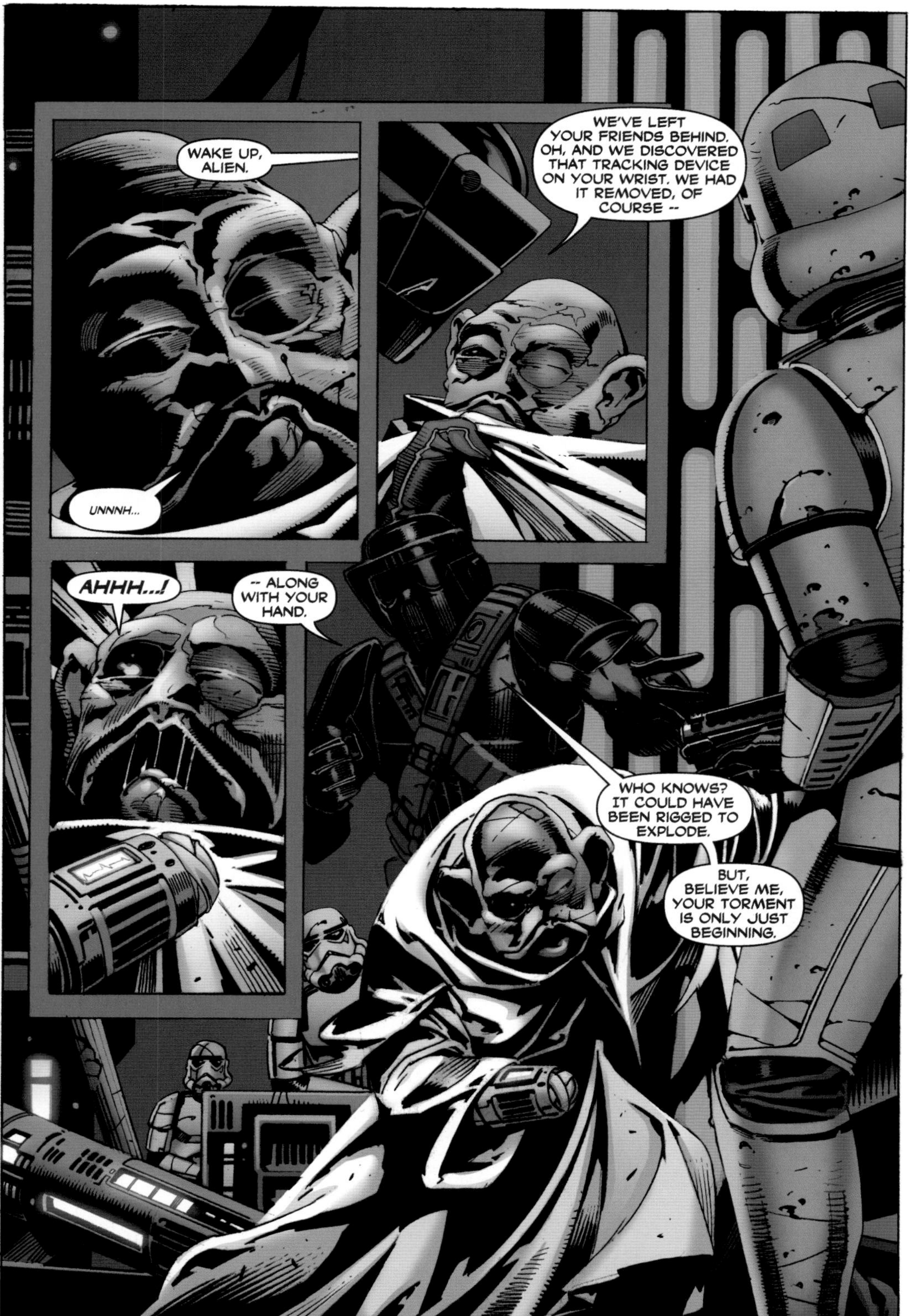
WAKE UP, ALIEN.
UNNNH...
WE'VE LEFT YOUR FRIENDS BEHIND. OH, AND WE DISCOVERED THAT TRACKING DEVICE ON YOUR WRIST. WE HAD IT REMOVED, OF COURSE --
AHHH...!
-- ALONG WITH YOUR HAND.
WHO KNOWS? IT COULD HAVE BEEN RIGGED TO EXPLODE.
BUT, BELIEVE ME, YOUR TORMENT IS ONLY JUST BEGINNING.

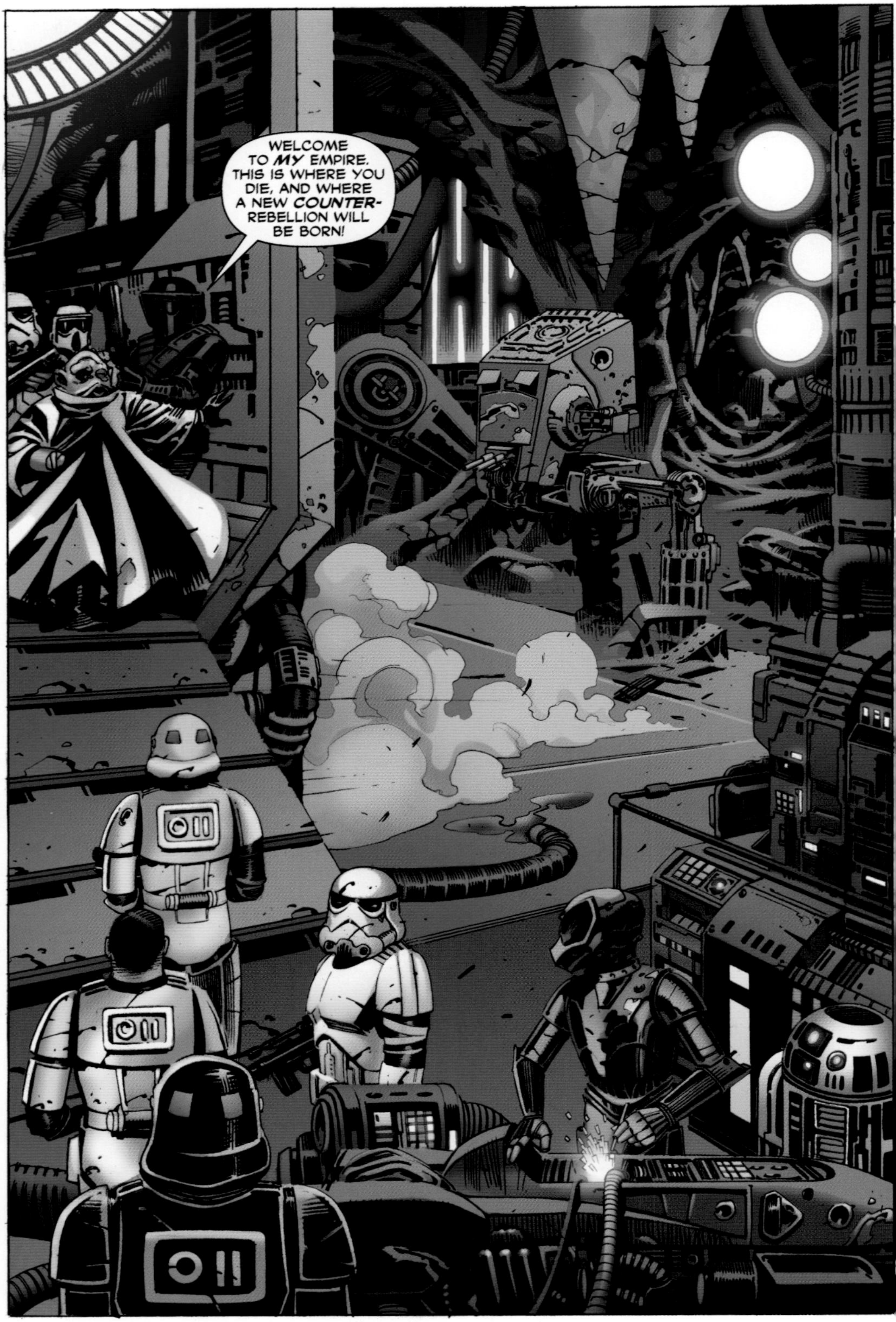
WELCOME TO *MY* EMPIRE. THIS IS WHERE YOU DIE, AND WHERE A NEW *COUNTER*-REBELLION WILL BE BORN!

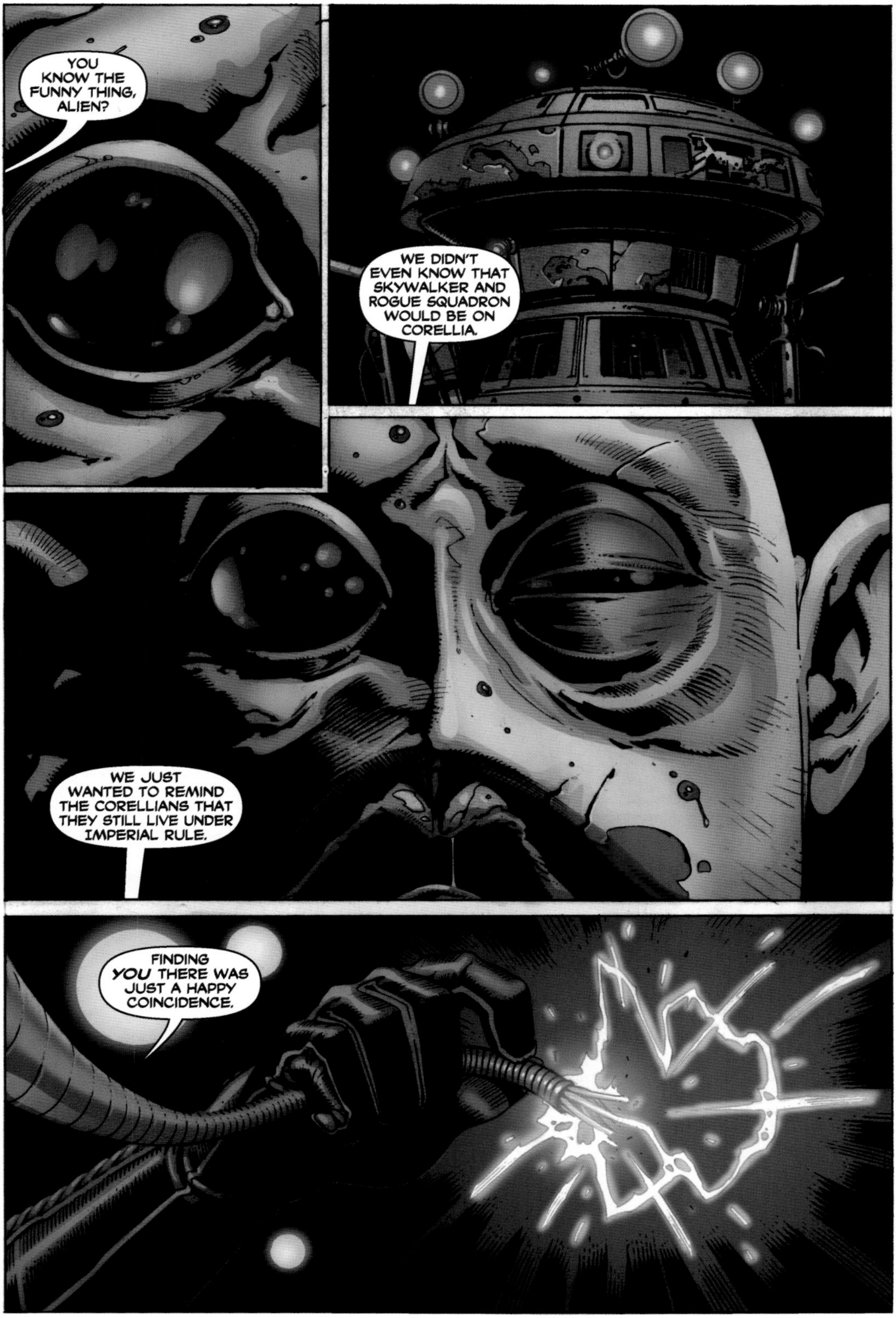
YOU KNOW THE FUNNY THING, ALIEN?
WE DIDN'T EVEN KNOW THAT SKYWALKER AND ROGUE SQUADRON WOULD BE ON CORELLIA.
WE JUST WANTED TO REMIND THE CORELLIANS THAT THEY STILL LIVE UNDER IMPERIAL RULE.
FINDING *YOU* THERE WAS JUST A HAPPY COINCIDENCE.

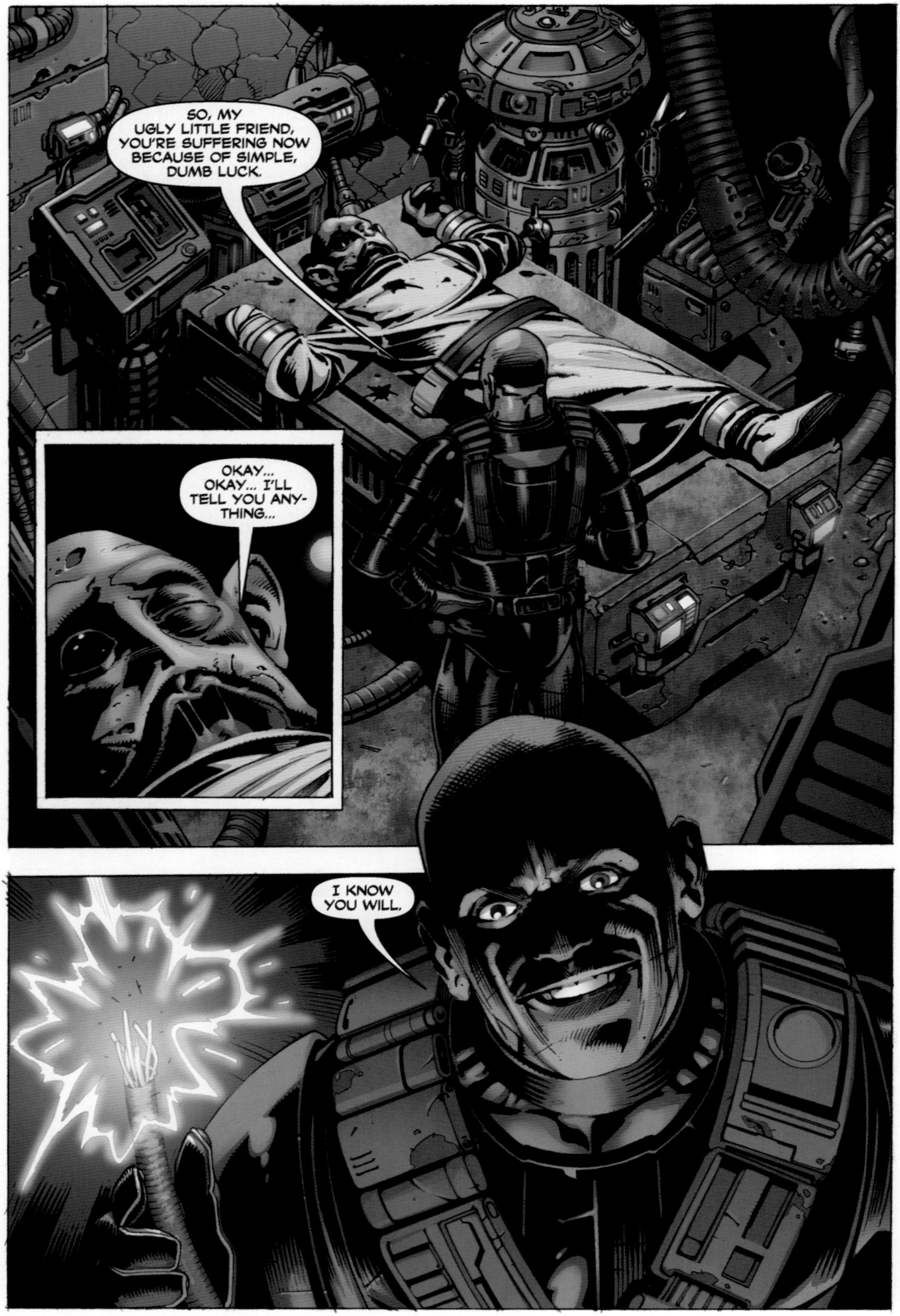

SO, MY UGLY LITTLE FRIEND, YOU'RE SUFFERING NOW BECAUSE OF SIMPLE, DUMB LUCK.
OKAY... OKAY... I'LL TELL YOU ANY-THING...
I KNOW YOU WILL.

WELCOME TO TRALUS, ROGUES...

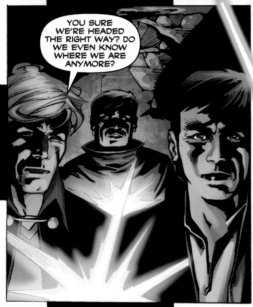

YOU SURE WE'RE HEADED THE RIGHT WAY? DO WE EVEN KNOW WHERE WE ARE ANYMORE?

ARTOO HAS BEEN MAPPING OUR PROGRESS AND HAS OUR POSITION LOCKED, TYCHO. WE'RE NOT LOST... YET.

GREAT, WE KNOW WHERE WE ARE, BUT WE STILL DON'T KNOW HOW TO FIND THE IMPERIALS.

ARTOO TRACKED THEM TO TRALUS, AND THE HUMANS ON THE SURFACE HAVE SEEN STORMTROOPERS USING THESE TUNNELS.

HOPEFULLY WE'LL FIND SOME CLUES DOWN --

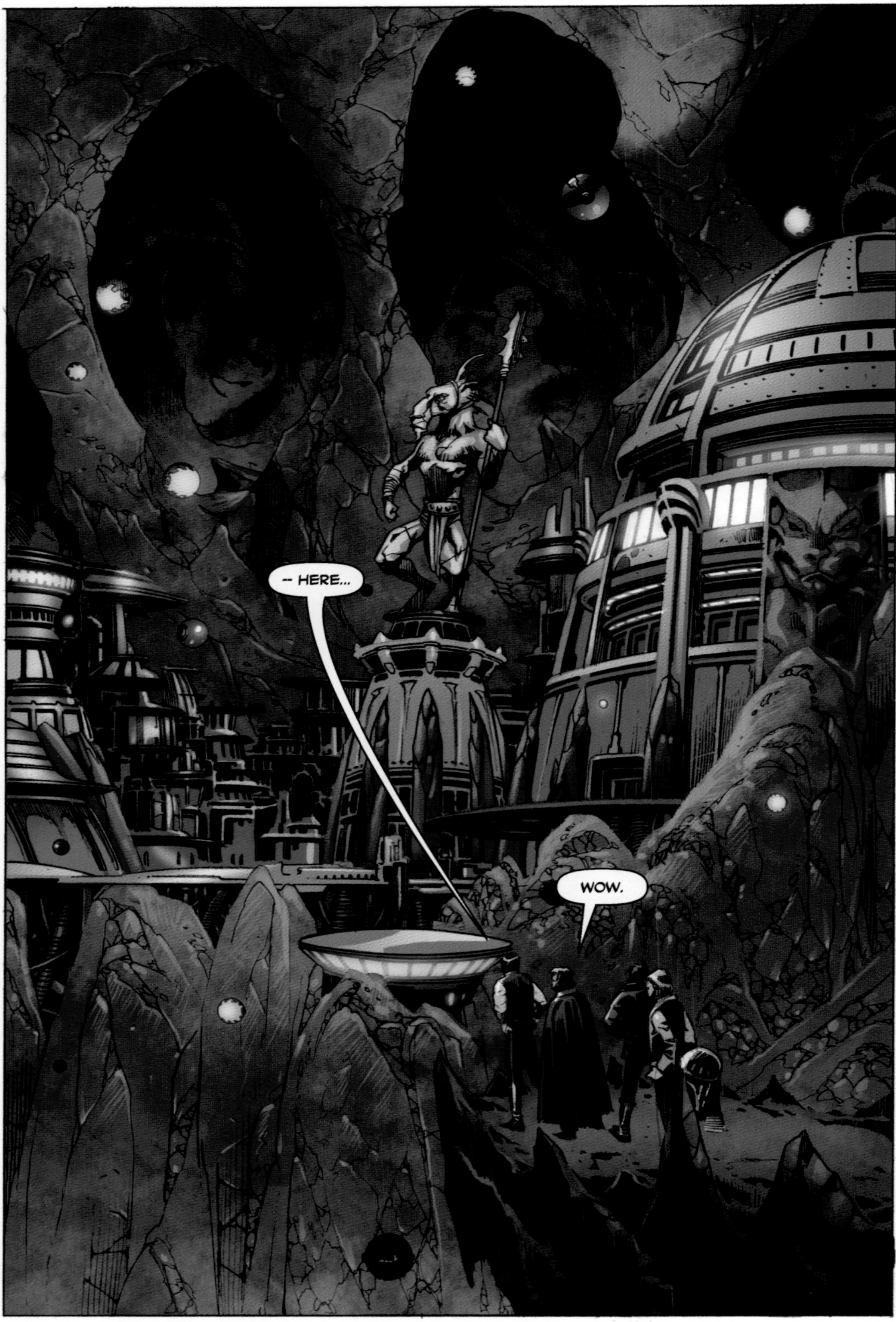
-- HERE...
WOW.

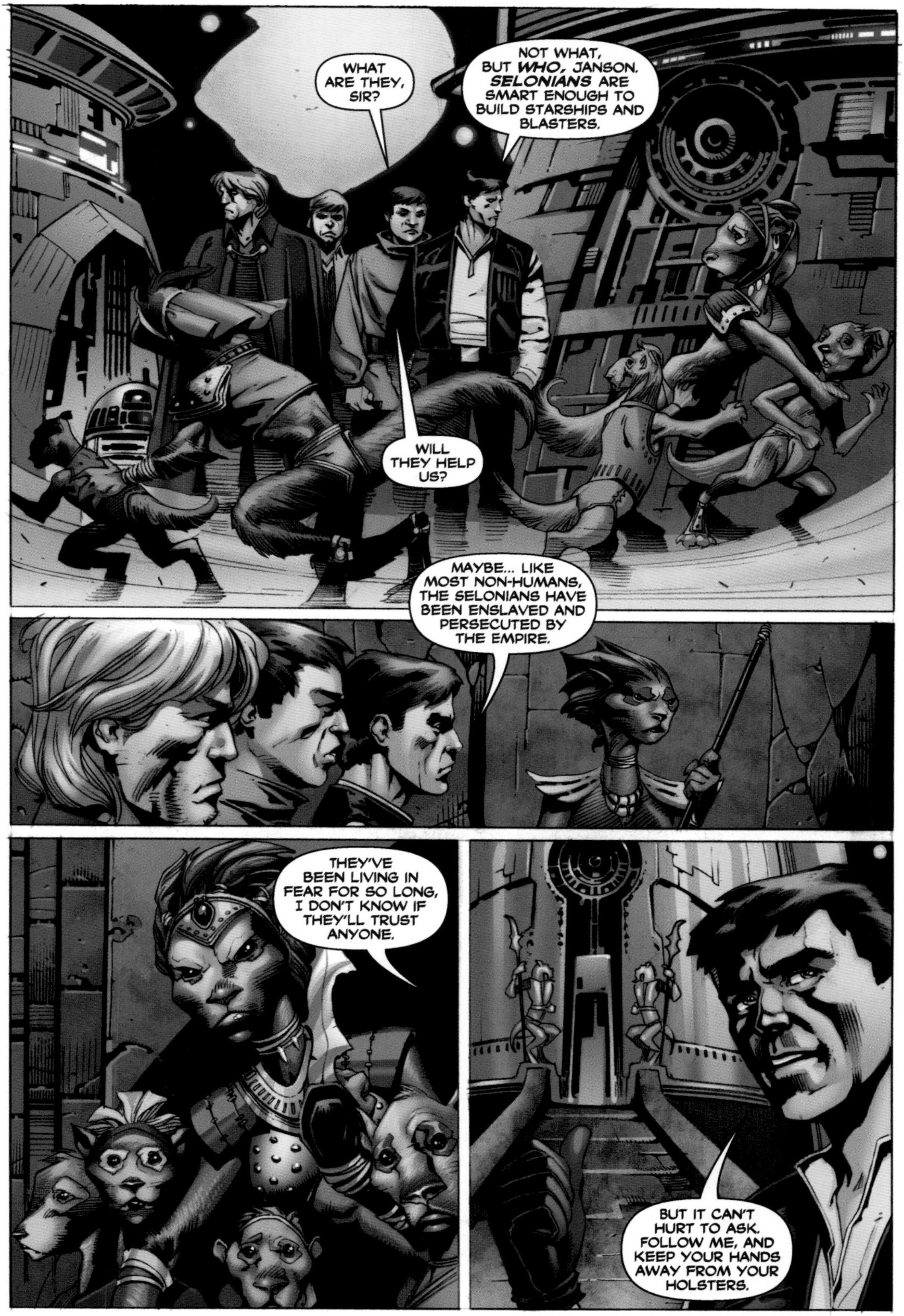
WHAT ARE THEY, SIR?
NOT WHAT, BUT *WHO,* JANSON. *SELONIANS* ARE SMART ENOUGH TO BUILD STARSHIPS AND BLASTERS.
WILL THEY HELP US?
MAYBE... LIKE MOST NON-HUMANS, THE SELONIANS HAVE BEEN ENSLAVED AND PERSECUTED BY THE EMPIRE.
THEY'VE BEEN LIVING IN FEAR FOR SO LONG, I DON'T KNOW IF THEY'LL TRUST ANYONE.
BUT IT CAN'T HURT TO ASK. FOLLOW ME, AND KEEP YOUR HANDS AWAY FROM YOUR HOLSTERS.

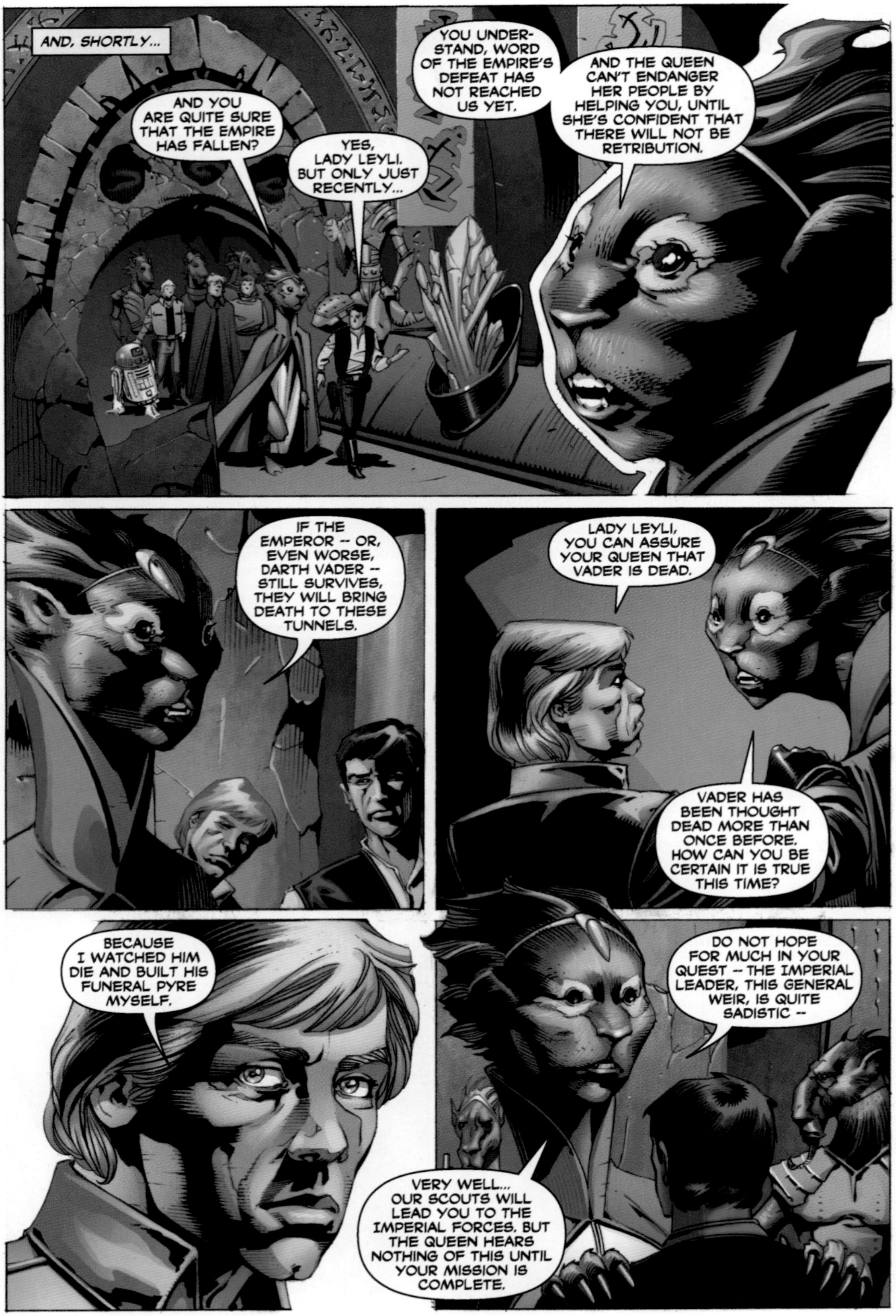
AND, SHORTLY...
AND YOU ARE QUITE SURE THAT THE EMPIRE HAS FALLEN?
YES, LADY LEYLI. BUT ONLY JUST RECENTLY...
YOU UNDERSTAND, WORD OF THE EMPIRE'S DEFEAT HAS NOT REACHED US YET.
AND THE QUEEN CAN'T ENDANGER HER PEOPLE BY HELPING YOU, UNTIL SHE'S CONFIDENT THAT THERE WILL NOT BE RETRIBUTION.
IF THE EMPEROR -- OR, EVEN WORSE, DARTH VADER -- STILL SURVIVES, THEY WILL BRING DEATH TO THESE TUNNELS.
LADY LEYLI, YOU CAN ASSURE YOUR QUEEN THAT VADER IS DEAD.
VADER HAS BEEN THOUGHT DEAD MORE THAN ONCE BEFORE. HOW CAN YOU BE CERTAIN IT IS TRUE THIS TIME?
BECAUSE I WATCHED HIM DIE AND BUILT HIS FUNERAL PYRE MYSELF.
DO NOT HOPE FOR MUCH IN YOUR QUEST -- THE IMPERIAL LEADER, THIS GENERAL WEIR, IS QUITE SADISTIC --
VERY WELL... OUR SCOUTS WILL LEAD YOU TO THE IMPERIAL FORCES. BUT THE QUEEN HEARS NOTHING OF THIS UNTIL YOUR MISSION IS COMPLETE.

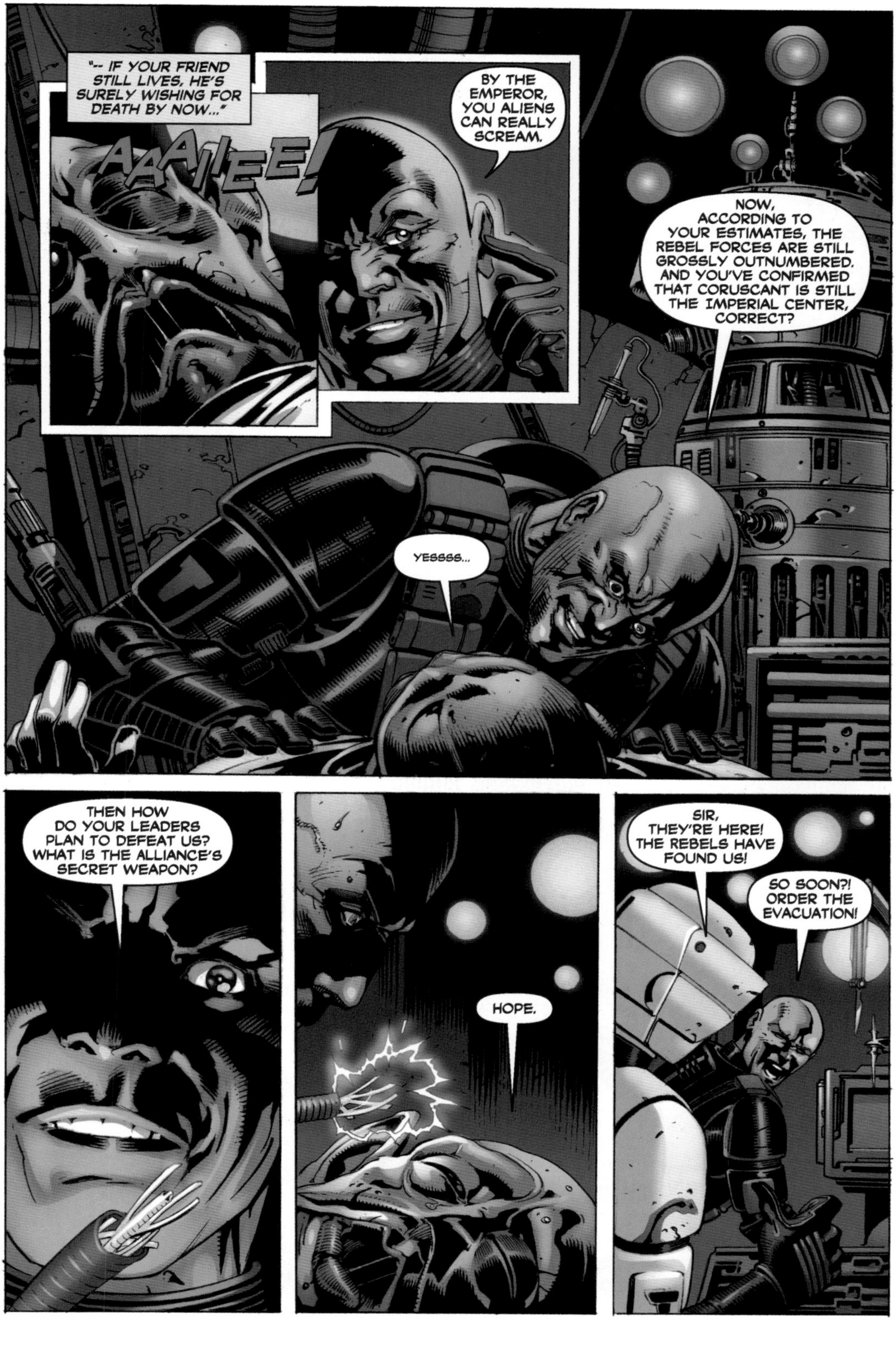
"-- IF YOUR FRIEND STILL LIVES, HE'S SURELY WISHING FOR DEATH BY NOW..."
AAAIIEE!
BY THE EMPEROR, YOU ALIENS CAN REALLY SCREAM.
NOW, ACCORDING TO YOUR ESTIMATES, THE REBEL FORCES ARE STILL GROSSLY OUTNUMBERED. AND YOU'VE CONFIRMED THAT CORUSCANT IS STILL THE IMPERIAL CENTER, CORRECT?
YESSSS...
THEN HOW DO YOUR LEADERS PLAN TO DEFEAT US? WHAT IS THE ALLIANCE'S SECRET WEAPON?
HOPE.
SIR, THEY'RE HERE! THE REBELS HAVE FOUND US!
SO SOON?! ORDER THE EVACUATION!

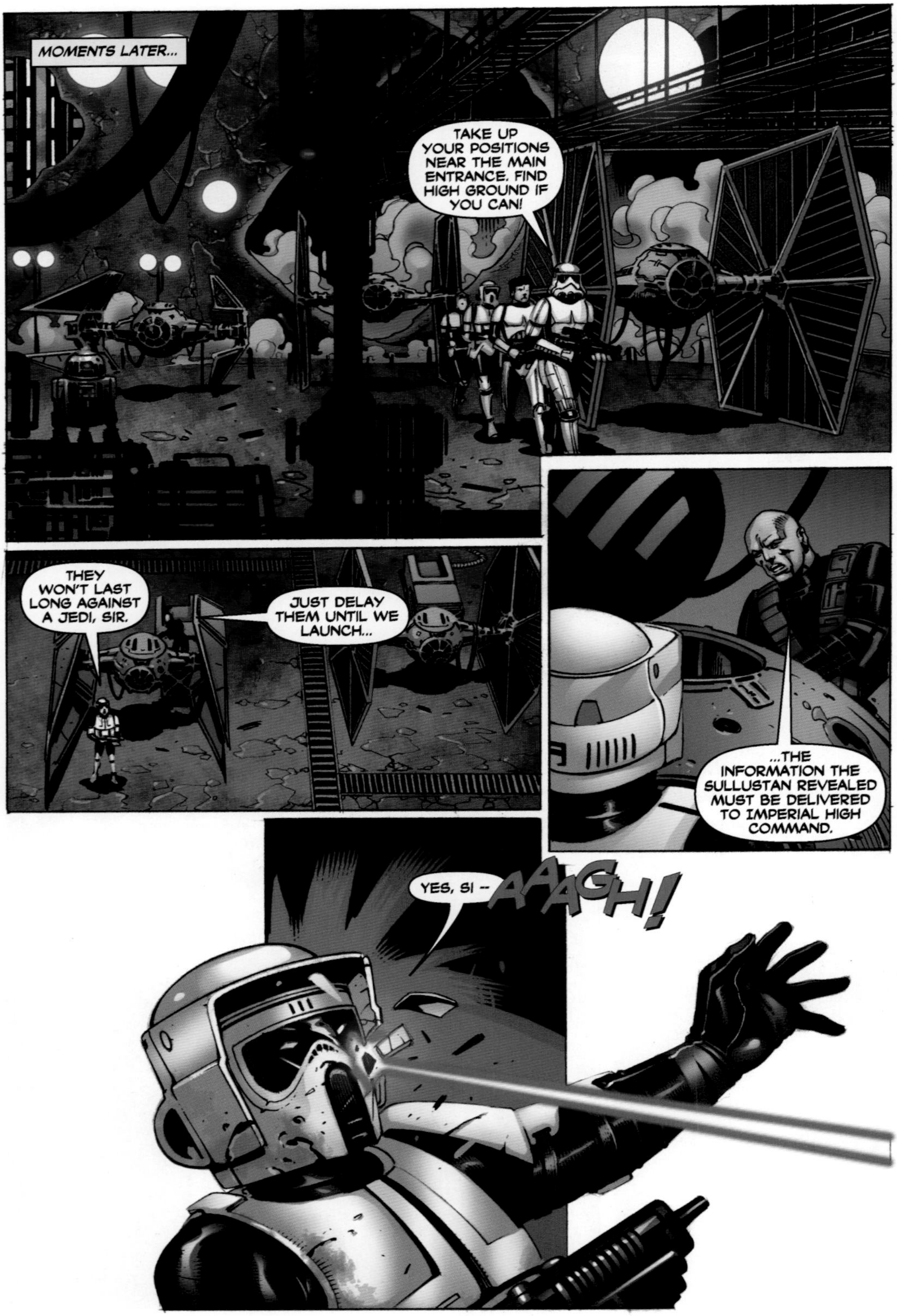
MOMENTS LATER...
TAKE UP YOUR POSITIONS NEAR THE MAIN ENTRANCE. FIND HIGH GROUND IF YOU CAN!
THEY WON'T LAST LONG AGAINST A JEDI, SIR.
JUST DELAY THEM UNTIL WE LAUNCH...
...THE INFORMATION THE SULLUSTAN REVEALED MUST BE DELIVERED TO IMPERIAL HIGH COMMAND.
YES, SI --
AAAGH!

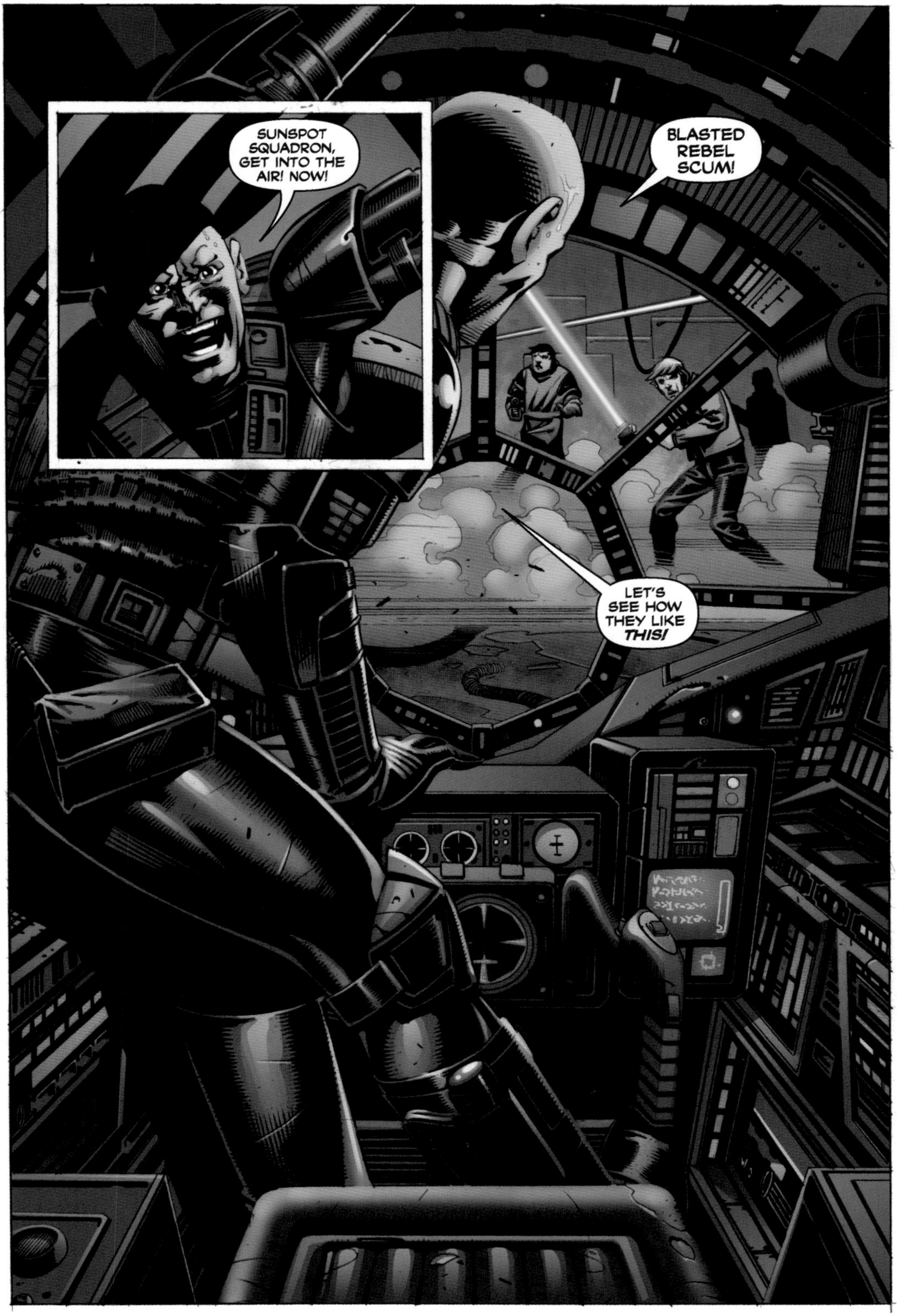
SUNSPOT SQUADRON, GET INTO THE AIR! NOW!
BLASTED REBEL SCUM!
LET'S SEE HOW THEY LIKE *THIS!*

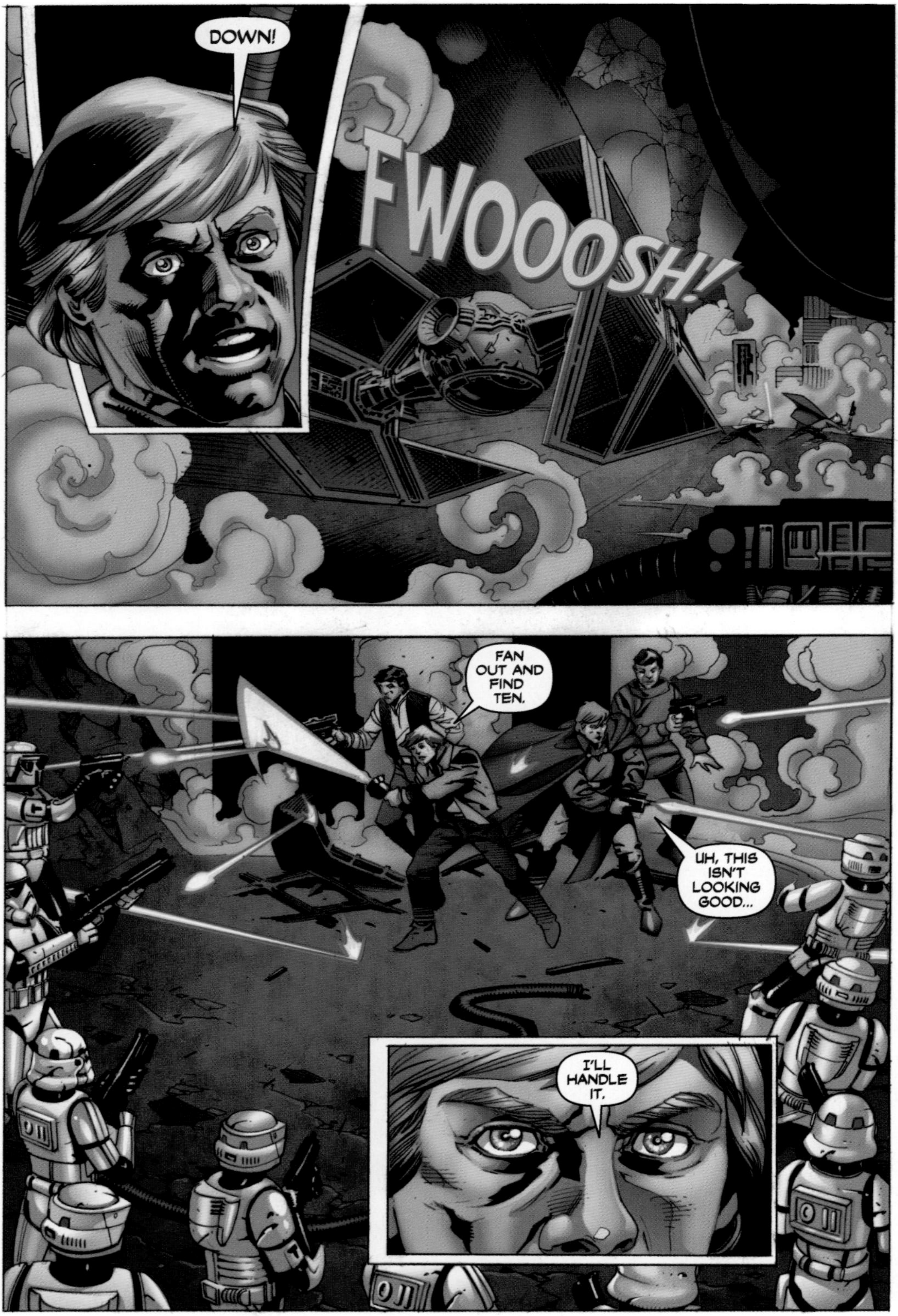
DOWN!
FWOOOSH!
FAN OUT AND FIND TEN.
UH, THIS ISN'T LOOKING GOOD...
I'LL HANDLE IT.

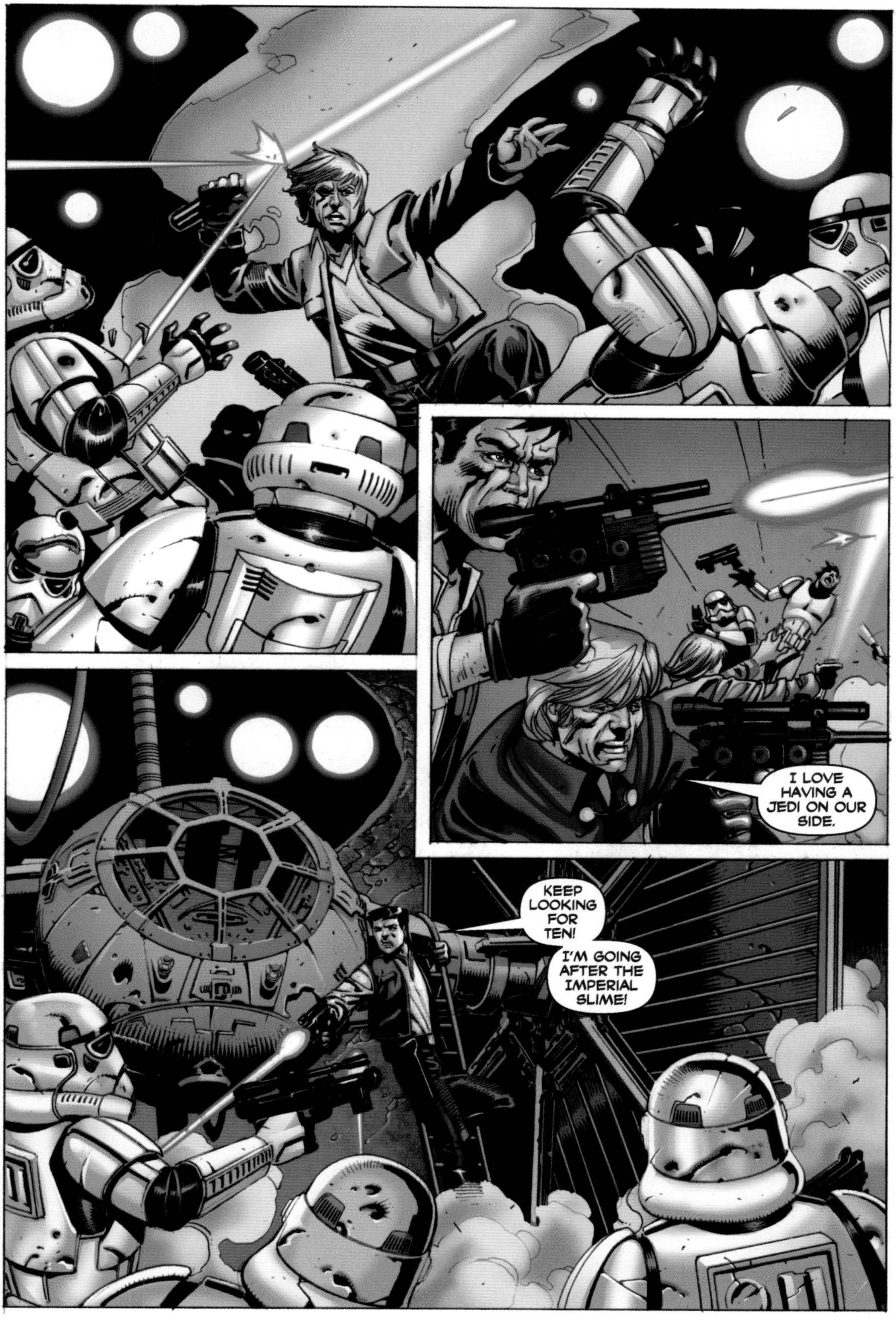
I LOVE HAVING A JEDI ON OUR SIDE.
KEEP LOOKING FOR TEN!
I'M GOING AFTER THE IMPERIAL SLIME!

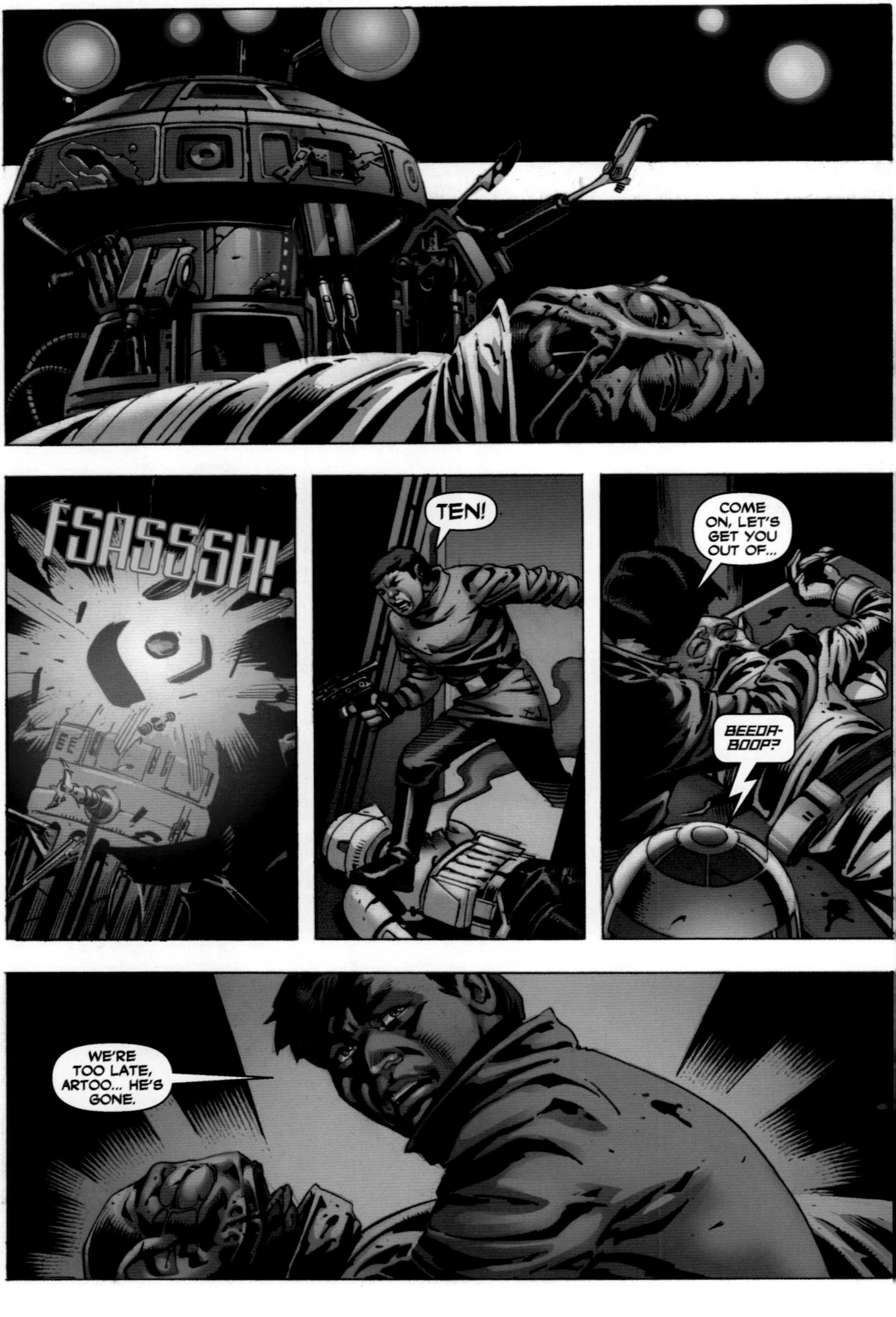
FSASSSH!
TEN!
COME ON, LET'S GET YOU OUT OF...
BEEDA-BOOP?
WE'RE TOO LATE, ARTOO... HE'S GONE.

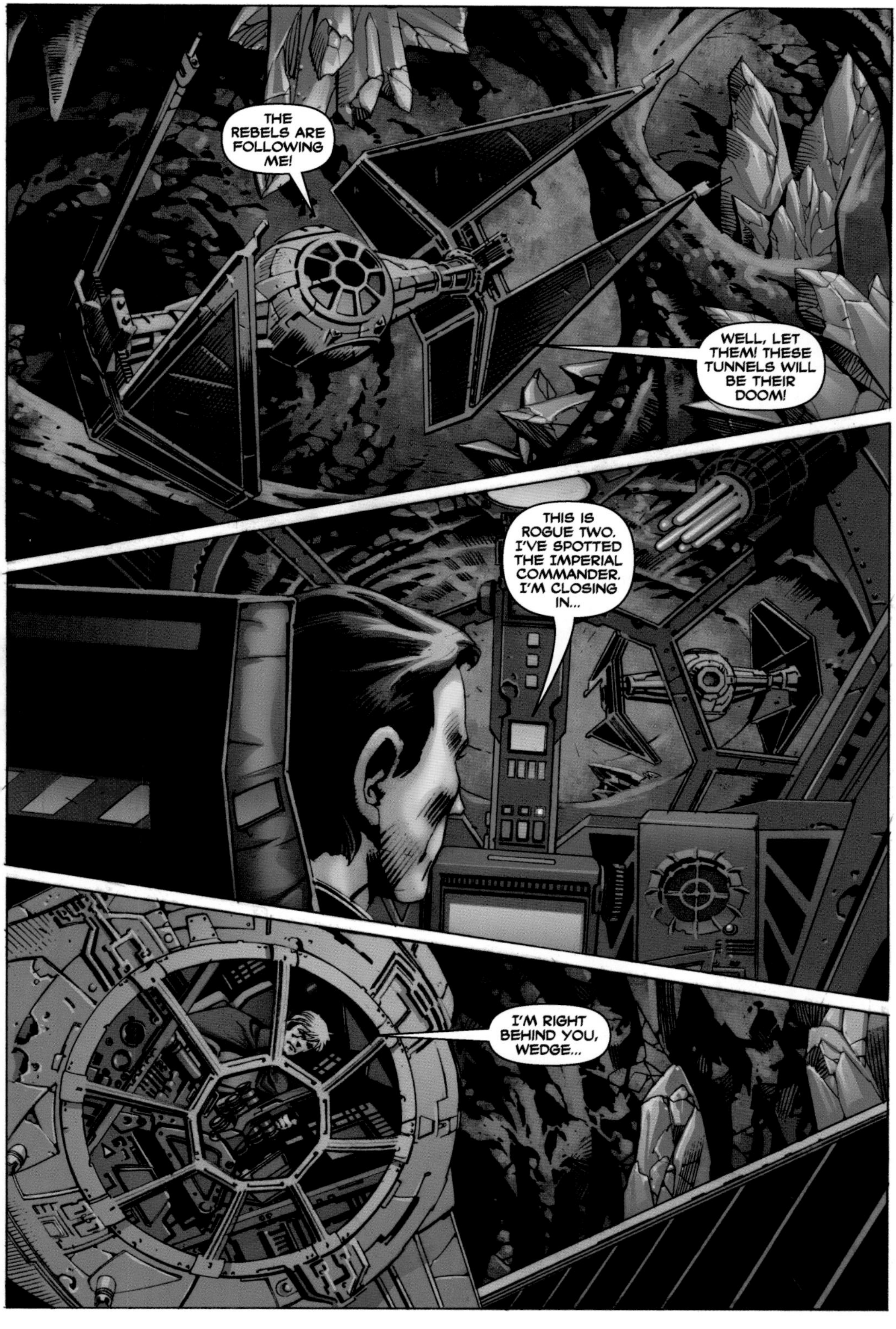
THE REBELS ARE FOLLOWING ME!
WELL, LET THEM! THESE TUNNELS WILL BE THEIR DOOM!
THIS IS ROGUE TWO. I'VE SPOTTED THE IMPERIAL COMMANDER. I'M CLOSING IN...
I'M RIGHT BEHIND YOU, WEDGE...

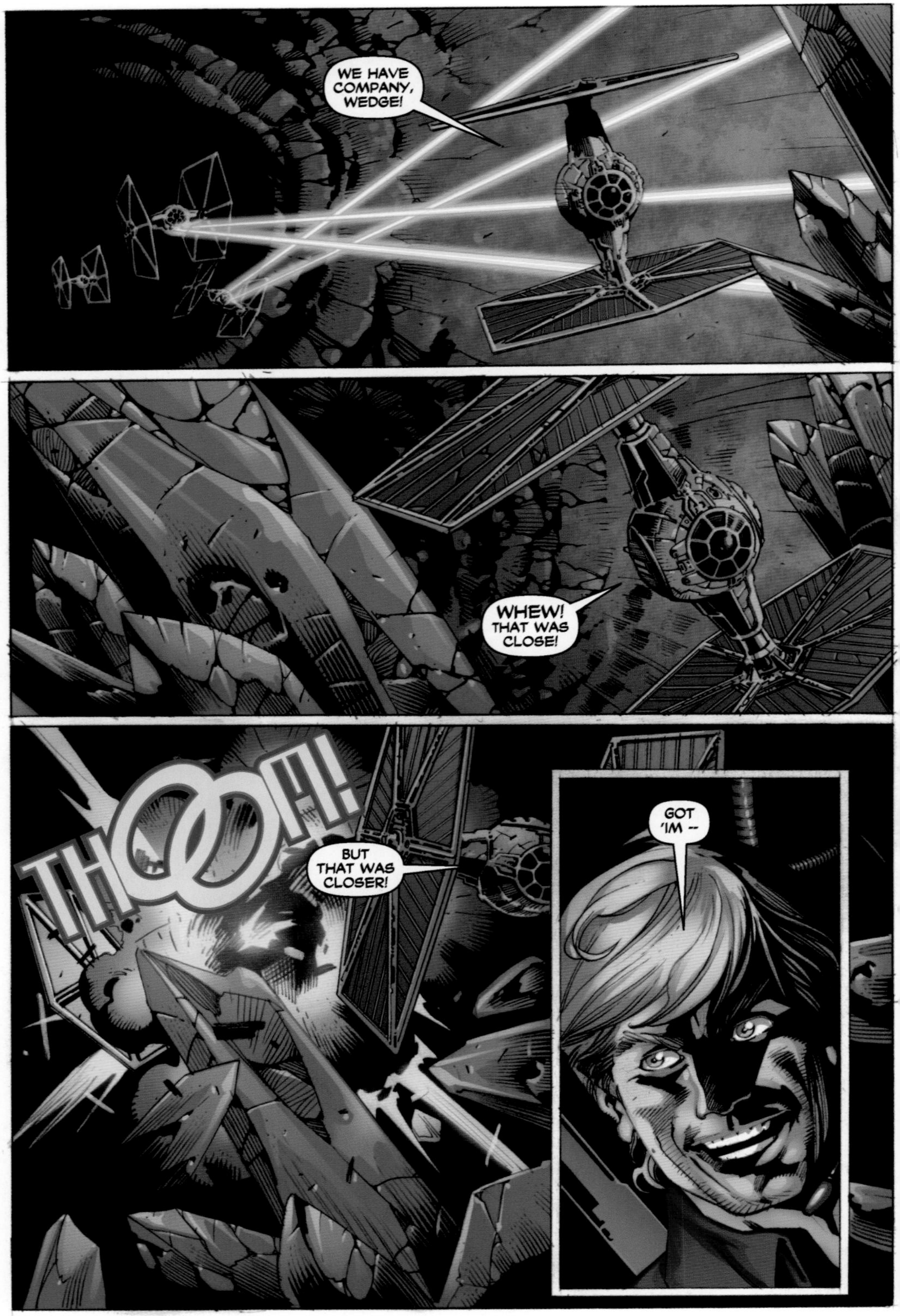
WE HAVE COMPANY, WEDGE!
WHEW! THAT WAS CLOSE!
THOOM!
BUT THAT WAS CLOSER!
GOT 'IM --

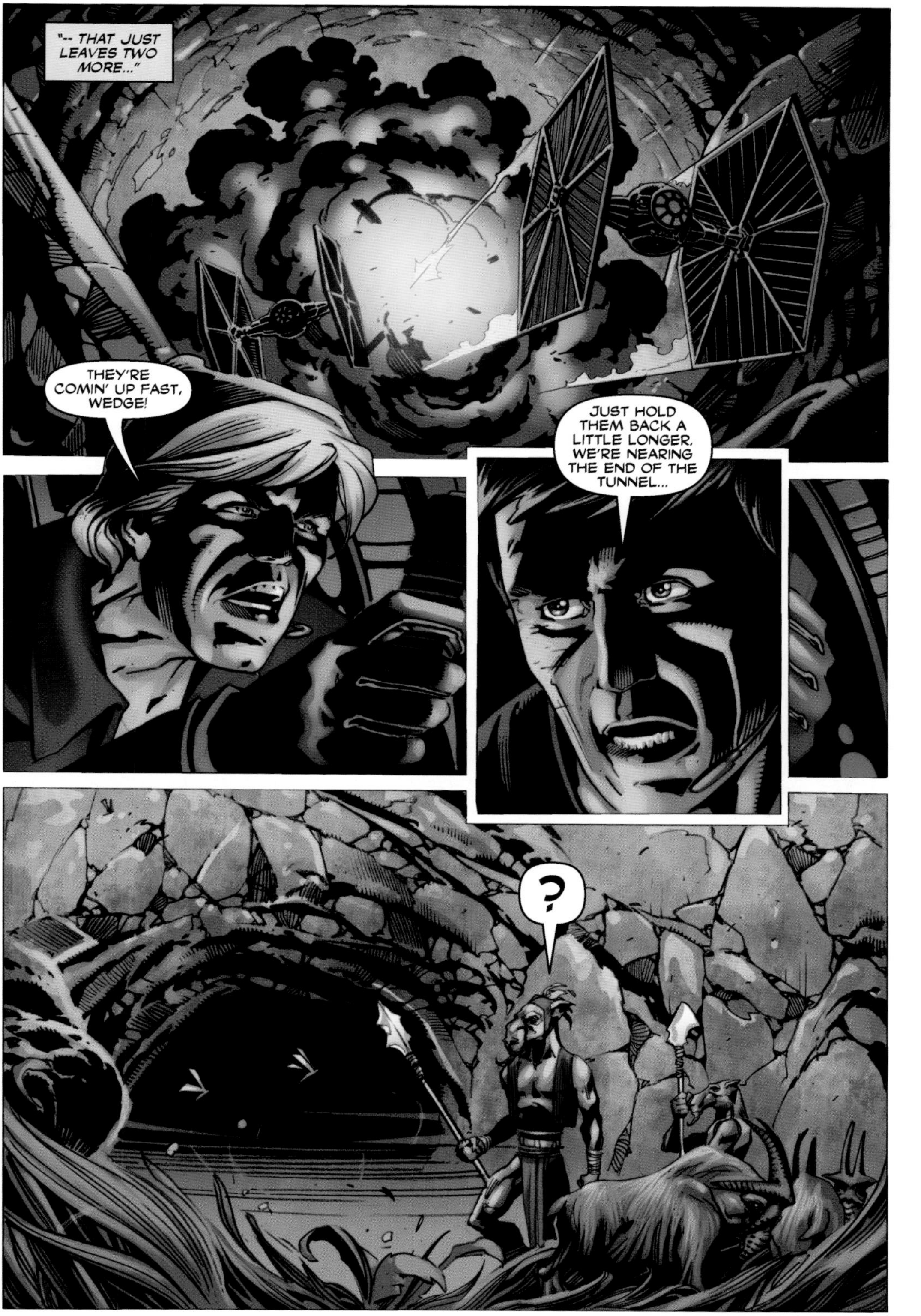
"-- THAT JUST LEAVES TWO MORE..."
THEY'RE COMIN' UP FAST, WEDGE!
JUST HOLD THEM BACK A LITTLE LONGER. WE'RE NEARING THE END OF THE TUNNEL...
?

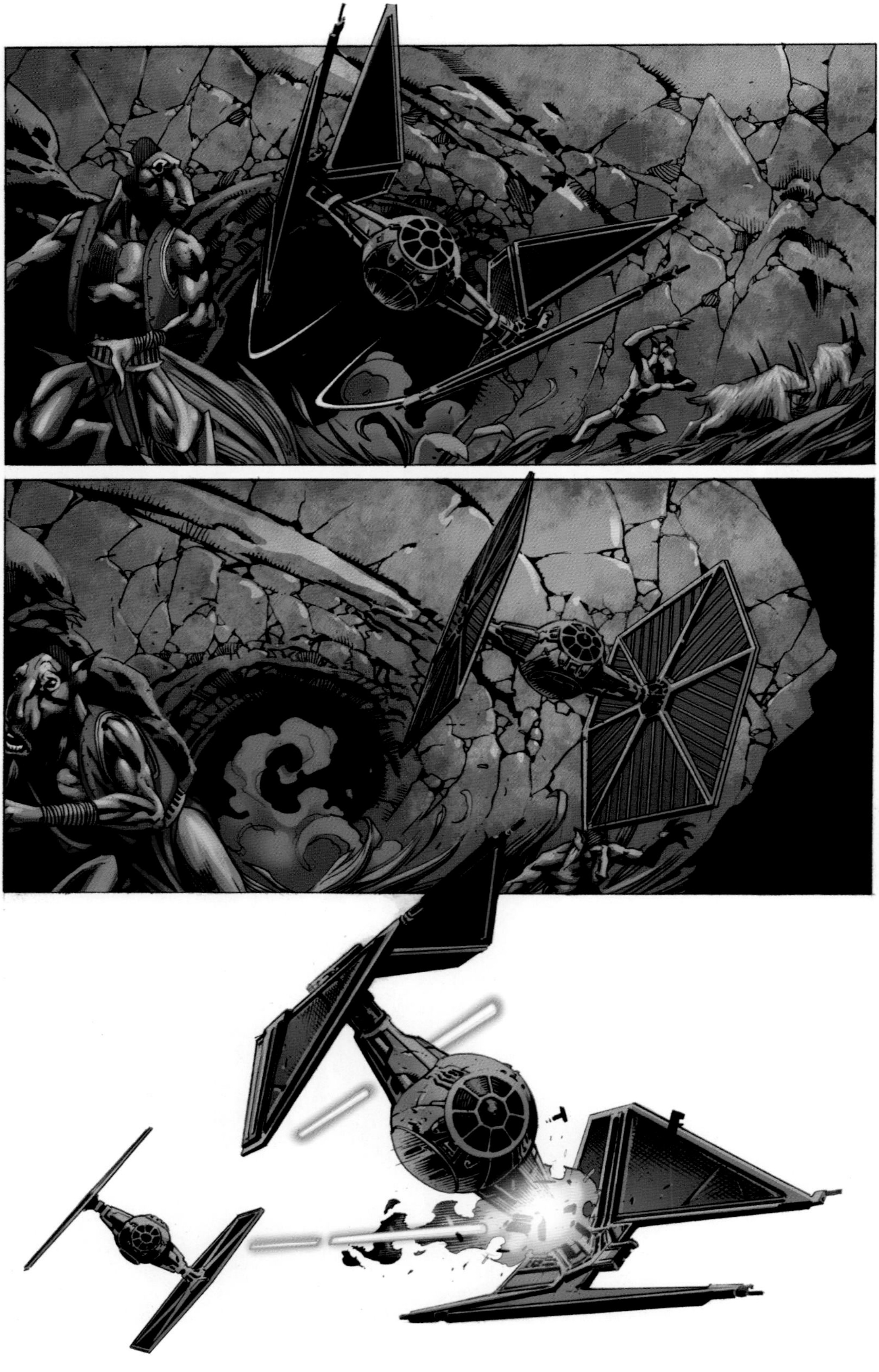

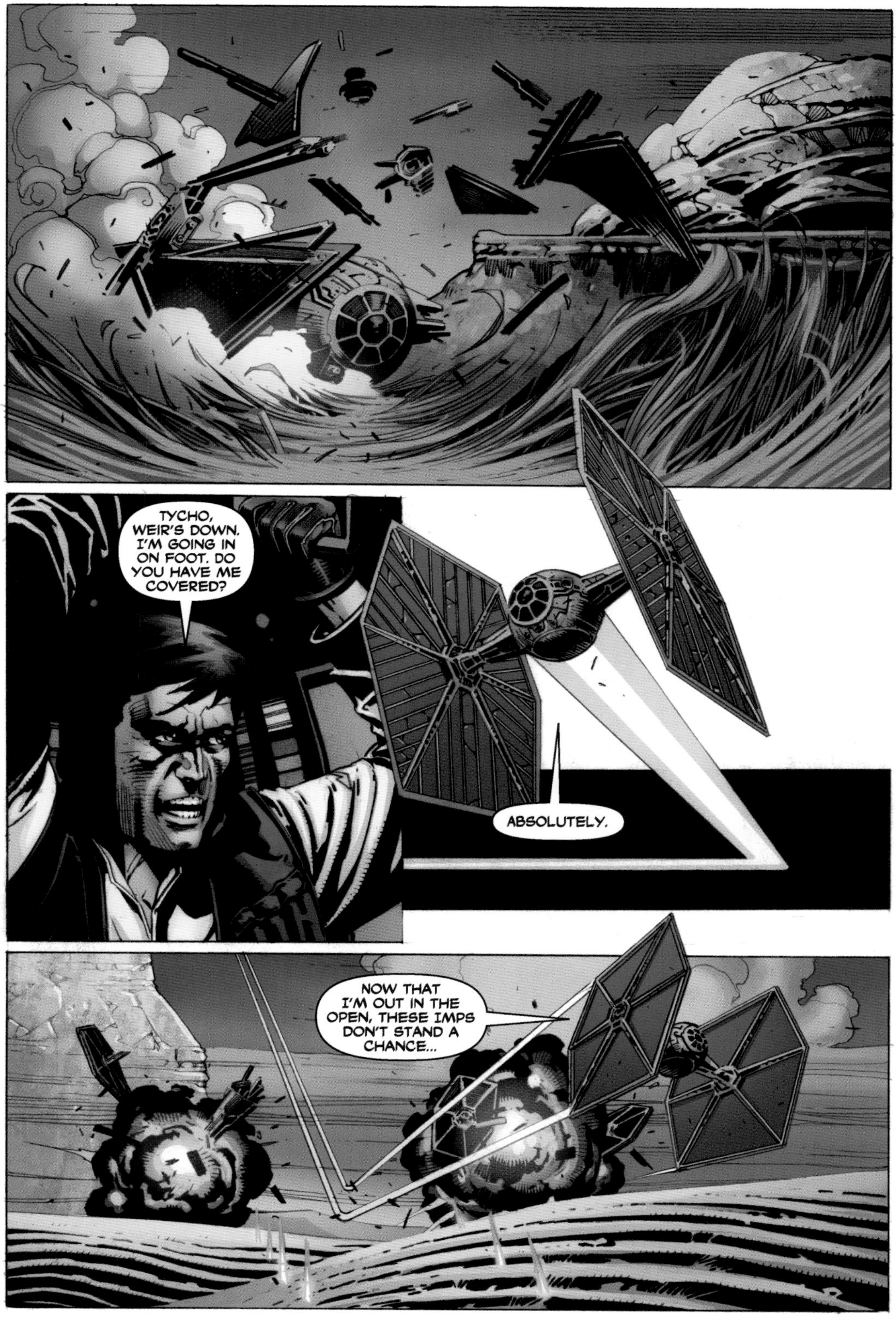
TYCHO, WEIR'S DOWN. I'M GOING IN ON FOOT. DO YOU HAVE ME COVERED?
ABSOLUTELY.
NOW THAT I'M OUT IN THE OPEN, THESE IMPS DON'T STAND A CHANCE...

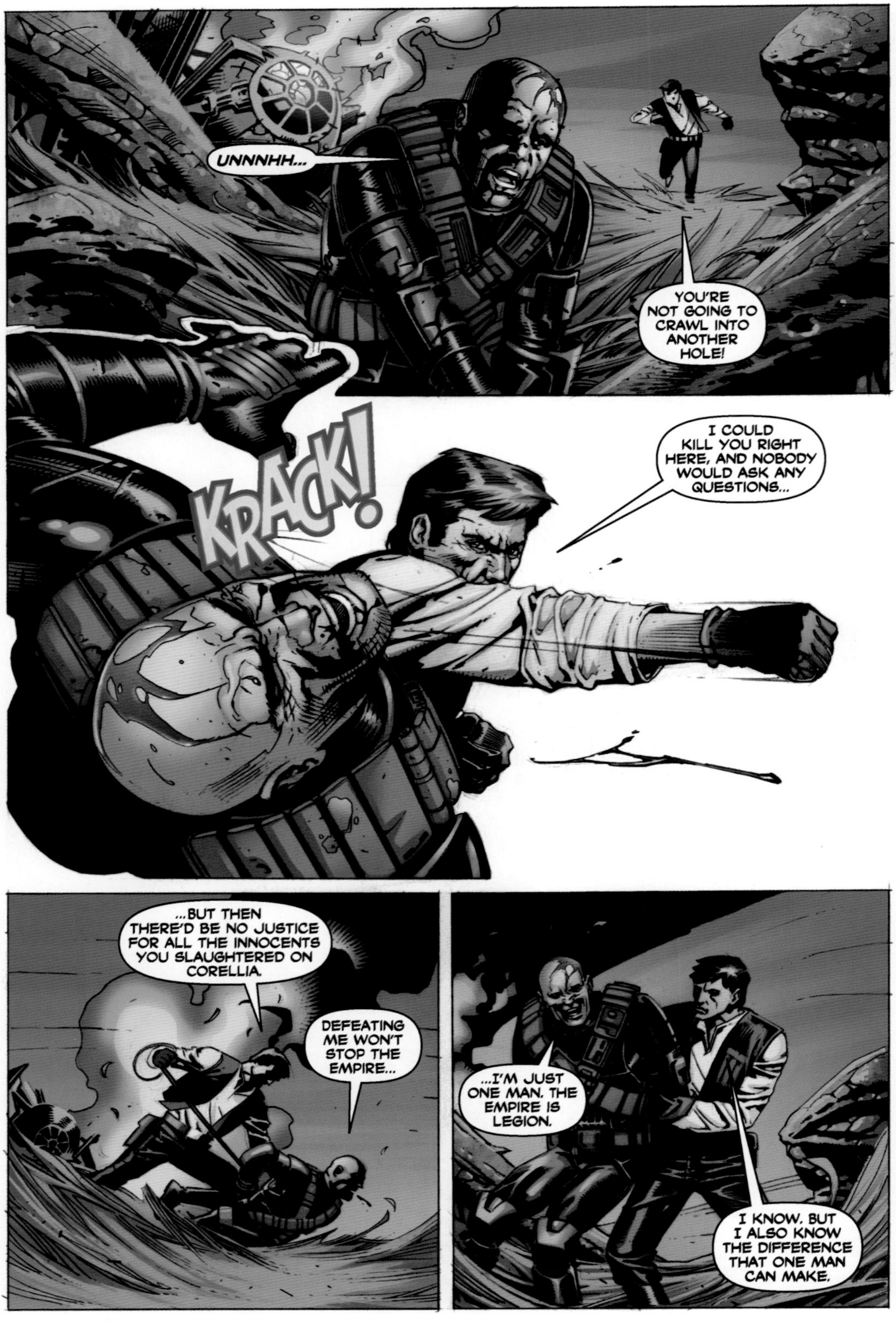
UNNNHH...
YOU'RE NOT GOING TO CRAWL INTO ANOTHER HOLE!
I COULD KILL YOU RIGHT HERE, AND NOBODY WOULD ASK ANY QUESTIONS...
KRACK!
...BUT THEN THERE'D BE NO JUSTICE FOR ALL THE INNOCENTS YOU SLAUGHTERED ON CORELLIA.
DEFEATING ME WON'T STOP THE EMPIRE...
...I'M JUST ONE MAN. THE EMPIRE IS LEGION.
I KNOW. BUT I ALSO KNOW THE DIFFERENCE THAT ONE MAN CAN MAKE.

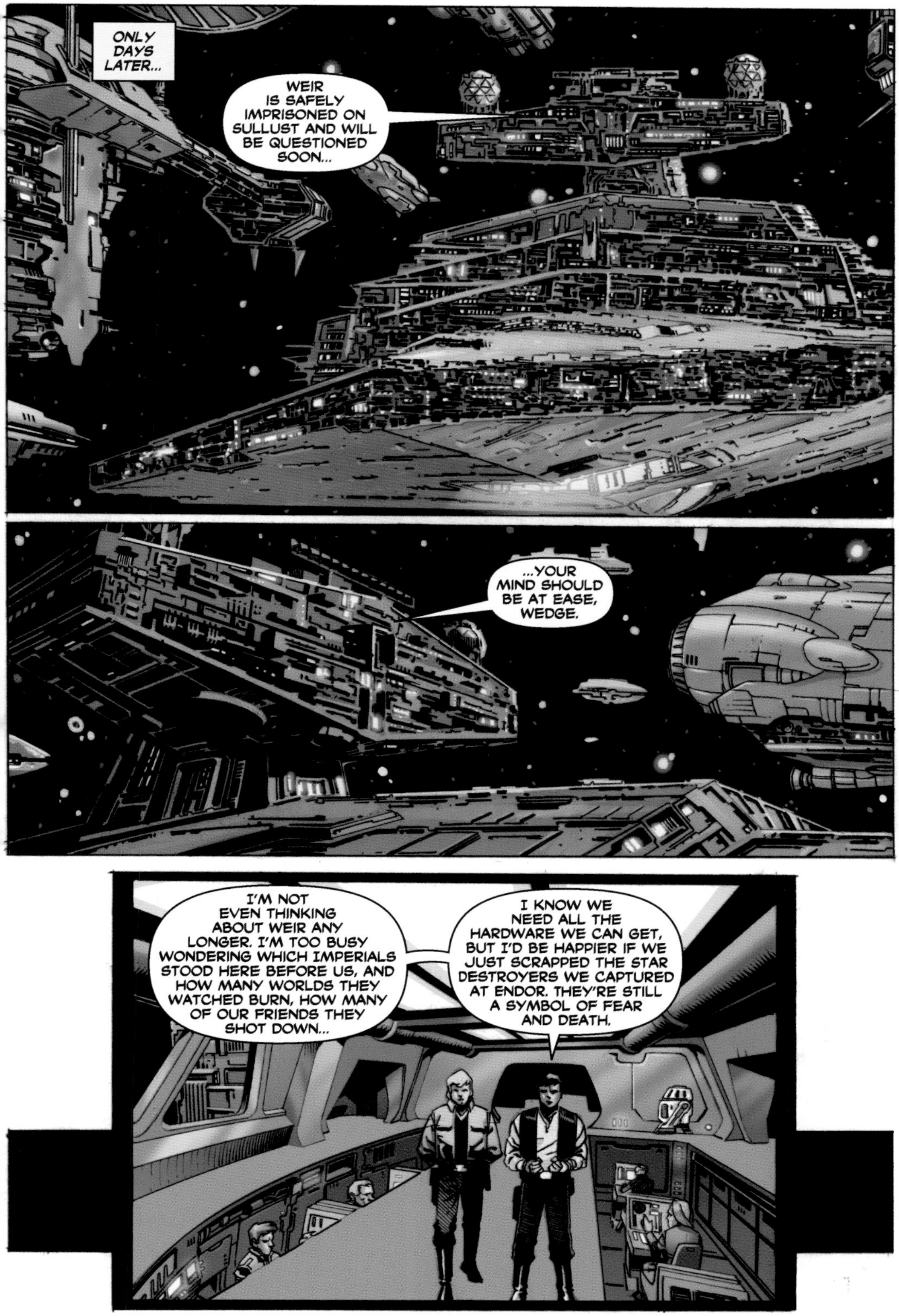
ONLY DAYS LATER...
WEIR IS SAFELY IMPRISONED ON SULLUST AND WILL BE QUESTIONED SOON...
...YOUR MIND SHOULD BE AT EASE, WEDGE.
I'M NOT EVEN THINKING ABOUT WEIR ANY LONGER. I'M TOO BUSY WONDERING WHICH IMPERIALS STOOD HERE BEFORE US, AND HOW MANY WORLDS THEY WATCHED BURN, HOW MANY OF OUR FRIENDS THEY SHOT DOWN...
I KNOW WE NEED ALL THE HARDWARE WE CAN GET, BUT I'D BE HAPPIER IF WE JUST SCRAPPED THE STAR DESTROYERS WE CAPTURED AT ENDOR. THEY'RE STILL A SYMBOL OF FEAR AND DEATH.

I THOUGHT I WAS THE MOROSE ONE.

SORRY. IT'S JUST THAT, AFTER EVERY MAJOR VICTORY, I HOPE THE FIGHTING IS OVER. BUT IT'LL NEVER BE OVER...

EVEN AFTER WE DEFEAT THE IMPERIALS, THERE WILL BE SOMEONE ... ANOTHER THREAT TO PEACE...

SOUNDS LIKE YOU'RE HANDING ME YOUR RESIGNATION.

ACTUALLY, I'M TRYING TO FIND A WAY TO TELL YOU I'VE NEVER BEEN MORE COMMITTED. WE HAVE TO KEEP FIGHTING SO THAT OTHERS DON'T HAVE TO.

I'D BE LYING IF I DIDN'T TELL YOU I'M RELIEVED. THE NEW REPUBLIC -- THE GALAXY -- STILL NEEDS ROGUE SQUADRON. BUT IT ALSO NEEDS A NEW JEDI ORDER...

NOW WHO'S GIVING HIS RESIGNATION SPEECH?

NOT YET... BUT I DON'T KNOW HOW MUCH TIME I CAN DEVOTE TO FLYING COMBAT MISSIONS. I NEED TO KNOW THAT THE SQUADRON IS BEING LED BY SOMEONE WITH A GOOD RIGHT HOOK...

THEN TELL ME MY NEXT MISSION, COMMANDER.

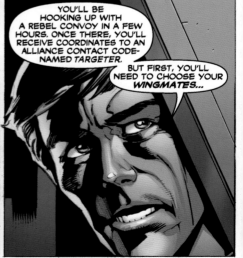

YOU'LL BE HOOKING UP WITH A REBEL CONVOY IN A FEW HOURS. ONCE THERE, YOU'LL RECEIVE COORDINATES TO AN ALLIANCE CONTACT CODE-NAMED TARGETER.

BUT FIRST, YOU'LL NEED TO CHOOSE YOUR WINGMATES...

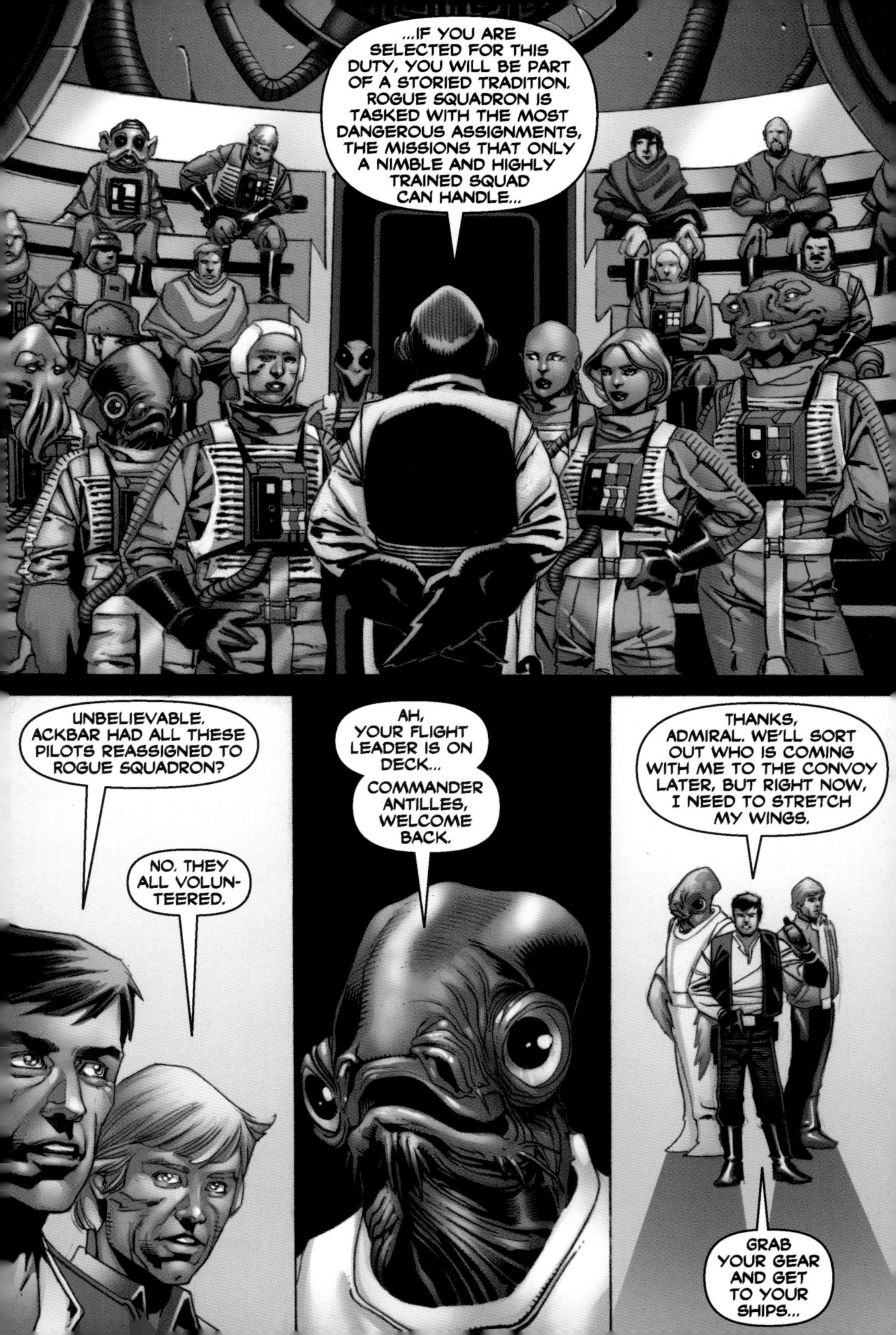
...IF YOU ARE SELECTED FOR THIS DUTY, YOU WILL BE PART OF A STORIED TRADITION. ROGUE SQUADRON IS TASKED WITH THE MOST DANGEROUS ASSIGNMENTS, THE MISSIONS THAT ONLY A NIMBLE AND HIGHLY TRAINED SQUAD CAN HANDLE...
UNBELIEVABLE. ACKBAR HAD ALL THESE PILOTS REASSIGNED TO ROGUE SQUADRON?
NO. THEY ALL VOLUNTEERED.
AH, YOUR FLIGHT LEADER IS ON DECK...
COMMANDER ANTILLES, WELCOME BACK.
THANKS, ADMIRAL. WE'LL SORT OUT WHO IS COMING WITH ME TO THE CONVOY LATER, BUT RIGHT NOW, I NEED TO STRETCH MY WINGS.
GRAB YOUR GEAR AND GET TO YOUR SHIPS...

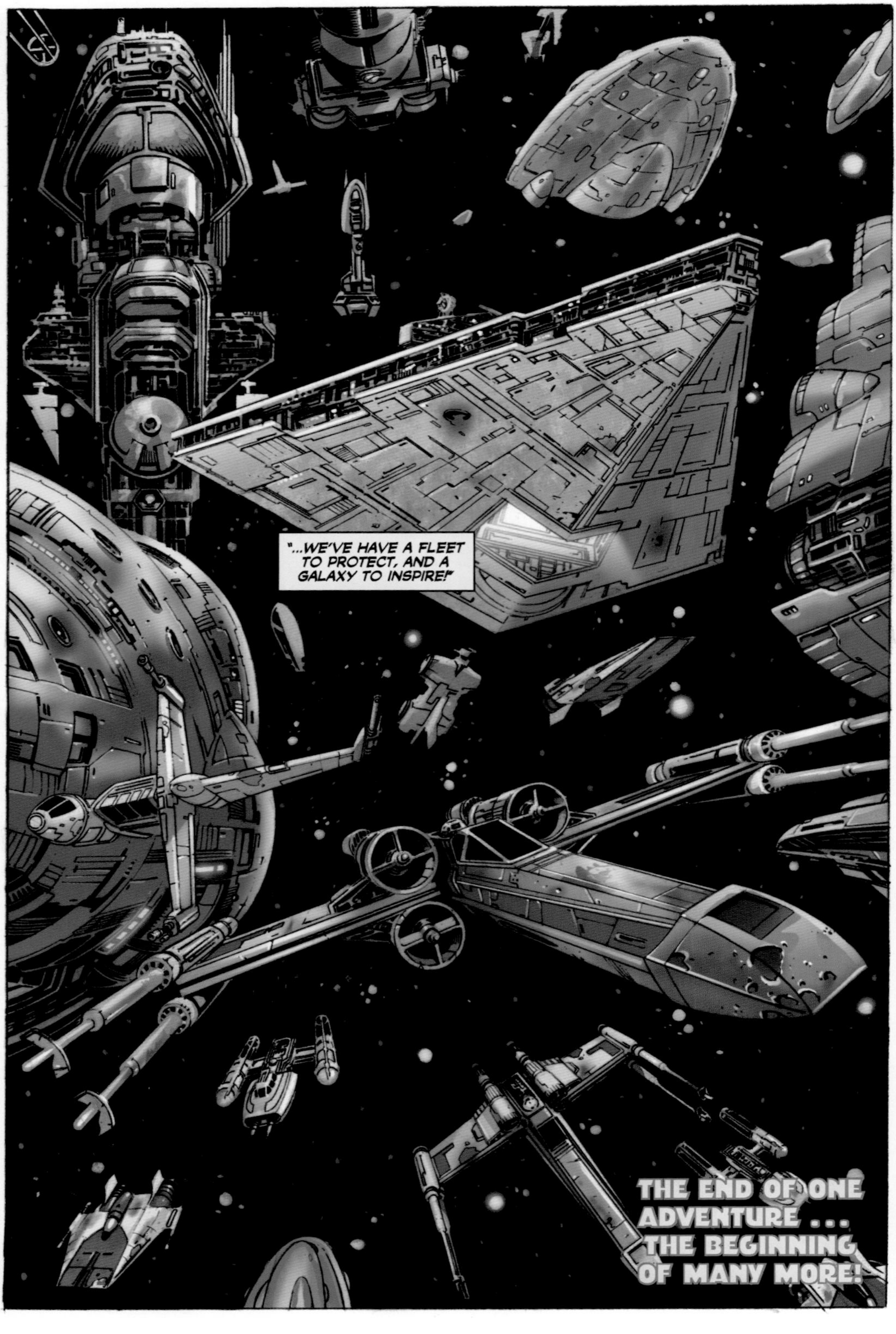
"...WE'VE HAVE A FLEET TO PROTECT, AND A GALAXY TO INSPIRE!"
THE END OF ONE ADVENTURE . . . THE BEGINNING OF MANY MORE!

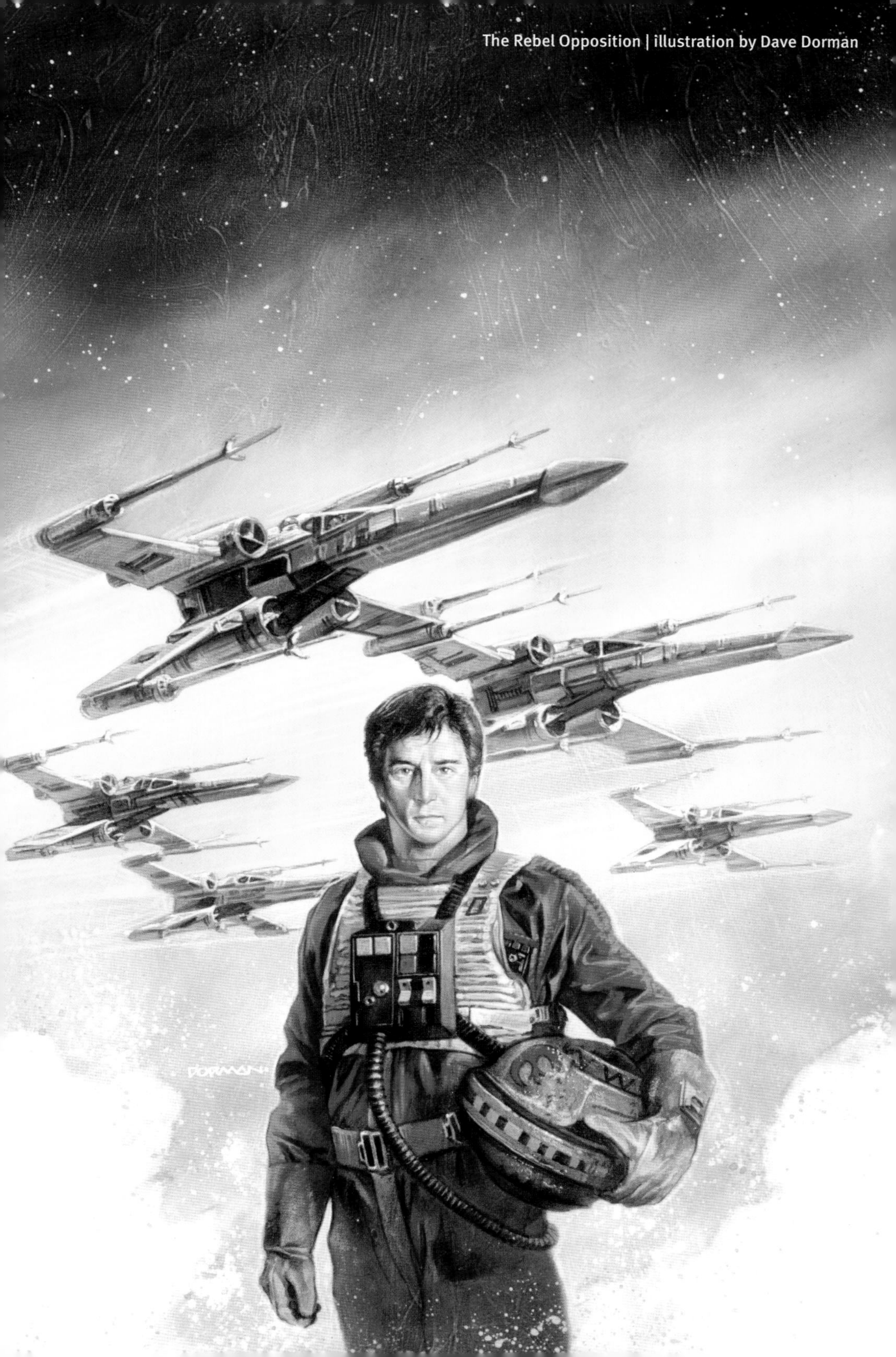
DORMAN

The Rebel Opposition | illustration by Dave Dorman

APPROXIMATELY ONE MONTH AFTER THE BATTLE
OF ENDOR . . .

story by Michael A. Stackpole
script by Mike Baron
pencils by Allen Nunis
inks by Andy Mushynsky
colors by Dave Nestelle
letters by Steve Dutro

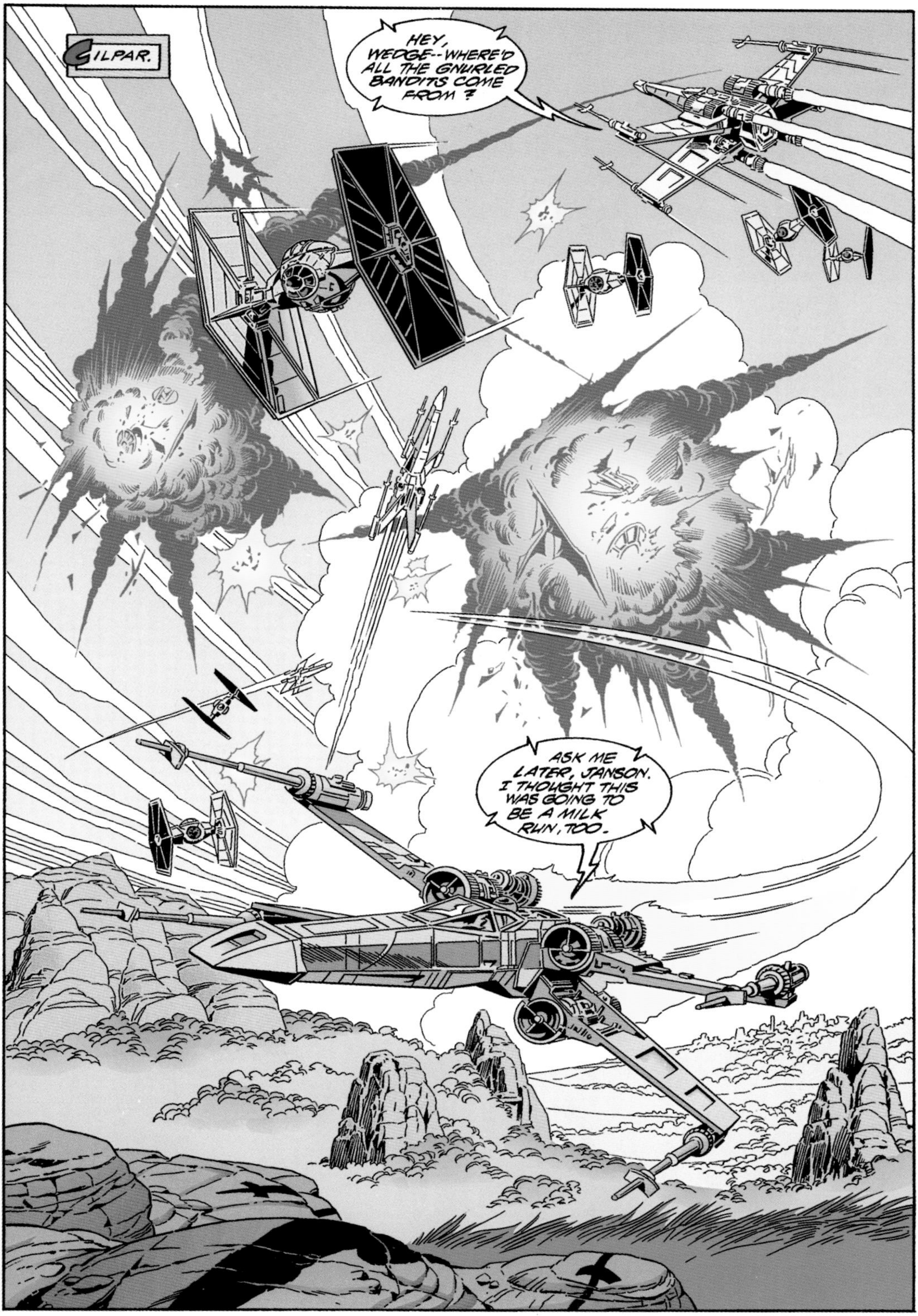
GILPAR.
HEY, WEDGE--WHERE'D ALL THE GNURLED BANDITS COME FROM ?
ASK ME LATER, JANSON. I THOUGHT THIS WAS GOING TO BE A MILK RUN, TOO.

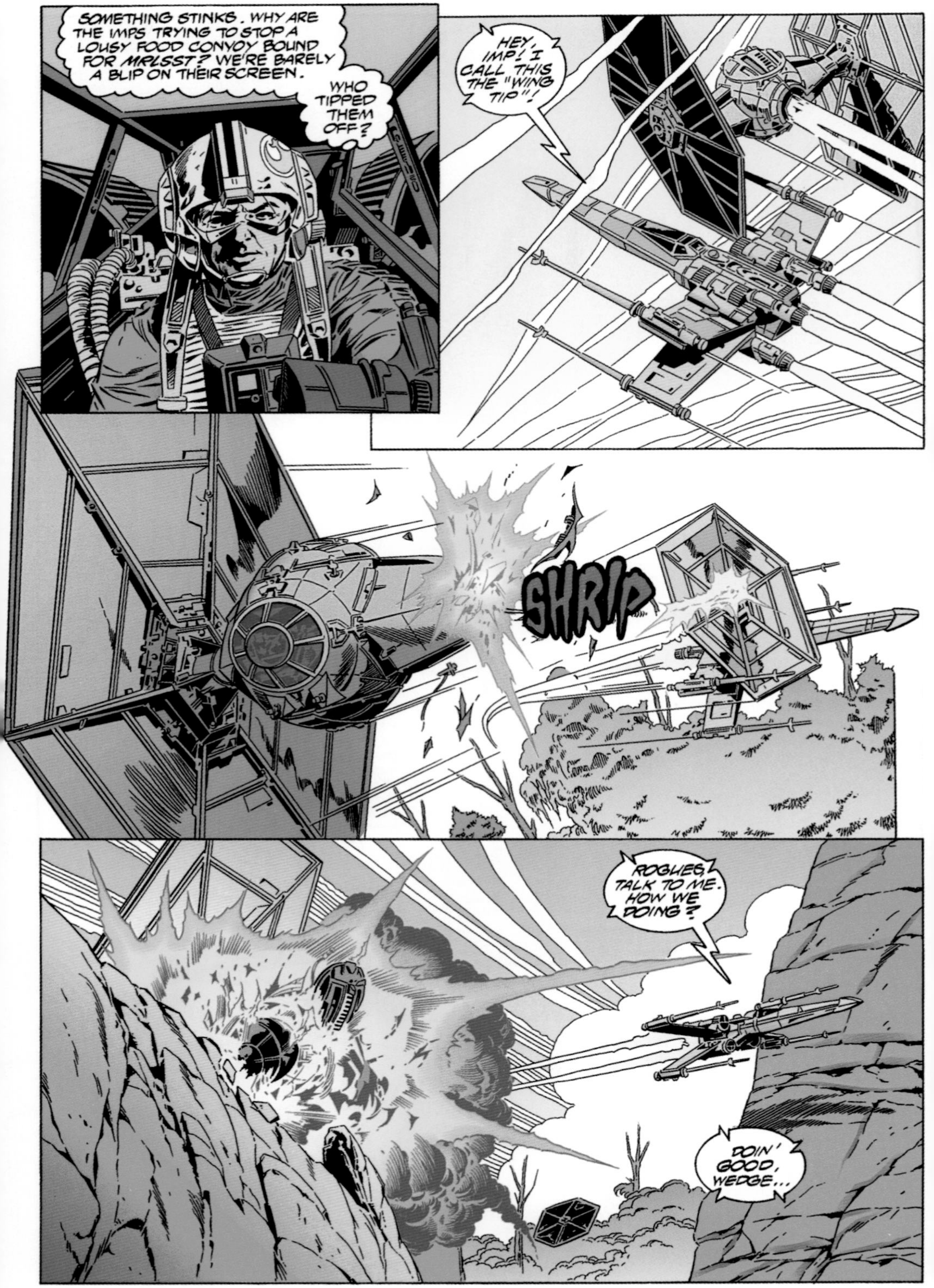
SOMETHING STINKS. WHY ARE THE IMPS TRYING TO STOP A LOUSY FOOD CONVOY BOUND FOR MRLSST? WE'RE BARELY A BLIP ON THEIR SCREEN.
WHO TIPPED THEM OFF?
HEY, IMP! I CALL THIS THE "WING TIP"!
SHRIP
ROGUES, TALK TO ME. HOW WE DOING?
DOIN' GOOD, WEDGE...

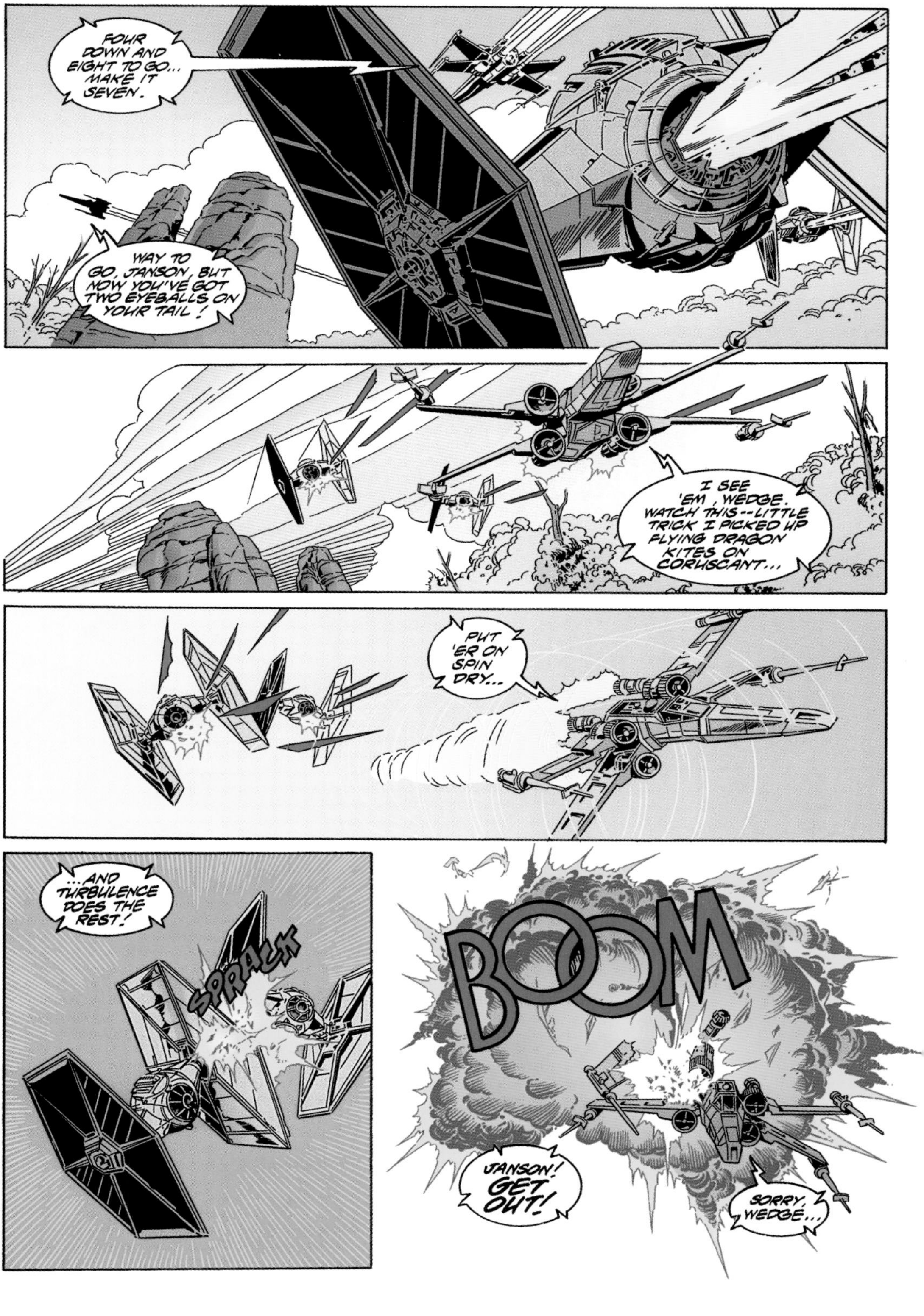
FOUR DOWN AND EIGHT TO GO... MAKE IT SEVEN.
WAY TO GO, JANSON, BUT NOW YOU'VE GOT TWO EYEBALLS ON YOUR TAIL!
I SEE 'EM, WEDGE. WATCH THIS--LITTLE TRICK I PICKED UP FLYING DRAGON KITES ON CORUSCANT...
PUT 'ER ON SPIN DRY...
...AND TURBULENCE DOES THE REST!
SPRACK
BOOM
JANSON! GET OUT!
SORRY, WEDGE...

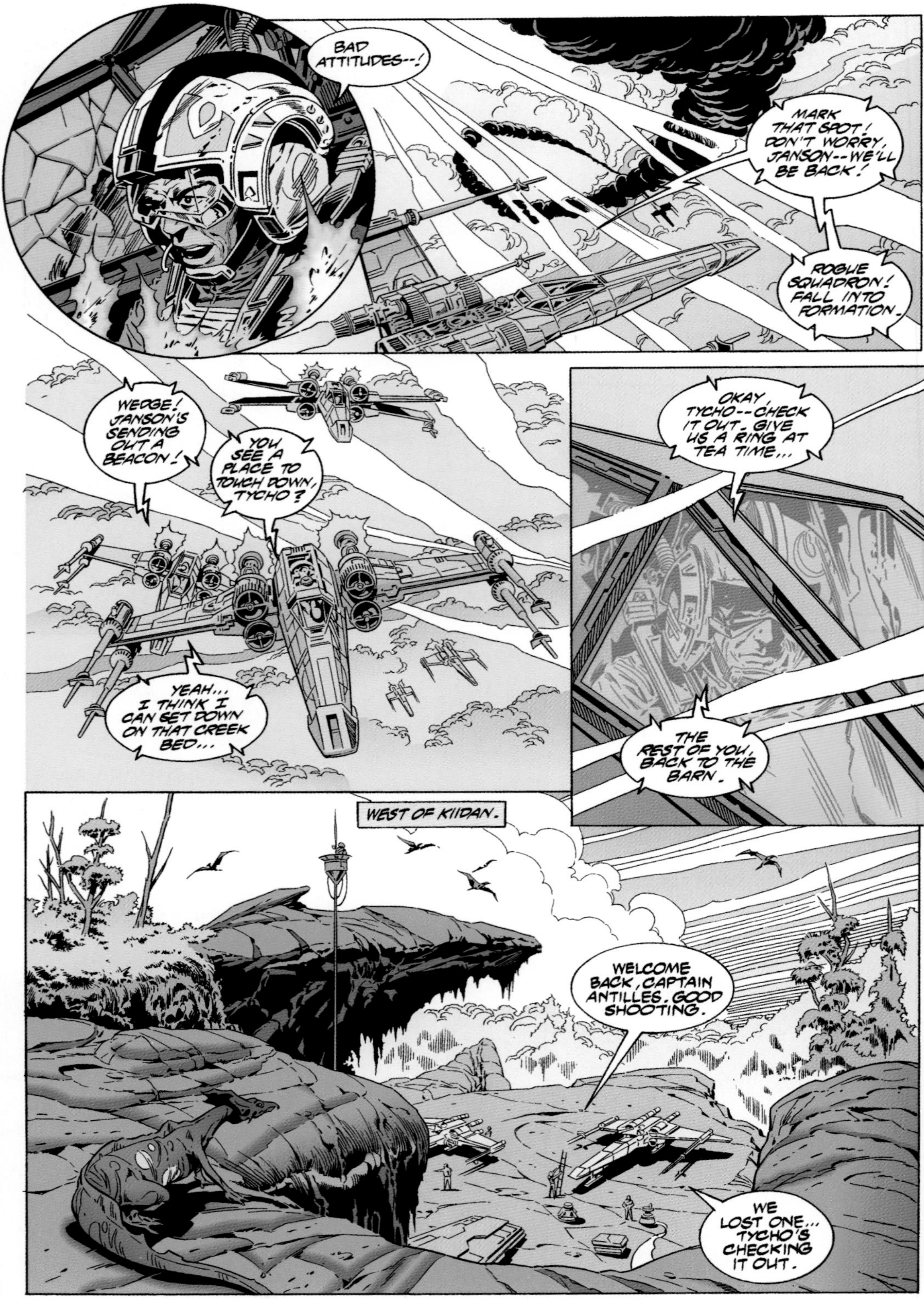
BAD ATTITUDES--!
MARK THAT SPOT! DON'T WORRY, JANSON--WE'LL BE BACK!
ROGUE SQUADRON! FALL INTO FORMATION.
WEDGE! JANSON'S SENDING OUT A BEACON!
YOU SEE A PLACE TO TOUCH DOWN, TYCHO?
YEAH... I THINK I CAN GET DOWN ON THAT CREEK BED...
OKAY, TYCHO--CHECK IT OUT. GIVE US A RING AT TEA TIME...
THE REST OF YOU, BACK TO THE BARN.
WEST OF KIIDAN.
WELCOME BACK, CAPTAIN ANTILLES. GOOD SHOOTING.
WE LOST ONE... TYCHO'S CHECKING IT OUT.

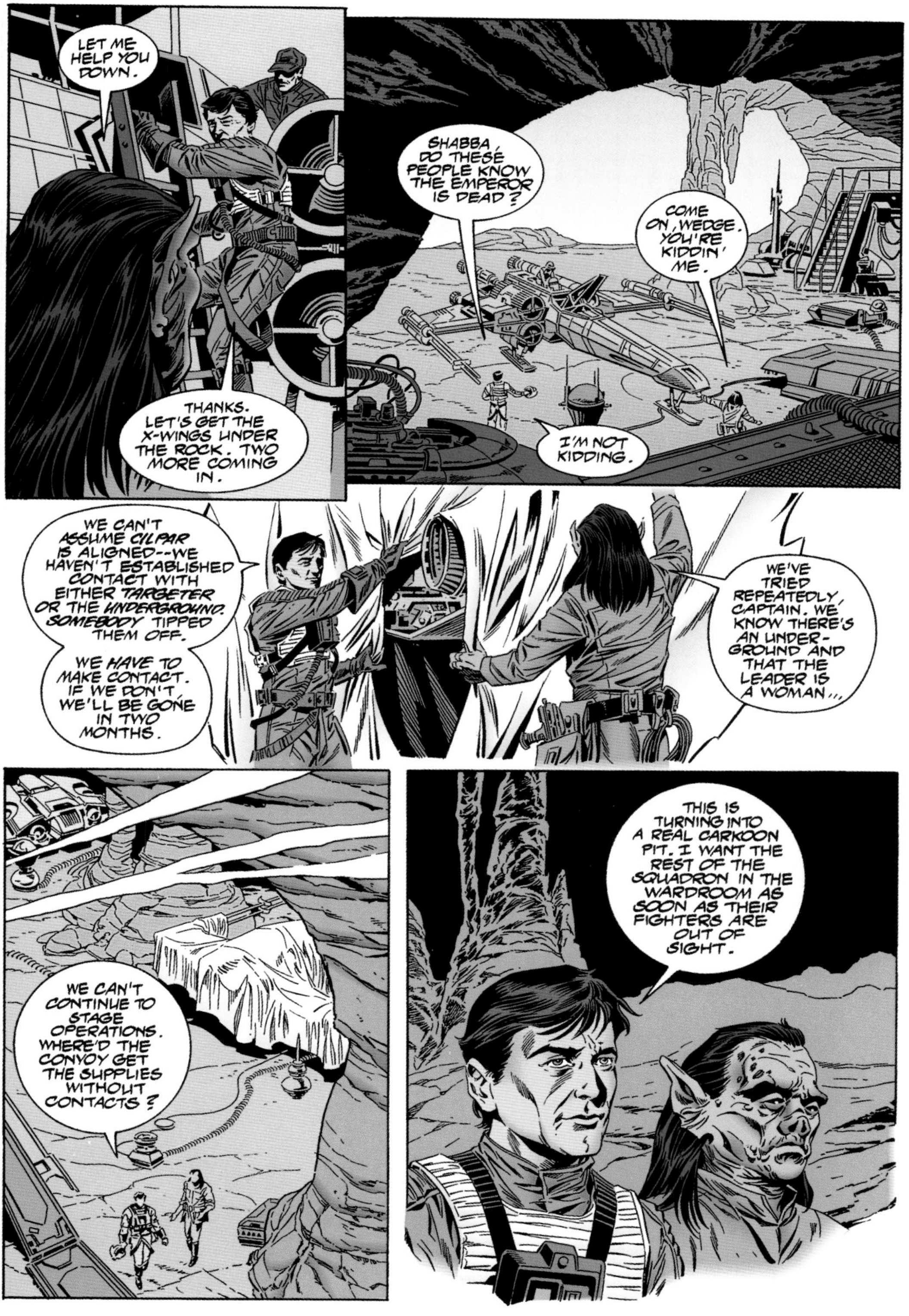
LET ME HELP YOU DOWN.
THANKS. LET'S GET THE X-WINGS UNDER THE ROCK. TWO MORE COMING IN.
SHABBA, DO THESE PEOPLE KNOW THE EMPEROR IS DEAD?
COME ON, WEDGE. YOU'RE KIDDIN' ME.
I'M NOT KIDDING.
WE CAN'T ASSUME CILPAR IS ALIGNED--WE HAVEN'T ESTABLISHED CONTACT WITH EITHER TARGETER OR THE UNDERGROUND. SOMEBODY TIPPED THEM OFF.
WE HAVE TO MAKE CONTACT. IF WE DON'T, WE'LL BE GONE IN TWO MONTHS.
WE'VE TRIED REPEATEDLY, CAPTAIN. WE KNOW THERE'S AN UNDER-GROUND AND THAT THE LEADER IS A WOMAN...
WE CAN'T CONTINUE TO STAGE OPERATIONS. WHERE'D THE CONVOY GET THE SUPPLIES WITHOUT CONTACTS?
THIS IS TURNING INTO A REAL CARKOON PIT. I WANT THE REST OF THE SQUADRON IN THE WARDROOM AS SOON AS THEIR FIGHTERS ARE OUT OF SIGHT.

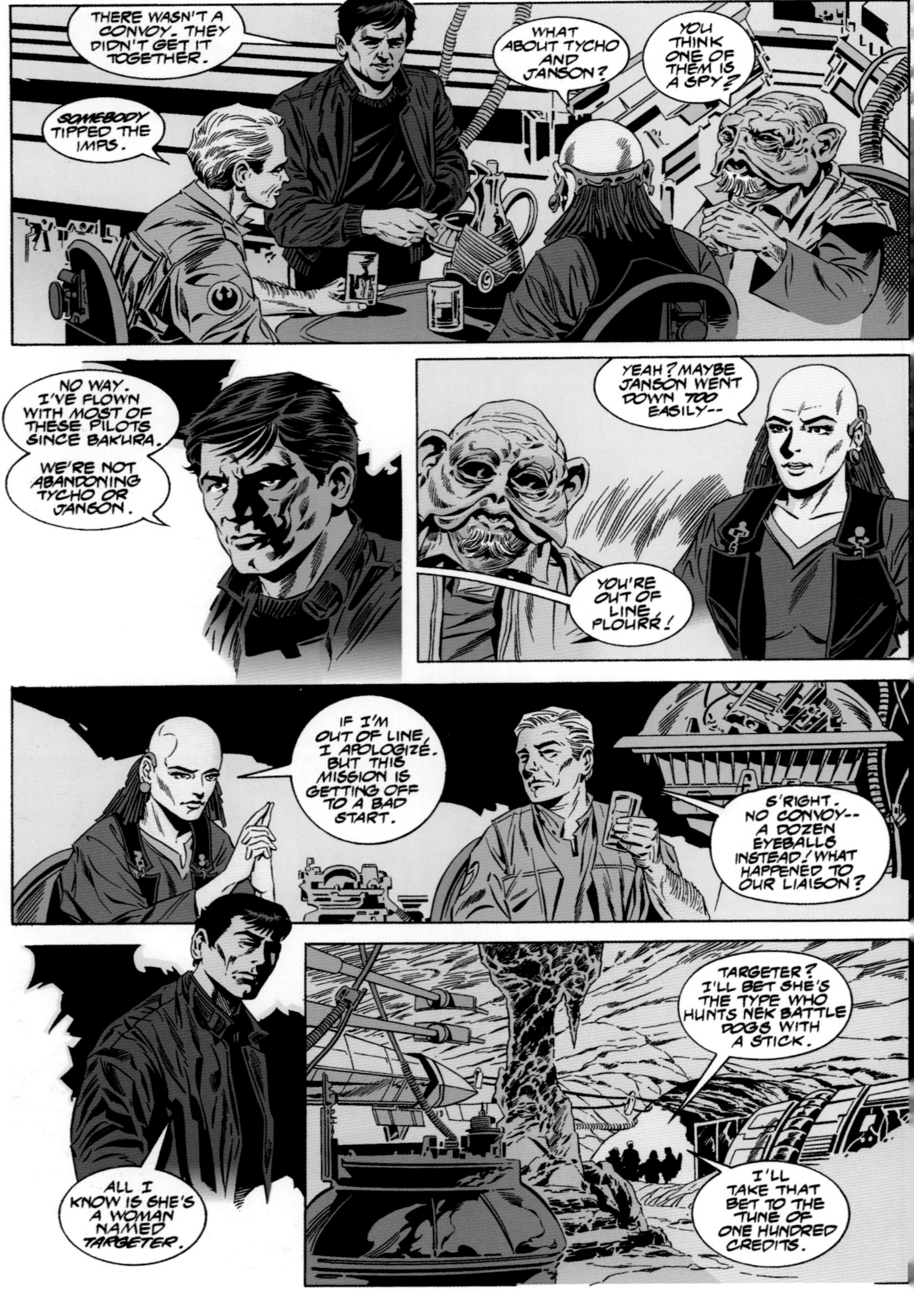
THERE WASN'T A CONVOY. THEY DIDN'T GET IT TOGETHER.
SOMEBODY TIPPED THE IMPS.
WHAT ABOUT TYCHO AND JANSON?
YOU THINK ONE OF THEM IS A SPY?
NO WAY. I'VE FLOWN WITH MOST OF THESE PILOTS SINCE BAKURA.
WE'RE NOT ABANDONING TYCHO OR JANSON.
YEAH? MAYBE JANSON WENT DOWN TOO EASILY--
YOU'RE OUT OF LINE, PLOURR!
IF I'M OUT OF LINE, I APOLOGIZE. BUT THIS MISSION IS GETTING OFF TO A BAD START.
S'RIGHT. NO CONVOY-- A DOZEN EYEBALLS INSTEAD! WHAT HAPPENED TO OUR LIAISON?
ALL I KNOW IS SHE'S A WOMAN NAMED TARGETER.
TARGETER? I'LL BET SHE'S THE TYPE WHO HUNTS NEK BATTLE DOGS WITH A STICK.
I'LL TAKE THAT BET TO THE TUNE OF ONE HUNDRED CREDITS.

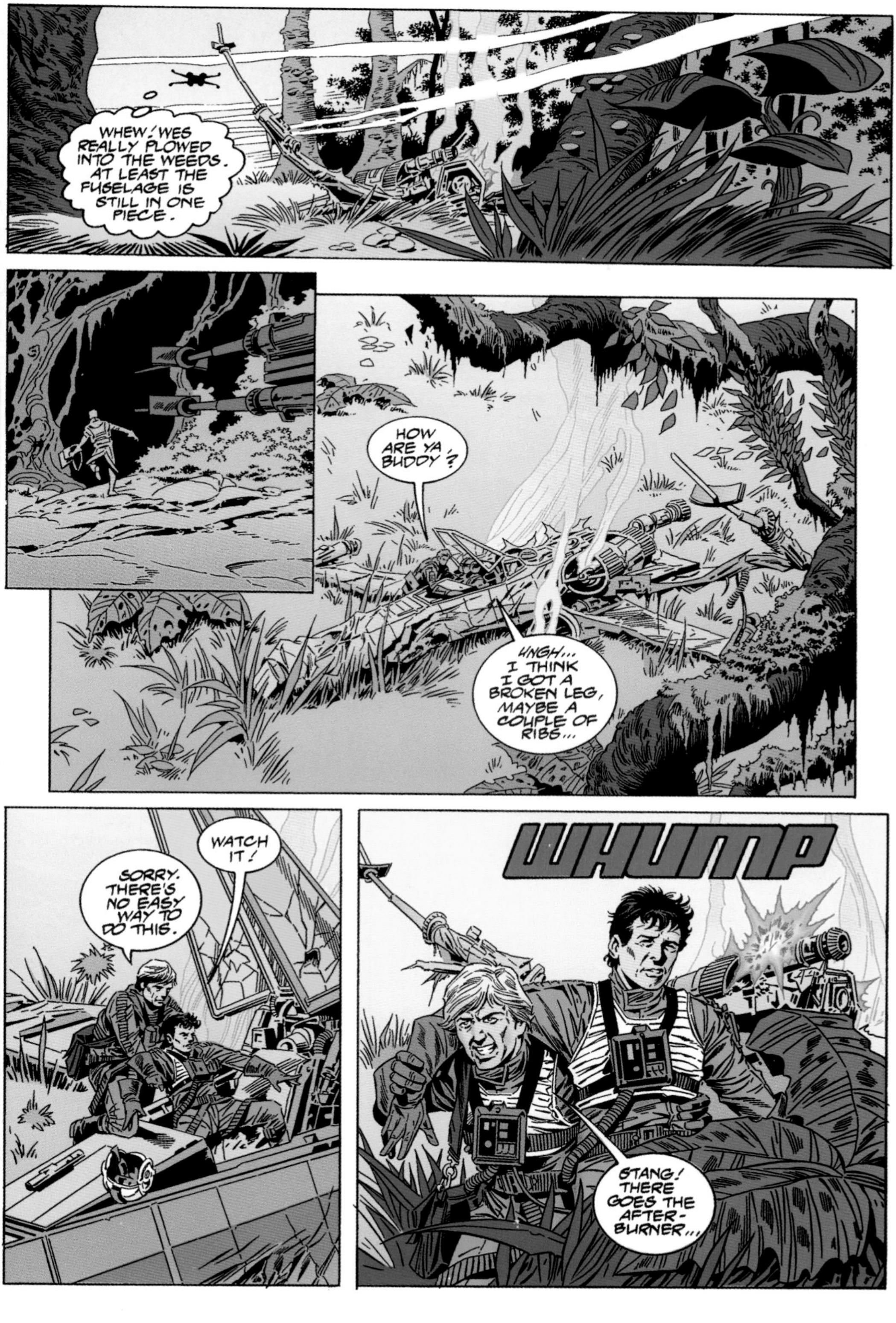
WHEW! WES REALLY PLOWED INTO THE WEEDS. AT LEAST THE FUSELAGE IS STILL IN ONE PIECE.
HOW ARE YA BUDDY?
UNGH... I THINK I GOT A BROKEN LEG, MAYBE A COUPLE OF RIBS...
SORRY. THERE'S NO EASY WAY TO DO THIS.
WATCH IT!
WHUMP
STANG! THERE GOES THE AFTER-BURNER...

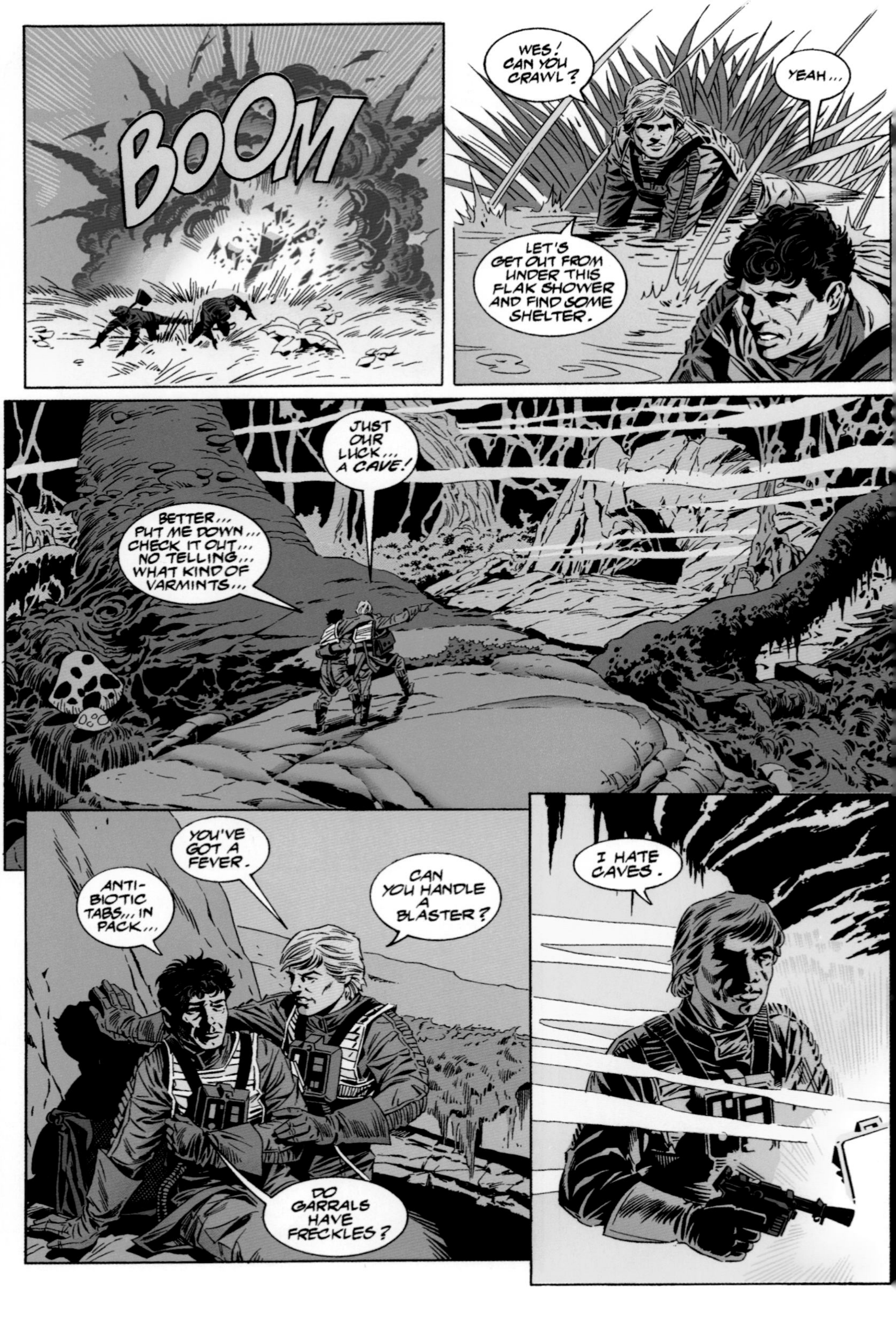
BOOM
WES! CAN YOU CRAWL?
YEAH...
LET'S GET OUT FROM UNDER THIS FLAK SHOWER AND FIND SOME SHELTER.
JUST OUR LUCK... A CAVE!
BETTER... PUT ME DOWN... CHECK IT OUT... NO TELLING... WHAT KIND OF VARMINTS...
YOU'VE GOT A FEVER.
ANTI-BIOTIC TABS... IN PACK...
CAN YOU HANDLE A BLASTER?
DO GARRALS HAVE FRECKLES?
I HATE CAVES.

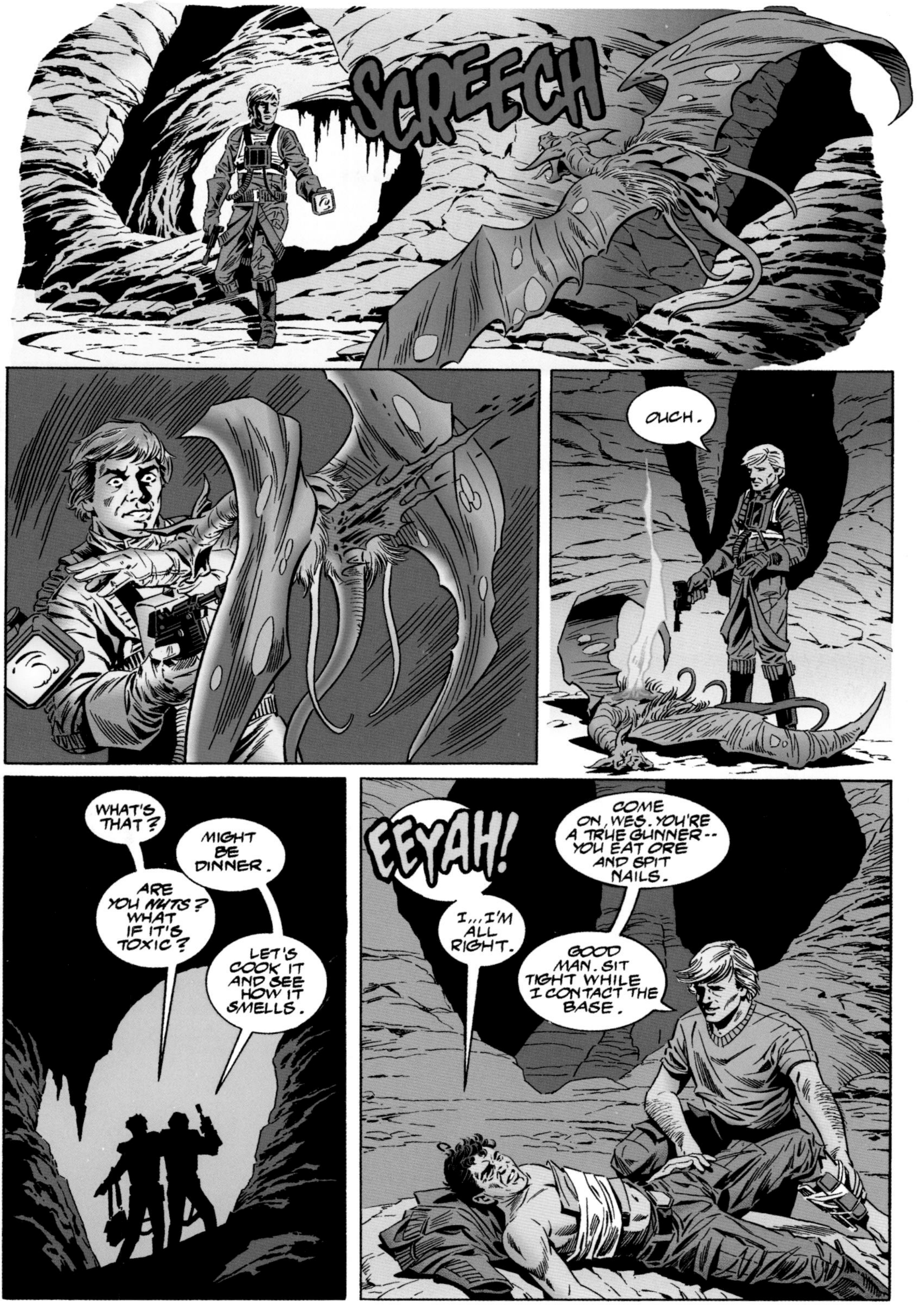
SCREECH
OUCH.
WHAT'S THAT?
MIGHT BE DINNER.
ARE YOU NUTS? WHAT IF IT'S TOXIC?
LET'S COOK IT AND SEE HOW IT SMELLS.
EEYAH!
COME ON, WES. YOU'RE A TRUE GUNNER-- YOU EAT ORE AND SPIT NAILS.
I... I'M ALL RIGHT.
GOOD MAN. SIT TIGHT WHILE I CONTACT THE BASE.

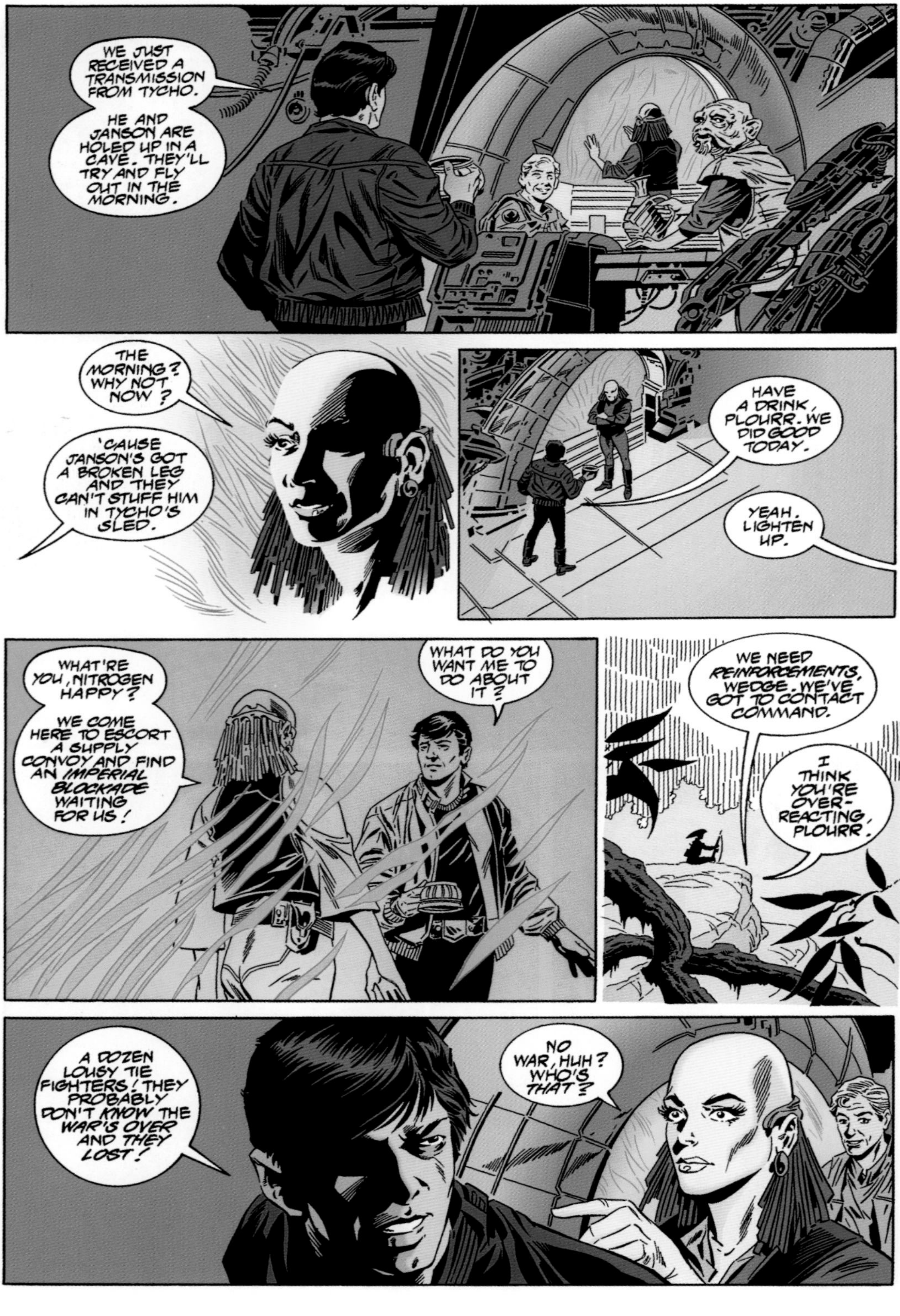
WE JUST RECEIVED A TRANSMISSION FROM TYCHO.
HE AND JANSON ARE HOLED UP IN A CAVE. THEY'LL TRY AND FLY OUT IN THE MORNING.
THE MORNING? WHY NOT NOW?
'CAUSE JANSON'S GOT A BROKEN LEG AND THEY CAN'T STUFF HIM IN TYCHO'S SLED.
HAVE A DRINK, PLOURR. WE DID GOOD TODAY.
YEAH. LIGHTEN UP.
WHAT'RE YOU, NITROGEN HAPPY?
WE COME HERE TO ESCORT A SUPPLY CONVOY AND FIND AN *IMPERIAL BLOCKADE* WAITING FOR US!
WHAT DO YOU WANT ME TO DO ABOUT IT?
WE NEED *REINFORCEMENTS*, WEDGE. WE'VE GOT TO CONTACT COMMAND.
I THINK YOU'RE OVER-REACTING, PLOURR.
A DOZEN LOUSY TIE FIGHTERS! THEY PROBABLY DON'T *KNOW* THE *WAR'S OVER* AND *THEY LOST*!
NO WAR, HUH? WHO'S *THAT*?

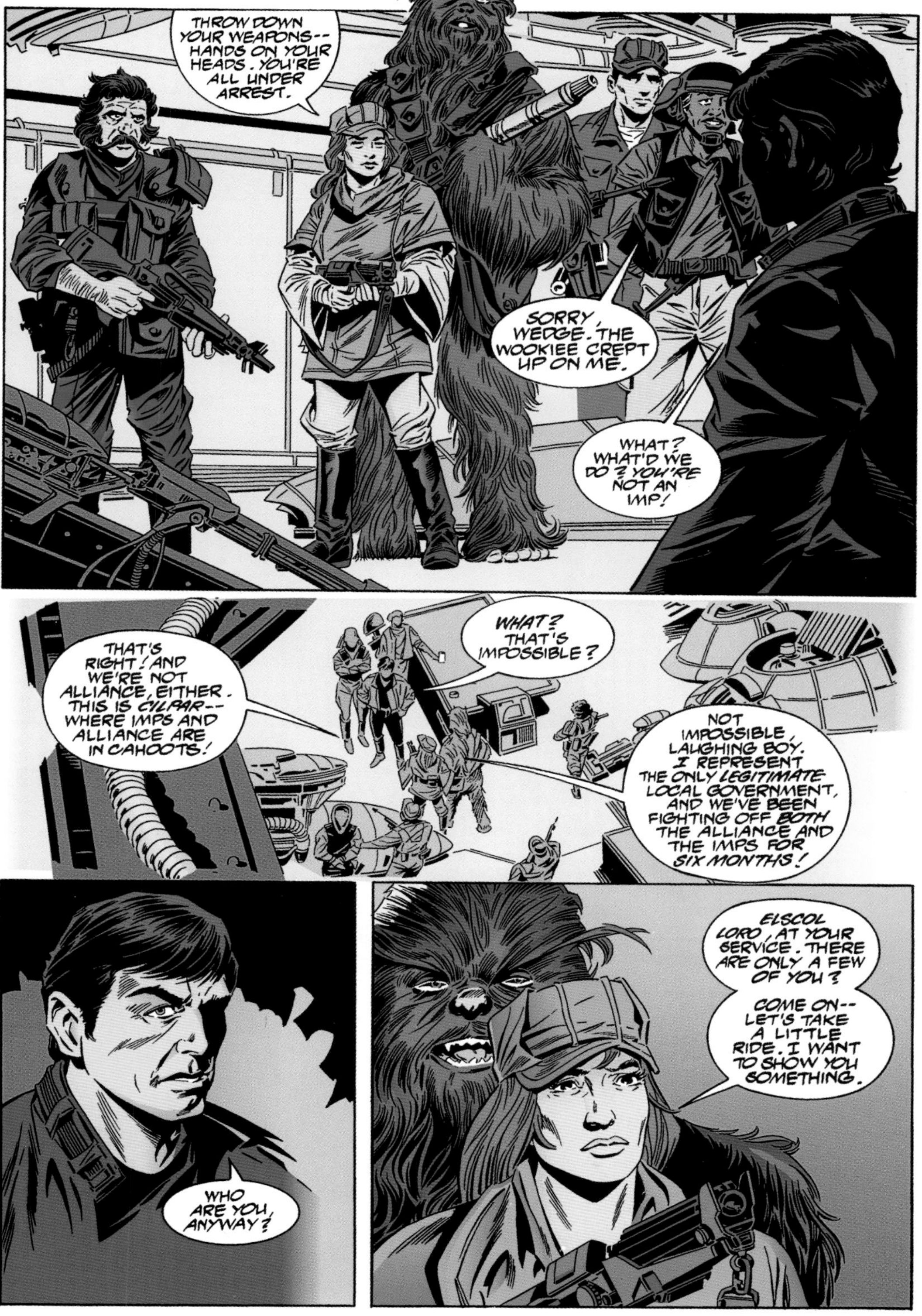
THROW DOWN YOUR WEAPONS-- HANDS ON YOUR HEADS. YOU'RE ALL UNDER ARREST.
SORRY, WEDGE. THE WOOKIEE CREPT UP ON ME.
WHAT? WHAT'D WE DO? YOU'RE NOT AN IMP!
WHAT? THAT'S IMPOSSIBLE?
THAT'S RIGHT! AND WE'RE NOT ALLIANCE, EITHER. THIS IS CILPAR-- WHERE IMPS AND ALLIANCE ARE IN CAHOOTS!
NOT IMPOSSIBLE, LAUGHING BOY. I REPRESENT THE ONLY LEGITIMATE LOCAL GOVERNMENT, AND WE'VE BEEN FIGHTING OFF BOTH THE ALLIANCE AND THE IMPS FOR SIX MONTHS!
WHO ARE YOU, ANYWAY?
ELSCOL LORO, AT YOUR SERVICE. THERE ARE ONLY A FEW OF YOU?
COME ON-- LET'S TAKE A LITTLE RIDE. I WANT TO SHOW YOU SOMETHING.

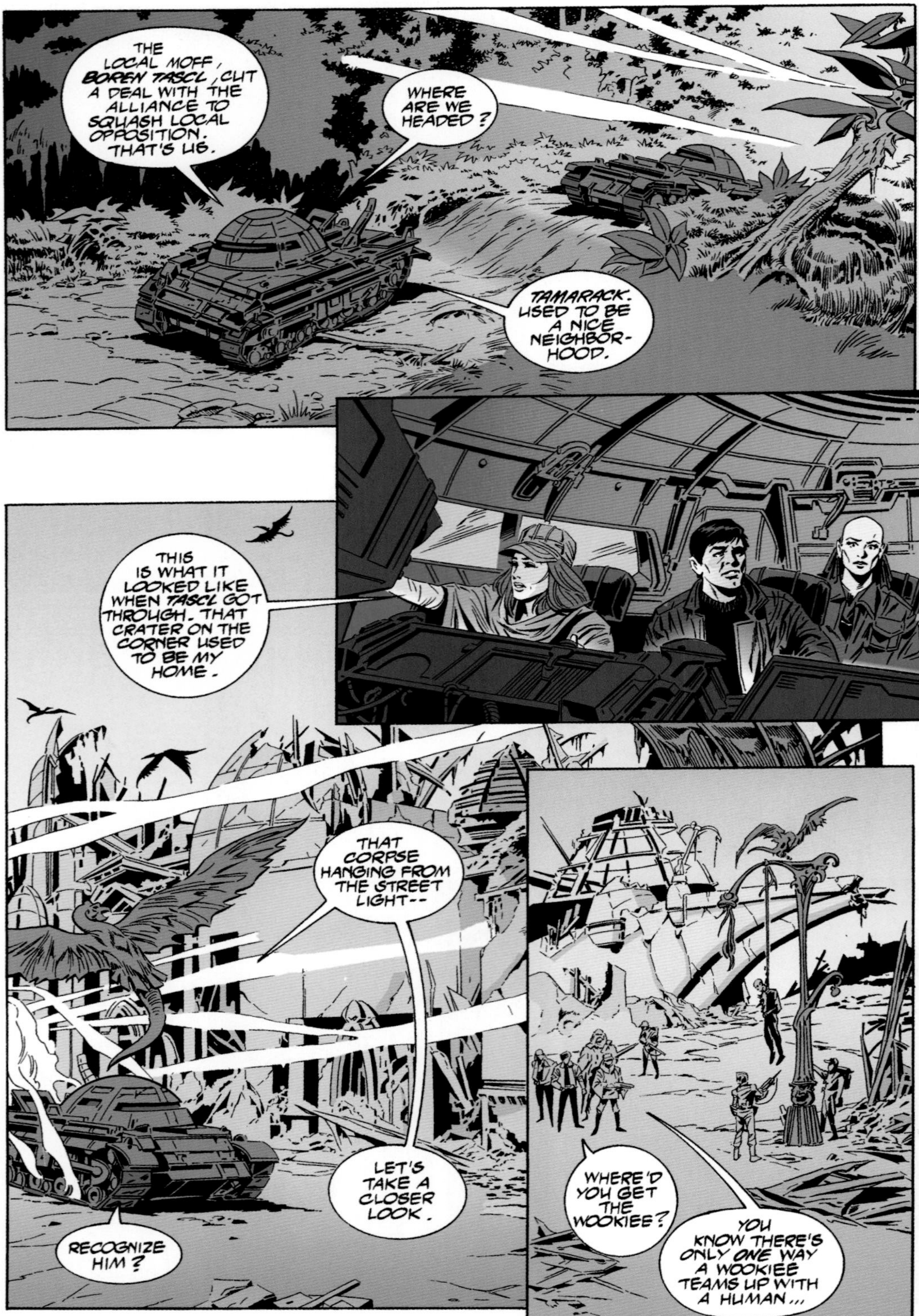
THE LOCAL MOFF, BOREN TASCL, CUT A DEAL WITH THE ALLIANCE TO SQUASH LOCAL OPPOSITION. THAT'S US.
WHERE ARE WE HEADED?
TAMARACK. USED TO BE A NICE NEIGHBORHOOD.
THIS IS WHAT IT LOOKED LIKE WHEN TASCL GOT THROUGH. THAT CRATER ON THE CORNER USED TO BE MY HOME.
THAT CORPSE HANGING FROM THE STREET LIGHT--
RECOGNIZE HIM?
LET'S TAKE A CLOSER LOOK.
WHERE'D YOU GET THE WOOKIEE?
YOU KNOW THERE'S ONLY ONE WAY A WOOKIEE TEAMS UP WITH A HUMAN...

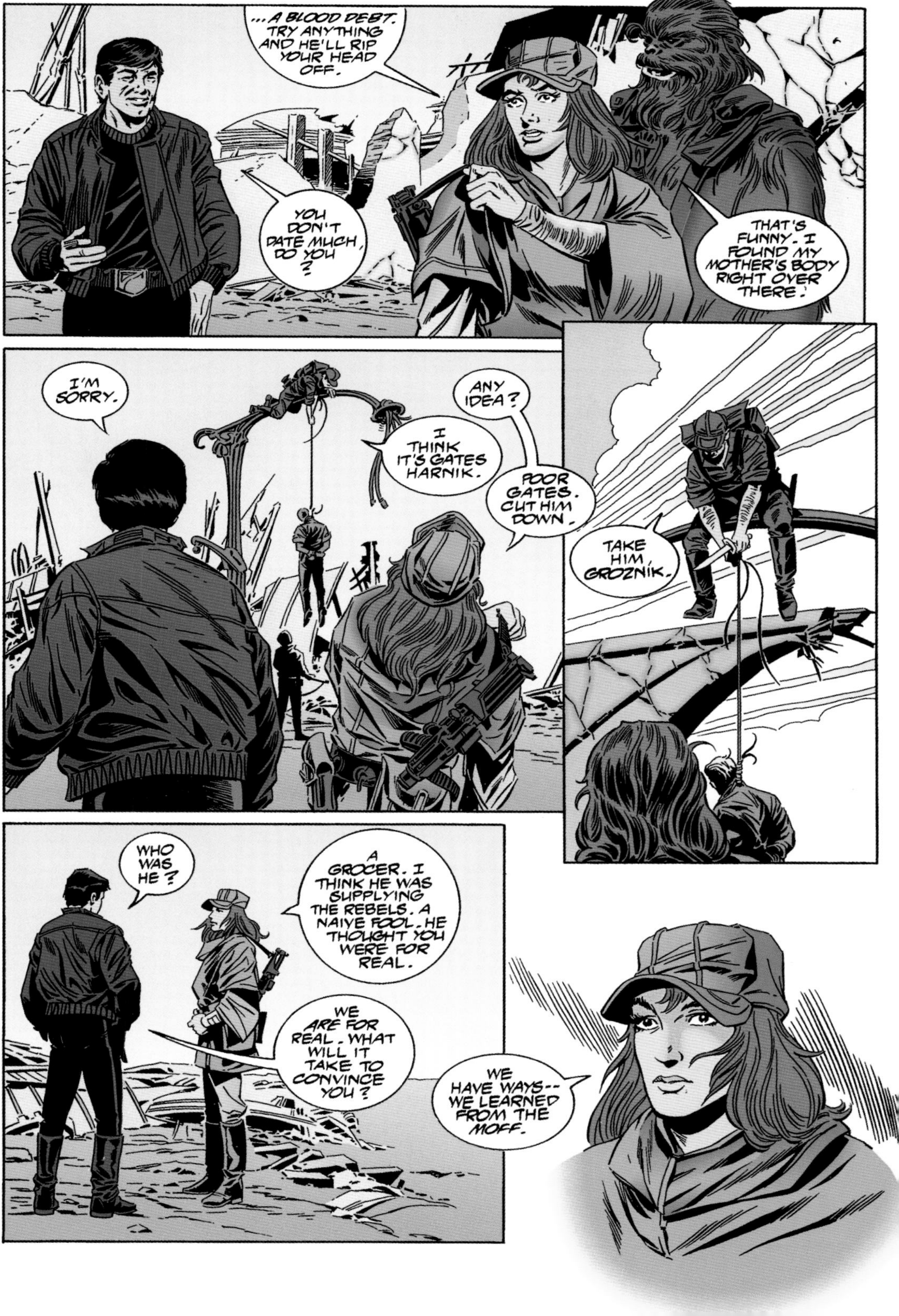
...A BLOOD DEBT. TRY ANYTHING AND HE'LL RIP YOUR HEAD OFF.
YOU DON'T DATE MUCH, DO YOU?
THAT'S FUNNY. I FOUND MY MOTHER'S BODY RIGHT OVER THERE.
I'M SORRY.
I THINK IT'S GATES HARNIK.
ANY IDEA?
POOR GATES. CUT HIM DOWN.
TAKE HIM, GROZNIK.
WHO WAS HE?
A GROCER. I THINK HE WAS SUPPLYING THE REBELS. A NAIVE FOOL. HE THOUGHT YOU WERE FOR REAL.
WE ARE FOR REAL. WHAT WILL IT TAKE TO CONVINCE YOU?
WE HAVE WAYS-- WE LEARNED FROM THE MOFF.

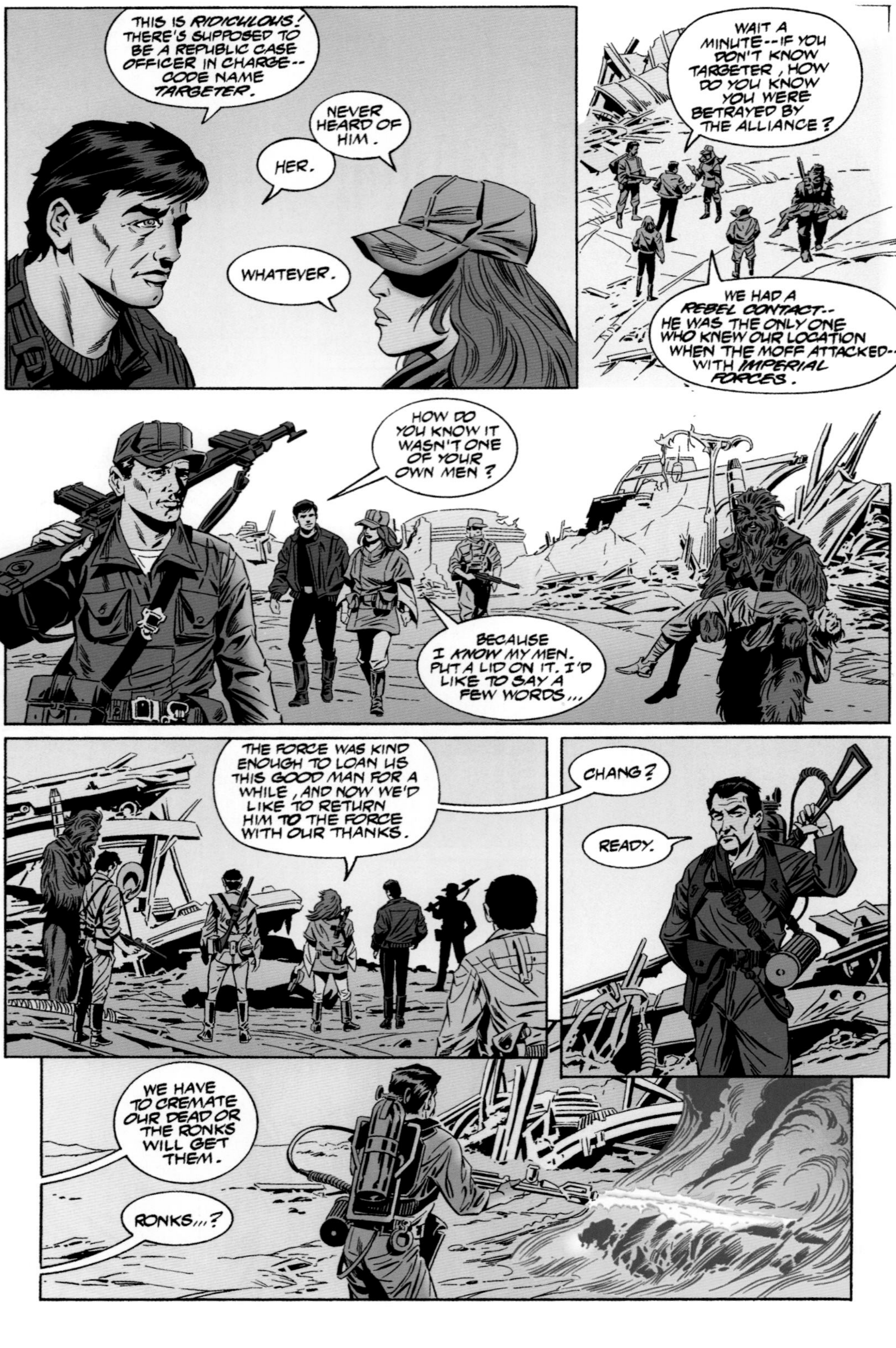
THIS IS RIDICULOUS! THERE'S SUPPOSED TO BE A REPUBLIC CASE OFFICER IN CHARGE-- CODE NAME TARGETER.
NEVER HEARD OF HIM.
HER.
WHATEVER.
WAIT A MINUTE--IF YOU DON'T KNOW TARGETER, HOW DO YOU KNOW YOU WERE BETRAYED BY THE ALLIANCE?
WE HAD A REBEL CONTACT-- HE WAS THE ONLY ONE WHO KNEW OUR LOCATION WHEN THE MOFF ATTACKED-- WITH IMPERIAL FORCES.
HOW DO YOU KNOW IT WASN'T ONE OF YOUR OWN MEN?
BECAUSE I KNOW MY MEN. PUT A LID ON IT. I'D LIKE TO SAY A FEW WORDS...
THE FORCE WAS KIND ENOUGH TO LOAN US THIS GOOD MAN FOR A WHILE, AND NOW WE'D LIKE TO RETURN HIM TO THE FORCE WITH OUR THANKS.
CHANG?
READY.
WE HAVE TO CREMATE OUR DEAD OR THE RONKS WILL GET THEM.
RONKS...?

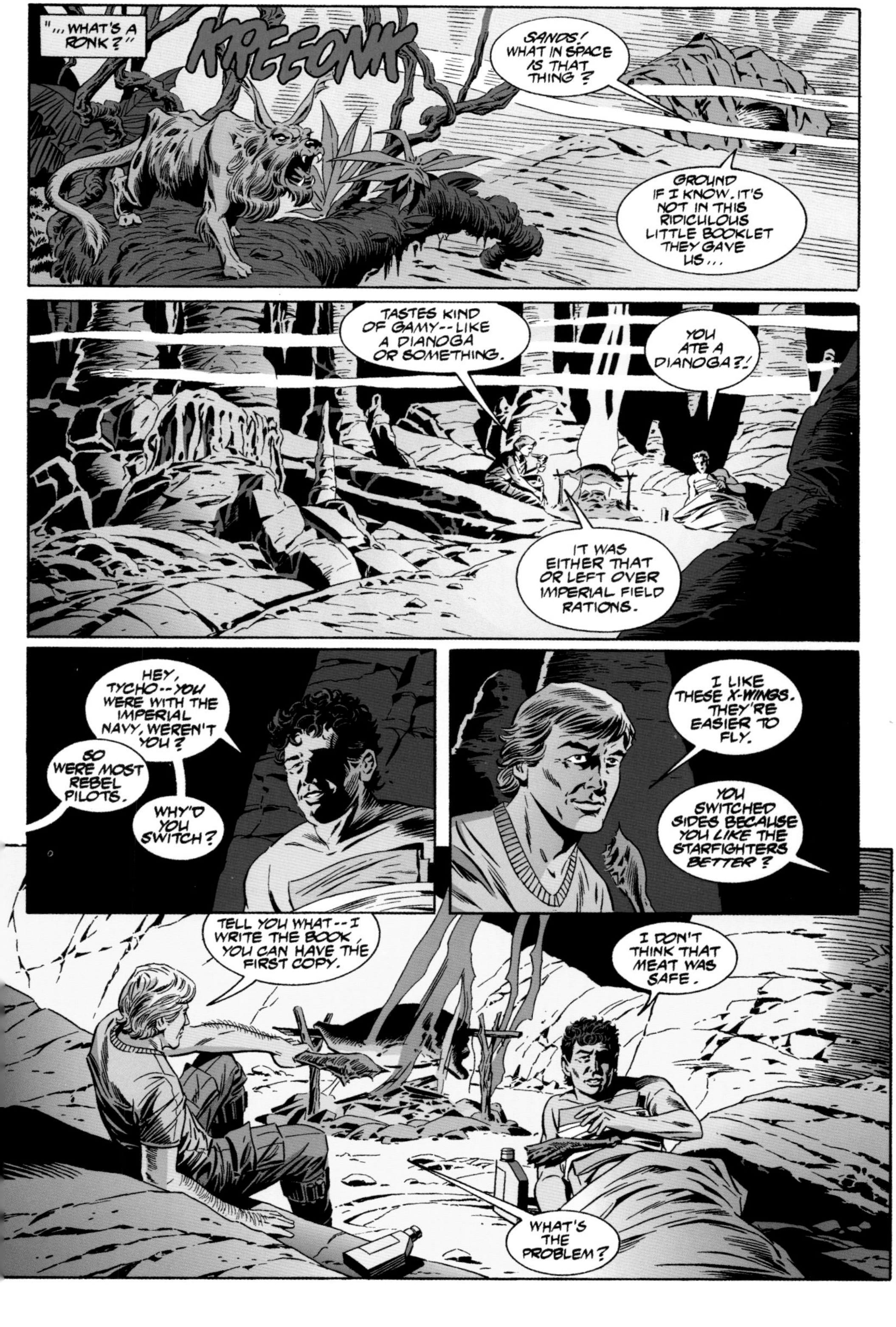
"...WHAT'S A RONK?"
KREEONK
SANDS! WHAT IN SPACE IS THAT THING?
GROUND IF I KNOW. IT'S NOT IN THIS RIDICULOUS LITTLE BOOKLET THEY GAVE US...
TASTES KIND OF GAMY--LIKE A DIANOGA OR SOMETHING.
YOU ATE A DIANOGA?!
IT WAS EITHER THAT OR LEFT OVER IMPERIAL FIELD RATIONS.
HEY, TYCHO--YOU WERE WITH THE IMPERIAL NAVY, WEREN'T YOU?
SO WERE MOST REBEL PILOTS.
WHY'D YOU SWITCH?
I LIKE THESE X-WINGS. THEY'RE EASIER TO FLY.
YOU SWITCHED SIDES BECAUSE YOU LIKE THE STARFIGHTERS BETTER?
TELL YOU WHAT--I WRITE THE BOOK, YOU CAN HAVE THE FIRST COPY.
I DON'T THINK THAT MEAT WAS SAFE.
WHAT'S THE PROBLEM?

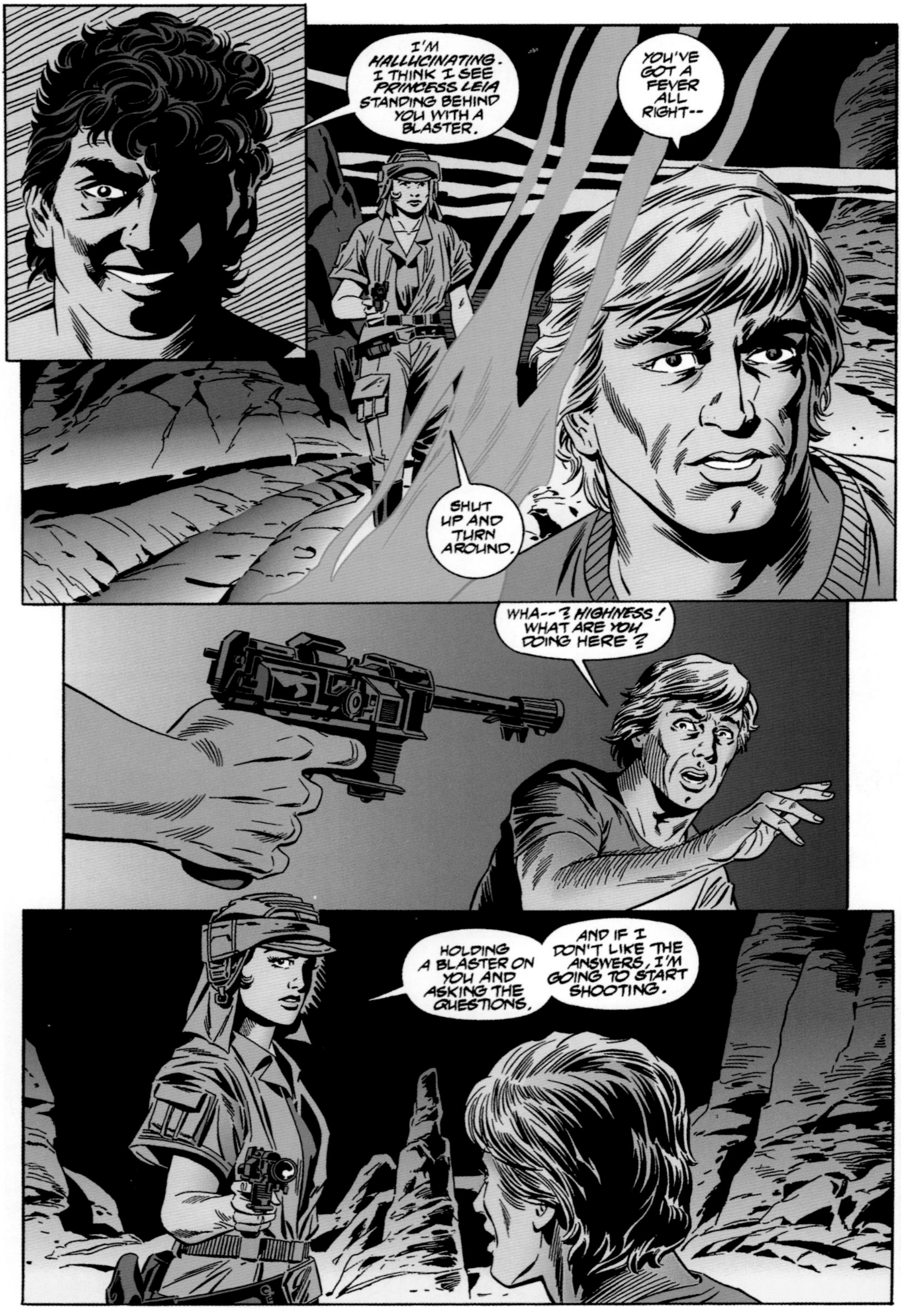
I'M HALLUCINATING. I THINK I SEE PRINCESS LEIA STANDING BEHIND YOU WITH A BLASTER.
YOU'VE GOT A FEVER ALL RIGHT--
SHUT UP AND TURN AROUND.
WHA--? HIGHNESS! WHAT ARE YOU DOING HERE?
HOLDING A BLASTER ON YOU AND ASKING THE QUESTIONS.
AND IF I DON'T LIKE THE ANSWERS, I'M GOING TO START SHOOTING.

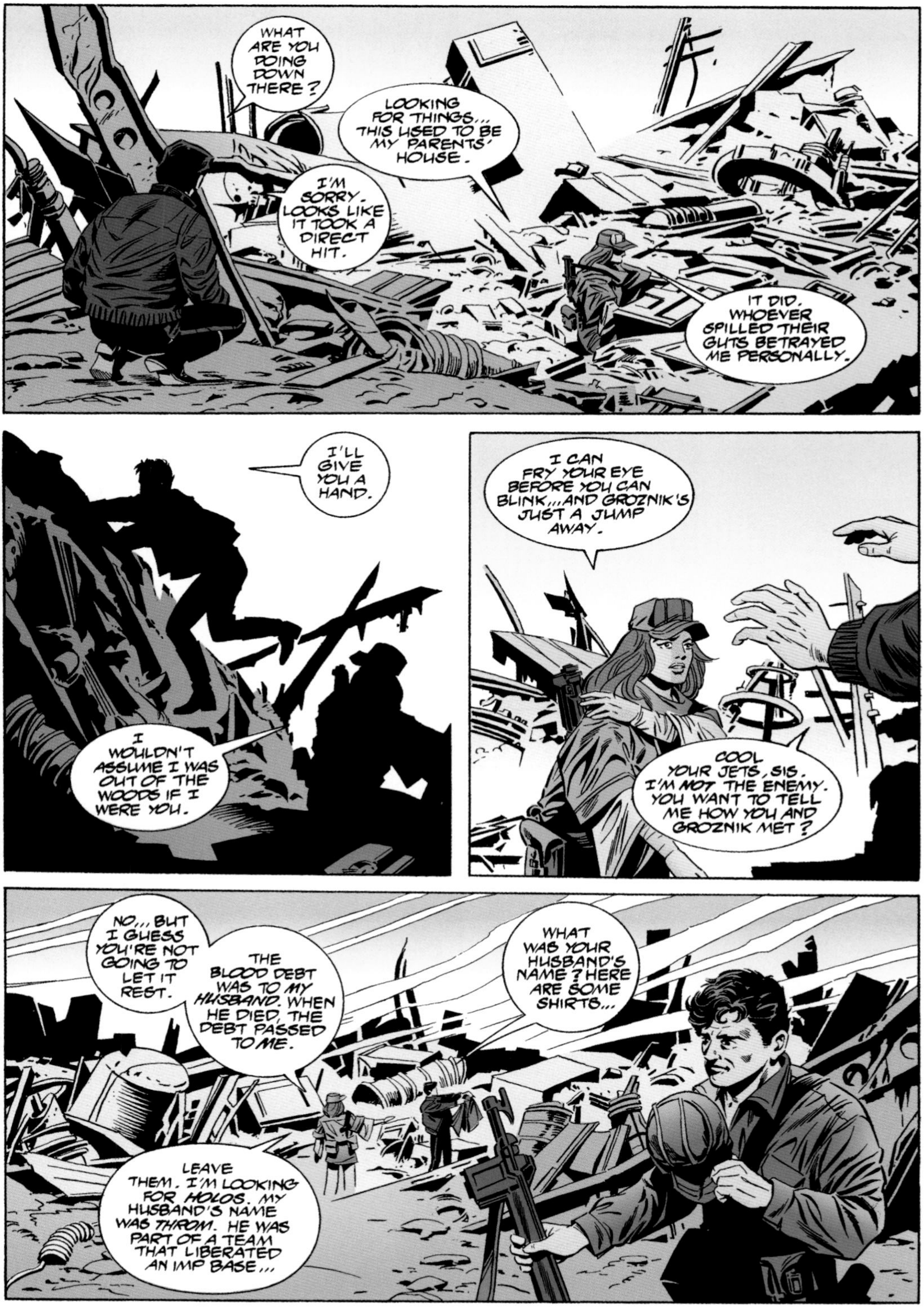
WHAT ARE YOU DOING DOWN THERE?
LOOKING FOR THINGS... THIS USED TO BE MY PARENTS' HOUSE.
I'M SORRY. LOOKS LIKE IT TOOK A DIRECT HIT.
IT DID. WHOEVER SPILLED THEIR GUTS BETRAYED ME PERSONALLY.
I'LL GIVE YOU A HAND.
I WOULDN'T ASSUME I WAS OUT OF THE WOODS IF I WERE YOU.
I CAN FRY YOUR EYE BEFORE YOU CAN BLINK... AND GROZNIK'S JUST A JUMP AWAY.
COOL YOUR JETS, SIS. I'M NOT THE ENEMY. YOU WANT TO TELL ME HOW YOU AND GROZNIK MET?
NO... BUT I GUESS YOU'RE NOT GOING TO LET IT REST.
THE BLOOD DEBT WAS TO MY HUSBAND. WHEN HE DIED, THE DEBT PASSED TO ME.
WHAT WAS YOUR HUSBAND'S NAME? HERE ARE SOME SHIRTS...
LEAVE THEM. I'M LOOKING FOR HOLOS. MY HUSBAND'S NAME WAS THROM. HE WAS PART OF A TEAM THAT LIBERATED AN IMP BASE...

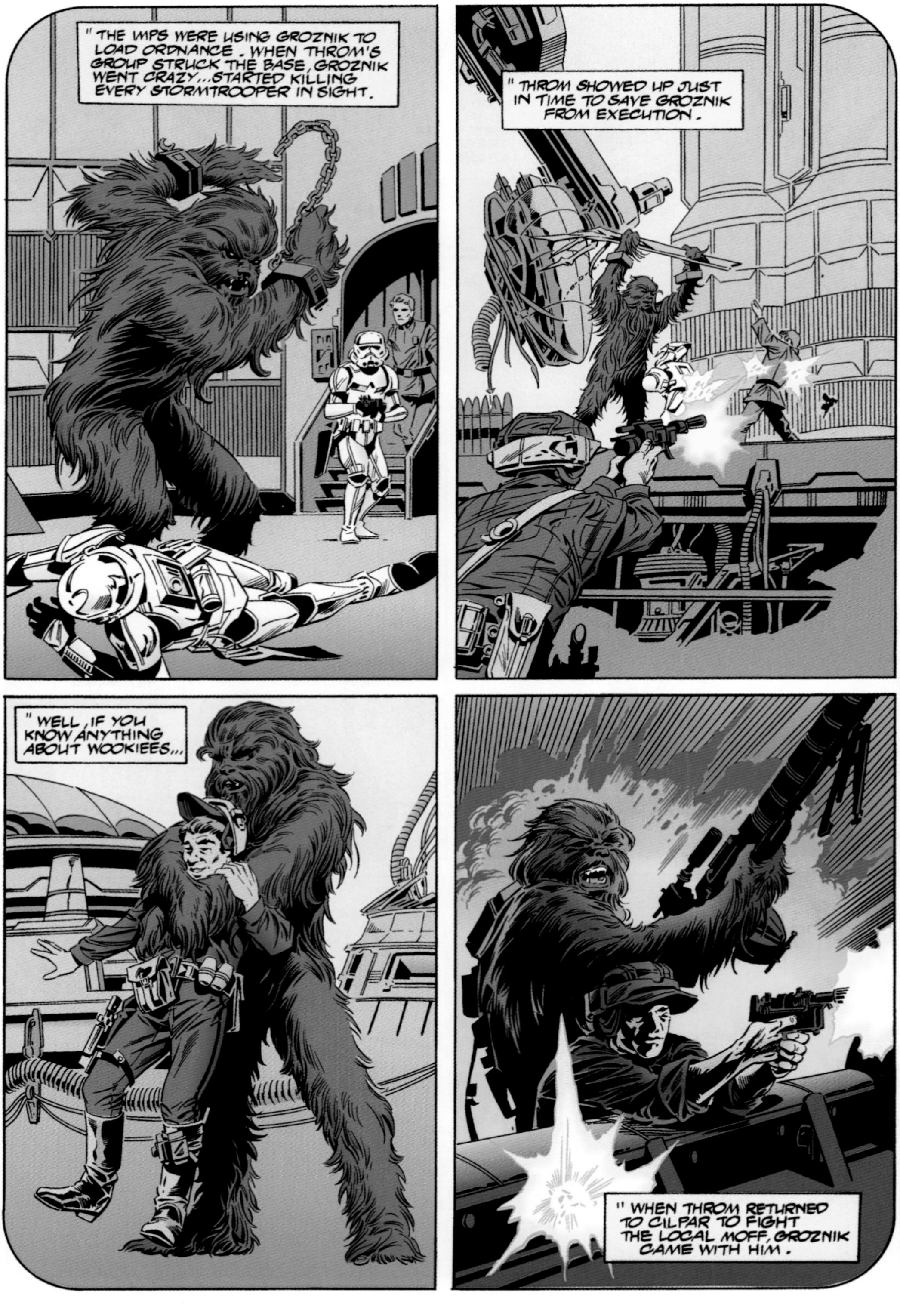
"THE IMPS WERE USING GROZNIK TO LOAD ORDNANCE. WHEN THROM'S GROUP STRUCK THE BASE, GROZNIK WENT CRAZY...STARTED KILLING EVERY STORMTROOPER IN SIGHT.
"THROM SHOWED UP JUST IN TIME TO SAVE GROZNIK FROM EXECUTION.
"WELL, IF YOU KNOW ANYTHING ABOUT WOOKIEES...
"WHEN THROM RETURNED TO CILPAR TO FIGHT THE LOCAL MOFF, GROZNIK CAME WITH HIM.

"ONCE THROM GOT THE ALLIANCE'S ATTENTION, THE IMPS WENT CRAZY.

"THEY FINALLY GOT HIM AT THE *BATTLE OF THE CLIFFS*.

"GROZNIK WAS DEVASTATED. NO OPPORTUNITY TO REPAY THE DEBT.

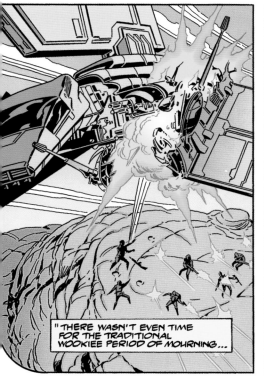

"THERE WASN'T EVEN TIME FOR THE TRADITIONAL WOOKIEE PERIOD OF MOURNING...

"THROM HAD TOLD HIM ABOUT ME, AND HE IMMEDIATELY TRANSFERRED HIS ALLEGIANCE. I GUESS I'M STUCK WITH HIM."

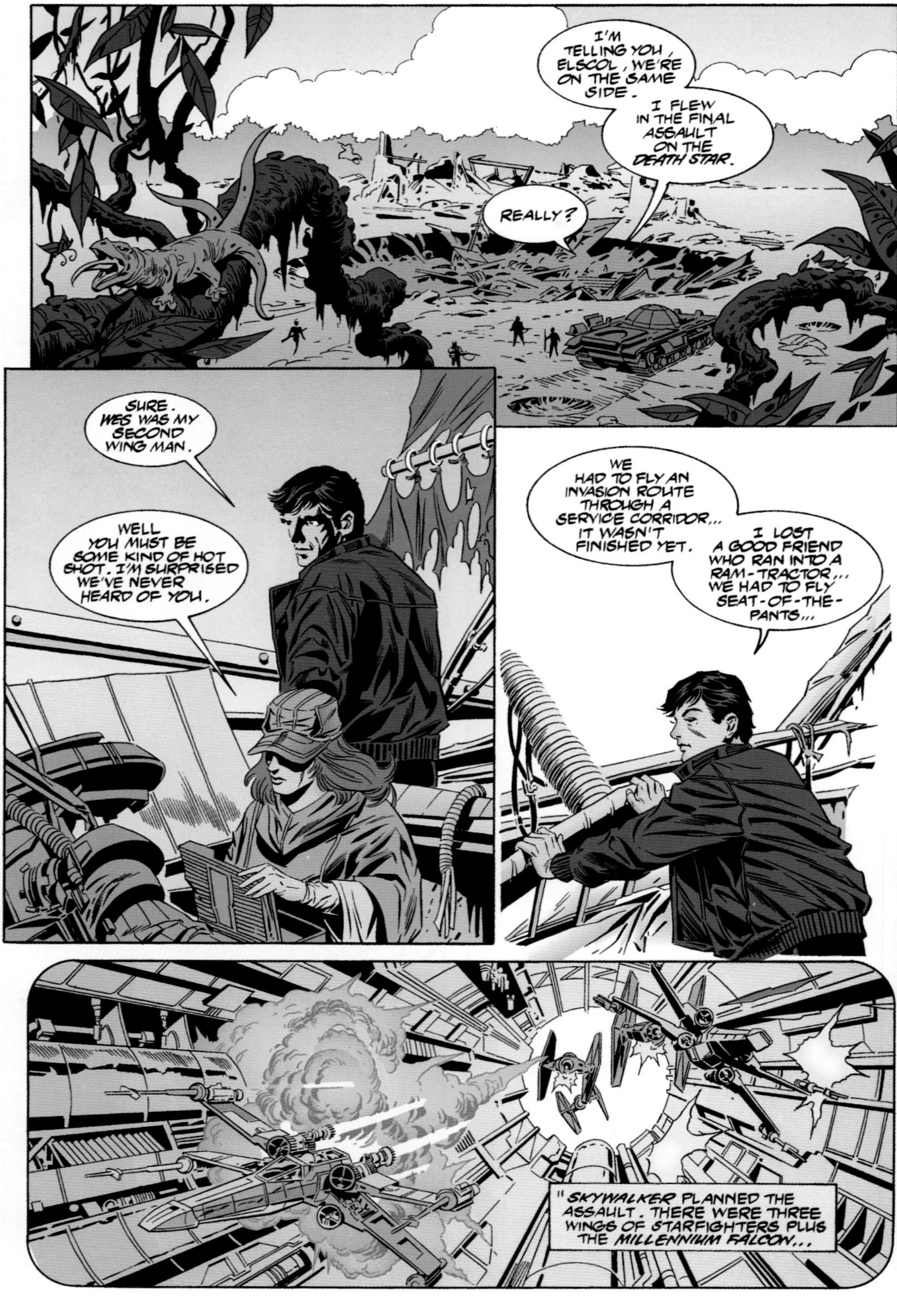
I'M TELLING YOU, ELSCOL, WE'RE ON THE SAME SIDE.
I FLEW IN THE FINAL ASSAULT ON THE DEATH STAR.
REALLY?
SURE. WES WAS MY SECOND WING MAN.
WELL YOU MUST BE SOME KIND OF HOT SHOT. I'M SURPRISED WE'VE NEVER HEARD OF YOU.
WE HAD TO FLY AN INVASION ROUTE THROUGH A SERVICE CORRIDOR... IT WASN'T FINISHED YET.
I LOST A GOOD FRIEND WHO RAN INTO A RAM-TRACTOR... WE HAD TO FLY SEAT-OF-THE-PANTS...
"SKYWALKER PLANNED THE ASSAULT. THERE WERE THREE WINGS OF STARFIGHTERS PLUS THE MILLENNIUM FALCON...

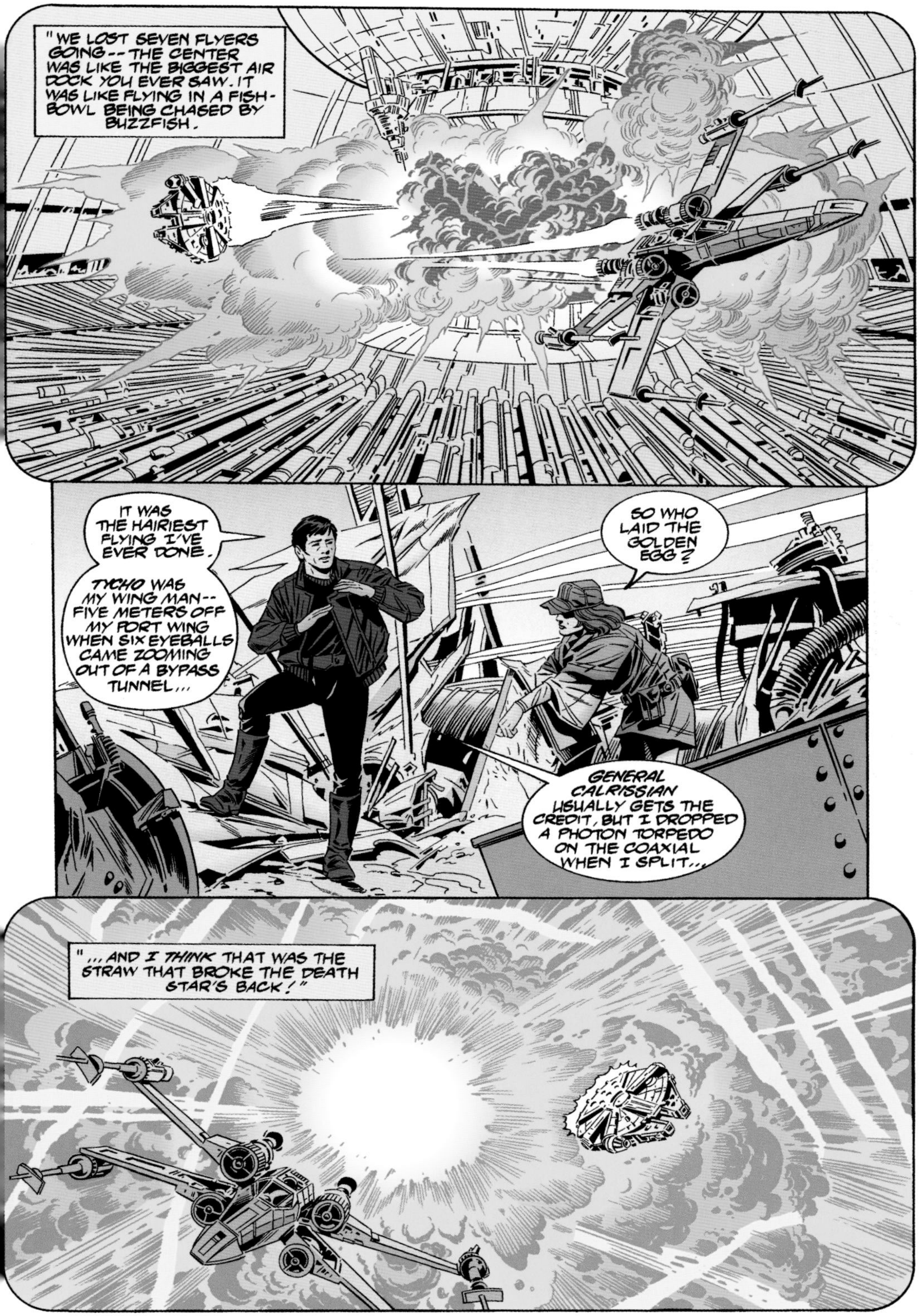
"WE LOST SEVEN FLYERS GOING -- THE CENTER WAS LIKE THE BIGGEST AIR DOCK YOU EVER SAW. IT WAS LIKE FLYING IN A FISH-BOWL BEING CHASED BY BUZZFISH.
IT WAS THE HAIRIEST FLYING I'VE EVER DONE.
TYCHO WAS MY WING MAN-- FIVE METERS OFF MY PORT WING WHEN SIX EYEBALLS CAME ZOOMING OUT OF A BYPASS TUNNEL...
SO WHO LAID THE GOLDEN EGG?
GENERAL CALRISSIAN USUALLY GETS THE CREDIT, BUT I DROPPED A PHOTON TORPEDO ON THE COAXIAL WHEN I SPLIT...
"...AND I THINK THAT WAS THE STRAW THAT BROKE THE DEATH STAR'S BACK!"

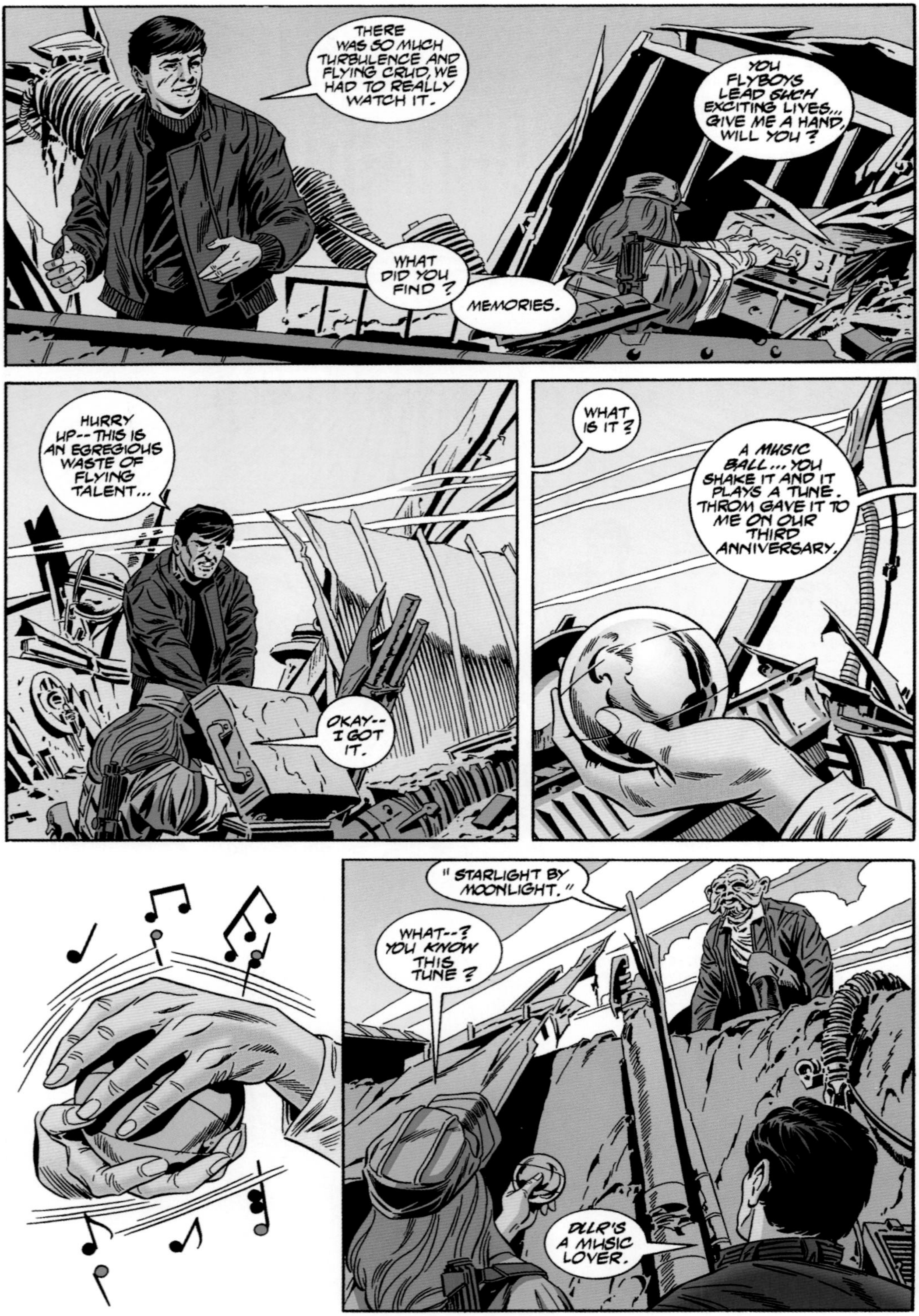
THERE WAS SO MUCH TURBULENCE AND FLYING CRUD, WE HAD TO REALLY WATCH IT.
YOU FLYBOYS LEAD SUCH EXCITING LIVES... GIVE ME A HAND, WILL YOU?
WHAT DID YOU FIND?
MEMORIES.
HURRY UP-- THIS IS AN EGREGIOUS WASTE OF FLYING TALENT...
OKAY-- I GOT IT.
WHAT IS IT?
A MUSIC BALL... YOU SHAKE IT AND IT PLAYS A TUNE. THROM GAVE IT TO ME ON OUR THIRD ANNIVERSARY.
"STARLIGHT BY MOONLIGHT."
WHAT--? YOU KNOW THIS TUNE?
DLLR'S A MUSIC LOVER.

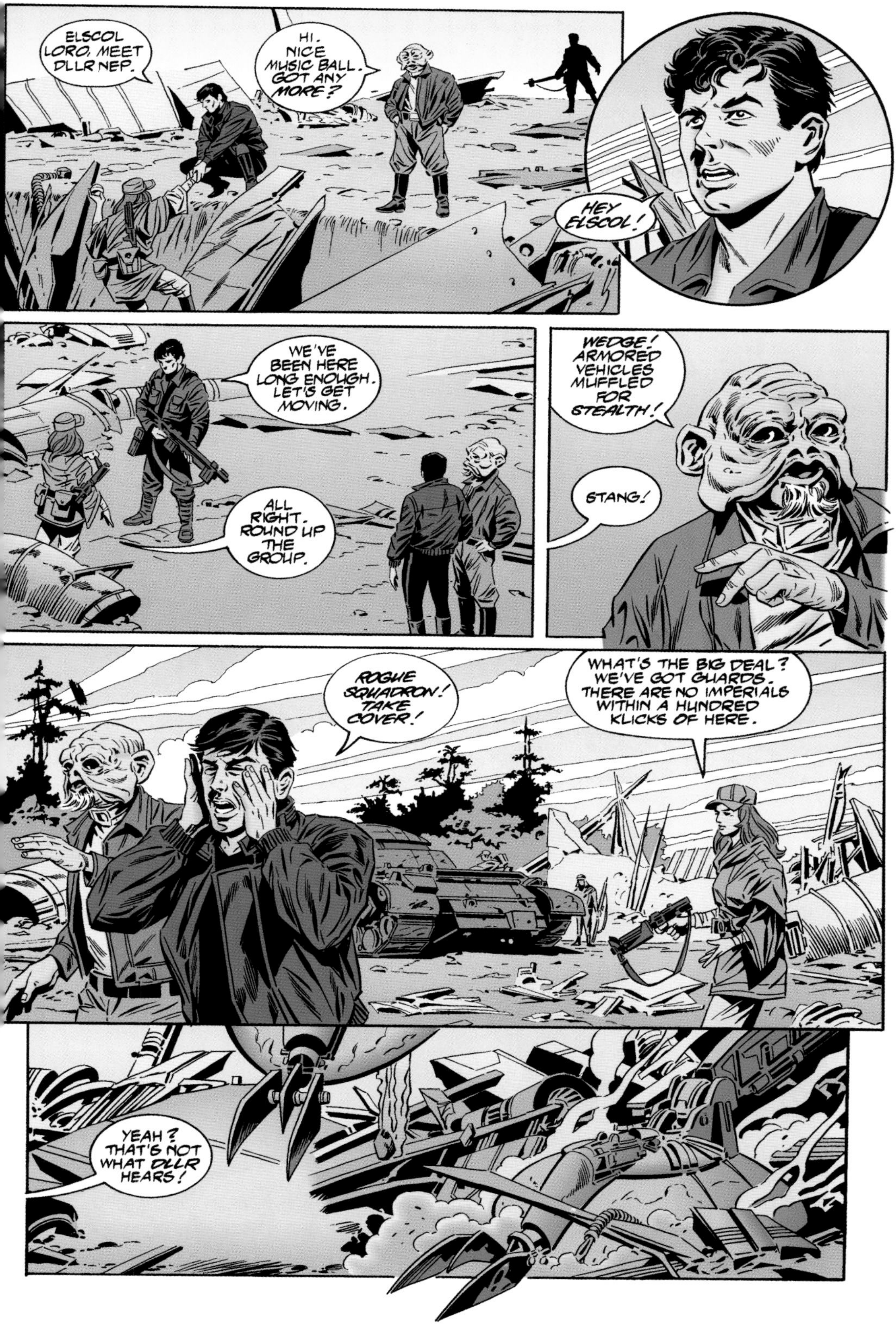
ELSCOL LORO, MEET DLLR NEP.
HI. NICE MUSIC BALL. GOT ANY MORE?
HEY ELSCOL!
WE'VE BEEN HERE LONG ENOUGH. LET'S GET MOVING.
ALL RIGHT. ROUND UP THE GROUP.
WEDGE! ARMORED VEHICLES MUFFLED FOR STEALTH!
STANG!
ROGUE SQUADRON! TAKE COVER!
WHAT'S THE BIG DEAL? WE'VE GOT GUARDS. THERE ARE NO IMPERIALS WITHIN A HUNDRED KLICKS OF HERE.
YEAH? THAT'S NOT WHAT DLLR HEARS!

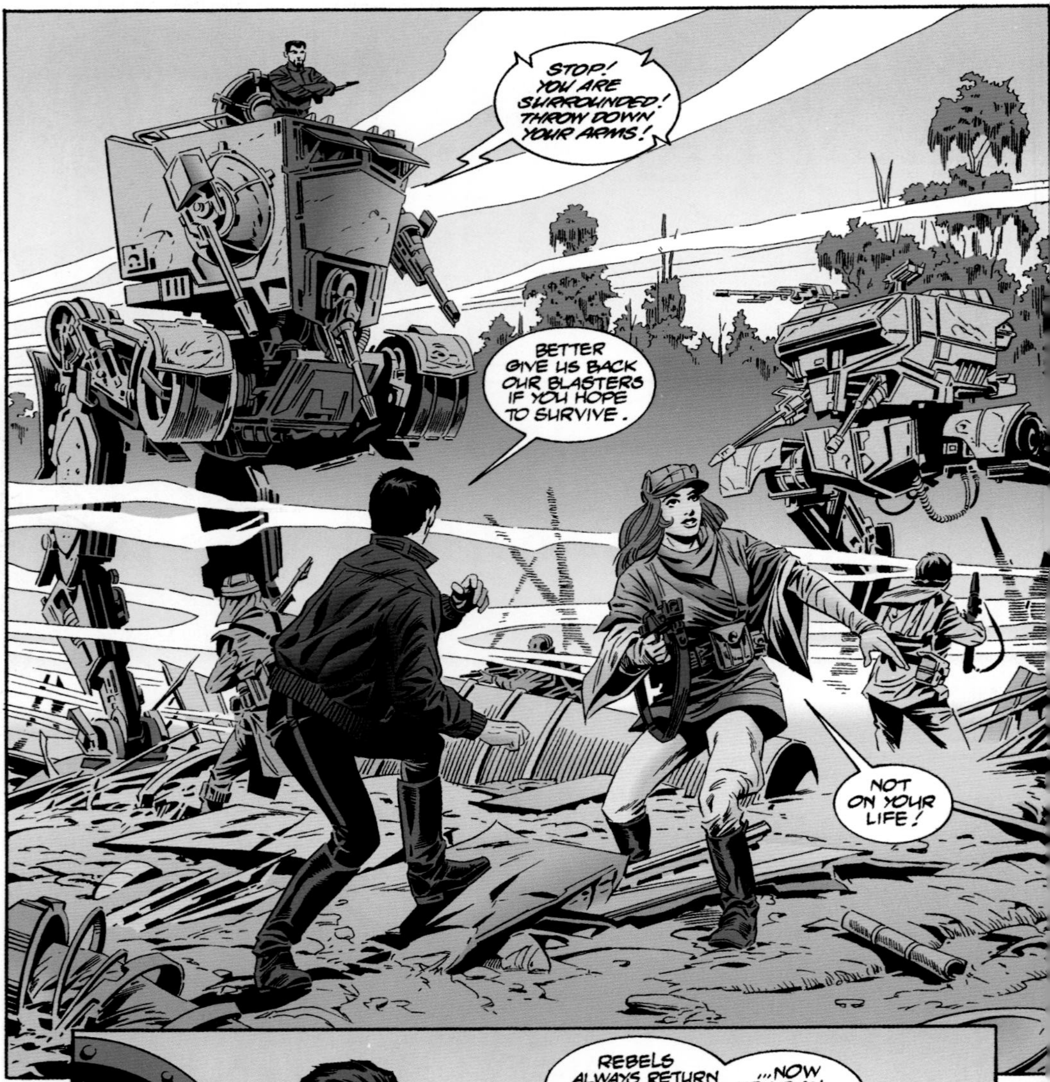
STOP! YOU ARE SURROUNDED! THROW DOWN YOUR ARMS!
BETTER GIVE US BACK OUR BLASTERS IF YOU HOPE TO SURVIVE.
NOT ON YOUR LIFE!
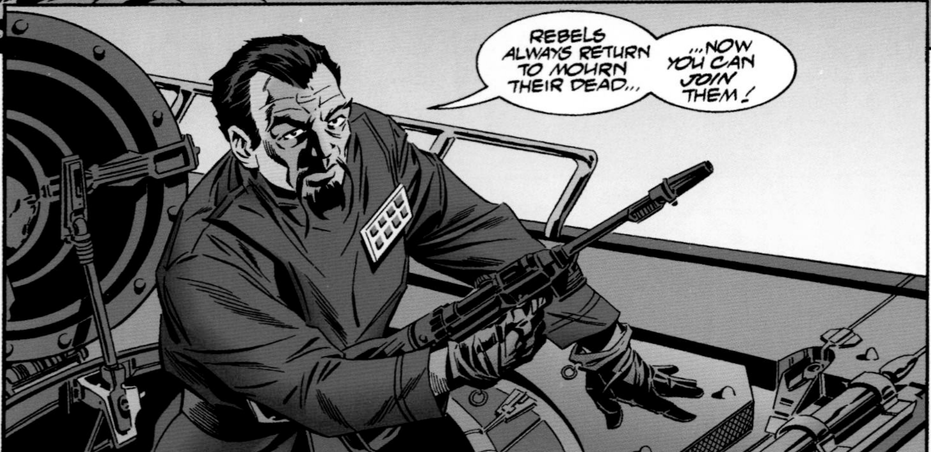
REBELS ALWAYS RETURN TO MOURN THEIR DEAD...
...NOW YOU CAN JOIN THEM!

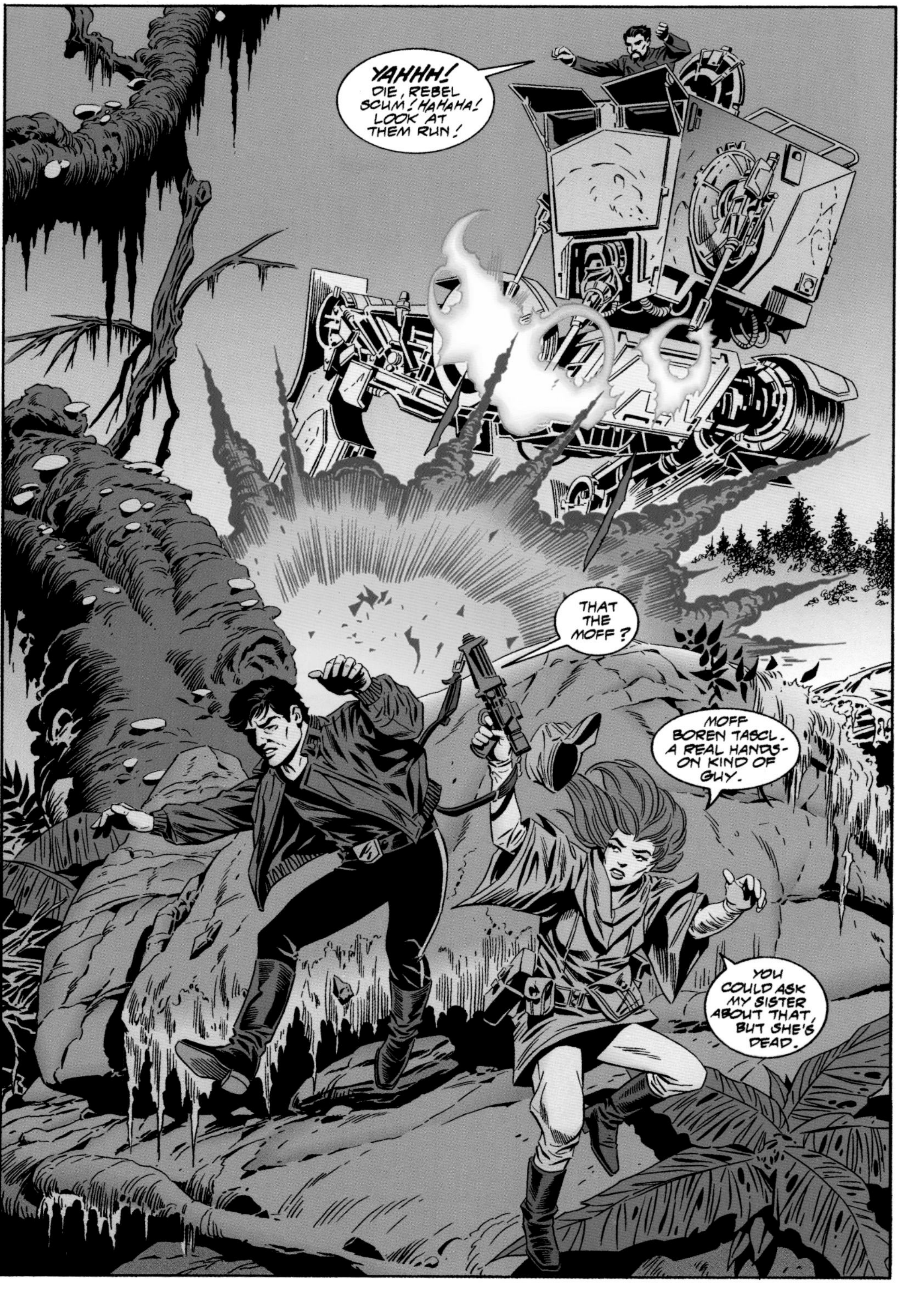
YAHHH! DIE, REBEL SCUM! HAHAHA! LOOK AT THEM RUN!
THAT THE MOFF?
MOFF BOREN TASCL. A REAL HANDS-ON KIND OF GUY.
YOU COULD ASK MY SISTER ABOUT THAT, BUT SHE'S DEAD.

WHAT IS THIS PLACE?

WE DON'T KNOW--IT PREDATES THE SETTLEMENT. OBVIOUSLY SOME KIND OF TEMPLE...

ELSCOL-- WE MUST HAVE TRIPPED AN ALARM.

WHAT'S TO STOP THEM FROM BRINGING THIS TEMPLE DOWN ON OUR HEADS?

THE ROCK. WE TRIED TO DISMANTLE THIS THING A COUPLE YEARS AGO.

DISMANTLE A NATIVE TEMPLE?

THAT'S RIGHT. WE NEEDED MONEY. --WE HAD A DEAL TO SELL THE WORKS TO TALON KARRDE...BUT WE COULDN'T PUT A CHIP IN THE STANG THING.

GIVE US BACK OUR WEAPONS.

FORGET IT.

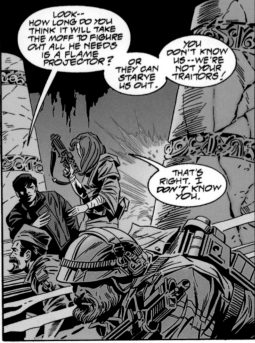

LOOK-- HOW LONG DO YOU THINK IT WILL TAKE THE MOFF TO FIGURE OUT ALL HE NEEDS IS A FLAME PROJECTOR?

OR THEY CAN STARVE US OUT.

YOU DON'T KNOW US--WE'RE NOT YOUR TRAITORS!

THAT'S RIGHT. I DON'T KNOW YOU.

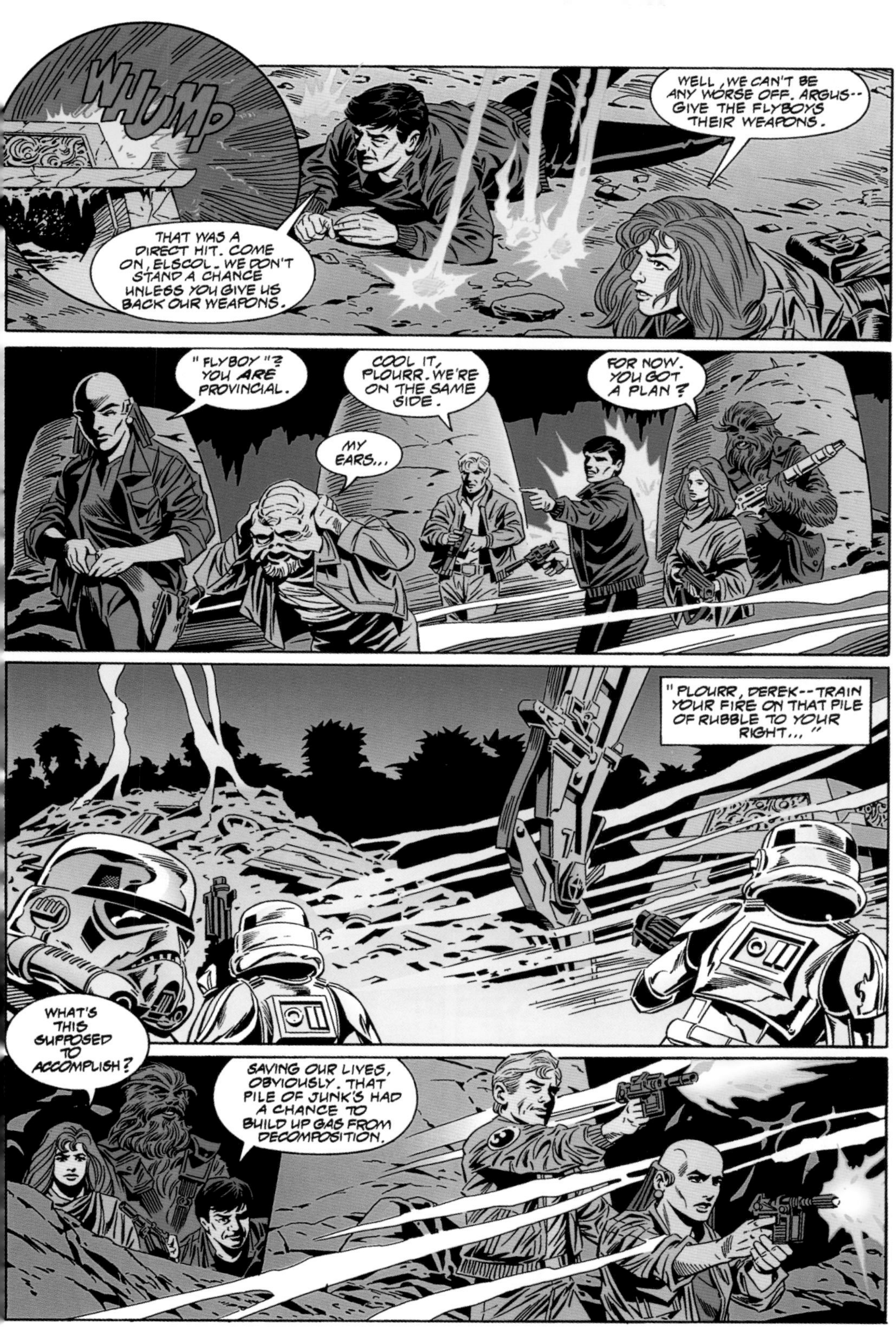
WHUMP
THAT WAS A DIRECT HIT. COME ON, ELSCOL. WE DON'T STAND A CHANCE UNLESS YOU GIVE US BACK OUR WEAPONS.
WELL, WE CAN'T BE ANY WORSE OFF. ARGUS-- GIVE THE FLYBOYS THEIR WEAPONS.
"FLYBOY"? YOU ARE PROVINCIAL.
COOL IT, PLOURR. WE'RE ON THE SAME SIDE.
MY EARS...
FOR NOW. YOU GOT A PLAN?
"PLOURR, DEREK--TRAIN YOUR FIRE ON THAT PILE OF RUBBLE TO YOUR RIGHT..."
WHAT'S THIS SUPPOSED TO ACCOMPLISH?
SAVING OUR LIVES, OBVIOUSLY. THAT PILE OF JUNK'S HAD A CHANCE TO BUILD UP GAS FROM DECOMPOSITION.

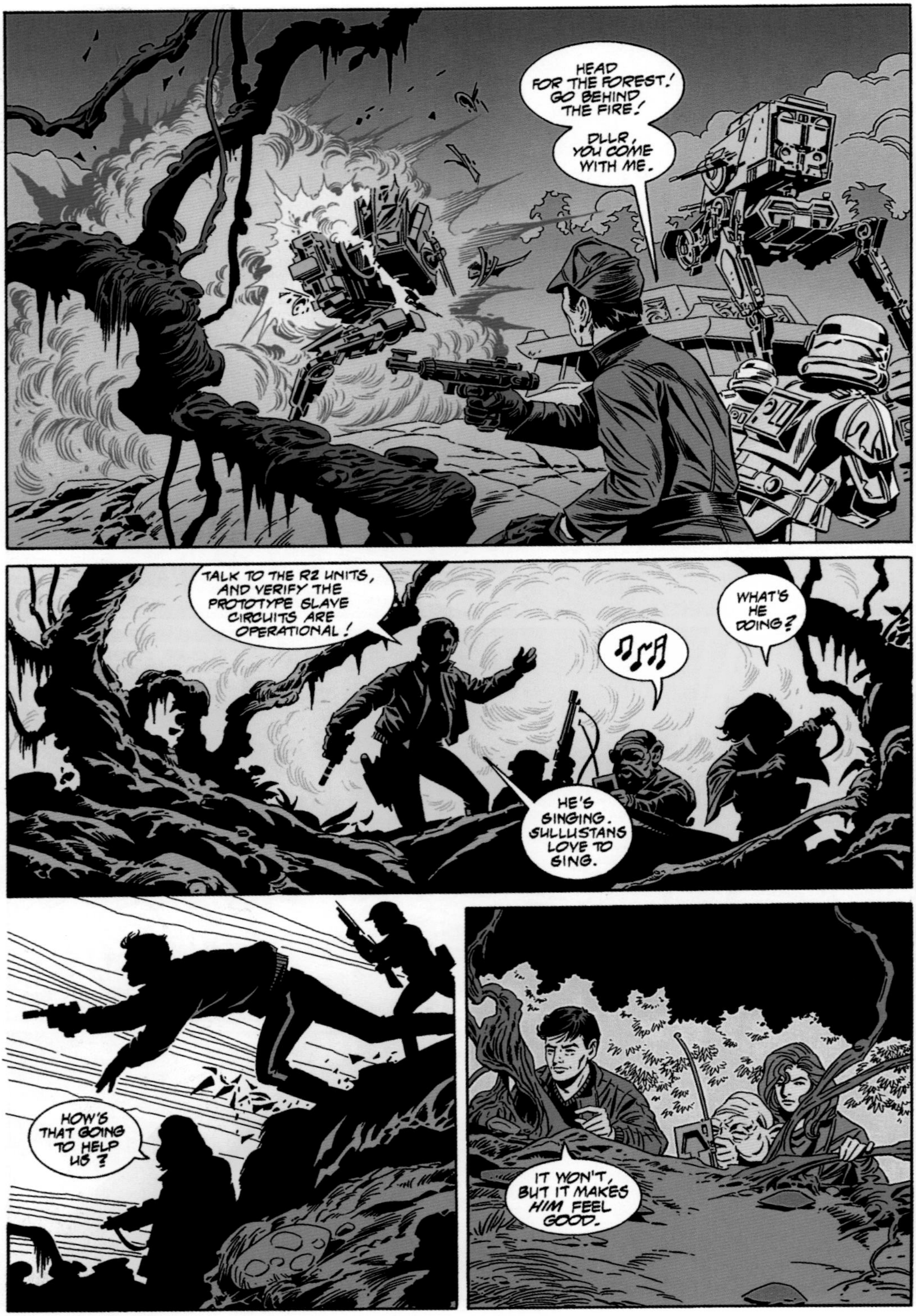

HEAD FOR THE FOREST! GO BEHIND THE FIRE!
DLLR, YOU COME WITH ME.
TALK TO THE R2 UNITS, AND VERIFY THE PROTOTYPE SLAVE CIRCUITS ARE OPERATIONAL!
WHAT'S HE DOING?
HE'S SINGING. SULLUSTANS LOVE TO SING.
HOW'S THAT GOING TO HELP US?
IT WON'T, BUT IT MAKES *HIM* FEEL GOOD.

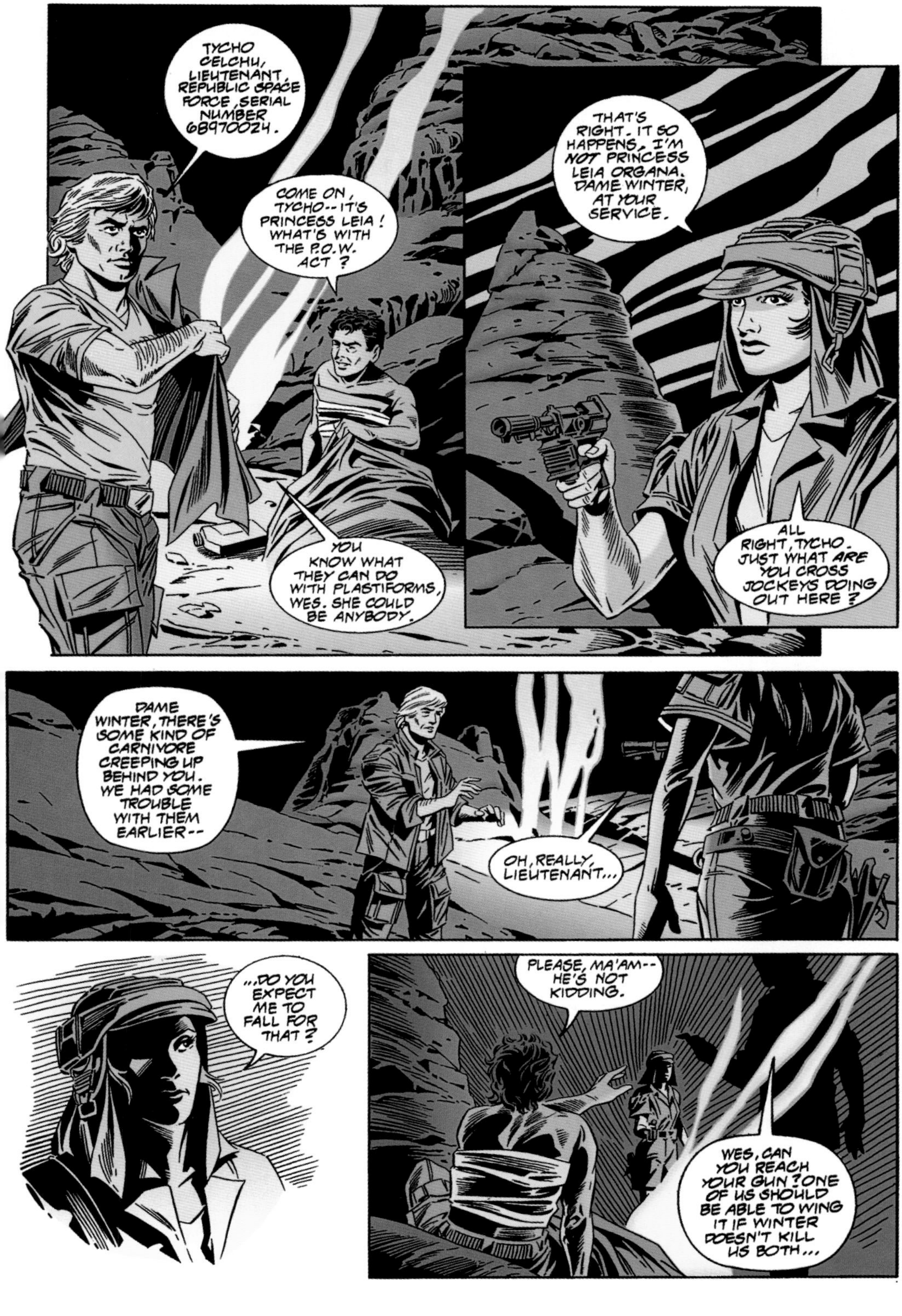
TYCHO CELCHU, LIEUTENANT, REPUBLIC SPACE FORCE, SERIAL NUMBER 68970024.
COME ON, TYCHO-- IT'S PRINCESS LEIA! WHAT'S WITH THE P.O.W. ACT?
YOU KNOW WHAT THEY CAN DO WITH PLASTIFORMS, WES. SHE COULD BE ANYBODY.
THAT'S RIGHT. IT SO HAPPENS, I'M NOT PRINCESS LEIA ORGANA. DAME WINTER, AT YOUR SERVICE.
ALL RIGHT, TYCHO. JUST WHAT ARE YOU CROSS JOCKEYS DOING OUT HERE?
DAME WINTER, THERE'S SOME KIND OF CARNIVORE CREEPING UP BEHIND YOU. WE HAD SOME TROUBLE WITH THEM EARLIER--
OH, REALLY, LIEUTENANT...
...DO YOU EXPECT ME TO FALL FOR THAT?
PLEASE, MA'AM-- HE'S NOT KIDDING.
WES, CAN YOU REACH YOUR GUN? ONE OF US SHOULD BE ABLE TO WING IT IF WINTER DOESN'T KILL US BOTH...

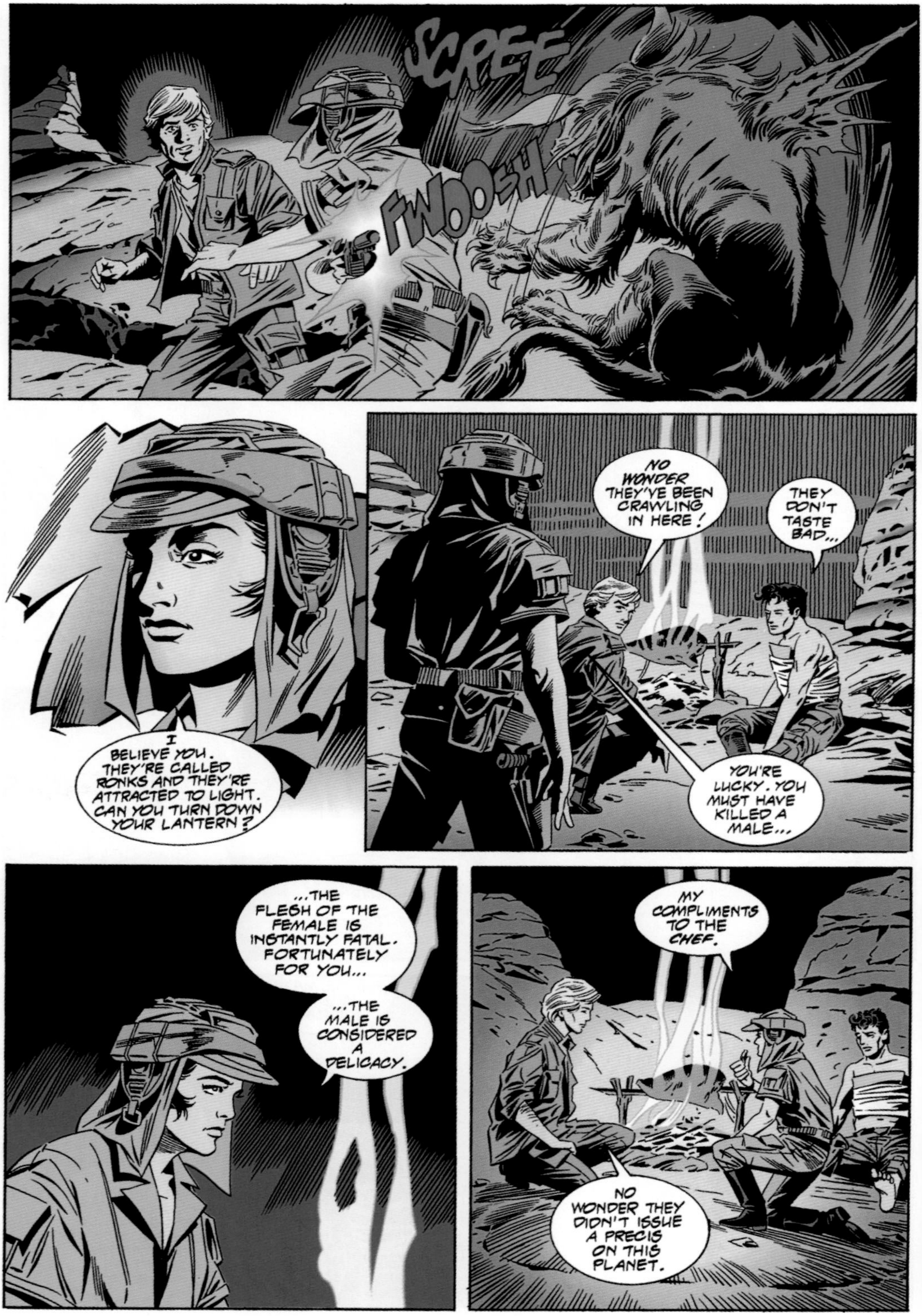
SCREEE
FWOOSH
I BELIEVE YOU. THEY'RE CALLED RONKS AND THEY'RE ATTRACTED TO LIGHT. CAN YOU TURN DOWN YOUR LANTERN?
NO WONDER THEY'VE BEEN CRAWLING IN HERE!
THEY DON'T TASTE BAD...
YOU'RE LUCKY. YOU MUST HAVE KILLED A MALE...
...THE FLESH OF THE FEMALE IS INSTANTLY FATAL. FORTUNATELY FOR YOU...
...THE MALE IS CONSIDERED A DELICACY.
MY COMPLIMENTS TO THE CHEF.
NO WONDER THEY DIDN'T ISSUE A PRECIS ON THIS PLANET.

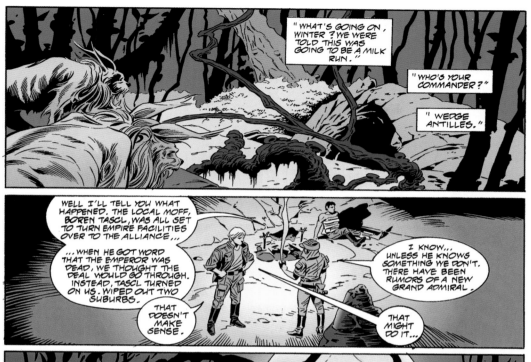

"WHAT'S GOING ON, WINTER? WE WERE TOLD THIS WAS GOING TO BE A MILK RUN."

"WHO'S YOUR COMMANDER?"

"WEDGE ANTILLES."

WELL I'LL TELL YOU WHAT HAPPENED. THE LOCAL MOFF, BOREN TASCL, WAS ALL SET TO TURN EMPIRE FACILITIES OVER TO THE ALLIANCE...

...WHEN HE GOT WORD THAT THE EMPEROR WAS DEAD, WE THOUGHT THE DEAL WOULD GO THROUGH. INSTEAD, TASCL TURNED ON US. WIPED OUT TWO SUBURBS.

THAT DOESN'T MAKE SENSE.

I KNOW... UNLESS HE KNOWS SOMETHING WE DON'T. THERE HAVE BEEN RUMORS OF A NEW GRAND ADMIRAL.

THAT MIGHT DO IT...

"...BUT WE STILL DON'T KNOW THE FULL EXTENT OF THE EMPIRE'S RESOURCES."

SO... WE NEED TO KNOW WHAT THE MOFF KNOWS. I CAN'T GO BACK-- THEY KNOW ME NOW. BUT YOU--YOU COULD PASS FOR AN IMP.

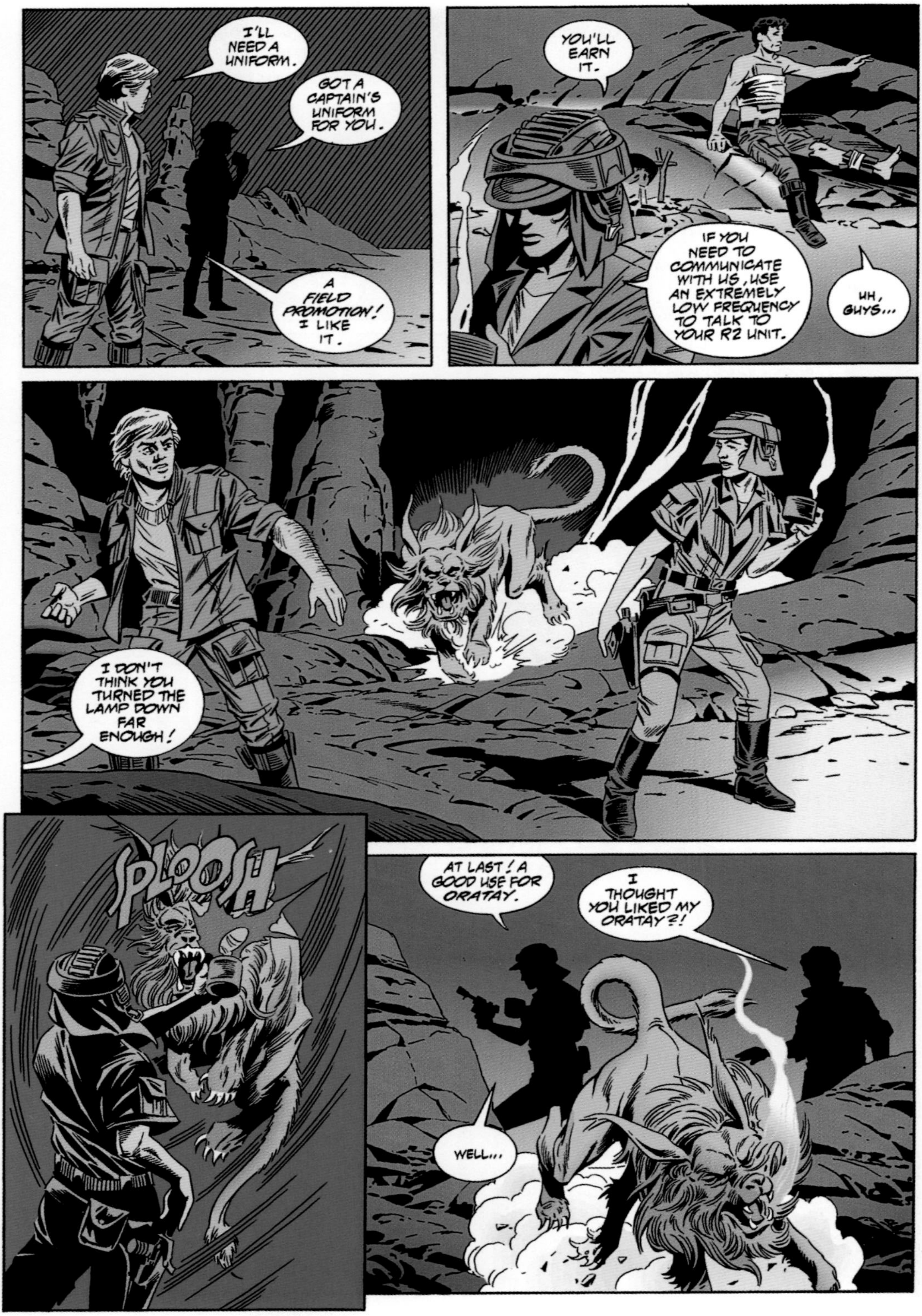
I'LL NEED A UNIFORM.
GOT A CAPTAIN'S UNIFORM FOR YOU.
A FIELD PROMOTION! I LIKE IT.
YOU'LL EARN IT.
IF YOU NEED TO COMMUNICATE WITH US, USE AN EXTREMELY LOW FREQUENCY TO TALK TO YOUR R2 UNIT.
UH, GUYS...
I DON'T THINK YOU TURNED THE LAMP DOWN FAR ENOUGH!
SPLOOSH
AT LAST! A GOOD USE FOR ORATAY.
I THOUGHT YOU LIKED MY ORATAY?!
WELL...

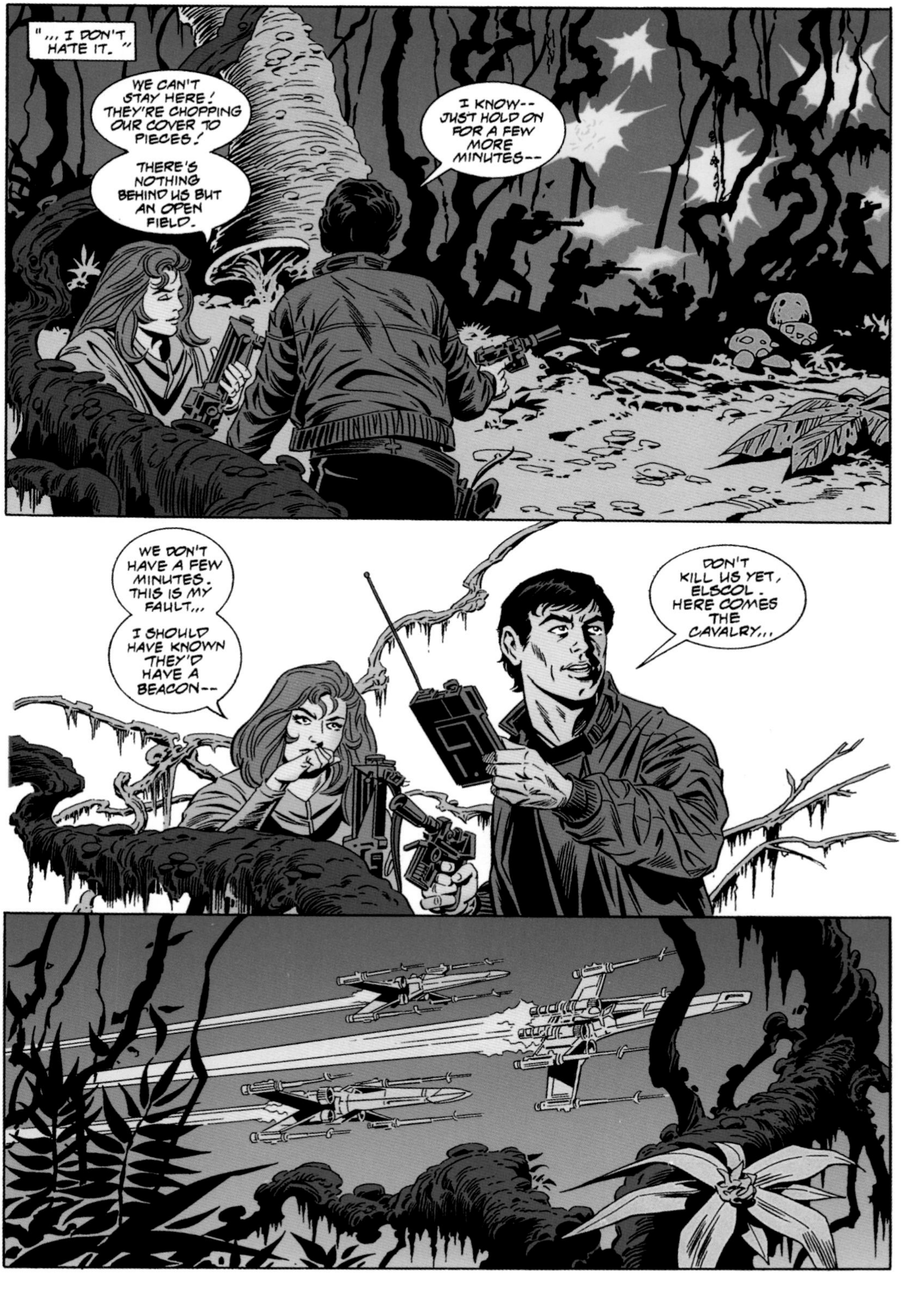
"... I DON'T HATE IT."
WE CAN'T STAY HERE! THEY'RE CHOPPING OUR COVER TO PIECES!
THERE'S NOTHING BEHIND US BUT AN OPEN FIELD.
I KNOW-- JUST HOLD ON FOR A FEW MORE MINUTES--
WE DON'T HAVE A FEW MINUTES. THIS IS MY FAULT...
I SHOULD HAVE KNOWN THEY'D HAVE A BEACON--
DON'T KILL US YET, ELSCOL. HERE COMES THE CAVALRY...

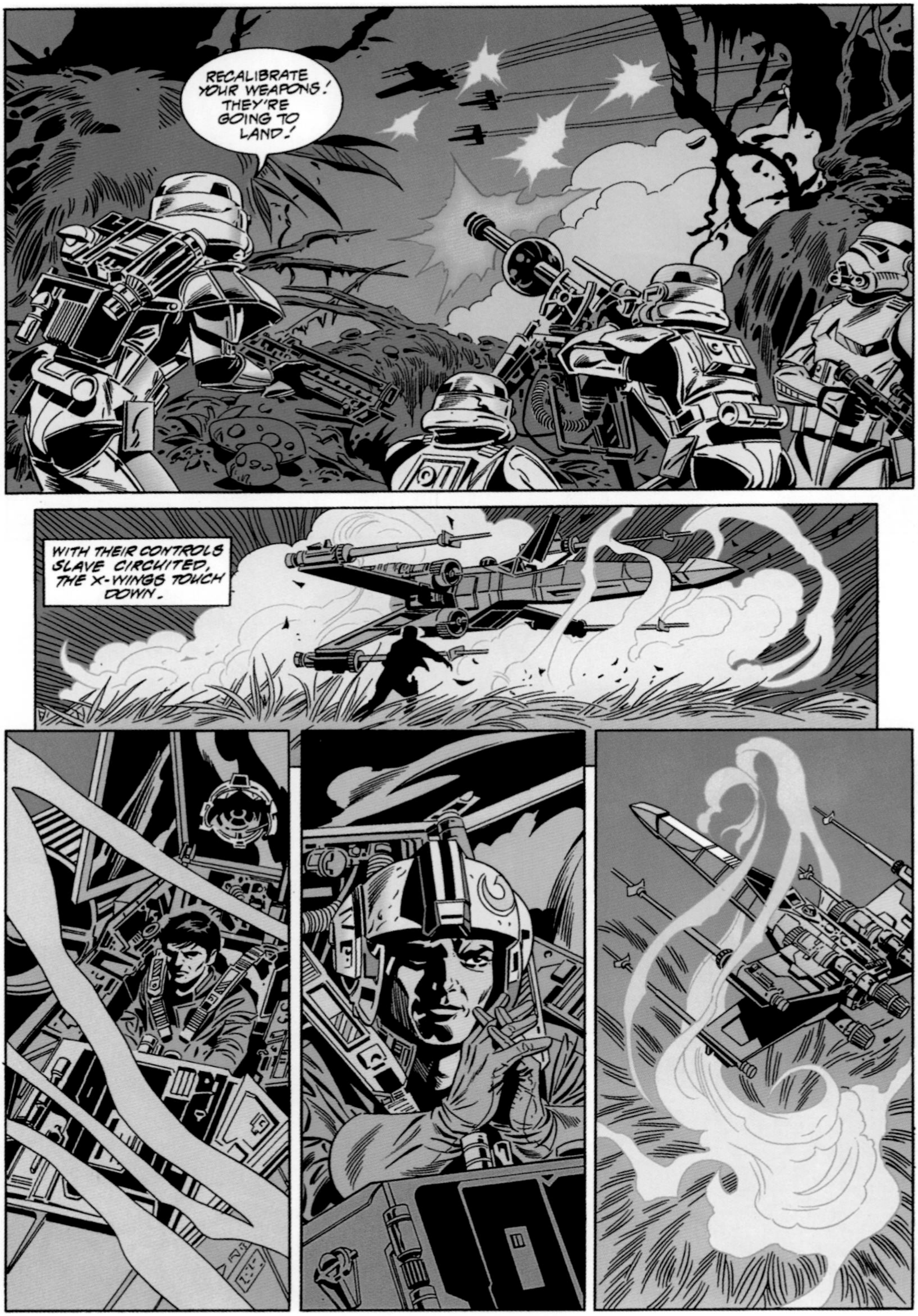

RECALIBRATE YOUR WEAPONS! THEY'RE GOING TO LAND!
WITH THEIR CONTROLS SLAVE CIRCUITED, THE X-WINGS TOUCH DOWN.

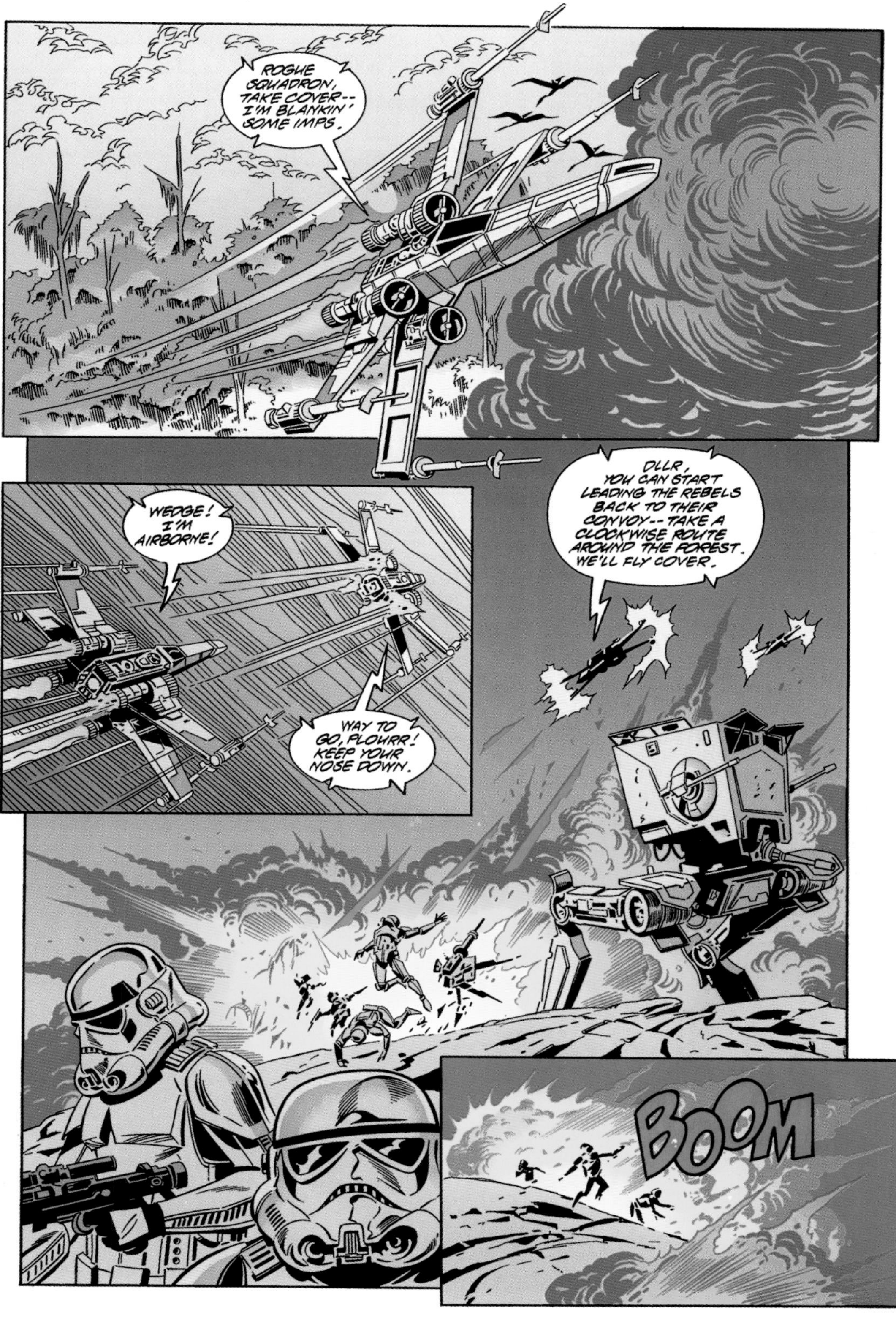

ROGUE SQUADRON, TAKE COVER-- I'M BLANKIN' SOME IMPS.
WEDGE! I'M AIRBORNE!
WAY TO GO, PLOURR! KEEP YOUR NOSE DOWN.
DLLR, YOU CAN START LEADING THE REBELS BACK TO THEIR CONVOY-- TAKE A CLOCKWISE ROUTE AROUND THE FOREST. WE'LL FLY COVER.
BOOM

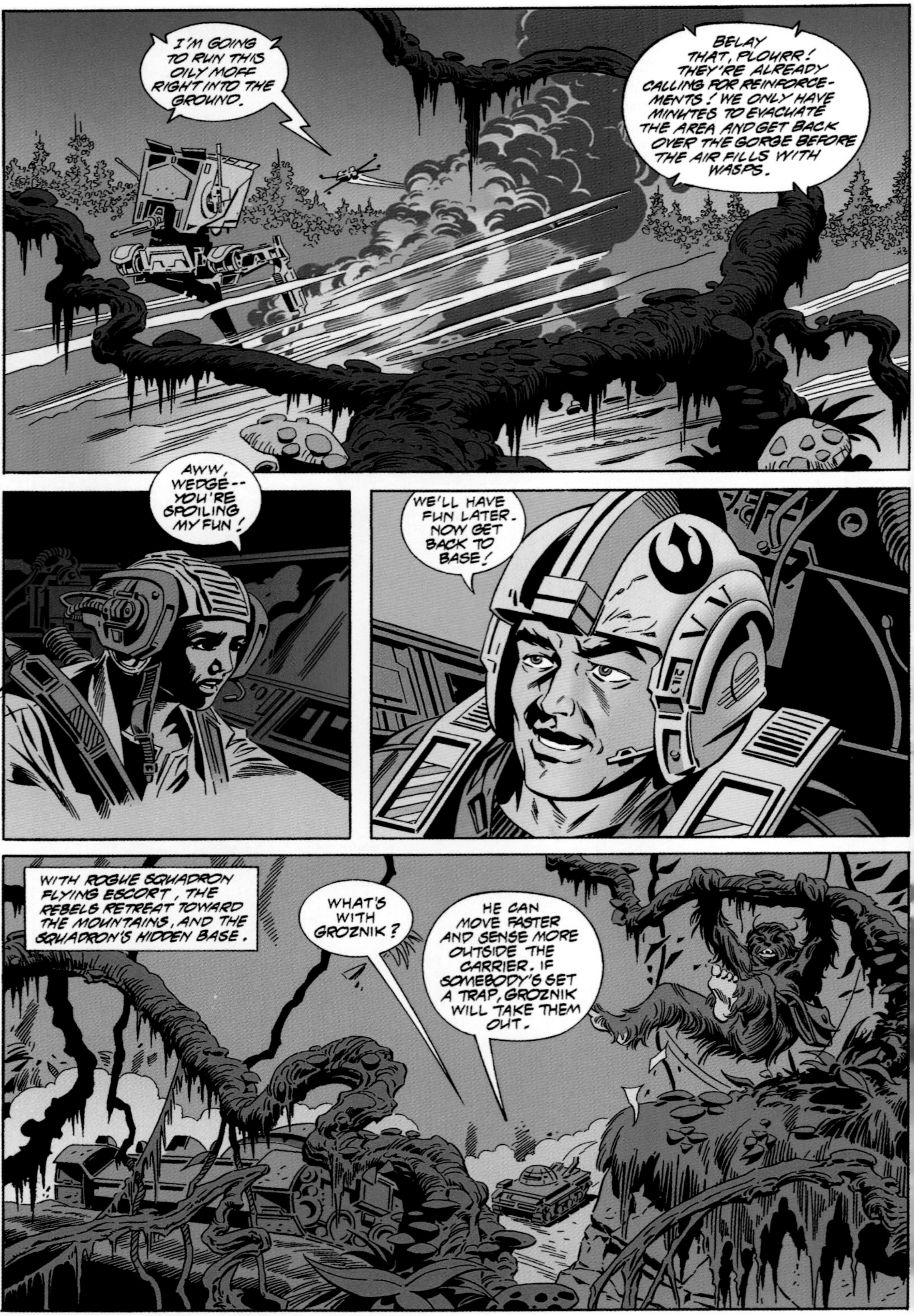
I'M GOING TO RUN THIS OILY MOFF RIGHT INTO THE GROUND.
BELAY THAT, PLOURR! THEY'RE ALREADY CALLING FOR REINFORCEMENTS! WE ONLY HAVE MINUTES TO EVACUATE THE AREA AND GET BACK OVER THE GORGE BEFORE THE AIR FILLS WITH WASPS.
AWW, WEDGE--YOU'RE SPOILING MY FUN!
WE'LL HAVE FUN LATER. NOW GET BACK TO BASE!
WITH ROGUE SQUADRON FLYING ESCORT, THE REBELS RETREAT TOWARD THE MOUNTAINS, AND THE SQUADRON'S HIDDEN BASE.
WHAT'S WITH GROZNIK?
HE CAN MOVE FASTER AND SENSE MORE OUTSIDE THE CARRIER. IF SOMEBODY'S SET A TRAP, GROZNIK WILL TAKE THEM OUT.

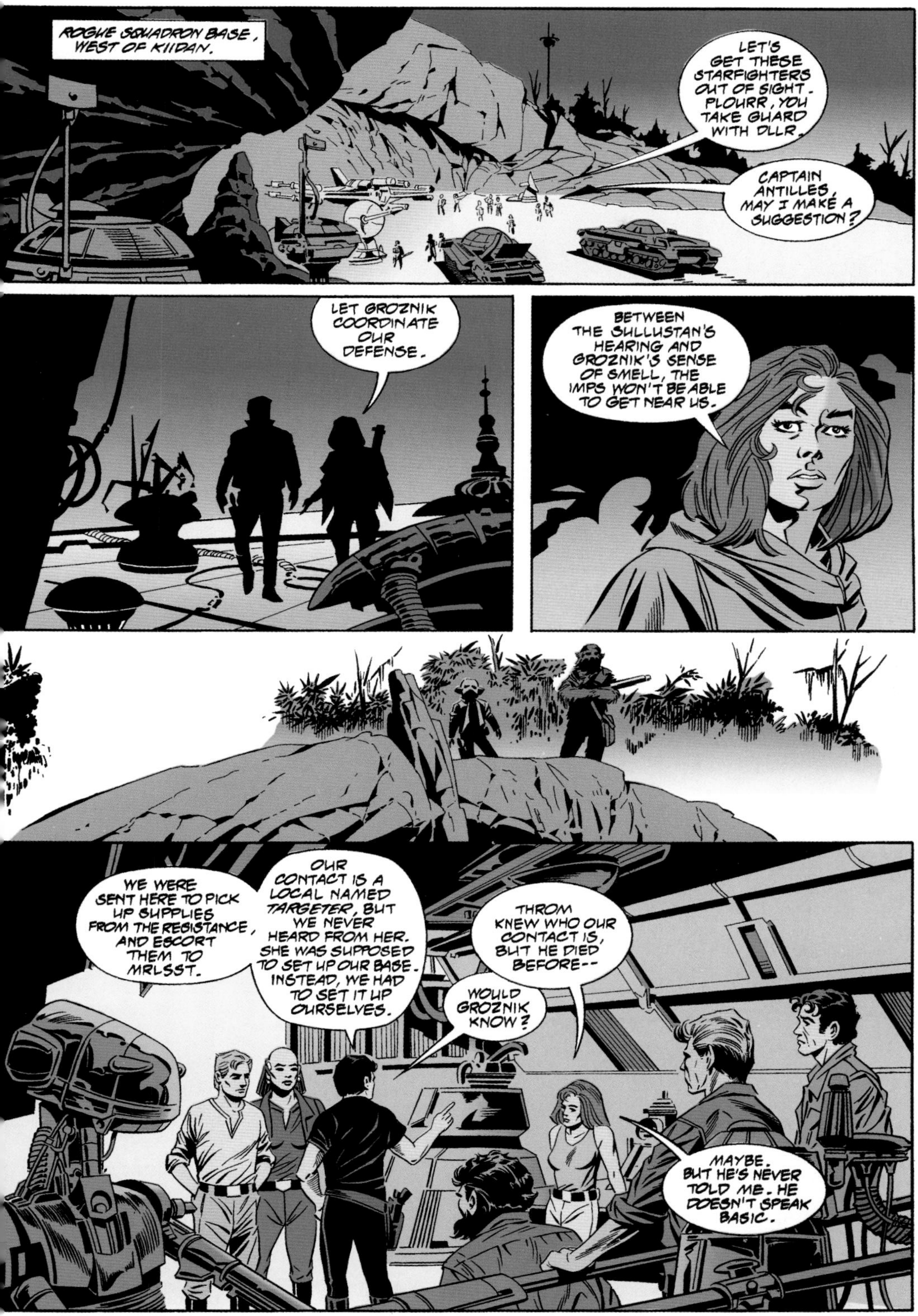
ROGUE SQUADRON BASE, WEST OF KIIDAN.
LET'S GET THESE STARFIGHTERS OUT OF SIGHT. PLOURR, YOU TAKE GUARD WITH DLLR.
CAPTAIN ANTILLES, MAY I MAKE A SUGGESTION?
LET GROZNIK COORDINATE OUR DEFENSE.
BETWEEN THE SULLUSTAN'S HEARING AND GROZNIK'S SENSE OF SMELL, THE IMPS WON'T BE ABLE TO GET NEAR US.
WE WERE SENT HERE TO PICK UP SUPPLIES FROM THE RESISTANCE, AND ESCORT THEM TO MRLSST.
OUR CONTACT IS A LOCAL NAMED TARGETER, BUT WE NEVER HEARD FROM HER. SHE WAS SUPPOSED TO SET UP OUR BASE. INSTEAD, WE HAD TO SET IT UP OURSELVES.
THROM KNEW WHO OUR CONTACT IS, BUT HE DIED BEFORE--
WOULD GROZNIK KNOW?
MAYBE. BUT HE'S NEVER TOLD ME. HE DOESN'T SPEAK BASIC.

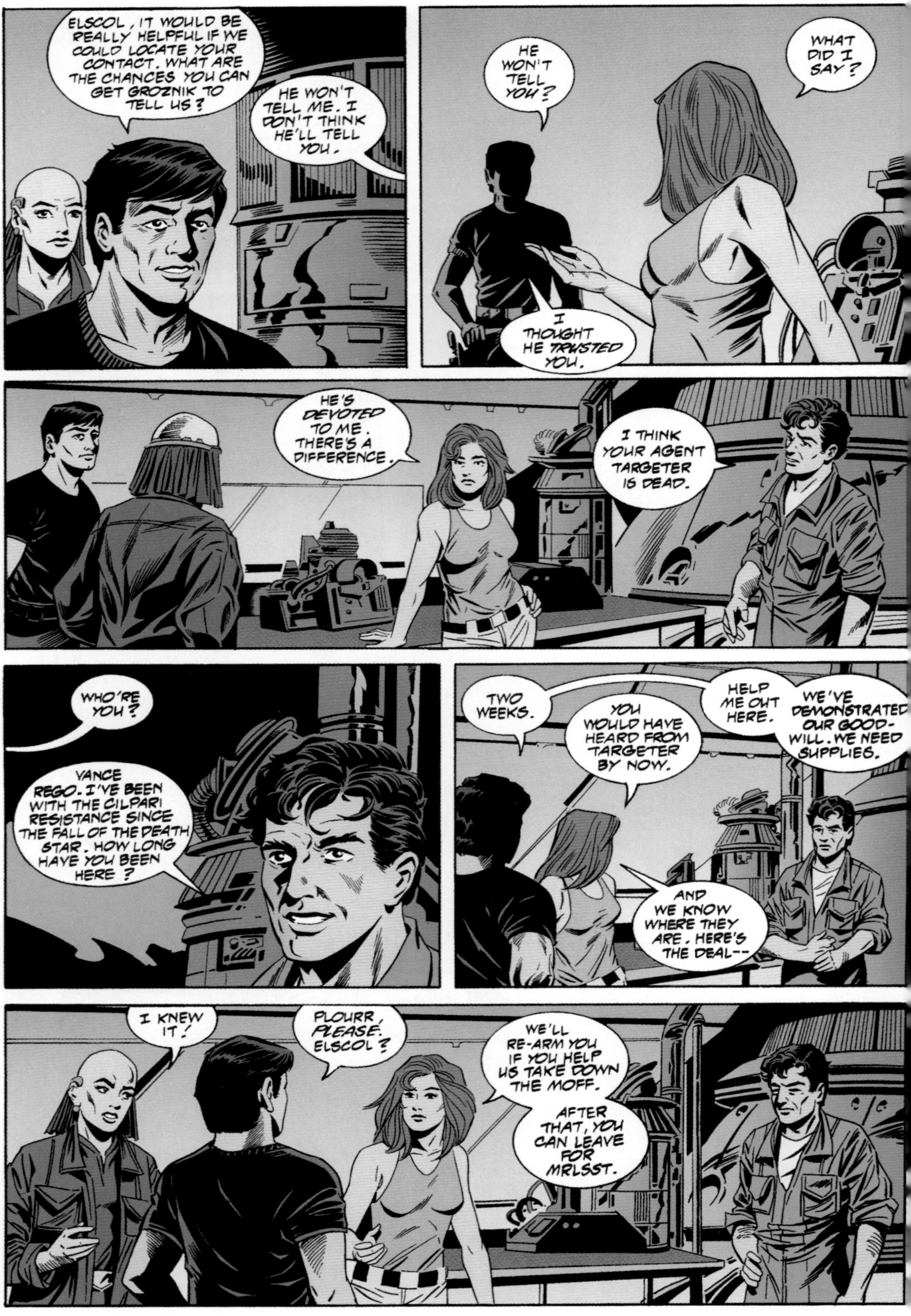
ELSCOL, IT WOULD BE REALLY HELPFUL IF WE COULD LOCATE YOUR CONTACT. WHAT ARE THE CHANCES YOU CAN GET GROZNIK TO TELL US?
HE WON'T TELL ME. I DON'T THINK HE'LL TELL YOU.
HE WON'T TELL YOU?
WHAT DID I SAY?
I THOUGHT HE TRUSTED YOU.
HE'S DEVOTED TO ME. THERE'S A DIFFERENCE.
I THINK YOUR AGENT TARGETER IS DEAD.
WHO'RE YOU?
VANCE REGO. I'VE BEEN WITH THE CILPARI RESISTANCE SINCE THE FALL OF THE DEATH STAR. HOW LONG HAVE YOU BEEN HERE?
TWO WEEKS.
YOU WOULD HAVE HEARD FROM TARGETER BY NOW.
HELP ME OUT HERE.
WE'VE DEMONSTRATED OUR GOOD-WILL. WE NEED SUPPLIES.
AND WE KNOW WHERE THEY ARE. HERE'S THE DEAL--
I KNEW IT!
PLOURR, PLEASE. ELSCOL?
WE'LL RE-ARM YOU IF YOU HELP US TAKE DOWN THE MOFF.
AFTER THAT, YOU CAN LEAVE FOR MRLSST.

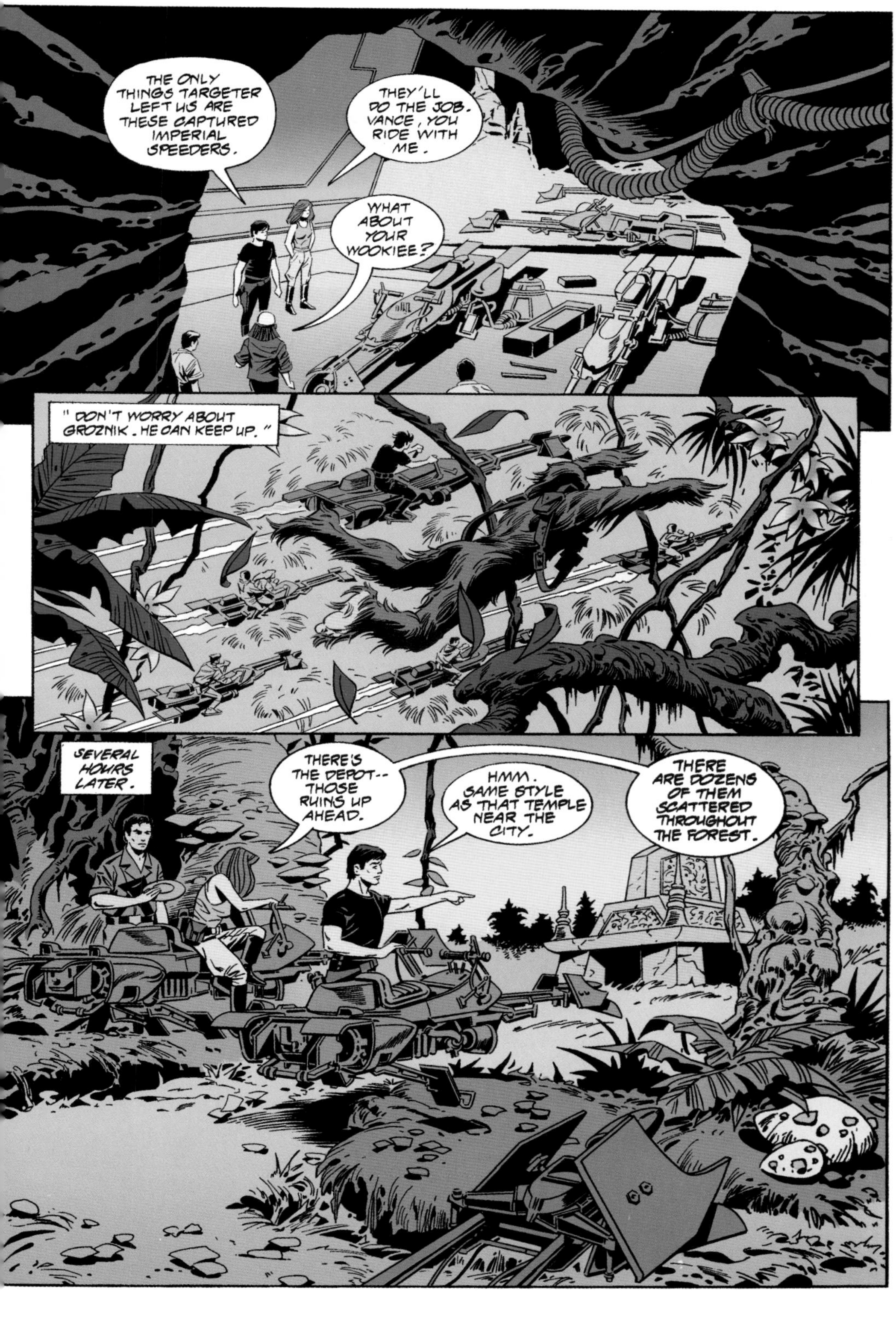
THE ONLY THINGS TARGETER LEFT US ARE THESE CAPTURED IMPERIAL SPEEDERS.
THEY'LL DO THE JOB. VANCE, YOU RIDE WITH ME.
WHAT ABOUT YOUR WOOKIEE?
"DON'T WORRY ABOUT GROZNIK. HE CAN KEEP UP."
SEVERAL HOURS LATER.
THERE'S THE DEPOT-- THOSE RUINS UP AHEAD.
HMM. SAME STYLE AS THAT TEMPLE NEAR THE CITY.
THERE ARE DOZENS OF THEM SCATTERED THROUGHOUT THE FOREST.

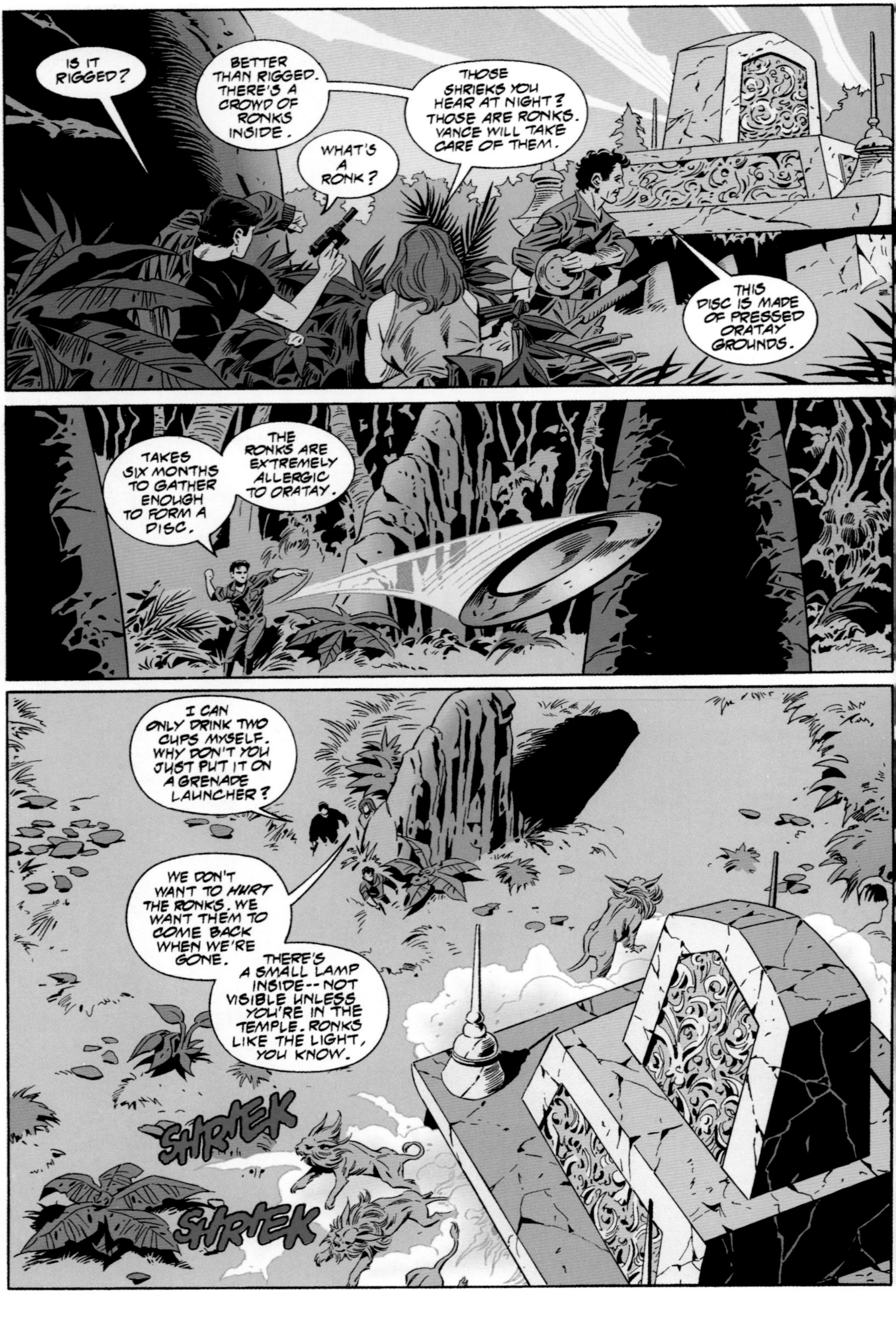
IS IT RIGGED?
BETTER THAN RIGGED. THERE'S A CROWD OF RONKS INSIDE.
WHAT'S A RONK?
THOSE SHRIEKS YOU HEAR AT NIGHT? THOSE ARE RONKS. VANCE WILL TAKE CARE OF THEM.
THIS DISC IS MADE OF PRESSED ORATAY GROUNDS.
TAKES SIX MONTHS TO GATHER ENOUGH TO FORM A DISC.
THE RONKS ARE EXTREMELY ALLERGIC TO ORATAY.
I CAN ONLY DRINK TWO CUPS MYSELF. WHY DON'T YOU JUST PUT IT ON A GRENADE LAUNCHER?
WE DON'T WANT TO HURT THE RONKS. WE WANT THEM TO COME BACK WHEN WE'RE GONE.
THERE'S A SMALL LAMP INSIDE-- NOT VISIBLE UNLESS YOU'RE IN THE TEMPLE. RONKS LIKE THE LIGHT, YOU KNOW.
SHRIEK
SHRIEK

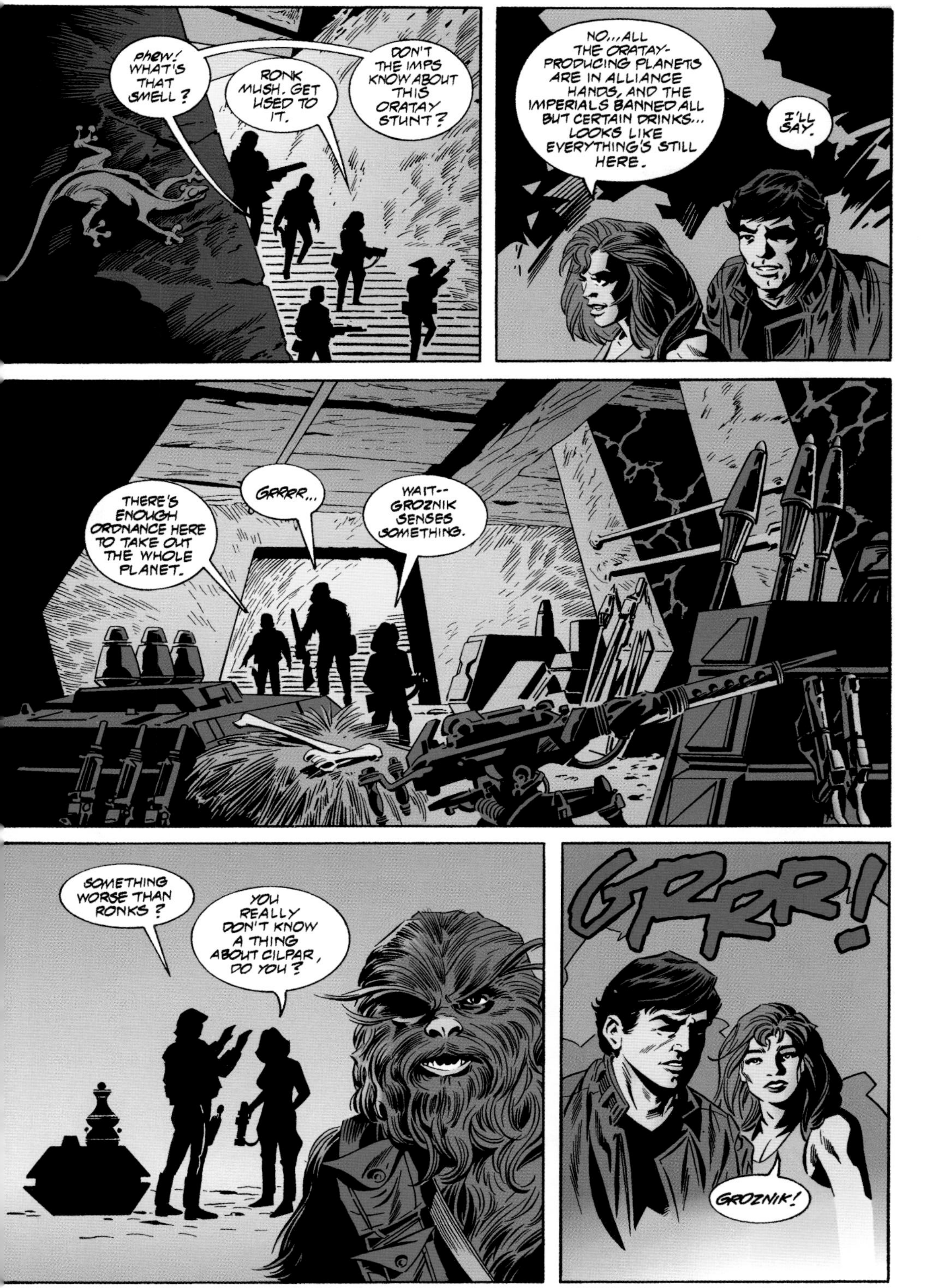
phew! WHAT'S THAT SMELL?
RONK MUSH. GET USED TO IT.
DON'T THE IMPS KNOW ABOUT THIS ORATAY STUNT?
NO...ALL THE ORATAY-PRODUCING PLANETS ARE IN ALLIANCE HANDS, AND THE IMPERIALS BANNED ALL BUT CERTAIN DRINKS... LOOKS LIKE EVERYTHING'S STILL HERE.
I'LL SAY.
THERE'S ENOUGH ORDNANCE HERE TO TAKE OUT THE WHOLE PLANET.
GRRRR...
WAIT-- GROZNIK SENSES SOMETHING.
SOMETHING WORSE THAN RONKS?
YOU REALLY DON'T KNOW A THING ABOUT CILPAR, DO YOU?
GRRR!
GROZNIK!

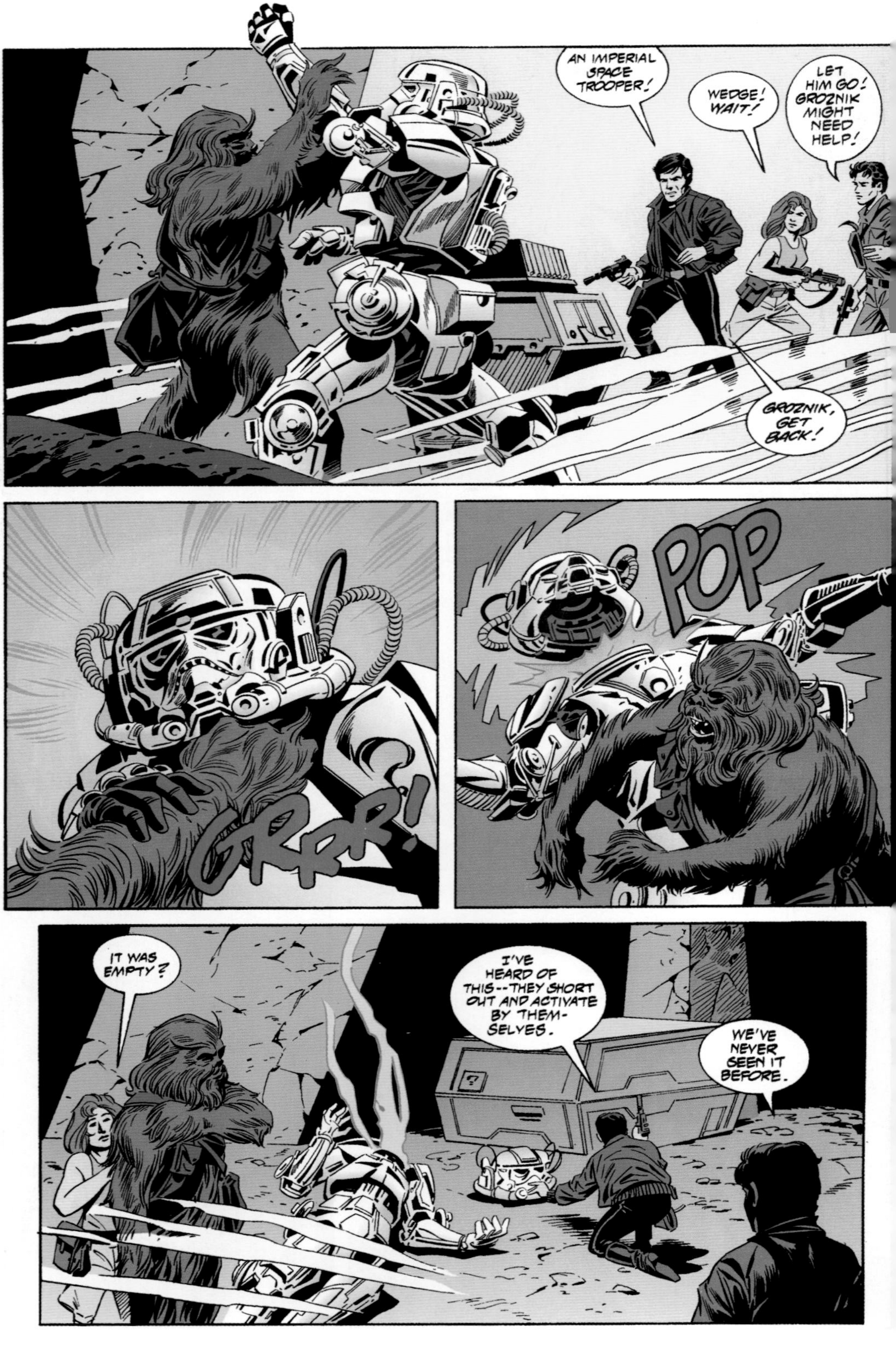
AN IMPERIAL SPACE TROOPER!
WEDGE! WAIT!
LET HIM GO! GROZNIK MIGHT NEED HELP!
GROZNIK, GET BACK!
GRRR!
POP
IT WAS EMPTY?
I'VE HEARD OF THIS--THEY SHORT OUT AND ACTIVATE BY THEM-SELVES.
WE'VE NEVER SEEN IT BEFORE.

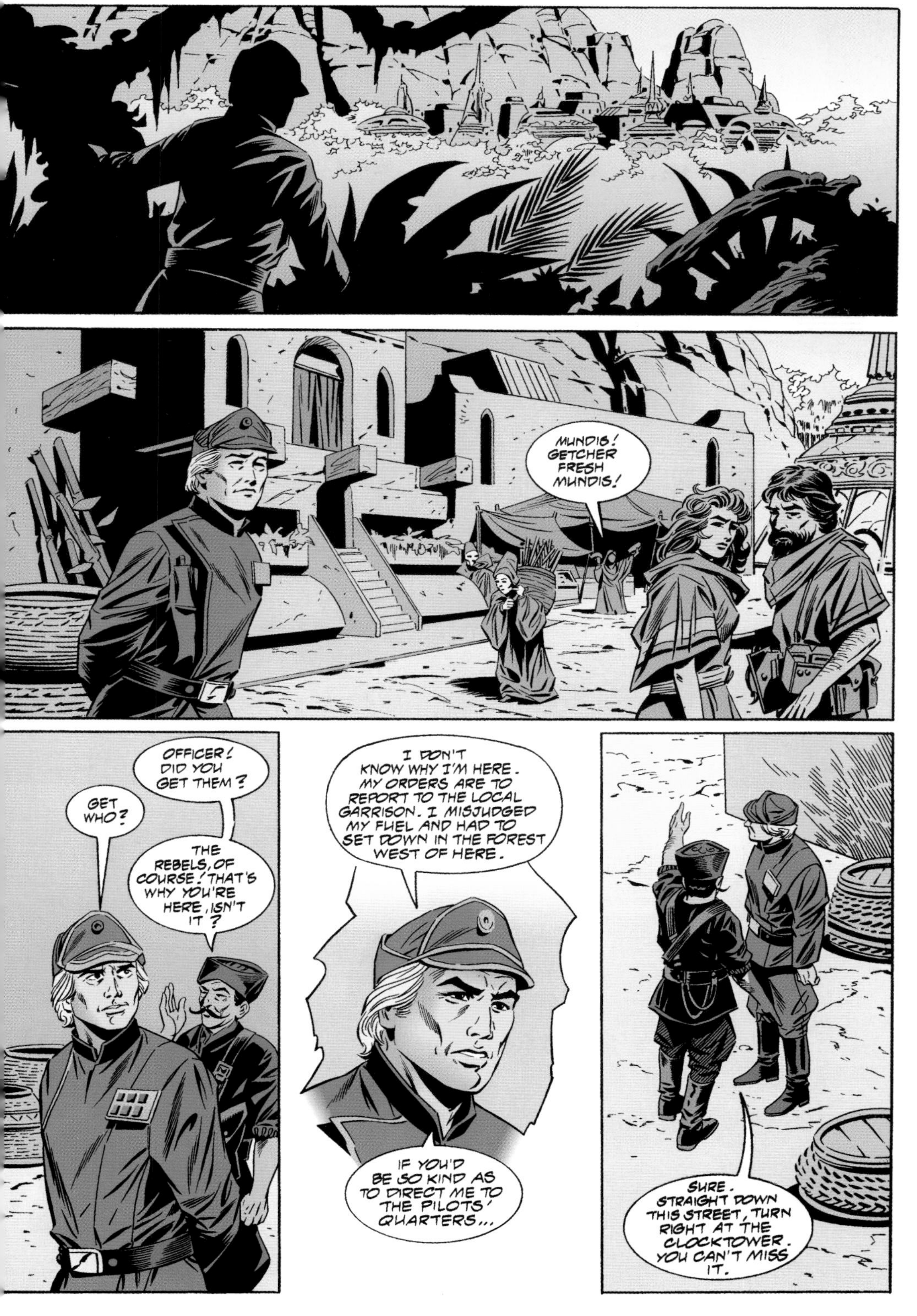
MUNDIS! GETCHER FRESH MUNDIS!
OFFICER! DID YOU GET THEM?
GET WHO?
THE REBELS, OF COURSE! THAT'S WHY YOU'RE HERE, ISN'T IT?
I DON'T KNOW WHY I'M HERE. MY ORDERS ARE TO REPORT TO THE LOCAL GARRISON. I MISJUDGED MY FUEL AND HAD TO SET DOWN IN THE FOREST WEST OF HERE.
IF YOU'D BE SO KIND AS TO DIRECT ME TO THE PILOTS' QUARTERS...
SURE. STRAIGHT DOWN THIS STREET, TURN RIGHT AT THE CLOCKTOWER. YOU CAN'T MISS IT.

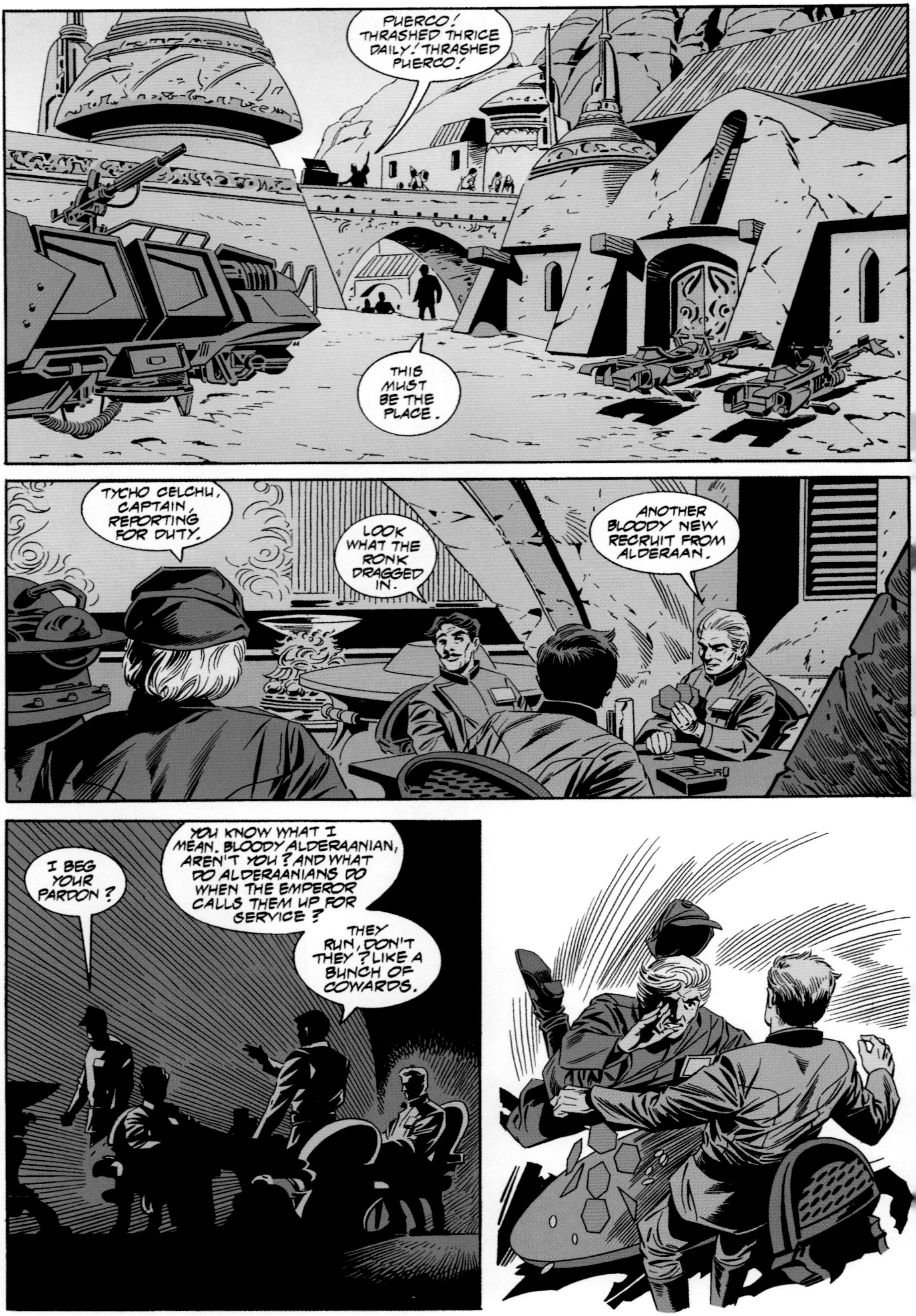
PUERCO! THRASHED THRICE DAILY! THRASHED PUERCO!
THIS MUST BE THE PLACE.
TYCHO CELCHU, CAPTAIN, REPORTING FOR DUTY.
LOOK WHAT THE RONK DRAGGED IN.
ANOTHER BLOODY NEW RECRUIT FROM ALDERAAN.
I BEG YOUR PARDON?
YOU KNOW WHAT I MEAN. BLOODY ALDERAANIAN, AREN'T YOU? AND WHAT DO ALDERAANIANS DO WHEN THE EMPEROR CALLS THEM UP FOR SERVICE?
THEY RUN, DON'T THEY? LIKE A BUNCH OF COWARDS.

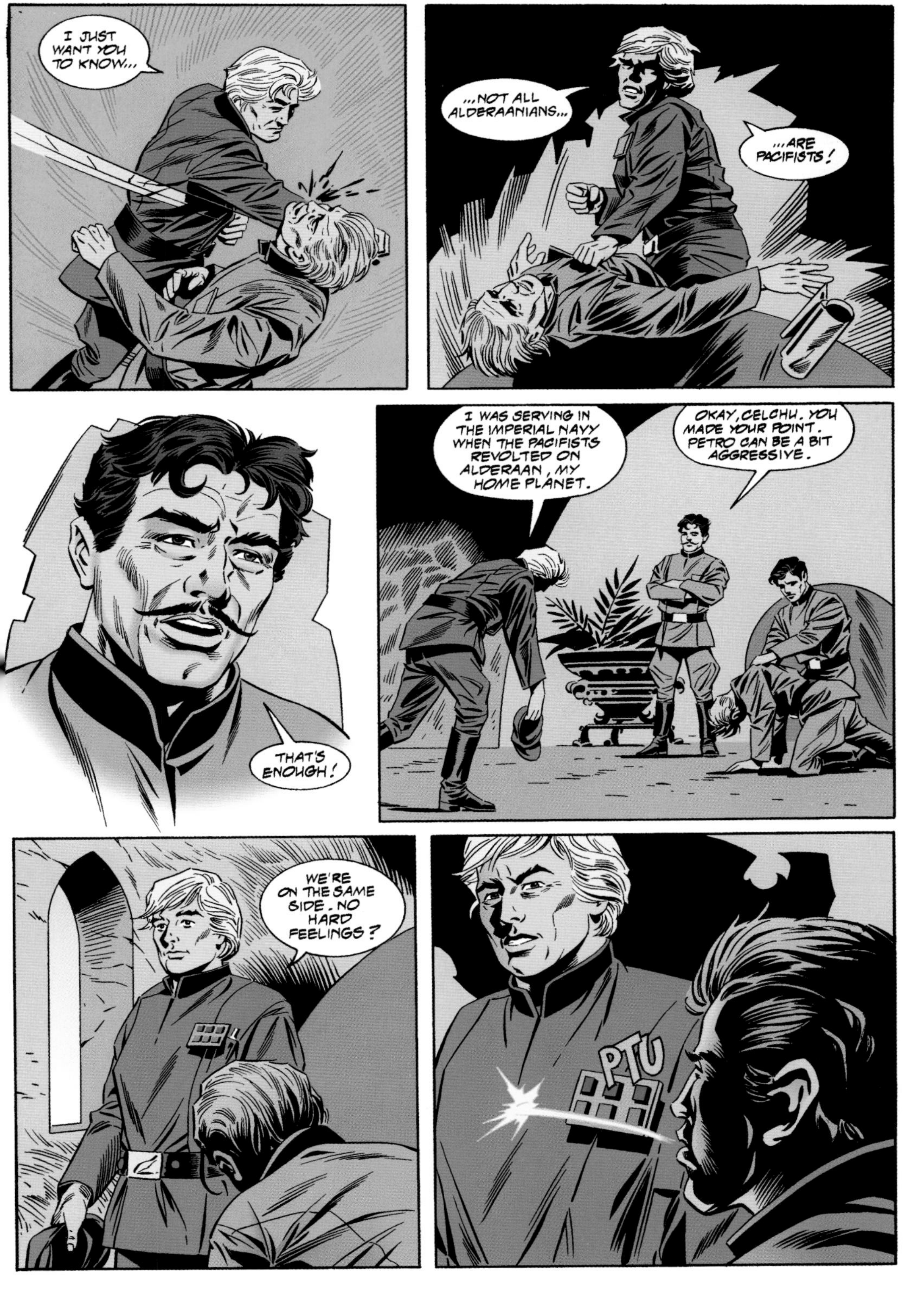
I JUST WANT YOU TO KNOW...
...NOT ALL ALDERAANIANS...
...ARE PACIFISTS!
THAT'S ENOUGH!
I WAS SERVING IN THE IMPERIAL NAVY WHEN THE PACIFISTS REVOLTED ON ALDERAAN, MY HOME PLANET.
OKAY, CELCHU. YOU MADE YOUR POINT. PETRO CAN BE A BIT AGGRESSIVE.
WE'RE ON THE SAME SIDE. NO HARD FEELINGS?
PTU

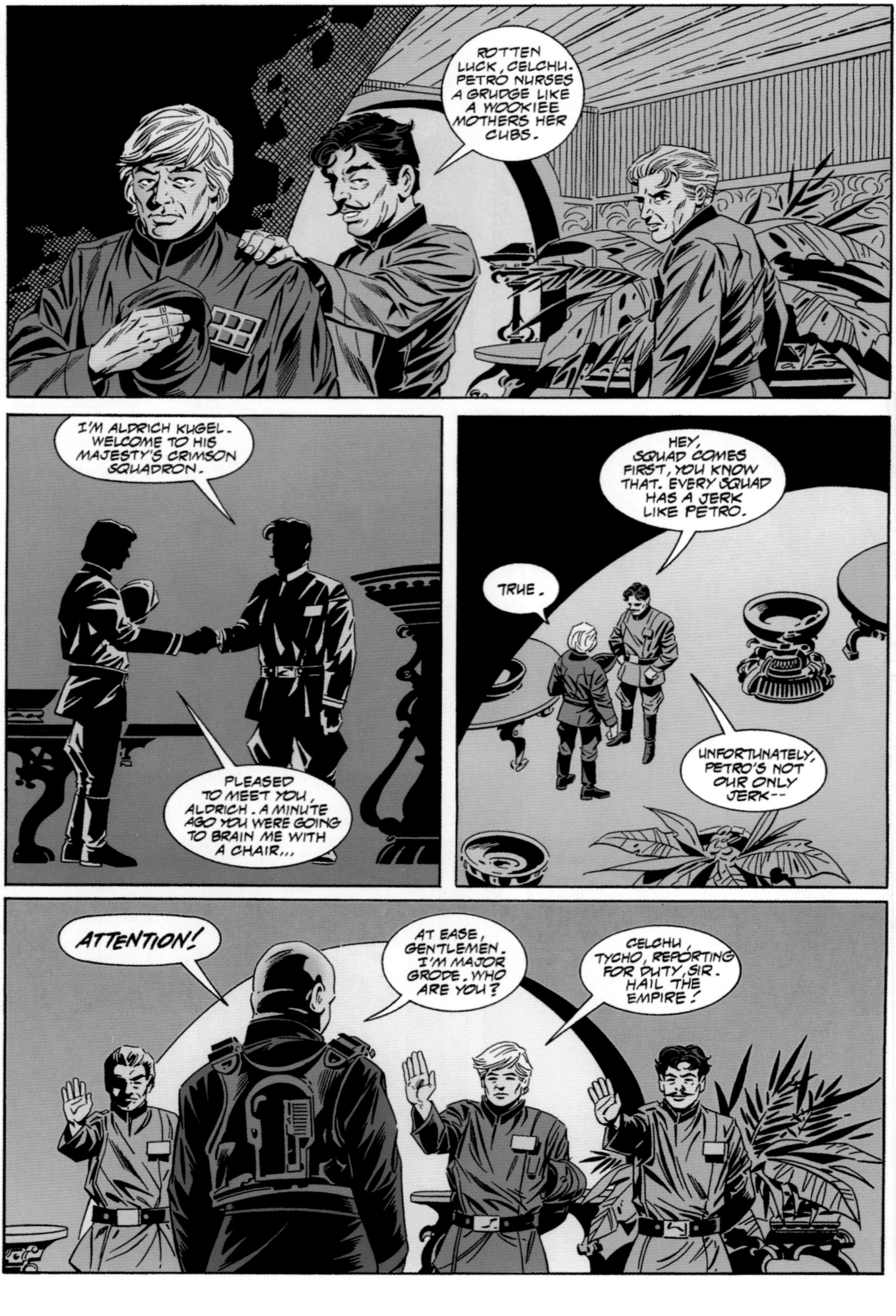
ROTTEN LUCK, CELCHU. PETRO NURSES A GRUDGE LIKE A WOOKIEE MOTHERS HER CUBS.
I'M ALDRICH KUGEL. WELCOME TO HIS MAJESTY'S CRIMSON SQUADRON.
PLEASED TO MEET YOU, ALDRICH. A MINUTE AGO YOU WERE GOING TO BRAIN ME WITH A CHAIR...
HEY, SQUAD COMES FIRST, YOU KNOW THAT. EVERY SQUAD HAS A JERK LIKE PETRO.
TRUE.
UNFORTUNATELY, PETRO'S NOT OUR ONLY JERK--
ATTENTION!
AT EASE, GENTLEMEN. I'M MAJOR GRODE. WHO ARE YOU?
CELCHU, TYCHO, REPORTING FOR DUTY, SIR. HAIL THE EMPIRE!

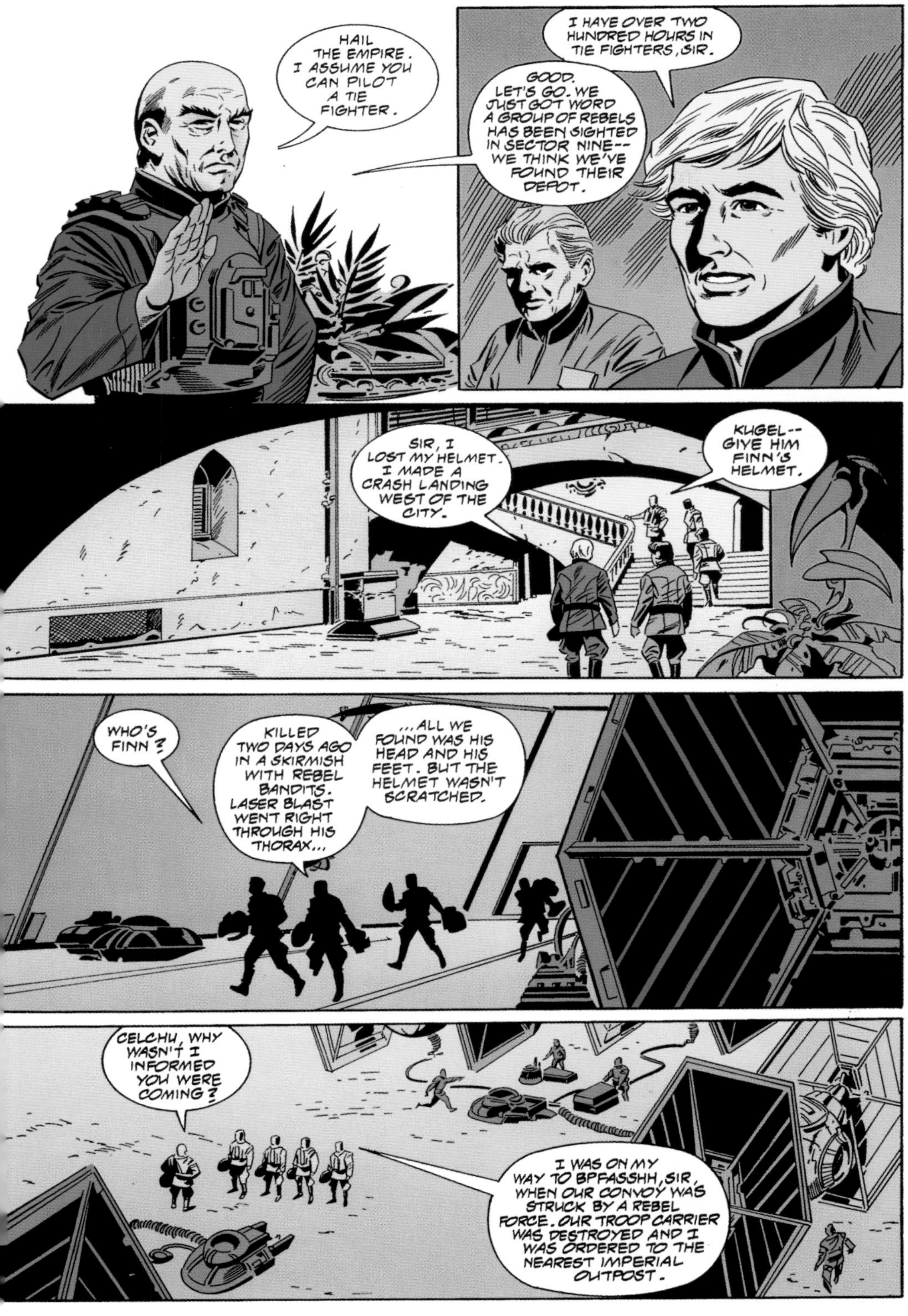
HAIL THE EMPIRE. I ASSUME YOU CAN PILOT A TIE FIGHTER.
I HAVE OVER TWO HUNDRED HOURS IN TIE FIGHTERS, SIR.
GOOD. LET'S GO. WE JUST GOT WORD A GROUP OF REBELS HAS BEEN SIGHTED IN SECTOR NINE-- WE THINK WE'VE FOUND THEIR DEPOT.
SIR, I LOST MY HELMET. I MADE A CRASH LANDING WEST OF THE CITY.
KUGEL-- GIVE HIM FINN'S HELMET.
WHO'S FINN?
KILLED TWO DAYS AGO IN A SKIRMISH WITH REBEL BANDITS. LASER BLAST WENT RIGHT THROUGH HIS THORAX...
...ALL WE FOUND WAS HIS HEAD AND HIS FEET. BUT THE HELMET WASN'T SCRATCHED.
CELCHU, WHY WASN'T I INFORMED YOU WERE COMING?
I WAS ON MY WAY TO BPFASSHH, SIR, WHEN OUR CONVOY WAS STRUCK BY A REBEL FORCE. OUR TROOP CARRIER WAS DESTROYED AND I WAS ORDERED TO THE NEAREST IMPERIAL OUTPOST.

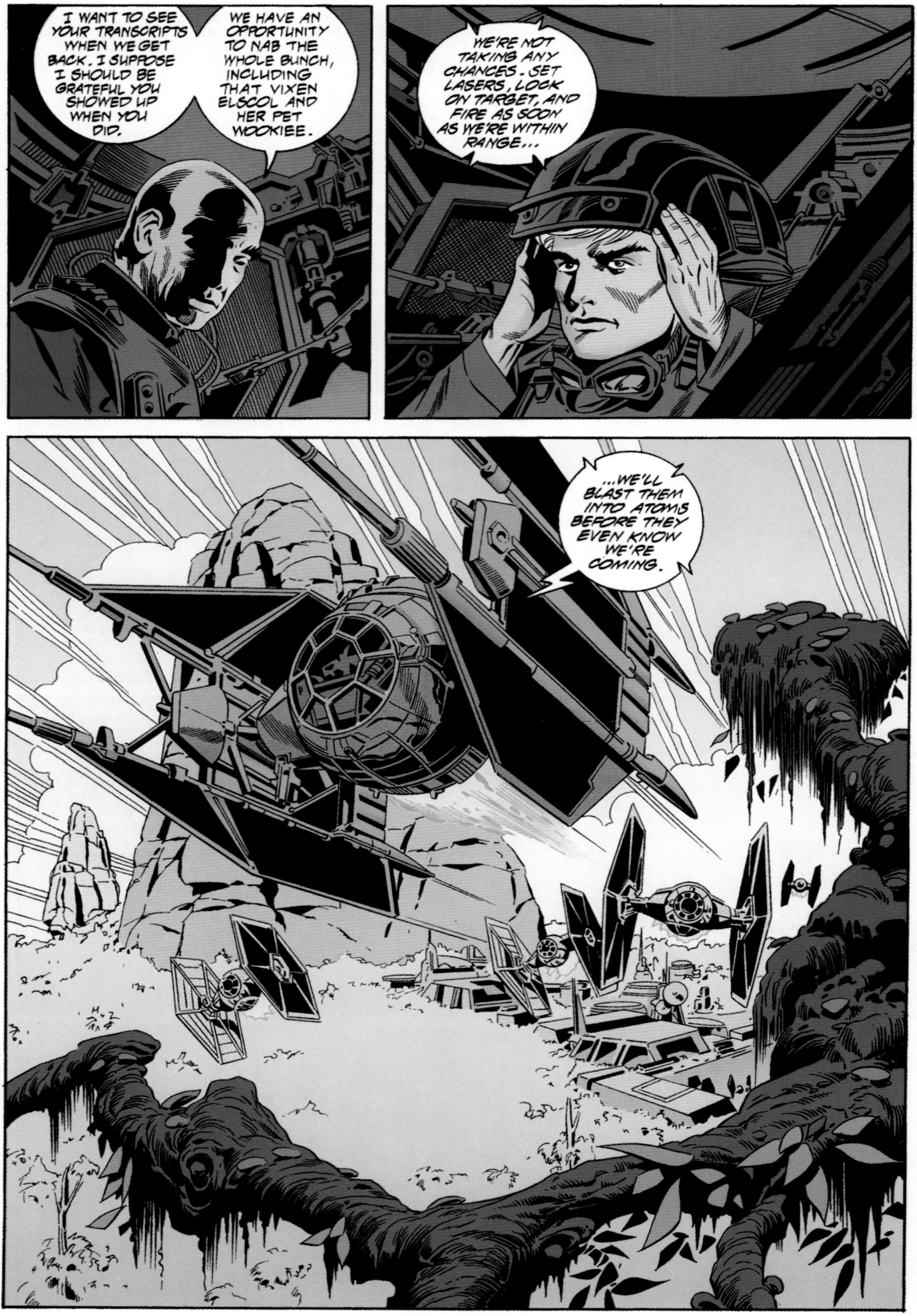
I WANT TO SEE YOUR TRANSCRIPTS WHEN WE GET BACK. I SUPPOSE I SHOULD BE GRATEFUL YOU SHOWED UP WHEN YOU DID.
WE HAVE AN OPPORTUNITY TO NAB THE WHOLE BUNCH, INCLUDING THAT VIXEN ELSCOL AND HER PET WOOKIEE.
WE'RE NOT TAKING ANY CHANCES. SET LASERS, LOCK ON TARGET, AND FIRE AS SOON AS WE'RE WITHIN RANGE...
...WE'LL BLAST THEM INTO ATOMS BEFORE THEY EVEN KNOW WE'RE COMING.

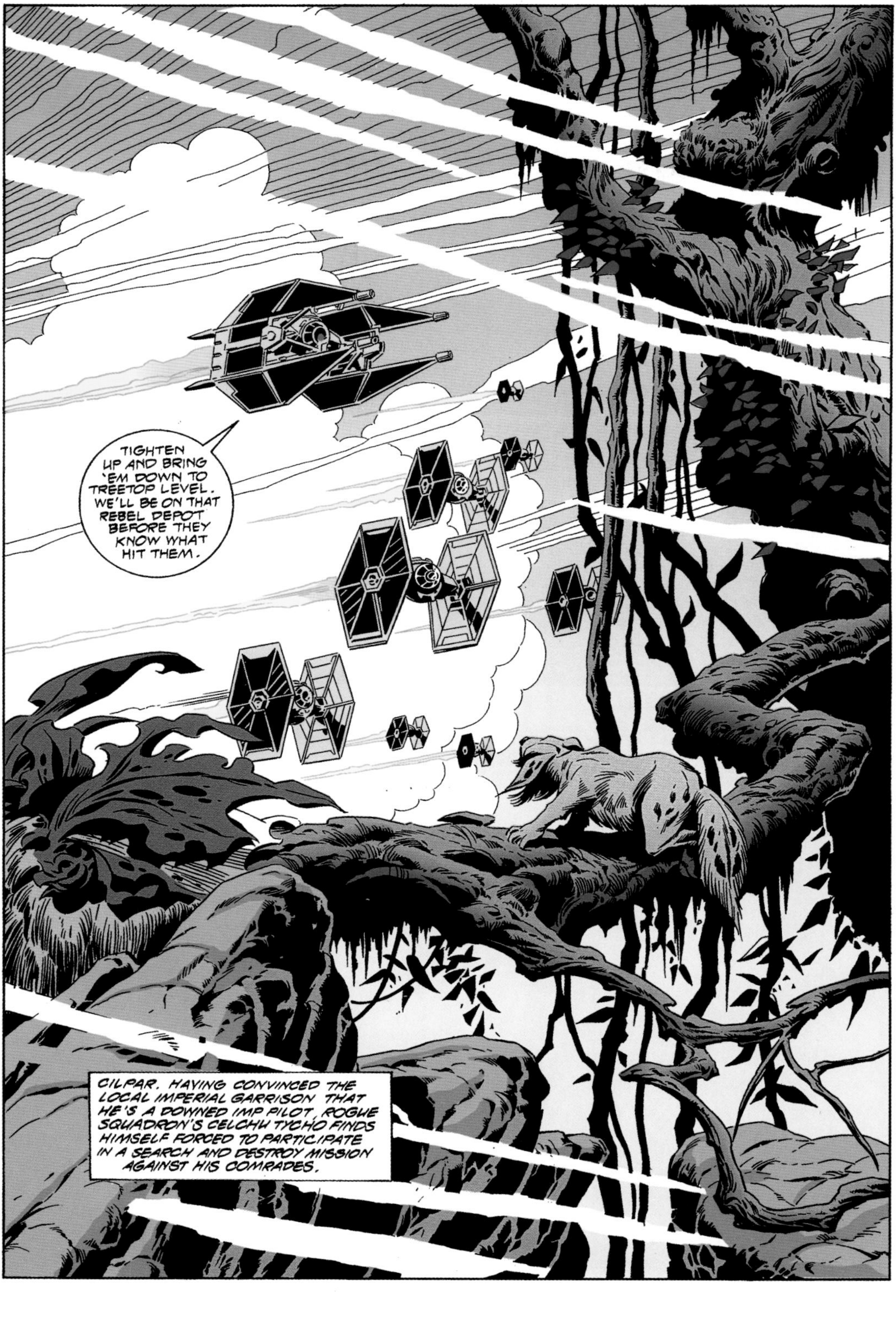
TIGHTEN UP AND BRING 'EM DOWN TO TREETOP LEVEL. WE'LL BE ON THAT REBEL DEPOT BEFORE THEY KNOW WHAT HIT THEM.
CILPAR. HAVING CONVINCED THE LOCAL IMPERIAL GARRISON THAT HE'S A DOWNED IMP PILOT, ROGUE SQUADRON'S CELCHU TYCHO FINDS HIMSELF FORCED TO PARTICIPATE IN A SEARCH AND DESTROY MISSION AGAINST HIS COMRADES.

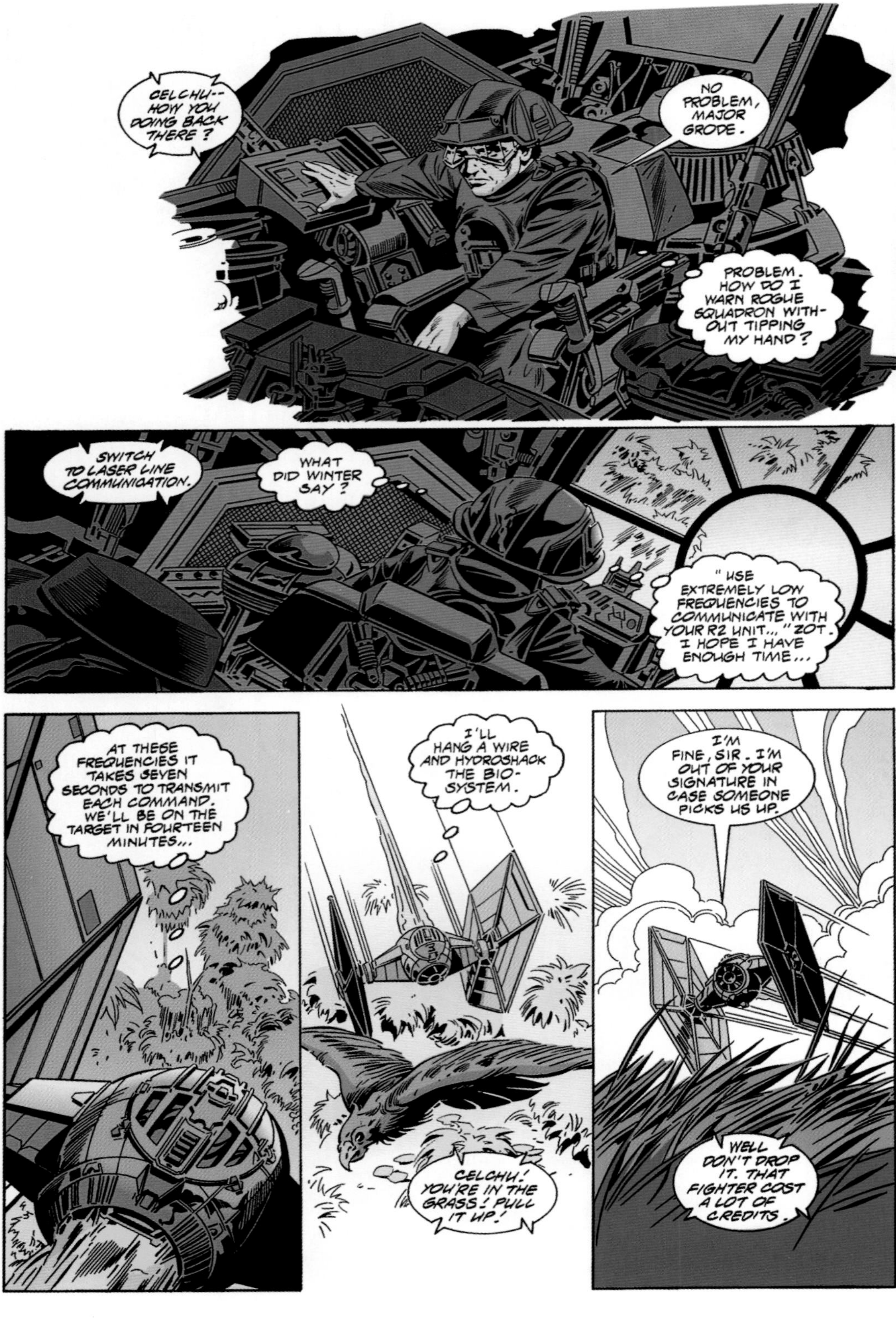
CELCHU-- HOW YOU DOING BACK THERE?
NO PROBLEM, MAJOR GRODE.
PROBLEM. HOW DO I WARN ROGUE SQUADRON WITHOUT TIPPING MY HAND?
SWITCH TO LASER LINE COMMUNICATION.
WHAT DID WINTER SAY?
"USE EXTREMELY LOW FREQUENCIES TO COMMUNICATE WITH YOUR R2 UNIT..." ZOT. I HOPE I HAVE ENOUGH TIME...
AT THESE FREQUENCIES IT TAKES SEVEN SECONDS TO TRANSMIT EACH COMMAND. WE'LL BE ON THE TARGET IN FOURTEEN MINUTES...
I'LL HANG A WIRE AND HYDROSHACK THE BIO-SYSTEM.
CELCHU! YOU'RE IN THE GRASS! PULL IT UP!
I'M FINE, SIR. I'M OUT OF YOUR SIGNATURE IN CASE SOMEONE PICKS US UP.
WELL DON'T DROP IT. THAT FIGHTER COST A LOT OF CREDITS.

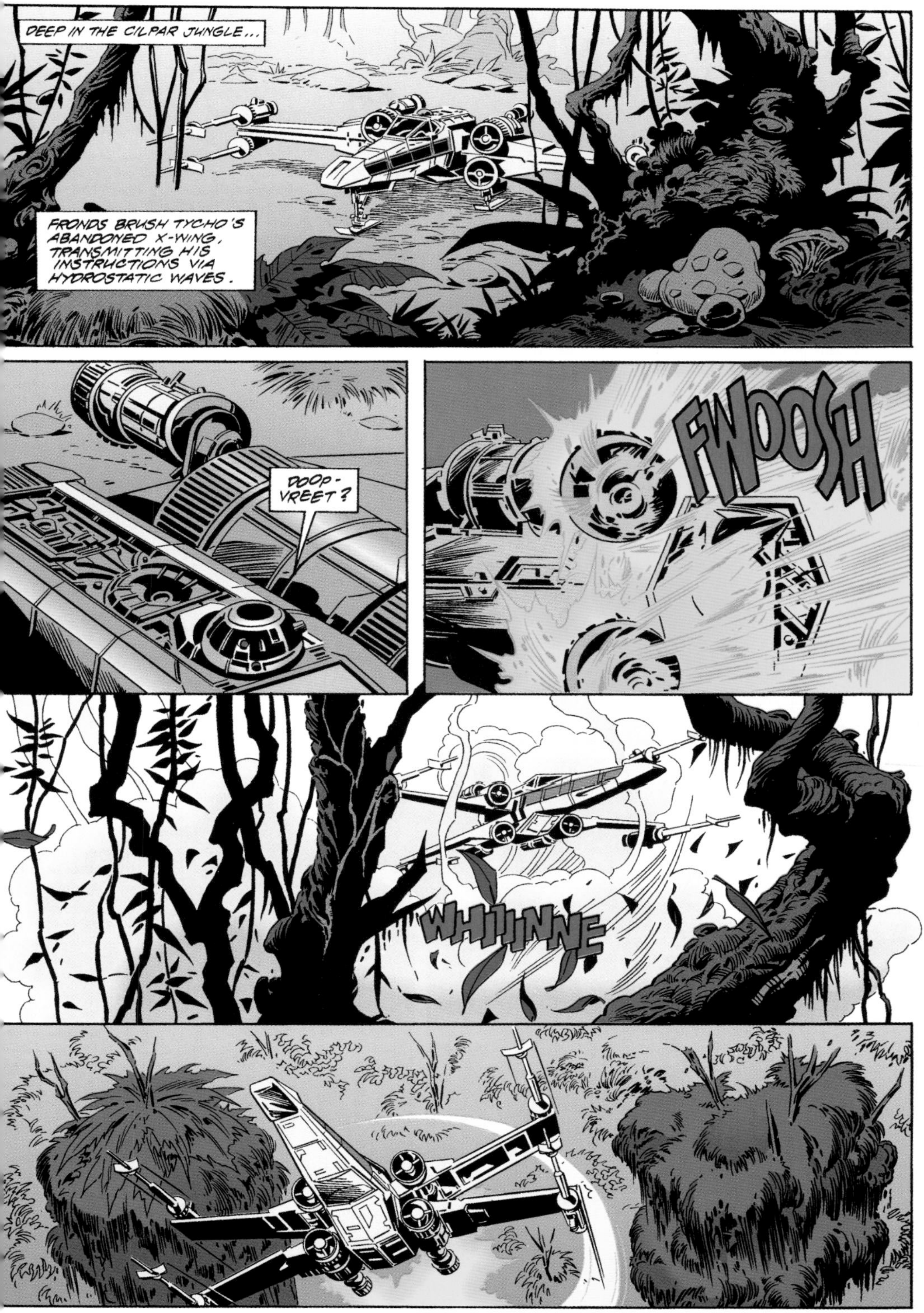
DEEP IN THE CILPAR JUNGLE...
FRONDS BRUSH TYCHO'S ABANDONED X-WING, TRANSMITTING HIS INSTRUCTIONS VIA HYDROSTATIC WAVES.
DOOP-VREET?
FWOOSH
WHIIIINNE

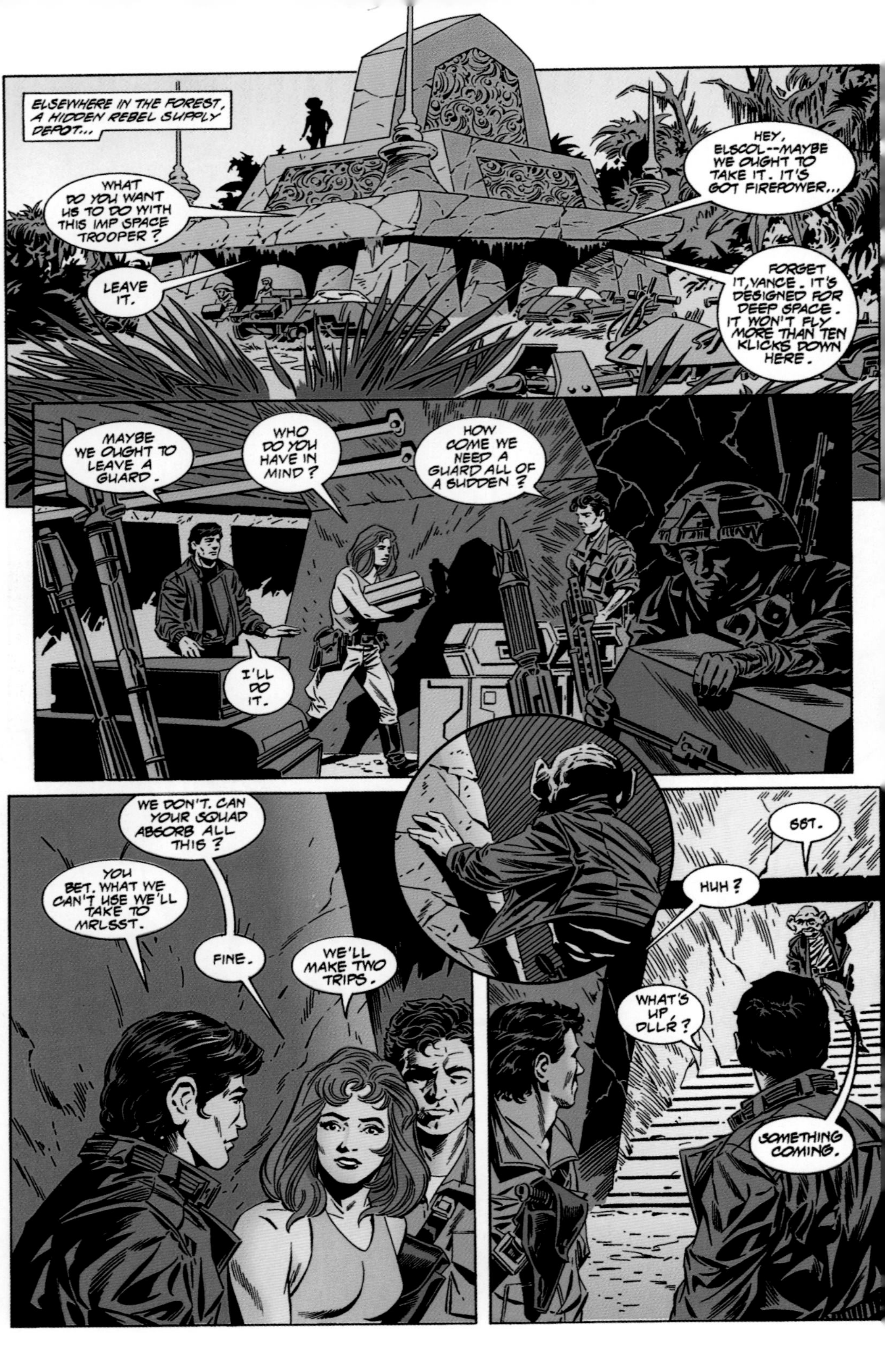
ELSEWHERE IN THE FOREST, A HIDDEN REBEL SUPPLY DEPOT...
WHAT DO YOU WANT US TO DO WITH THIS IMP SPACE TROOPER?
LEAVE IT.
HEY, ELSCOL--MAYBE WE OUGHT TO TAKE IT. IT'S GOT FIREPOWER...
FORGET IT, VANCE. IT'S DESIGNED FOR DEEP SPACE. IT WON'T FLY MORE THAN TEN KLICKS DOWN HERE.
MAYBE WE OUGHT TO LEAVE A GUARD.
WHO DO YOU HAVE IN MIND?
HOW COME WE NEED A GUARD ALL OF A SUDDEN?
I'LL DO IT.
WE DON'T. CAN YOUR SQUAD ABSORB ALL THIS?
YOU BET. WHAT WE CAN'T USE WE'LL TAKE TO MRLSST.
FINE.
WE'LL MAKE TWO TRIPS.
SST.
HUH?
WHAT'S UP, DLLR?
SOMETHING COMING.

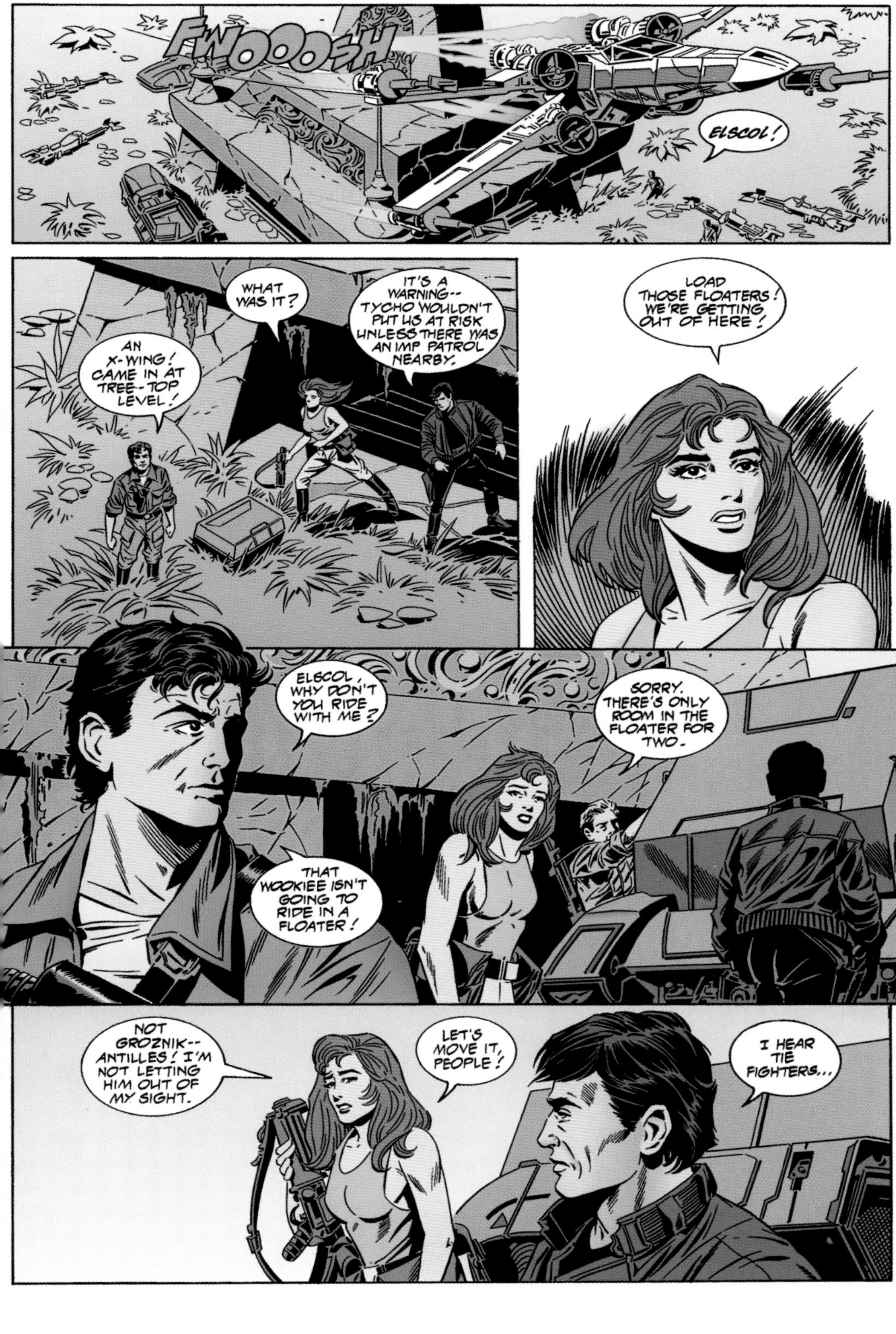
FWOOOOSH
ELSCOL!
WHAT WAS IT?
AN X-WING! CAME IN AT TREE-TOP LEVEL!
IT'S A WARNING-- TYCHO WOULDN'T PUT US AT RISK UNLESS THERE WAS AN IMP PATROL NEARBY.
LOAD THOSE FLOATERS! WE'RE GETTING OUT OF HERE!
ELSCOL, WHY DON'T YOU RIDE WITH ME?
SORRY. THERE'S ONLY ROOM IN THE FLOATER FOR TWO.
THAT WOOKIEE ISN'T GOING TO RIDE IN A FLOATER!
NOT GROZNIK-- ANTILLES! I'M NOT LETTING HIM OUT OF MY SIGHT.
LET'S MOVE IT, PEOPLE!
I HEAR TIE FIGHTERS...

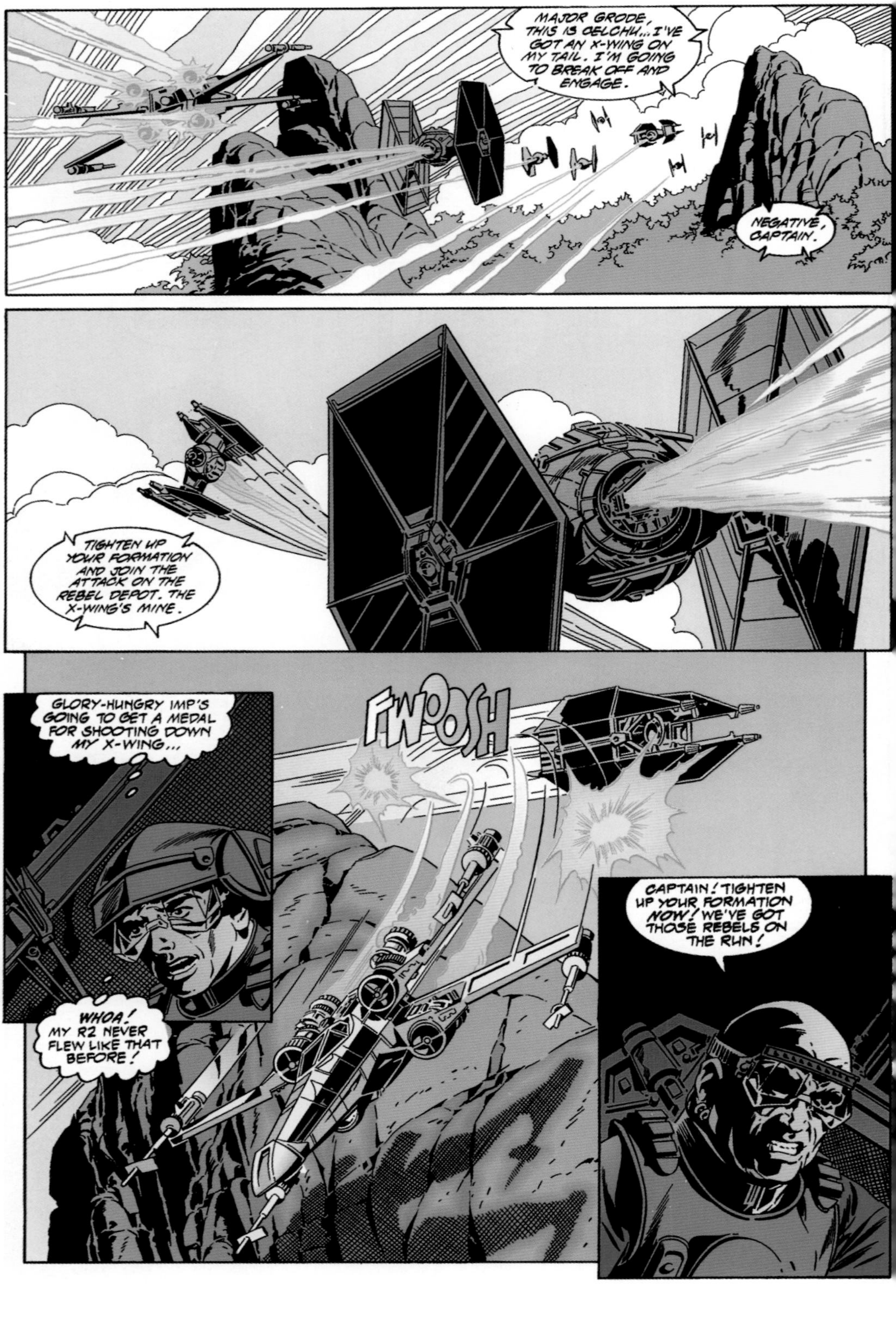
MAJOR GRODE, THIS IS OELCHU... I'VE GOT AN X-WING ON MY TAIL. I'M GOING TO BREAK OFF AND ENGAGE.
NEGATIVE, CAPTAIN.
TIGHTEN UP YOUR FORMATION AND JOIN THE ATTACK ON THE REBEL DEPOT. THE X-WING'S MINE.
GLORY-HUNGRY IMP'S GOING TO GET A MEDAL FOR SHOOTING DOWN MY X-WING...
FWOOSH
WHOA! MY R2 NEVER FLEW LIKE THAT BEFORE!
CAPTAIN! TIGHTEN UP YOUR FORMATION NOW! WE'VE GOT THOSE REBELS ON THE RUN!

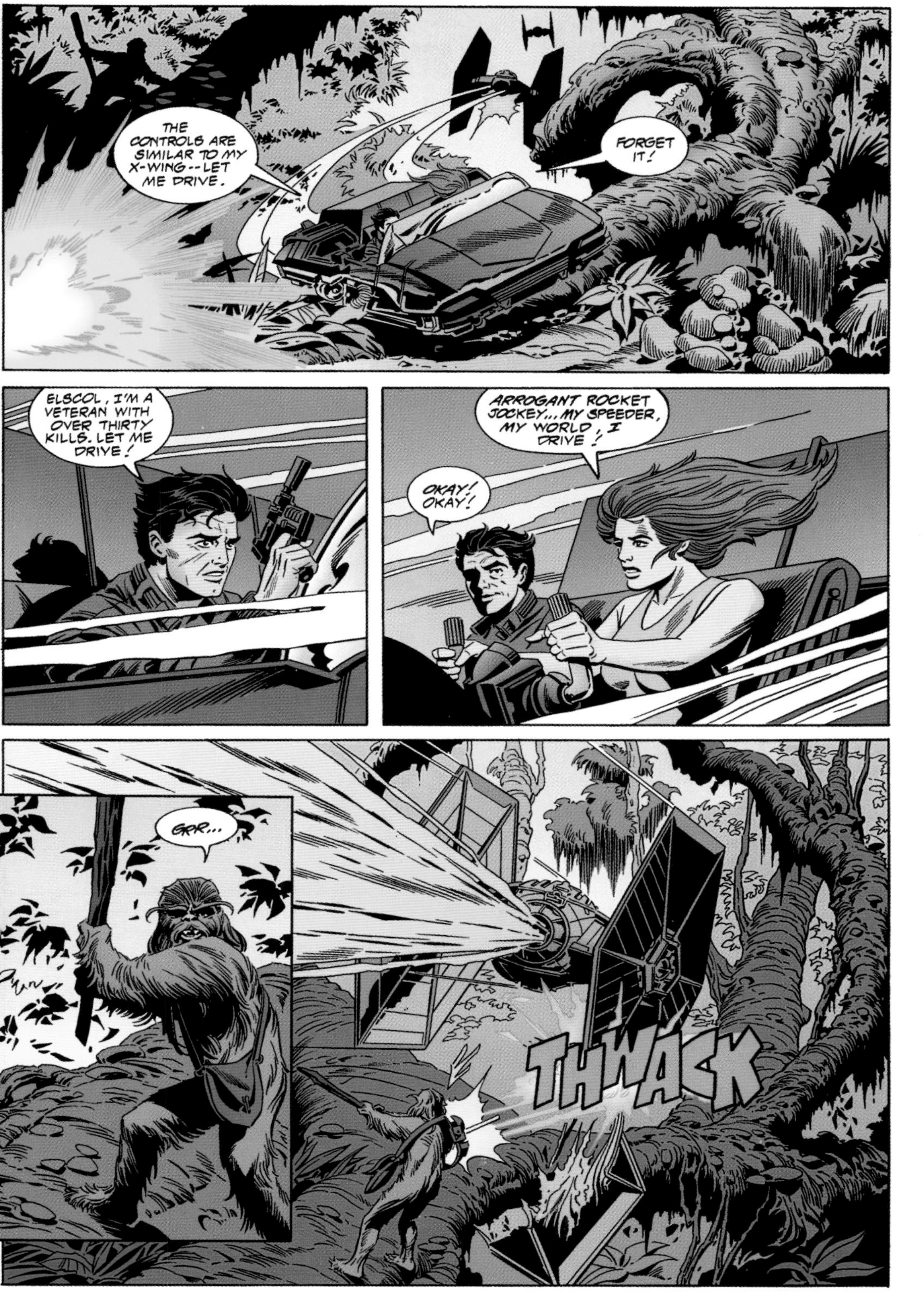
THE CONTROLS ARE SIMILAR TO MY X-WING--LET ME DRIVE.
FORGET IT!
ELSCOL, I'M A VETERAN WITH OVER THIRTY KILLS. LET ME DRIVE!
ARROGANT ROCKET JOCKEY... MY SPEEDER, MY WORLD, I DRIVE!
OKAY! OKAY!
GRR...
THWACK

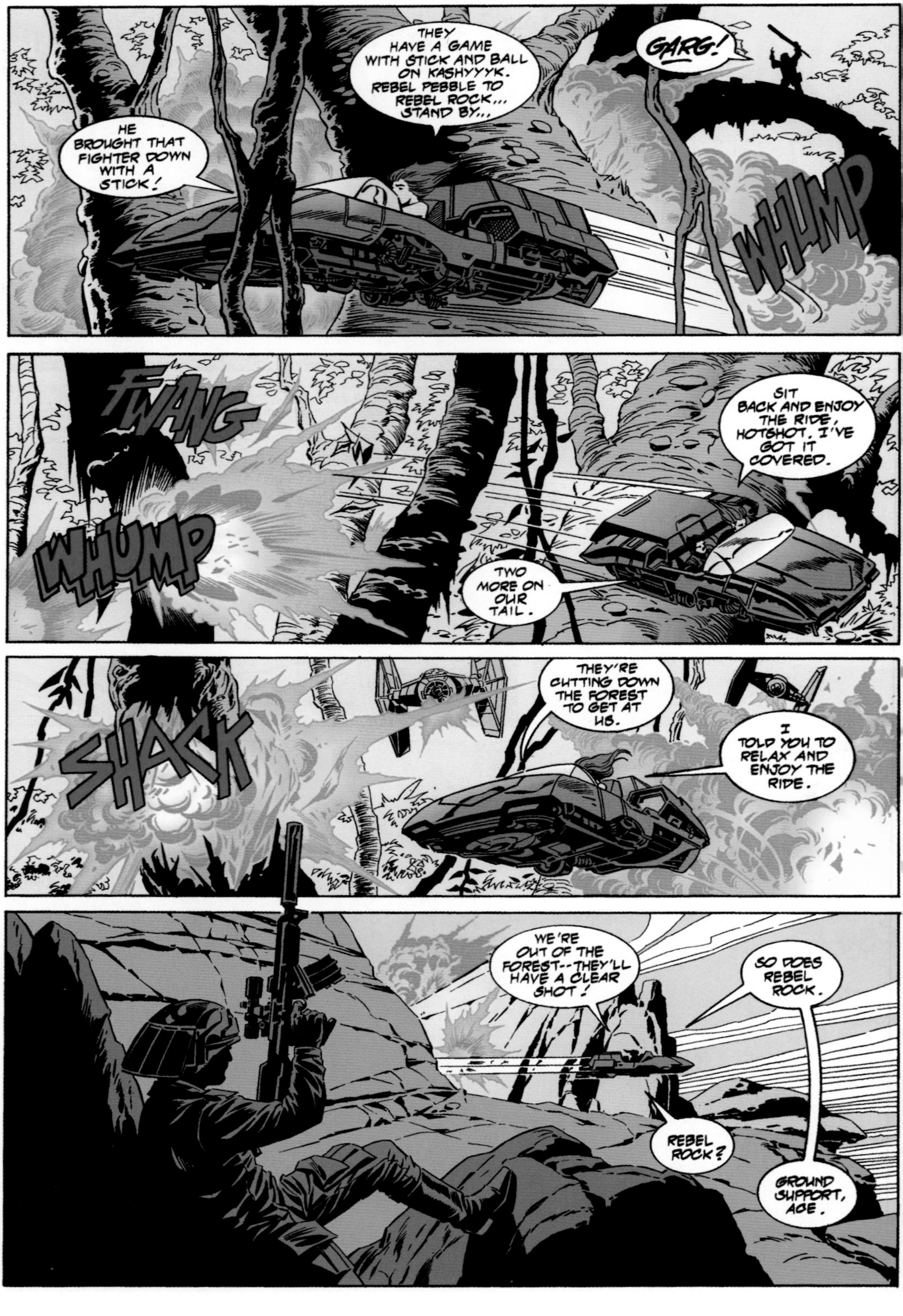
HE BROUGHT THAT FIGHTER DOWN WITH A STICK!
THEY HAVE A GAME WITH STICK AND BALL ON KASHYYYK. REBEL PEBBLE TO REBEL ROCK... STAND BY...
GARG!
WHUMP
FWANG
WHUMP
SIT BACK AND ENJOY THE RIDE, HOTSHOT. I'VE GOT IT COVERED.
TWO MORE ON OUR TAIL.
SHACK
THEY'RE CUTTING DOWN THE FOREST TO GET AT US.
I TOLD YOU TO RELAX AND ENJOY THE RIDE.
WE'RE OUT OF THE FOREST--THEY'LL HAVE A CLEAR SHOT!
SO DOES REBEL ROCK.
REBEL ROCK?
GROUND SUPPORT, ACE.

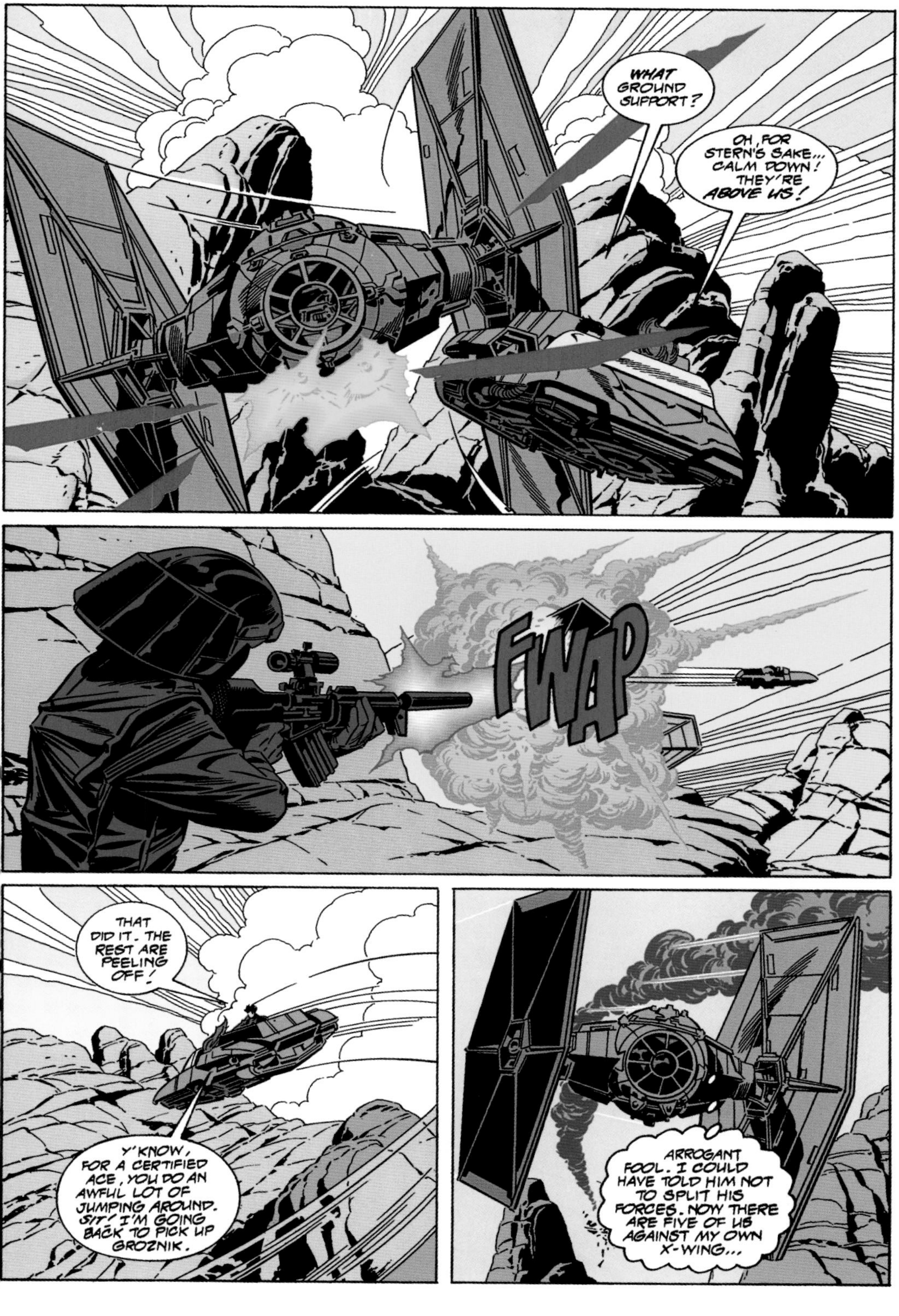
WHAT GROUND SUPPORT?
OH, FOR STERN'S SAKE... CALM DOWN! THEY'RE ABOVE US!
FWAP
THAT DID IT. THE REST ARE PEELING OFF!
Y'KNOW, FOR A CERTIFIED ACE, YOU DO AN AWFUL LOT OF JUMPING AROUND. SIT! I'M GOING BACK TO PICK UP GROZNIK.
ARROGANT FOOL. I COULD HAVE TOLD HIM NOT TO SPLIT HIS FORCES. NOW THERE ARE FIVE OF US AGAINST MY OWN X-WING...

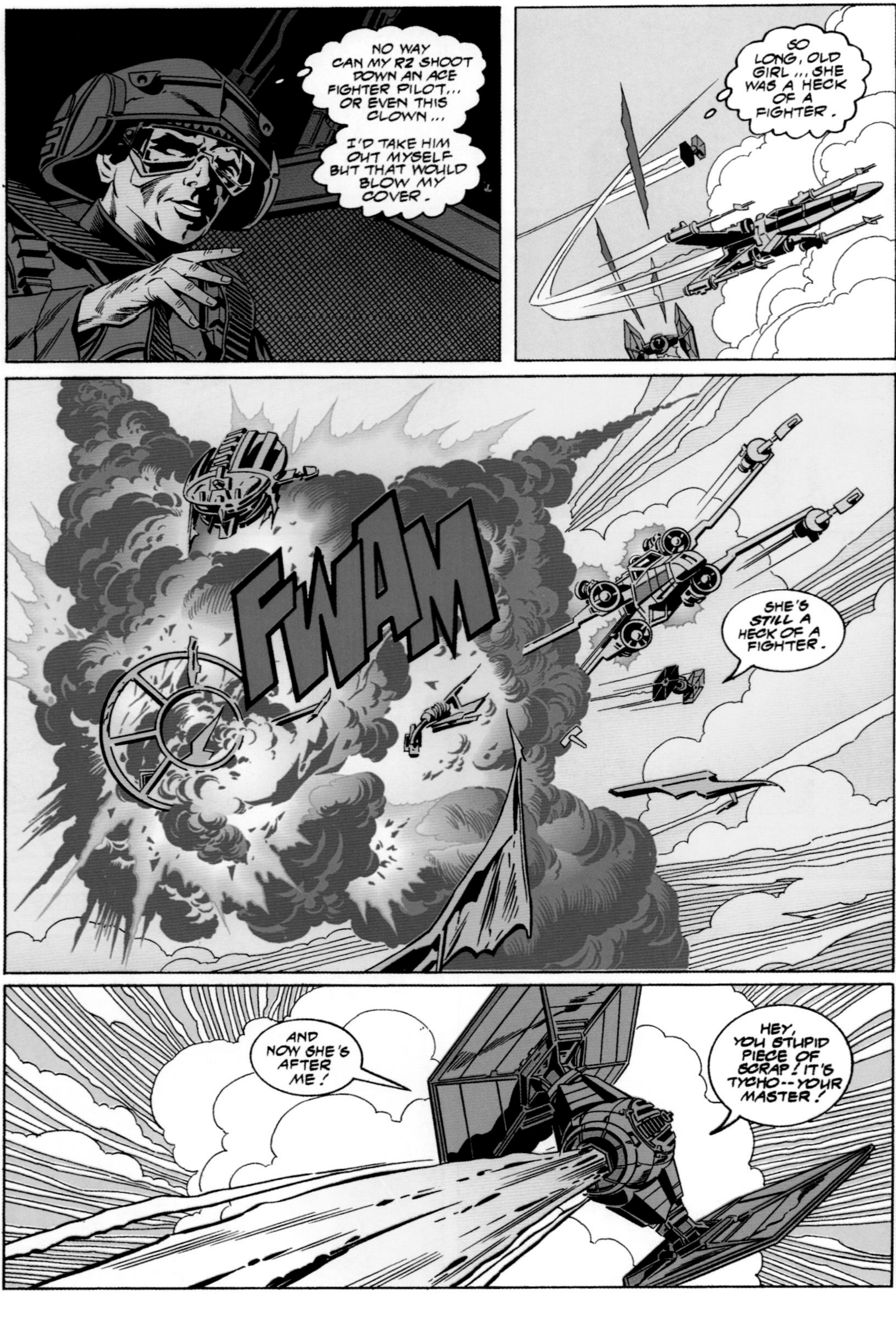
NO WAY CAN MY R2 SHOOT DOWN AN ACE FIGHTER PILOT... OR EVEN THIS CLOWN...
I'D TAKE HIM OUT MYSELF BUT THAT WOULD BLOW MY COVER.
SO LONG, OLD GIRL... SHE WAS A HECK OF A FIGHTER.
FWAM
SHE'S STILL A HECK OF A FIGHTER.
AND NOW SHE'S AFTER ME!
HEY, YOU STUPID PIECE OF SCRAP! IT'S TYCHO--YOUR MASTER!

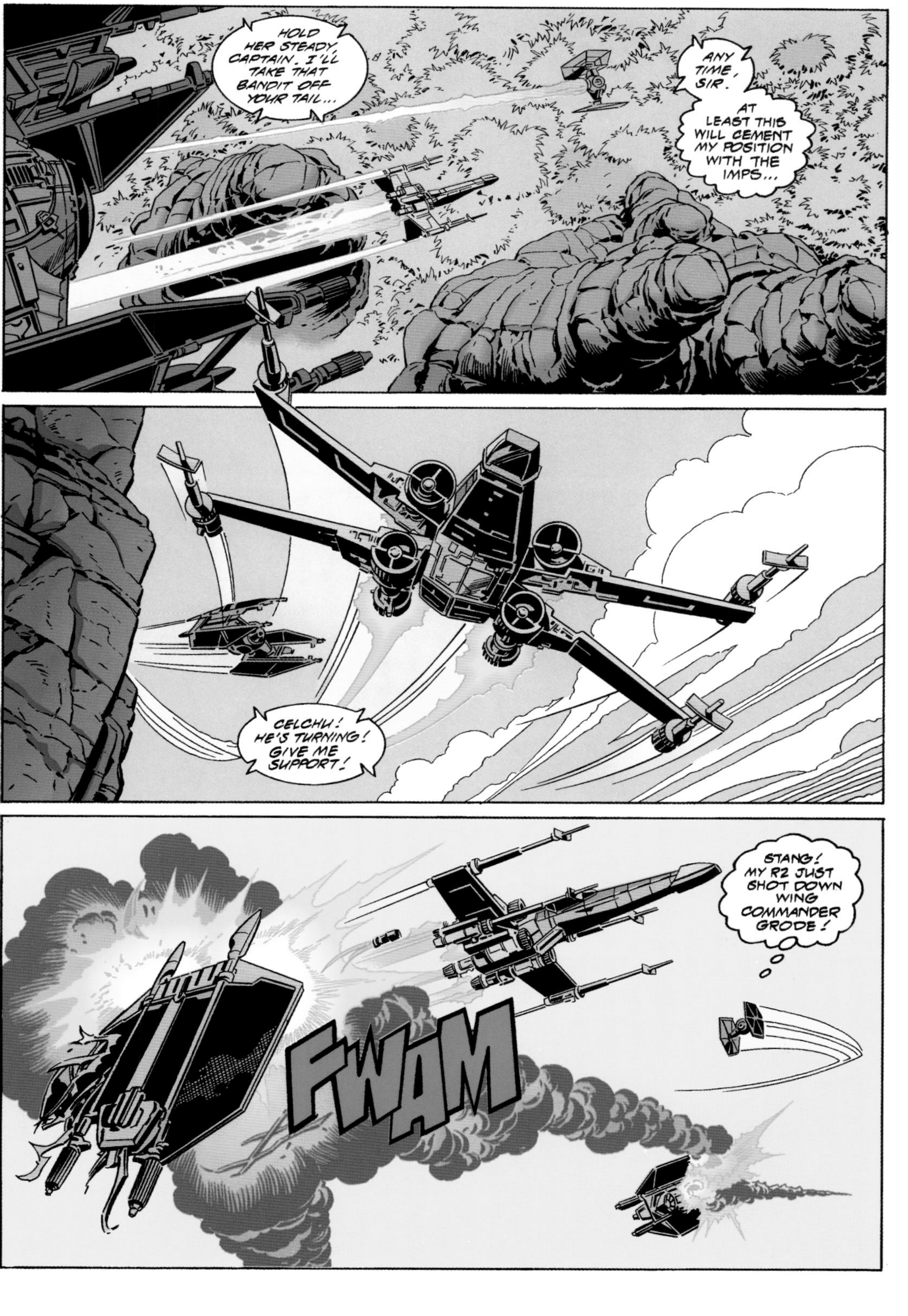

HOLD HER STEADY, CAPTAIN. I'LL TAKE THAT BANDIT OFF YOUR TAIL...
ANY TIME, SIR.
AT LEAST THIS WILL CEMENT MY POSITION WITH THE IMPS...
CELCHU! HE'S TURNING! GIVE ME SUPPORT!
STANG! MY R2 JUST SHOT DOWN WING COMMANDER GRODE!
FWAM

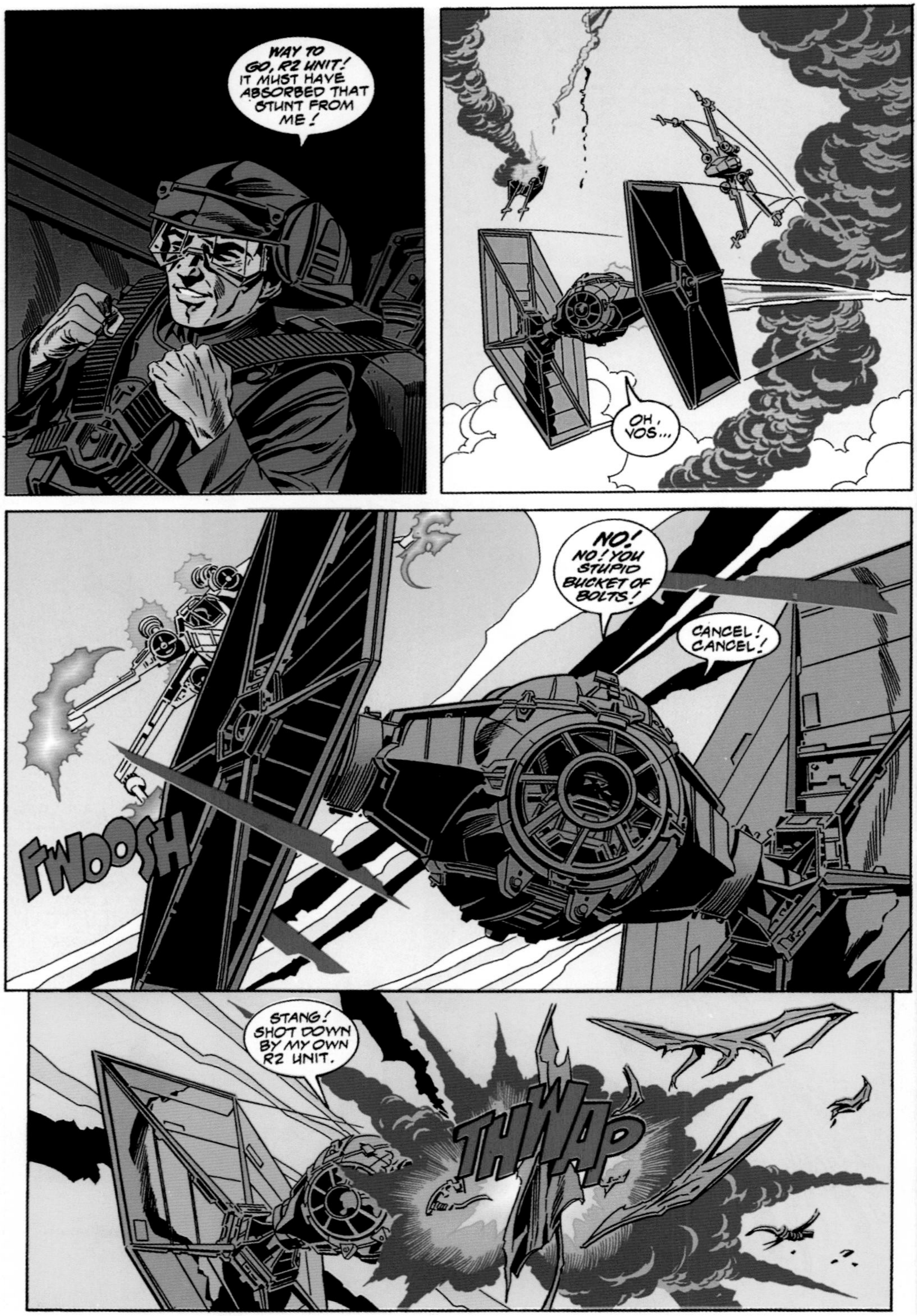

WAY TO GO, R2 UNIT! IT MUST HAVE ABSORBED THAT STUNT FROM ME!
OH, VOS...
NO! NO! YOU STUPID BUCKET OF BOLTS!
CANCEL! CANCEL!
FWOOSH
STANG! SHOT DOWN BY MY OWN R2 UNIT.
THWAP

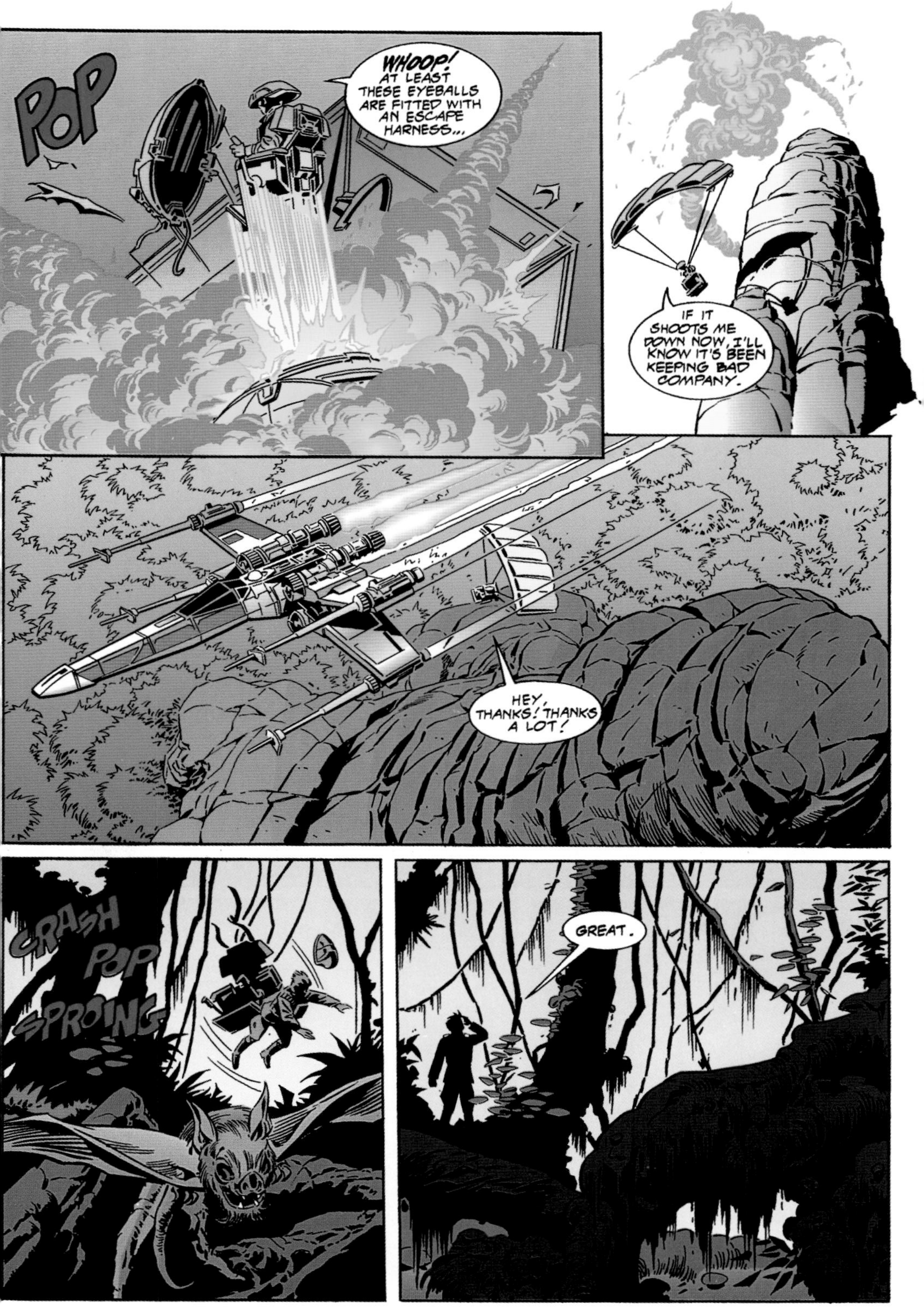
POP
WHOOP! AT LEAST THESE EYEBALLS ARE FITTED WITH AN ESCAPE HARNESS...
IF IT SHOOTS ME DOWN NOW, I'LL KNOW IT'S BEEN KEEPING BAD COMPANY.
HEY, THANKS! THANKS A LOT!
CRASH
POP
SPROING
GREAT.

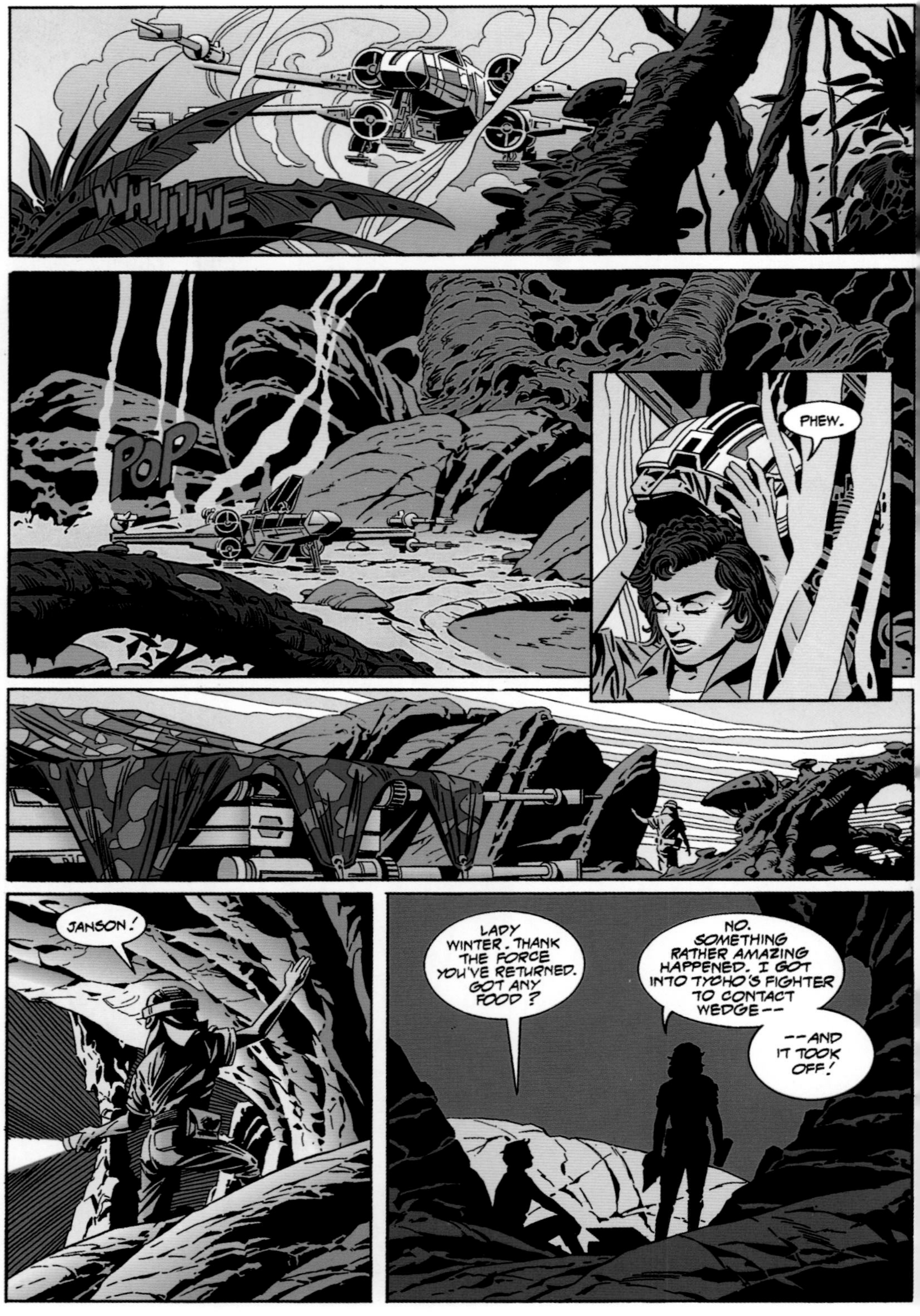
WHIIIINE
POP
PHEW.
JANSON!
LADY WINTER. THANK THE FORCE YOU'VE RETURNED. GOT ANY FOOD?
NO. SOMETHING RATHER AMAZING HAPPENED. I GOT INTO TYCHO'S FIGHTER TO CONTACT WEDGE--
--AND IT TOOK OFF!

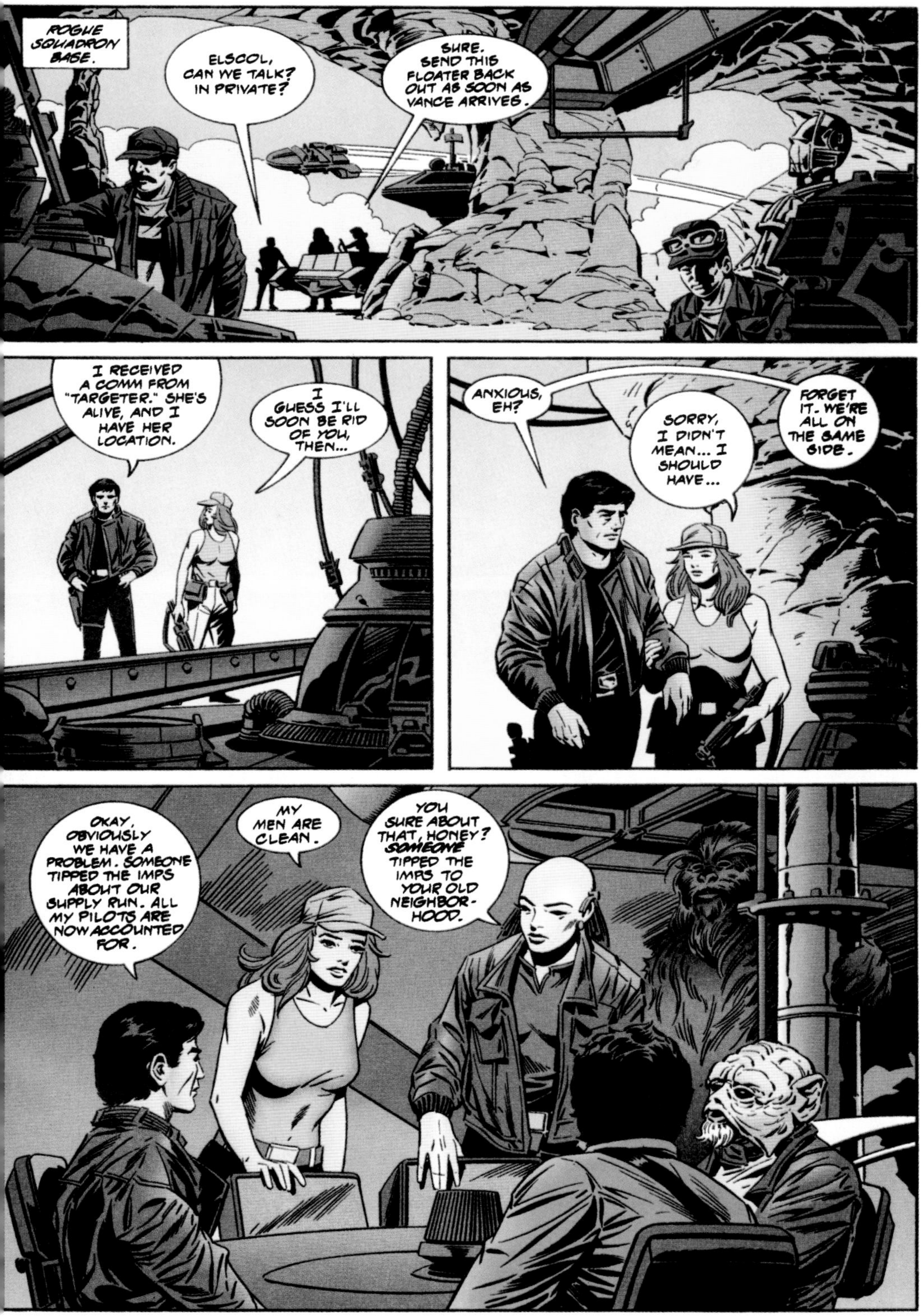
ROGUE SQUADRON BASE.
ELSCOL, CAN WE TALK? IN PRIVATE?
SURE. SEND THIS FLOATER BACK OUT AS SOON AS VANCE ARRIVES.
I RECEIVED A COMM FROM "TARGETER." SHE'S ALIVE, AND I HAVE HER LOCATION.
I GUESS I'LL SOON BE RID OF YOU, THEN...
ANXIOUS, EH?
SORRY, I DIDN'T MEAN... I SHOULD HAVE...
FORGET IT. WE'RE ALL ON THE SAME SIDE.
OKAY, OBVIOUSLY WE HAVE A PROBLEM. SOMEONE TIPPED THE IMPS ABOUT OUR SUPPLY RUN. ALL MY PILOTS ARE NOW ACCOUNTED FOR.
MY MEN ARE CLEAN.
YOU SURE ABOUT THAT, HONEY? SOMEONE TIPPED THE IMPS TO YOUR OLD NEIGHBOR-HOOD.

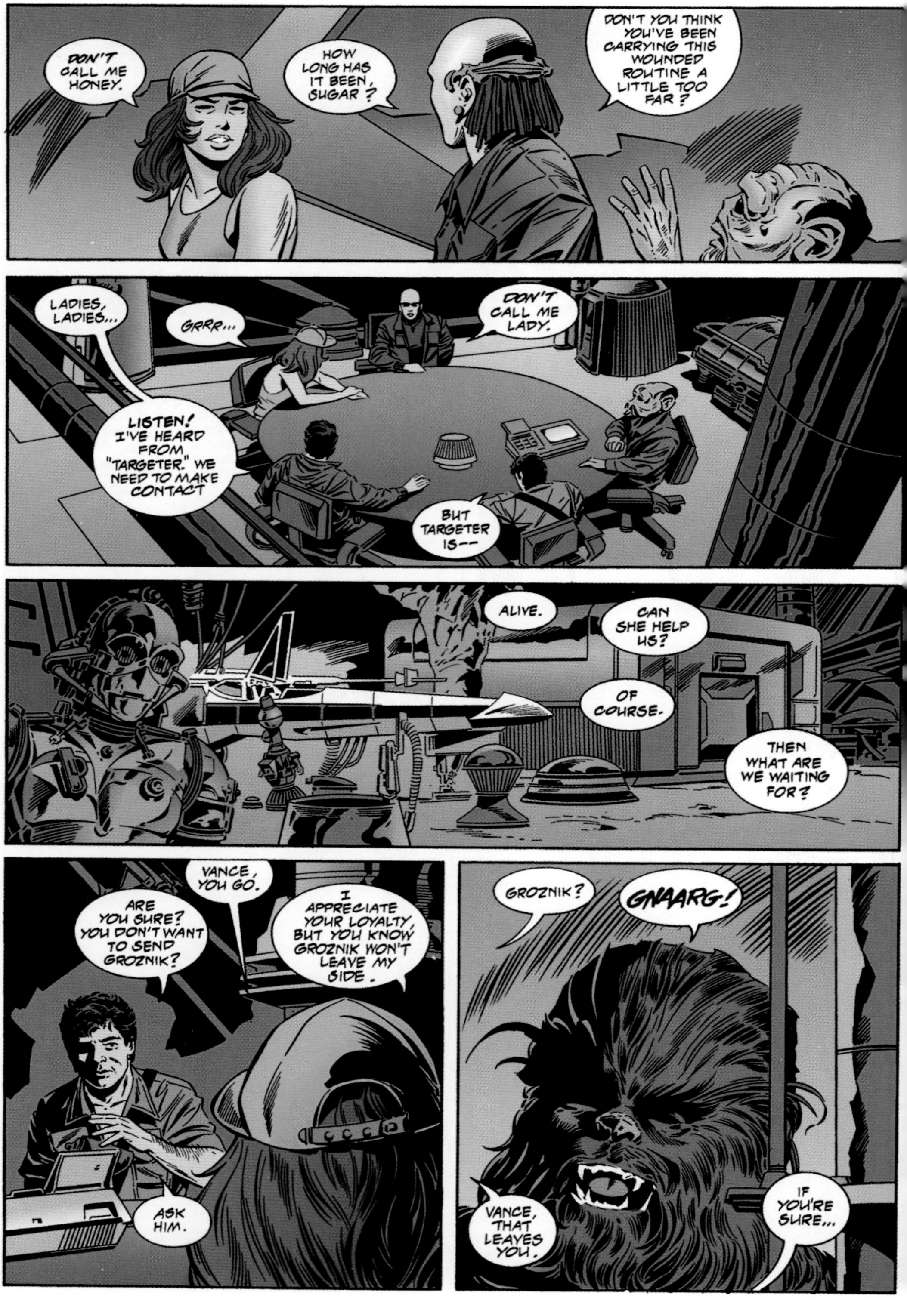
DON'T CALL ME HONEY.
HOW LONG HAS IT BEEN, SUGAR?
DON'T YOU THINK YOU'VE BEEN CARRYING THIS WOUNDED ROUTINE A LITTLE TOO FAR?
LADIES, LADIES...
GRRR...
DON'T CALL ME LADY.
LISTEN! I'VE HEARD FROM "TARGETER." WE NEED TO MAKE CONTACT
BUT TARGETER IS--
ALIVE.
CAN SHE HELP US?
OF COURSE.
THEN WHAT ARE WE WAITING FOR?
VANCE, YOU GO.
ARE YOU SURE? YOU DON'T WANT TO SEND GROZNIK?
I APPRECIATE YOUR LOYALTY, BUT YOU KNOW GROZNIK WON'T LEAVE MY SIDE.
ASK HIM.
GROZNIK?
GNAARG!
VANCE, THAT LEAVES YOU.
IF YOU'RE SURE...

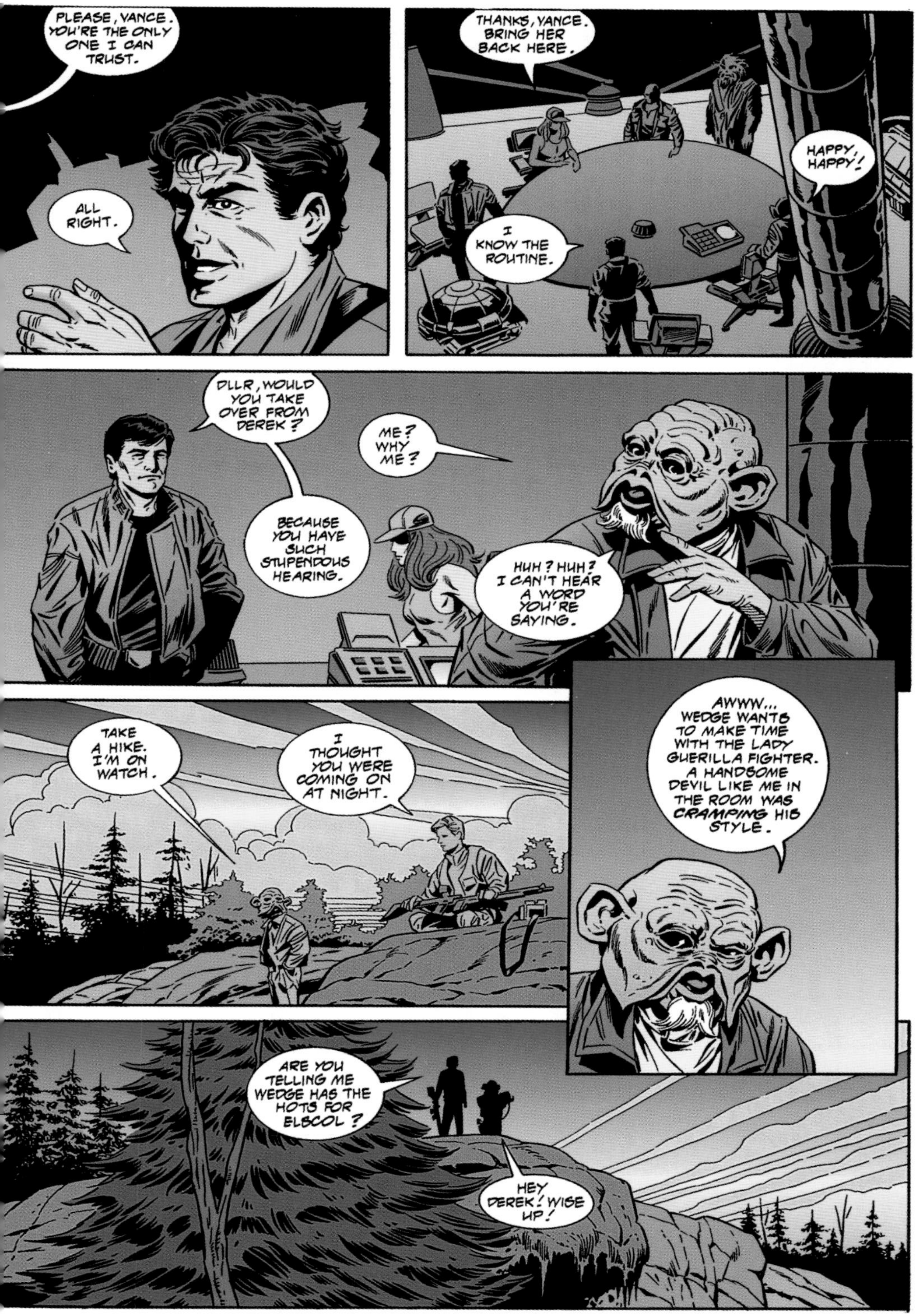
PLEASE, VANCE. YOU'RE THE ONLY ONE I CAN TRUST.
ALL RIGHT.
THANKS, VANCE. BRING HER BACK HERE.
I KNOW THE ROUTINE.
HAPPY, HAPPY!
DLLR, WOULD YOU TAKE OVER FROM DEREK?
ME? WHY ME?
BECAUSE YOU HAVE SUCH STUPENDOUS HEARING.
HUH? HUH? I CAN'T HEAR A WORD YOU'RE SAYING.
AWWW... WEDGE WANTS TO MAKE TIME WITH THE LADY GUERILLA FIGHTER. A HANDSOME DEVIL LIKE ME IN THE ROOM WAS CRAMPING HIS STYLE.
TAKE A HIKE. I'M ON WATCH.
I THOUGHT YOU WERE COMING ON AT NIGHT.
ARE YOU TELLING ME WEDGE HAS THE HOTS FOR ELSCOL?
HEY DEREK! WISE UP!

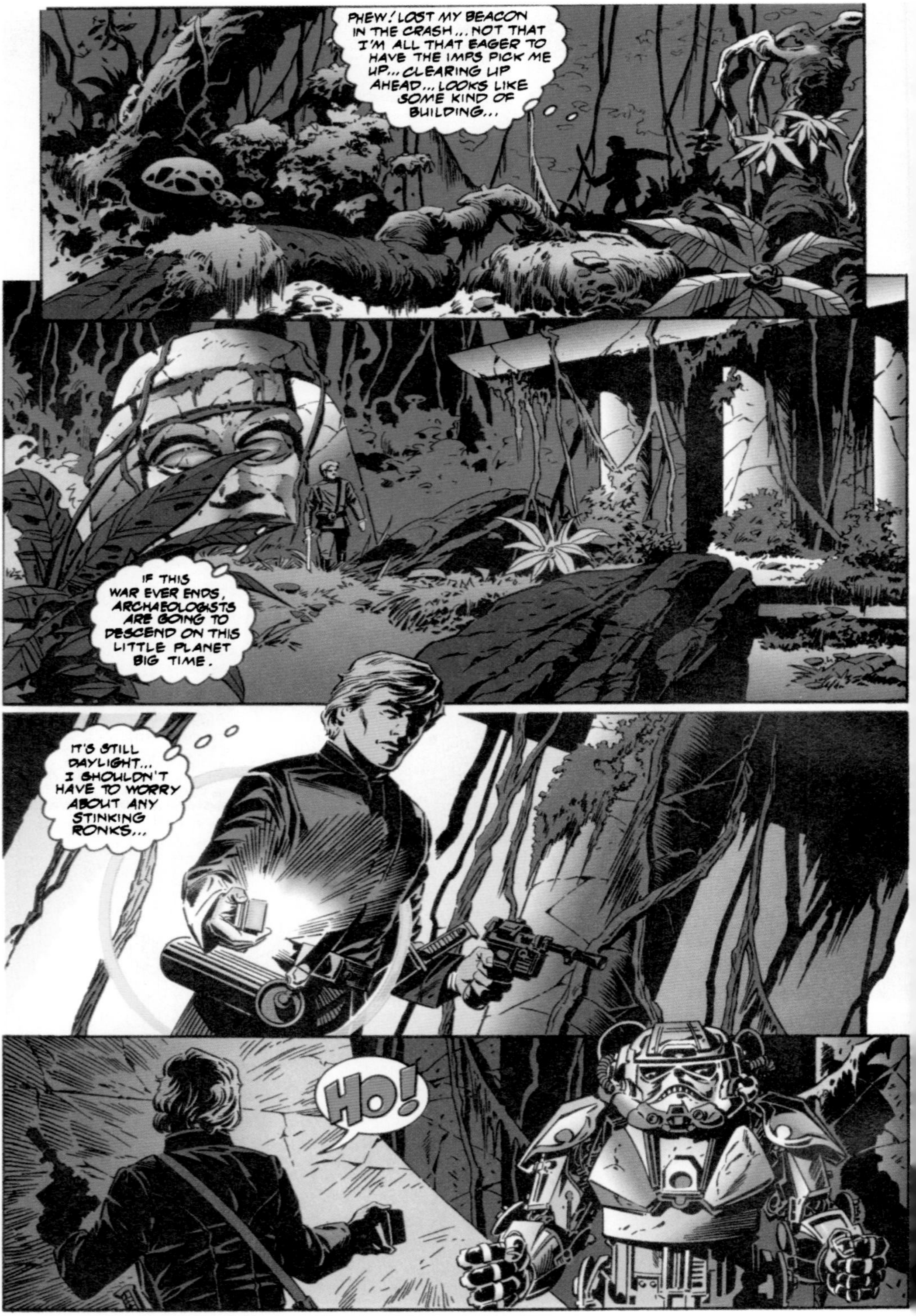

PHEW! LOST MY BEACON IN THE CRASH... NOT THAT I'M ALL THAT EAGER TO HAVE THE IMPS PICK ME UP... CLEARING UP AHEAD... LOOKS LIKE SOME KIND OF BUILDING...
IF THIS WAR EVER ENDS, ARCHAEOLOGISTS ARE GOING TO DESCEND ON THIS LITTLE PLANET BIG TIME.
IT'S STILL DAYLIGHT... I SHOULDN'T HAVE TO WORRY ABOUT ANY STINKING RONKS...
HO!

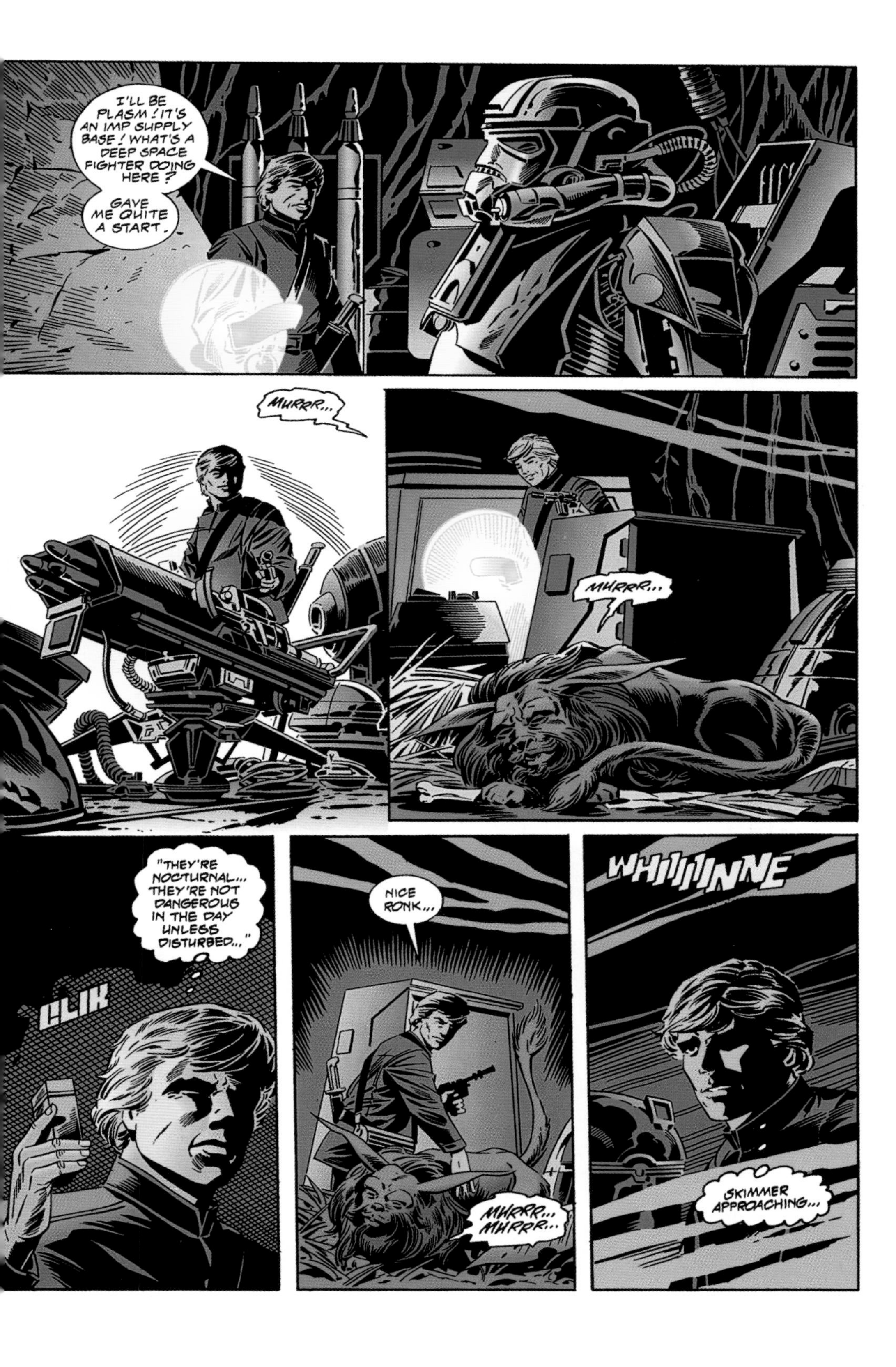
I'LL BE PLASM! IT'S AN IMP SUPPLY BASE! WHAT'S A DEEP SPACE FIGHTER DOING HERE?
GAVE ME QUITE A START.
MURRR...
MURRR...
"THEY'RE NOCTURNAL... THEY'RE NOT DANGEROUS IN THE DAY UNLESS DISTURBED..."
CLIK
NICE RONK...
MURRR... MURRR...
WHIIIIINNE
SKIMMER APPROACHING...

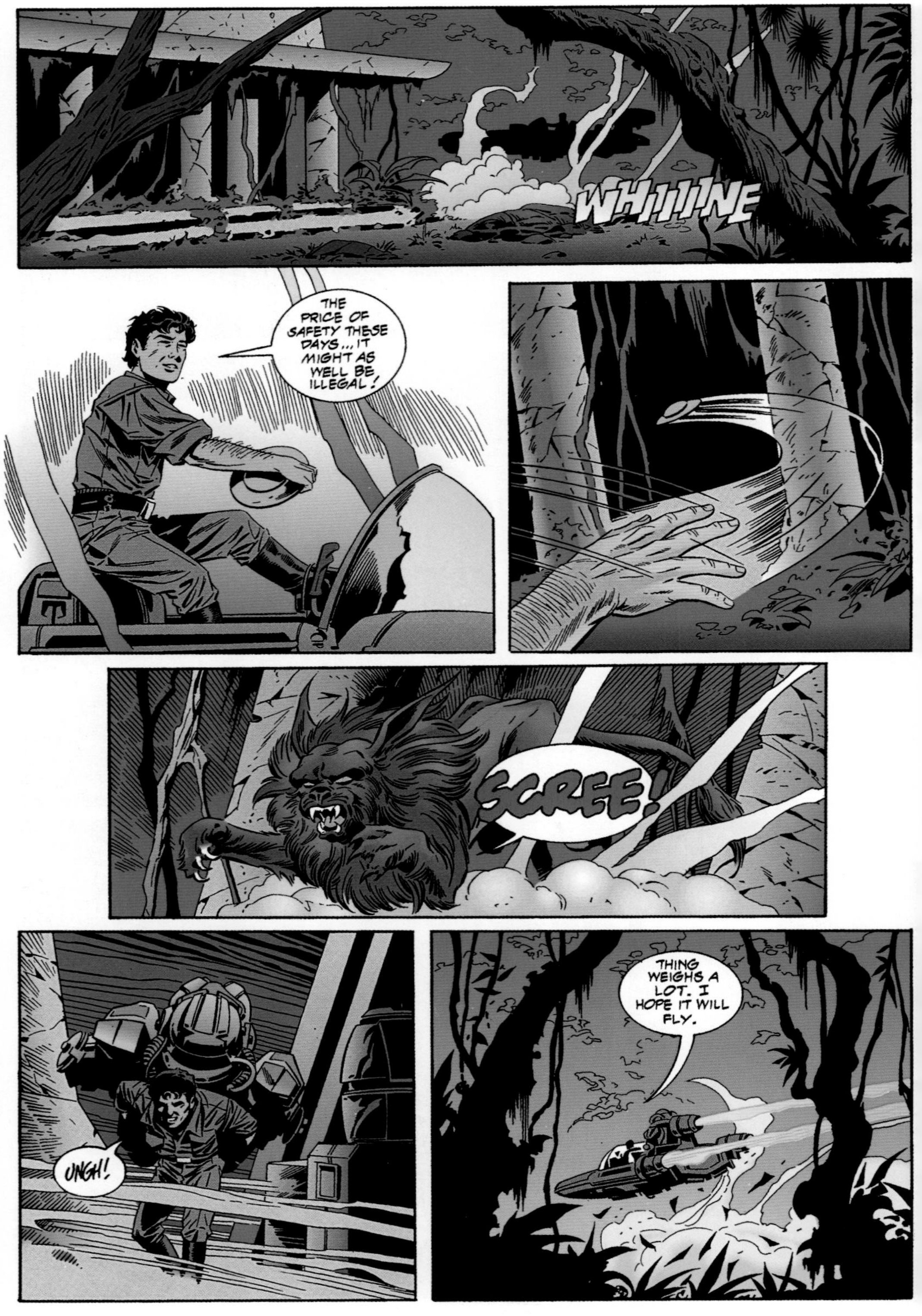
WHIIIINE
THE PRICE OF SAFETY THESE DAYS... IT MIGHT AS WELL BE ILLEGAL!
SCREE!
UNGH!
THING WEIGHS A LOT. I HOPE IT WILL FLY.

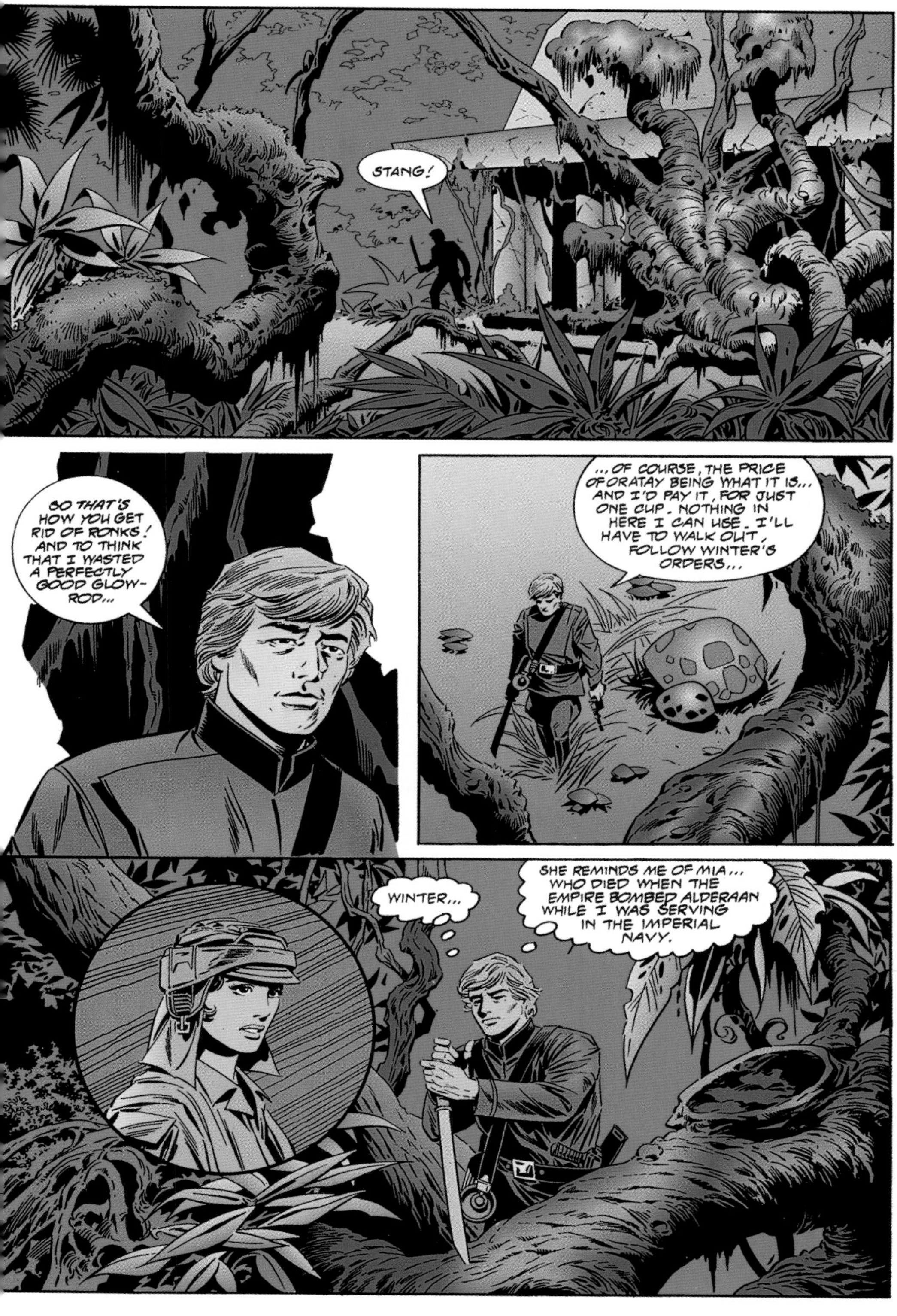
STANG!
SO THAT'S HOW YOU GET RID OF RONKS! AND TO THINK THAT I WASTED A PERFECTLY GOOD GLOW-ROD...
...OF COURSE, THE PRICE OF ORATAY BEING WHAT IT IS... AND I'D PAY IT, FOR JUST ONE CUP. NOTHING IN HERE I CAN USE. I'LL HAVE TO WALK OUT, FOLLOW WINTER'S ORDERS...
WINTER...
SHE REMINDS ME OF MIA... WHO DIED WHEN THE EMPIRE BOMBED ALDERAAN WHILE I WAS SERVING IN THE IMPERIAL NAVY.

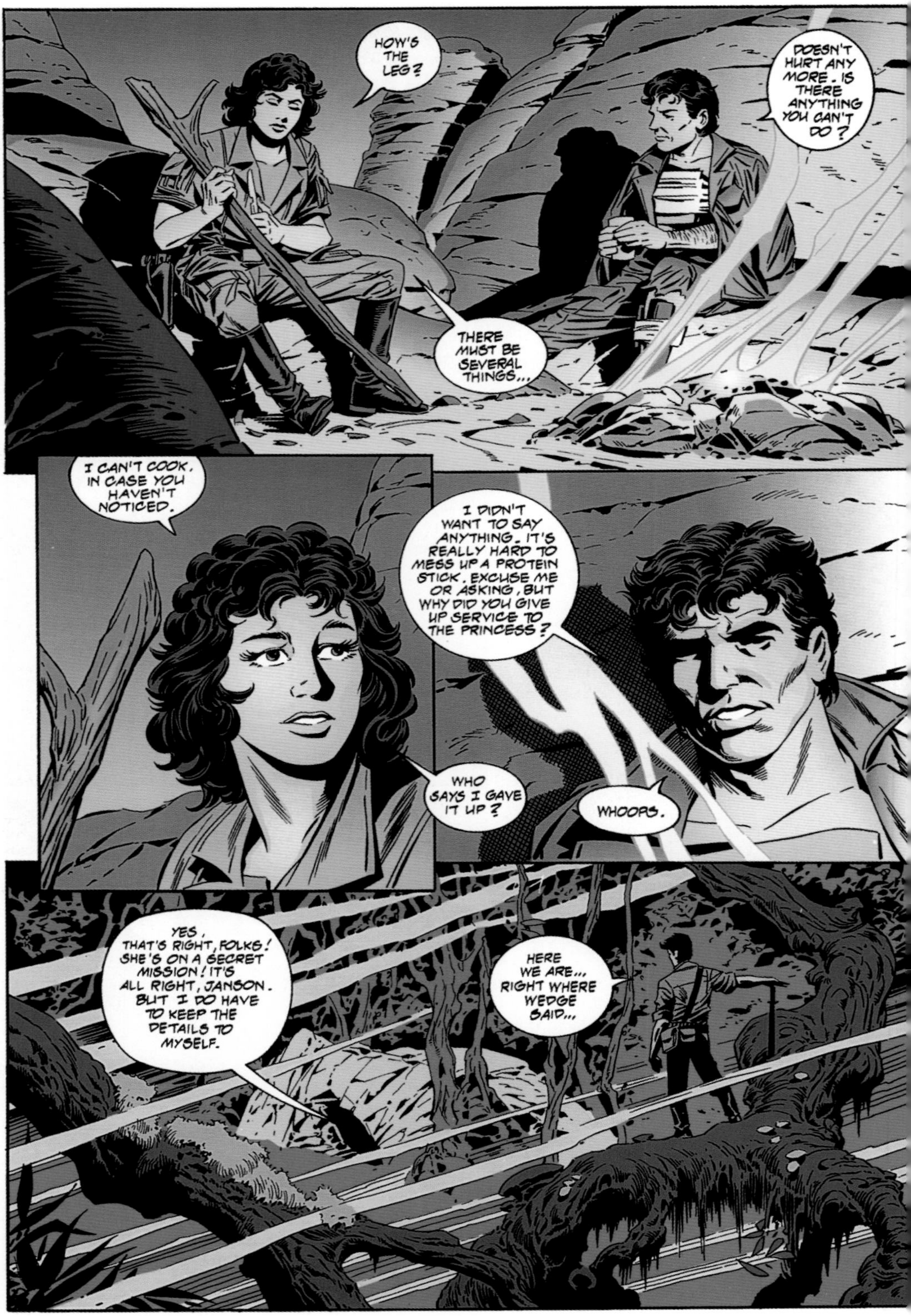
HOW'S THE LEG?
DOESN'T HURT ANY MORE. IS THERE ANYTHING YOU CAN'T DO?
THERE MUST BE SEVERAL THINGS...
I CAN'T COOK, IN CASE YOU HAVEN'T NOTICED.
I DIDN'T WANT TO SAY ANYTHING. IT'S REALLY HARD TO MESS UP A PROTEIN STICK. EXCUSE ME OR ASKING, BUT WHY DID YOU GIVE UP SERVICE TO THE PRINCESS?
WHO SAYS I GAVE IT UP?
WHOOPS.
YES, THAT'S RIGHT, FOLKS! SHE'S ON A SECRET MISSION! IT'S ALL RIGHT, JANSON. BUT I DO HAVE TO KEEP THE DETAILS TO MYSELF.
HERE WE ARE... RIGHT WHERE WEDGE SAID...

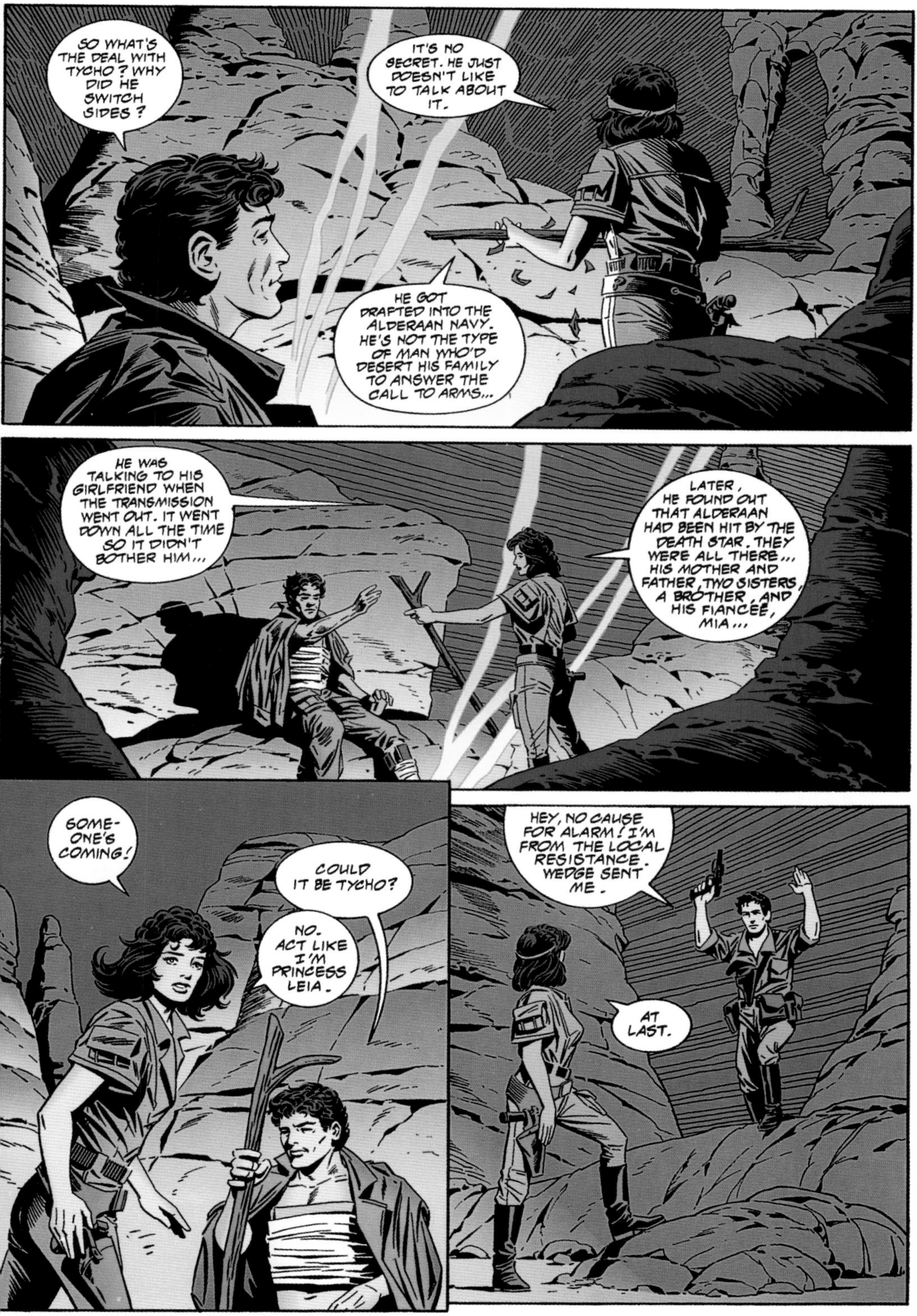
SO WHAT'S THE DEAL WITH TYCHO? WHY DID HE SWITCH SIDES?
IT'S NO SECRET. HE JUST DOESN'T LIKE TO TALK ABOUT IT.
HE GOT DRAFTED INTO THE ALDERAAN NAVY. HE'S NOT THE TYPE OF MAN WHO'D DESERT HIS FAMILY TO ANSWER THE CALL TO ARMS...
HE WAS TALKING TO HIS GIRLFRIEND WHEN THE TRANSMISSION WENT OUT. IT WENT DOWN ALL THE TIME SO IT DIDN'T BOTHER HIM...
LATER, HE FOUND OUT THAT ALDERAAN HAD BEEN HIT BY THE DEATH STAR. THEY WERE ALL THERE... HIS MOTHER AND FATHER, TWO SISTERS, A BROTHER, AND HIS FIANCÉE, MIA...
SOME-ONE'S COMING!
COULD IT BE TYCHO?
NO. ACT LIKE I'M PRINCESS LEIA.
HEY, NO CAUSE FOR ALARM! I'M FROM THE LOCAL RESISTANCE. WEDGE SENT ME.
AT LAST.

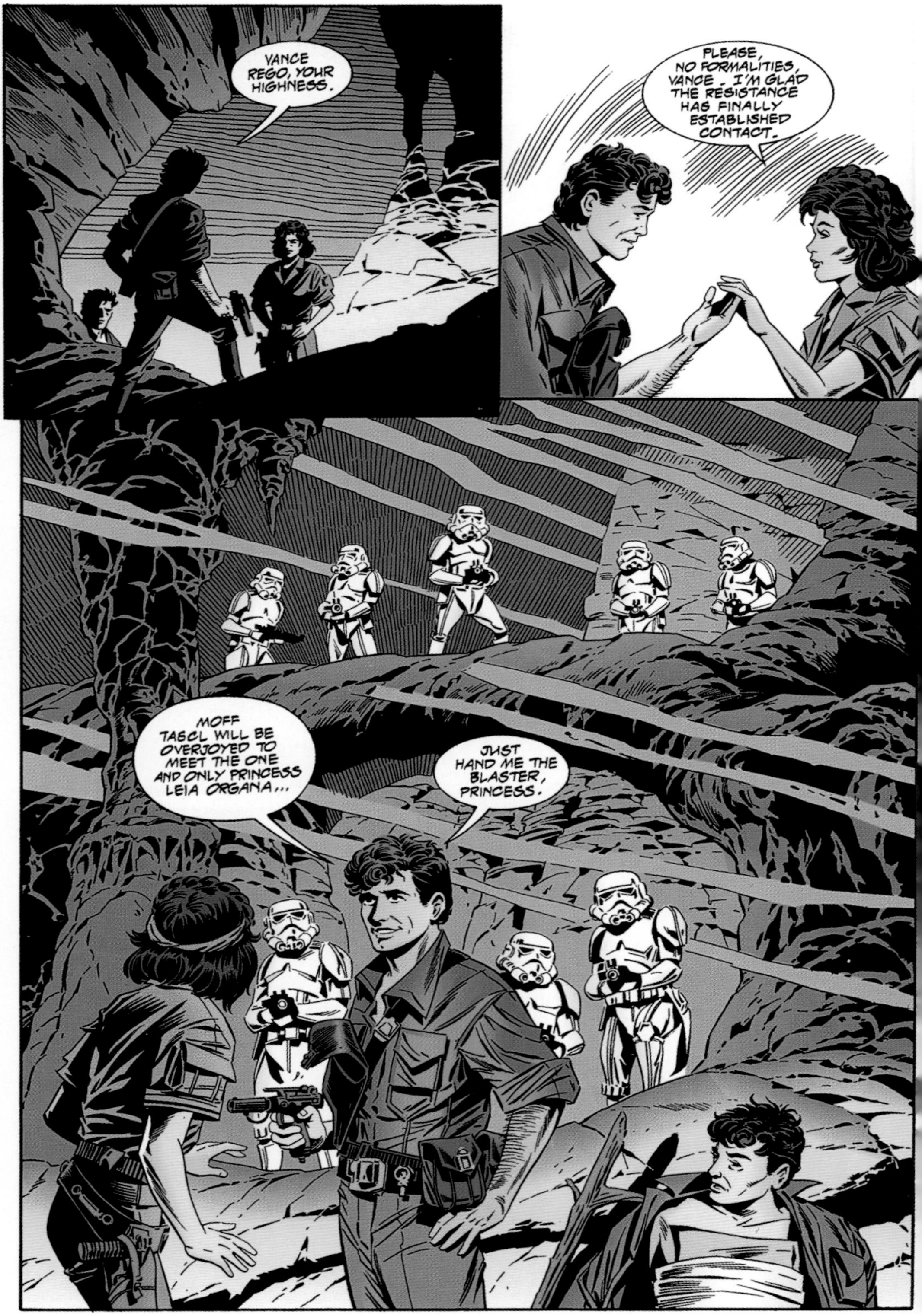
VANCE REGO, YOUR HIGHNESS.
PLEASE, NO FORMALITIES, VANCE. I'M GLAD THE RESISTANCE HAS FINALLY ESTABLISHED CONTACT.
MOFF TASCL WILL BE OVERJOYED TO MEET THE ONE AND ONLY PRINCESS LEIA ORGANA...
JUST HAND ME THE BLASTER, PRINCESS.

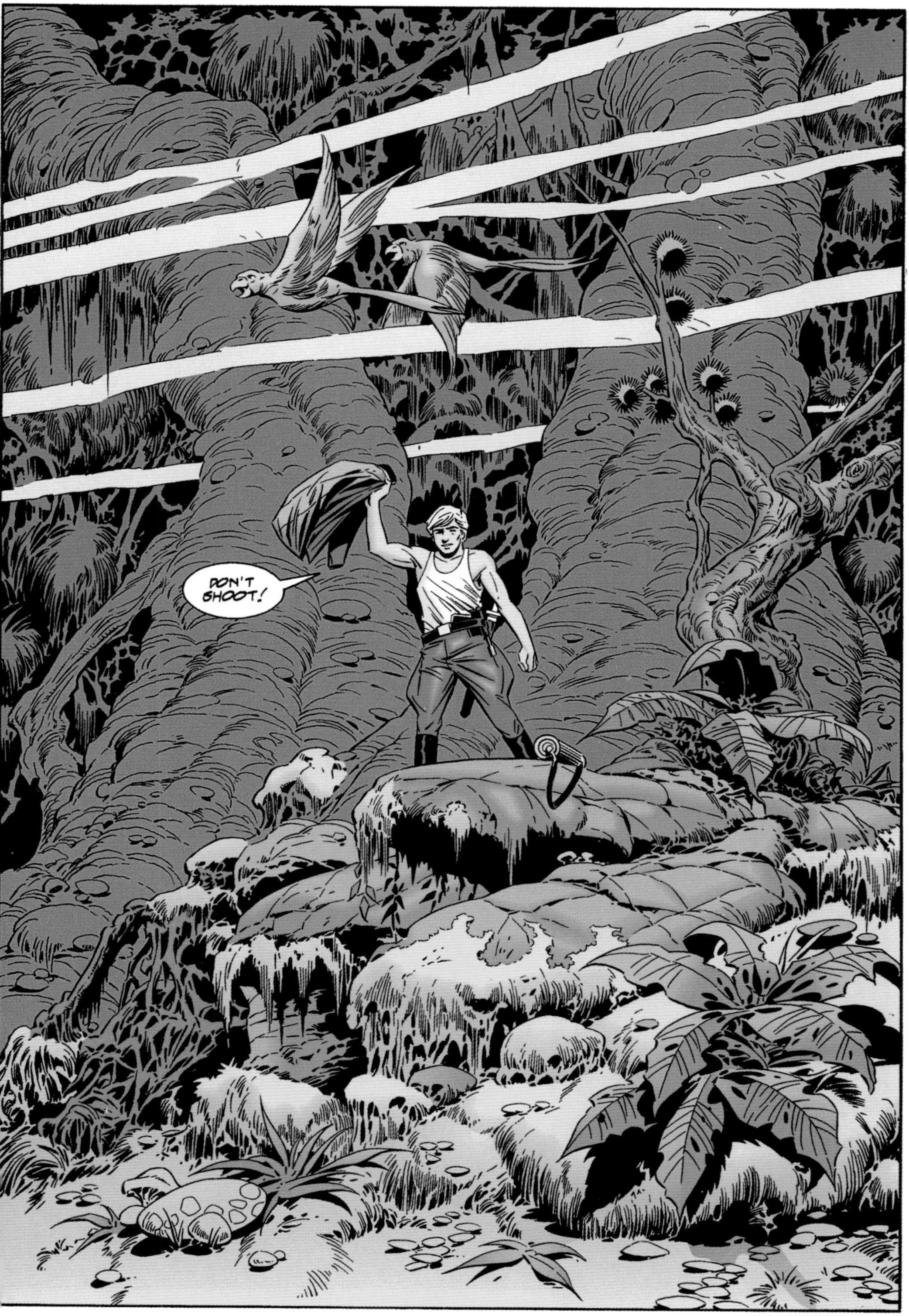
DON'T SHOOT!

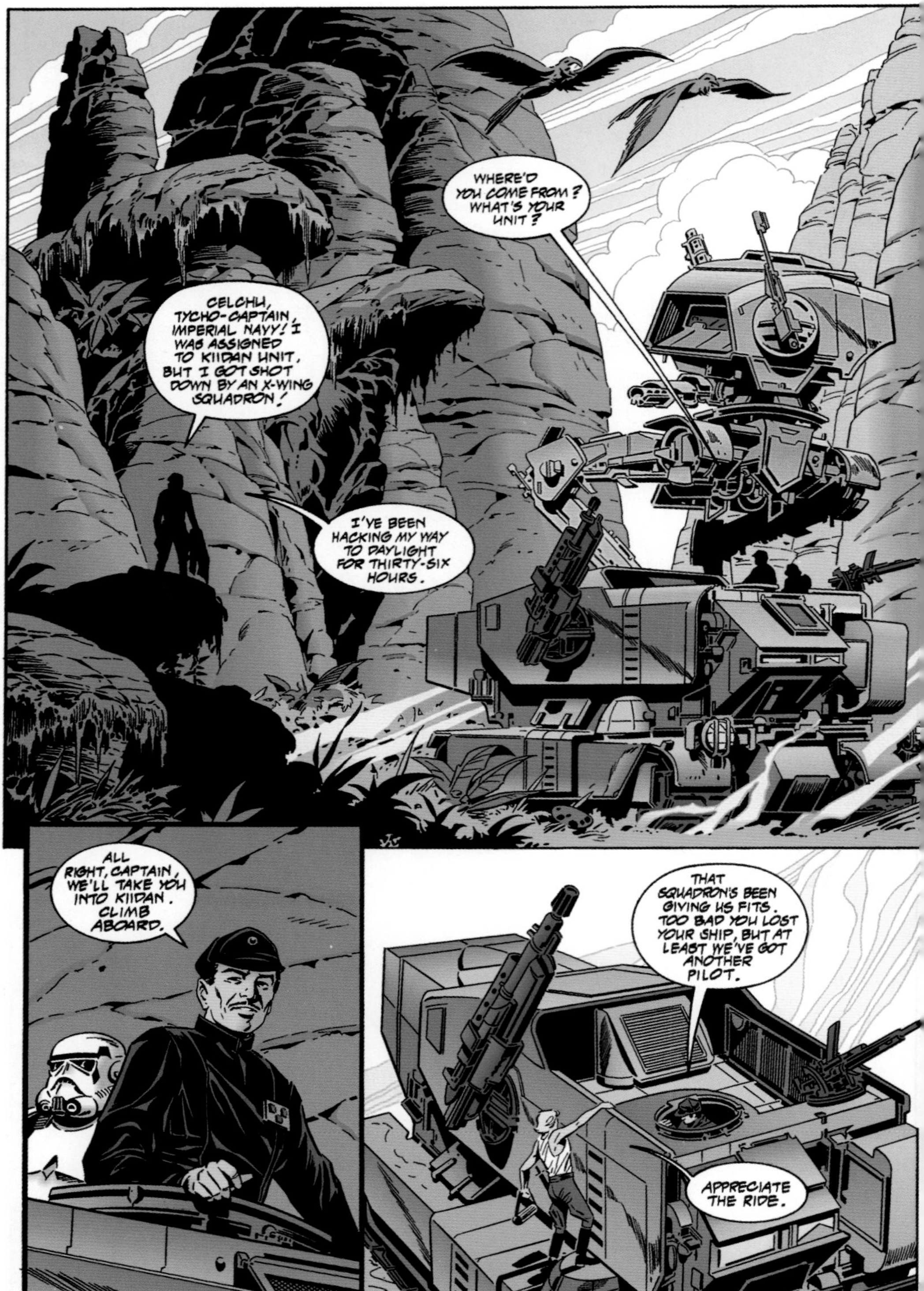
WHERE'D YOU COME FROM? WHAT'S YOUR UNIT?
CELCHU, TYCHO-CAPTAIN, IMPERIAL NAVY! I WAS ASSIGNED TO KIIDAN UNIT, BUT I GOT SHOT DOWN BY AN X-WING SQUADRON!
I'VE BEEN HACKING MY WAY TO DAYLIGHT FOR THIRTY-SIX HOURS.
ALL RIGHT, CAPTAIN, WE'LL TAKE YOU INTO KIIDAN. CLIMB ABOARD.
THAT SQUADRON'S BEEN GIVING US FITS. TOO BAD YOU LOST YOUR SHIP, BUT AT LEAST WE'VE GOT ANOTHER PILOT.
APPRECIATE THE RIDE.

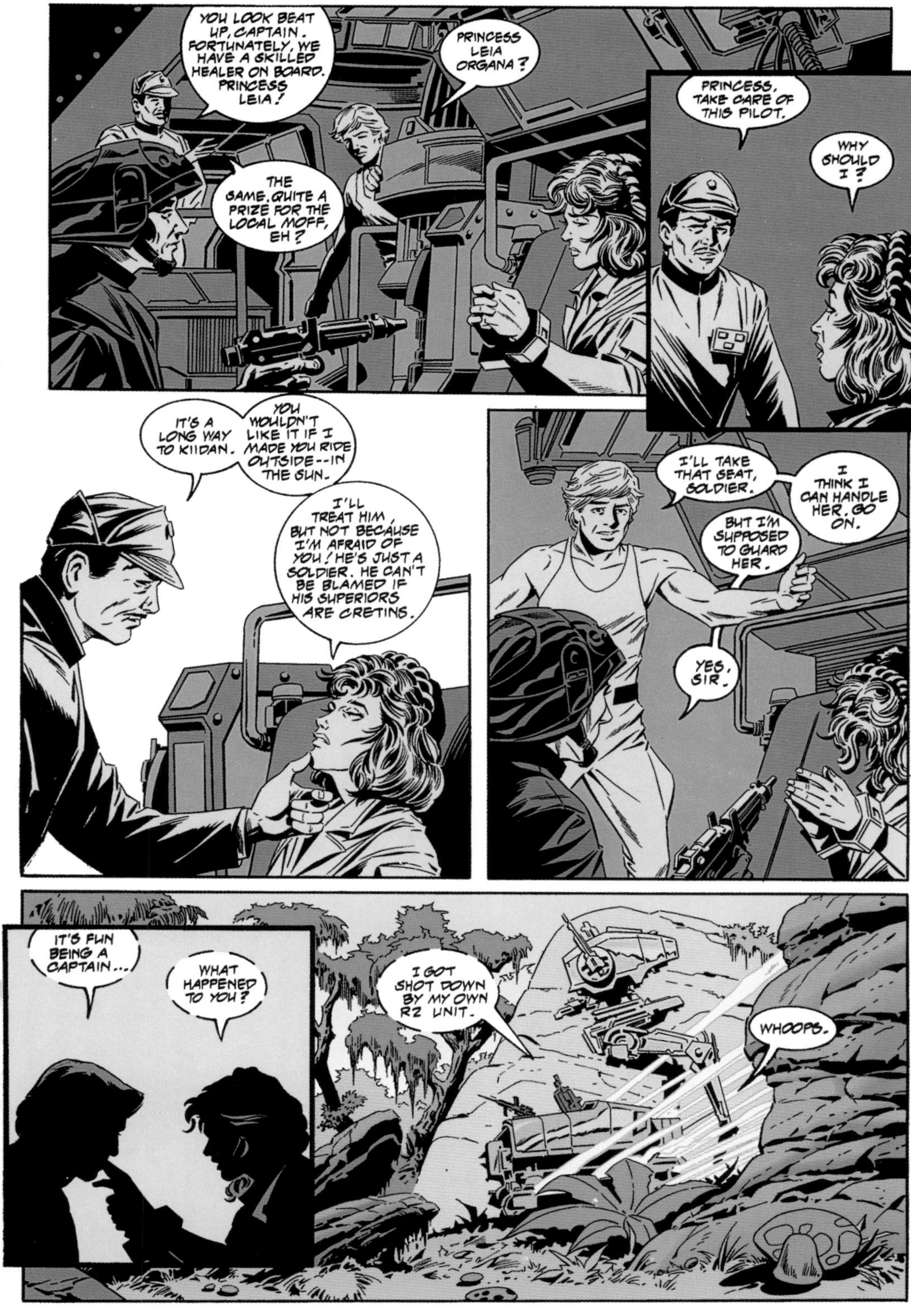
YOU LOOK BEAT UP, CAPTAIN. FORTUNATELY, WE HAVE A SKILLED HEALER ON BOARD. PRINCESS LEIA!
PRINCESS LEIA ORGANA?
THE SAME. QUITE A PRIZE FOR THE LOCAL MOFF, EH?
PRINCESS, TAKE CARE OF THIS PILOT.
WHY SHOULD I?
IT'S A LONG WAY TO KIIDAN.
YOU WOULDN'T LIKE IT IF I MADE YOU RIDE OUTSIDE--IN THE SUN.
I'LL TREAT HIM, BUT NOT BECAUSE I'M AFRAID OF YOU! HE'S JUST A SOLDIER. HE CAN'T BE BLAMED IF HIS SUPERIORS ARE CRETINS.
I'LL TAKE THAT SEAT, SOLDIER.
BUT I'M SUPPOSED TO GUARD HER.
I THINK I CAN HANDLE HER. GO ON.
YES, SIR.
IT'S FUN BEING A CAPTAIN...
WHAT HAPPENED TO YOU?
I GOT SHOT DOWN BY MY OWN R2 UNIT.
WHOOPS.

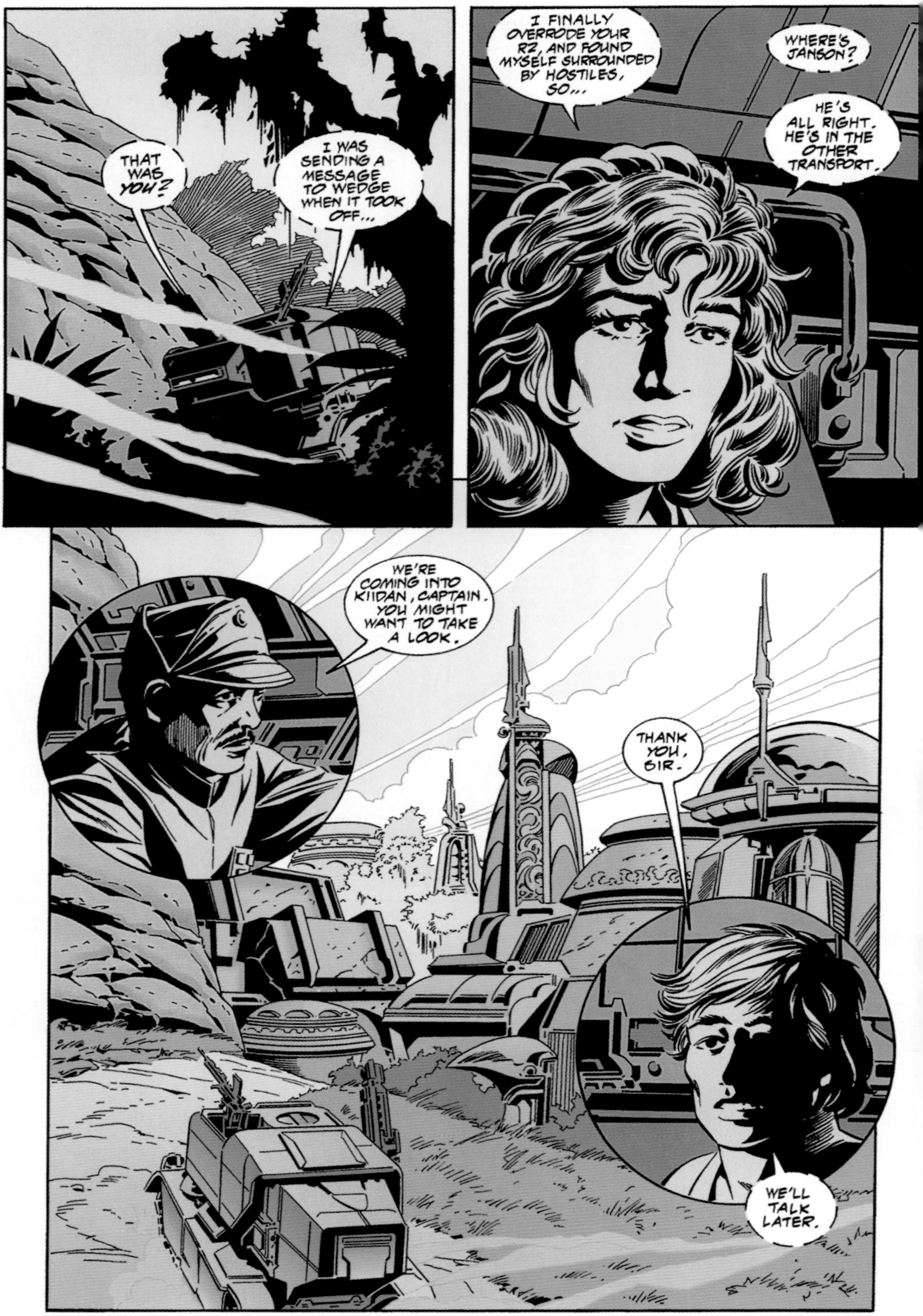
THAT WAS YOU?
I WAS SENDING A MESSAGE TO WEDGE WHEN IT TOOK OFF...
I FINALLY OVERRODE YOUR R2, AND FOUND MYSELF SURROUNDED BY HOSTILES, SO...
WHERE'S JANSON?
HE'S ALL RIGHT. HE'S IN THE OTHER TRANSPORT.
WE'RE COMING INTO KIIDAN, CAPTAIN. YOU MIGHT WANT TO TAKE A LOOK.
THANK YOU, SIR.
WE'LL TALK LATER.

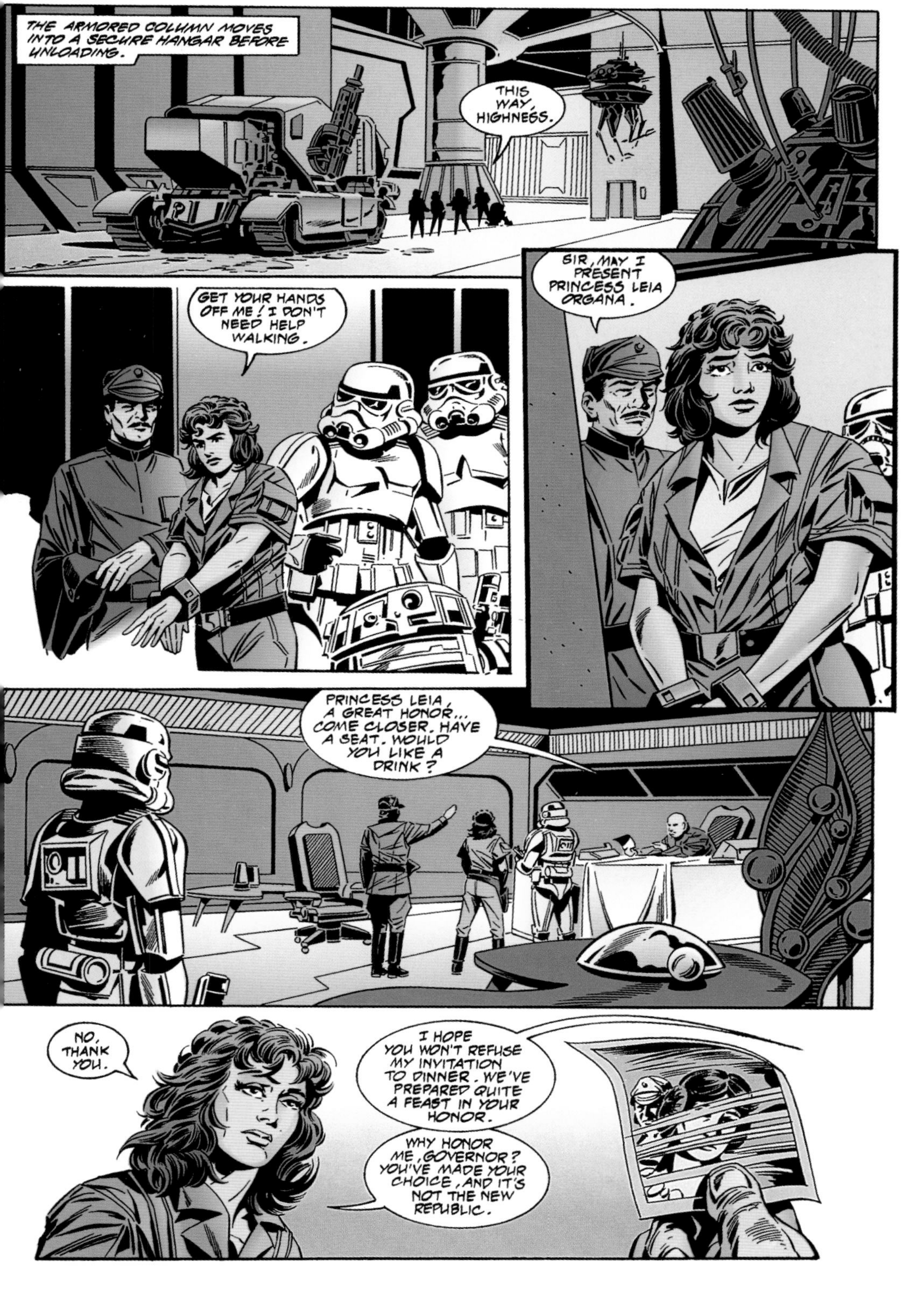
THE ARMORED COLUMN MOVES INTO A SECURE HANGAR BEFORE UNLOADING.
THIS WAY, HIGHNESS.
GET YOUR HANDS OFF ME! I DON'T NEED HELP WALKING.
SIR, MAY I PRESENT PRINCESS LEIA ORGANA.
PRINCESS LEIA, A GREAT HONOR... COME CLOSER. HAVE A SEAT. WOULD YOU LIKE A DRINK?
NO, THANK YOU.
I HOPE YOU WON'T REFUSE MY INVITATION TO DINNER. WE'VE PREPARED QUITE A FEAST IN YOUR HONOR.
WHY HONOR ME, GOVERNOR? YOU'VE MADE YOUR CHOICE, AND IT'S NOT THE NEW REPUBLIC.

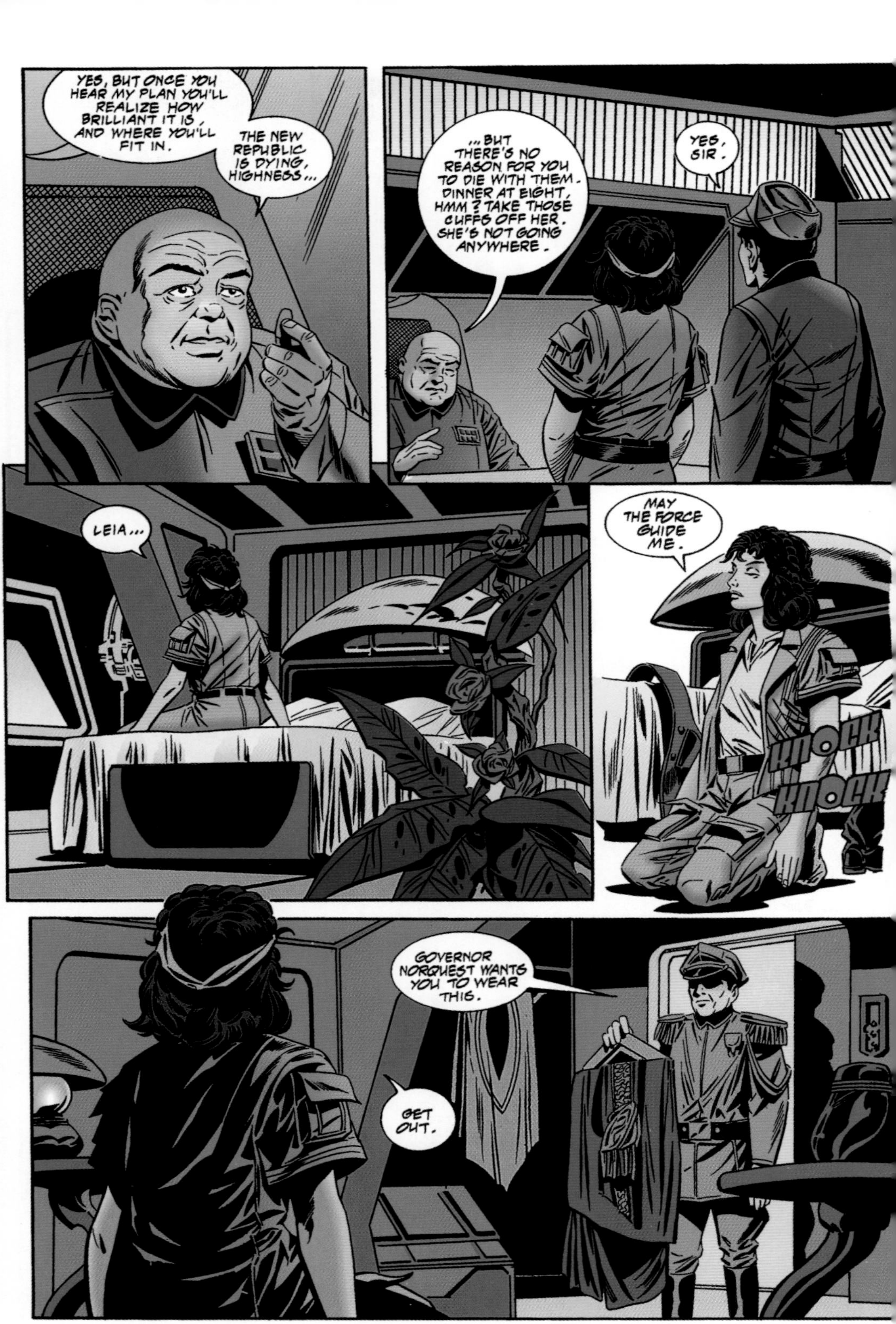
YES, BUT ONCE YOU HEAR MY PLAN YOU'LL REALIZE HOW BRILLIANT IT IS, AND WHERE YOU'LL FIT IN.
THE NEW REPUBLIC IS DYING, HIGHNESS...
...BUT THERE'S NO REASON FOR YOU TO DIE WITH THEM. DINNER AT EIGHT, HMM? TAKE THOSE CUFFS OFF HER. SHE'S NOT GOING ANYWHERE.
YES, SIR.
LEIA...
MAY THE FORCE GUIDE ME.
KNOCK
KNOCK
GOVERNOR NORQUEST WANTS YOU TO WEAR THIS.
GET OUT.

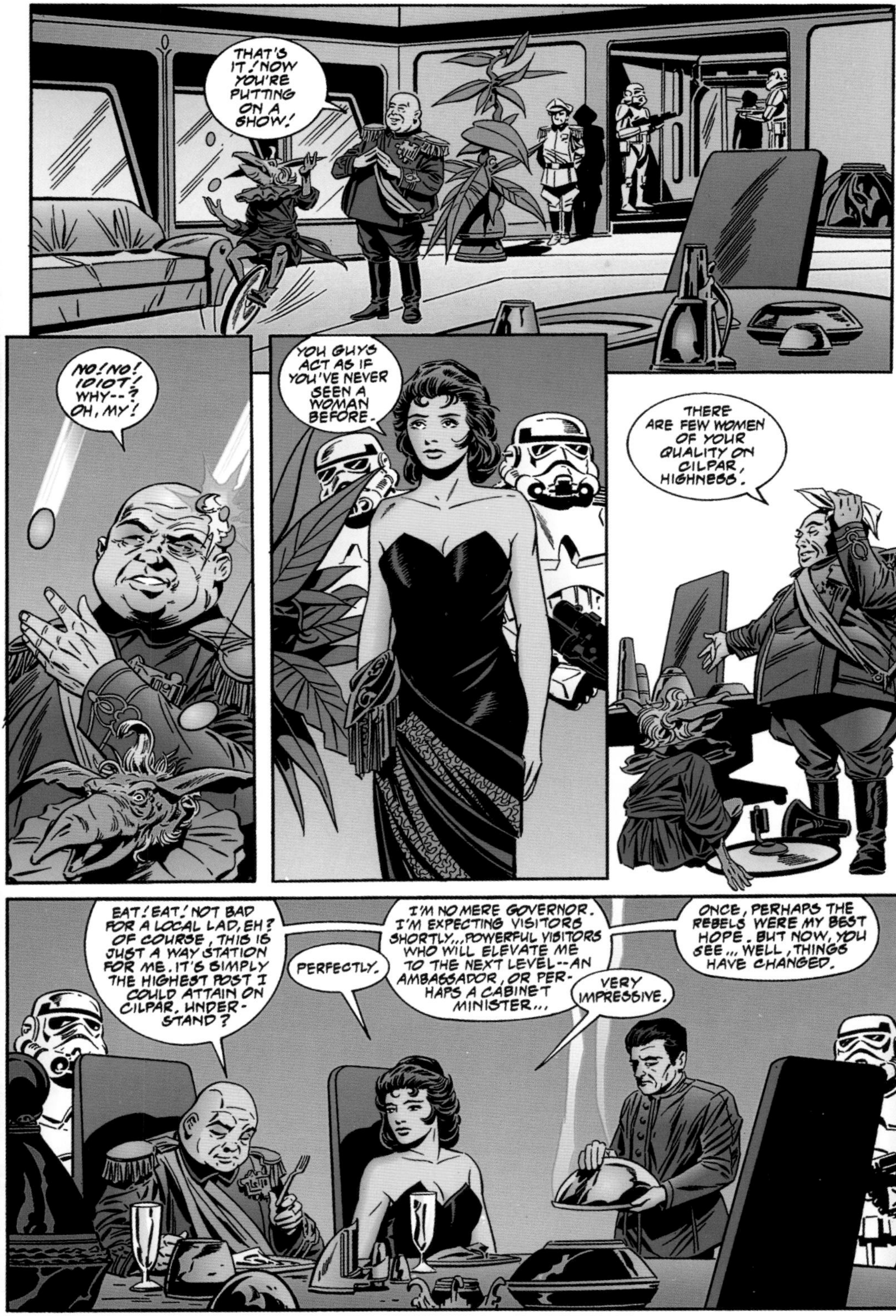
THAT'S IT! NOW YOU'RE PUTTING ON A SHOW!
NO! NO! IDIOT! WHY--? OH, MY!
YOU GUYS ACT AS IF YOU'VE NEVER SEEN A WOMAN BEFORE.
THERE ARE FEW WOMEN OF YOUR QUALITY ON CILPAR, HIGHNESS.
EAT! EAT! NOT BAD FOR A LOCAL LAD, EH? OF COURSE, THIS IS JUST A WAY STATION FOR ME. IT'S SIMPLY THE HIGHEST POST I COULD ATTAIN ON CILPAR. UNDER-STAND?
PERFECTLY.
I'M NO MERE GOVERNOR. I'M EXPECTING VISITORS SHORTLY... POWERFUL VISITORS WHO WILL ELEVATE ME TO THE NEXT LEVEL--AN AMBASSADOR, OR PER-HAPS A CABINET MINISTER...
VERY IMPRESSIVE.
ONCE, PERHAPS THE REBELS WERE MY BEST HOPE. BUT NOW, YOU SEE... WELL, THINGS HAVE CHANGED.

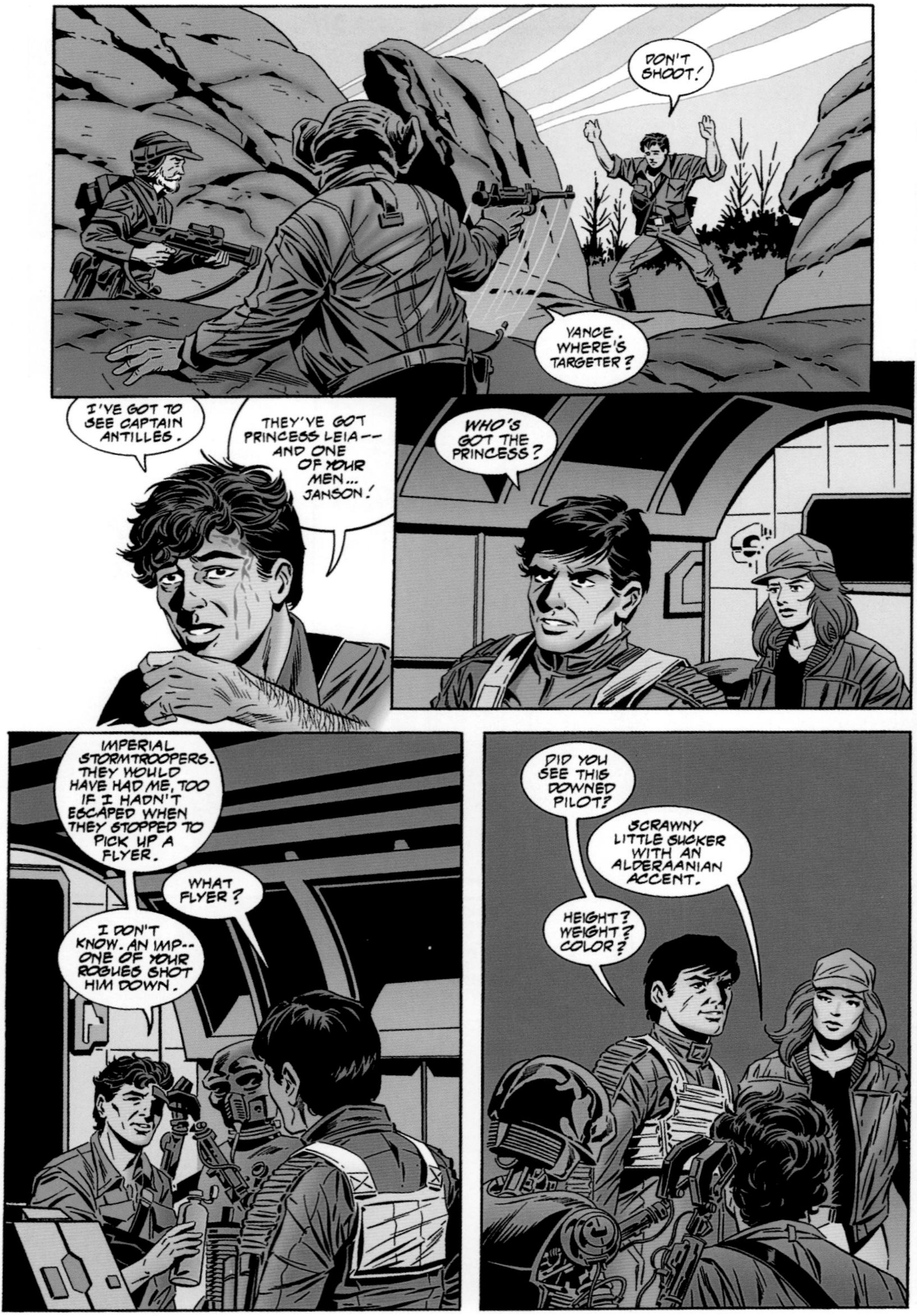
DON'T SHOOT!
YANCE. WHERE'S TARGETER?
I'VE GOT TO SEE CAPTAIN ANTILLES.
THEY'VE GOT PRINCESS LEIA -- AND ONE OF YOUR MEN... JANSON!
WHO'S GOT THE PRINCESS?
IMPERIAL STORMTROOPERS. THEY WOULD HAVE HAD ME, TOO IF I HADN'T ESCAPED WHEN THEY STOPPED TO PICK UP A FLYER.
WHAT FLYER?
I DON'T KNOW. AN IMP-- ONE OF YOUR ROGUES SHOT HIM DOWN.
DID YOU SEE THIS DOWNED PILOT?
SCRAWNY LITTLE SUCKER WITH AN ALDERAANIAN ACCENT.
HEIGHT? WEIGHT? COLOR?

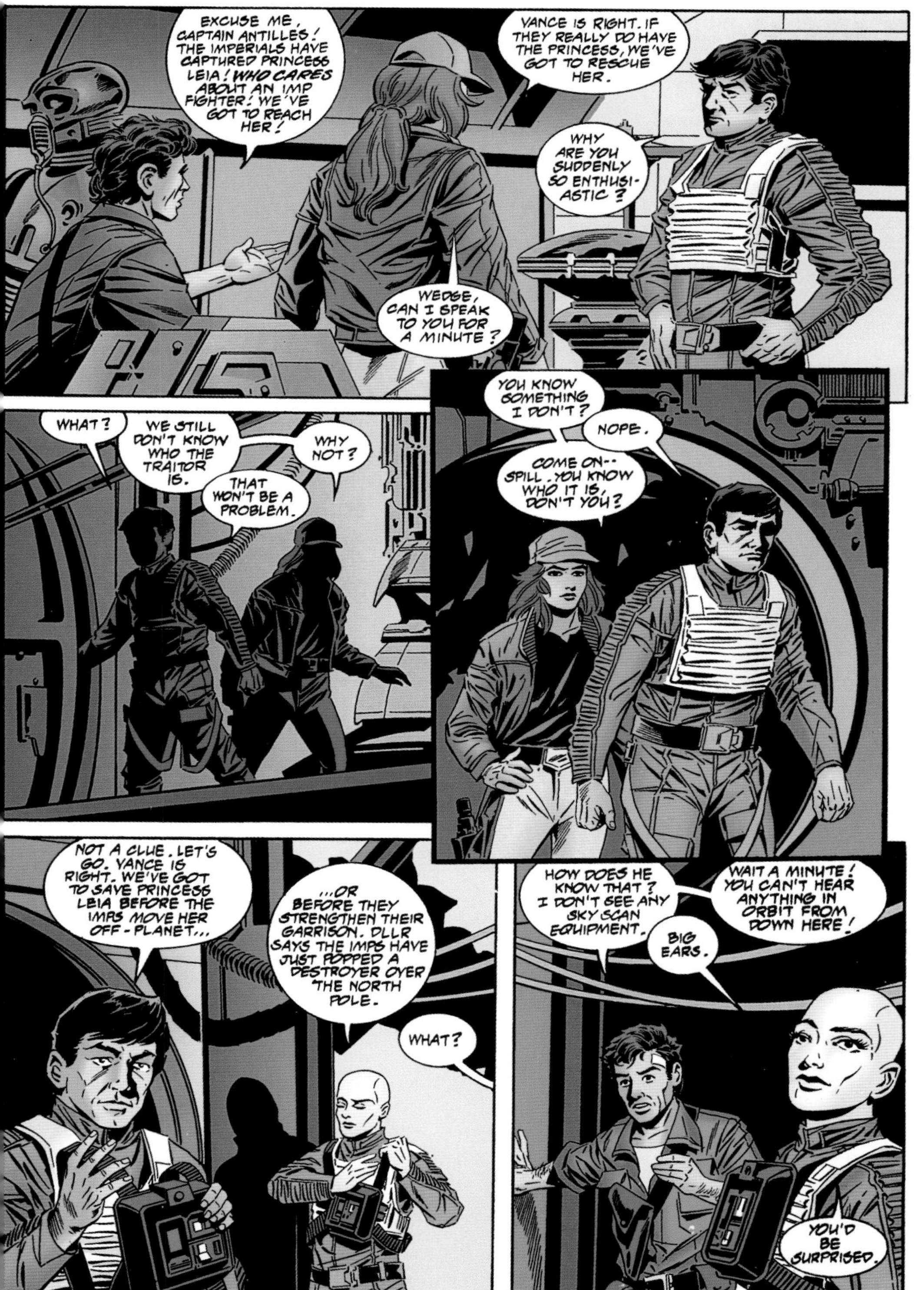
EXCUSE ME, CAPTAIN ANTILLES! THE IMPERIALS HAVE CAPTURED PRINCESS LEIA! WHO CARES ABOUT AN IMP FIGHTER! WE'VE GOT TO REACH HER!
VANCE IS RIGHT. IF THEY REALLY DO HAVE THE PRINCESS, WE'VE GOT TO RESCUE HER.
WHY ARE YOU SUDDENLY SO ENTHUSIASTIC?
WEDGE, CAN I SPEAK TO YOU FOR A MINUTE?
WHAT?
WE STILL DON'T KNOW WHO THE TRAITOR IS.
WHY NOT?
THAT WON'T BE A PROBLEM.
YOU KNOW SOMETHING I DON'T?
NOPE.
COME ON-- SPILL. YOU KNOW WHO IT IS, DON'T YOU?
NOT A CLUE. LET'S GO. VANCE IS RIGHT. WE'VE GOT TO SAVE PRINCESS LEIA BEFORE THE IMPS MOVE HER OFF-PLANET...
...OR BEFORE THEY STRENGTHEN THEIR GARRISON. DLLR SAYS THE IMPS HAVE JUST POPPED A DESTROYER OVER THE NORTH POLE.
WHAT?
HOW DOES HE KNOW THAT? I DON'T SEE ANY SKY SCAN EQUIPMENT.
BIG EARS.
WAIT A MINUTE! YOU CAN'T HEAR ANYTHING IN ORBIT FROM DOWN HERE!
YOU'D BE SURPRISED.

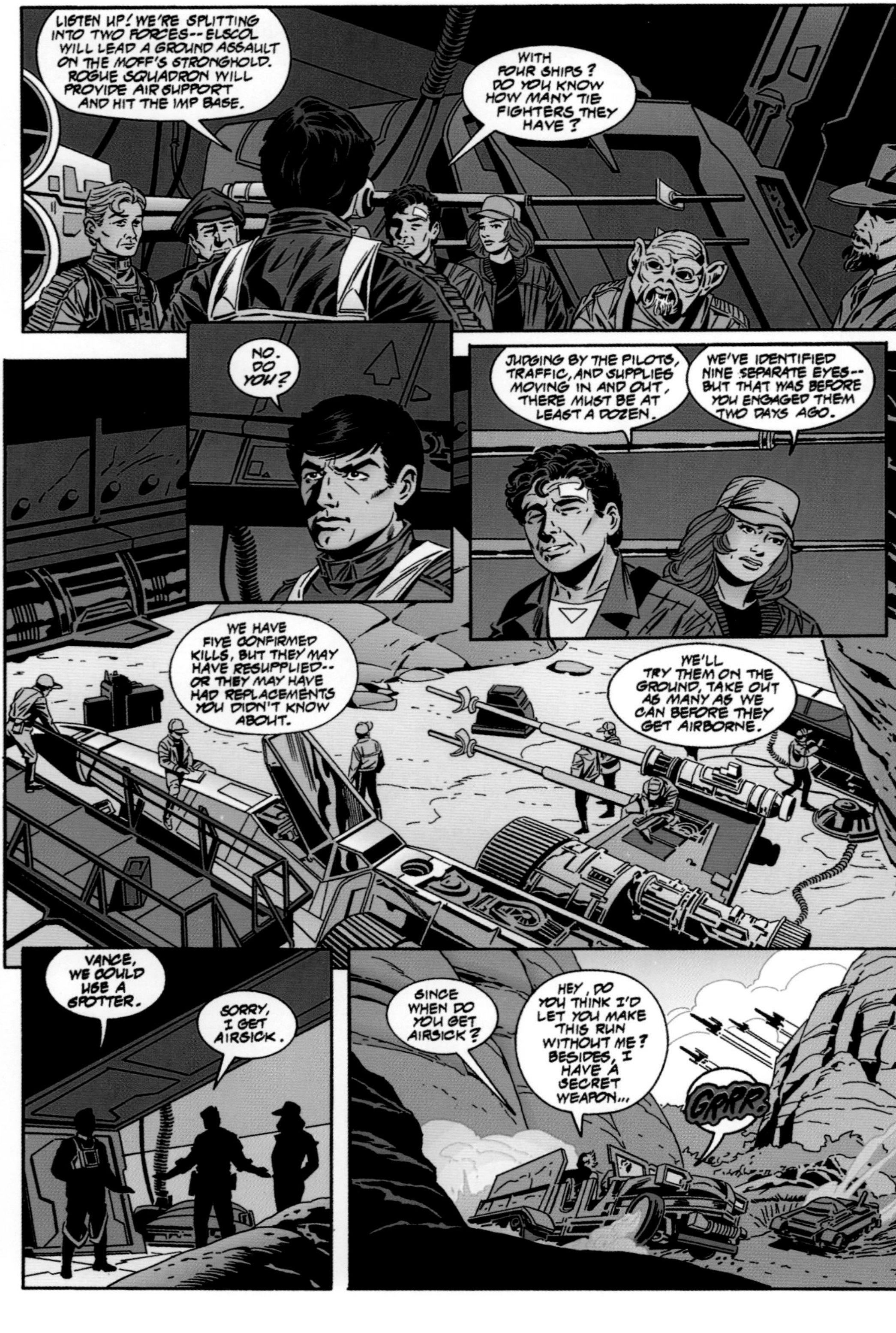
LISTEN UP! WE'RE SPLITTING INTO TWO FORCES--ELSCOL WILL LEAD A GROUND ASSAULT ON THE MOFF'S STRONGHOLD. ROGUE SQUADRON WILL PROVIDE AIR SUPPORT AND HIT THE IMP BASE.
WITH FOUR SHIPS? DO YOU KNOW HOW MANY TIE FIGHTERS THEY HAVE?
NO. DO YOU?
JUDGING BY THE PILOTS, TRAFFIC, AND SUPPLIES MOVING IN AND OUT, THERE MUST BE AT LEAST A DOZEN.
WE'VE IDENTIFIED NINE SEPARATE EYES--BUT THAT WAS BEFORE YOU ENGAGED THEM TWO DAYS AGO.
WE HAVE FIVE CONFIRMED KILLS, BUT THEY MAY HAVE RESUPPLIED--OR THEY MAY HAVE HAD REPLACEMENTS YOU DIDN'T KNOW ABOUT.
WE'LL TRY THEM ON THE GROUND, TAKE OUT AS MANY AS WE CAN BEFORE THEY GET AIRBORNE.
VANCE, WE COULD USE A SPOTTER.
SORRY, I GET AIRSICK.
SINCE WHEN DO YOU GET AIRSICK?
HEY, DO YOU THINK I'D LET YOU MAKE THIS RUN WITHOUT ME? BESIDES, I HAVE A SECRET WEAPON...
GRRR.

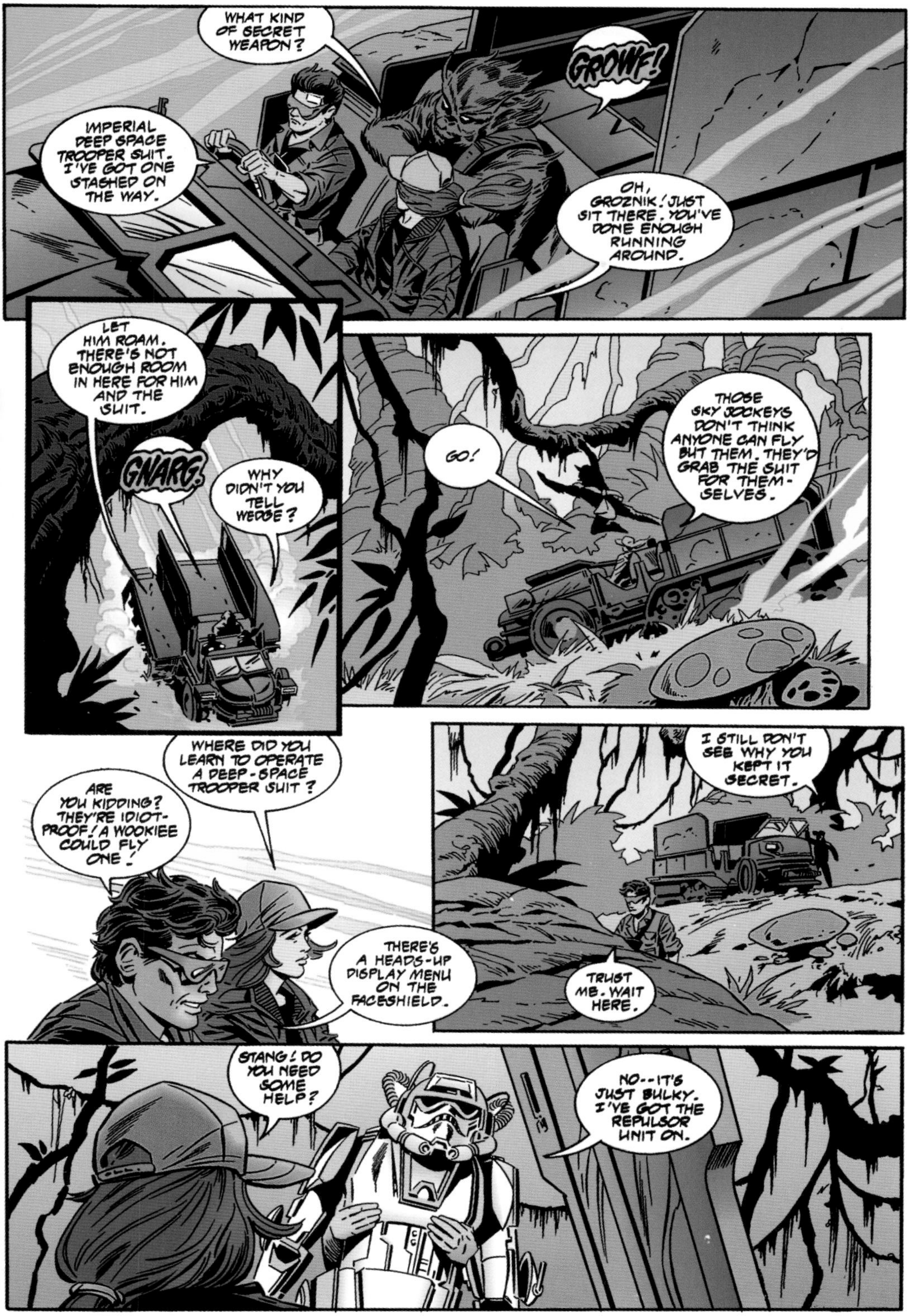
WHAT KIND OF SECRET WEAPON?
GROWF!
IMPERIAL DEEP SPACE TROOPER SUIT. I'VE GOT ONE STASHED ON THE WAY.
OH, GROZNIK! JUST SIT THERE. YOU'VE DONE ENOUGH RUNNING AROUND.
LET HIM ROAM. THERE'S NOT ENOUGH ROOM IN HERE FOR HIM AND THE SUIT.
GNARG.
WHY DIDN'T YOU TELL WEDGE?
THOSE SKY JOCKEYS DON'T THINK ANYONE CAN FLY BUT THEM. THEY'D GRAB THE SUIT FOR THEM-SELVES.
GO!
I STILL DON'T SEE WHY YOU KEPT IT SECRET.
TRUST ME. WAIT HERE.
WHERE DID YOU LEARN TO OPERATE A DEEP-SPACE TROOPER SUIT?
ARE YOU KIDDING? THEY'RE IDIOT-PROOF! A WOOKIEE COULD FLY ONE!
THERE'S A HEADS-UP DISPLAY MENU ON THE FACESHIELD.
STANG! DO YOU NEED SOME HELP?
NO--IT'S JUST BULKY. I'VE GOT THE REPULSOR UNIT ON.

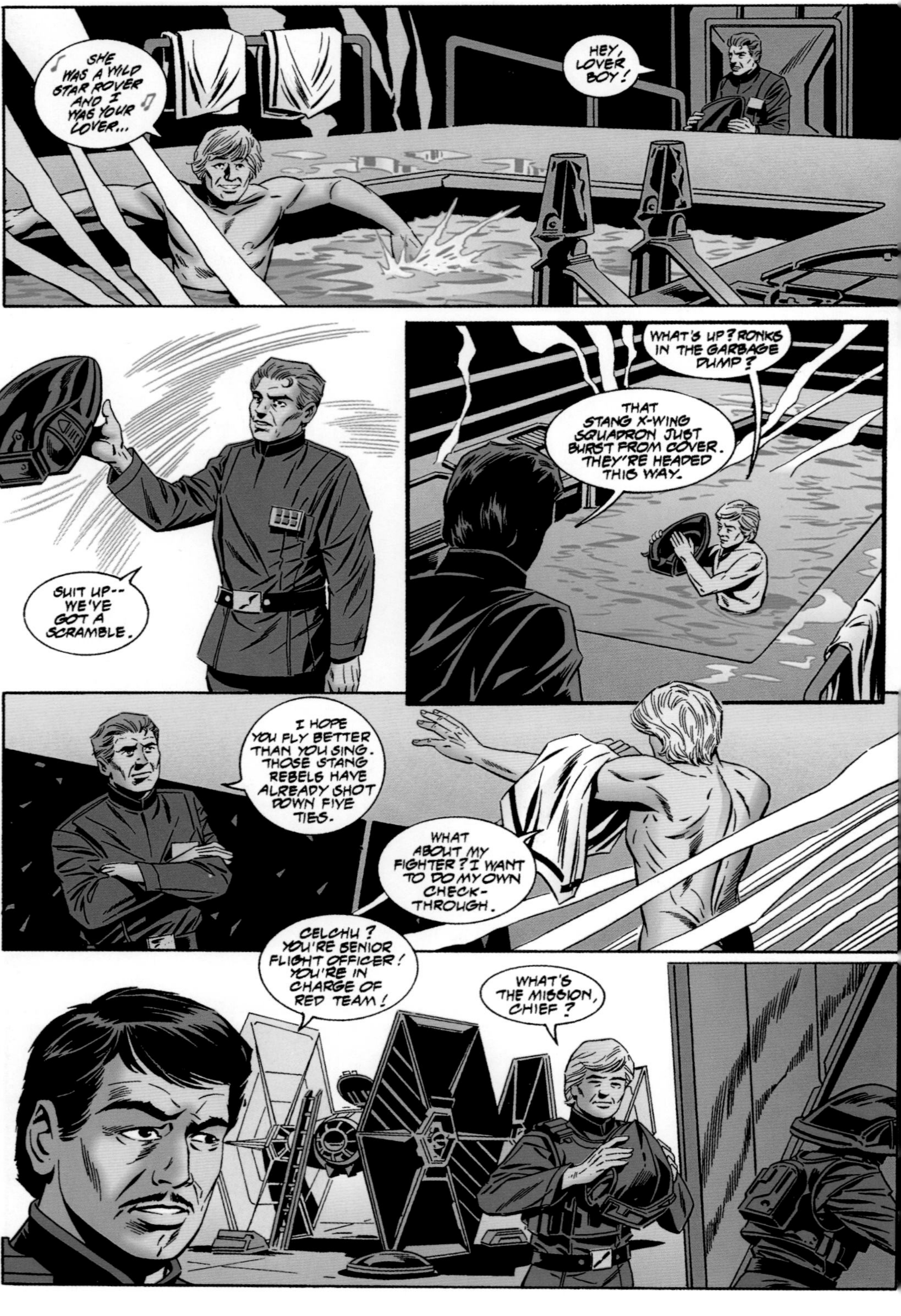
SHE WAS A WILD STAR ROVER AND I WAS YOUR LOVER...
HEY, LOVER BOY!
SUIT UP-- WE'VE GOT A SCRAMBLE.
WHAT'S UP? RONKS IN THE GARBAGE DUMP?
THAT STANG X-WING SQUADRON JUST BURST FROM COVER. THEY'RE HEADED THIS WAY.
I HOPE YOU FLY BETTER THAN YOU SING. THOSE STANG REBELS HAVE ALREADY SHOT DOWN FIVE TIES.
WHAT ABOUT MY FIGHTER? I WANT TO DO MY OWN CHECK-THROUGH.
CELCHU? YOU'RE SENIOR FLIGHT OFFICER! YOU'RE IN CHARGE OF RED TEAM!
WHAT'S THE MISSION, CHIEF?

WE'RE SPLITTING INTO TWO FLIGHTS. YOU LEAD RED SQUAD AGAINST AN ARMORED COLUMN ADVANCING TOWARD K'IIDAN THROUGH THE EMPEROR'S FOREST...

PETRO WILL LEAD THE AIR ASSAULT ON THE X-WING SQUADRON.

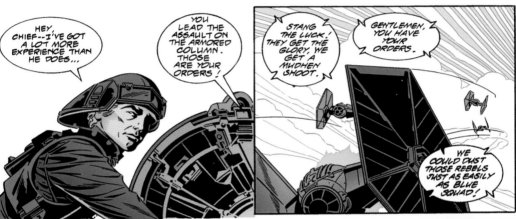

HEY, CHIEF--I'VE GOT A LOT MORE EXPERIENCE THAN HE DOES...

YOU LEAD THE ASSAULT ON THE ARMORED COLUMN. THOSE ARE YOUR ORDERS!

STANG THE LUCK! THEY GET THE GLORY, WE GET A MUDHEN SHOOT.

GENTLEMEN, YOU HAVE YOUR ORDERS.

WE COULD DUST THOSE REBELS JUST AS EASILY AS BLUE SQUAD!

NO DOUBT. IF THAT'S THE WAY YOU FEEL ABOUT IT, YOU CAN START WITH ME... ...BECAUSE I SURVIVED ENDOR AS A REBEL!

WHAT?!

TYCHO TO ROGUE LEADER! WEDGE! DON'T SHOOT! I'M IN THE LEAD EYEBALL!

I READ YOU, TYCHO. MAINTAIN BEARING AND...

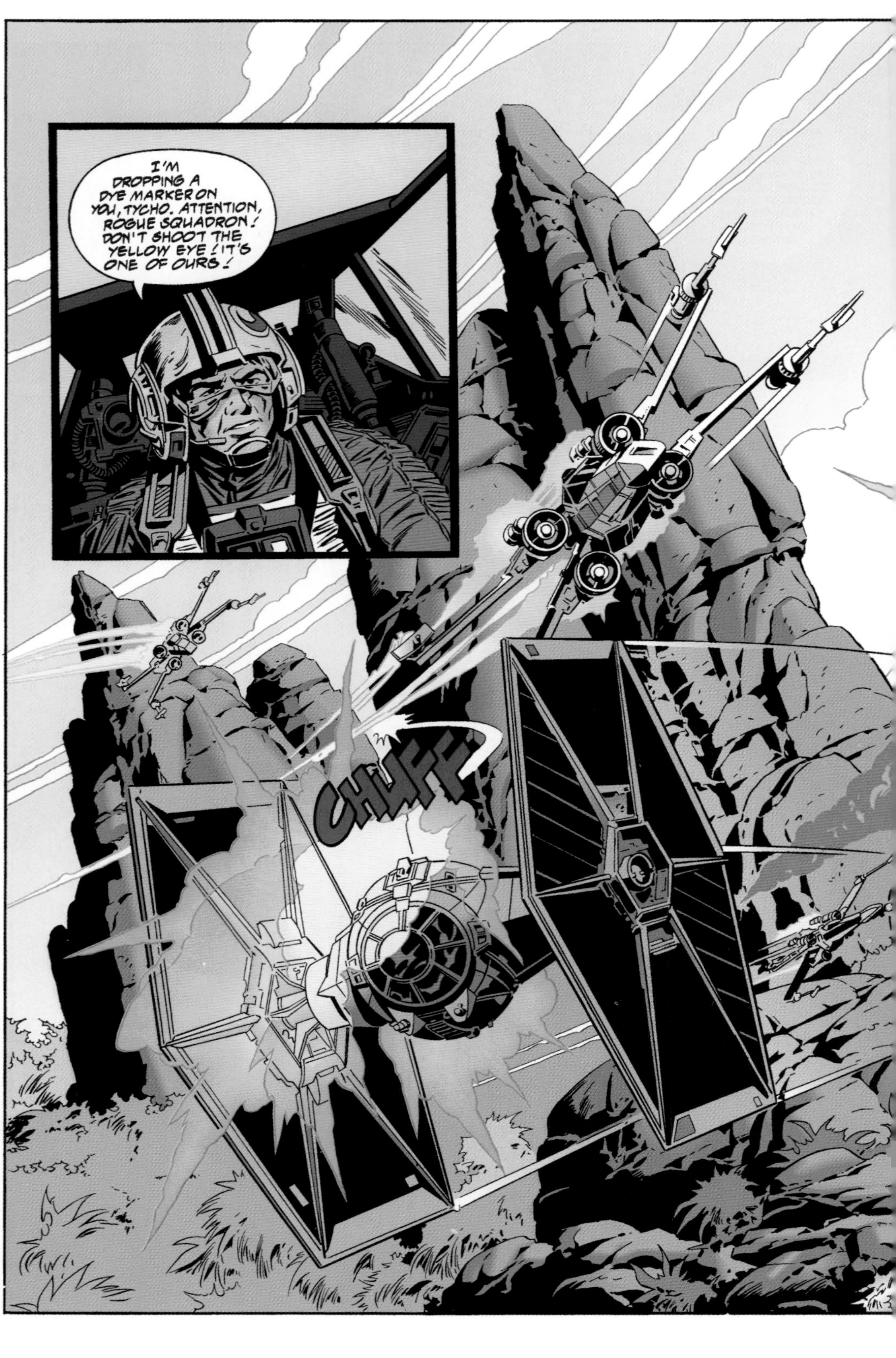
I'M DROPPING A DYE MARKER ON YOU, TYCHO. ATTENTION, ROGUE SQUADRON! DON'T SHOOT THE YELLOW EYE! IT'S ONE OF OURS!
CHUFF

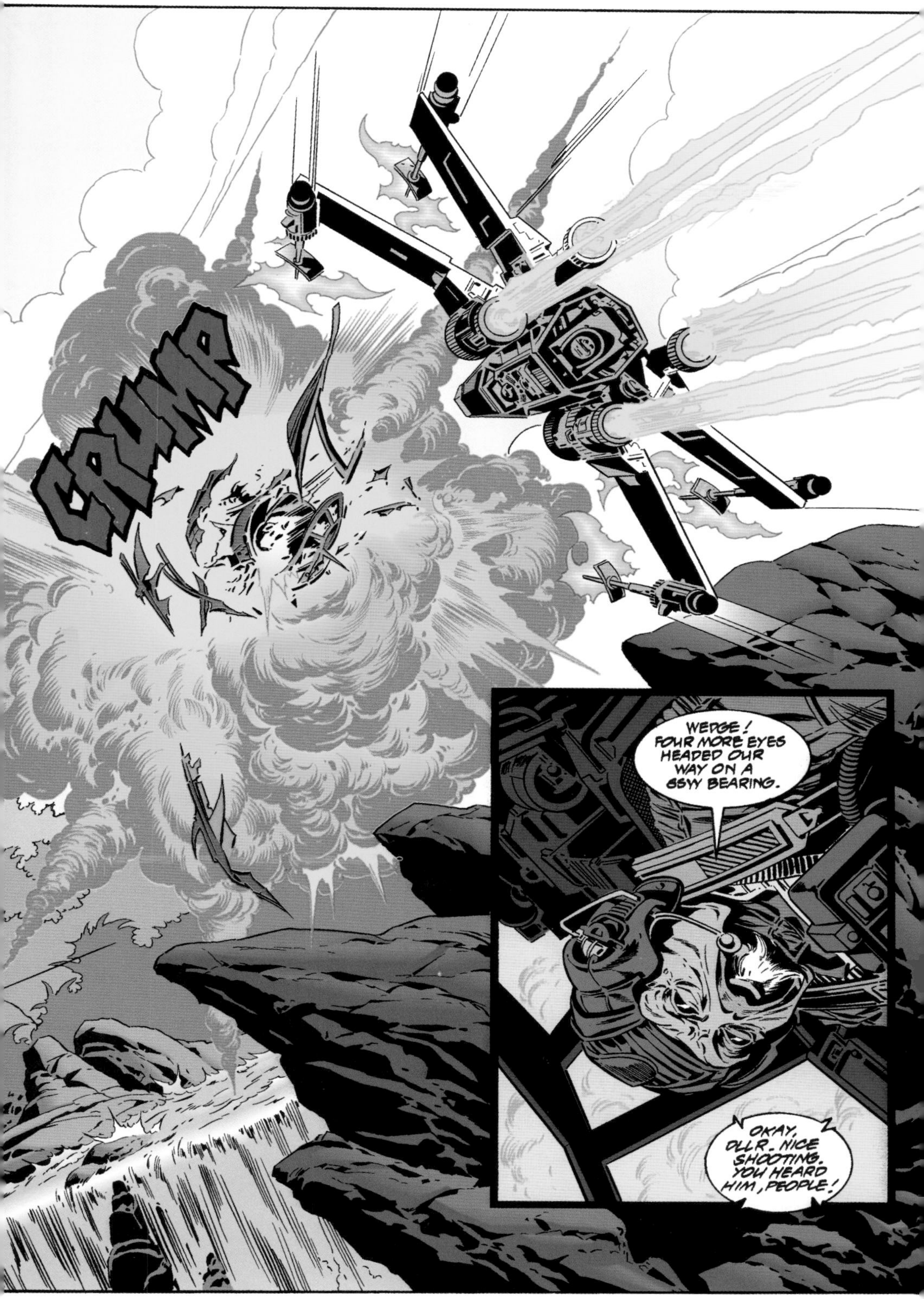
CRUMP
WEDGE! FOUR MORE EYES HEADED OUR WAY ON A 65YY BEARING.
OKAY, OLL R. NICE SHOOTING. YOU HEARD HIM, PEOPLE!

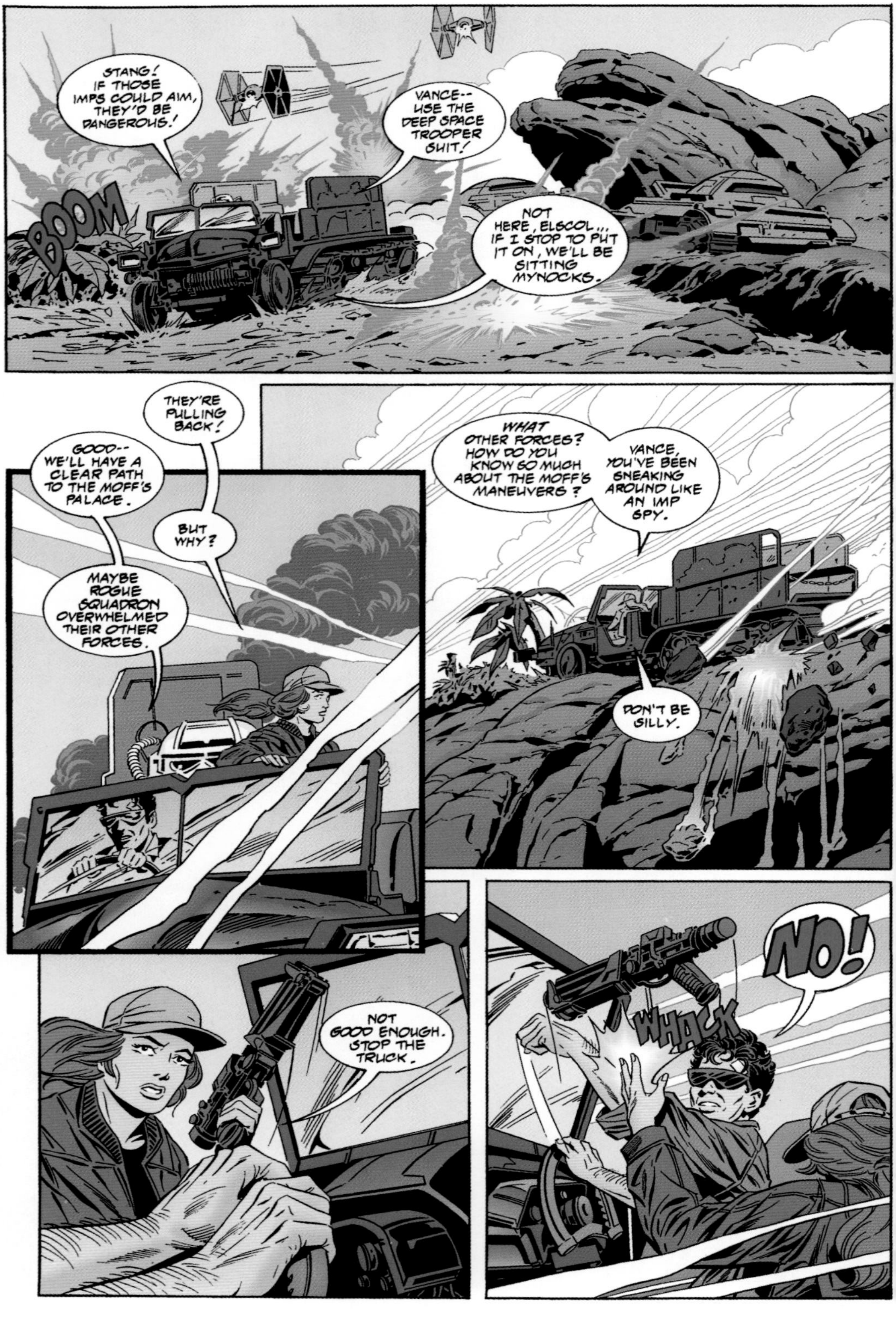
STANG! IF THOSE IMPS COULD AIM, THEY'D BE DANGEROUS!
BOOM
VANCE-- USE THE DEEP SPACE TROOPER SUIT!
NOT HERE, ELSCOL... IF I STOP TO PUT IT ON, WE'LL BE SITTING MYNOCKS.
THEY'RE PULLING BACK!
GOOD-- WE'LL HAVE A CLEAR PATH TO THE MOFF'S PALACE.
BUT WHY?
MAYBE ROGUE SQUADRON OVERWHELMED THEIR OTHER FORCES.
WHAT OTHER FORCES? HOW DO YOU KNOW SO MUCH ABOUT THE MOFF'S MANEUVERS?
VANCE, YOU'VE BEEN SNEAKING AROUND LIKE AN IMP SPY.
DON'T BE SILLY.
NOT GOOD ENOUGH. STOP THE TRUCK.
WHACK
NO!

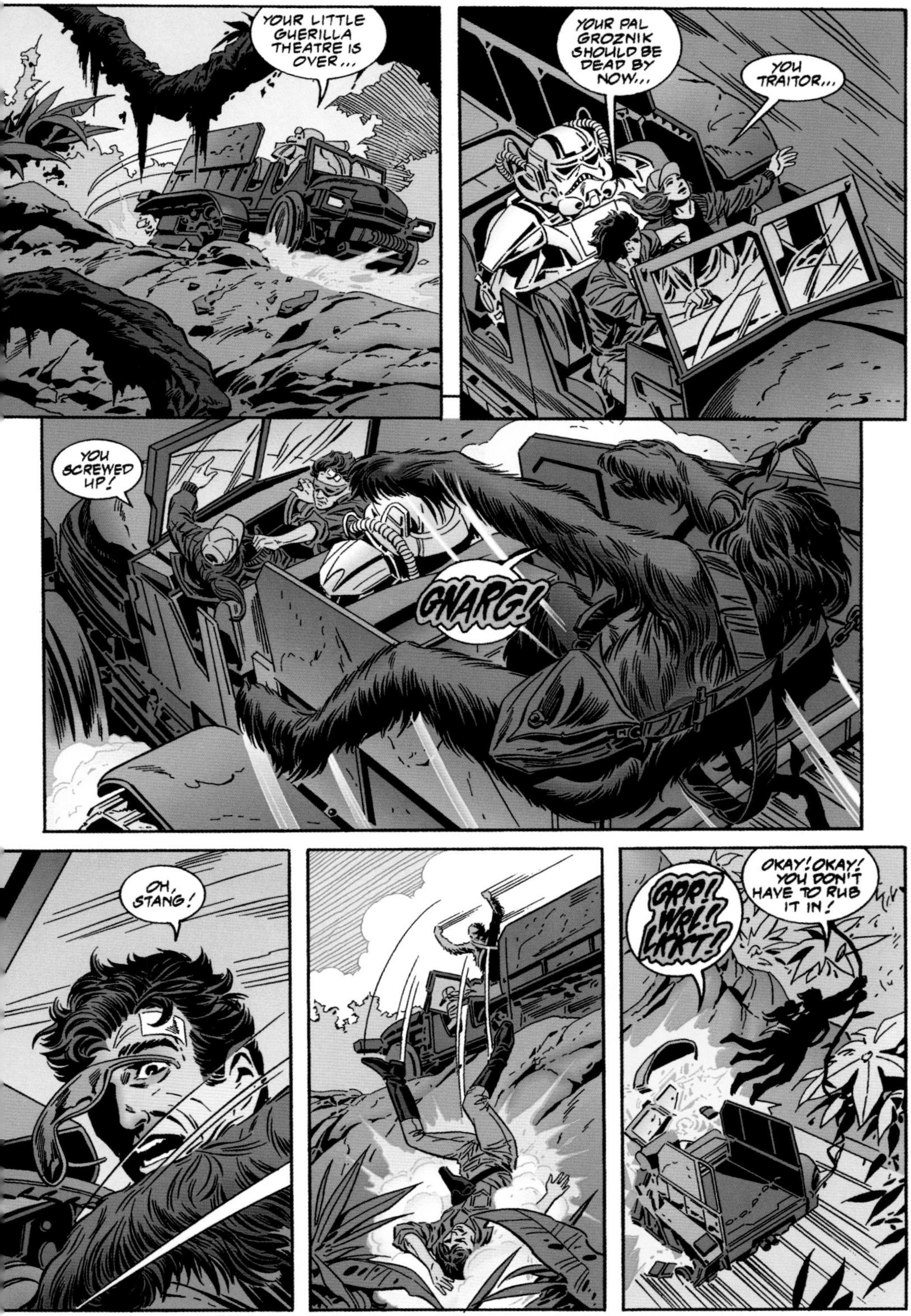
YOUR LITTLE GUERILLA THEATRE IS OVER...
YOUR PAL GROZNIK SHOULD BE DEAD BY NOW...
YOU TRAITOR...
YOU SCREWED UP!
GNARG!
OH, STANG!
GRR! WRL! LKKT!
OKAY! OKAY! YOU DON'T HAVE TO RUB IT IN!

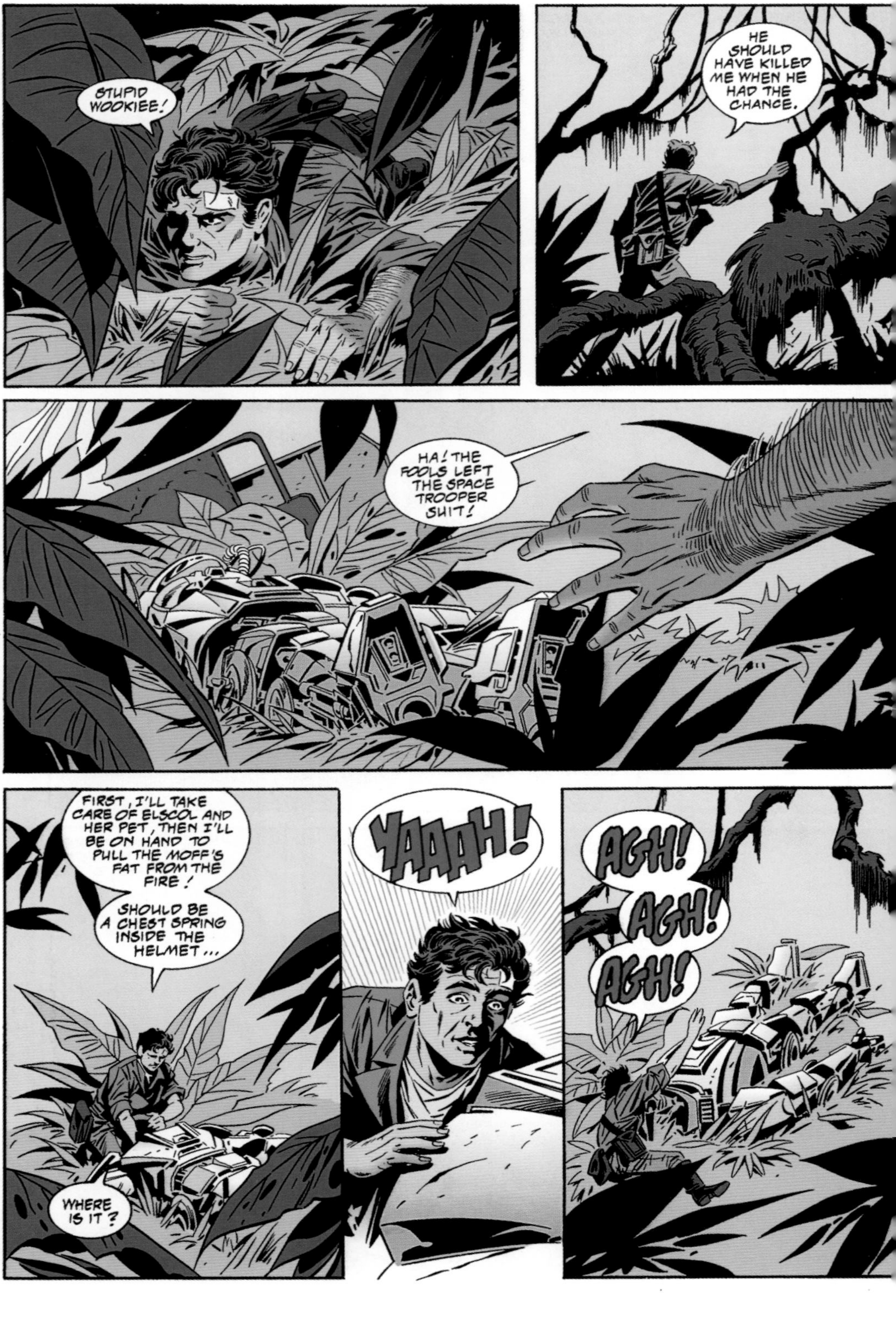
STUPID WOOKIEE!
HE SHOULD HAVE KILLED ME WHEN HE HAD THE CHANCE.
HA! THE FOOLS LEFT THE SPACE TROOPER SUIT!
FIRST, I'LL TAKE CARE OF ELSCOL AND HER PET, THEN I'LL BE ON HAND TO PULL THE MOFF'S FAT FROM THE FIRE!
SHOULD BE A CHEST SPRING INSIDE THE HELMET...
WHERE IS IT?
YAAAH!
AGH!
AGH!
AGH!

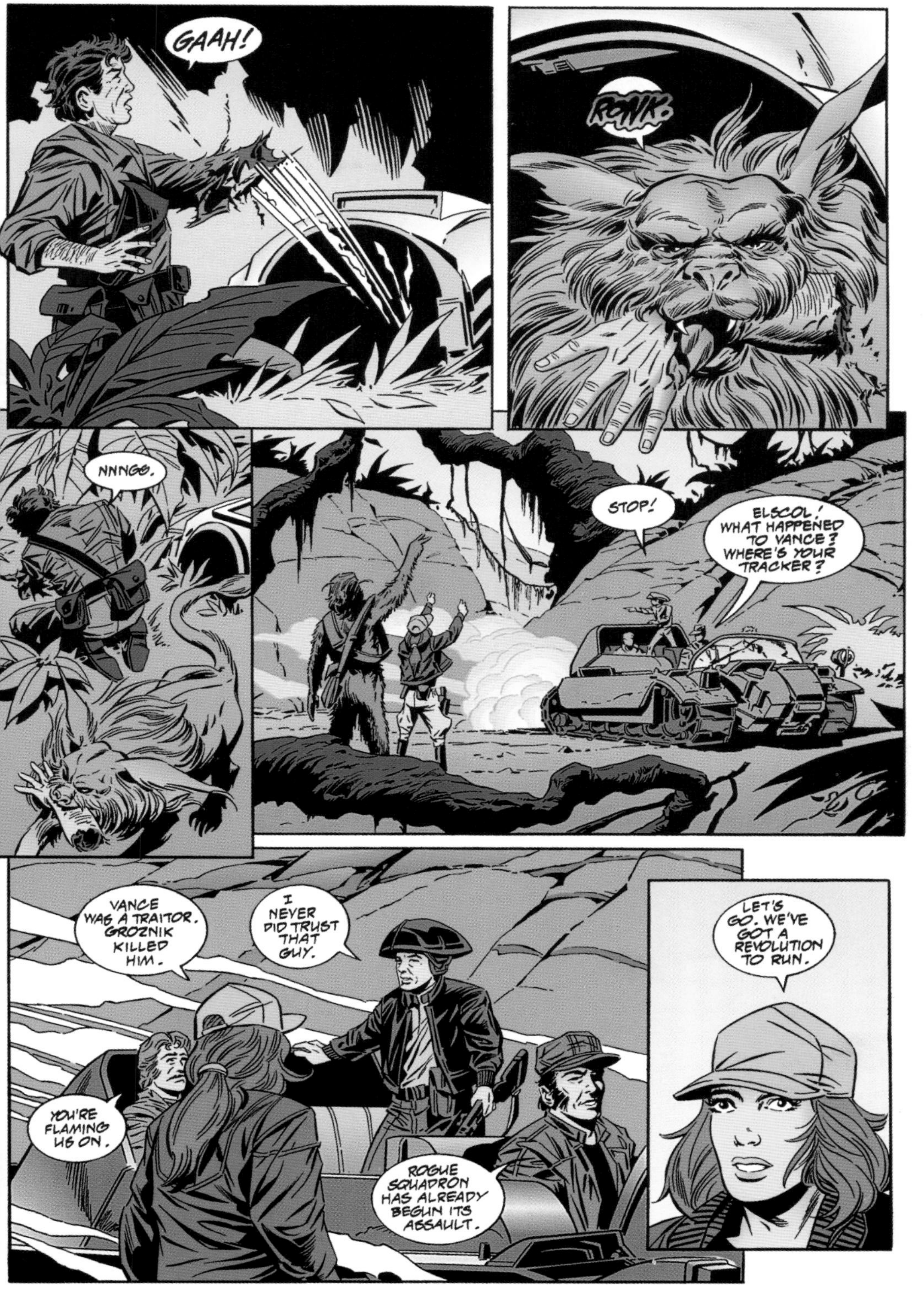
GAAH!
RONK.
NNNGG.
STOP!
ELSCOL! WHAT HAPPENED TO VANCE? WHERE'S YOUR TRACKER?
VANCE WAS A TRAITOR. GROZNIK KILLED HIM.
I NEVER DID TRUST THAT GUY.
YOU'RE FLAMING US ON.
ROGUE SQUADRON HAS ALREADY BEGUN ITS ASSAULT.
LET'S GO. WE'VE GOT A REVOLUTION TO RUN.

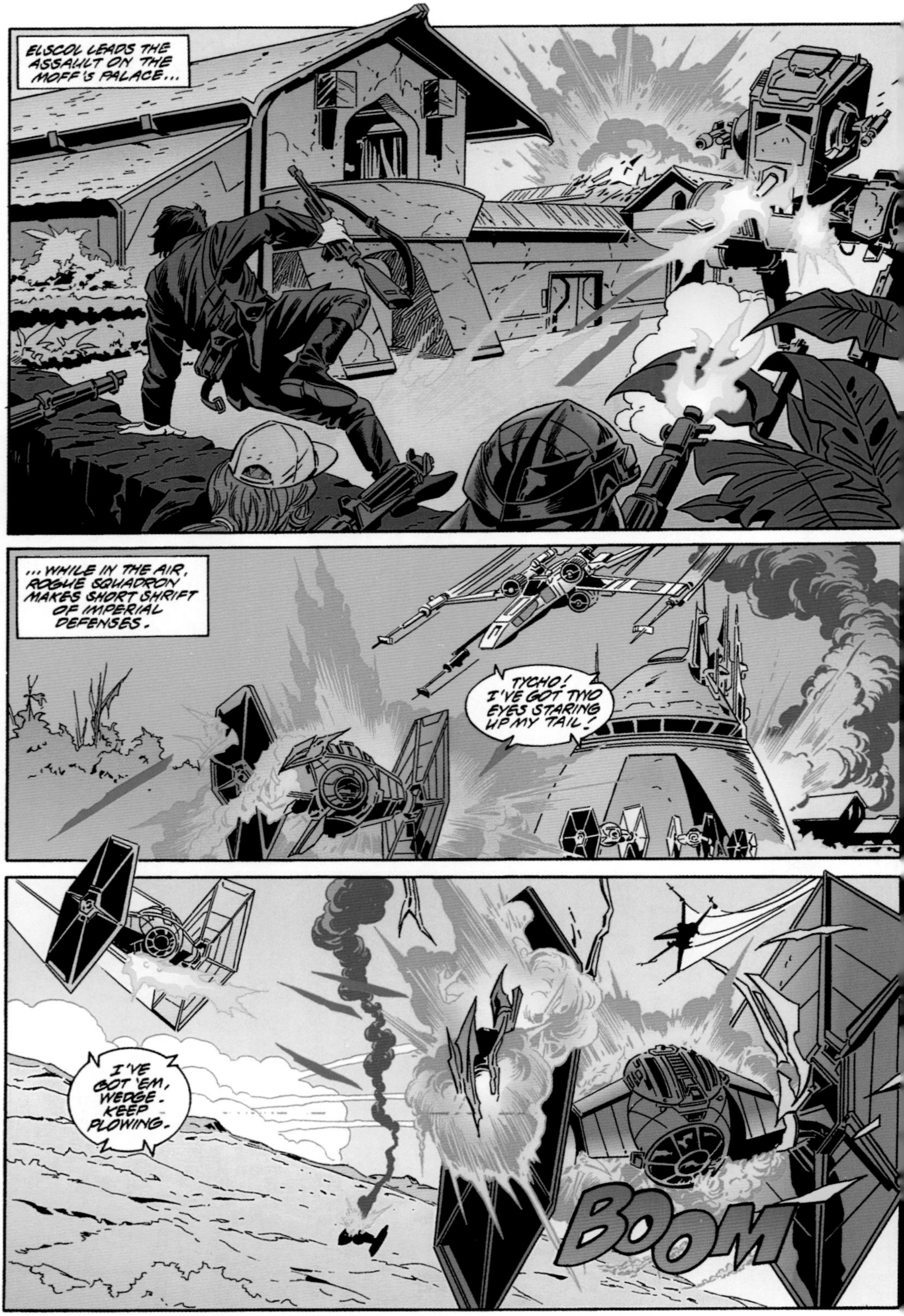

ELSCOL LEADS THE ASSAULT ON THE MOFF'S PALACE...
...WHILE IN THE AIR, ROGUE SQUADRON MAKES SHORT SHRIFT OF IMPERIAL DEFENSES.
TYCHO! I'VE GOT TWO EYES STARING UP MY TAIL!
I'VE GOT 'EM, WEDGE. KEEP PLOWING.
BOOM

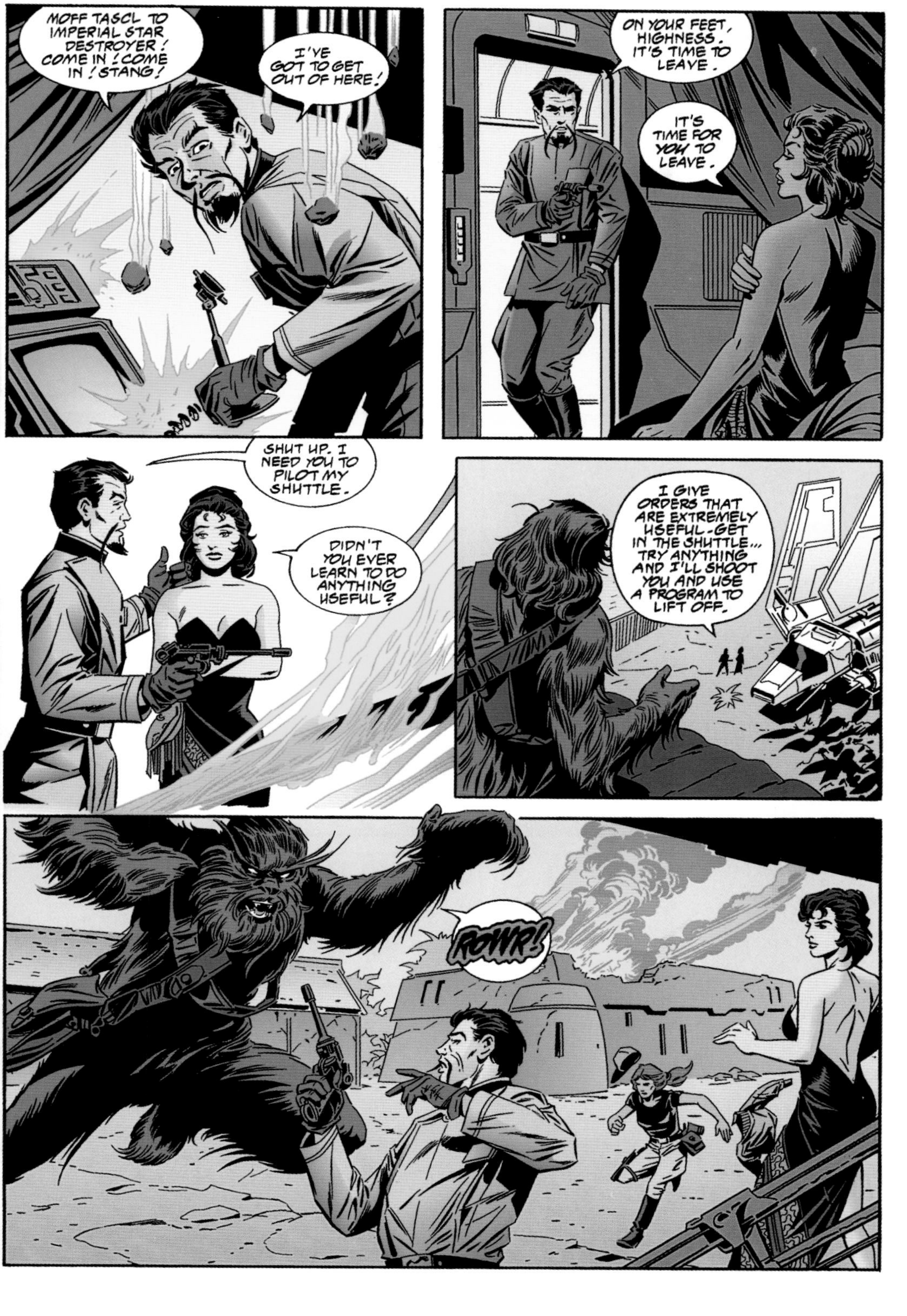
MOFF TASCL TO IMPERIAL STAR DESTROYER! COME IN! COME IN! STANG!
I'VE GOT TO GET OUT OF HERE!
ON YOUR FEET, HIGHNESS. IT'S TIME TO LEAVE.
IT'S TIME FOR YOU TO LEAVE.
SHUT UP. I NEED YOU TO PILOT MY SHUTTLE.
DIDN'T YOU EVER LEARN TO DO ANYTHING USEFUL?
I GIVE ORDERS THAT ARE EXTREMELY USEFUL-GET IN THE SHUTTLE... TRY ANYTHING AND I'LL SHOOT YOU AND USE A PROGRAM TO LIFT OFF.
ROWR!

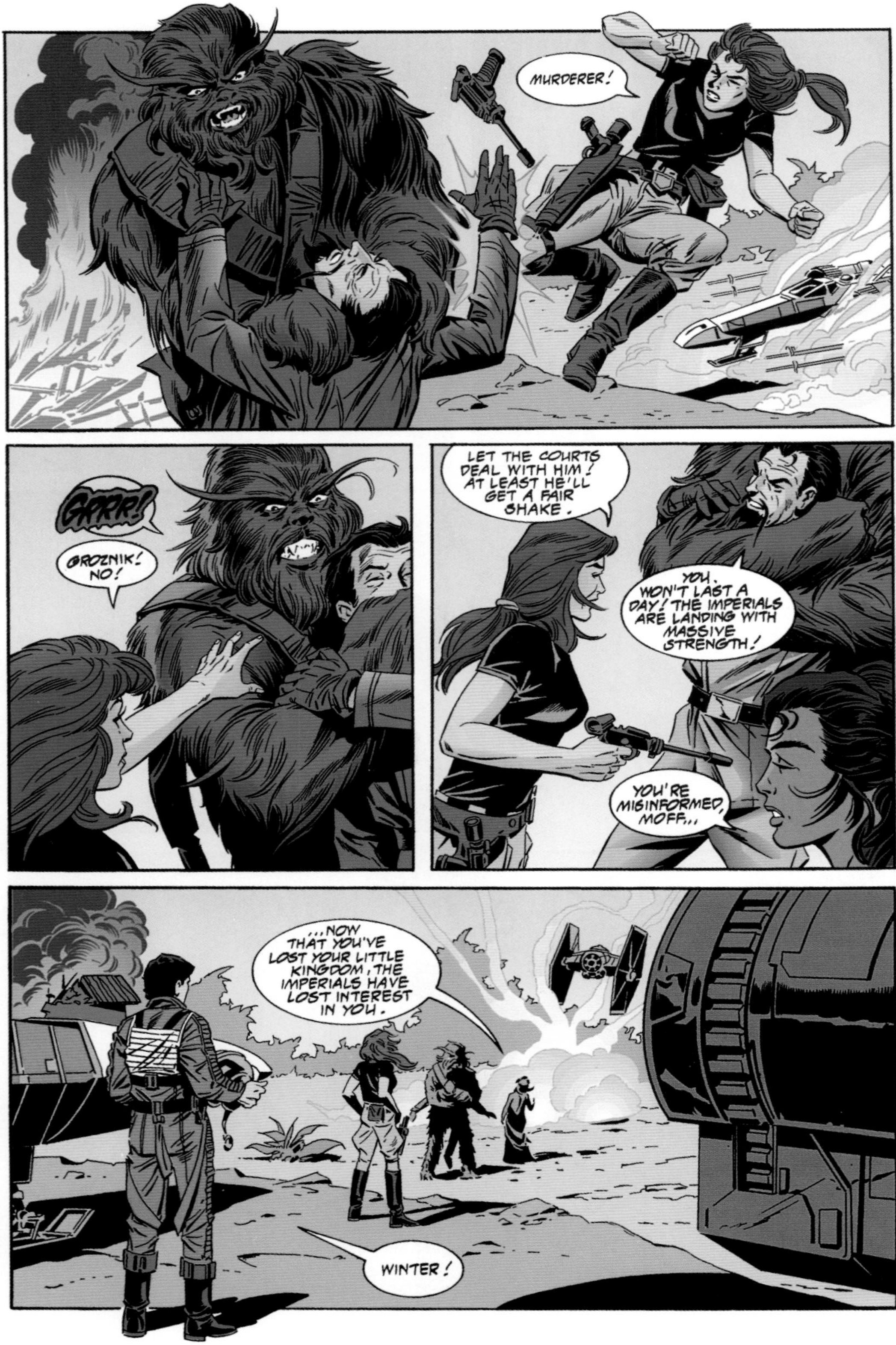
MURDERER!
GRRR!
GROZNIK! NO!
LET THE COURTS DEAL WITH HIM! AT LEAST HE'LL GET A FAIR SHAKE.
YOU. WON'T LAST A DAY! THE IMPERIALS ARE LANDING WITH MASSIVE STRENGTH!
YOU'RE MISINFORMED, MOFF...
...NOW THAT YOU'VE LOST YOUR LITTLE KINGDOM, THE IMPERIALS HAVE LOST INTEREST IN YOU.
WINTER!

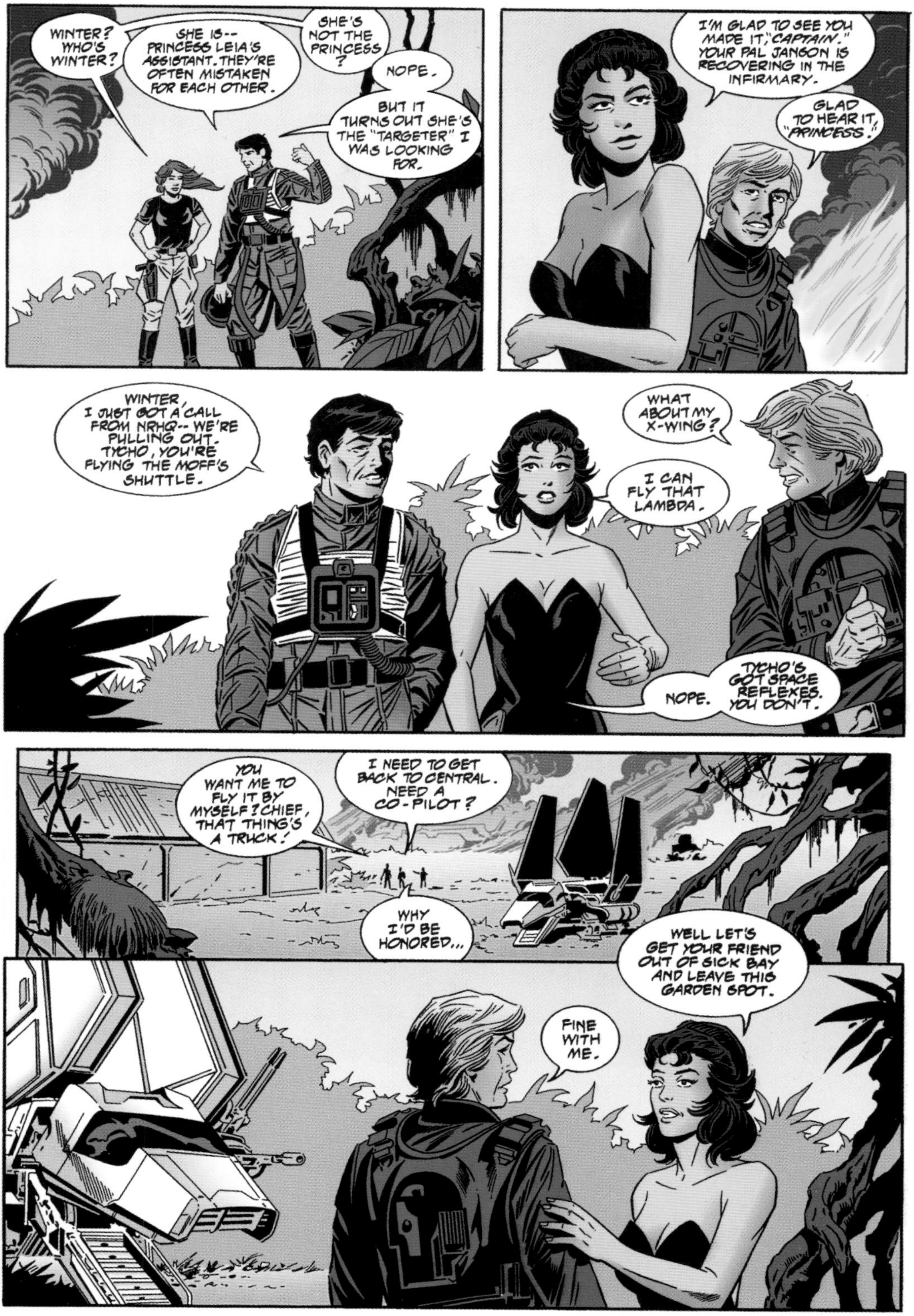

WINTER? WHO'S WINTER?
SHE IS-- PRINCESS LEIA'S ASSISTANT. THEY'RE OFTEN MISTAKEN FOR EACH OTHER.
SHE'S NOT THE PRINCESS?
NOPE.
BUT IT TURNS OUT SHE'S THE "TARGETER" I WAS LOOKING FOR.
I'M GLAD TO SEE YOU MADE IT, "CAPTAIN." YOUR PAL JANSON IS RECOVERING IN THE INFIRMARY.
GLAD TO HEAR IT, "PRINCESS."
WINTER, I JUST GOT A CALL FROM NRHQ-- WE'RE PULLING OUT. TYCHO, YOU'RE FLYING THE MOFF'S SHUTTLE.
WHAT ABOUT MY X-WING?
I CAN FLY THAT LAMBDA.
NOPE.
TYCHO'S GOT SPACE REFLEXES. YOU DON'T.
YOU WANT ME TO FLY IT BY MYSELF? CHIEF, THAT THING'S A TRUCK!
I NEED TO GET BACK TO CENTRAL. NEED A CO-PILOT?
WHY I'D BE HONORED...
WELL LET'S GET YOUR FRIEND OUT OF SICK BAY AND LEAVE THIS GARDEN SPOT.
FINE WITH ME.

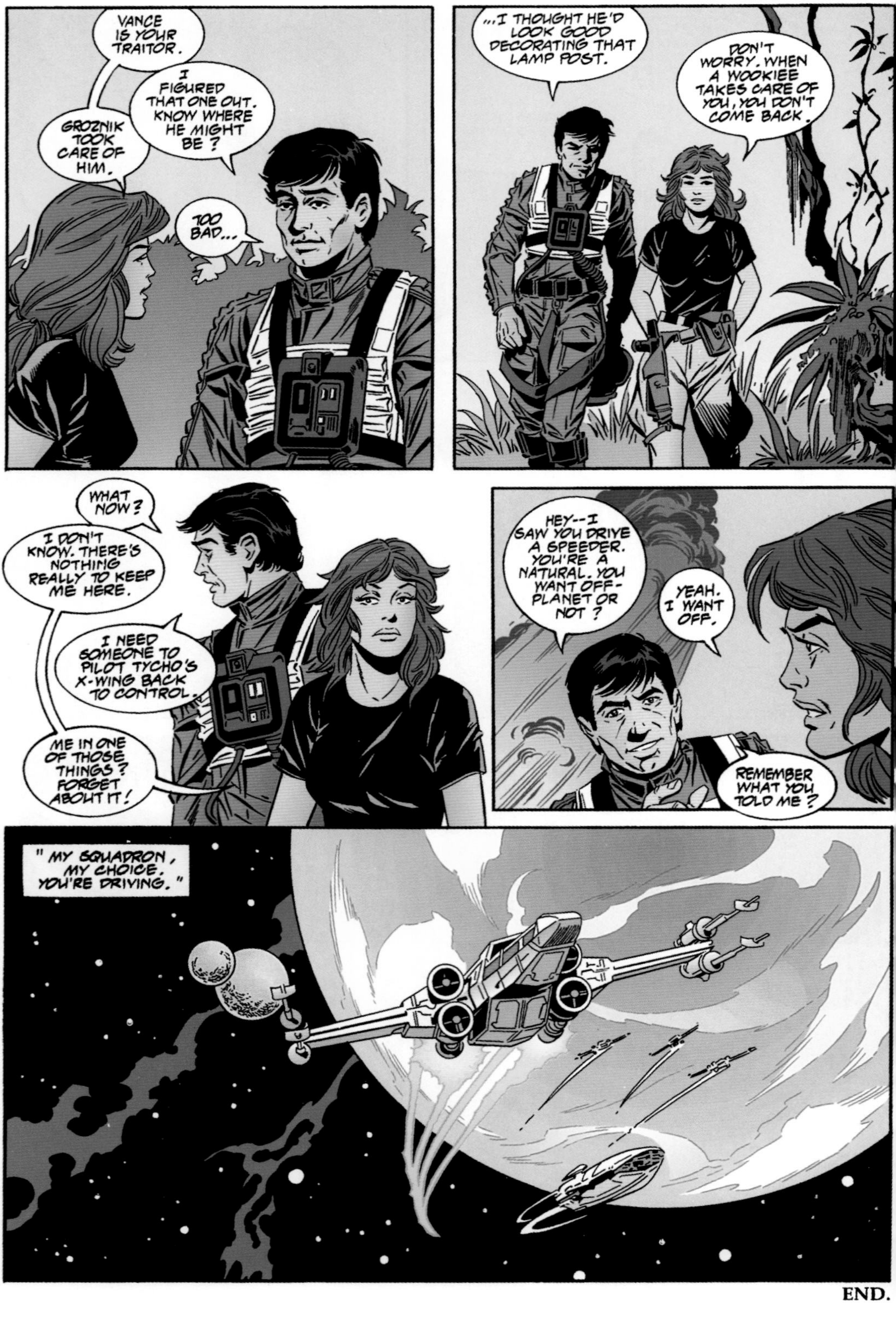
VANCE IS YOUR TRAITOR.
GROZNIK TOOK CARE OF HIM.
I FIGURED THAT ONE OUT. KNOW WHERE HE MIGHT BE?
TOO BAD...
...I THOUGHT HE'D LOOK GOOD DECORATING THAT LAMP POST.
DON'T WORRY. WHEN A WOOKIEE TAKES CARE OF YOU, YOU DON'T COME BACK.
WHAT NOW?
I DON'T KNOW. THERE'S NOTHING REALLY TO KEEP ME HERE.
I NEED SOMEONE TO PILOT TYCHO'S X-WING BACK TO CONTROL.
ME IN ONE OF THOSE THINGS? FORGET ABOUT IT!
HEY--I SAW YOU DRIVE A SPEEDER. YOU'RE A NATURAL. YOU WANT OFF-PLANET OR NOT?
YEAH. I WANT OFF.
REMEMBER WHAT YOU TOLD ME?
"MY SQUADRON, MY CHOICE. YOU'RE DRIVING."

END.

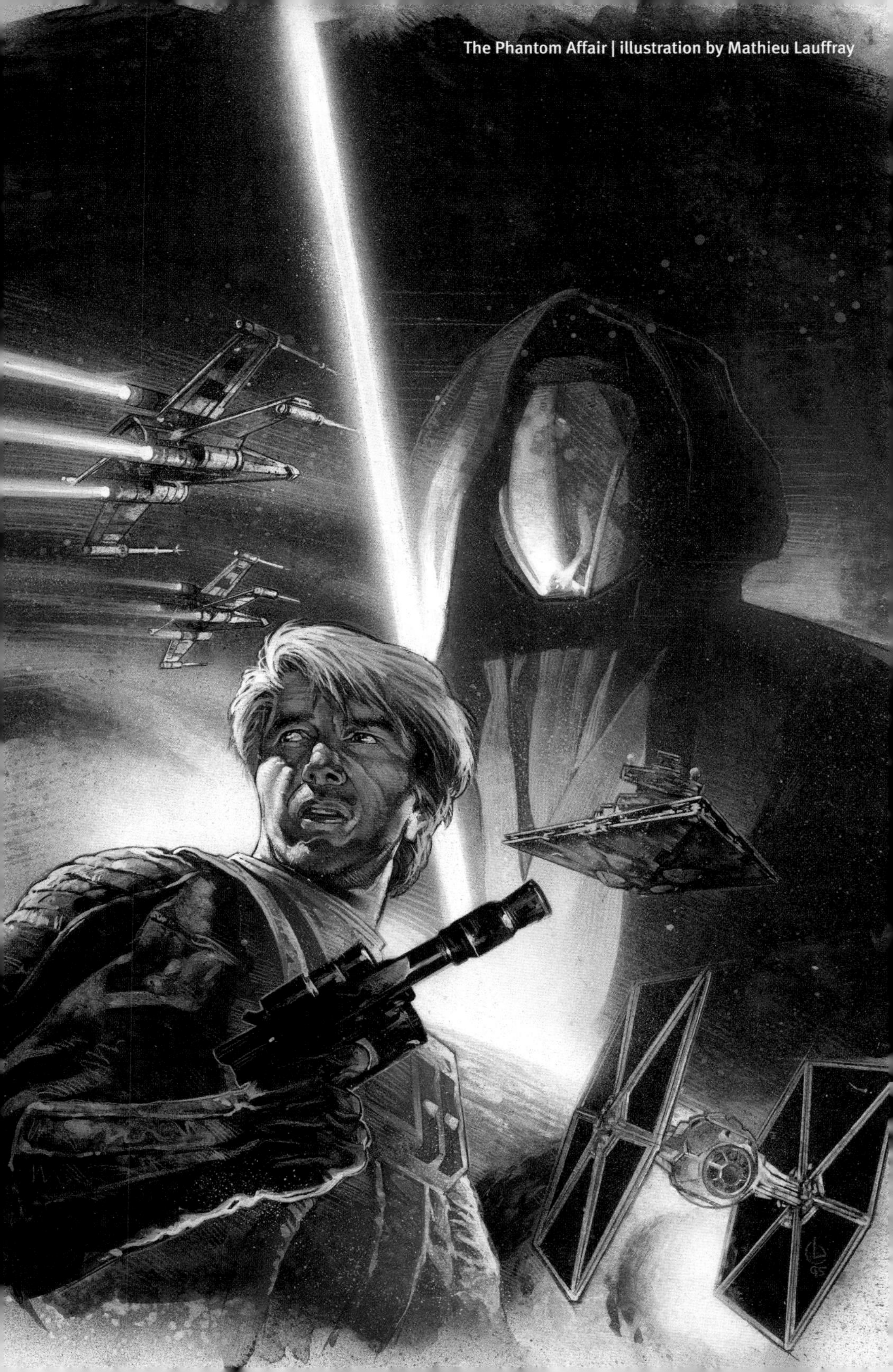
The Phantom Affair | illustration by Mathieu Lauffray

APPROXIMATELY TWO MONTHS AFTER THE BATTLE
OF ENDOR . . .

story by Michael A. Stackpole
script by Darko Macan
art by Edvin Biukovic, Gary Erskine, and John Nadeau
with Jordi Ensign
letters by Edvin Biukovic, Dave Cooper, and Annie Parkhouse
colors by Dave Nestelle

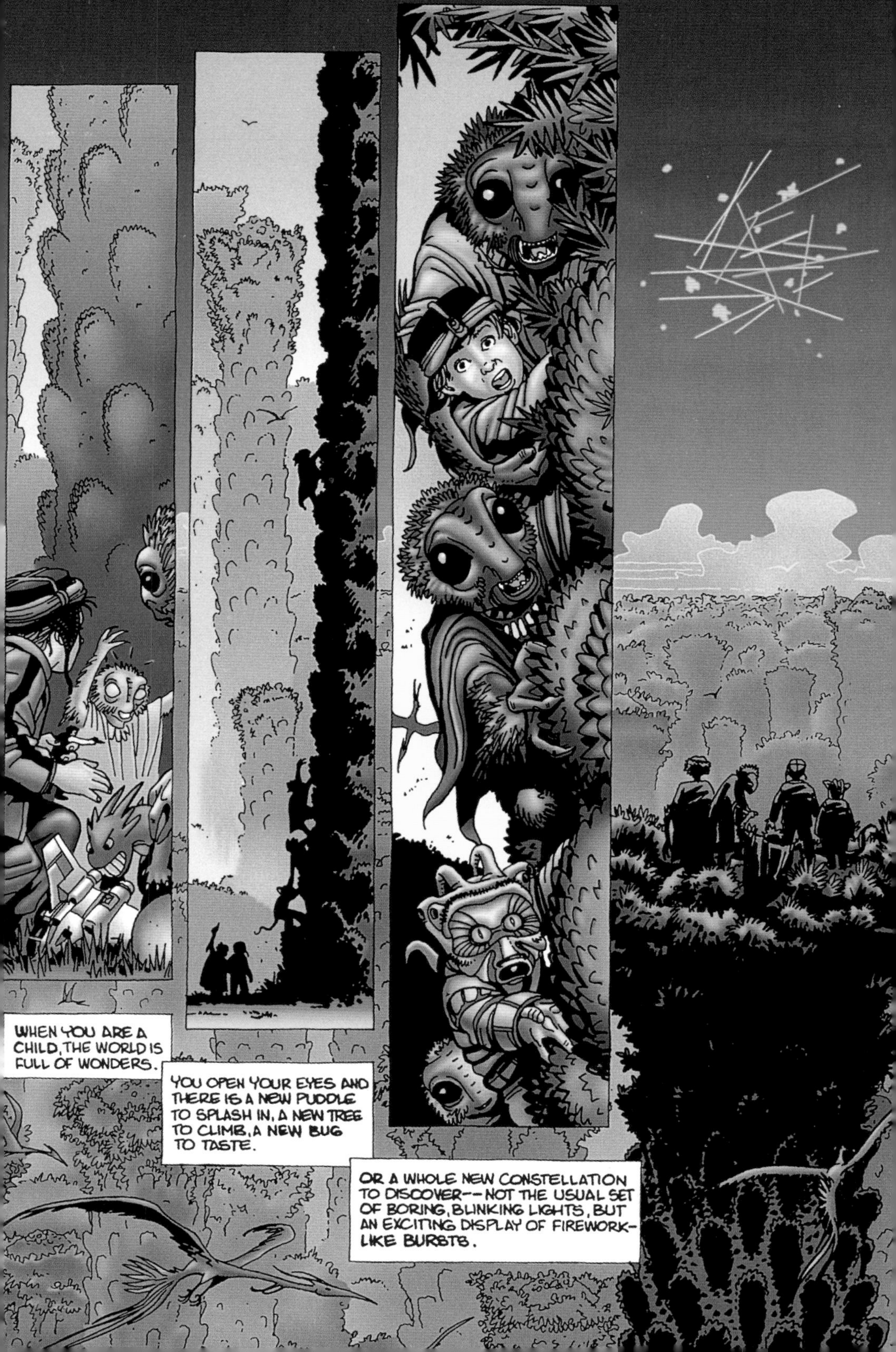
WHEN YOU ARE A CHILD, THE WORLD IS FULL OF WONDERS.
YOU OPEN YOUR EYES AND THERE IS A NEW PUDDLE TO SPLASH IN, A NEW TREE TO CLIMB, A NEW BUG TO TASTE.
OR A WHOLE NEW CONSTELLATION TO DISCOVER-- NOT THE USUAL SET OF BORING, BLINKING LIGHTS, BUT AN EXCITING DISPLAY OF FIREWORK-LIKE BURSTS.

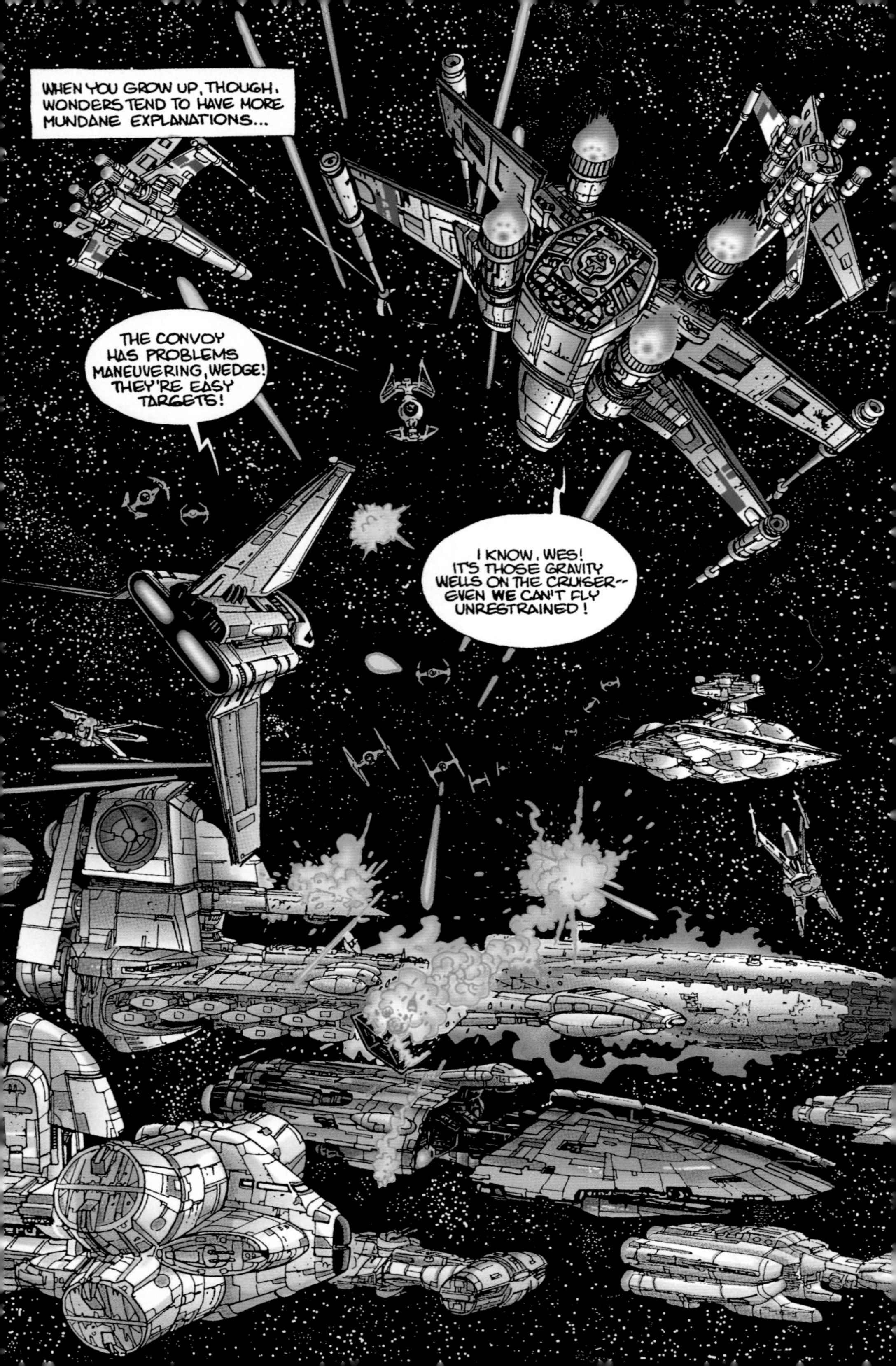
WHEN YOU GROW UP, THOUGH, WONDERS TEND TO HAVE MORE MUNDANE EXPLANATIONS...
THE CONVOY HAS PROBLEMS MANEUVERING, WEDGE! THEY'RE EASY TARGETS!
I KNOW, WES! IT'S THOSE GRAVITY WELLS ON THE CRUISER-- EVEN WE CAN'T FLY UNRESTRAINED!

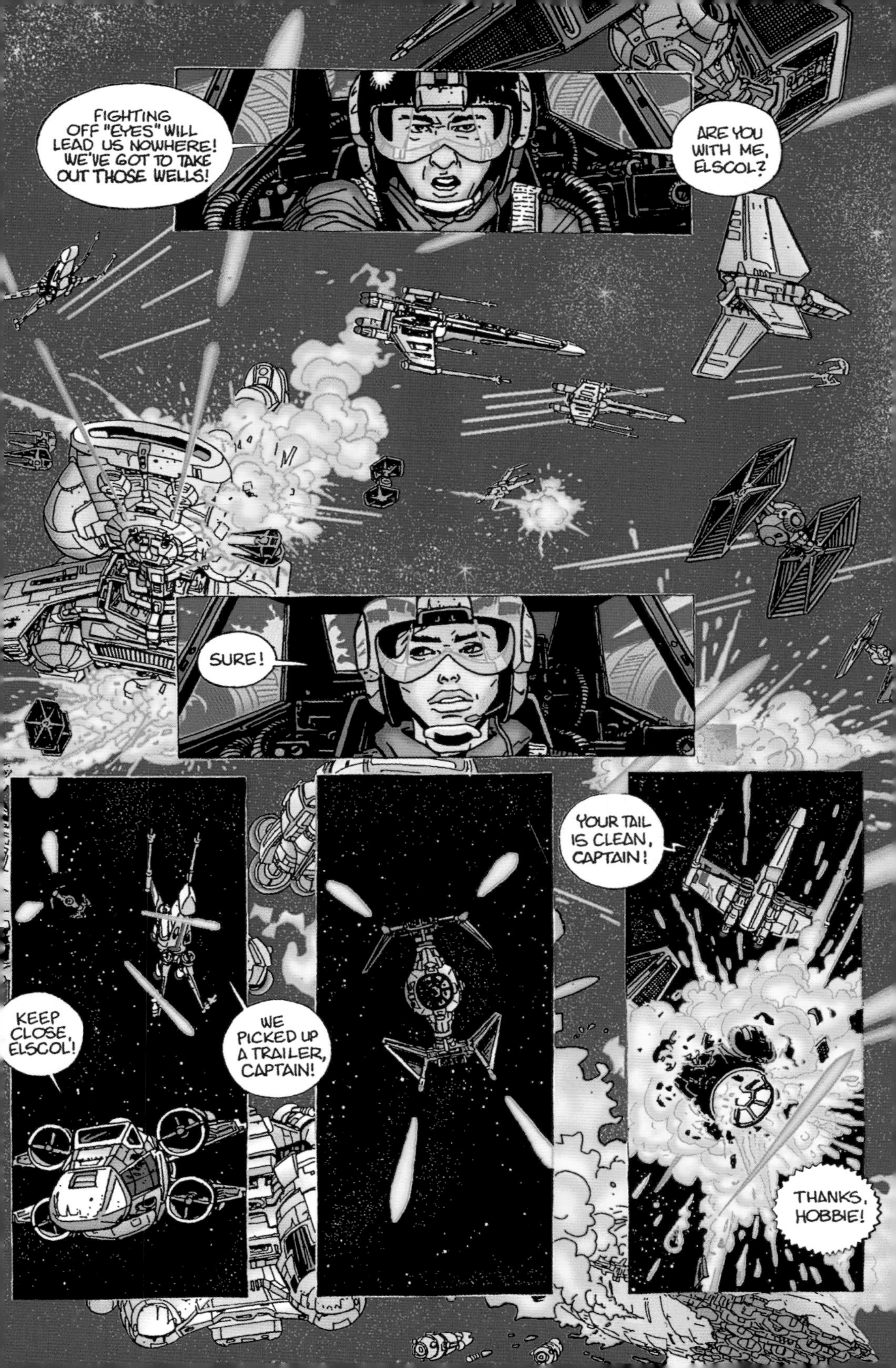
FIGHTING OFF "EYES" WILL LEAD US NOWHERE! WE'VE GOT TO TAKE OUT THOSE WELLS!
ARE YOU WITH ME, ELSCOL?
SURE!
KEEP CLOSE, ELSCOL!
WE PICKED UP A TRAILER, CAPTAIN!
YOUR TAIL IS CLEAN, CAPTAIN!
THANKS, HOBBIE!

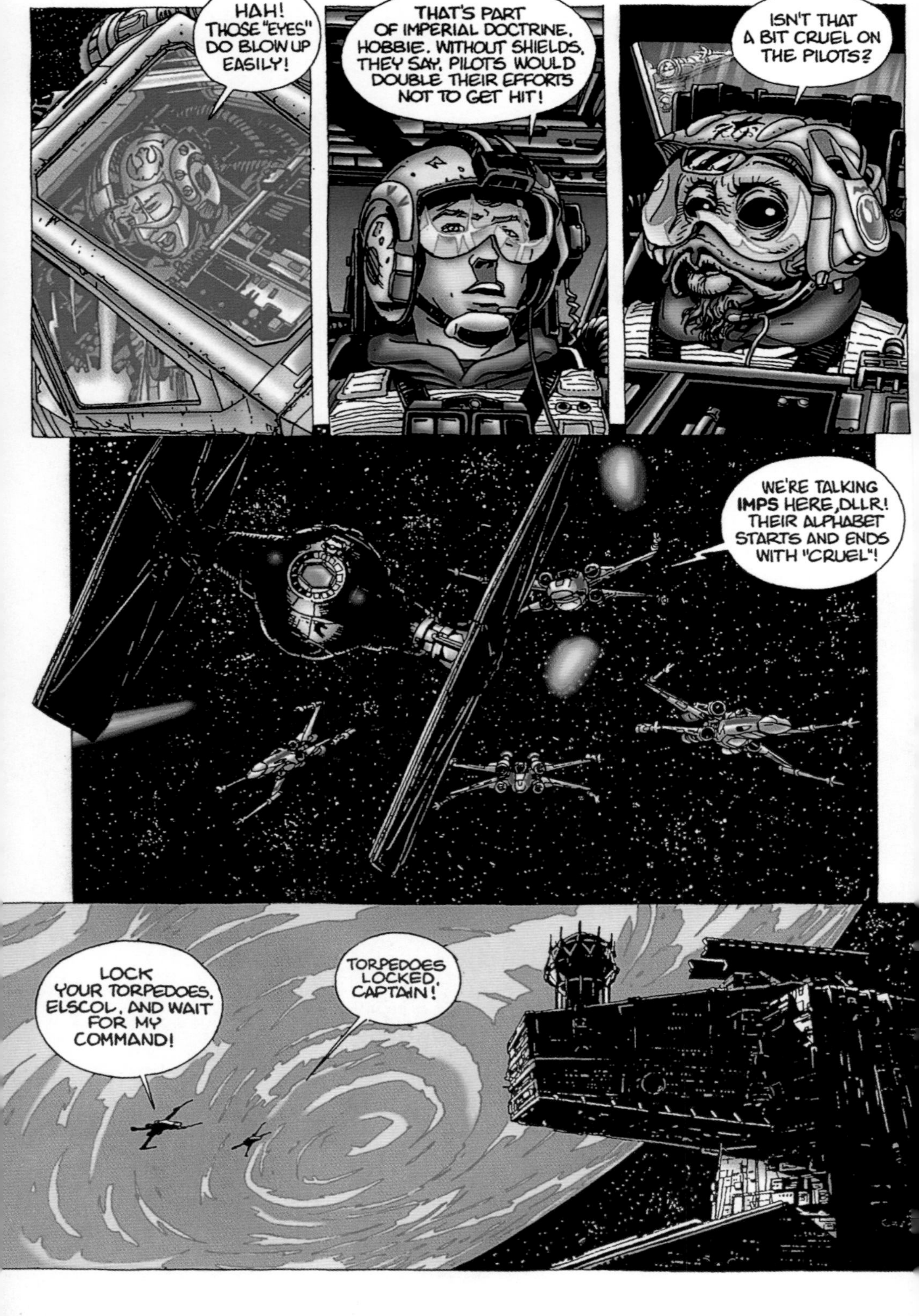
HAH! THOSE "EYES" DO BLOW UP EASILY!
THAT'S PART OF IMPERIAL DOCTRINE, HOBBIE. WITHOUT SHIELDS, THEY SAY, PILOTS WOULD DOUBLE THEIR EFFORTS NOT TO GET HIT!
ISN'T THAT A BIT CRUEL ON THE PILOTS?
WE'RE TALKING **IMPS** HERE, DLLR! THEIR ALPHABET STARTS AND ENDS WITH "CRUEL"!
LOCK YOUR TORPEDOES, ELSCOL, AND WAIT FOR MY COMMAND!
TORPEDOES LOCKED, CAPTAIN!

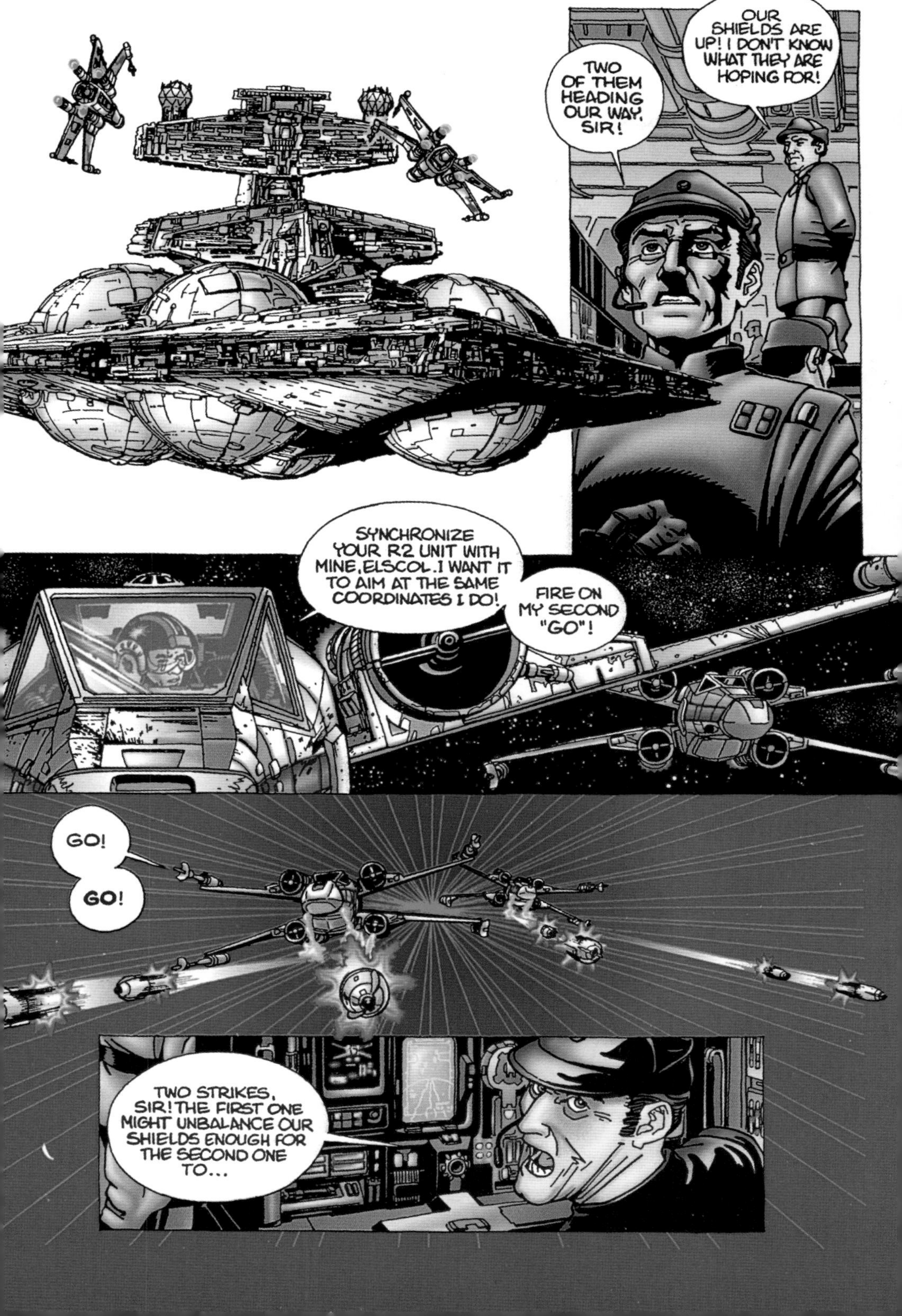
TWO OF THEM HEADING OUR WAY, SIR!
OUR SHIELDS ARE UP! I DON'T KNOW WHAT THEY ARE HOPING FOR!
SYNCHRONIZE YOUR R2 UNIT WITH MINE, ELSCOL. I WANT IT TO AIM AT THE SAME COORDINATES I DO!
FIRE ON MY SECOND "GO"!
GO!
GO!
TWO STRIKES, SIR! THE FIRST ONE MIGHT UNBALANCE OUR SHIELDS ENOUGH FOR THE SECOND ONE TO...

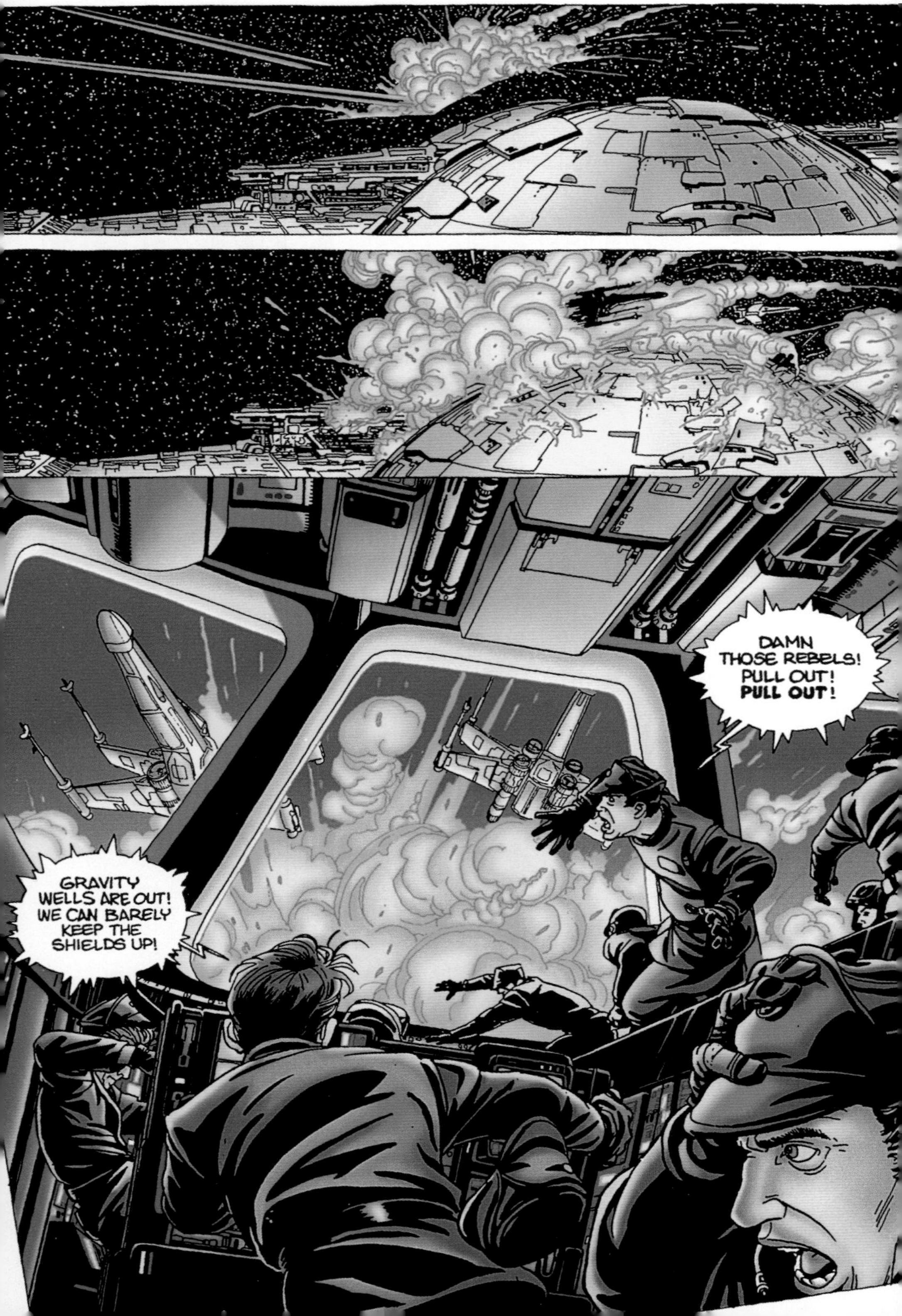

DAMN THOSE REBELS! PULL OUT! **PULL OUT**!
GRAVITY WELLS ARE OUT! WE CAN BARELY KEEP THE SHIELDS UP!

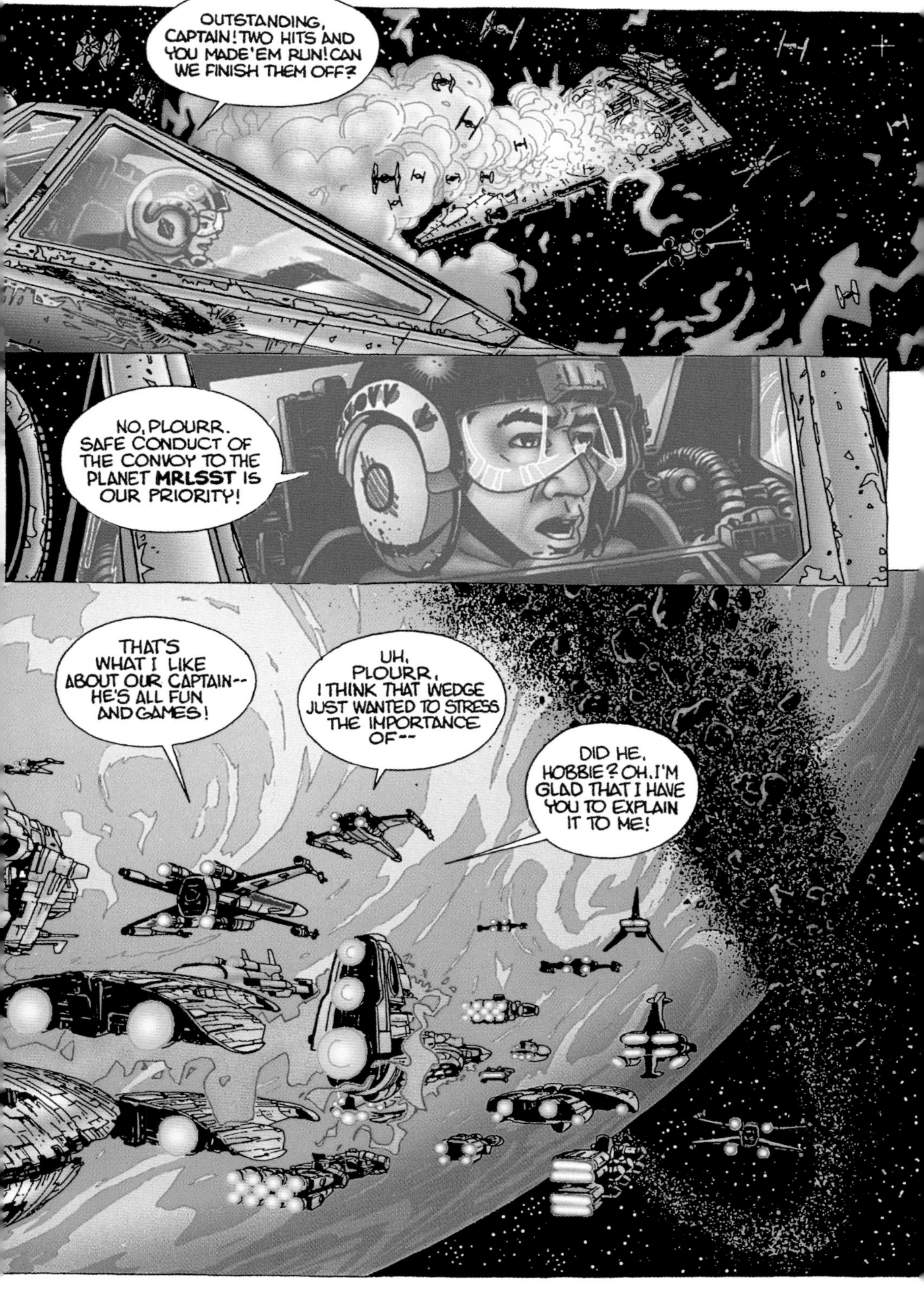
OUTSTANDING, CAPTAIN! TWO HITS AND YOU MADE'EM RUN! CAN WE FINISH THEM OFF?
NO, PLOURR. SAFE CONDUCT OF THE CONVOY TO THE PLANET MRLSST IS OUR PRIORITY!
THAT'S WHAT I LIKE ABOUT OUR CAPTAIN-- HE'S ALL FUN AND GAMES!
UH, PLOURR, I THINK THAT WEDGE JUST WANTED TO STRESS THE IMPORTANCE OF--
DID HE, HOBBIE? OH, I'M GLAD THAT I HAVE YOU TO EXPLAIN IT TO ME!

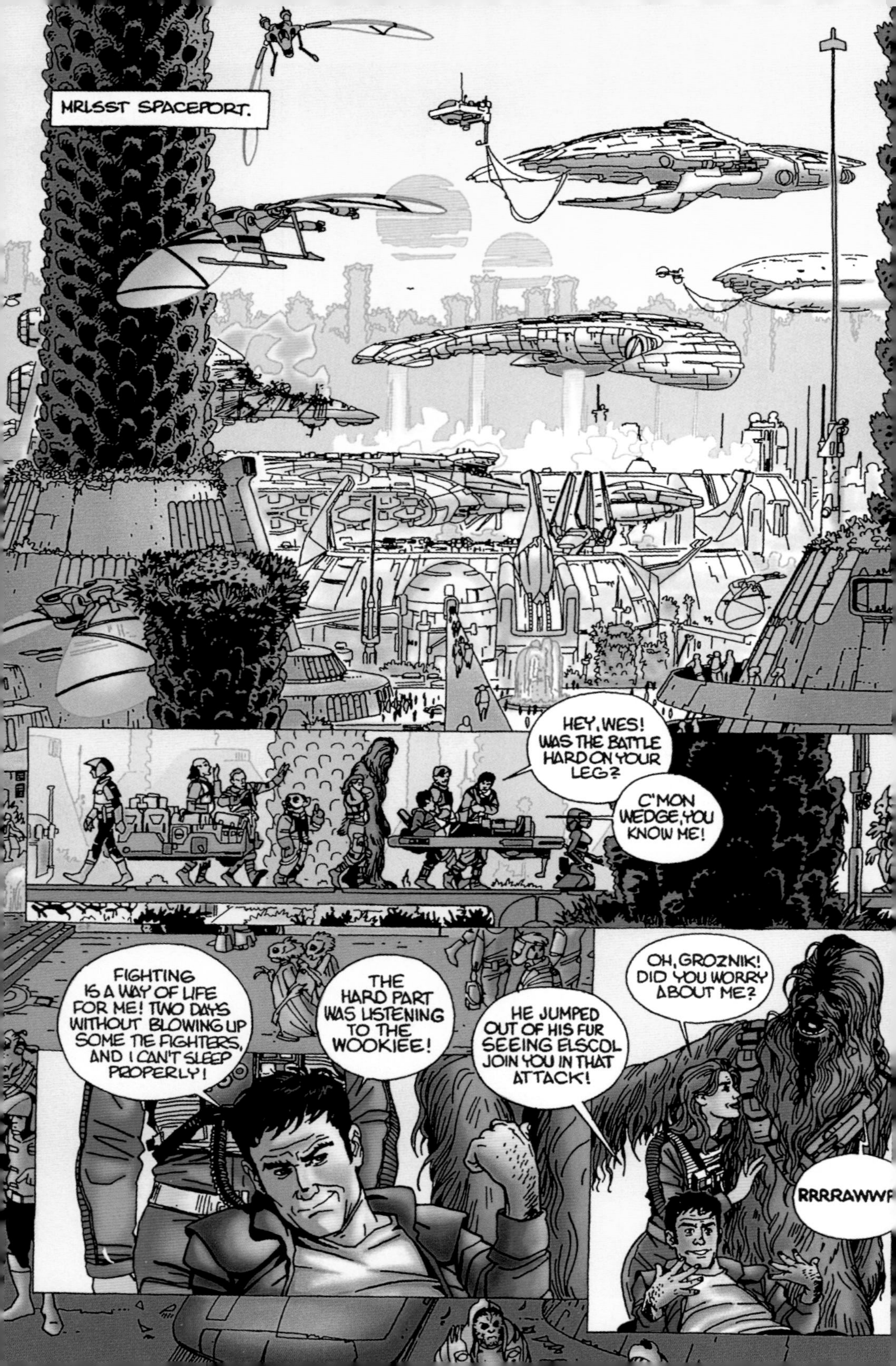
MRLSST SPACEPORT.
HEY, WES! WAS THE BATTLE HARD ON YOUR LEG?
C'MON WEDGE, YOU KNOW ME!
FIGHTING IS A WAY OF LIFE FOR ME! TWO DAYS WITHOUT BLOWING UP SOME TIE FIGHTERS, AND I CAN'T SLEEP PROPERLY!
THE HARD PART WAS LISTENING TO THE WOOKIEE!
HE JUMPED OUT OF HIS FUR SEEING ELSCOL JOIN YOU IN THAT ATTACK!
OH, GROZNIK! DID YOU WORRY ABOUT ME?
RRRRAWWR

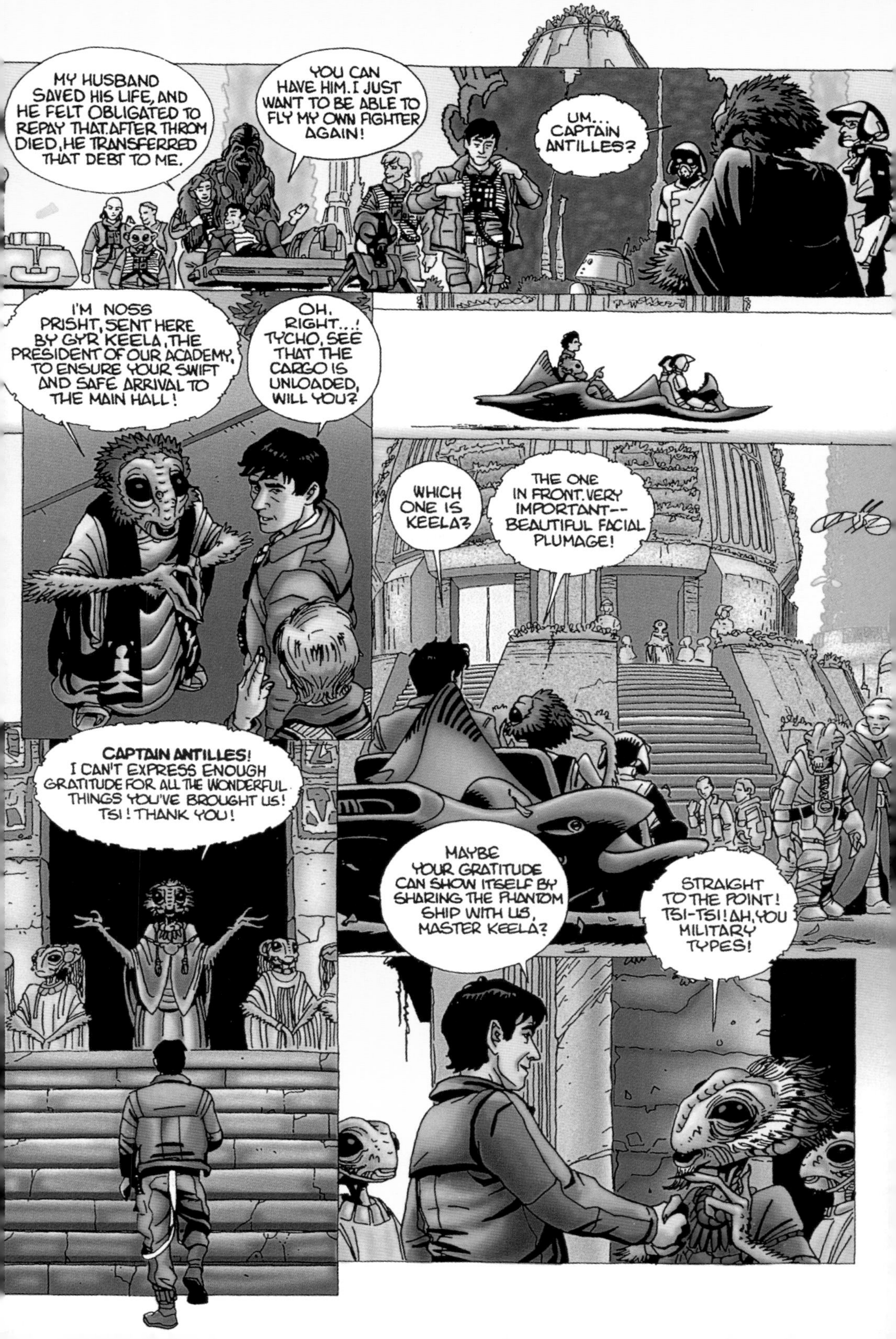
MY HUSBAND SAVED HIS LIFE, AND HE FELT OBLIGATED TO REPAY THAT. AFTER THROM DIED, HE TRANSFERRED THAT DEBT TO ME.
YOU CAN HAVE HIM. I JUST WANT TO BE ABLE TO FLY MY OWN FIGHTER AGAIN!
UM... CAPTAIN ANTILLES?
I'M NOSS PRISHT, SENT HERE BY GYR KEELA, THE PRESIDENT OF OUR ACADEMY, TO ENSURE YOUR SWIFT AND SAFE ARRIVAL TO THE MAIN HALL!
OH. RIGHT...! TYCHO, SEE THAT THE CARGO IS UNLOADED, WILL YOU?
WHICH ONE IS KEELA?
THE ONE IN FRONT. VERY IMPORTANT-- BEAUTIFUL FACIAL PLUMAGE!
CAPTAIN ANTILLES! I CAN'T EXPRESS ENOUGH GRATITUDE FOR ALL THE WONDERFUL THINGS YOU'VE BROUGHT US! TSI! THANK YOU!
MAYBE YOUR GRATITUDE CAN SHOW ITSELF BY SHARING THE PHANTOM SHIP WITH US, MASTER KEELA?
STRAIGHT TO THE POINT! TSI-TSI! AH, YOU MILITARY TYPES!

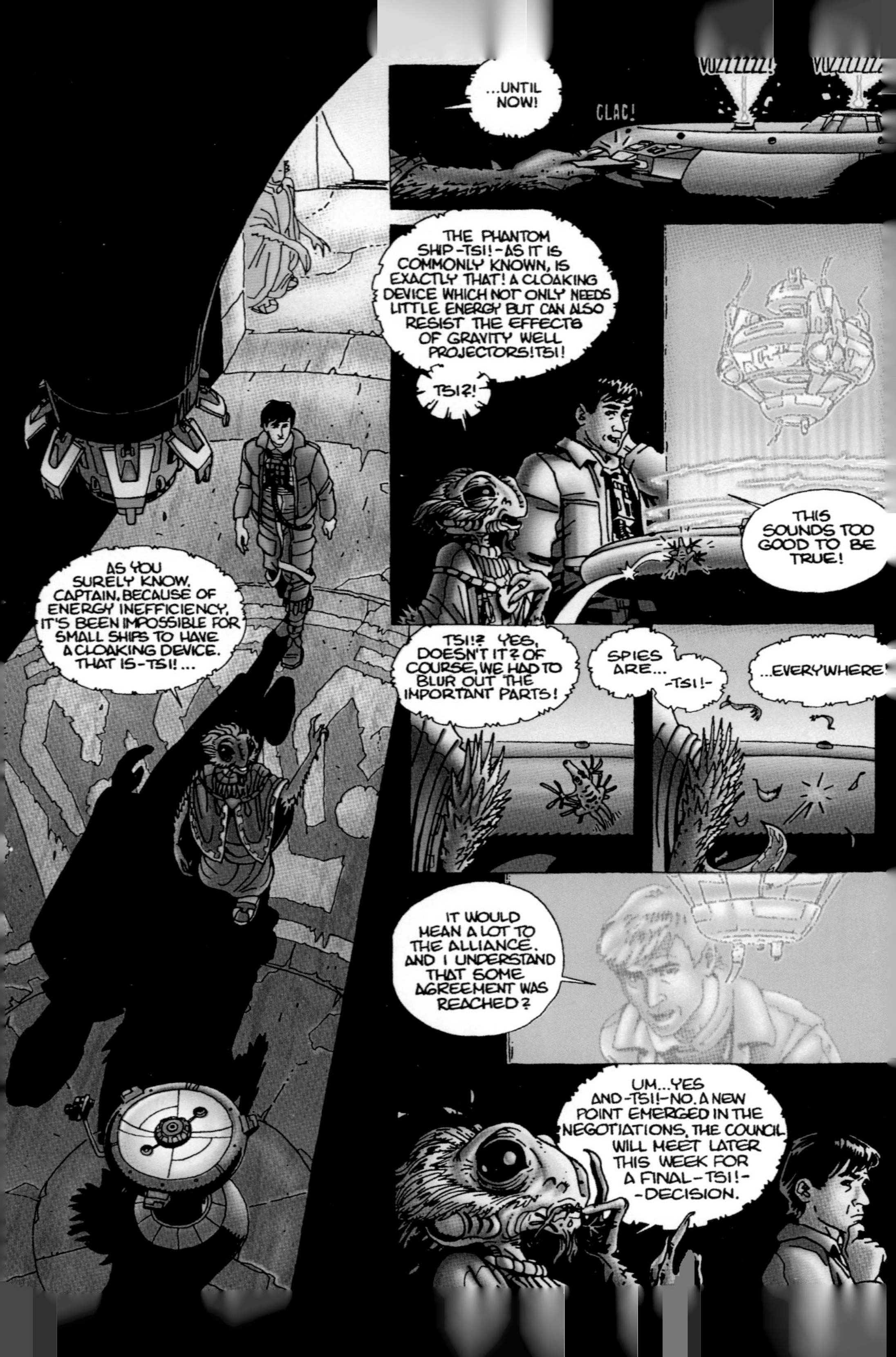

...UNTIL NOW!
CLAC!
VUZZZZZZ!
THE PHANTOM SHIP -TSI!- AS IT IS COMMONLY KNOWN, IS EXACTLY THAT! A CLOAKING DEVICE WHICH NOT ONLY NEEDS LITTLE ENERGY BUT CAN ALSO RESIST THE EFFECTS OF GRAVITY WELL PROJECTORS! TSI!
TSI?!
THIS SOUNDS TOO GOOD TO BE TRUE!
AS YOU SURELY KNOW, CAPTAIN, BECAUSE OF ENERGY INEFFICIENCY, IT'S BEEN IMPOSSIBLE FOR SMALL SHIPS TO HAVE A CLOAKING DEVICE. THAT IS -TSI! ...
TSI!? YES, DOESN'T IT? OF COURSE, WE HAD TO BLUR OUT THE IMPORTANT PARTS!
SPIES ARE... -TSI!-
...EVERYWHERE!
IT WOULD MEAN A LOT TO THE ALLIANCE. AND I UNDERSTAND THAT SOME AGREEMENT WAS REACHED?
UM...YES AND -TSI!- NO. A NEW POINT EMERGED IN THE NEGOTIATIONS, THE COUNCIL WILL MEET LATER THIS WEEK FOR A FINAL -TSI!- -DECISION.

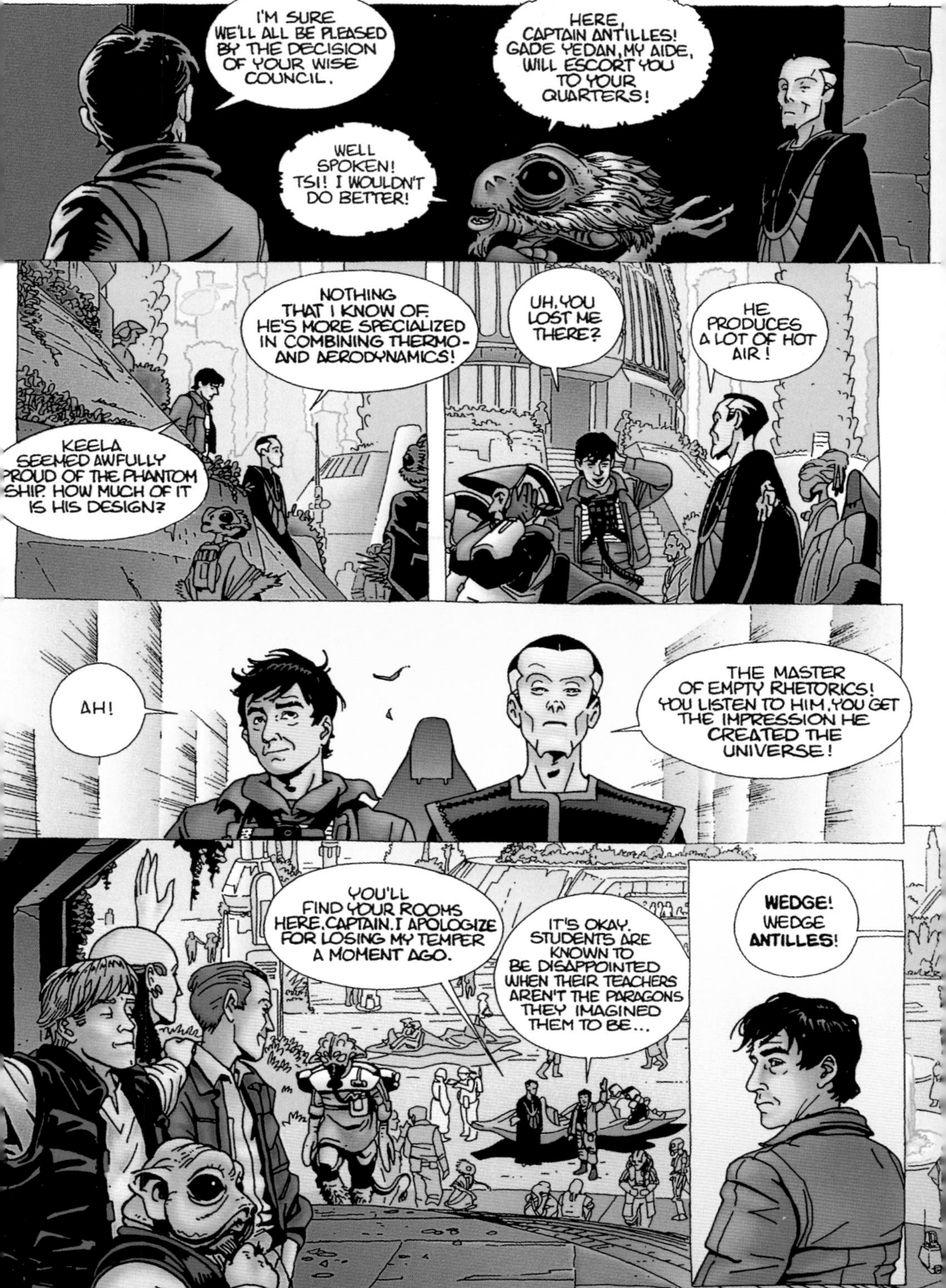
I'M SURE WE'LL ALL BE PLEASED BY THE DECISION OF YOUR WISE COUNCIL.
HERE, CAPTAIN ANTILLES! GADE YEDAN, MY AIDE, WILL ESCORT YOU TO YOUR QUARTERS!
WELL SPOKEN! TSI! I WOULDN'T DO BETTER!
KEELA SEEMED AWFULLY PROUD OF THE PHANTOM SHIP. HOW MUCH OF IT IS HIS DESIGN?
NOTHING THAT I KNOW OF. HE'S MORE SPECIALIZED IN COMBINING THERMO- AND AERODYNAMICS!
UH, YOU LOST ME THERE?
HE PRODUCES A LOT OF HOT AIR!
AH!
THE MASTER OF EMPTY RHETORICS! YOU LISTEN TO HIM, YOU GET THE IMPRESSION HE CREATED THE UNIVERSE!
YOU'LL FIND YOUR ROOMS HERE, CAPTAIN. I APOLOGIZE FOR LOSING MY TEMPER A MOMENT AGO.
IT'S OKAY. STUDENTS ARE KNOWN TO BE DISAPPOINTED WHEN THEIR TEACHERS AREN'T THE PARAGONS THEY IMAGINED THEM TO BE...
WEDGE! WEDGE ANTILLES!

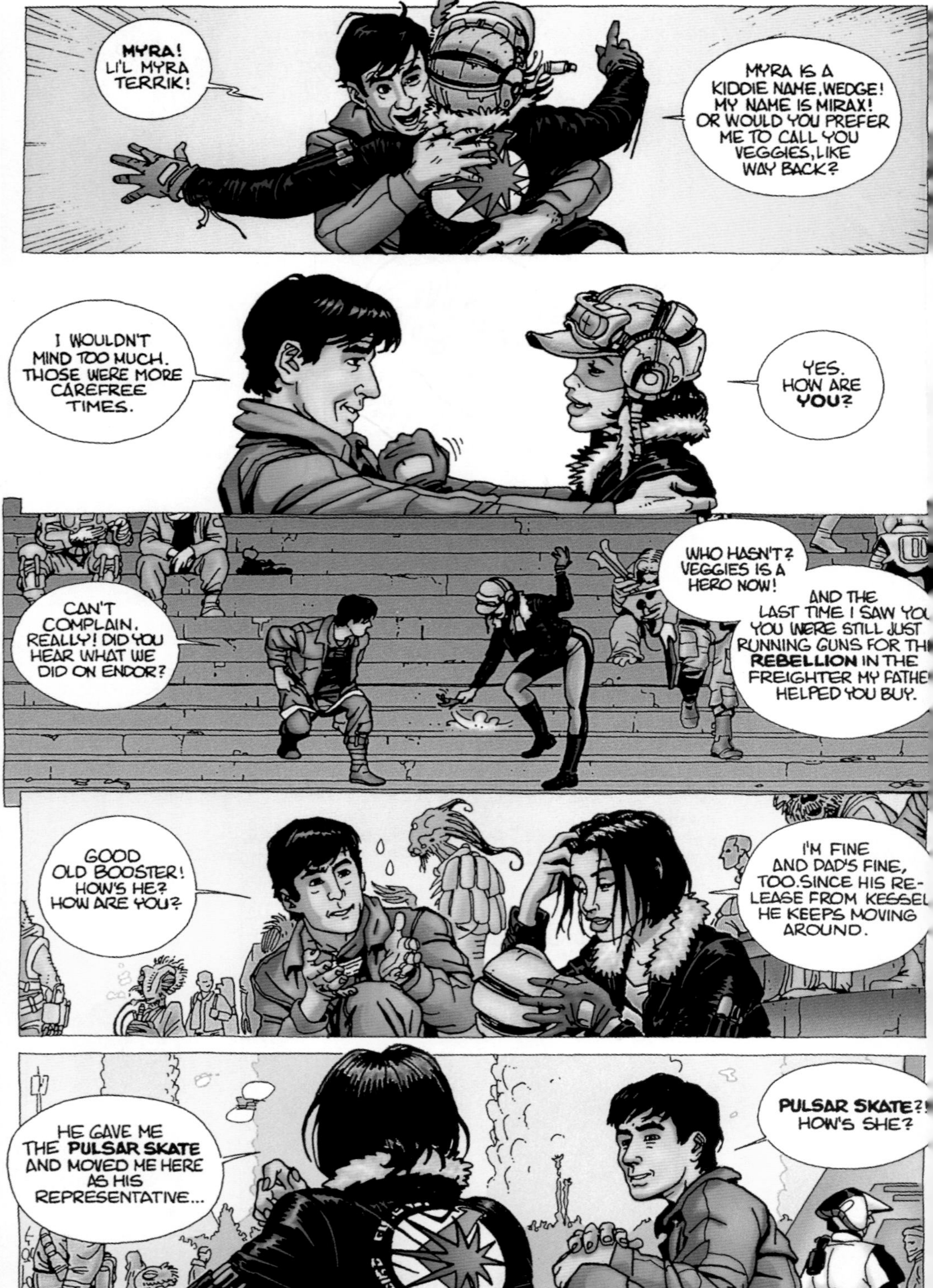

MYRA! LI'L MYRA TERRIK!
MYRA IS A KIDDIE NAME, WEDGE! MY NAME IS MIRAX! OR WOULD YOU PREFER ME TO CALL YOU VEGGIES, LIKE WAY BACK?
I WOULDN'T MIND TOO MUCH. THOSE WERE MORE CAREFREE TIMES.
YES. HOW ARE **YOU**?
CAN'T COMPLAIN. REALLY! DID YOU HEAR WHAT WE DID ON ENDOR?
WHO HASN'T? VEGGIES IS A HERO NOW!
AND THE LAST TIME I SAW YOU YOU WERE STILL JUST RUNNING GUNS FOR THE **REBELLION** IN THE FREIGHTER MY FATHER HELPED YOU BUY.
GOOD OLD BOOSTER! HOW'S HE? HOW ARE YOU?
I'M FINE AND DAD'S FINE, TOO. SINCE HIS RE-LEASE FROM KESSEL HE KEEPS MOVING AROUND.
HE GAVE ME THE **PULSAR SKATE** AND MOVED ME HERE AS HIS REPRESENTATIVE...
PULSAR SKATE?! HOW'S SHE?

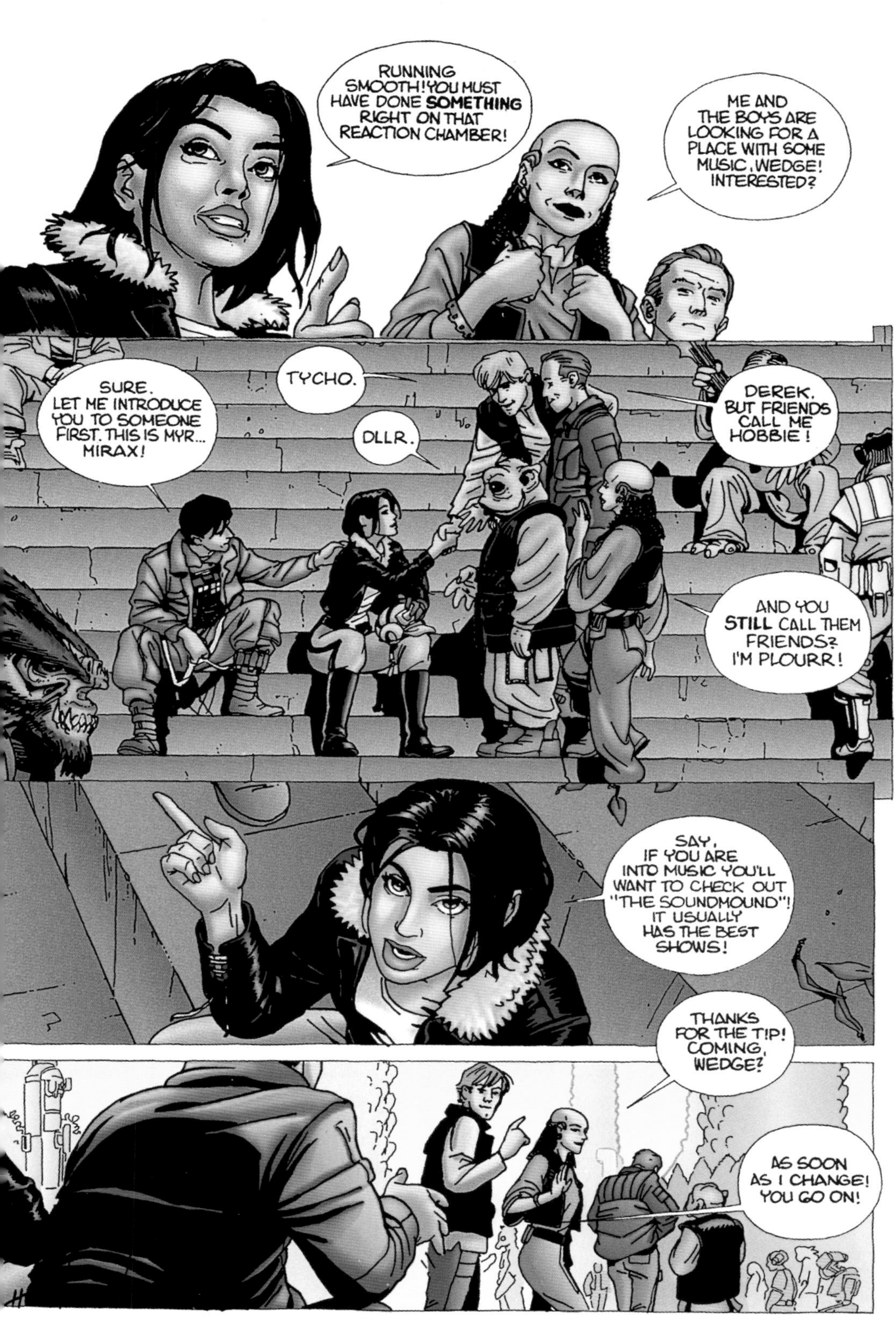
RUNNING SMOOTH! YOU MUST HAVE DONE **SOMETHING** RIGHT ON THAT REACTION CHAMBER!
ME AND THE BOYS ARE LOOKING FOR A PLACE WITH SOME MUSIC, WEDGE! INTERESTED?
SURE. LET ME INTRODUCE YOU TO SOMEONE FIRST. THIS IS MYR... MIRAX!
TYCHO.
DLLR.
DEREK. BUT FRIENDS CALL ME HOBBIE!
AND YOU **STILL** CALL THEM FRIENDS? I'M PLOURR!
SAY, IF YOU ARE INTO MUSIC YOU'LL WANT TO CHECK OUT "THE SOUNDMOUND"! IT USUALLY HAS THE BEST SHOWS!
THANKS FOR THE TIP! COMING, WEDGE?
AS SOON AS I CHANGE! YOU GO ON!

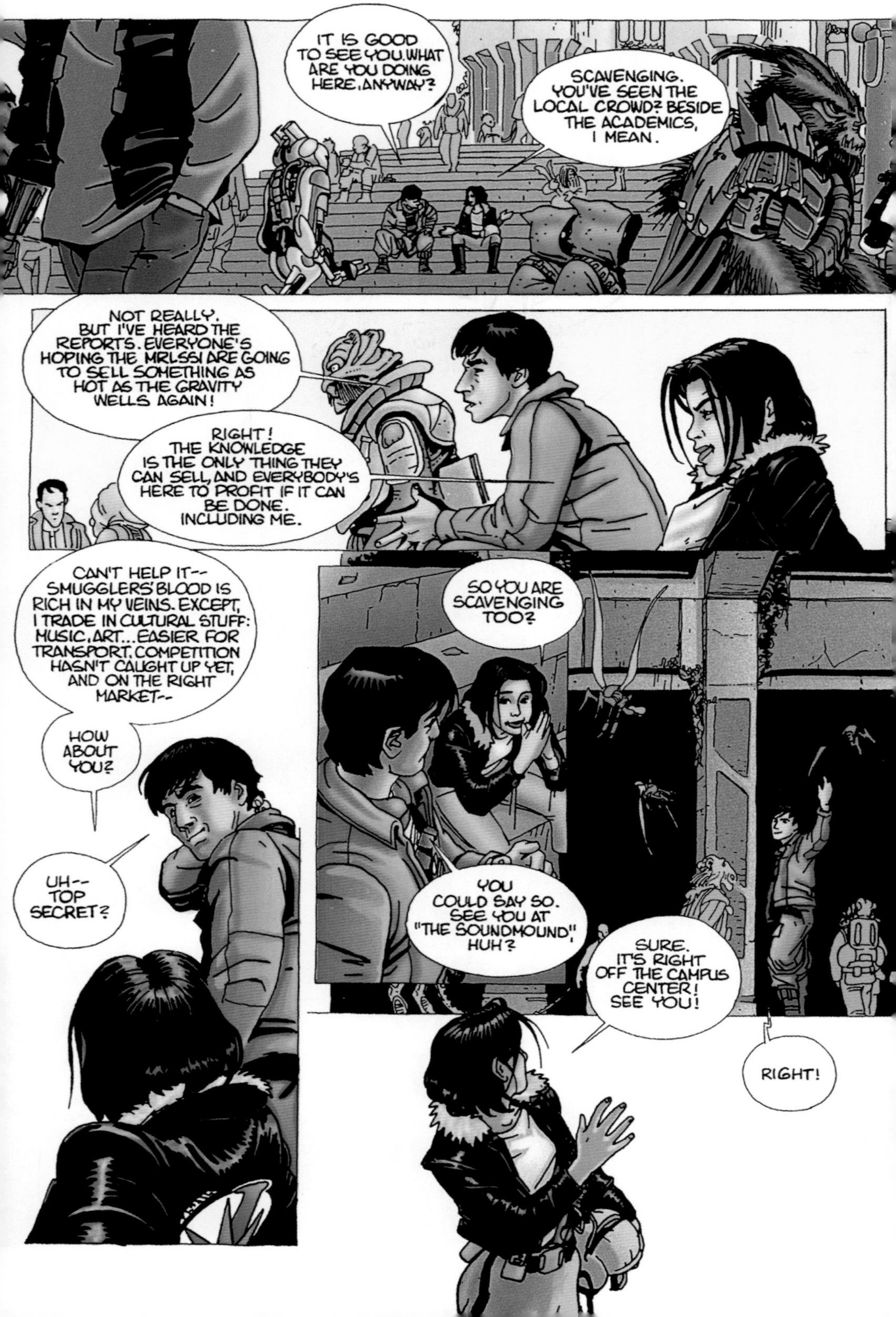

IT IS GOOD TO SEE YOU. WHAT ARE YOU DOING HERE, ANYWAY?
SCAVENGING. YOU'VE SEEN THE LOCAL CROWD? BESIDE THE ACADEMICS, I MEAN.
NOT REALLY. BUT I'VE HEARD THE REPORTS. EVERYONE'S HOPING THE MRLSSI ARE GOING TO SELL SOMETHING AS HOT AS THE GRAVITY WELLS AGAIN!
RIGHT! THE KNOWLEDGE IS THE ONLY THING THEY CAN SELL, AND EVERYBODY'S HERE TO PROFIT IF IT CAN BE DONE. INCLUDING ME.
CAN'T HELP IT-- SMUGGLERS' BLOOD IS RICH IN MY VEINS. EXCEPT, I TRADE IN CULTURAL STUFF: MUSIC, ART... EASIER FOR TRANSPORT, COMPETITION HASN'T CAUGHT UP YET, AND ON THE RIGHT MARKET--
HOW ABOUT YOU?
UH-- TOP SECRET?
SO YOU ARE SCAVENGING TOO?
YOU COULD SAY SO. SEE YOU AT "THE SOUNDMOUND", HUH?
SURE. IT'S RIGHT OFF THE CAMPUS CENTER! SEE YOU!
RIGHT!

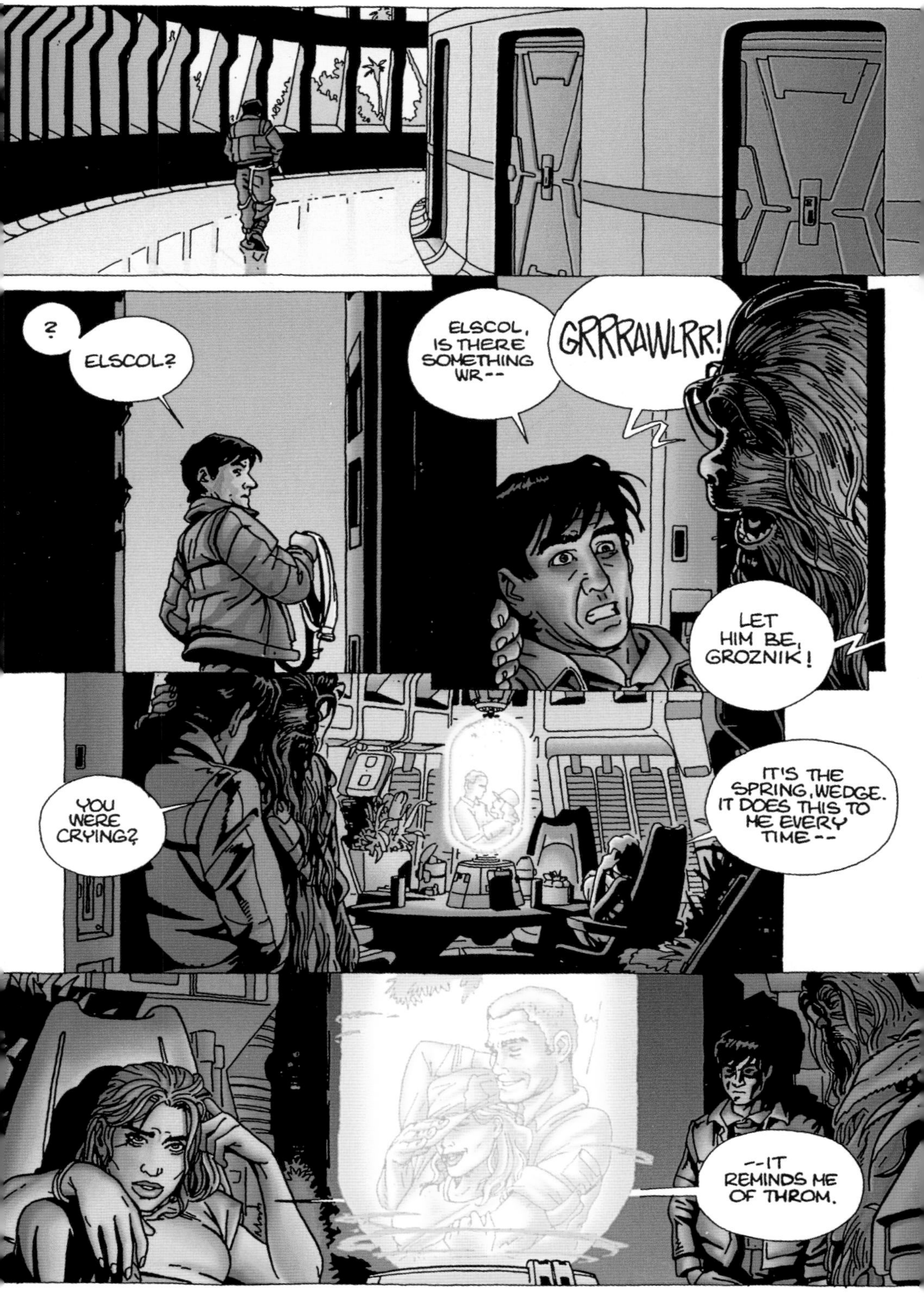
?
ELSCOL?
ELSCOL, IS THERE SOMETHING WR--
GRRRAWLRR!
LET HIM BE, GROZNIK!
YOU WERE CRYING?
IT'S THE SPRING, WEDGE. IT DOES THIS TO ME EVERY TIME--
--IT REMINDS ME OF THROM.

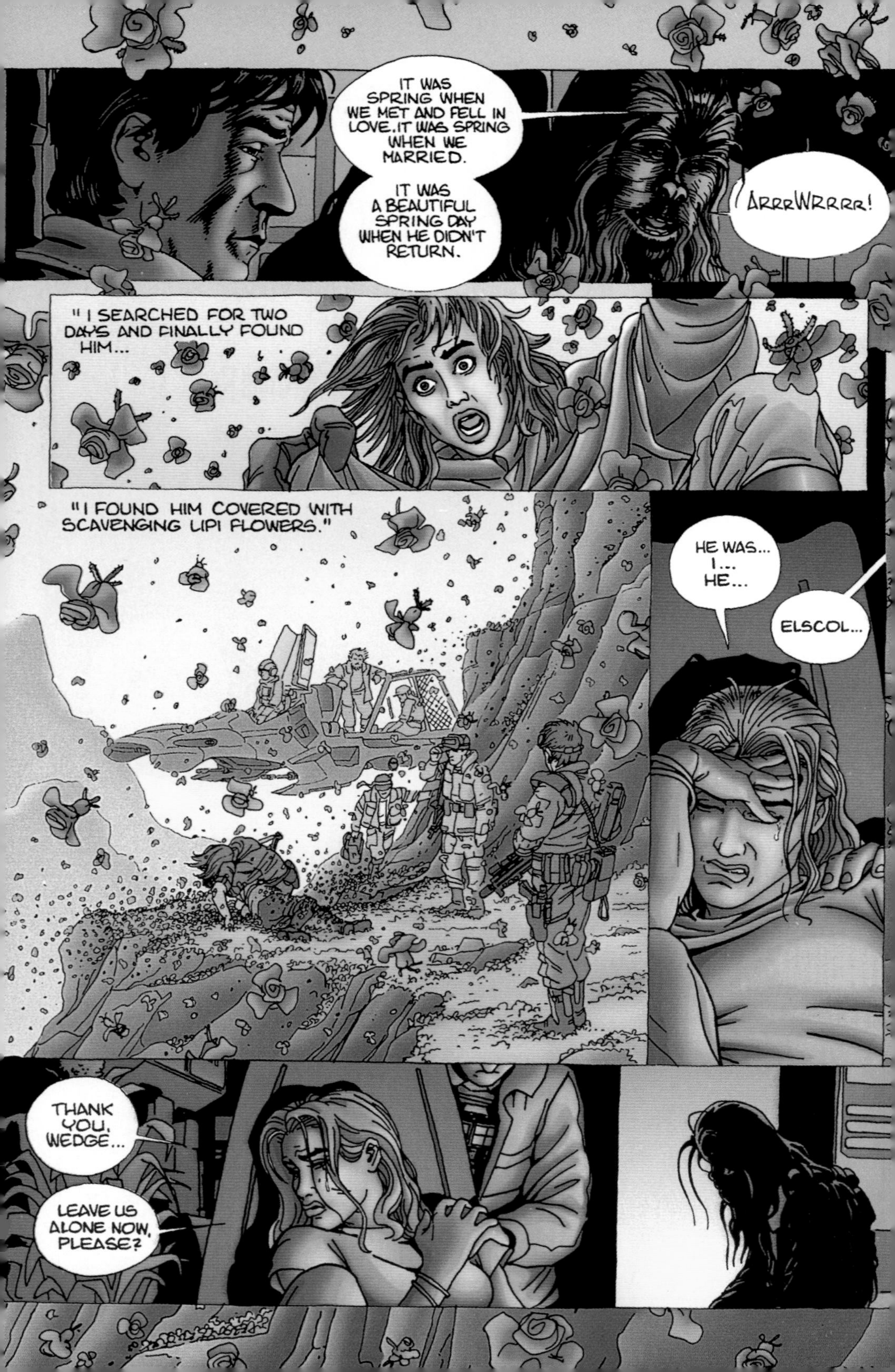
IT WAS SPRING WHEN WE MET AND FELL IN LOVE. IT WAS SPRING WHEN WE MARRIED.
IT WAS A BEAUTIFUL SPRING DAY WHEN HE DIDN'T RETURN.
ARRRWRRRR!
"I SEARCHED FOR TWO DAYS AND FINALLY FOUND HIM...
"I FOUND HIM COVERED WITH SCAVENGING LIPI FLOWERS."
HE WAS... I... HE...
ELSCOL...
THANK YOU, WEDGE...
LEAVE US ALONE NOW, PLEASE?

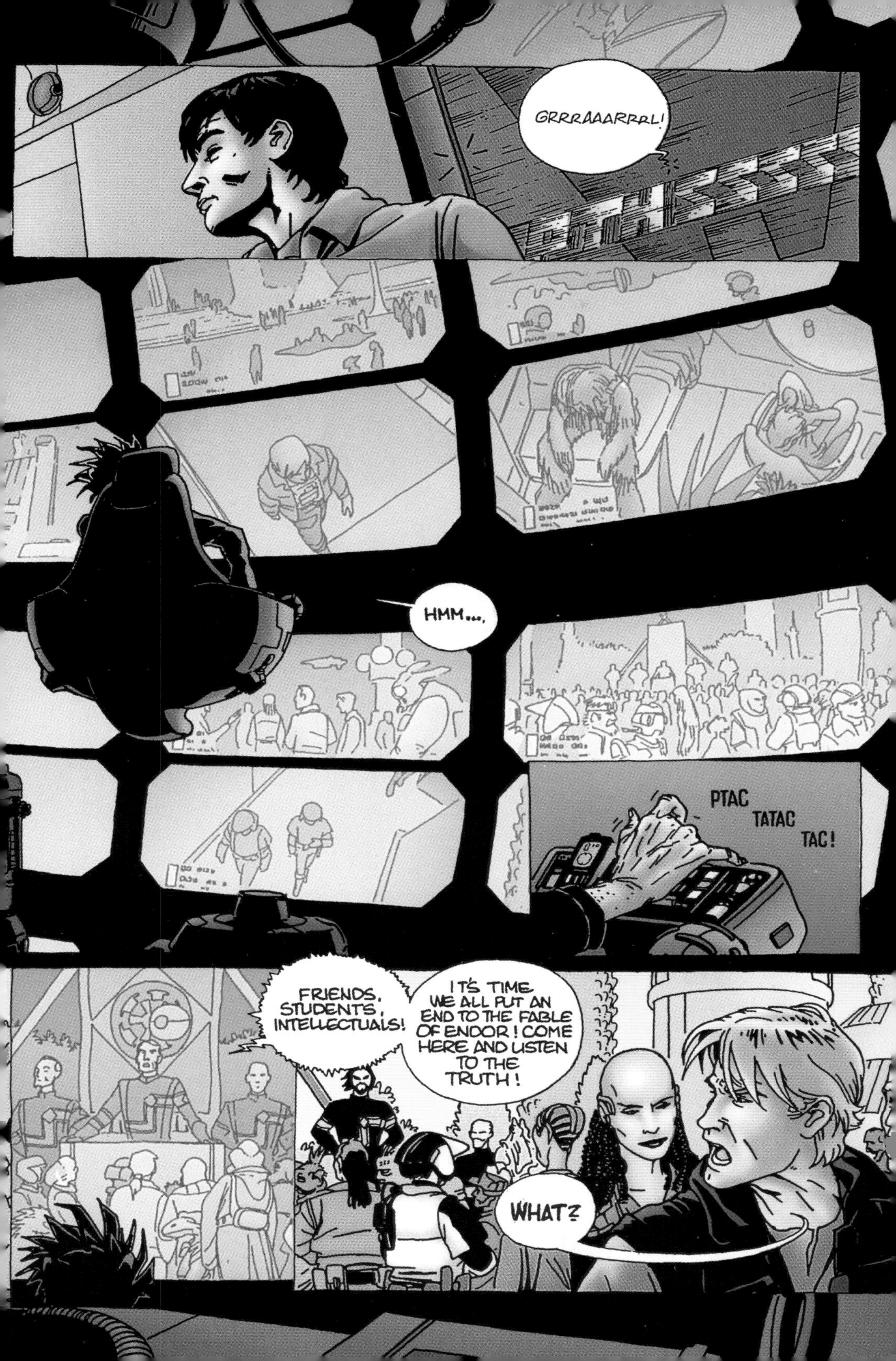
GRRRAAARRRL!
HMM...
PTAC
TATAC
TAC!
FRIENDS, STUDENTS, INTELLECTUALS!
IT'S TIME WE ALL PUT AN END TO THE FABLE OF ENDOR! COME HERE AND LISTEN TO THE TRUTH!
WHAT?

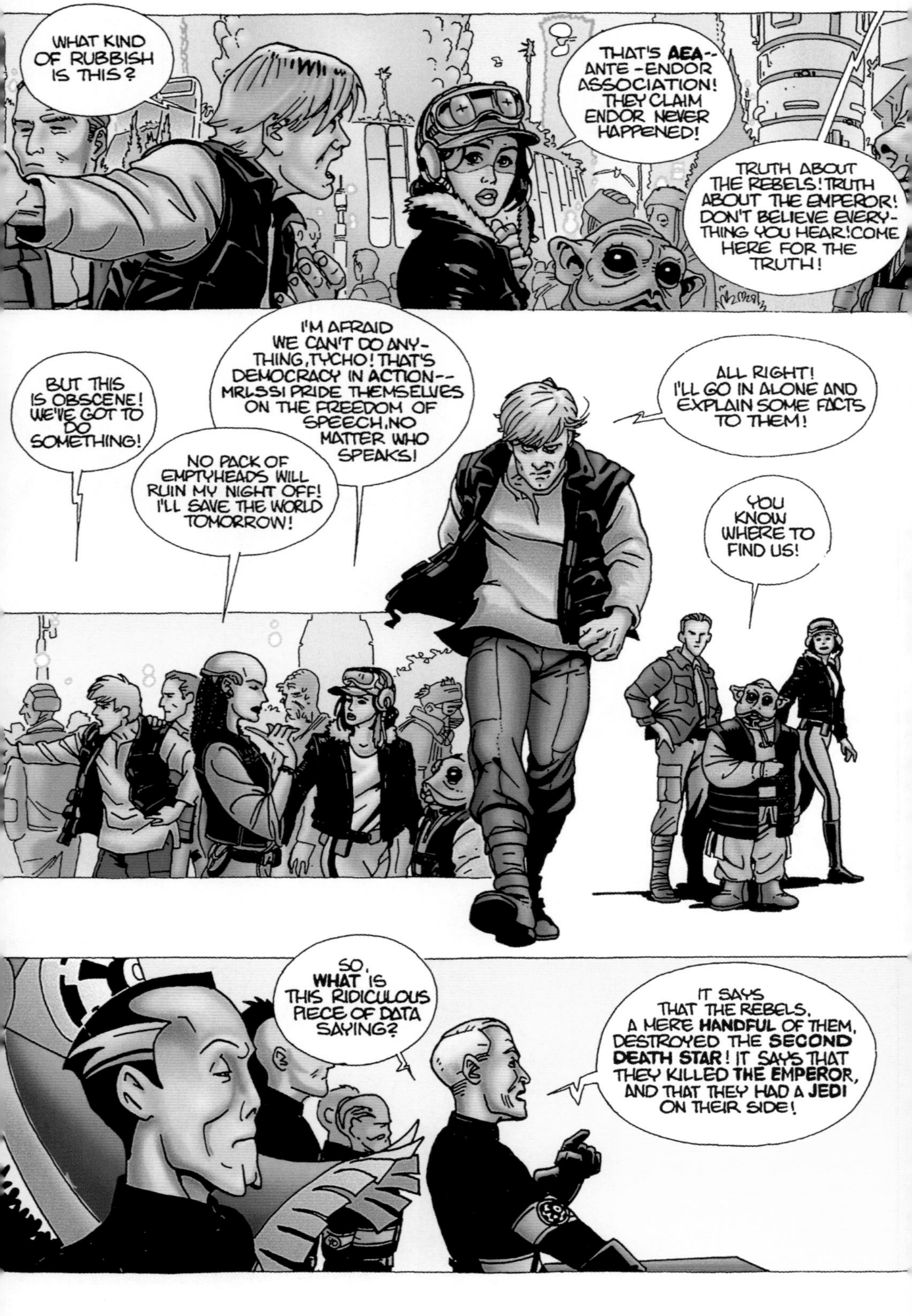
WHAT KIND OF RUBBISH IS THIS?
THAT'S **AEA**-- ANTE-ENDOR ASSOCIATION! THEY CLAIM ENDOR NEVER HAPPENED!
TRUTH ABOUT THE REBELS! TRUTH ABOUT THE EMPEROR! DON'T BELIEVE EVERY-THING YOU HEAR! COME HERE FOR THE TRUTH!
BUT THIS IS OBSCENE! WE'VE GOT TO DO SOMETHING!
I'M AFRAID WE CAN'T DO ANY-THING, TYCHO! THAT'S DEMOCRACY IN ACTION-- MRLSSI PRIDE THEMSELVES ON THE FREEDOM OF SPEECH, NO MATTER WHO SPEAKS!
NO PACK OF EMPTYHEADS WILL RUIN MY NIGHT OFF! I'LL SAVE THE WORLD TOMORROW!
ALL RIGHT! I'LL GO IN ALONE AND EXPLAIN SOME FACTS TO THEM!
YOU KNOW WHERE TO FIND US!
SO, **WHAT** IS THIS RIDICULOUS PIECE OF DATA SAYING?
IT SAYS THAT THE REBELS, A MERE **HANDFUL** OF THEM, DESTROYED THE **SECOND DEATH STAR**! IT SAYS THAT THEY KILLED **THE EMPEROR**, AND THAT THEY HAD A **JEDI** ON THEIR SIDE!

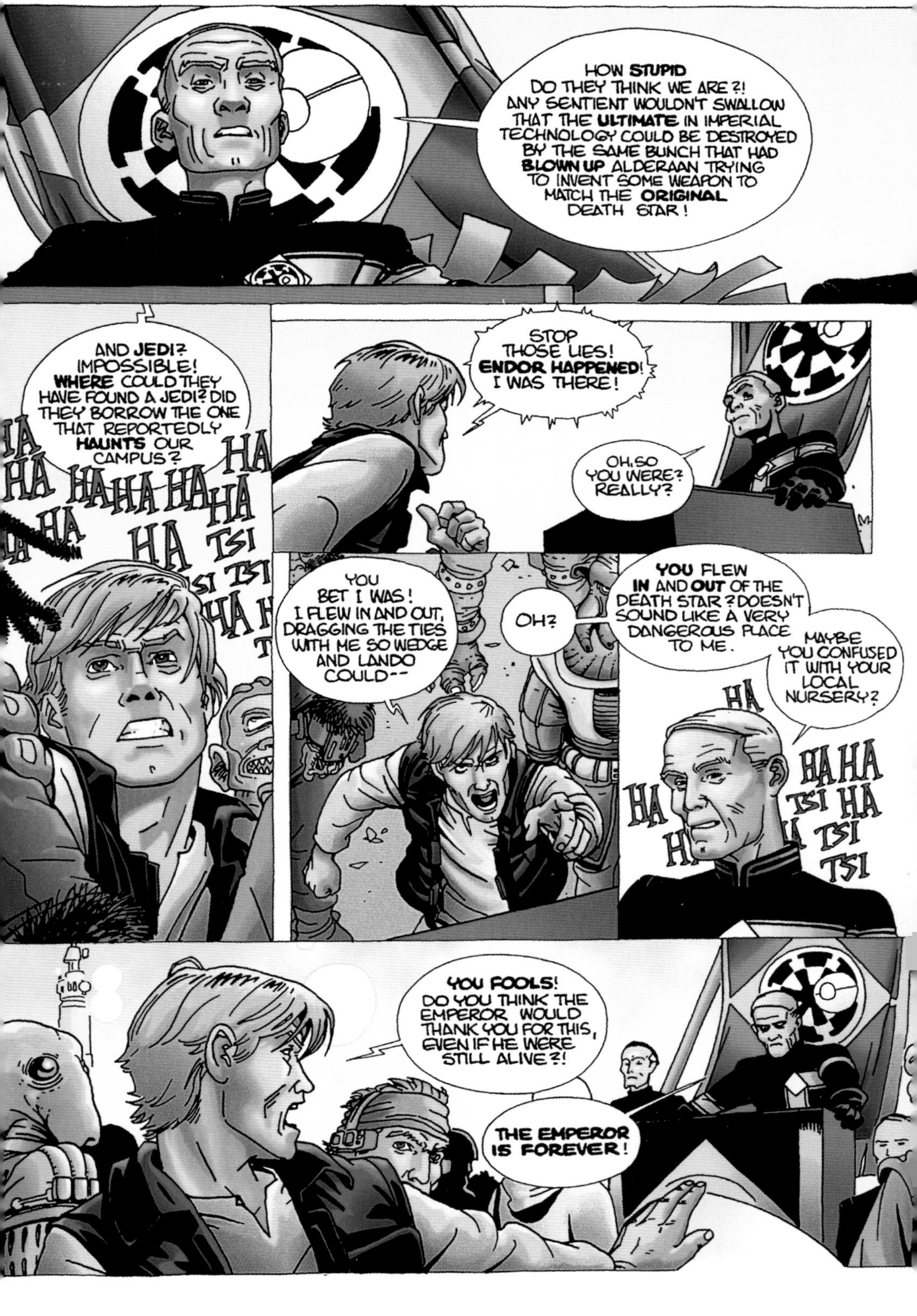

HOW STUPID DO THEY THINK WE ARE?! ANY SENTIENT WOULDN'T SWALLOW THAT THE ULTIMATE IN IMPERIAL TECHNOLOGY COULD BE DESTROYED BY THE SAME BUNCH THAT HAD BLOWN UP ALDERAAN TRYING TO INVENT SOME WEAPON TO MATCH THE ORIGINAL DEATH STAR!
AND JEDI? IMPOSSIBLE! WHERE COULD THEY HAVE FOUND A JEDI? DID THEY BORROW THE ONE THAT REPORTEDLY HAUNTS OUR CAMPUS?
HA HA HAHA HAHA HA HA HA HA TSI TSI TSI HA
STOP THOSE LIES! ENDOR HAPPENED! I WAS THERE!
OH, SO YOU WERE? REALLY?
YOU BET I WAS! I FLEW IN AND OUT, DRAGGING THE TIES WITH ME SO WEDGE AND LANDO COULD--
OH?
YOU FLEW IN AND OUT OF THE DEATH STAR? DOESN'T SOUND LIKE A VERY DANGEROUS PLACE TO ME.
MAYBE YOU CONFUSED IT WITH YOUR LOCAL NURSERY?
HA HAHA HA TSI HA TSI TSI
YOU FOOLS! DO YOU THINK THE EMPEROR WOULD THANK YOU FOR THIS, EVEN IF HE WERE STILL ALIVE?!
THE EMPEROR IS FOREVER!

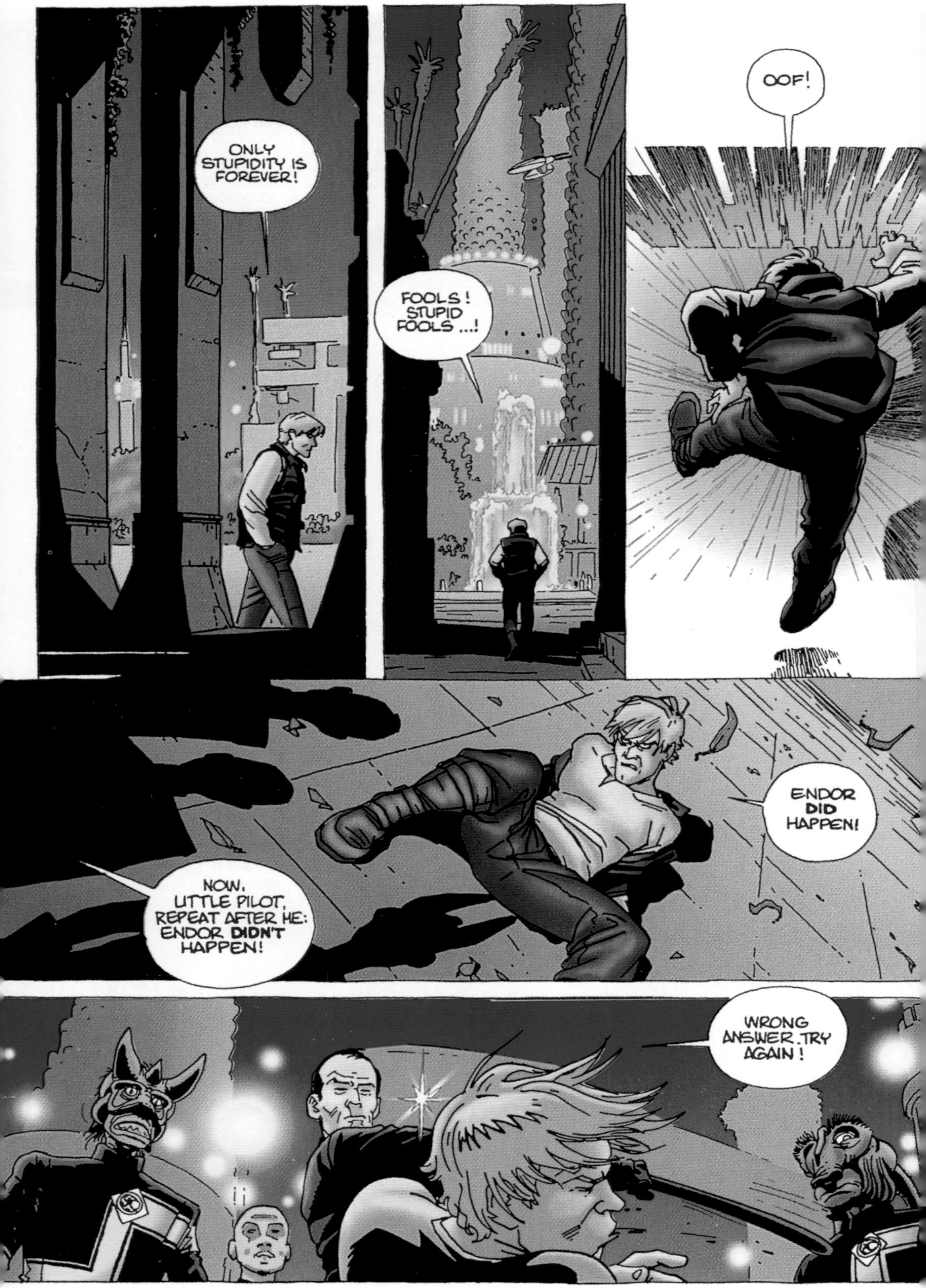
ONLY STUPIDITY IS FOREVER!
FOOLS! STUPID FOOLS ...!
OOF!
NOW, LITTLE PILOT, REPEAT AFTER ME: ENDOR **DIDN'T** HAPPEN!
ENDOR **DID** HAPPEN!
WRONG ANSWER. TRY AGAIN!

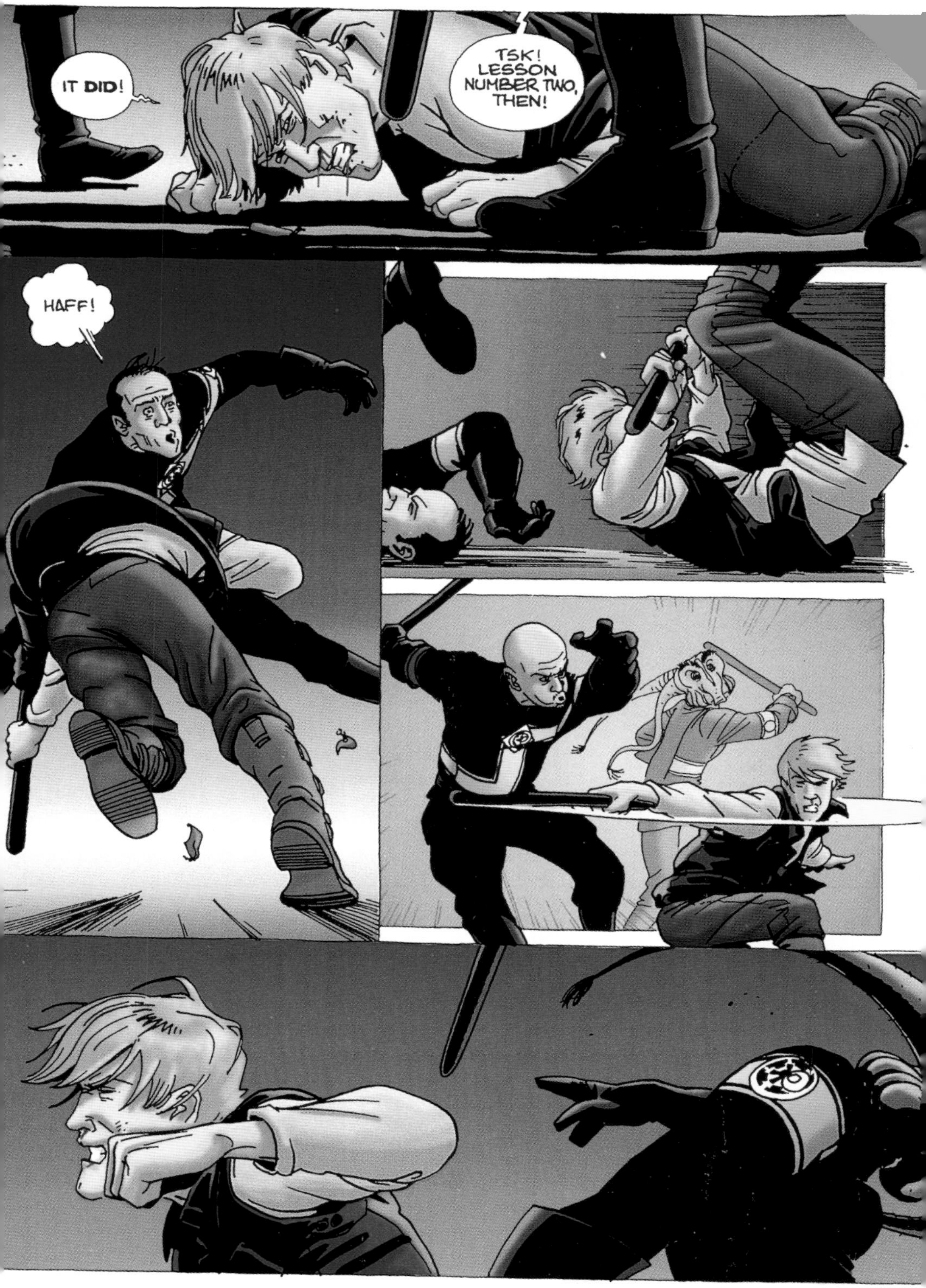
IT DID!
TSK! LESSON NUMBER TWO, THEN!
HAFF!

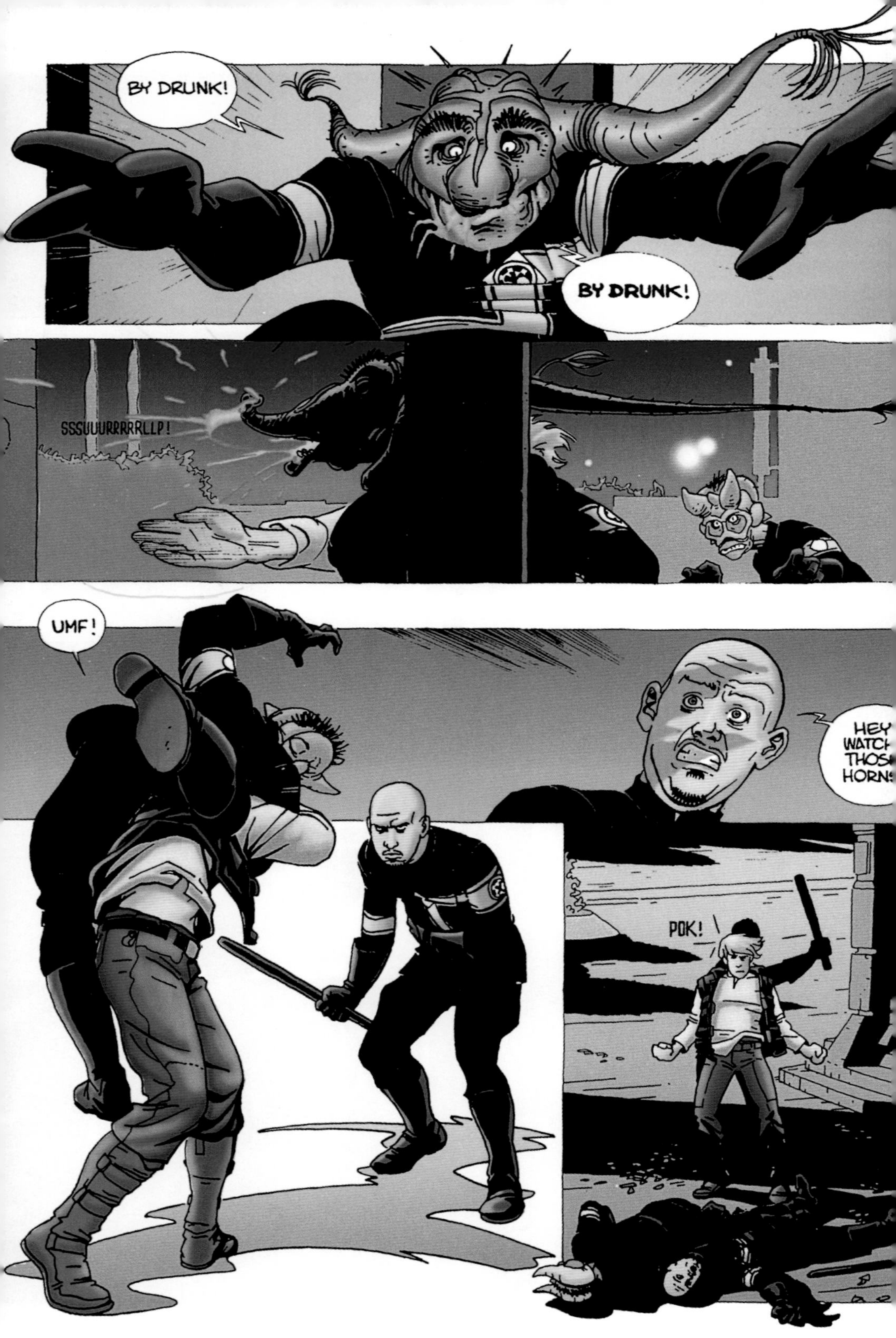
BY DRUNK!
BY DRUNK!
SSSUUURRRRRLLP!
UMF!
HEY WATCH THOS HORNS
POK!

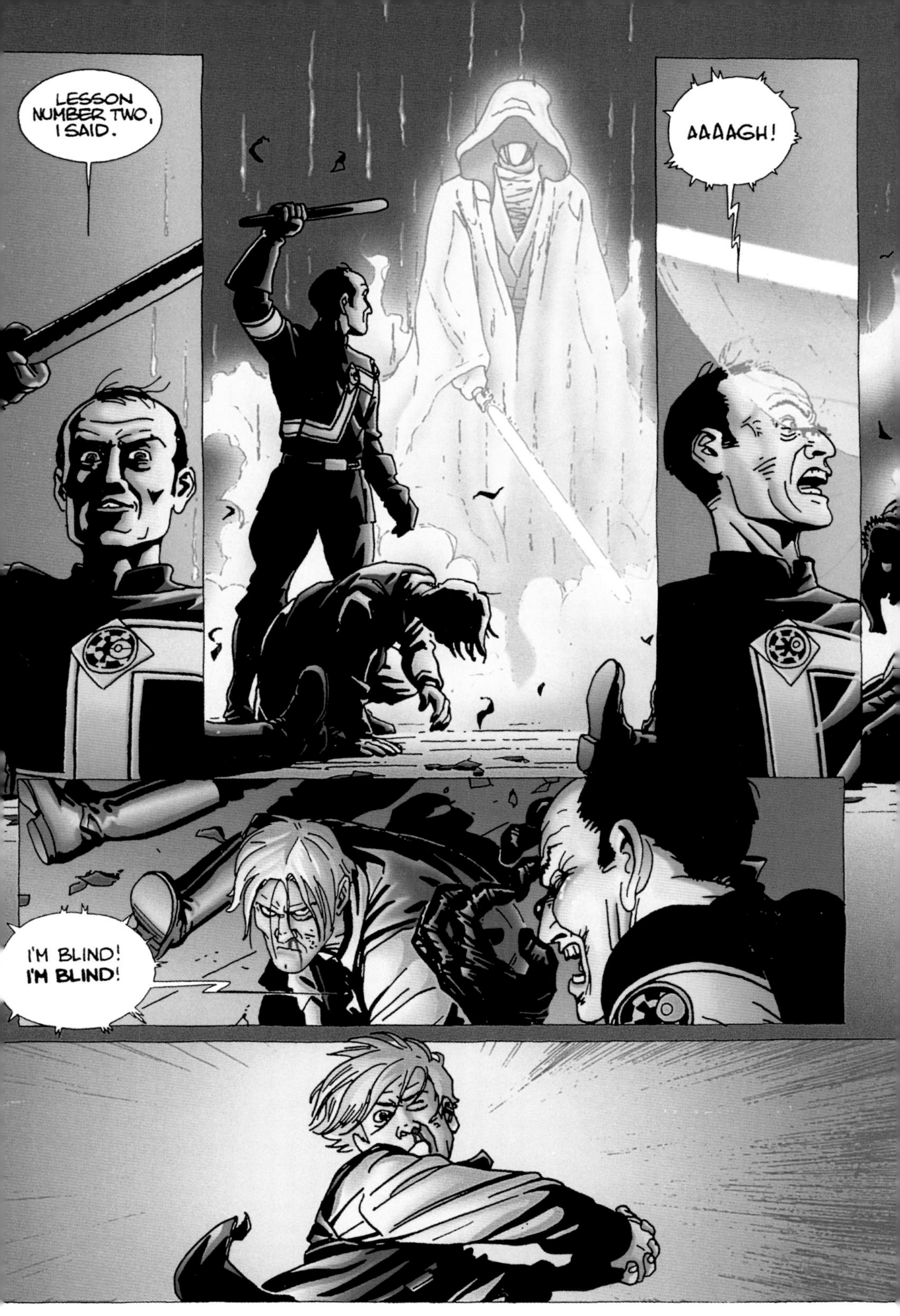
LESSON NUMBER TWO, I SAID.
AAAAGH!
I'M BLIND! I'M BLIND!

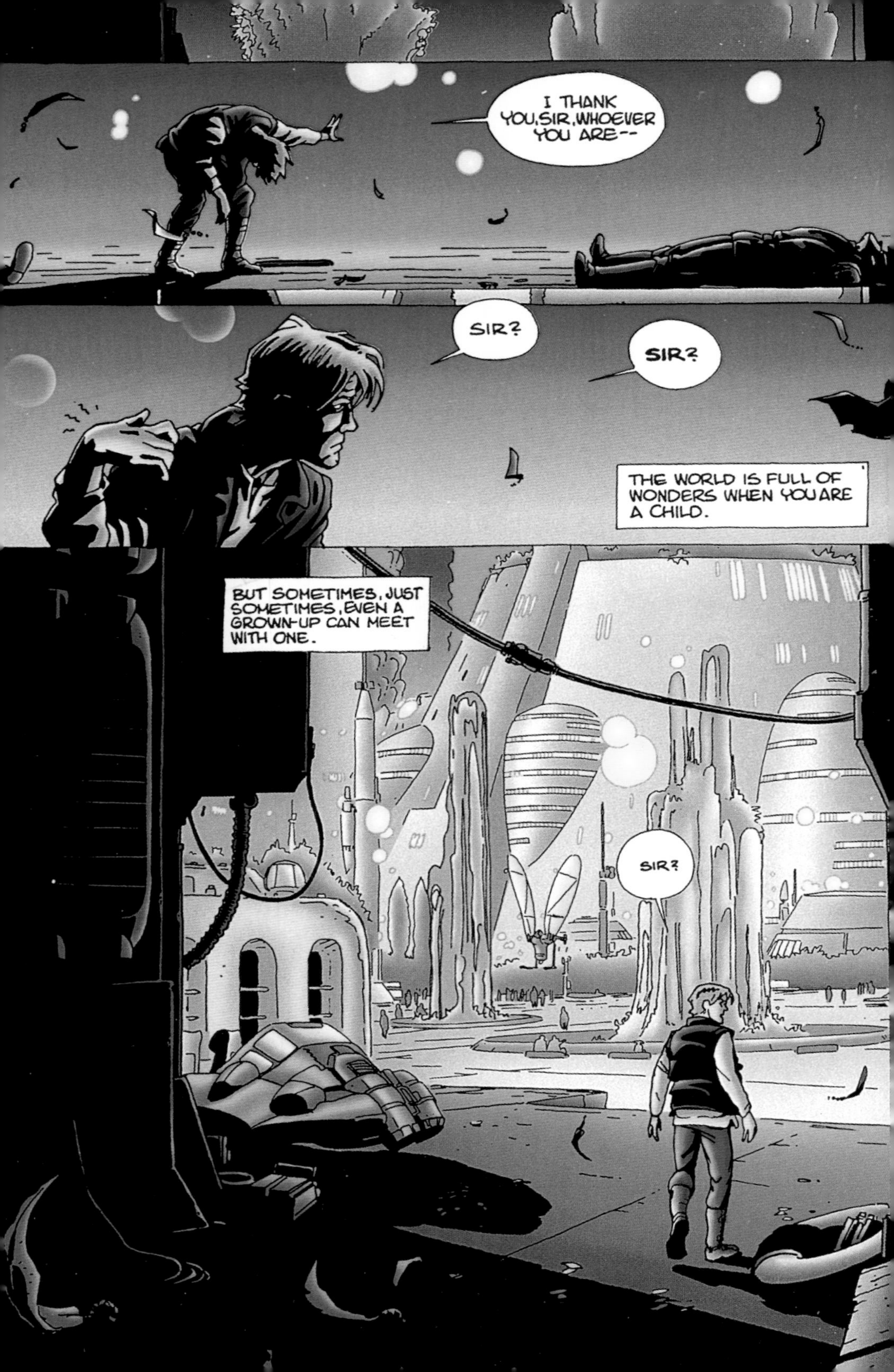
I THANK YOU, SIR, WHOEVER YOU ARE--
SIR?
SIR?
THE WORLD IS FULL OF WONDERS WHEN YOU ARE A CHILD.
BUT SOMETIMES, JUST SOMETIMES, EVEN A GROWN-UP CAN MEET WITH ONE.
SIR?

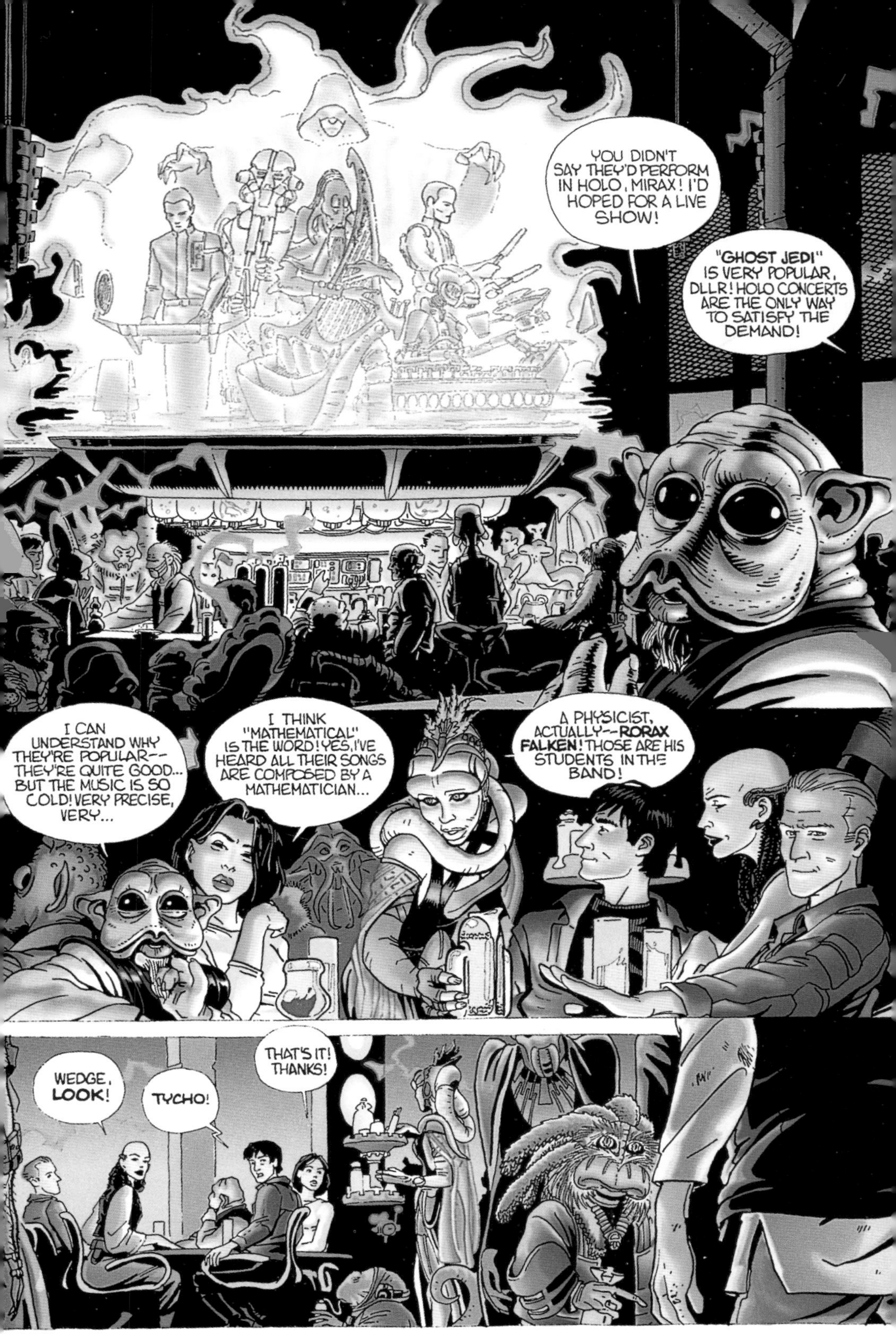
YOU DIDN'T SAY THEY'D PERFORM IN HOLO, MIRAX! I'D HOPED FOR A LIVE SHOW!
"GHOST JEDI" IS VERY POPULAR, DLLR! HOLO CONCERTS ARE THE ONLY WAY TO SATISFY THE DEMAND!
I CAN UNDERSTAND WHY THEY'RE POPULAR-- THEY'RE QUITE GOOD... BUT THE MUSIC IS SO COLD! VERY PRECISE, VERY...
I THINK "MATHEMATICAL" IS THE WORD! YES, I'VE HEARD ALL THEIR SONGS ARE COMPOSED BY A MATHEMATICIAN...
A PHYSICIST, ACTUALLY-- RORAX FALKEN! THOSE ARE HIS STUDENTS IN THE BAND!
WEDGE, LOOK!
TYCHO!
THAT'S IT! THANKS!

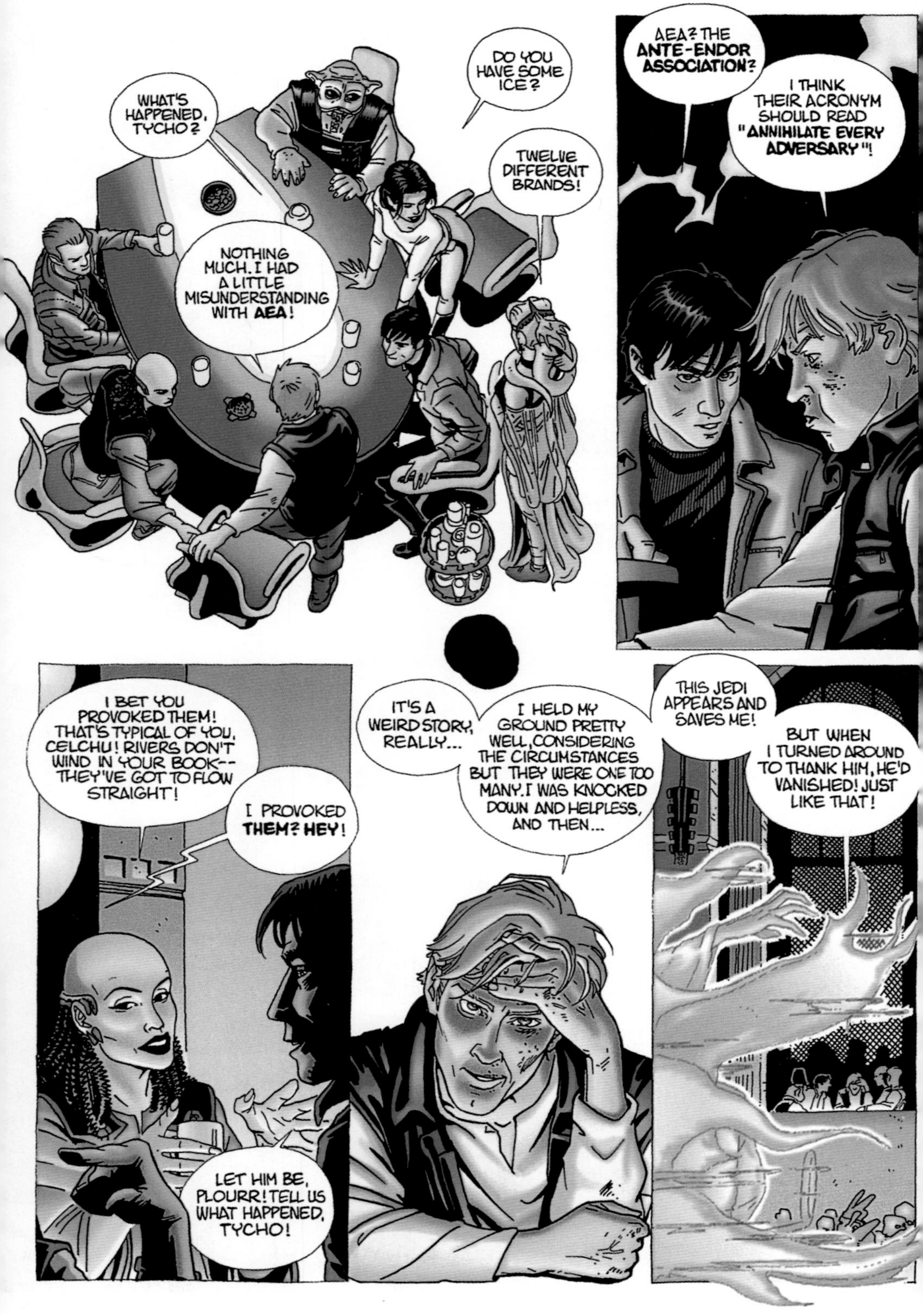

WHAT'S HAPPENED, TYCHO?
DO YOU HAVE SOME ICE?
TWELVE DIFFERENT BRANDS!
NOTHING MUCH. I HAD A LITTLE MISUNDERSTANDING WITH **AEA**!
AEA? THE **ANTE-ENDOR ASSOCIATION**?
I THINK THEIR ACRONYM SHOULD READ **"ANNIHILATE EVERY ADVERSARY"**!
I BET YOU PROVOKED THEM! THAT'S TYPICAL OF YOU, CELCHU! RIVERS DON'T WIND IN YOUR BOOK-- THEY'VE GOT TO FLOW STRAIGHT!
I PROVOKED **THEM? HEY**!
LET HIM BE, PLOURR! TELL US WHAT HAPPENED, TYCHO!
IT'S A WEIRD STORY, REALLY...
I HELD MY GROUND PRETTY WELL, CONSIDERING THE CIRCUMSTANCES BUT THEY WERE ONE TOO MANY. I WAS KNOCKED DOWN AND HELPLESS, AND THEN...
THIS JEDI APPEARS AND SAVES ME!
BUT WHEN I TURNED AROUND TO THANK HIM, HE'D VANISHED! JUST LIKE THAT!

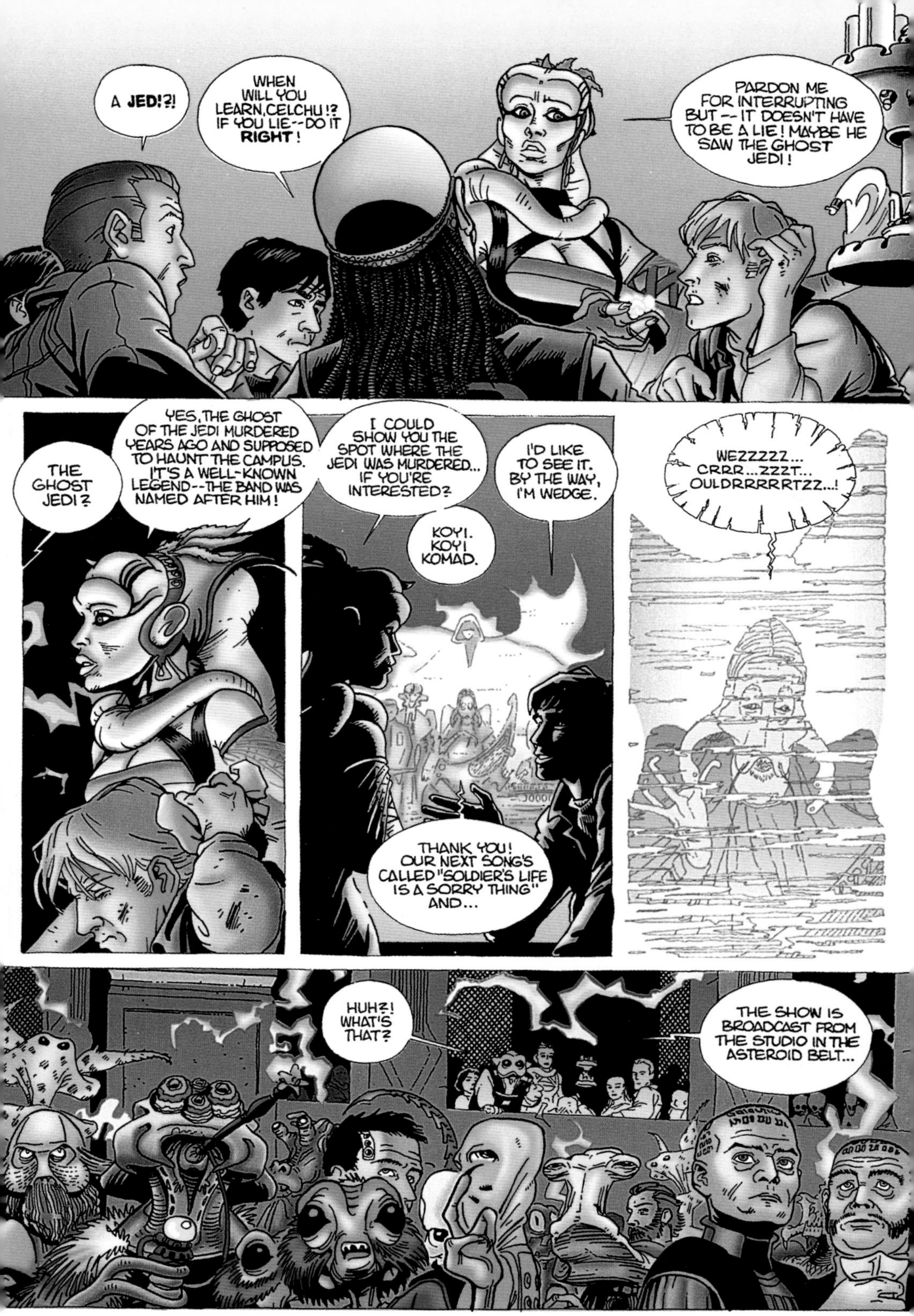
A JEDI!?!
WHEN WILL YOU LEARN, CELCHU!? IF YOU LIE--DO IT RIGHT!
PARDON ME FOR INTERRUPTING BUT -- IT DOESN'T HAVE TO BE A LIE! MAYBE HE SAW THE GHOST JEDI!
THE GHOST JEDI?
YES, THE GHOST OF THE JEDI MURDERED YEARS AGO AND SUPPOSED TO HAUNT THE CAMPUS. IT'S A WELL-KNOWN LEGEND--THE BAND WAS NAMED AFTER HIM!
I COULD SHOW YOU THE SPOT WHERE THE JEDI WAS MURDERED... IF YOU'RE INTERESTED?
I'D LIKE TO SEE IT. BY THE WAY, I'M WEDGE.
KOYI. KOYI KOMAD.
THANK YOU! OUR NEXT SONG'S CALLED "SOLDIER'S LIFE IS A SORRY THING" AND...
WEZZZZZ... CRRR...ZZZT... OULDRRRRRTZZ...!
HUH?! WHAT'S THAT?
THE SHOW IS BROADCAST FROM THE STUDIO IN THE ASTEROID BELT...

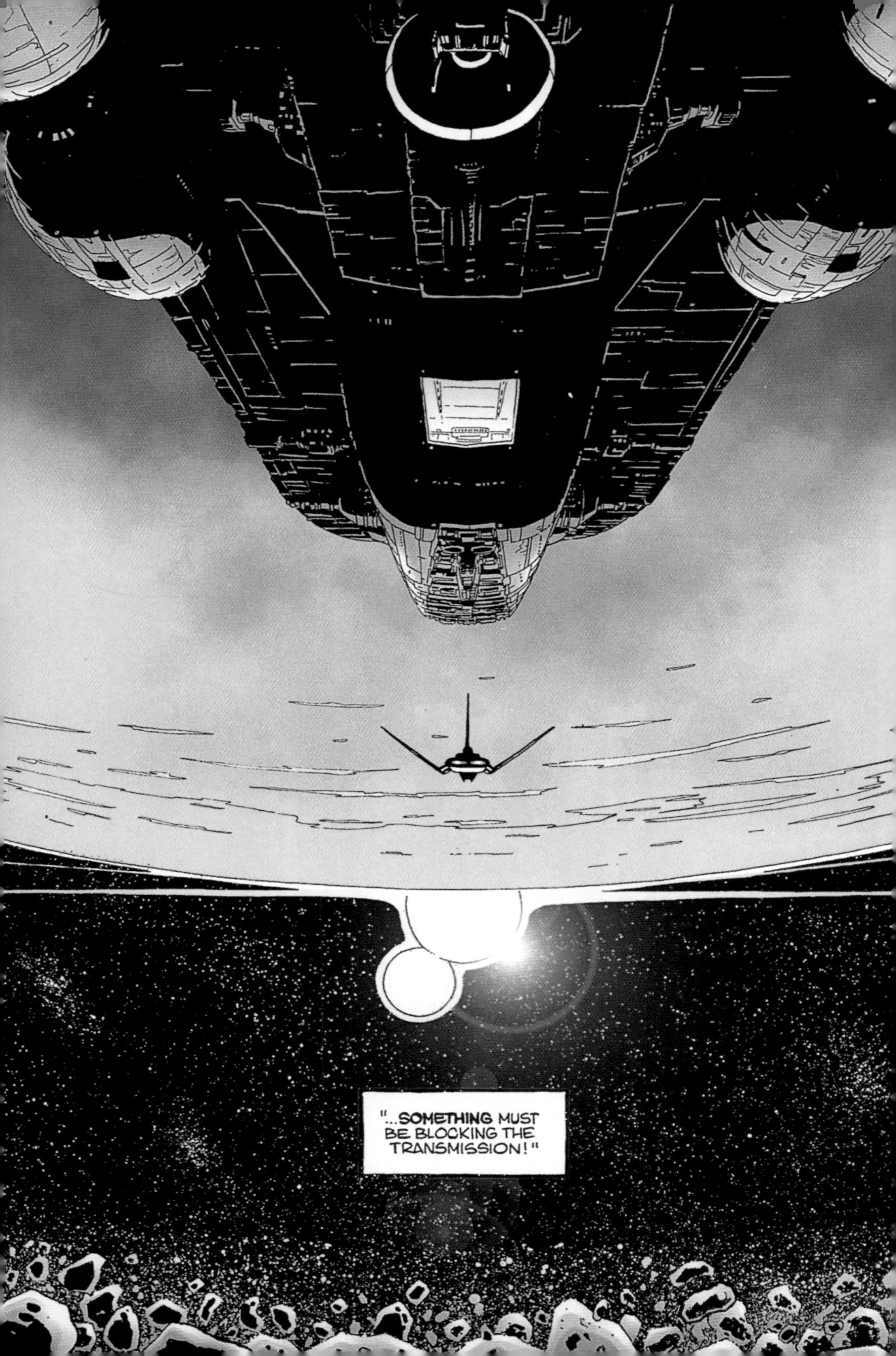
"...SOMETHING MUST BE BLOCKING THE TRANSMISSION!"

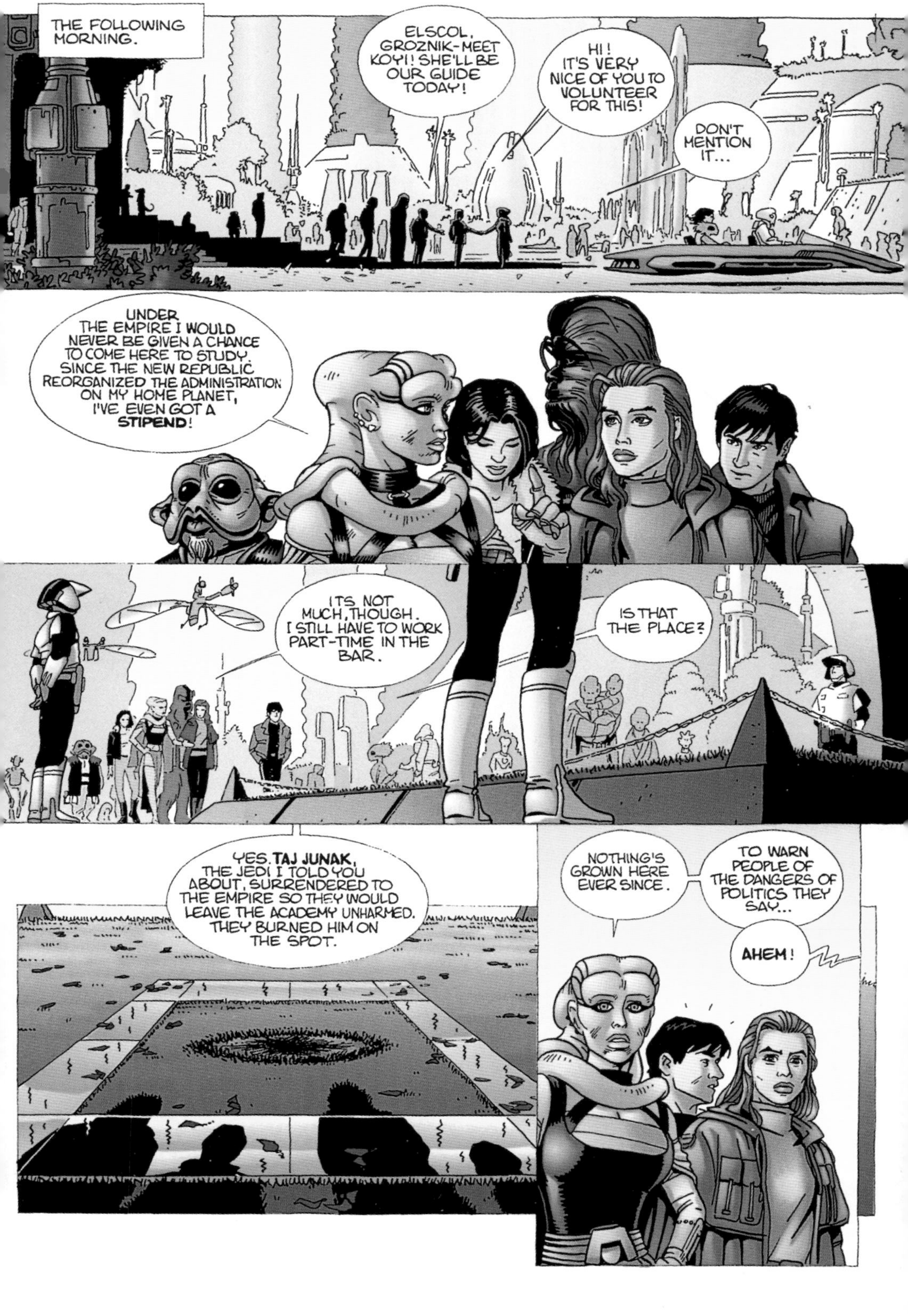
THE FOLLOWING MORNING.
ELSCOL, GROZNIK-MEET KOYI! SHE'LL BE OUR GUIDE TODAY!
HI! IT'S VERY NICE OF YOU TO VOLUNTEER FOR THIS!
DON'T MENTION IT...
UNDER THE EMPIRE I WOULD NEVER BE GIVEN A CHANCE TO COME HERE TO STUDY. SINCE THE NEW REPUBLIC REORGANIZED THE ADMINISTRATION ON MY HOME PLANET, I'VE EVEN GOT A **STIPEND**!
ITS NOT MUCH, THOUGH. I STILL HAVE TO WORK PART-TIME IN THE BAR.
IS THAT THE PLACE?
YES. **TAJ JUNAK**, THE JEDI I TOLD YOU ABOUT, SURRENDERED TO THE EMPIRE SO THEY WOULD LEAVE THE ACADEMY UNHARMED. THEY BURNED HIM ON THE SPOT.
NOTHING'S GROWN HERE EVER SINCE.
TO WARN PEOPLE OF THE DANGERS OF POLITICS THEY SAY...
AHEM!

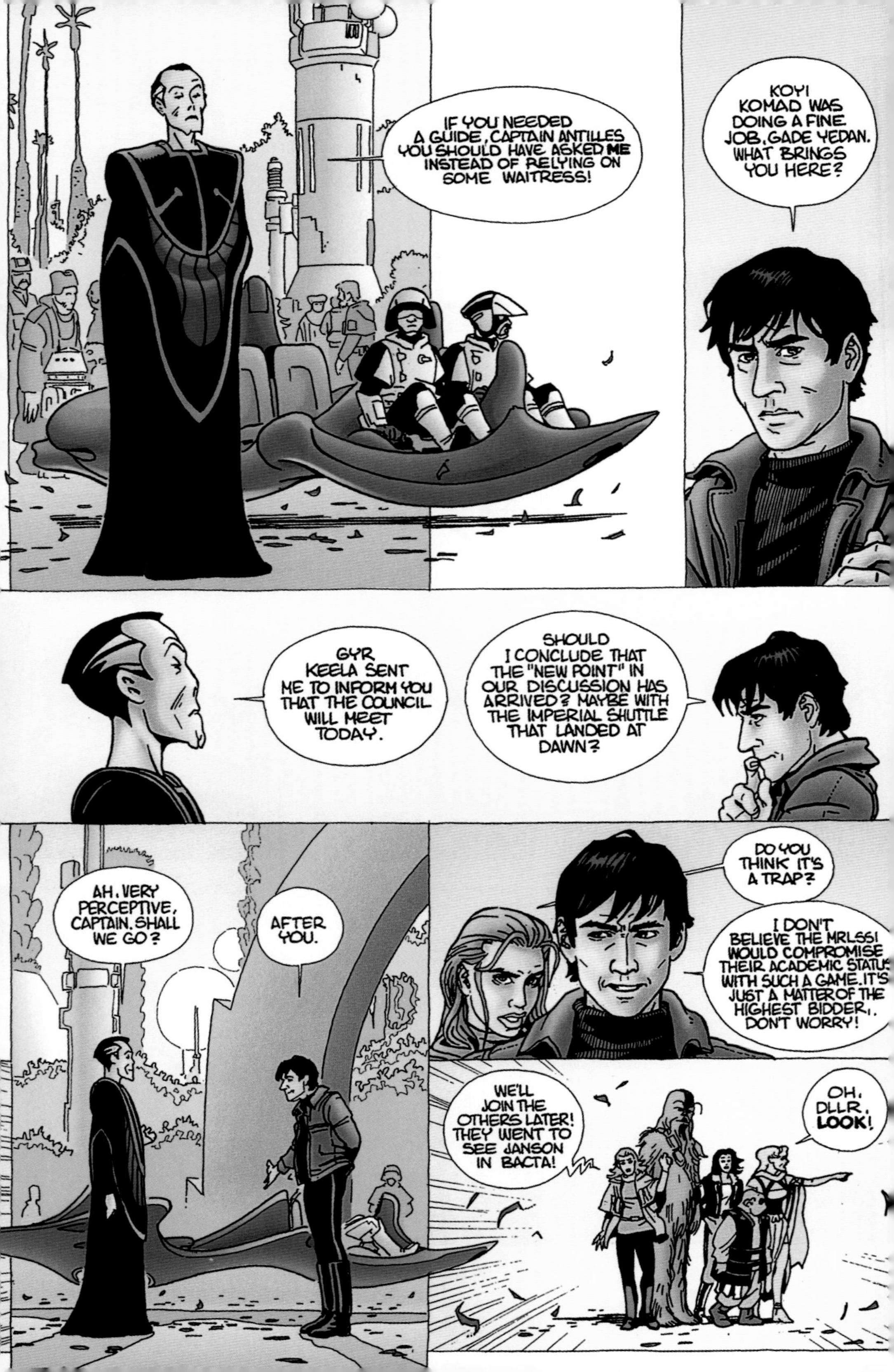
IF YOU NEEDED A GUIDE, CAPTAIN ANTILLES YOU SHOULD HAVE ASKED **ME** INSTEAD OF RELYING ON SOME WAITRESS!
KOYI KOMAD WAS DOING A FINE JOB, GADE YEDAN. WHAT BRINGS YOU HERE?
GYR KEELA SENT ME TO INFORM YOU THAT THE COUNCIL WILL MEET TODAY.
SHOULD I CONCLUDE THAT THE "NEW POINT" IN OUR DISCUSSION HAS ARRIVED? MAYBE WITH THE IMPERIAL SHUTTLE THAT LANDED AT DAWN?
AH, VERY PERCEPTIVE, CAPTAIN. SHALL WE GO?
AFTER YOU.
DO YOU THINK IT'S A TRAP?
I DON'T BELIEVE THE MRLSSI WOULD COMPROMISE THEIR ACADEMIC STATUS WITH SUCH A GAME. IT'S JUST A MATTER OF THE HIGHEST BIDDER... DON'T WORRY!
WE'LL JOIN THE OTHERS LATER! THEY WENT TO SEE JANSON IN BACTA!
OH, DLLR, **LOOK**!

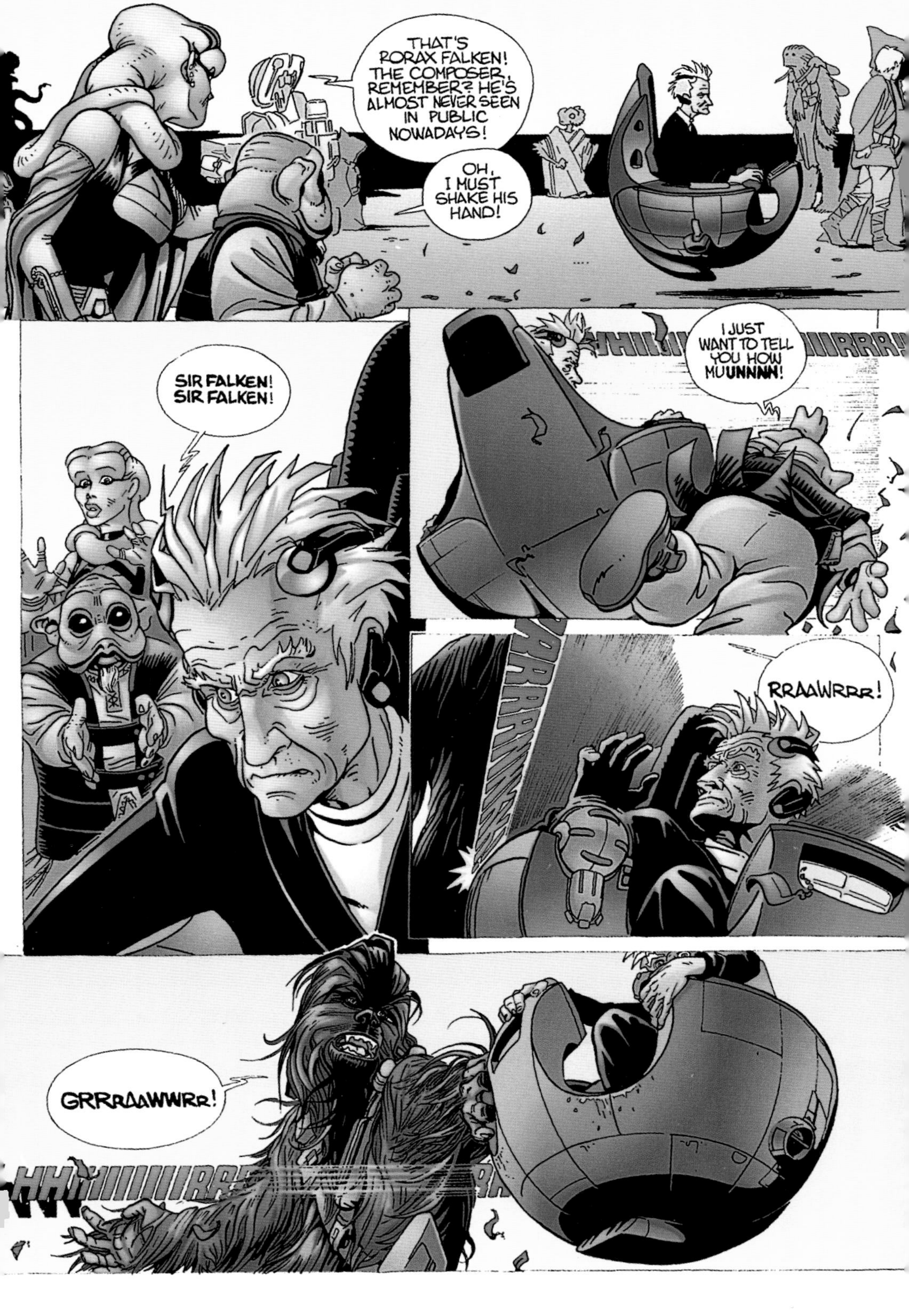
THAT'S RORAX FALKEN! THE COMPOSER, REMEMBER? HE'S ALMOST NEVER SEEN IN PUBLIC NOWADAYS!
OH, I MUST SHAKE HIS HAND!
SIR FALKEN! SIR FALKEN!
I JUST WANT TO TELL YOU HOW MUUNNNN!
RRAAWRRR!
GRRRAAWWRR!

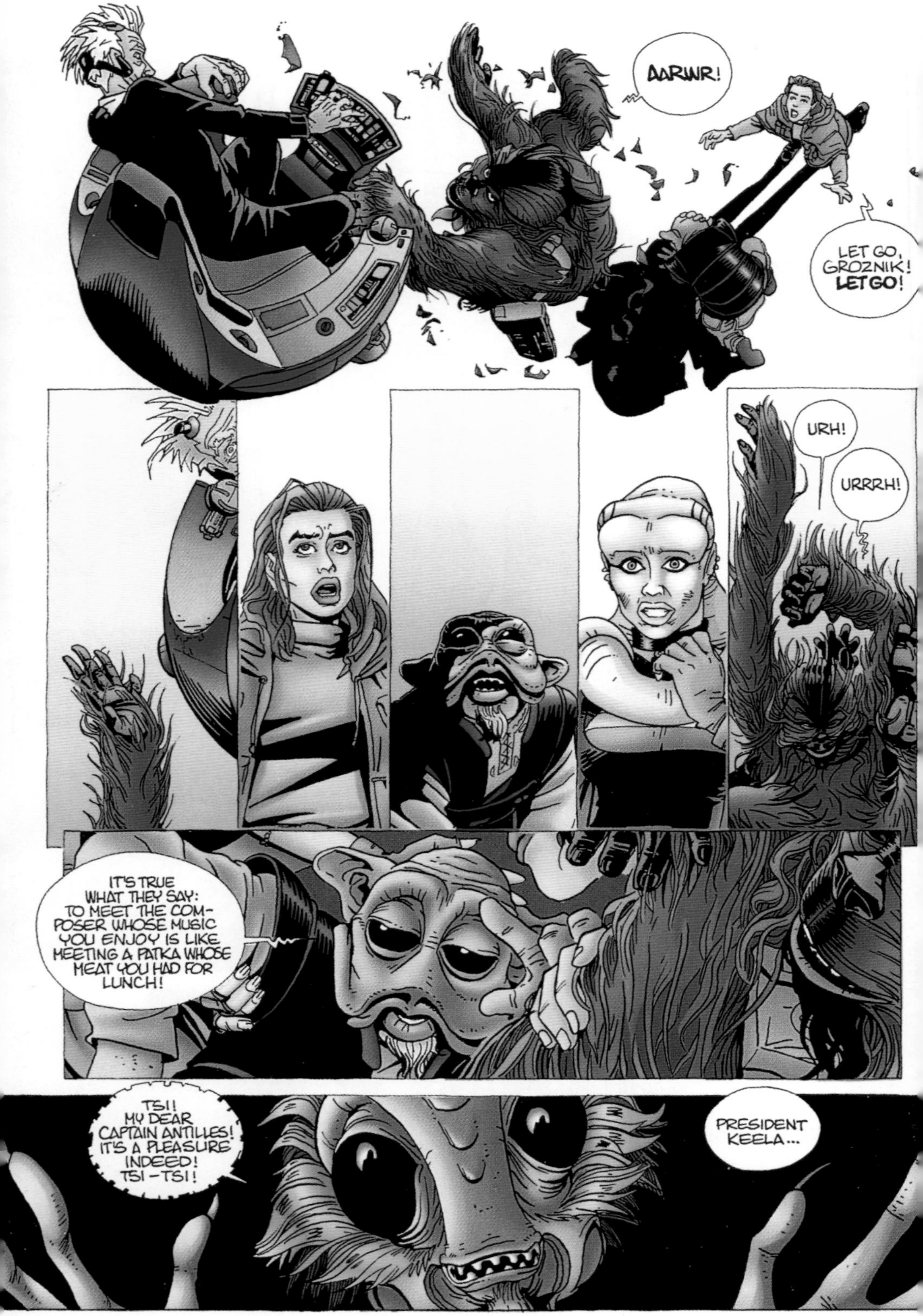
AARWR!
LET GO, GROZNIK! LET GO!
URH!
URRRH!
IT'S TRUE WHAT THEY SAY: TO MEET THE COMPOSER WHOSE MUSIC YOU ENJOY IS LIKE MEETING A PATKA WHOSE MEAT YOU HAD FOR LUNCH!
TSI! MY DEAR CAPTAIN ANTILLES! IT'S A PLEASURE INDEED! TSI-TSI!
PRESIDENT KEELA...

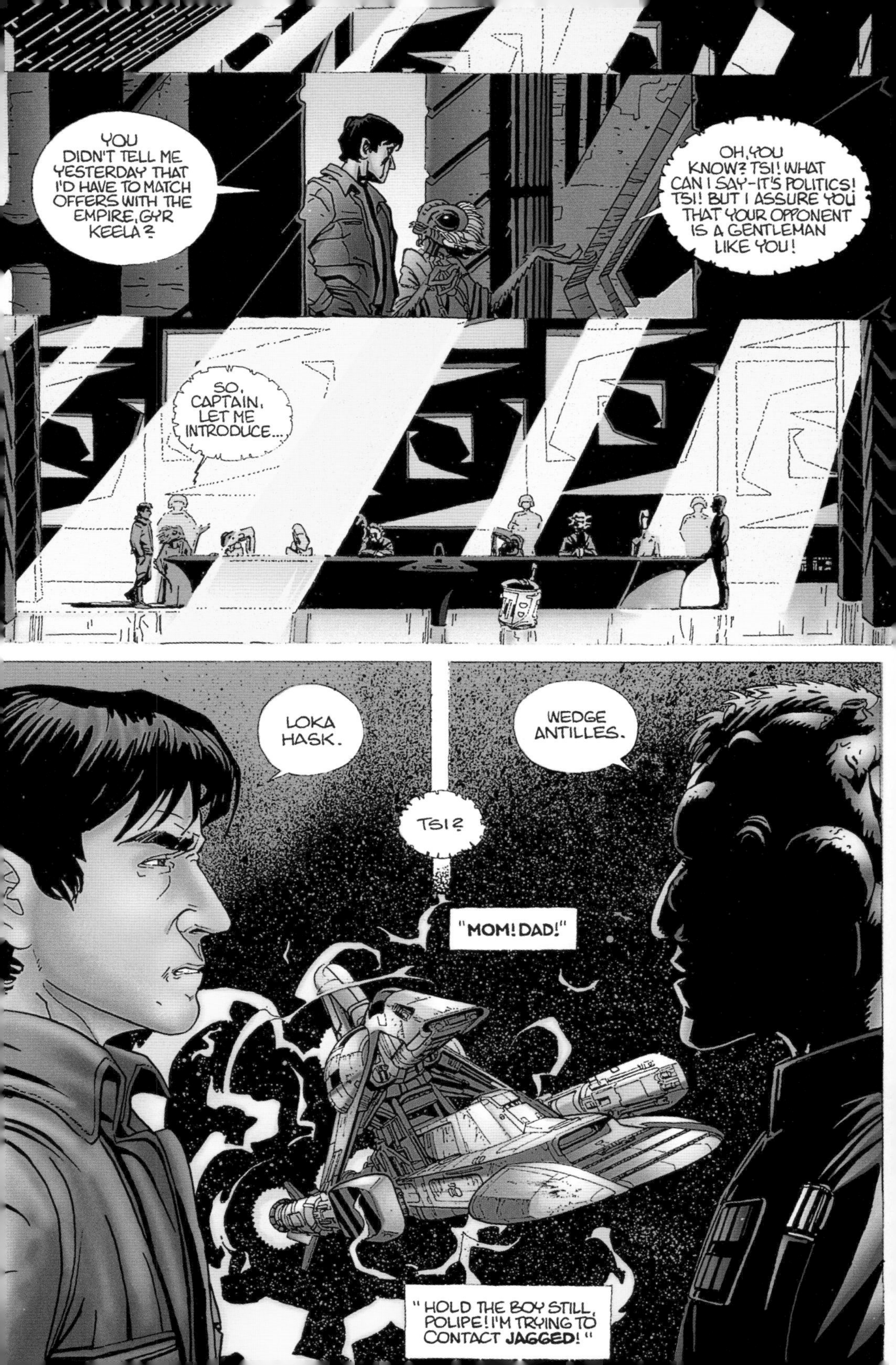
YOU DIDN'T TELL ME YESTERDAY THAT I'D HAVE TO MATCH OFFERS WITH THE EMPIRE, GYR KEELA?
OH, YOU KNOW? TSI! WHAT CAN I SAY--IT'S POLITICS! TSI! BUT I ASSURE YOU THAT YOUR OPPONENT IS A GENTLEMAN LIKE YOU!
SO, CAPTAIN, LET ME INTRODUCE...
LOKA HASK.
WEDGE ANTILLES.
TSI?
"MOM! DAD!"
"HOLD THE BOY STILL, POLIPE! I'M TRYING TO CONTACT JAGGED!"

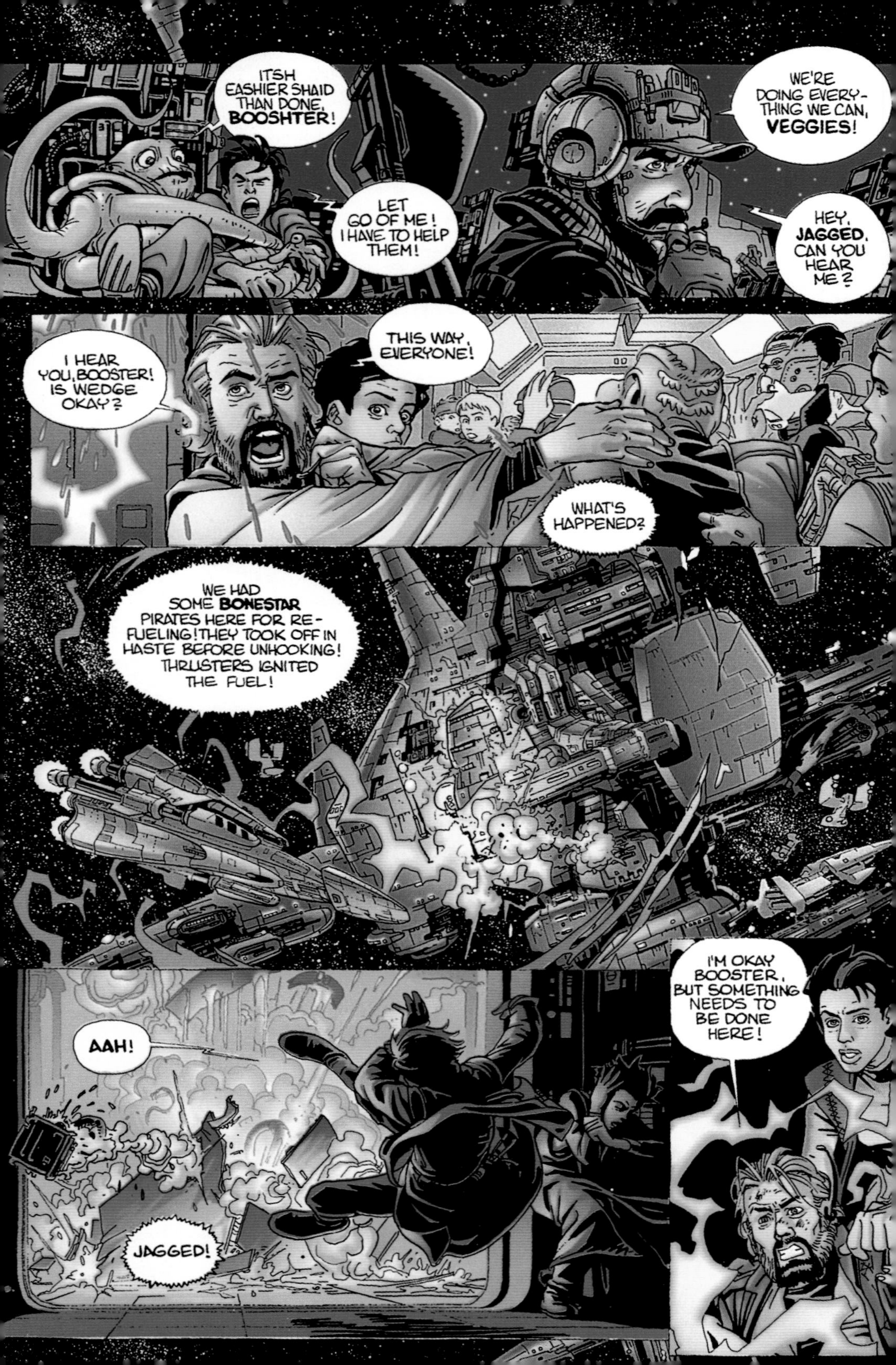
ITSH EASHIER SHAID THAN DONE, BOOSHTER!
LET GO OF ME! I HAVE TO HELP THEM!
WE'RE DOING EVERY-THING WE CAN, VEGGIES!
HEY, JAGGED, CAN YOU HEAR ME?
I HEAR YOU, BOOSTER! IS WEDGE OKAY?
THIS WAY, EVERYONE!
WHAT'S HAPPENED?
WE HAD SOME BONESTAR PIRATES HERE FOR RE-FUELING! THEY TOOK OFF IN HASTE BEFORE UNHOOKING! THRUSTERS IGNITED THE FUEL!
AAH!
JAGGED!
I'M OKAY BOOSTER, BUT SOMETHING NEEDS TO BE DONE HERE!

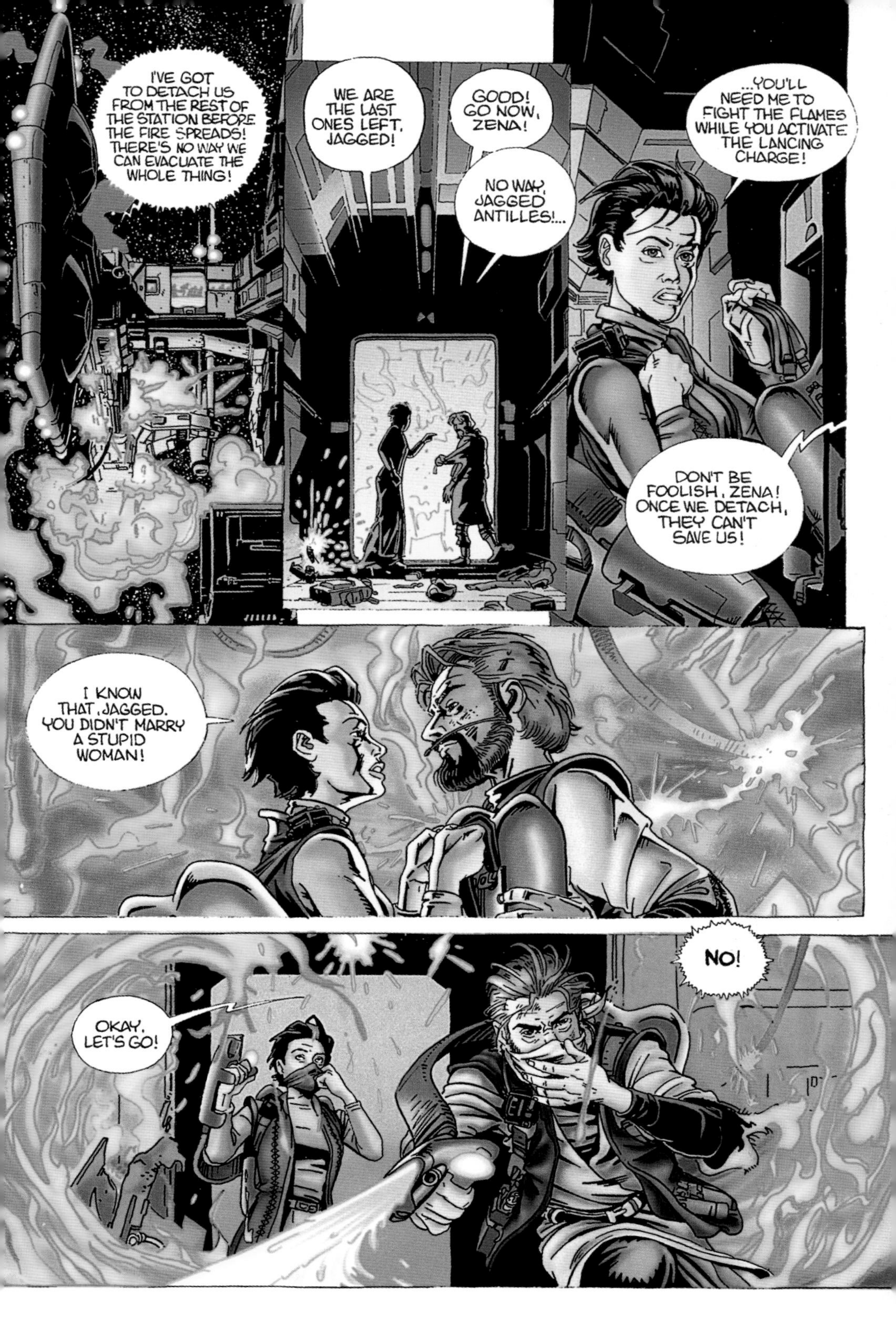
I'VE GOT TO DETACH US FROM THE REST OF THE STATION BEFORE THE FIRE SPREADS! THERE'S NO WAY WE CAN EVACUATE THE WHOLE THING!
WE ARE THE LAST ONES LEFT, JAGGED!
GOOD! GO NOW, ZENA!
NO WAY, JAGGED ANTILLES!...
...YOU'LL NEED ME TO FIGHT THE FLAMES WHILE YOU ACTIVATE THE LANCING CHARGE!
DON'T BE FOOLISH, ZENA! ONCE WE DETACH, THEY CAN'T SAVE US!
I KNOW THAT, JAGGED. YOU DIDN'T MARRY A STUPID WOMAN!
NO!
OKAY, LET'S GO!

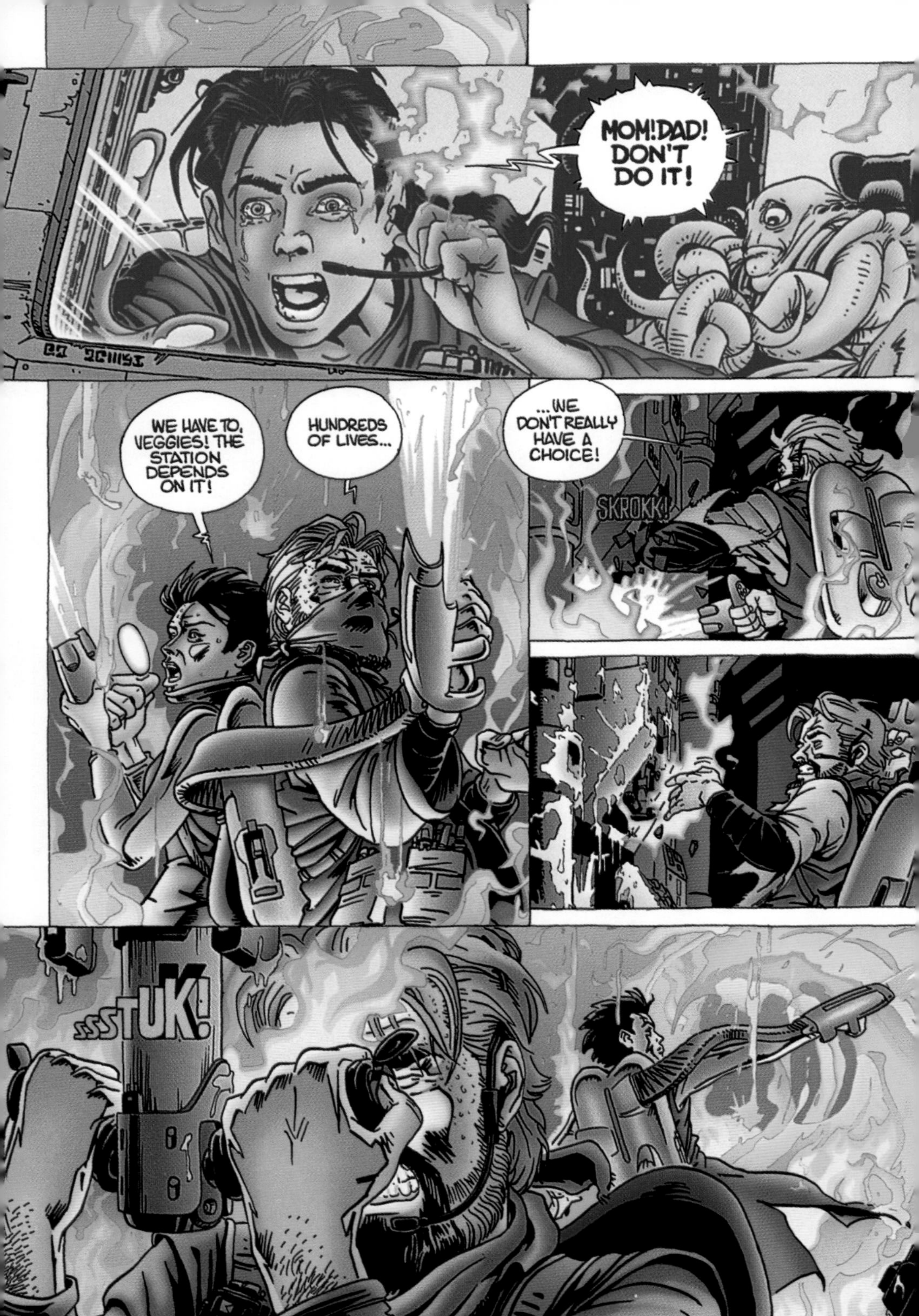
MOM! DAD! DON'T DO IT!
WE HAVE TO, VEGGIES! THE STATION DEPENDS ON IT!
HUNDREDS OF LIVES...
...WE DON'T REALLY HAVE A CHOICE!
SKROKK!
SSSTUK!

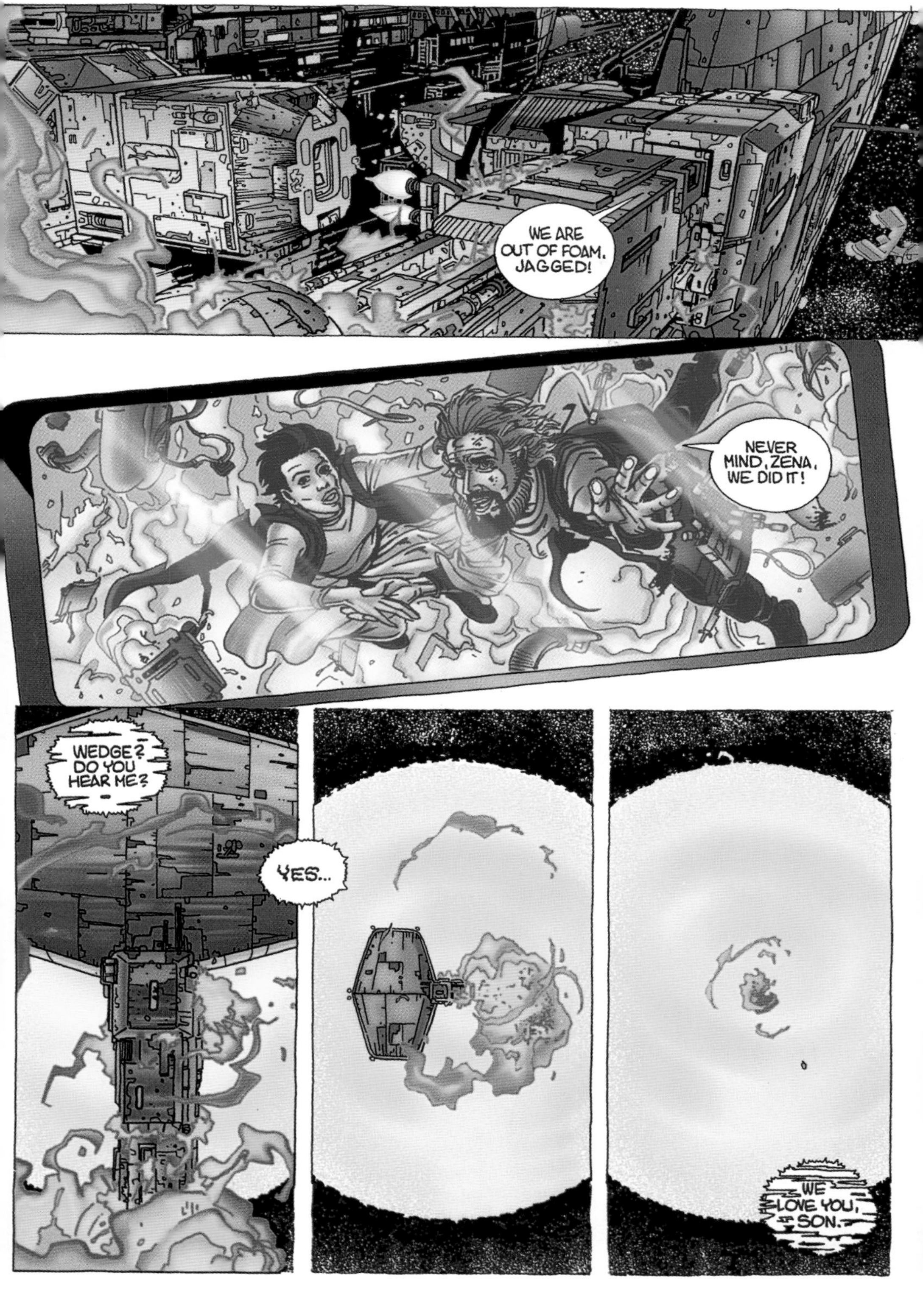
WE ARE OUT OF FOAM. JAGGED!
NEVER MIND, ZENA, WE DID IT!
WEDGE? DO YOU HEAR ME?
YES...
WE LOVE YOU, SON.

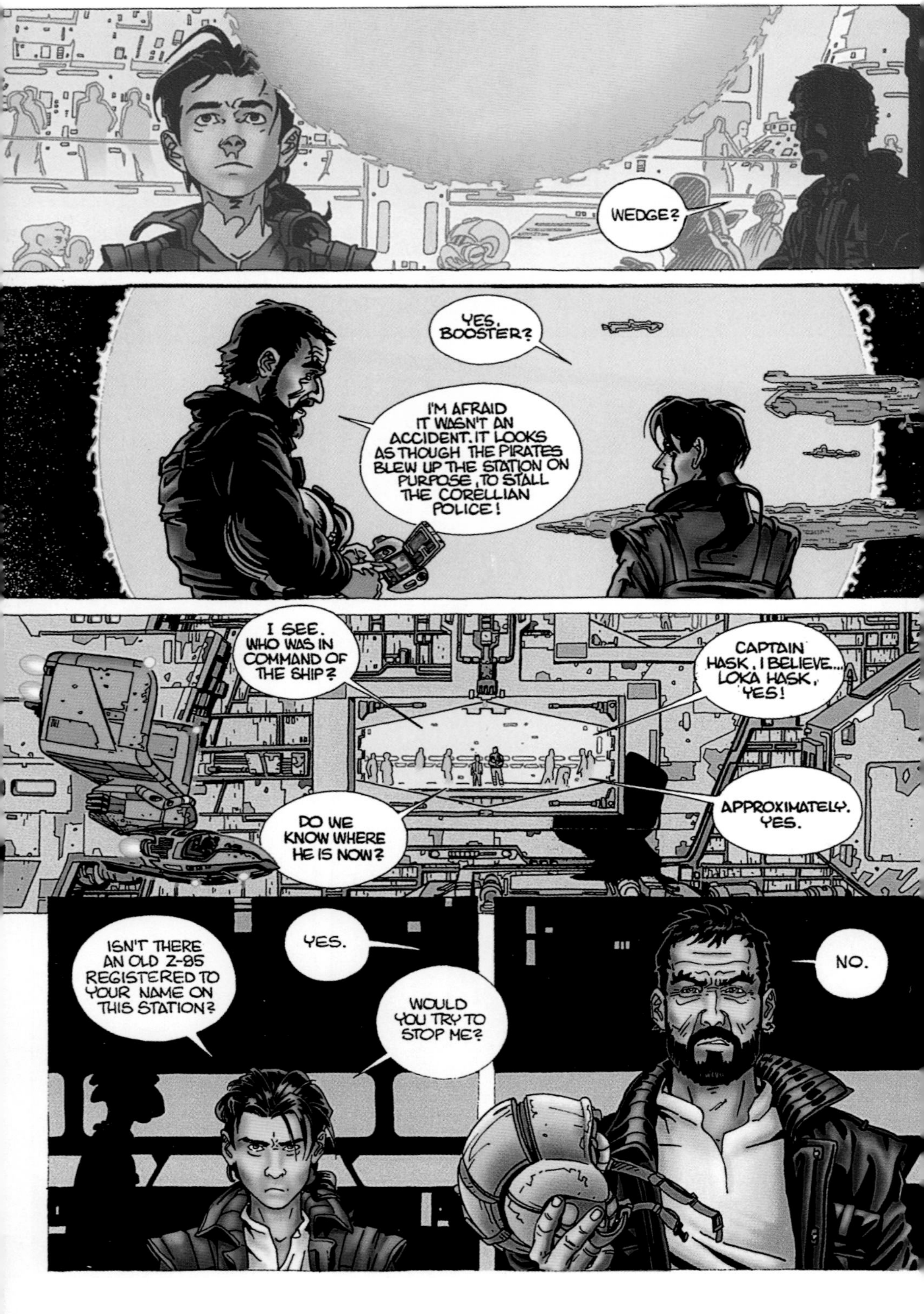
WEDGE?
YES, BOOSTER?
I'M AFRAID IT WASN'T AN ACCIDENT. IT LOOKS AS THOUGH THE PIRATES BLEW UP THE STATION ON PURPOSE, TO STALL THE CORELLIAN POLICE!
I SEE. WHO WAS IN COMMAND OF THE SHIP?
CAPTAIN HASK, I BELIEVE... LOKA HASK, YES!
DO WE KNOW WHERE HE IS NOW?
APPROXIMATELY. YES.
ISN'T THERE AN OLD Z-95 REGISTERED TO YOUR NAME ON THIS STATION?
YES.
WOULD YOU TRY TO STOP ME?
NO.

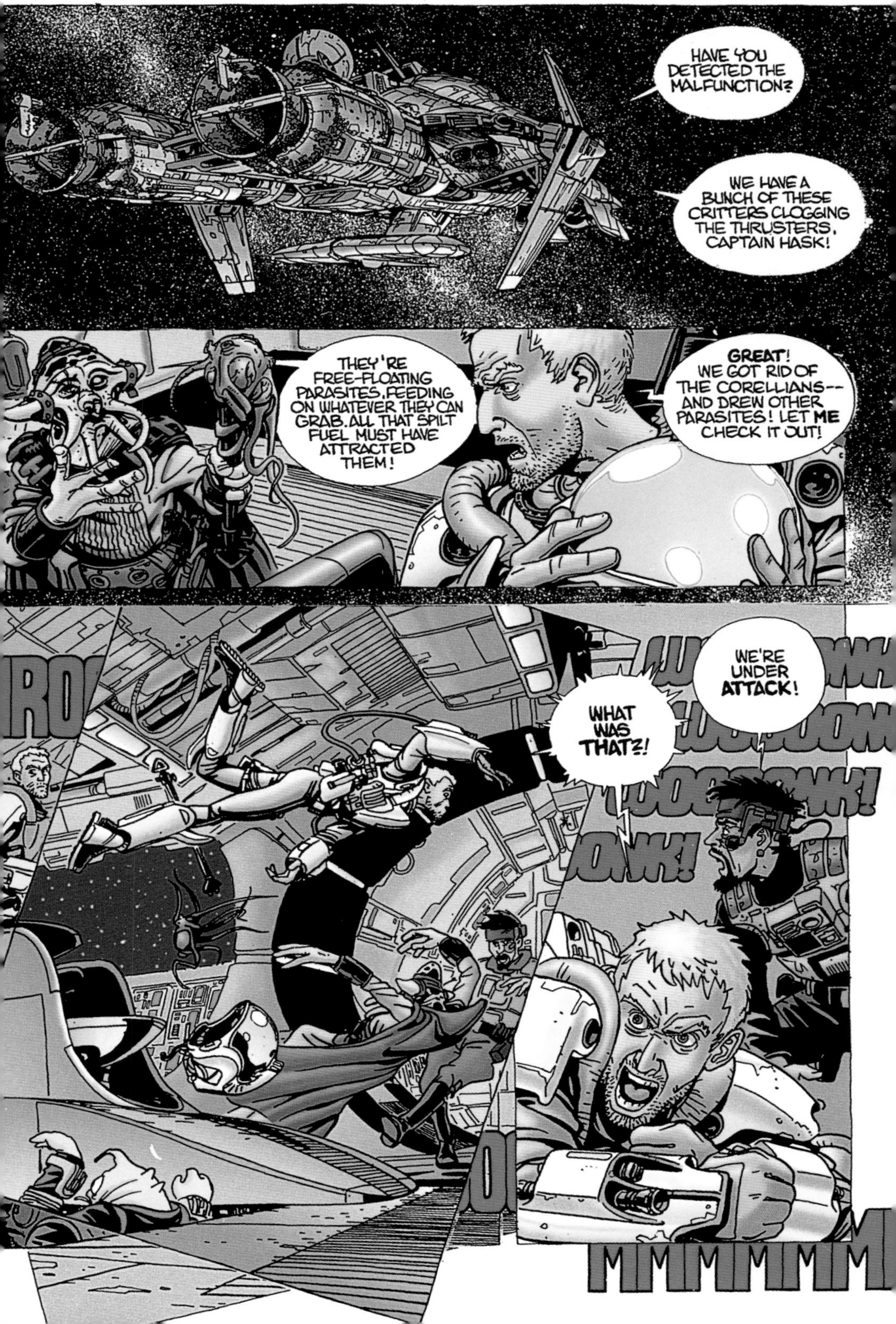
HAVE YOU DETECTED THE MALFUNCTION?
WE HAVE A BUNCH OF THESE CRITTERS CLOGGING THE THRUSTERS, CAPTAIN HASK!
THEY'RE FREE-FLOATING PARASITES, FEEDING ON WHATEVER THEY CAN GRAB. ALL THAT SPILT FUEL MUST HAVE ATTRACTED THEM!
GREAT! WE GOT RID OF THE CORELLIANS-- AND DREW OTHER PARASITES! LET ME CHECK IT OUT!
WE'RE UNDER ATTACK!
WHAT WAS THAT?!

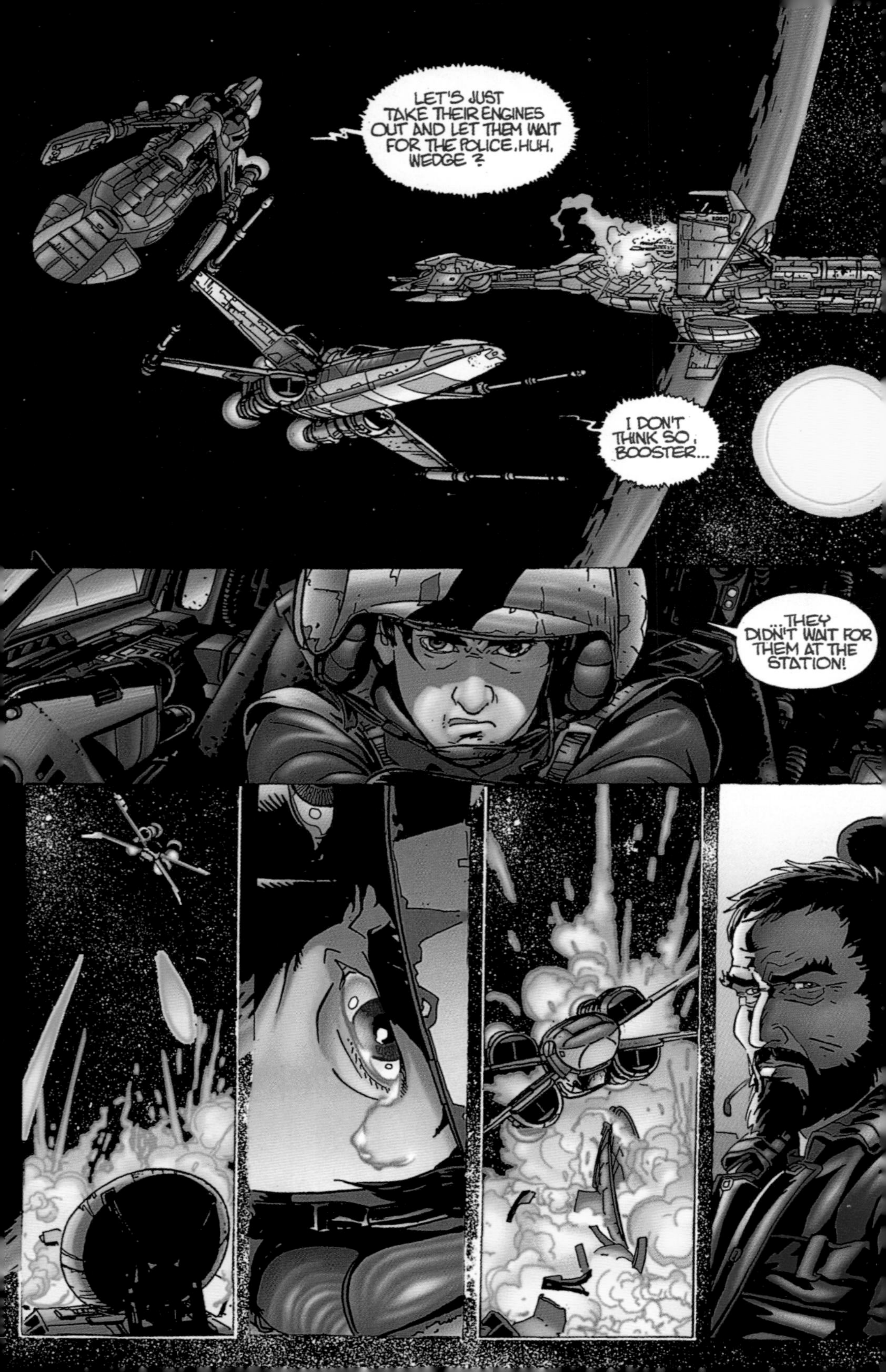
LET'S JUST TAKE THEIR ENGINES OUT AND LET THEM WAIT FOR THE POLICE, HUH, WEDGE ?
I DON'T THINK SO, BOOSTER...
...THEY DIDN'T WAIT FOR THEM AT THE STATION!

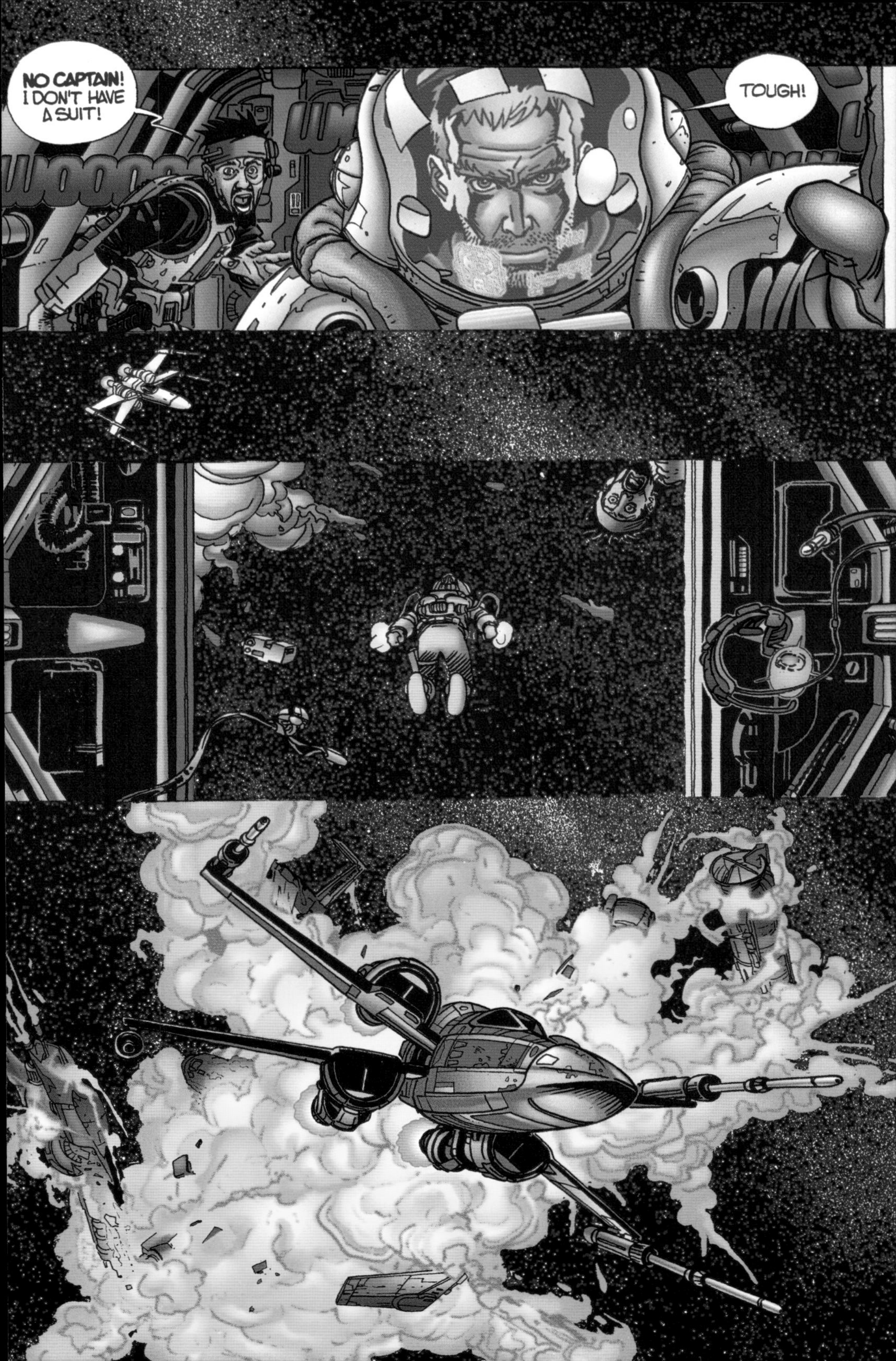
NO CAPTAIN! I DON'T HAVE A SUIT!
TOUGH!

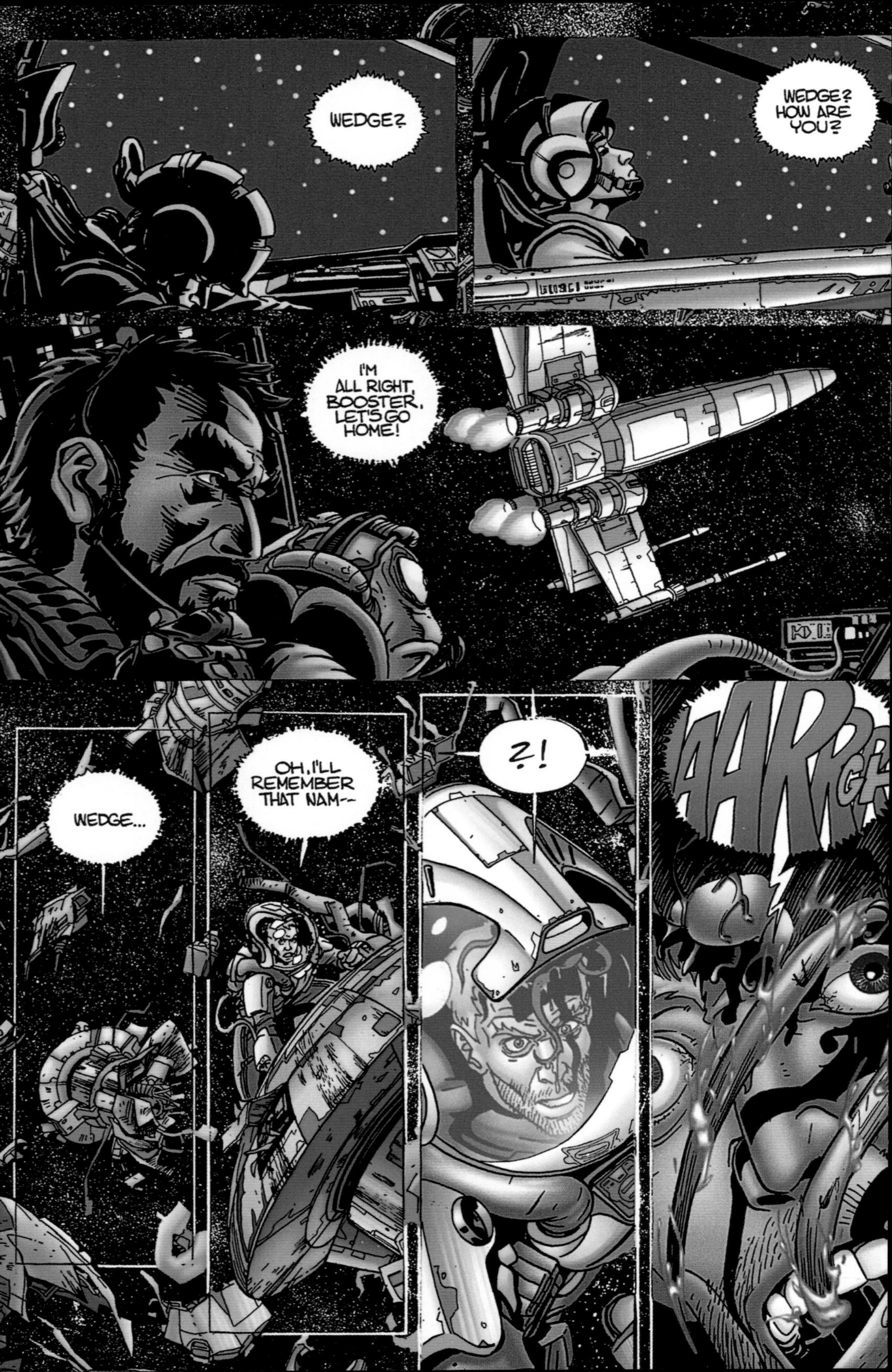

WEDGE?
WEDGE? HOW ARE YOU?
I'M ALL RIGHT, BOOSTER. LET'S GO HOME!
WEDGE...
OH, I'LL REMEMBER THAT NAM--
?!
AARRGH

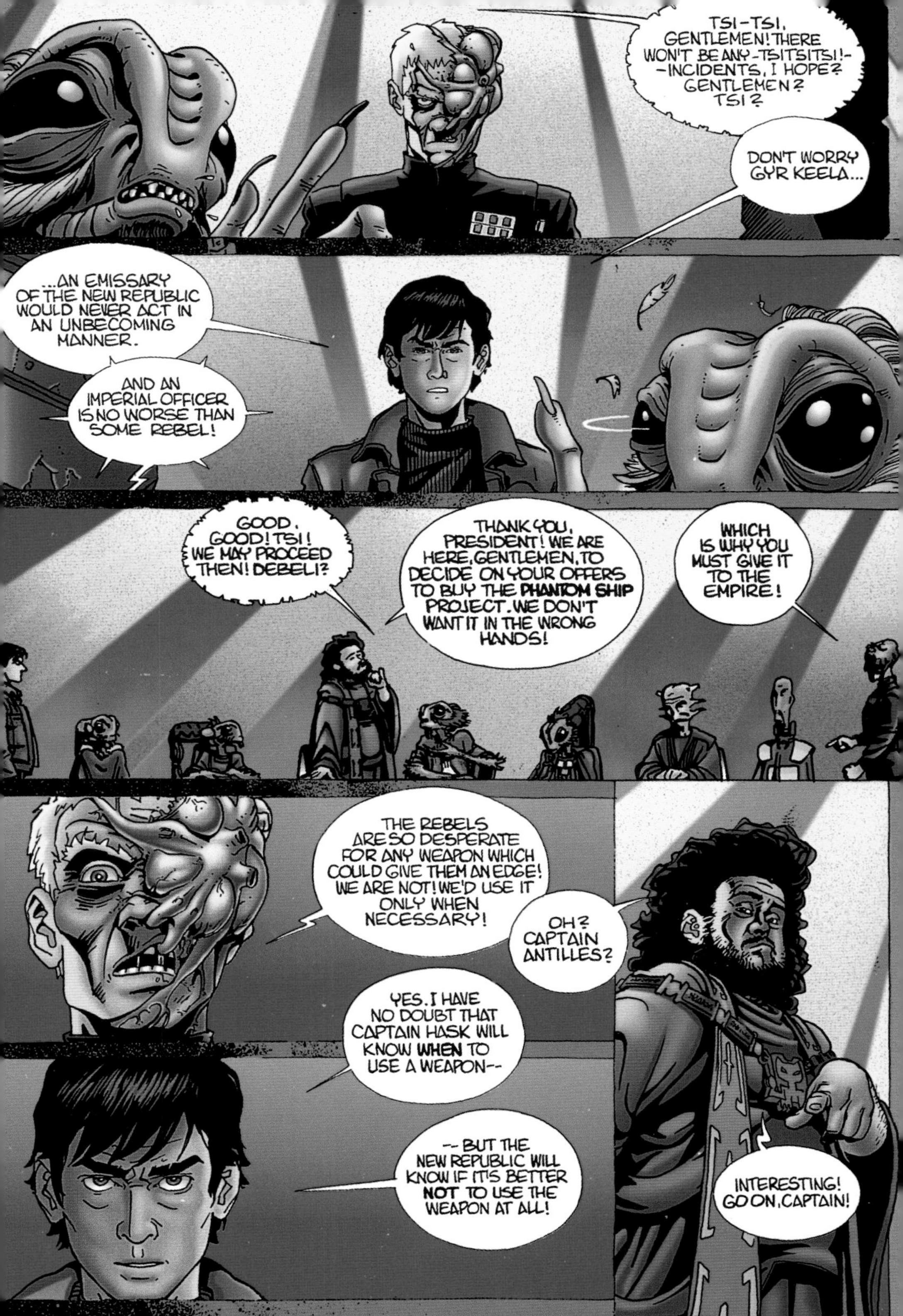
TSI-TSI, GENTLEMEN! THERE WON'T BE ANY-TSITSITSI!- -INCIDENTS, I HOPE? GENTLEMEN? TSI?
DON'T WORRY GYR KEELA...
...AN EMISSARY OF THE NEW REPUBLIC WOULD NEVER ACT IN AN UNBECOMING MANNER.
AND AN IMPERIAL OFFICER IS NO WORSE THAN SOME REBEL!
GOOD. GOOD! TSI! WE MAY PROCEED THEN! DEBELI?
THANK YOU, PRESIDENT! WE ARE HERE, GENTLEMEN, TO DECIDE ON YOUR OFFERS TO BUY THE PHANTOM SHIP PROJECT. WE DON'T WANT IT IN THE WRONG HANDS!
WHICH IS WHY YOU MUST GIVE IT TO THE EMPIRE!
THE REBELS ARE SO DESPERATE FOR ANY WEAPON WHICH COULD GIVE THEM AN EDGE! WE ARE NOT! WE'D USE IT ONLY WHEN NECESSARY!
OH? CAPTAIN ANTILLES?
YES. I HAVE NO DOUBT THAT CAPTAIN HASK WILL KNOW WHEN TO USE A WEAPON--
--BUT THE NEW REPUBLIC WILL KNOW IF IT'S BETTER NOT TO USE THE WEAPON AT ALL!
INTERESTING! GO ON, CAPTAIN!

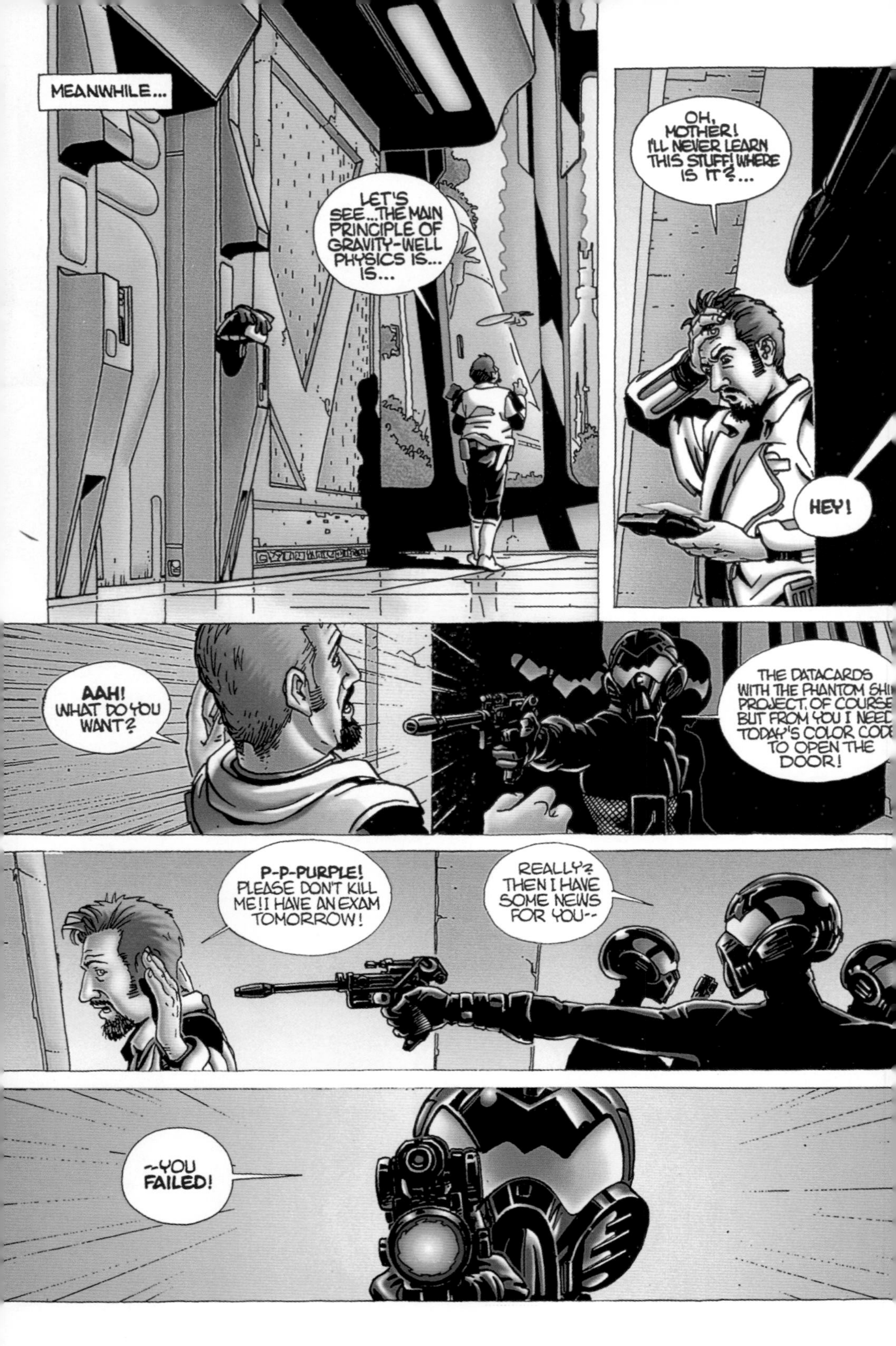
MEANWHILE...
LET'S SEE...THE MAIN PRINCIPLE OF GRAVITY-WELL PHYSICS IS... IS...
OH, MOTHER! I'LL NEVER LEARN THIS STUFF! WHERE IS IT?...
HEY!
AAH! WHAT DO YOU WANT?
THE DATACARDS WITH THE PHANTOM SHI PROJECT, OF COURSE BUT FROM YOU I NEED TODAY'S COLOR CODE TO OPEN THE DOOR!
P-P-PURPLE! PLEASE DON'T KILL ME! I HAVE AN EXAM TOMORROW!
REALLY? THEN I HAVE SOME NEWS FOR YOU--
--YOU FAILED!

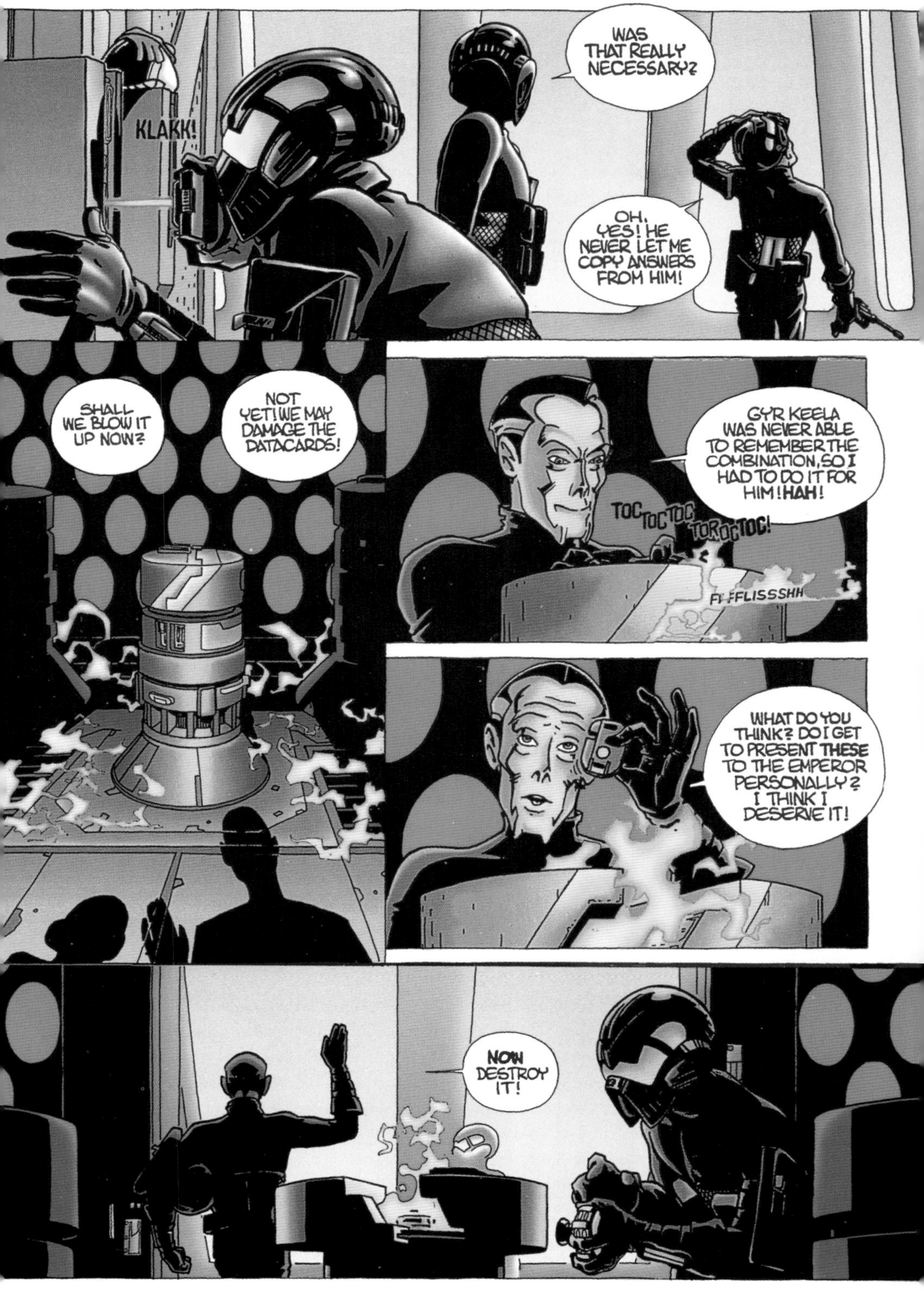
KLAKK!
WAS THAT REALLY NECESSARY?
OH, YES! HE NEVER LET ME COPY ANSWERS FROM HIM!
SHALL WE BLOW IT UP NOW?
NOT YET! WE MAY DAMAGE THE DATACARDS!
GYR KEELA WAS NEVER ABLE TO REMEMBER THE COMBINATION, SO I HAD TO DO IT FOR HIM! HAH!
TOC TOC TOC TOROC TOC!
FFFFLISSSHH
WHAT DO YOU THINK? DO I GET TO PRESENT THESE TO THE EMPEROR PERSONALLY? I THINK I DESERVE IT!
NOW DESTROY IT!

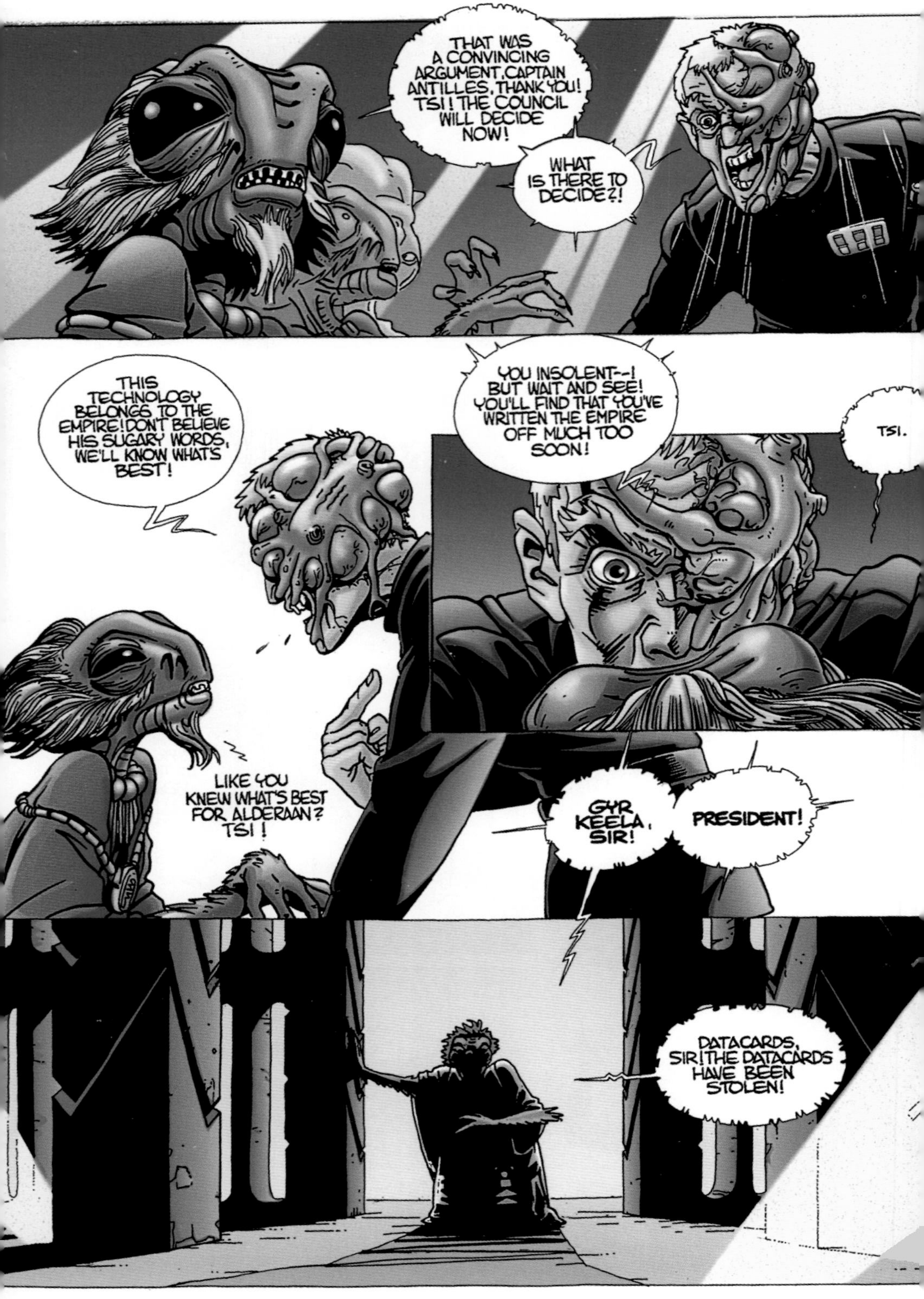
THAT WAS A CONVINCING ARGUMENT, CAPTAIN ANTILLES, THANK YOU! TSI! THE COUNCIL WILL DECIDE NOW!
WHAT IS THERE TO DECIDE?!
THIS TECHNOLOGY BELONGS TO THE EMPIRE! DON'T BELIEVE HIS SUGARY WORDS, WE'LL KNOW WHAT'S BEST!
YOU INSOLENT--! BUT WAIT AND SEE! YOU'LL FIND THAT YOU'VE WRITTEN THE EMPIRE OFF MUCH TOO SOON!
TSI.
LIKE YOU KNEW WHAT'S BEST FOR ALDERAAN? TSI!
GYR KEELA, SIR!
PRESIDENT!
DATACARDS, SIR! THE DATACARDS HAVE BEEN STOLEN!

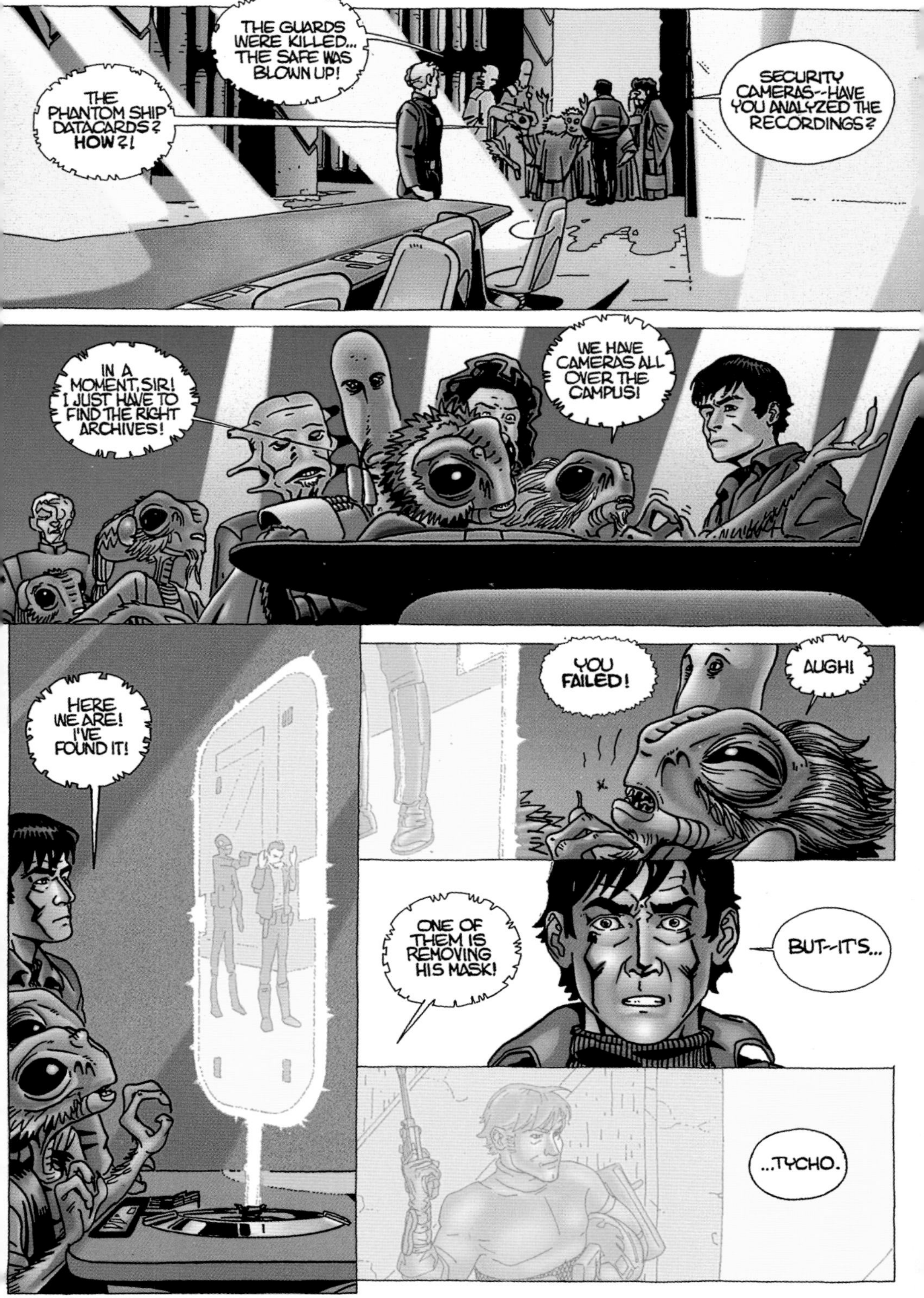

THE PHANTOM SHIP DATACARDS? HOW?!
THE GUARDS WERE KILLED... THE SAFE WAS BLOWN UP!
SECURITY CAMERAS--HAVE YOU ANALYZED THE RECORDINGS?
IN A MOMENT, SIR! I JUST HAVE TO FIND THE RIGHT ARCHIVES!
WE HAVE CAMERAS ALL OVER THE CAMPUS!
HERE WE ARE! I'VE FOUND IT!
YOU FAILED!
AUGH!
ONE OF THEM IS REMOVING HIS MASK!
BUT--IT'S...
...TYCHO.

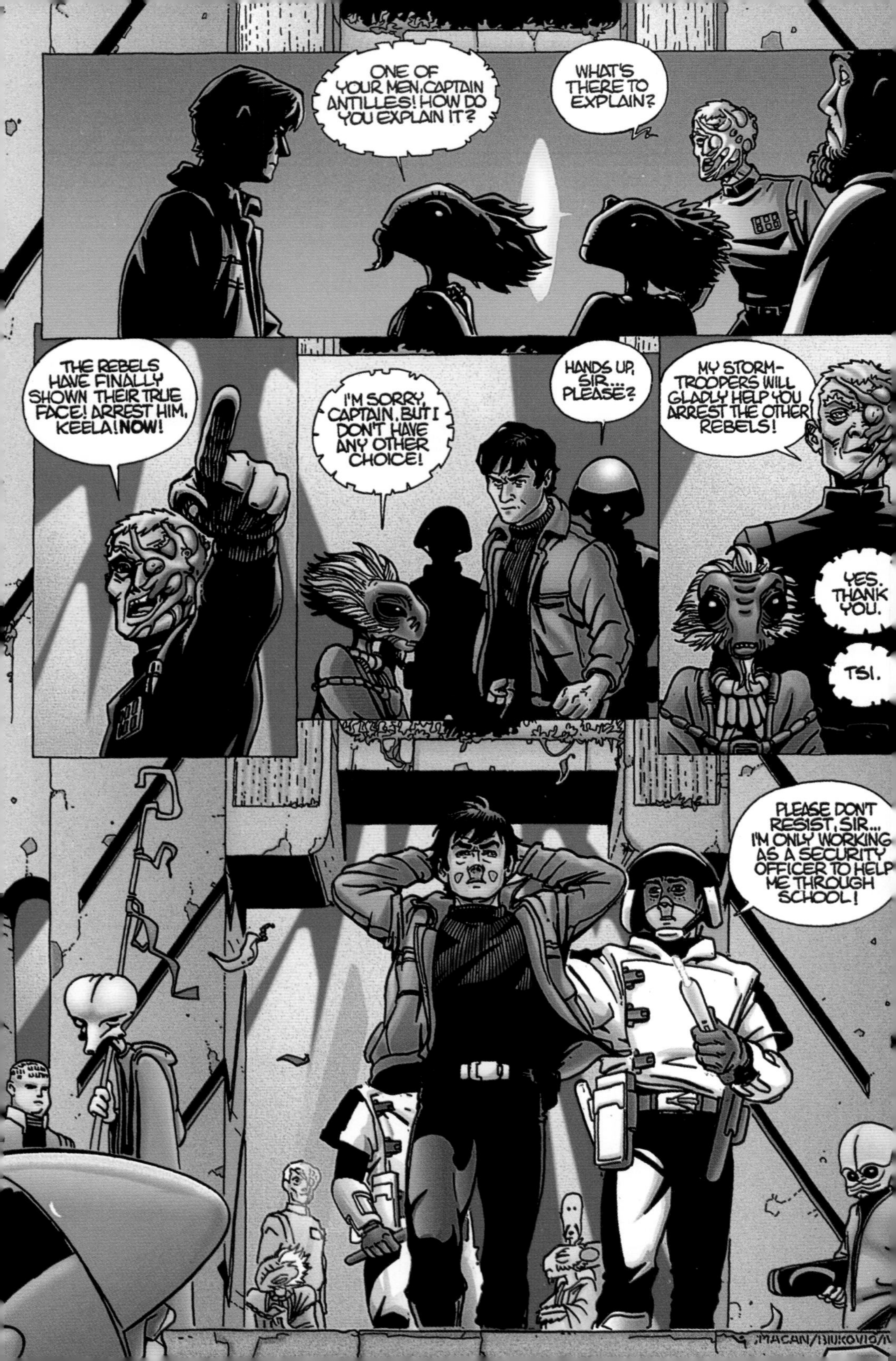

ONE OF YOUR MEN, CAPTAIN ANTILLES! HOW DO YOU EXPLAIN IT?
WHAT'S THERE TO EXPLAIN?
THE REBELS HAVE FINALLY SHOWN THEIR TRUE FACE! ARREST HIM, KEELA! NOW!
I'M SORRY, CAPTAIN, BUT I DON'T HAVE ANY OTHER CHOICE!
HANDS UP, SIR... PLEASE?
MY STORM-TROOPERS WILL GLADLY HELP YOU ARREST THE OTHER REBELS!
YES. THANK YOU.
TSI.
PLEASE DON'T RESIST, SIR... I'M ONLY WORKING AS A SECURITY OFFICER TO HELP ME THROUGH SCHOOL!
MACAN/BIUKOVIC/A

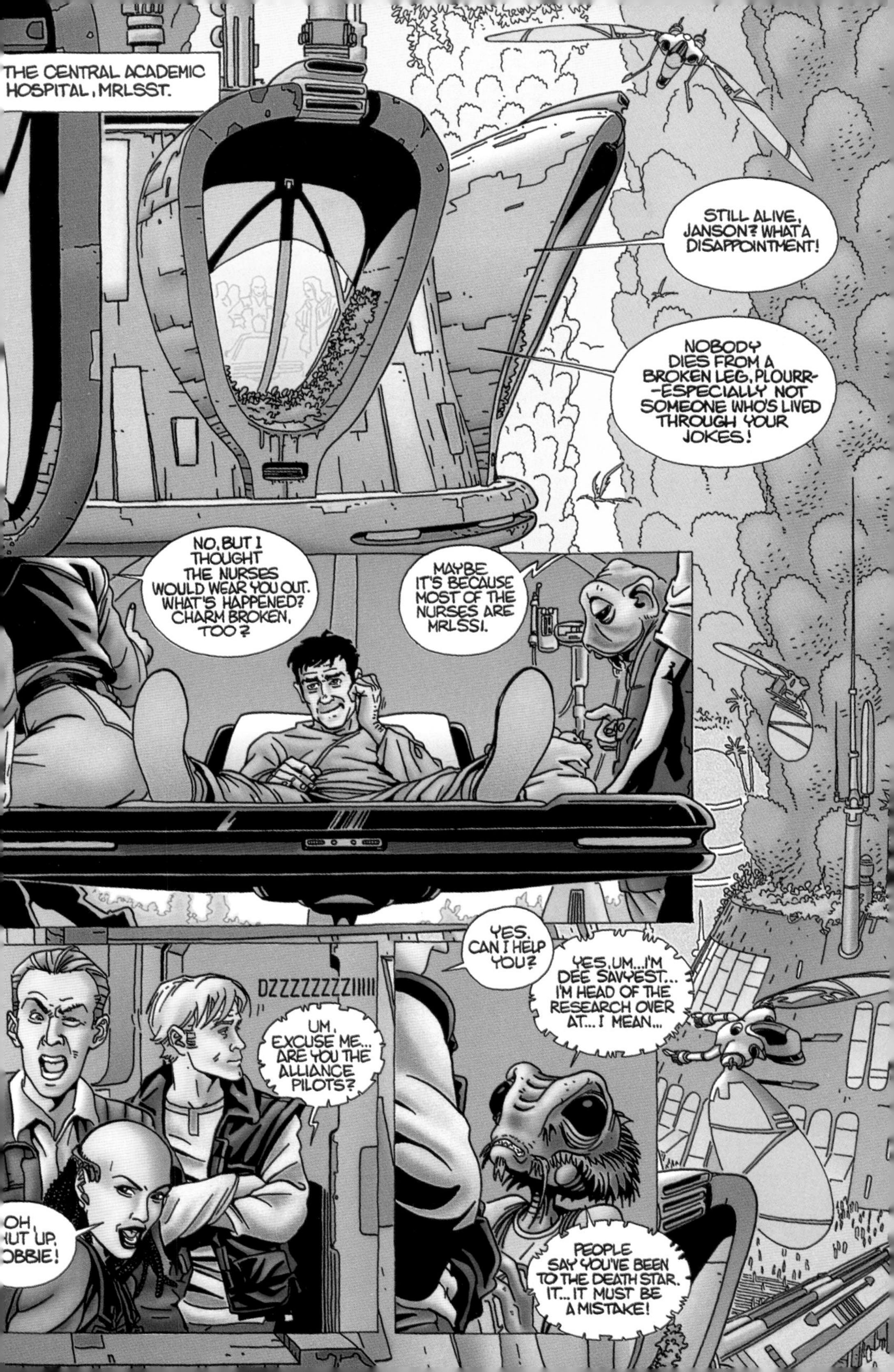
THE CENTRAL ACADEMIC HOSPITAL, MRLSST.
STILL ALIVE, JANSON? WHAT A DISAPPOINTMENT!
NOBODY DIES FROM A BROKEN LEG, PLOURR--ESPECIALLY NOT SOMEONE WHO'S LIVED THROUGH YOUR JOKES!
NO, BUT I THOUGHT THE NURSES WOULD WEAR YOU OUT. WHAT'S HAPPENED? CHARM BROKEN, TOO?
MAYBE IT'S BECAUSE MOST OF THE NURSES ARE MRLSSI.
DZZZZZZZZ!!!!!
UM, EXCUSE ME... ARE YOU THE ALLIANCE PILOTS?
OH, HUT UP, OBBIE!
YES. CAN I HELP YOU?
YES, UM...I'M DEE SAVYEST... I'M HEAD OF THE RESEARCH OVER AT... I MEAN...
PEOPLE SAY YOU'VE BEEN TO THE DEATH STAR. IT... IT MUST BE A MISTAKE!

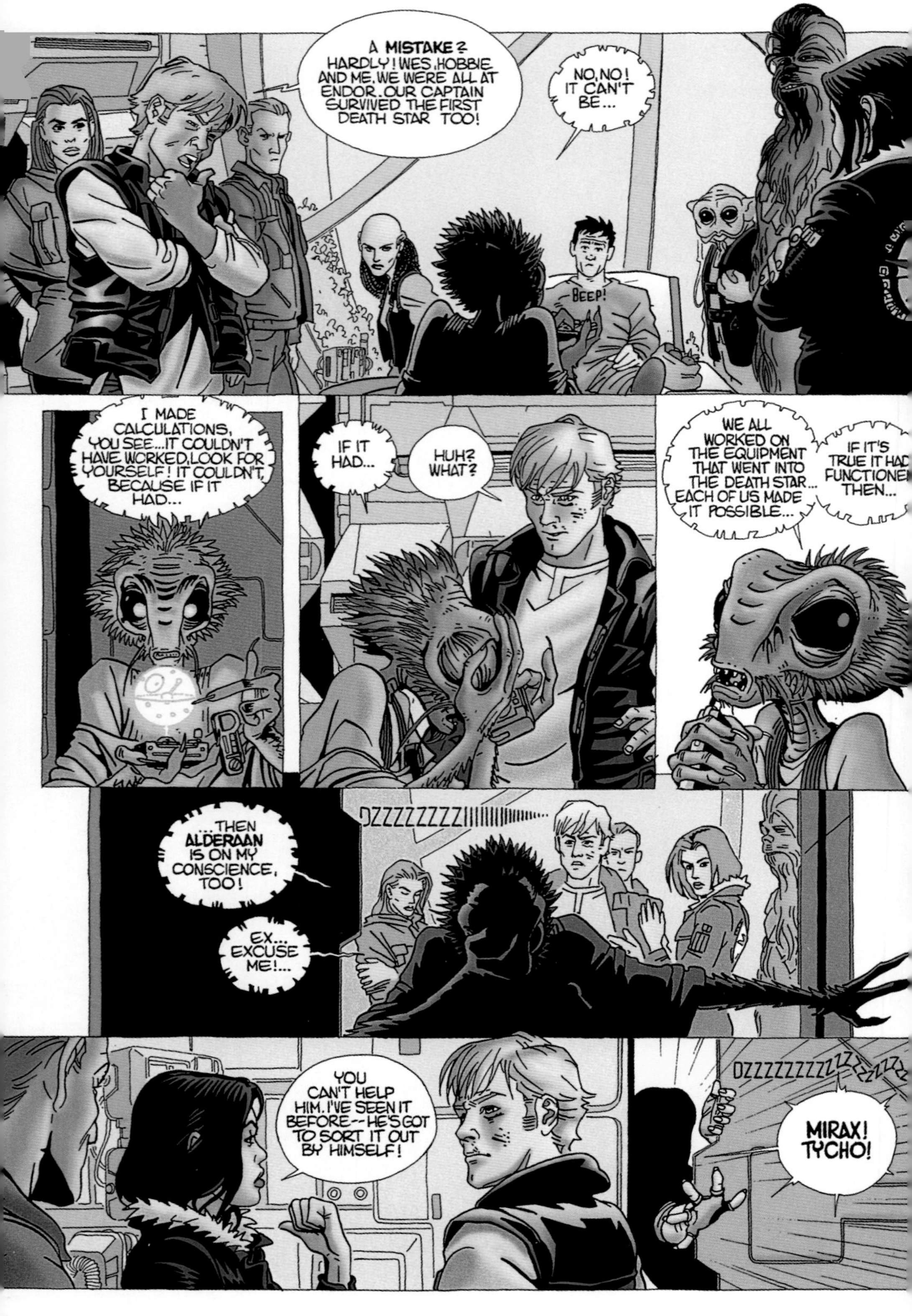

A MISTAKE? HARDLY! WES, HOBBIE AND ME, WE WERE ALL AT ENDOR. OUR CAPTAIN SURVIVED THE FIRST DEATH STAR TOO!
NO, NO! IT CAN'T BE...
BEEP!
I MADE CALCULATIONS, YOU SEE... IT COULDN'T HAVE WORKED, LOOK FOR YOURSELF! IT COULDN'T, BECAUSE IF IT HAD...
IF IT HAD...
HUH? WHAT?
WE ALL WORKED ON THE EQUIPMENT THAT WENT INTO THE DEATH STAR... EACH OF US MADE IT POSSIBLE...
IF IT'S TRUE IT HAD FUNCTIONED THEN...
...THEN ALDERAAN IS ON MY CONSCIENCE, TOO!
EX... EXCUSE ME!...
DZZZZZZZZ
YOU CAN'T HELP HIM. I'VE SEEN IT BEFORE-- HE'S GOT TO SORT IT OUT BY HIMSELF!
DZZZZZZZZZZZZZZZ
MIRAX! TYCHO!

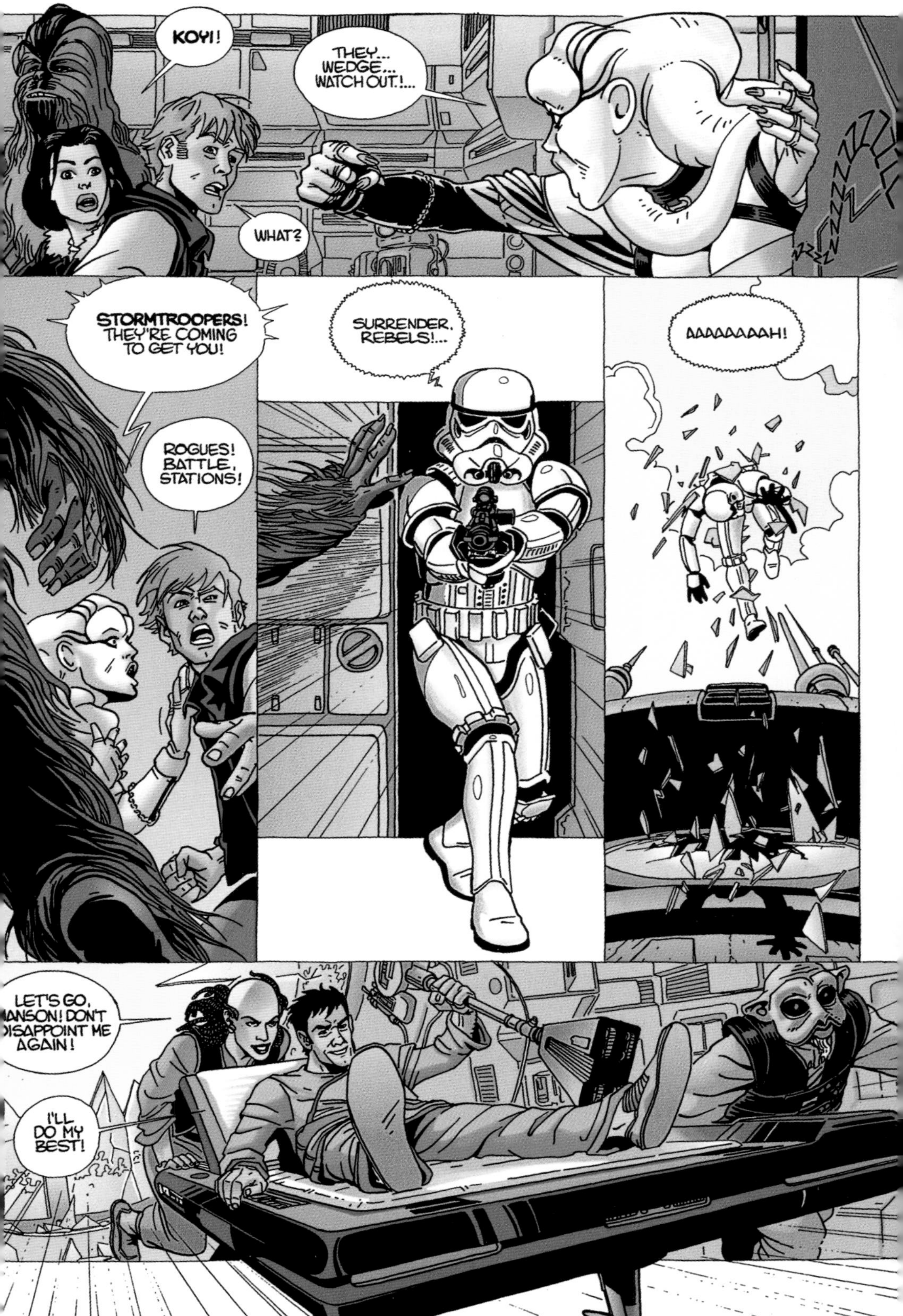
KOYI!
THEY... WEDGE... WATCH OUT.!...
WHAT?
STORMTROOPERS! THEY'RE COMING TO GET YOU!
ROGUES! BATTLE, STATIONS!
SURRENDER, REBELS!...
AAAAAAAAH!
LET'S GO, MANSON! DON'T DISAPPOINT ME AGAIN!
I'LL DO MY BEST!

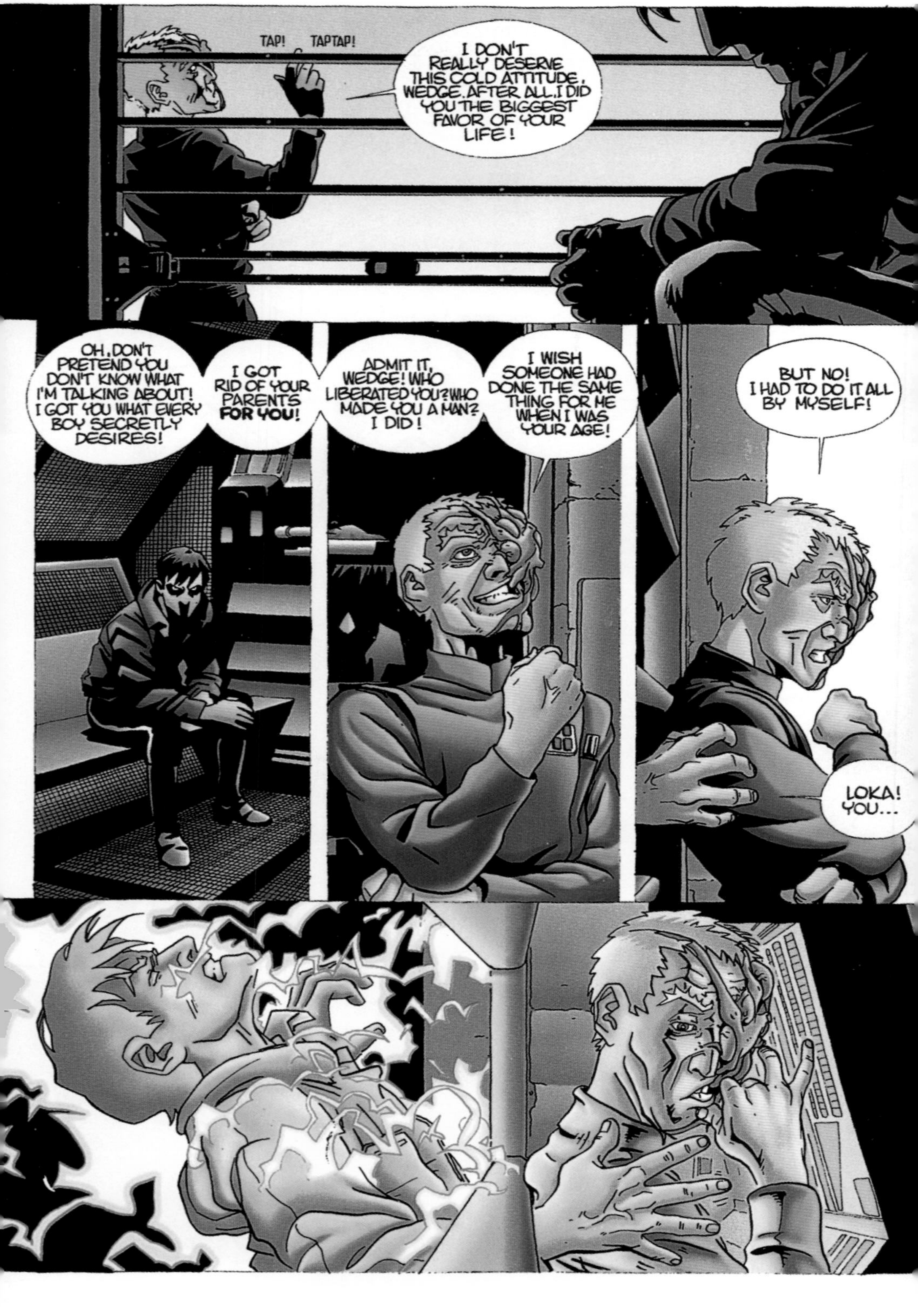
TAP! TAPTAP!
I DON'T REALLY DESERVE THIS COLD ATTITUDE, WEDGE. AFTER ALL, I DID YOU THE BIGGEST FAVOR OF YOUR LIFE!
OH, DON'T PRETEND YOU DON'T KNOW WHAT I'M TALKING ABOUT! I GOT YOU WHAT EVERY BOY SECRETLY DESIRES!
I GOT RID OF YOUR PARENTS **FOR YOU**!
ADMIT IT, WEDGE! WHO LIBERATED YOU? WHO MADE YOU A MAN? I DID!
I WISH SOMEONE HAD DONE THE SAME THING FOR ME WHEN I WAS YOUR AGE!
BUT NO! I HAD TO DO IT ALL BY MYSELF!
LOKA! YOU...

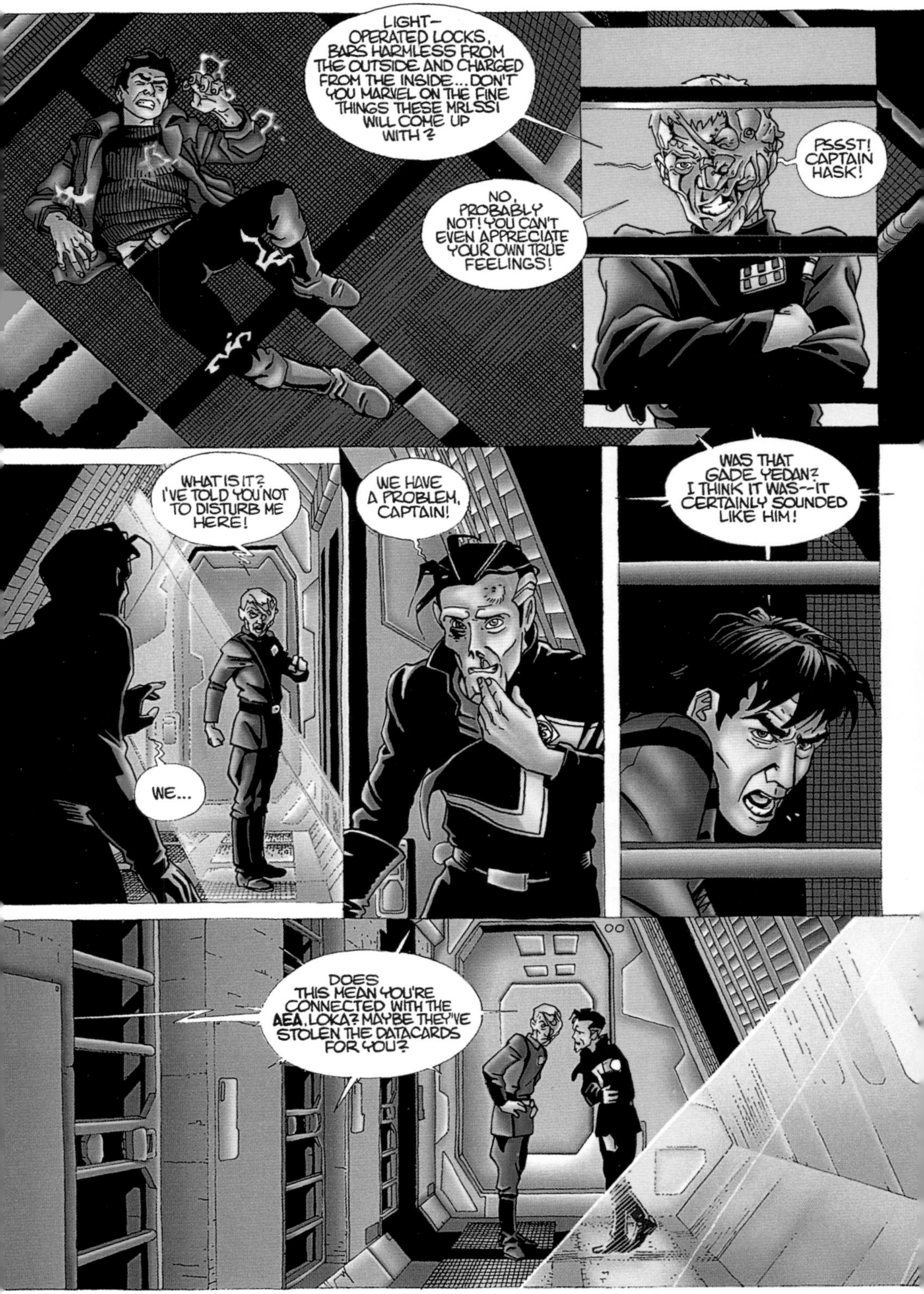
LIGHT-OPERATED LOCKS, BARS HARMLESS FROM THE OUTSIDE AND CHARGED FROM THE INSIDE... DON'T YOU MARVEL ON THE FINE THINGS THESE MRLSSI WILL COME UP WITH?
NO, PROBABLY NOT! YOU CAN'T EVEN APPRECIATE YOUR OWN TRUE FEELINGS!
PSSST! CAPTAIN HASK!
WHAT IS IT? I'VE TOLD YOU NOT TO DISTURB ME HERE!
WE...
WE HAVE A PROBLEM, CAPTAIN!
WAS THAT GADE YEDAN? I THINK IT WAS--IT CERTAINLY SOUNDED LIKE HIM!
DOES THIS MEAN YOU'RE CONNECTED WITH THE AEA, LOKA? MAYBE THEY'VE STOLEN THE DATACARDS FOR YOU?

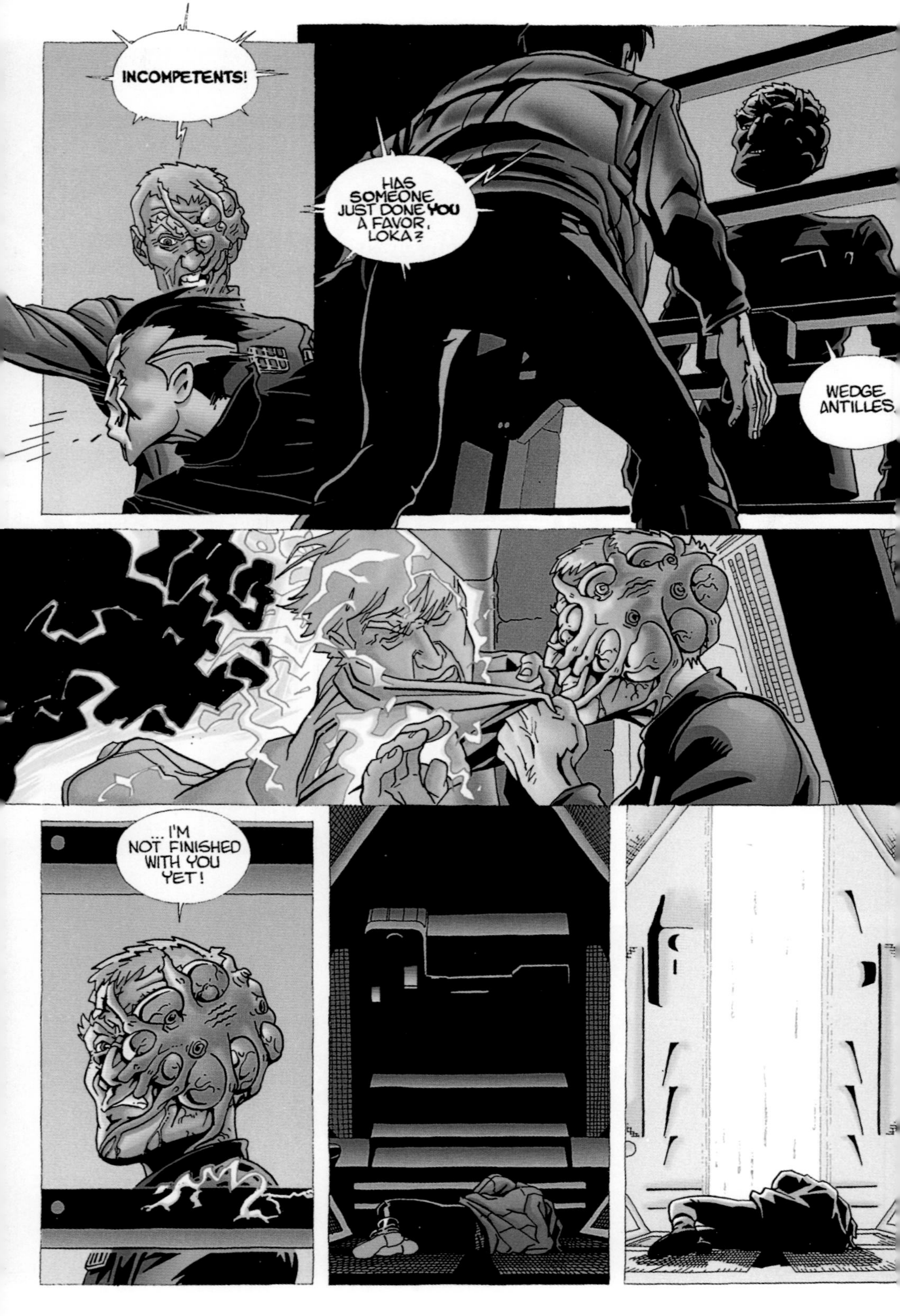
INCOMPETENTS!
HAS SOMEONE JUST DONE YOU A FAVOR, LOKA?
WEDGE ANTILLES.
...I'M NOT FINISHED WITH YOU YET!

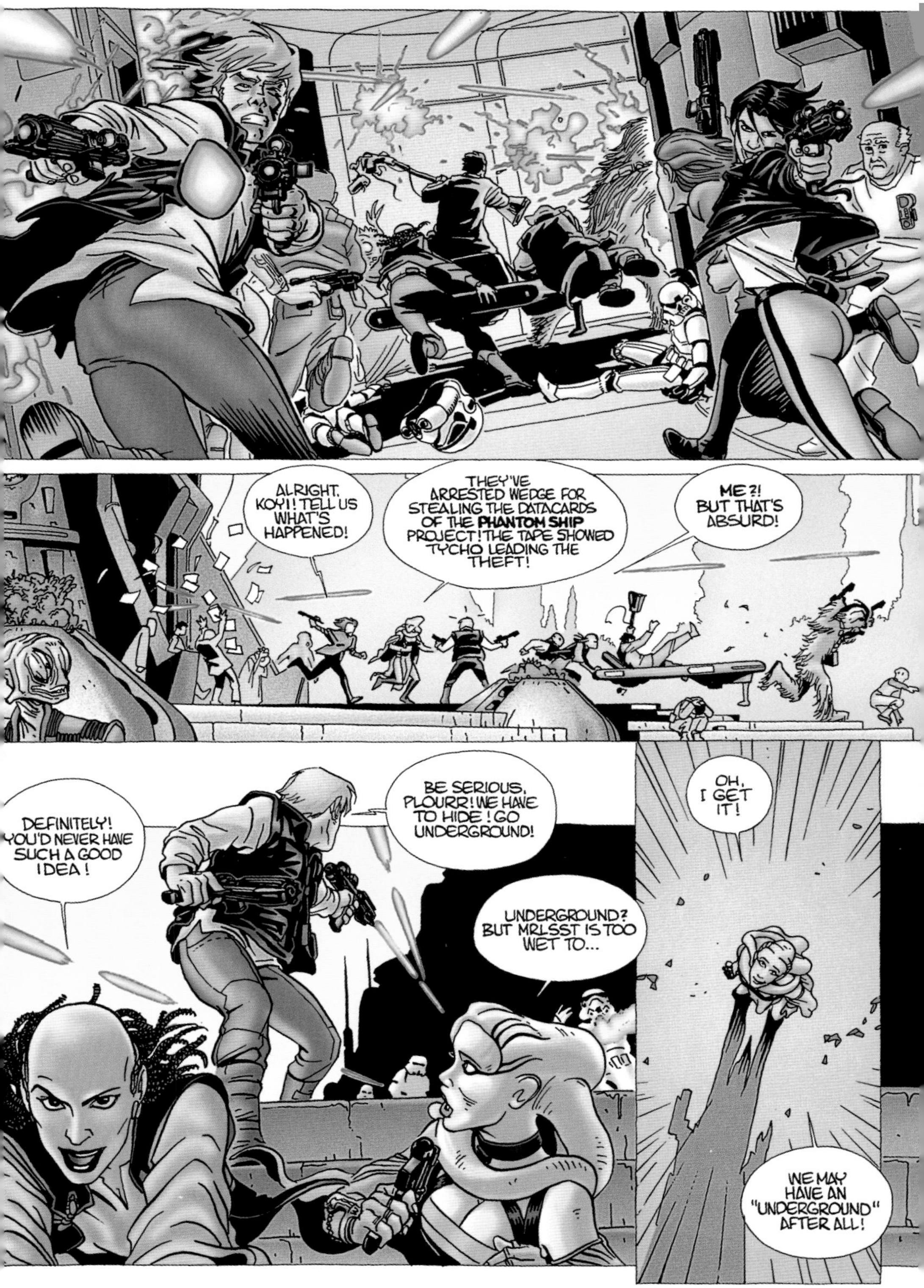

ALRIGHT, KOYI! TELL US WHAT'S HAPPENED!
THEY'VE ARRESTED WEDGE FOR STEALING THE DATACARDS OF THE **PHANTOM SHIP** PROJECT! THE TAPE SHOWED TYCHO LEADING THE THEFT!
ME?! BUT THAT'S ABSURD!
DEFINITELY! YOU'D NEVER HAVE SUCH A GOOD IDEA!
BE SERIOUS, PLOURR! WE HAVE TO HIDE! GO UNDERGROUND!
UNDERGROUND? BUT MRLSST IS TOO WET TO...
OH, I GET IT!
WE MAY HAVE AN "UNDERGROUND" AFTER ALL!

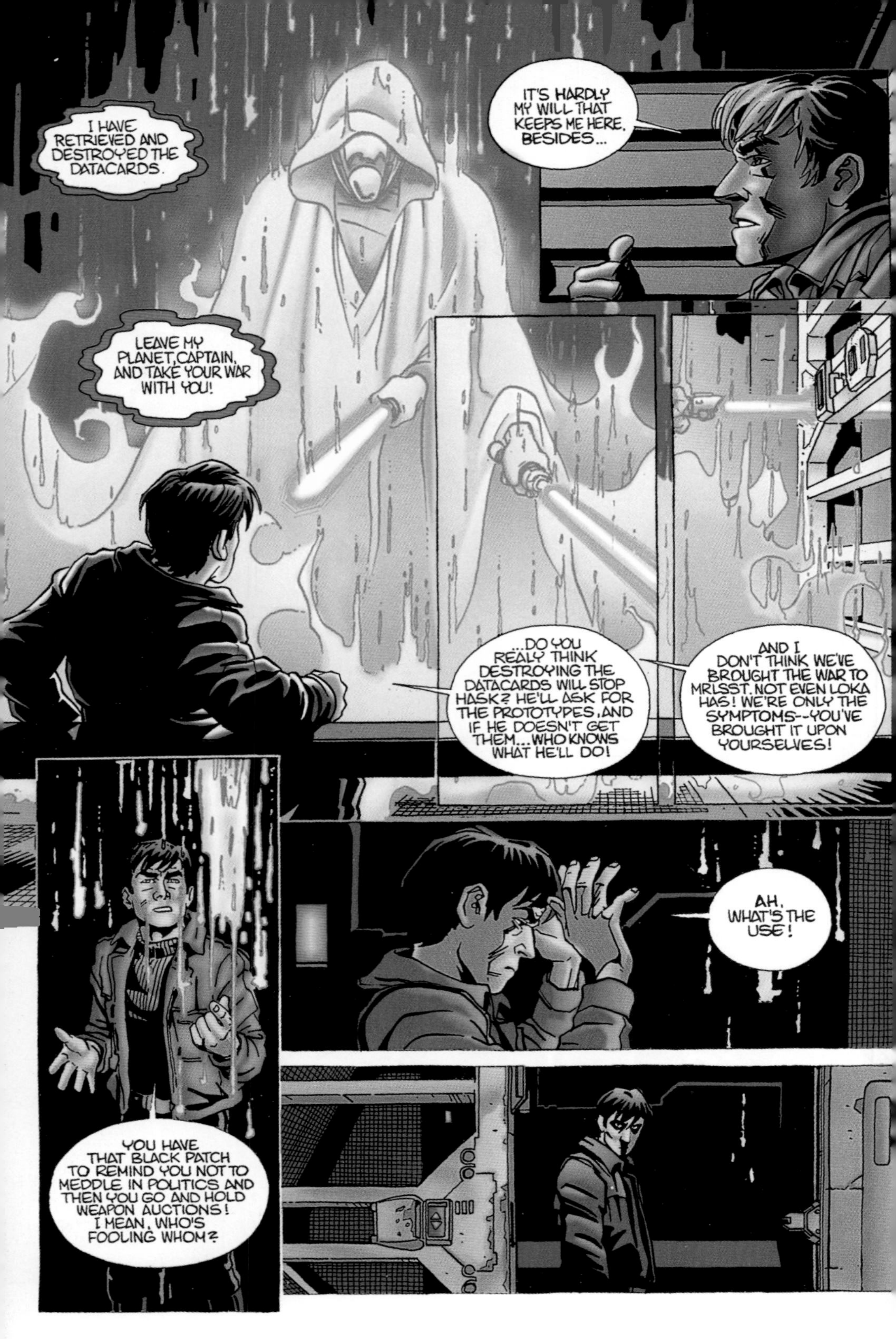
I HAVE RETRIEVED AND DESTROYED THE DATACARDS.
IT'S HARDLY MY WILL THAT KEEPS ME HERE. BESIDES...
LEAVE MY PLANET, CAPTAIN, AND TAKE YOUR WAR WITH YOU!
...DO YOU REALY THINK DESTROYING THE DATACARDS WILL STOP HASK? HE'LL ASK FOR THE PROTOTYPES, AND IF HE DOESN'T GET THEM... WHO KNOWS WHAT HE'LL DO!
AND I DON'T THINK WE'VE BROUGHT THE WAR TO MRLSST. NOT EVEN LOKA HAS! WE'RE ONLY THE SYMPTOMS--YOU'VE BROUGHT IT UPON YOURSELVES!
YOU HAVE THAT BLACK PATCH TO REMIND YOU NOT TO MEDDLE IN POLITICS AND THEN YOU GO AND HOLD WEAPON AUCTIONS! I MEAN, WHO'S FOOLING WHOM?
AH, WHAT'S THE USE!

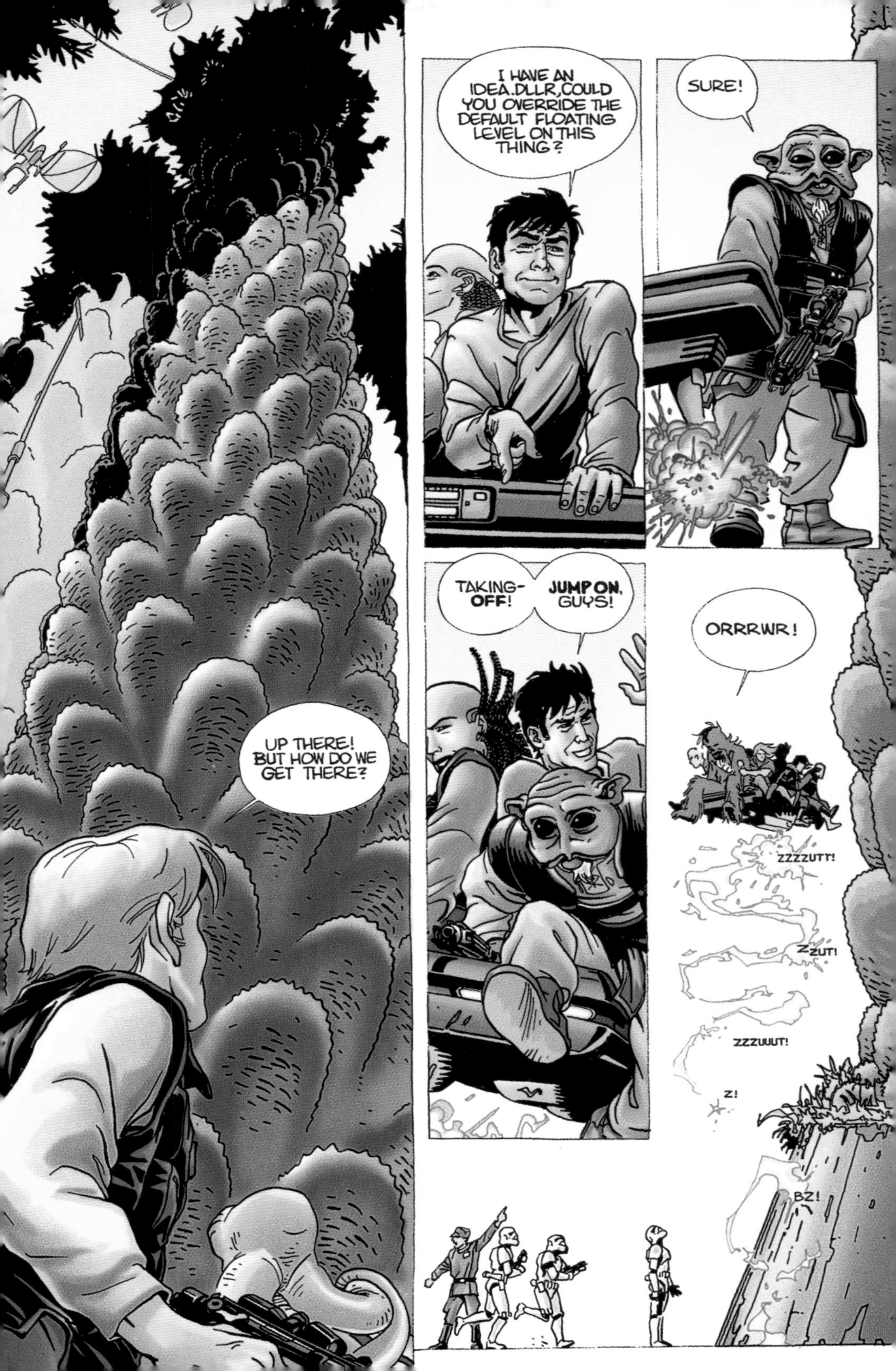
UP THERE! BUT HOW DO WE GET THERE?
I HAVE AN IDEA. DLLR, COULD YOU OVERRIDE THE DEFAULT FLOATING LEVEL ON THIS THING?
SURE!
TAKING-OFF!
JUMP ON, GUYS!
ORRRWR!
ZZZZUTT!
ZZUT!
ZZZUUUT!
Z!
BZ!

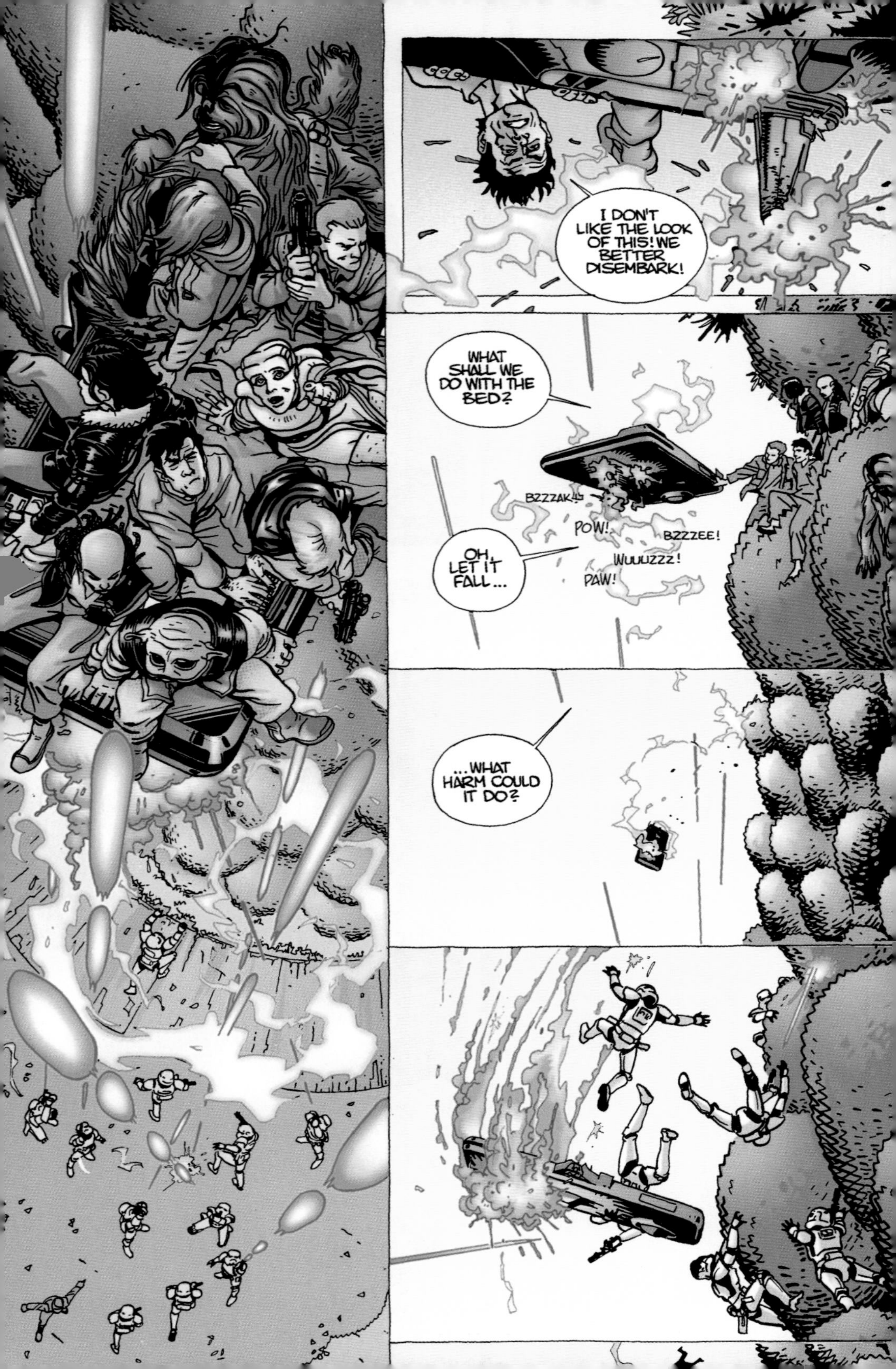

I DON'T LIKE THE LOOK OF THIS! WE BETTER DISEMBARK!
WHAT SHALL WE DO WITH THE BED?
BZZZAK!
POW!
BZZZEE!
OH, LET IT FALL...
WUUUZZZ!
PAW!
...WHAT HARM COULD IT DO?

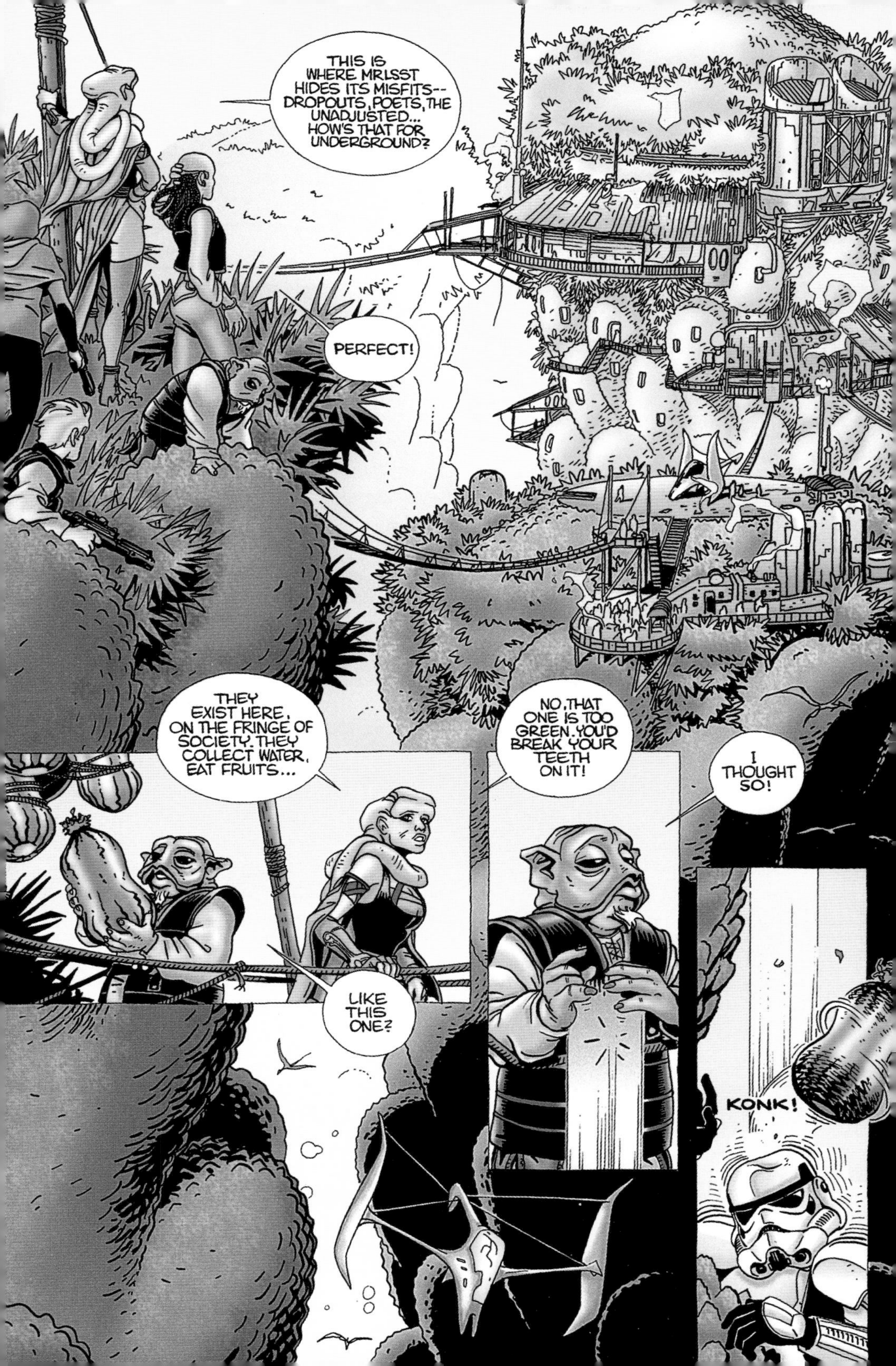
THIS IS WHERE MRLSST HIDES ITS MISFITS-- DROPOUTS, POETS, THE UNADJUSTED... HOW'S THAT FOR UNDERGROUND?
PERFECT!
THEY EXIST HERE, ON THE FRINGE OF SOCIETY. THEY COLLECT WATER, EAT FRUITS...
LIKE THIS ONE?
NO, THAT ONE IS TOO GREEN. YOU'D BREAK YOUR TEETH ON IT!
I THOUGHT SO!
KONK!

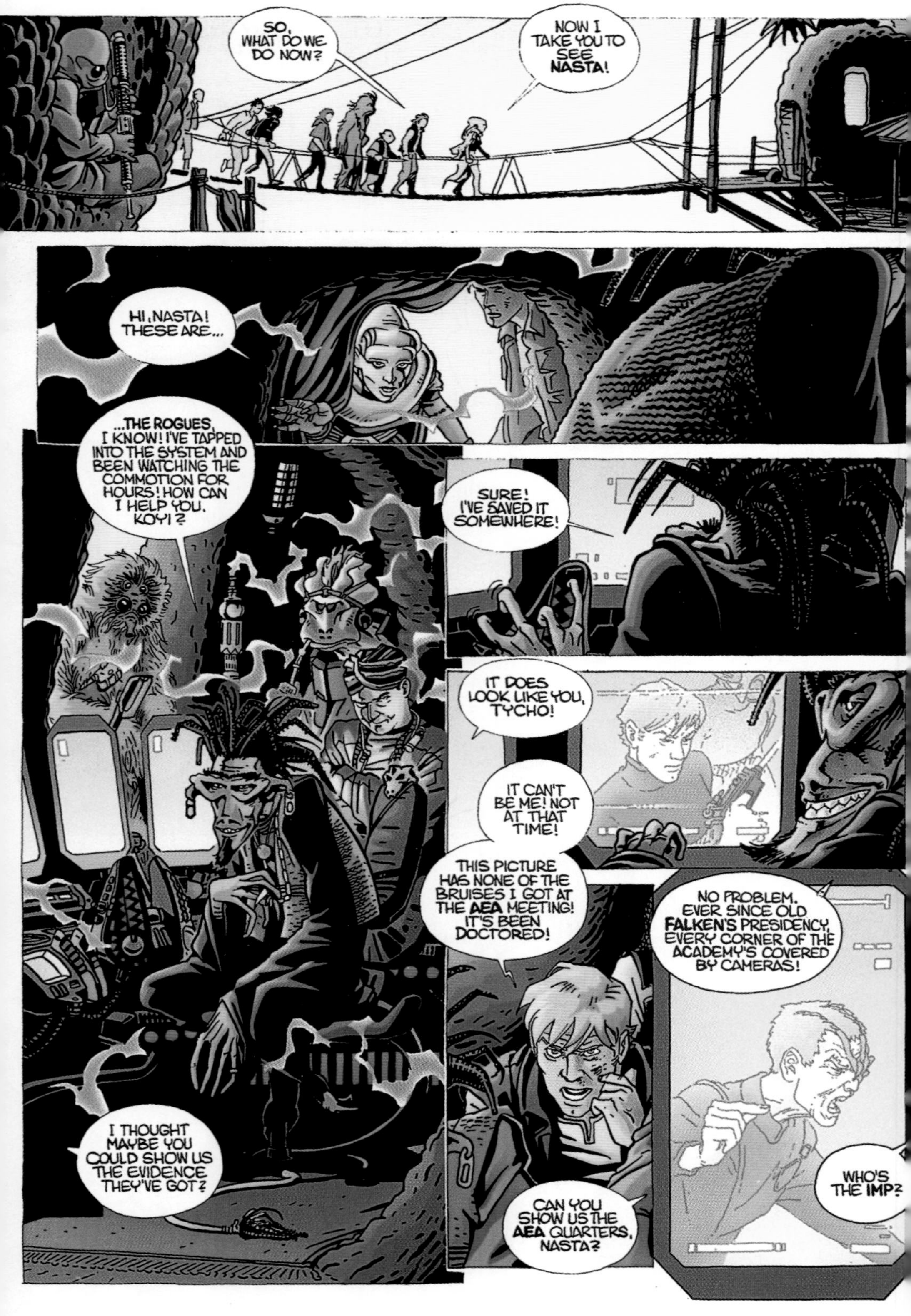
SO, WHAT DO WE DO NOW?
NOW I TAKE YOU TO SEE NASTA!
HI, NASTA! THESE ARE...
...THE ROGUES, I KNOW! I'VE TAPPED INTO THE SYSTEM AND BEEN WATCHING THE COMMOTION FOR HOURS! HOW CAN I HELP YOU, KOYI?
I THOUGHT MAYBE YOU COULD SHOW US THE EVIDENCE THEY'VE GOT?
SURE! I'VE SAVED IT SOMEWHERE!
IT DOES LOOK LIKE YOU, TYCHO!
IT CAN'T BE ME! NOT AT THAT TIME!
THIS PICTURE HAS NONE OF THE BRUISES I GOT AT THE AEA MEETING! IT'S BEEN DOCTORED!
CAN YOU SHOW US THE AEA QUARTERS, NASTA?
NO PROBLEM. EVER SINCE OLD FALKEN'S PRESIDENCY, EVERY CORNER OF THE ACADEMY'S COVERED BY CAMERAS!
WHO'S THE IMP?

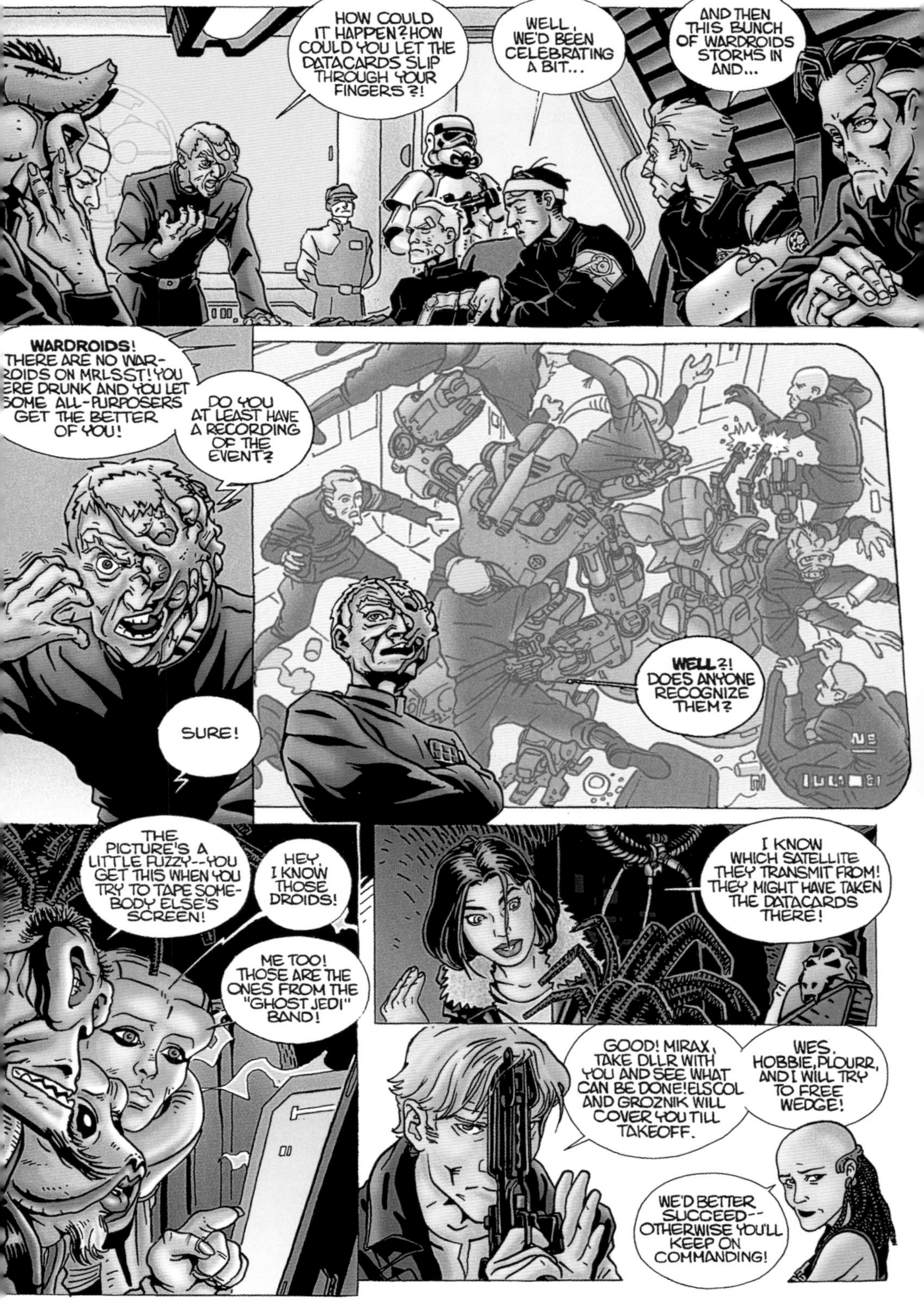
HOW COULD IT HAPPEN? HOW COULD YOU LET THE DATACARDS SLIP THROUGH YOUR FINGERS?!
WELL, WE'D BEEN CELEBRATING A BIT...
AND THEN THIS BUNCH OF WARDROIDS STORMS IN AND...
WARDROIDS! THERE ARE NO WAR-ROIDS ON MRLSST! YOU ERE DRUNK AND YOU LET SOME ALL-PURPOSERS GET THE BETTER OF YOU!
DO YOU AT LEAST HAVE A RECORDING OF THE EVENT?
SURE!
WELL?! DOES ANYONE RECOGNIZE THEM?
THE PICTURE'S A LITTLE FUZZY--YOU GET THIS WHEN YOU TRY TO TAPE SOMEBODY ELSE'S SCREEN!
HEY, I KNOW THOSE DROIDS!
ME TOO! THOSE ARE THE ONES FROM THE "GHOST JEDI" BAND!
I KNOW WHICH SATELLITE THEY TRANSMIT FROM! THEY MIGHT HAVE TAKEN THE DATACARDS THERE!
GOOD! MIRAX, TAKE DLLR WITH YOU AND SEE WHAT CAN BE DONE! ELSCOL AND GROZNIK WILL COVER YOU TILL TAKEOFF.
WES, HOBBIE, PLOURR, AND I WILL TRY TO FREE WEDGE!
WE'D BETTER SUCCEED--OTHERWISE YOU'LL KEEP ON COMMANDING!

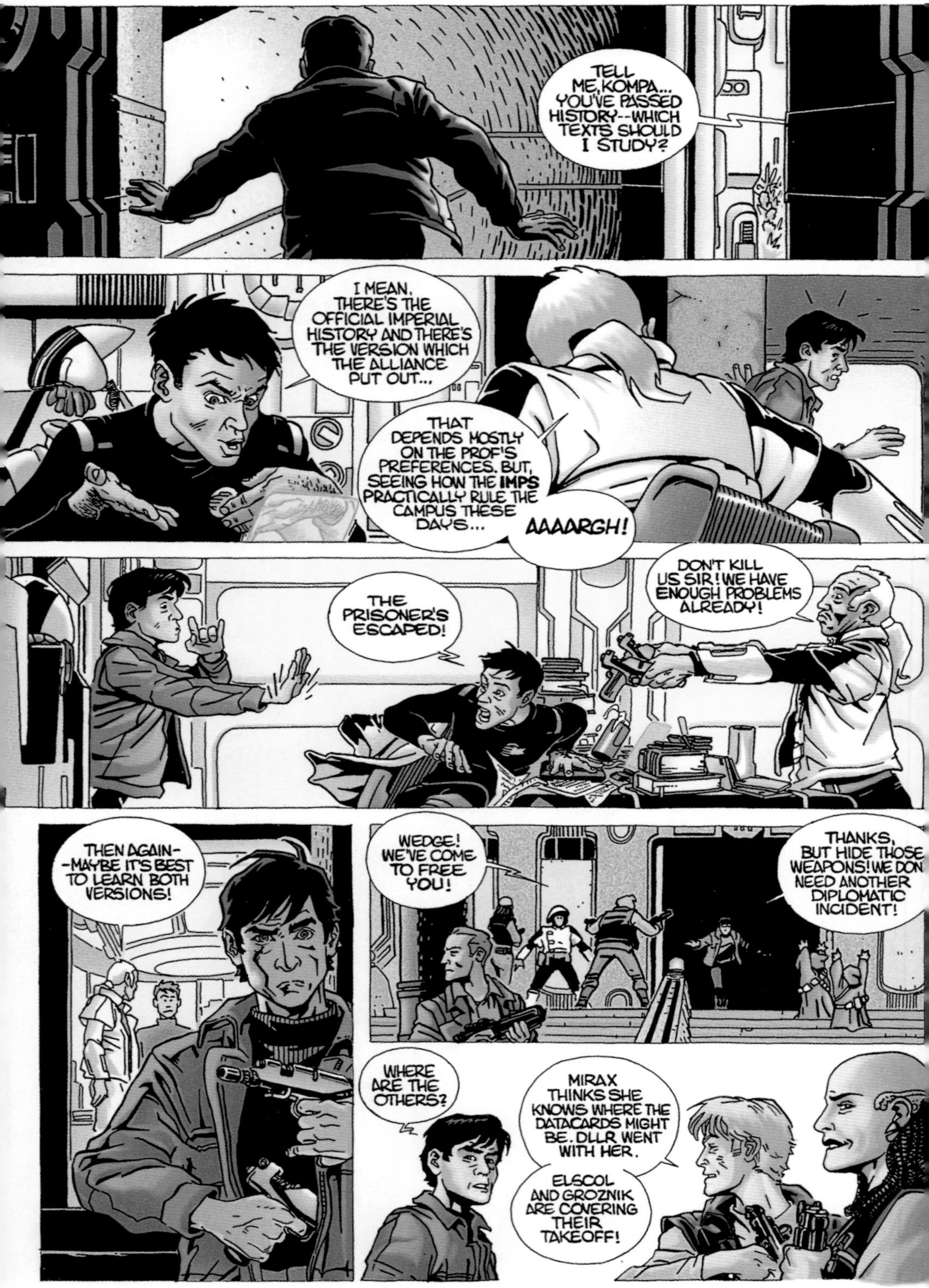
TELL ME, KOMPA... YOU'VE PASSED HISTORY--WHICH TEXTS SHOULD I STUDY?
I MEAN, THERE'S THE OFFICIAL IMPERIAL HISTORY AND THERE'S THE VERSION WHICH THE ALLIANCE PUT OUT...
THAT DEPENDS MOSTLY ON THE PROF'S PREFERENCES. BUT, SEEING HOW THE **IMPS** PRACTICALLY RULE THE CAMPUS THESE DAYS...
AAAARGH!
THE PRISONER'S ESCAPED!
DON'T KILL US SIR! WE HAVE ENOUGH PROBLEMS ALREADY!
THEN AGAIN--MAYBE IT'S BEST TO LEARN BOTH VERSIONS!
WEDGE! WE'VE COME TO FREE YOU!
THANKS, BUT HIDE THOSE WEAPONS! WE DON NEED ANOTHER DIPLOMATIC INCIDENT!
WHERE ARE THE OTHERS?
MIRAX THINKS SHE KNOWS WHERE THE DATACARDS MIGHT BE. DLLR WENT WITH HER.
ELSCOL AND GROZNIK ARE COVERING THEIR TAKEOFF!

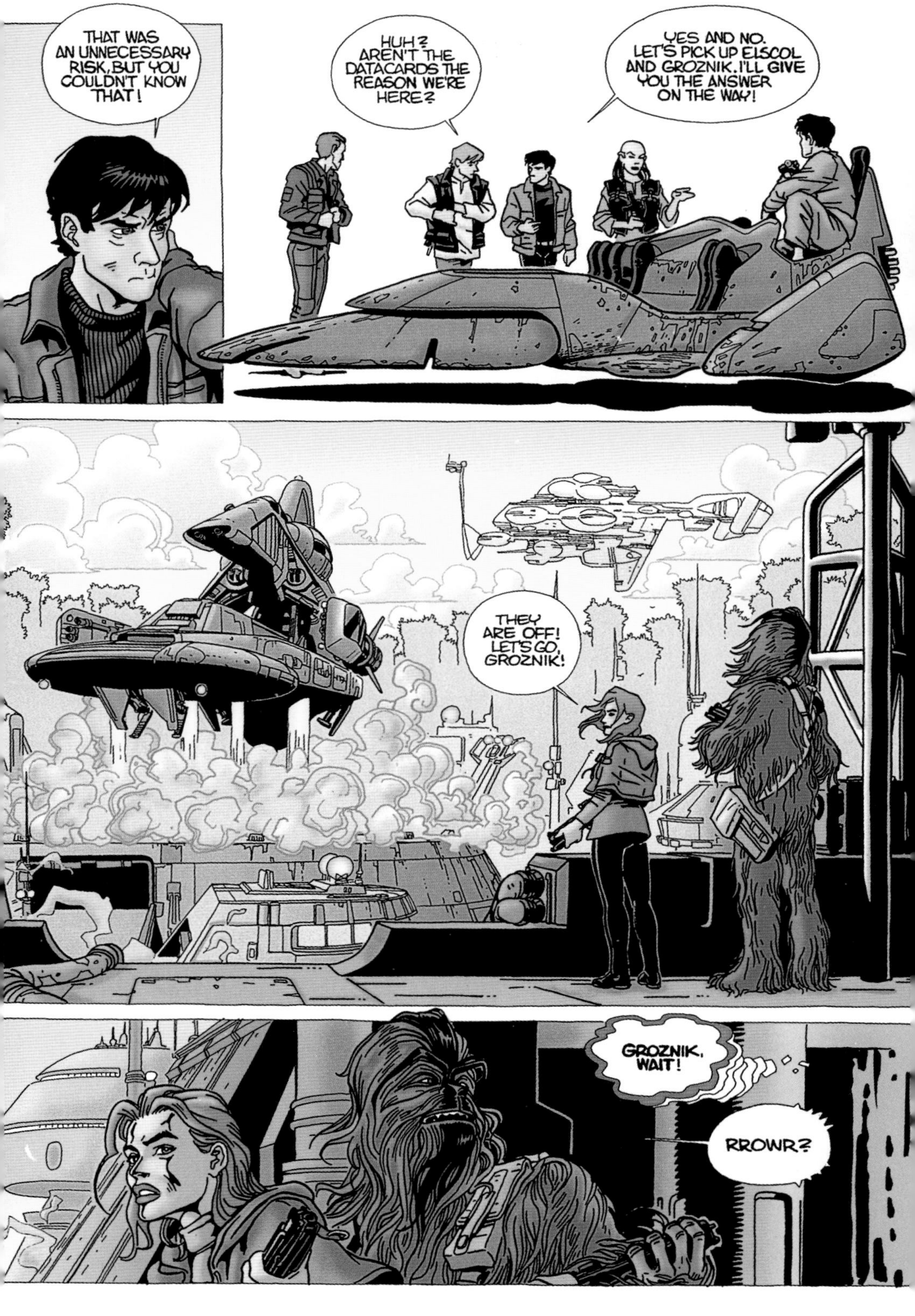
THAT WAS AN UNNECESSARY RISK, BUT YOU COULDN'T KNOW THAT!
HUH? AREN'T THE DATACARDS THE REASON WE'RE HERE?
YES AND NO. LET'S PICK UP ELSCOL AND GROZNIK. I'LL GIVE YOU THE ANSWER ON THE WAY!
THEY ARE OFF! LET'S GO, GROZNIK!
GROZNIK, WAIT!
RROWR?

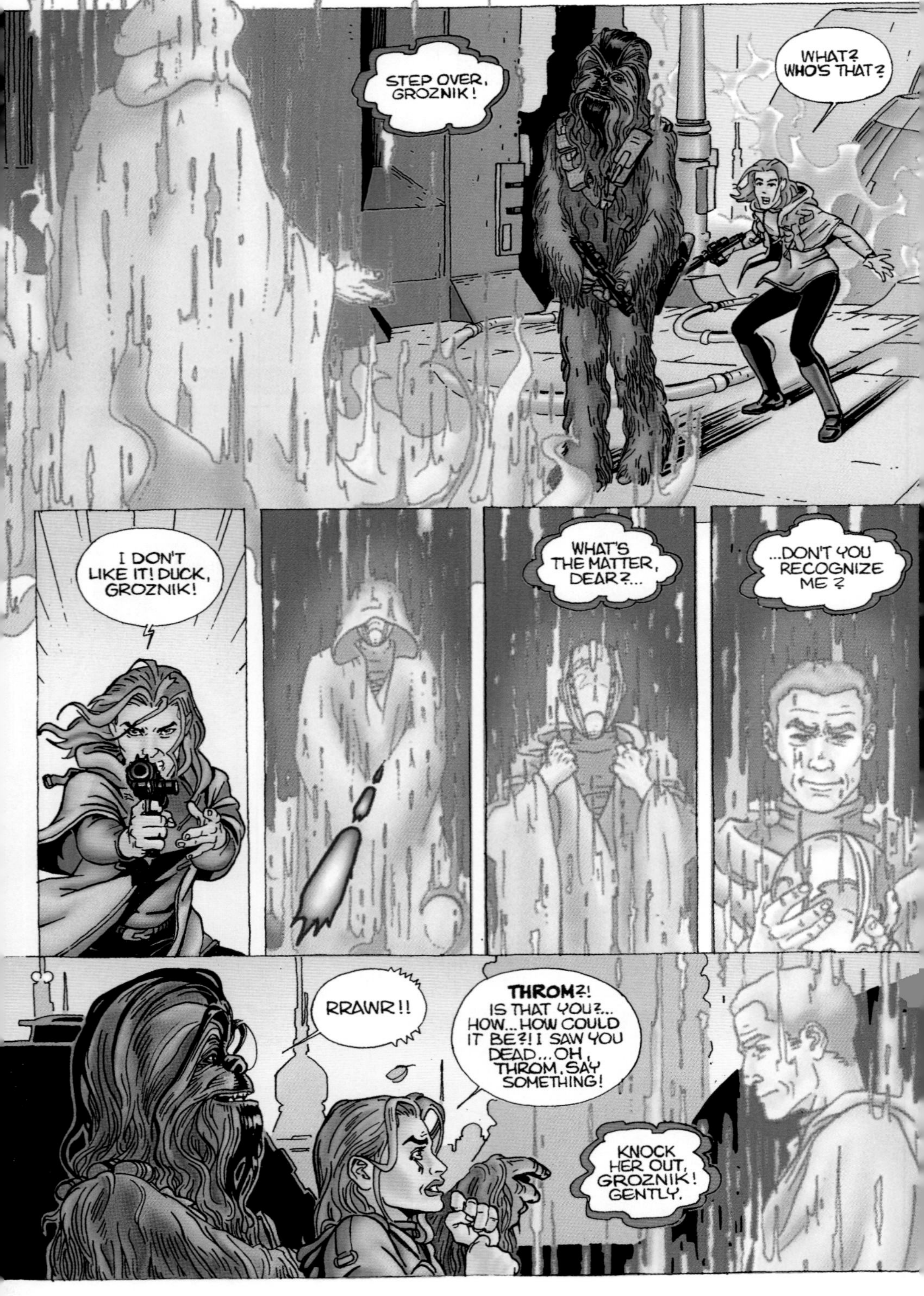
STEP OVER, GROZNIK!
WHAT? WHO'S THAT?
I DON'T LIKE IT! DUCK, GROZNIK!
WHAT'S THE MATTER, DEAR?...
...DON'T YOU RECOGNIZE ME?
RRAWR!!
THROM?! IS THAT YOU?... HOW... HOW COULD IT BE?! I SAW YOU DEAD... OH, THROM, SAY SOMETHING!
KNOCK HER OUT, GROZNIK! GENTLY.

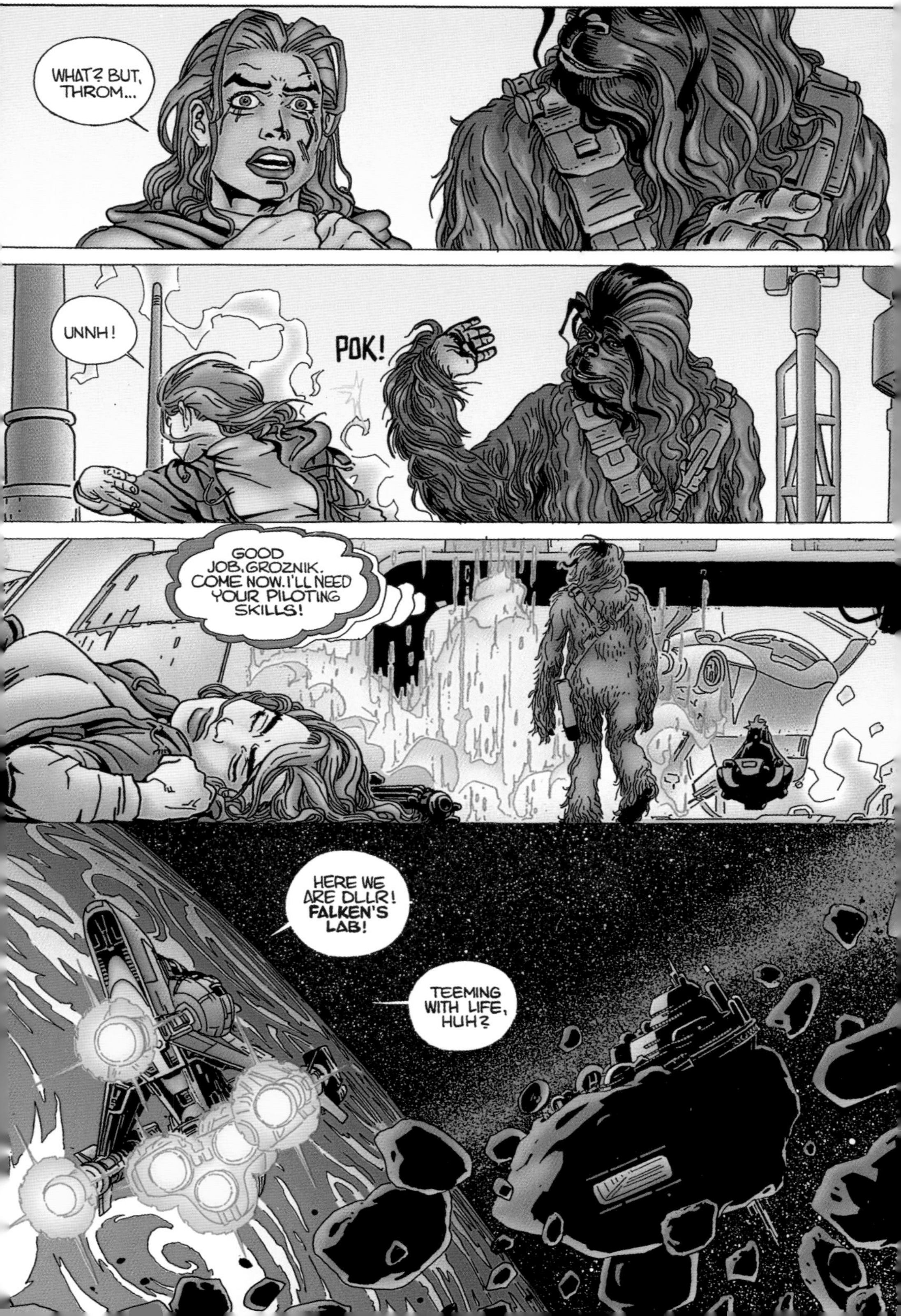
WHAT? BUT, THROM...
UNNH!
POK!
GOOD JOB, GROZNIK. COME NOW. I'LL NEED YOUR PILOTING SKILLS!
HERE WE ARE DLLR! FALKEN'S LAB!
TEEMING WITH LIFE, HUH?

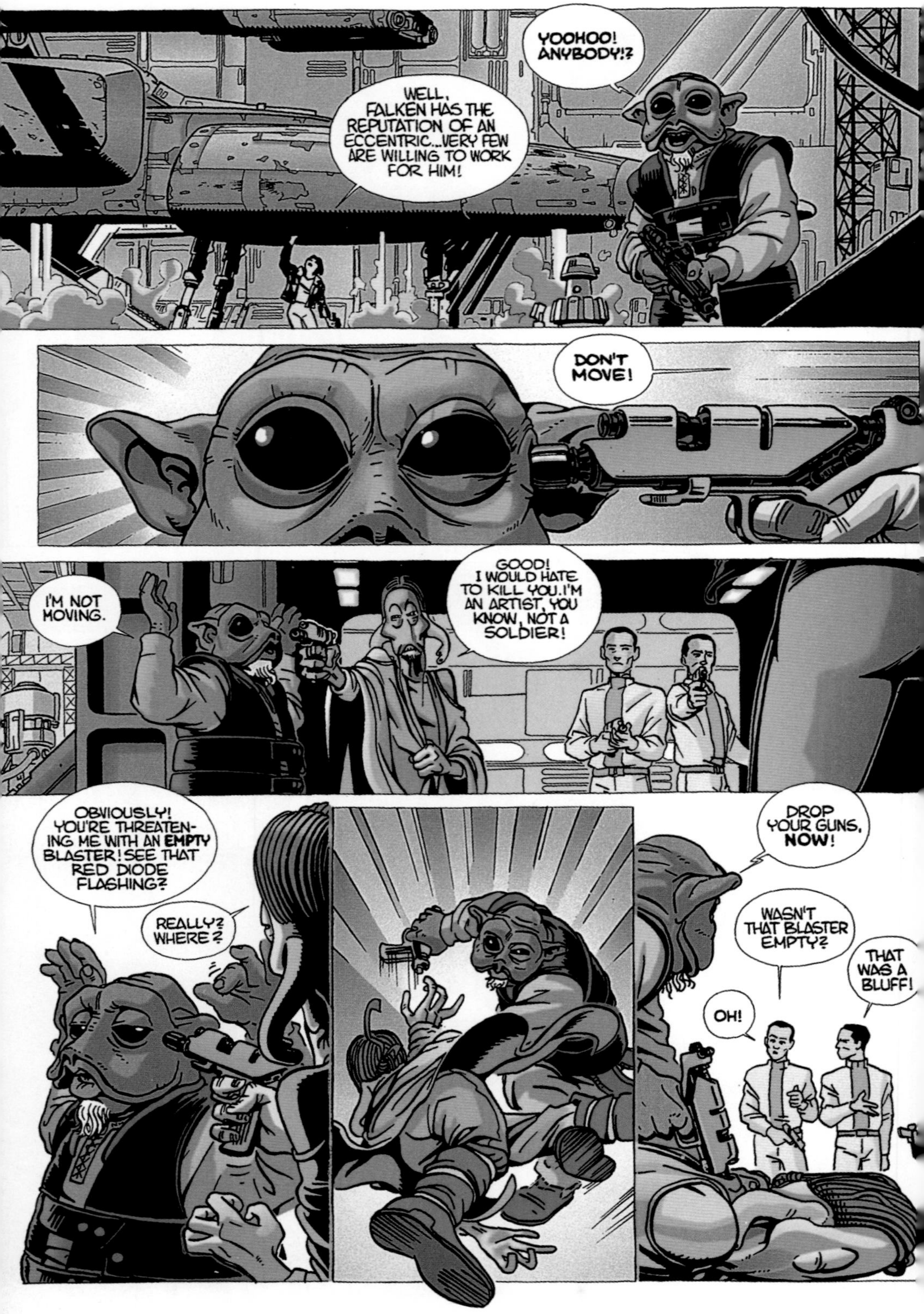

WELL, FALKEN HAS THE REPUTATION OF AN ECCENTRIC...VERY FEW ARE WILLING TO WORK FOR HIM!
YOOHOO! ANYBODY!?
DON'T MOVE!
I'M NOT MOVING.
GOOD! I WOULD HATE TO KILL YOU. I'M AN ARTIST, YOU KNOW, NOT A SOLDIER!
OBVIOUSLY! YOU'RE THREATENING ME WITH AN EMPTY BLASTER! SEE THAT RED DIODE FLASHING?
REALLY? WHERE?
DROP YOUR GUNS, NOW!
WASN'T THAT BLASTER EMPTY?
OH!
THAT WAS A BLUFF!

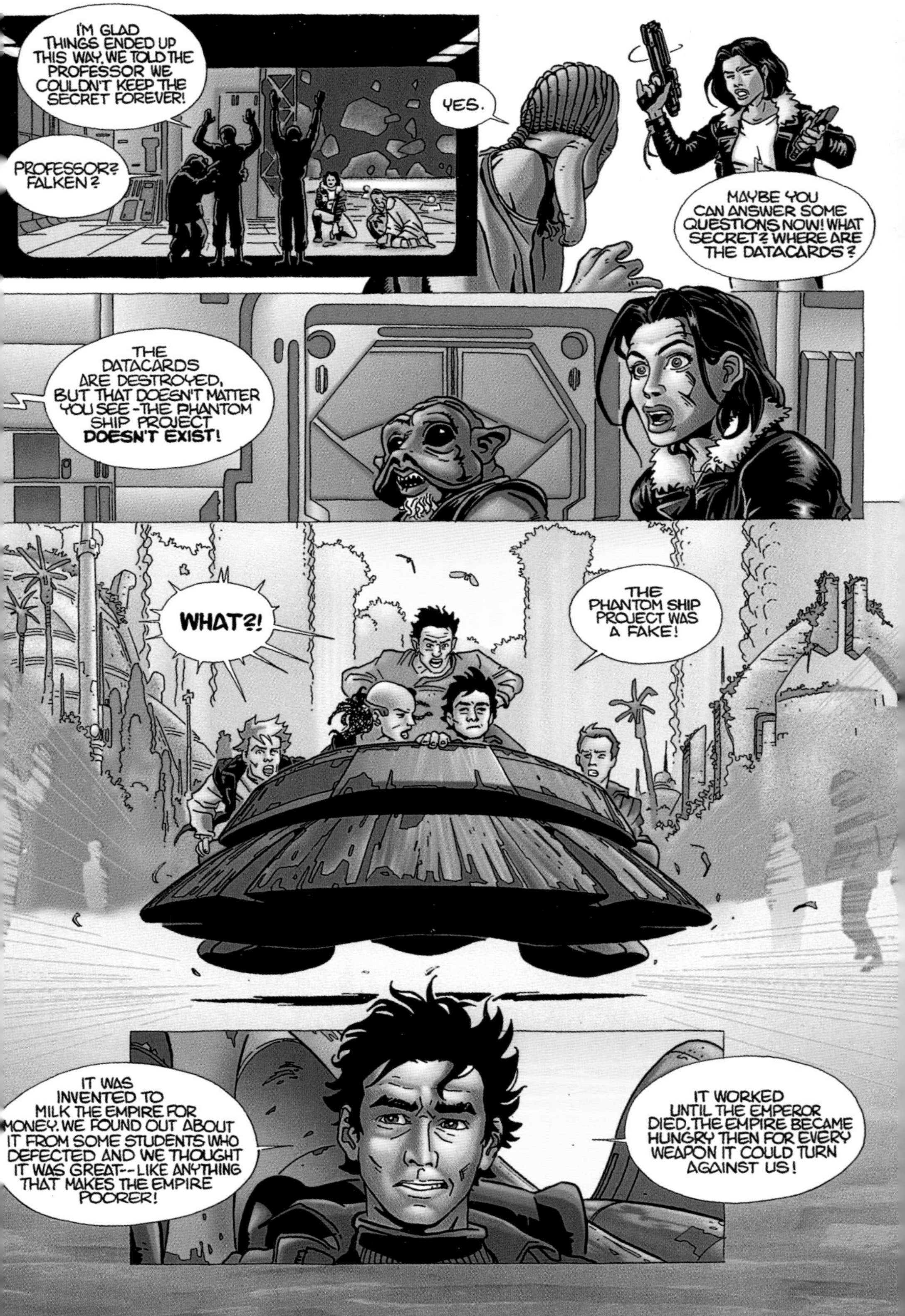
I'M GLAD THINGS ENDED UP THIS WAY. WE TOLD THE PROFESSOR WE COULDN'T KEEP THE SECRET FOREVER!
PROFESSOR? FALKEN?
YES.
MAYBE YOU CAN ANSWER SOME QUESTIONS NOW! WHAT SECRET? WHERE ARE THE DATACARDS?
THE DATACARDS ARE DESTROYED, BUT THAT DOESN'T MATTER YOU SEE -THE PHANTOM SHIP PROJECT **DOESN'T EXIST!**
WHAT?!
THE PHANTOM SHIP PROJECT WAS A FAKE!
IT WAS INVENTED TO MILK THE EMPIRE FOR MONEY. WE FOUND OUT ABOUT IT FROM SOME STUDENTS WHO DEFECTED AND WE THOUGHT IT WAS GREAT--LIKE ANYTHING THAT MAKES THE EMPIRE POORER!
IT WORKED UNTIL THE EMPEROR DIED. THE EMPIRE BECAME HUNGRY THEN FOR EVERY WEAPON IT COULD TURN AGAINST US!

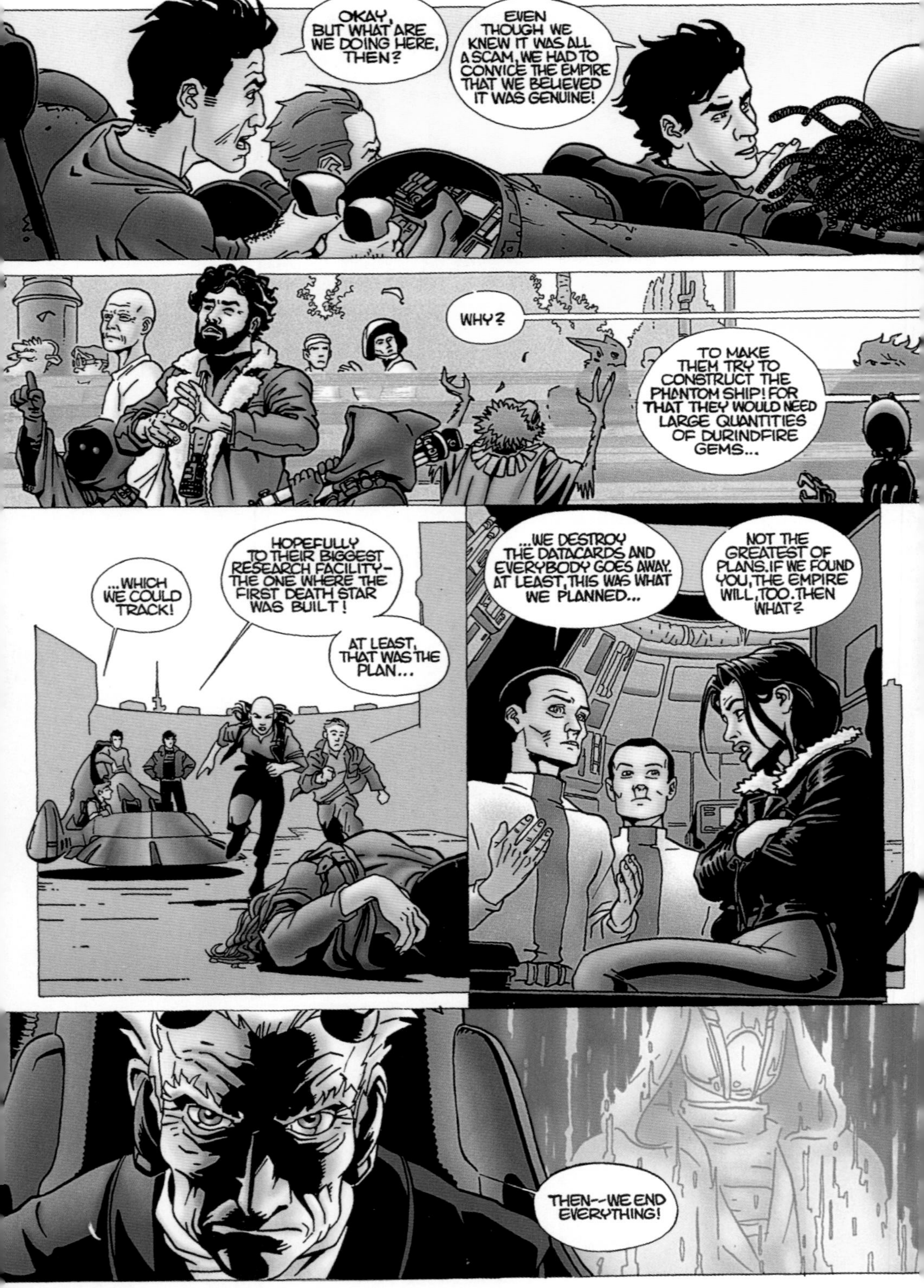
OKAY, BUT WHAT ARE WE DOING HERE, THEN?
EVEN THOUGH WE KNEW IT WAS ALL A SCAM, WE HAD TO CONVICE THE EMPIRE THAT WE BELIEVED IT WAS GENUINE!
WHY?
TO MAKE THEM TRY TO CONSTRUCT THE PHANTOM SHIP! FOR THAT THEY WOULD NEED LARGE QUANTITIES OF DURINDFIRE GEMS...
...WHICH WE COULD TRACK!
HOPEFULLY TO THEIR BIGGEST RESEARCH FACILITY-- THE ONE WHERE THE FIRST DEATH STAR WAS BUILT!
AT LEAST, THAT WAS THE PLAN...
...WE DESTROY THE DATACARDS AND EVERYBODY GOES AWAY. AT LEAST, THIS WAS WHAT WE PLANNED...
NOT THE GREATEST OF PLANS. IF WE FOUND YOU, THE EMPIRE WILL, TOO. THEN WHAT?
THEN--WE END EVERYTHING!

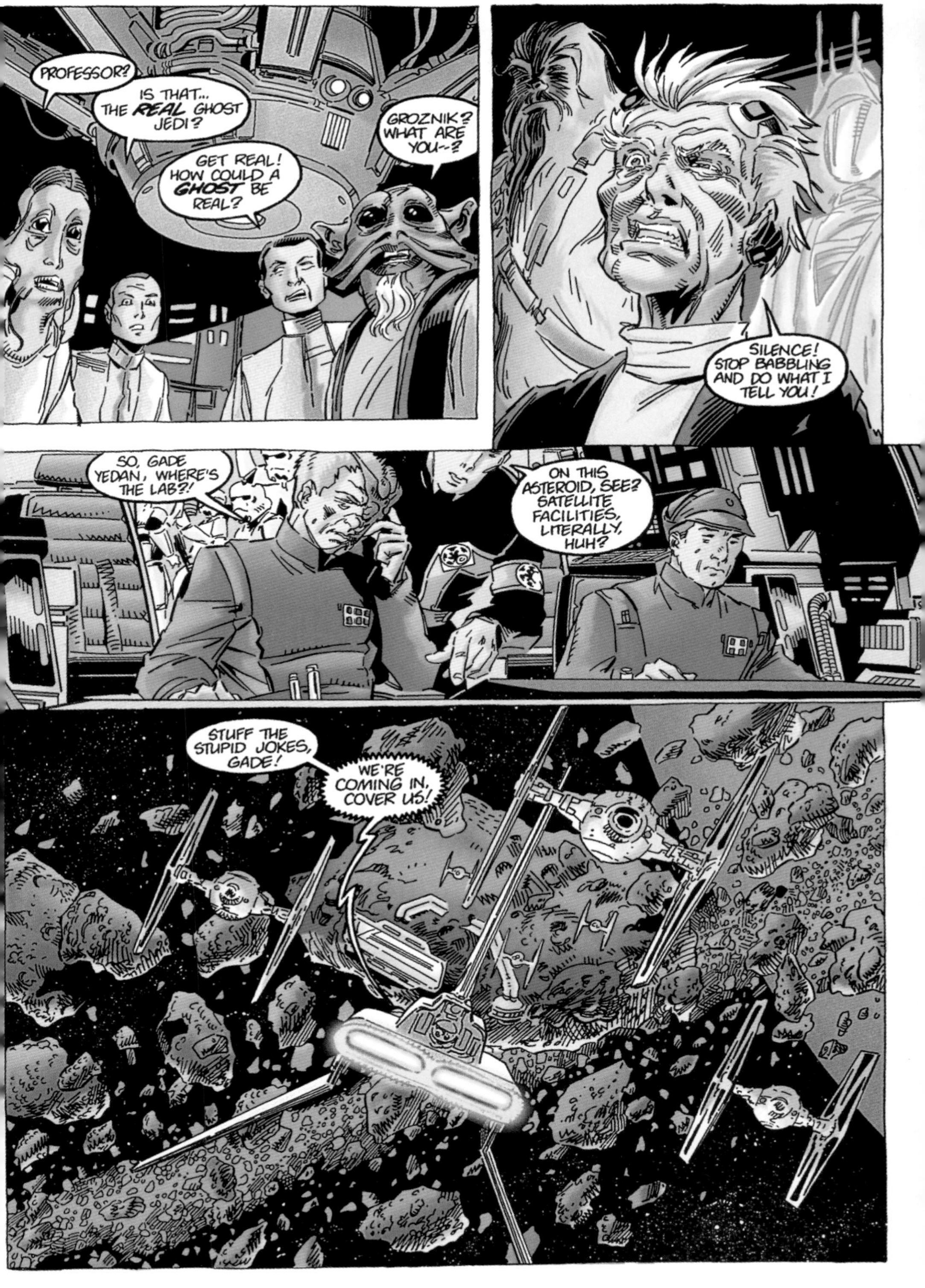
PROFESSOR?
IS THAT... THE REAL GHOST JEDI?
GROZNIK? WHAT ARE YOU--?
GET REAL! HOW COULD A GHOST BE REAL?
SILENCE! STOP BABBLING AND DO WHAT I TELL YOU!
SO, GADE YEDAN, WHERE'S THE LAB?!
ON THIS ASTEROID, SEE? SATELLITE FACILITIES, LITERALLY, HUH?
STUFF THE STUPID JOKES, GADE!
WE'RE COMING IN, COVER US!

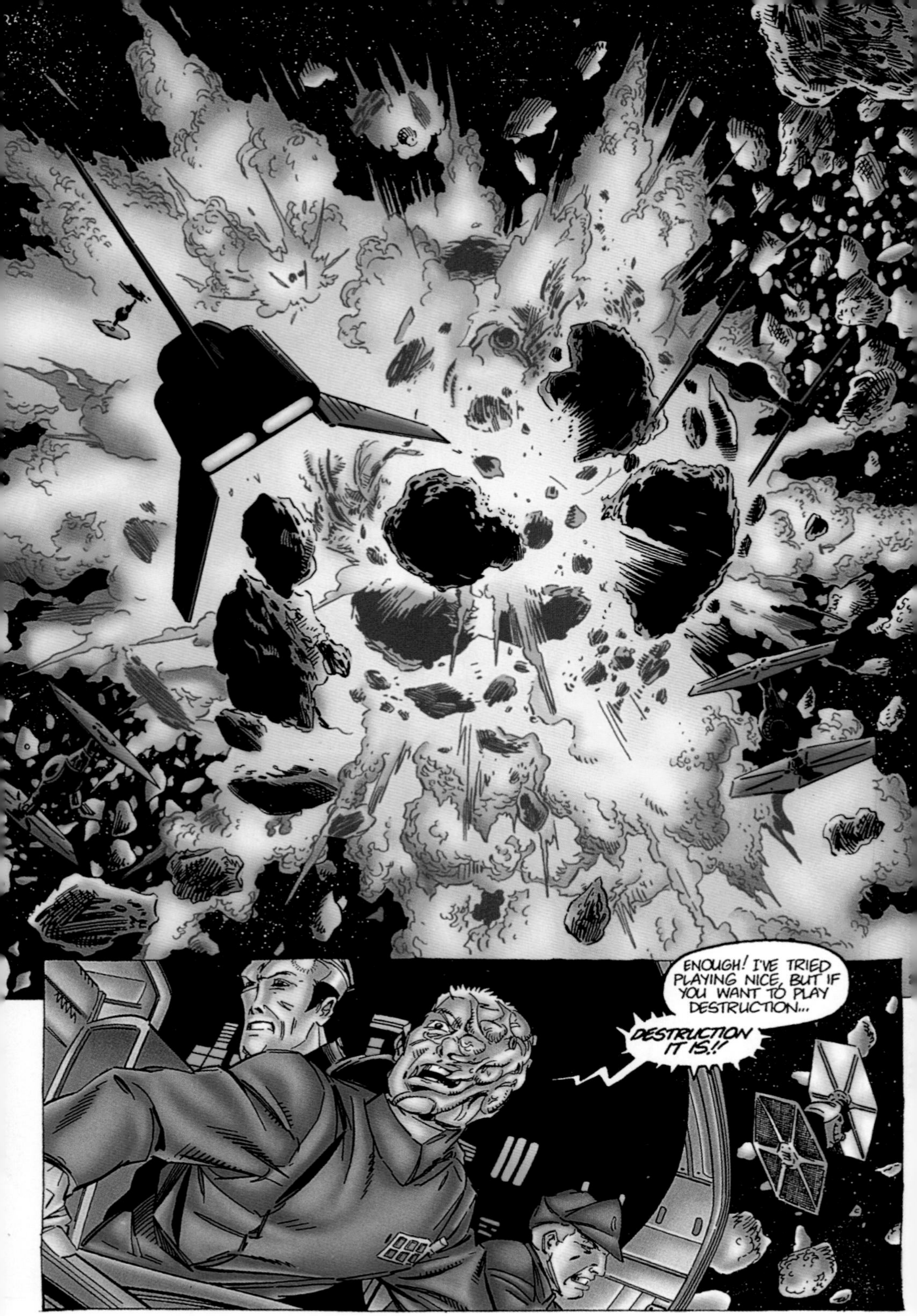
ENOUGH! I'VE TRIED PLAYING NICE, BUT IF YOU WANT TO PLAY DESTRUCTION...
DESTRUCTION IT IS!!

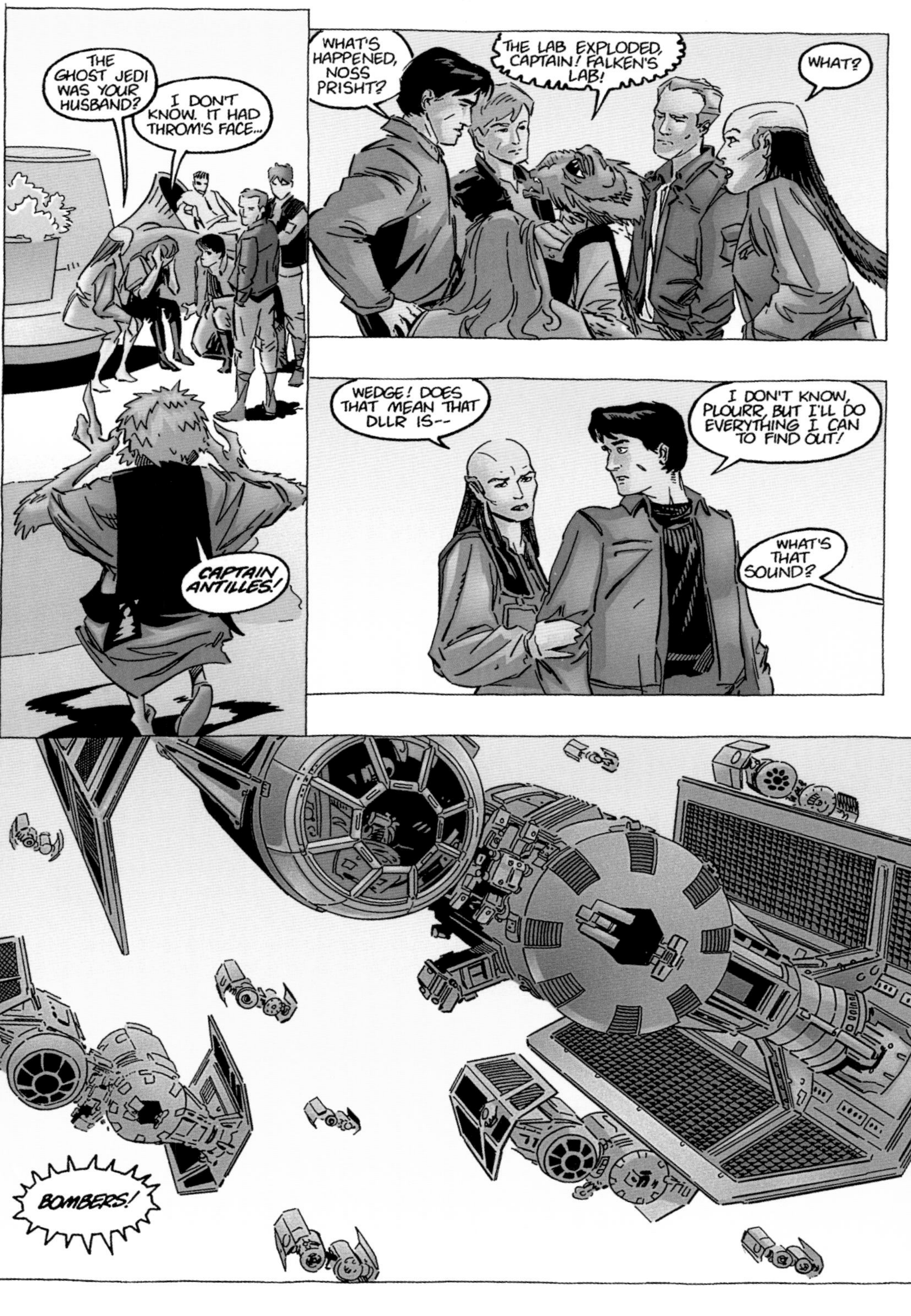
THE GHOST JEDI WAS YOUR HUSBAND?
I DON'T KNOW. IT HAD THROM'S FACE...
CAPTAIN ANTILLES!
WHAT'S HAPPENED, NOSS PRISHT?
THE LAB EXPLODED, CAPTAIN! FALKEN'S LAB!
WHAT?
WEDGE! DOES THAT MEAN THAT DLLR IS--
I DON'T KNOW, PLOURR, BUT I'LL DO EVERYTHING I CAN TO FIND OUT!
WHAT'S THAT SOUND?
BOMBERS!

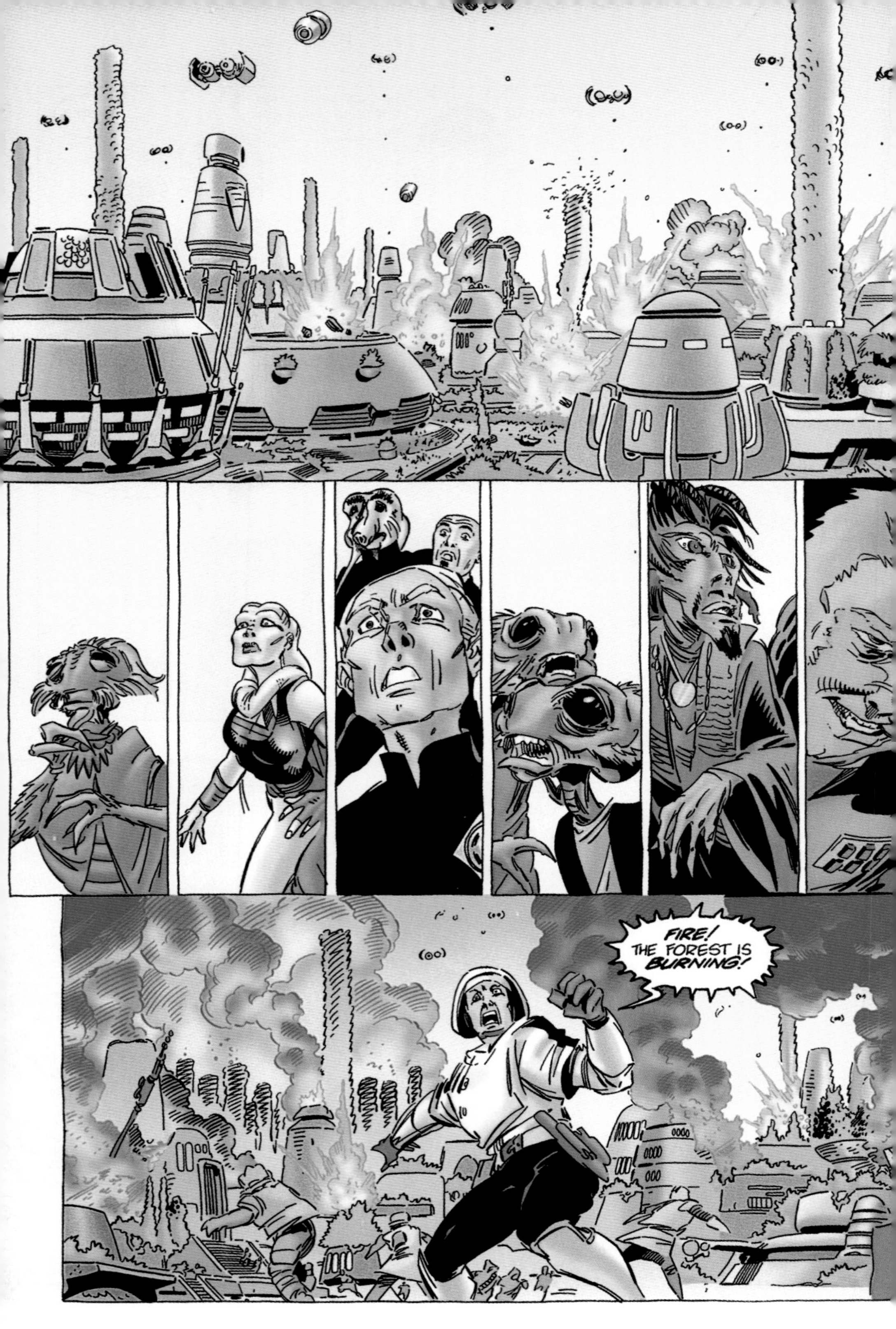
FIRE! THE FOREST IS BURNING!

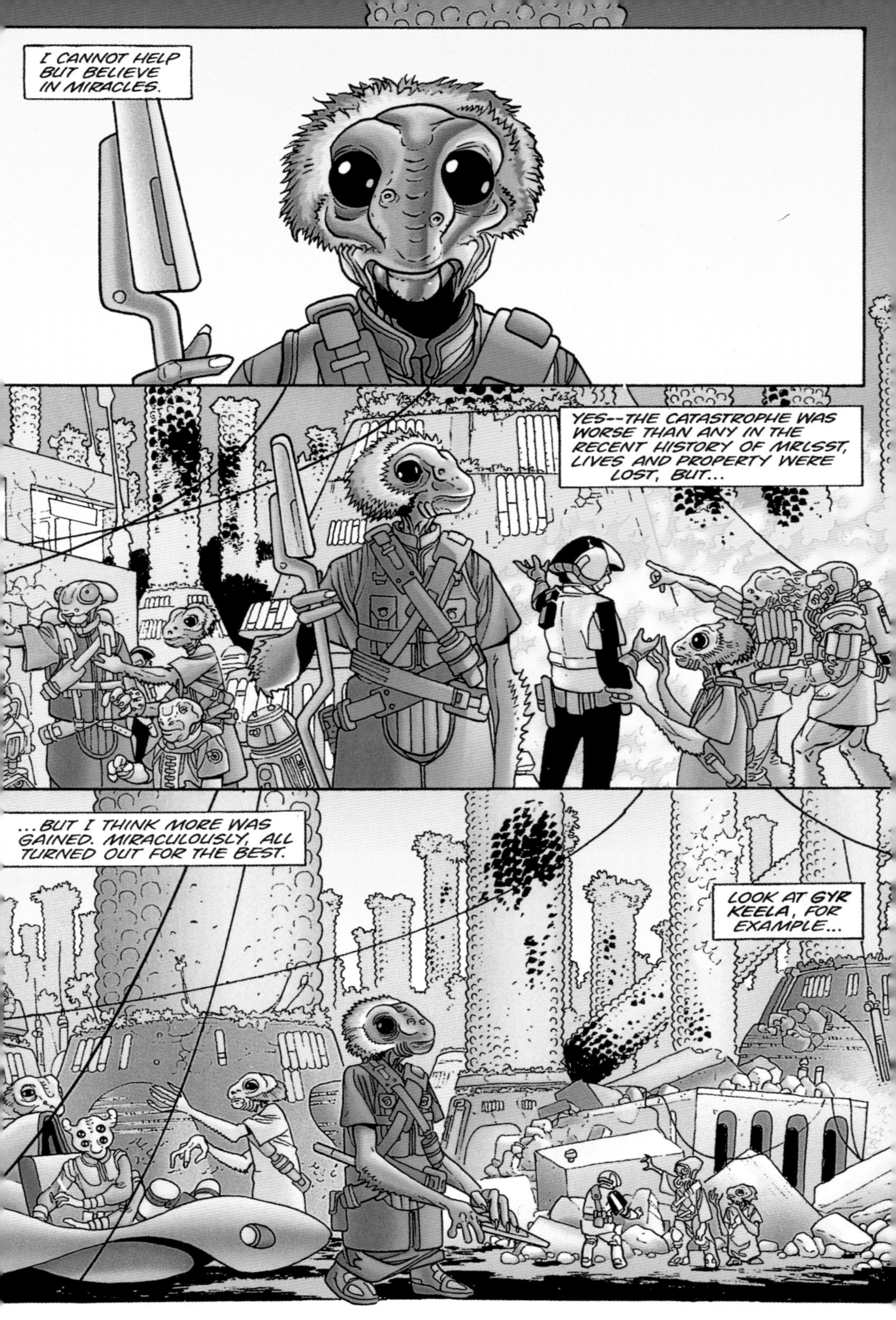
I CANNOT HELP BUT BELIEVE IN MIRACLES.
YES--THE CATASTROPHE WAS WORSE THAN ANY IN THE RECENT HISTORY OF MRLSST, LIVES AND PROPERTY WERE LOST, BUT...
...BUT I THINK MORE WAS GAINED. MIRACULOUSLY, ALL TURNED OUT FOR THE BEST.
LOOK AT GYR KEELA, FOR EXAMPLE...

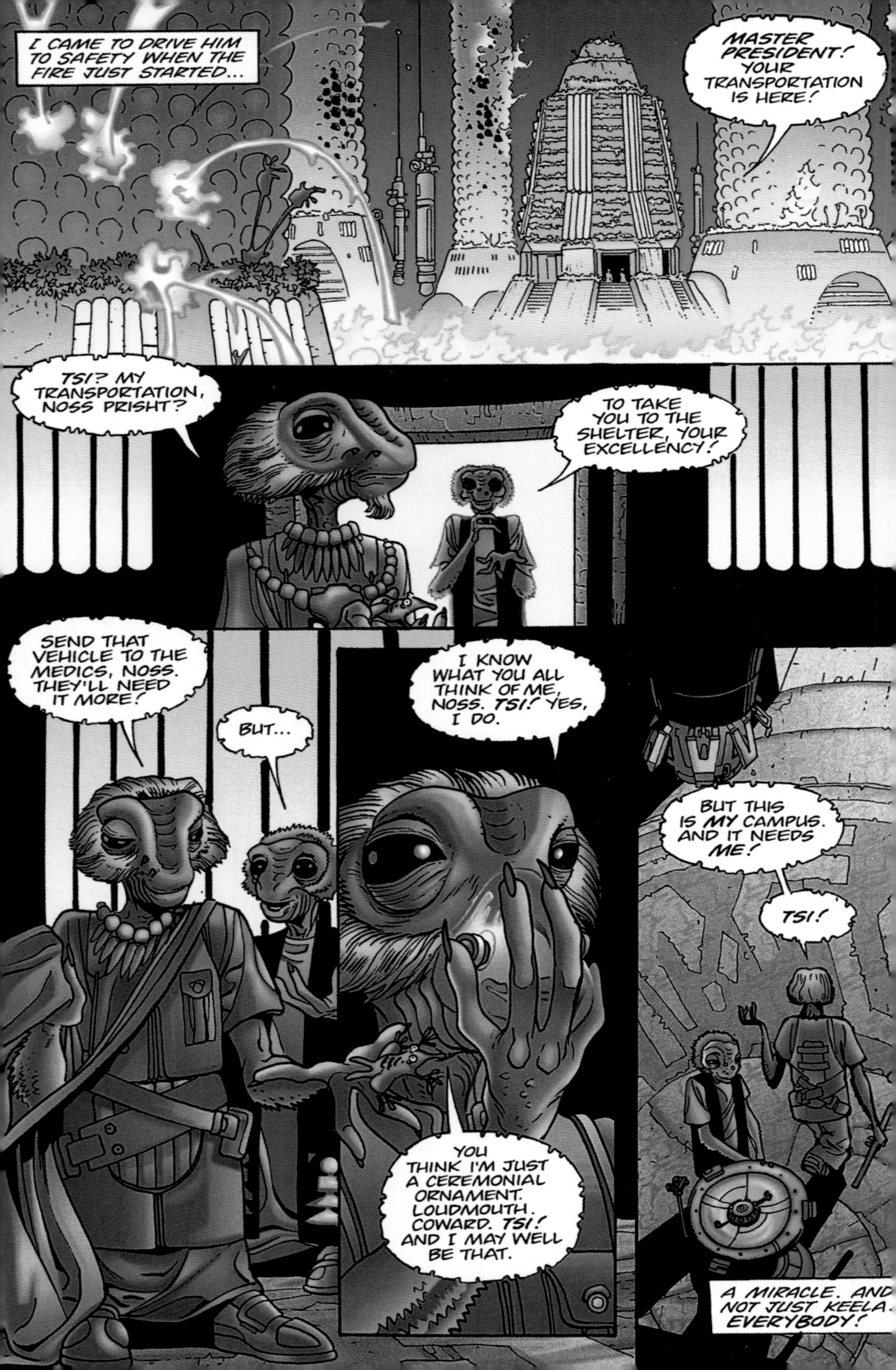

I CAME TO DRIVE HIM TO SAFETY WHEN THE FIRE JUST STARTED...
MASTER PRESIDENT! YOUR TRANSPORTATION IS HERE!
TSI? MY TRANSPORTATION, NOSS PRISHT?
TO TAKE YOU TO THE SHELTER, YOUR EXCELLENCY!
SEND THAT VEHICLE TO THE MEDICS, NOSS. THEY'LL NEED IT MORE!
BUT...
I KNOW WHAT YOU ALL THINK OF ME, NOSS. TSI! YES, I DO.
YOU THINK I'M JUST A CEREMONIAL ORNAMENT. LOUDMOUTH. COWARD. TSI! AND I MAY WELL BE THAT.
BUT THIS IS MY CAMPUS. AND IT NEEDS ME!
TSI!
A MIRACLE. AND NOT JUST KEELA. EVERYBODY!

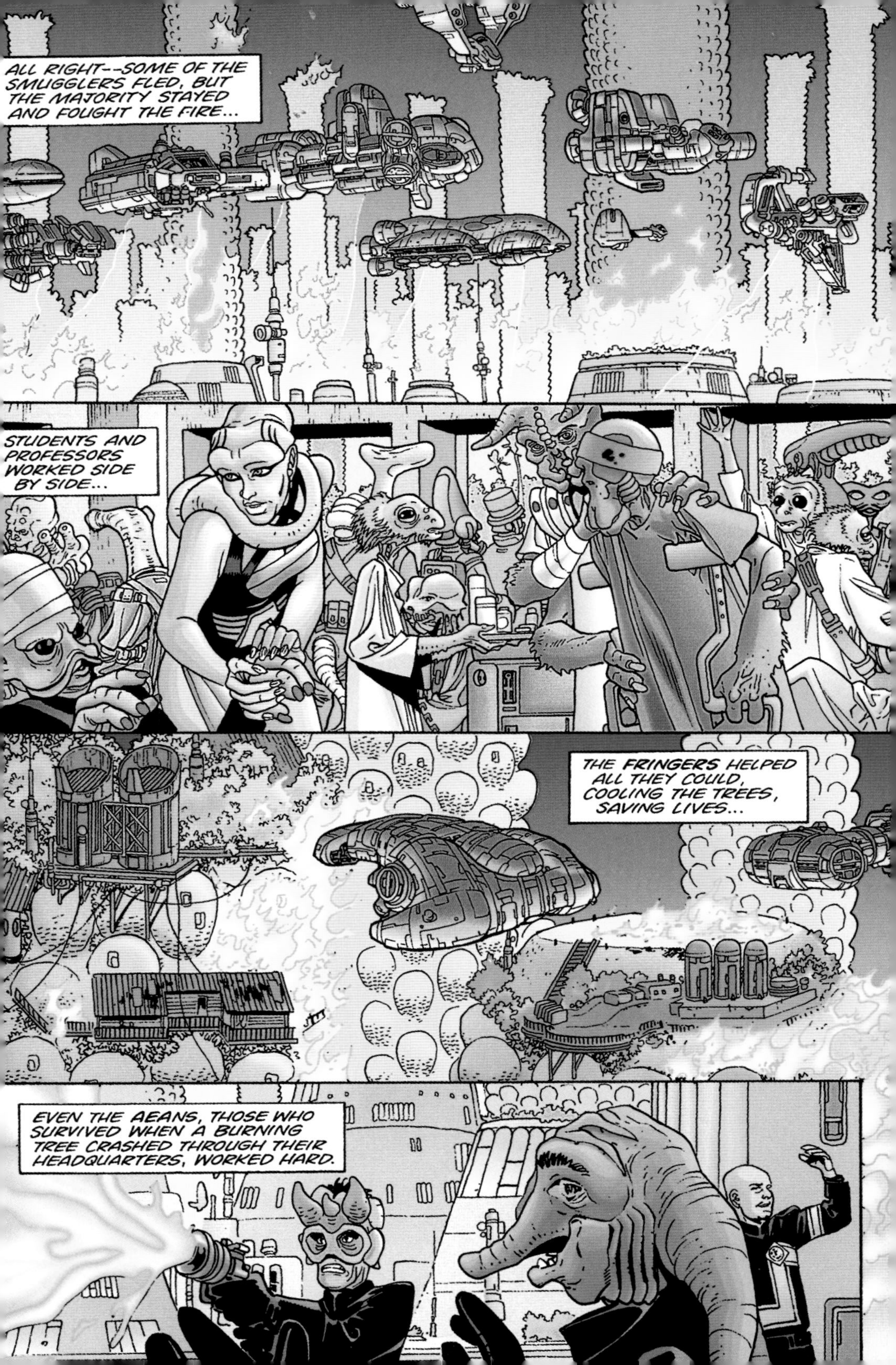
ALL RIGHT--SOME OF THE SMUGGLERS FLED, BUT THE MAJORITY STAYED AND FOUGHT THE FIRE...
STUDENTS AND PROFESSORS WORKED SIDE BY SIDE...
THE FRINGERS HELPED ALL THEY COULD, COOLING THE TREES, SAVING LIVES...
EVEN THE AEANS, THOSE WHO SURVIVED WHEN A BURNING TREE CRASHED THROUGH THEIR HEADQUARTERS, WORKED HARD.

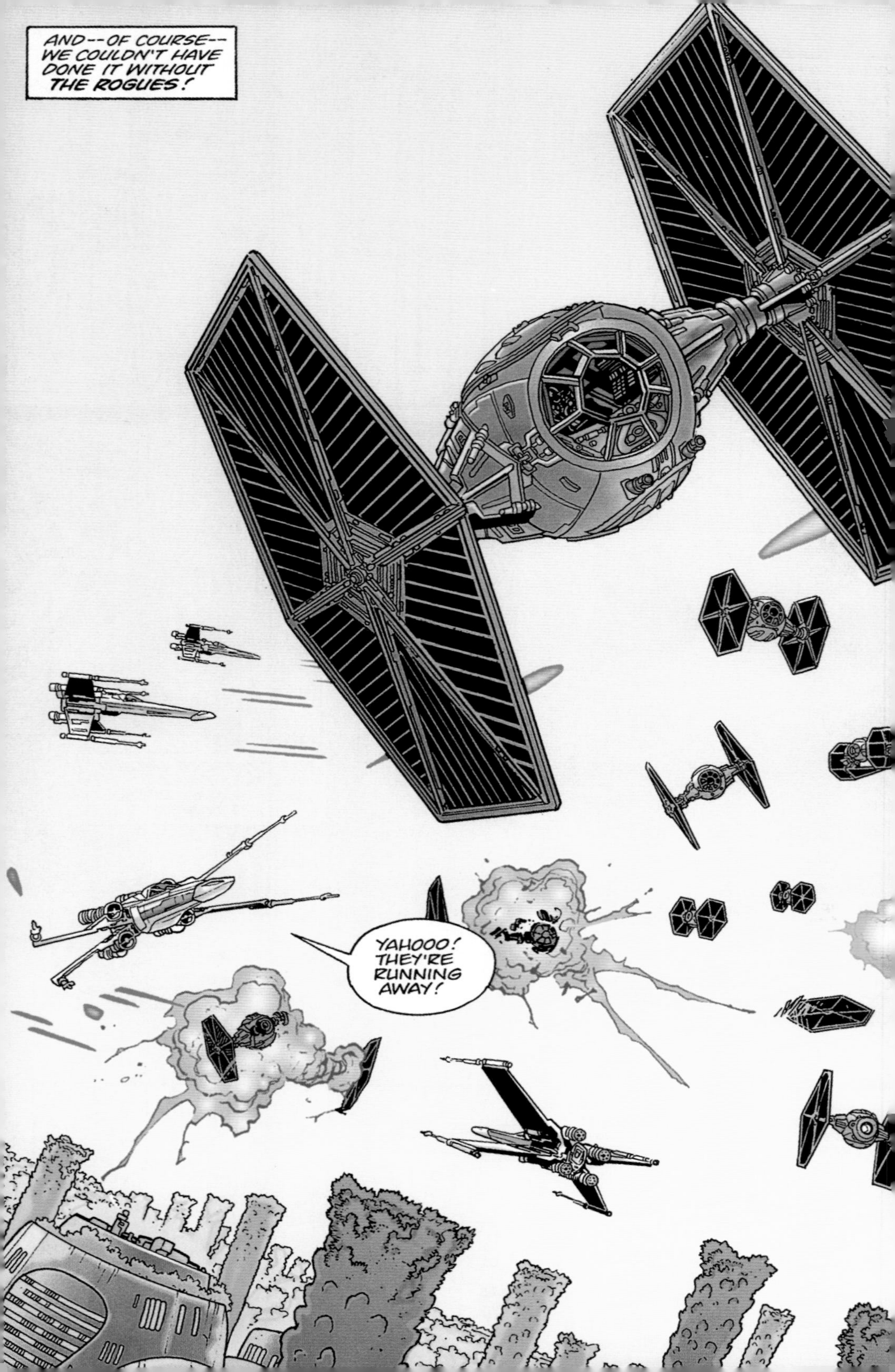
AND--OF COURSE--
WE COULDN'T HAVE
DONE IT WITHOUT
THE ROGUES!
YAHOOO!
THEY'RE
RUNNING
AWAY!

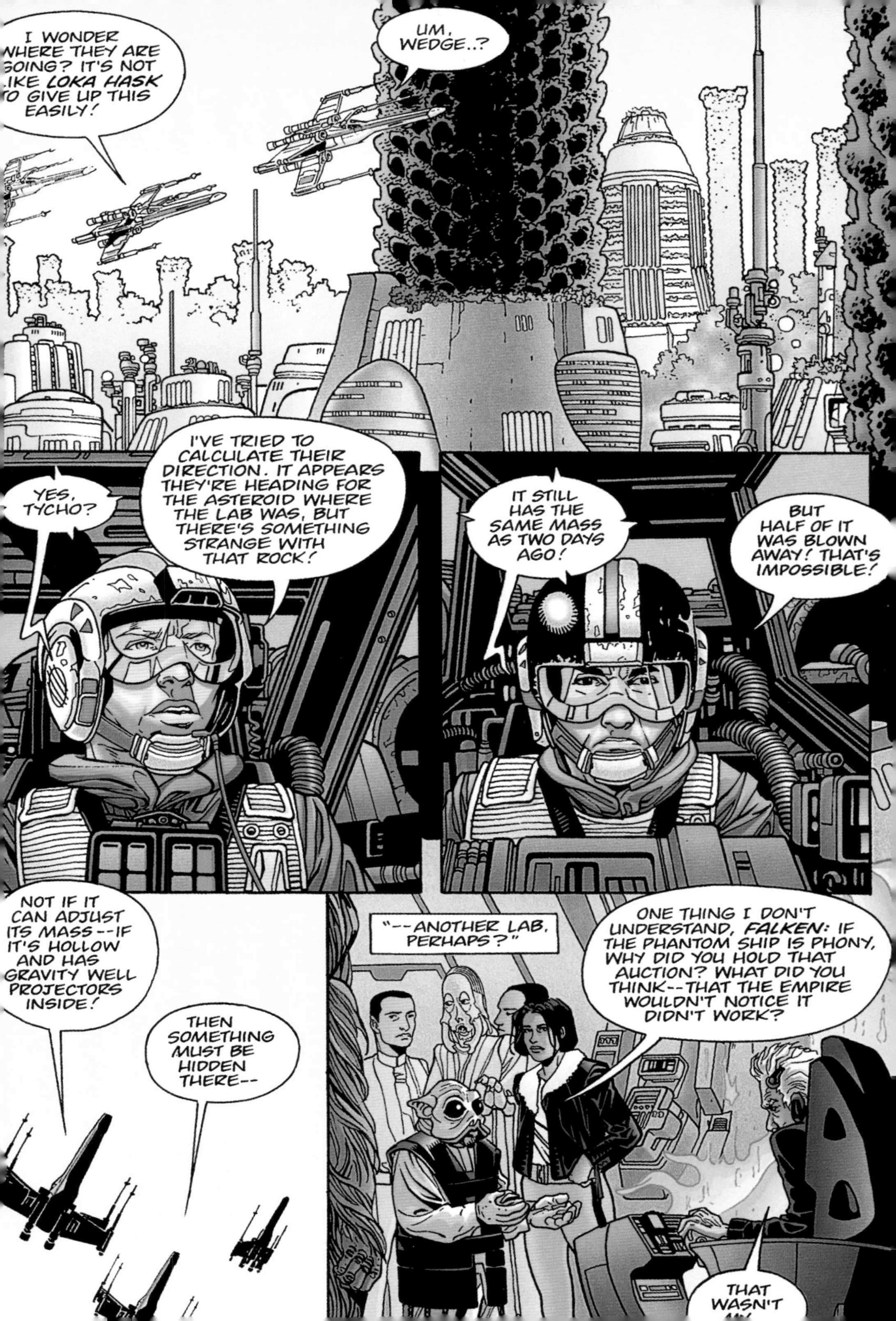
I WONDER WHERE THEY ARE GOING? IT'S NOT LIKE LOKA HASK TO GIVE UP THIS EASILY!
UM, WEDGE..?
YES, TYCHO?
I'VE TRIED TO CALCULATE THEIR DIRECTION. IT APPEARS THEY'RE HEADING FOR THE ASTEROID WHERE THE LAB WAS, BUT THERE'S SOMETHING STRANGE WITH THAT ROCK!
IT STILL HAS THE SAME MASS AS TWO DAYS AGO!
BUT HALF OF IT WAS BLOWN AWAY! THAT'S IMPOSSIBLE!
NOT IF IT CAN ADJUST ITS MASS--IF IT'S HOLLOW AND HAS GRAVITY WELL PROJECTORS INSIDE!
THEN SOMETHING MUST BE HIDDEN THERE--
"--ANOTHER LAB, PERHAPS?"
ONE THING I DON'T UNDERSTAND, FALKEN: IF THE PHANTOM SHIP IS PHONY, WHY DID YOU HOLD THAT AUCTION? WHAT DID YOU THINK--THAT THE EMPIRE WOULDN'T NOTICE IT DIDN'T WORK?
THAT WASN'T

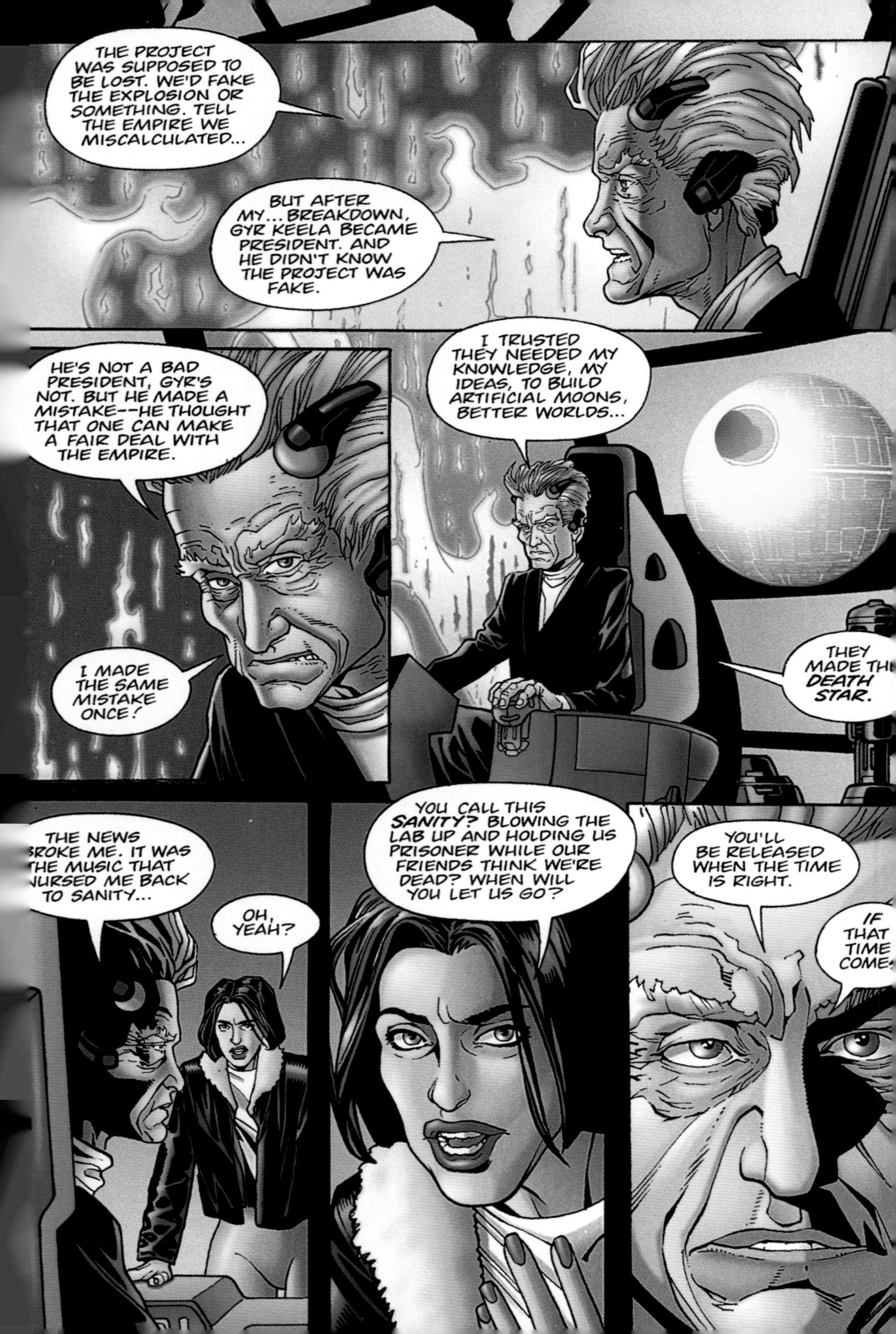
THE PROJECT WAS SUPPOSED TO BE LOST. WE'D FAKE THE EXPLOSION OR SOMETHING. TELL THE EMPIRE WE MISCALCULATED...
BUT AFTER MY... BREAKDOWN, GYR KEELA BECAME PRESIDENT. AND HE DIDN'T KNOW THE PROJECT WAS FAKE.
HE'S NOT A BAD PRESIDENT, GYR'S NOT. BUT HE MADE A MISTAKE--HE THOUGHT THAT ONE CAN MAKE A FAIR DEAL WITH THE EMPIRE.
I MADE THE SAME MISTAKE ONCE!
I TRUSTED THEY NEEDED MY KNOWLEDGE, MY IDEAS, TO BUILD ARTIFICIAL MOONS, BETTER WORLDS...
THEY MADE TH DEATH STAR.
THE NEWS BROKE ME. IT WAS THE MUSIC THAT NURSED ME BACK TO SANITY...
OH, YEAH?
YOU CALL THIS SANITY? BLOWING THE LAB UP AND HOLDING US PRISONER WHILE OUR FRIENDS THINK WE'RE DEAD? WHEN WILL YOU LET US GO?
YOU'LL BE RELEASED WHEN THE TIME IS RIGHT.
IF THAT TIME COME.

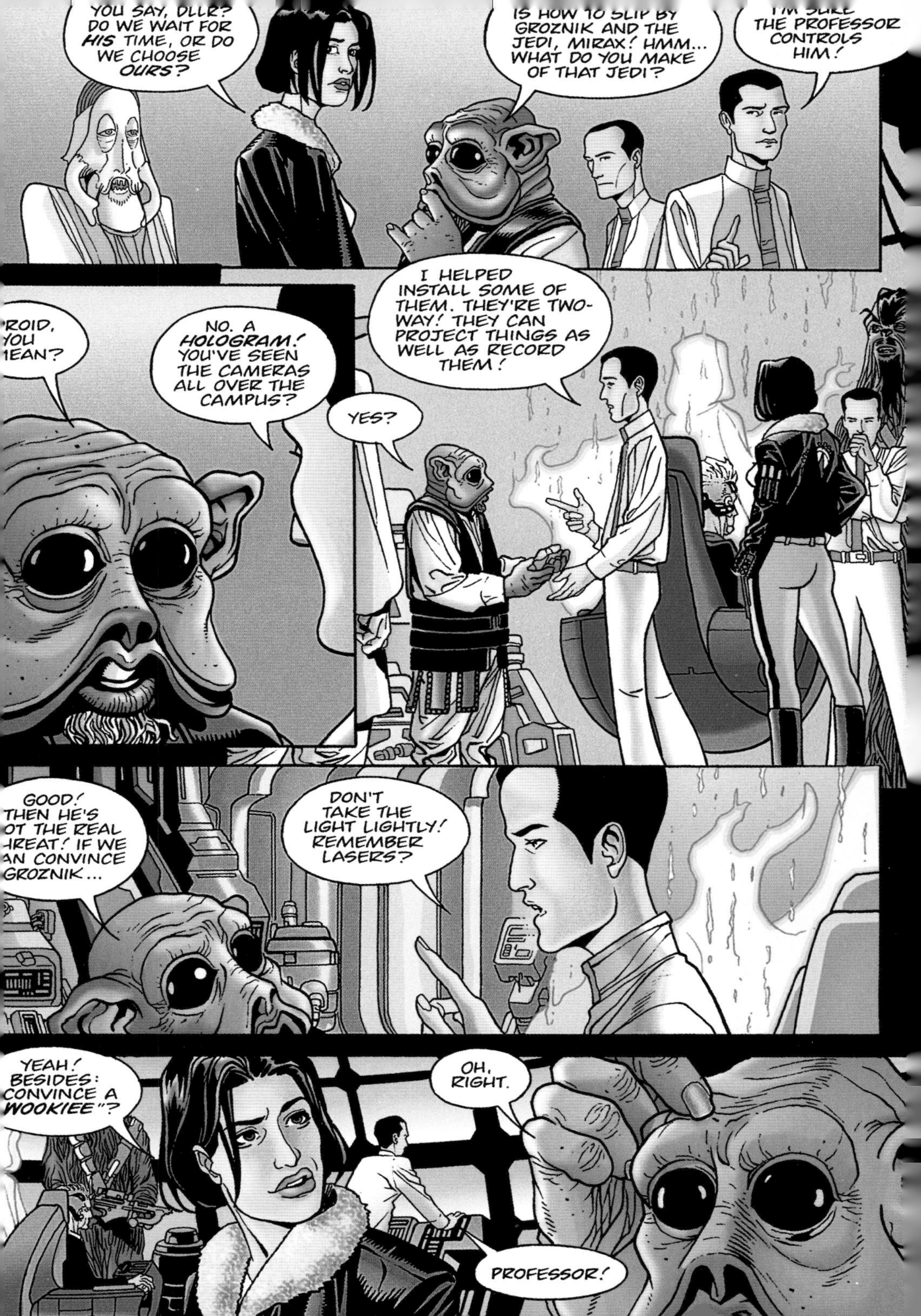
YOU SAY, DLLR? DO WE WAIT FOR HIS TIME, OR DO WE CHOOSE OURS?
IS HOW TO SLIP BY GROZNIK AND THE JEDI, MIRAX! HMM... WHAT DO YOU MAKE OF THAT JEDI?
THE PROFESSOR CONTROLS HIM!
ROID, YOU MEAN?
NO. A HOLOGRAM! YOU'VE SEEN THE CAMERAS ALL OVER THE CAMPUS?
YES?
I HELPED INSTALL SOME OF THEM. THEY'RE TWO-WAY! THEY CAN PROJECT THINGS AS WELL AS RECORD THEM!
GOOD! THEN HE'S OT THE REAL HREAT! IF WE AN CONVINCE GROZNIK...
DON'T TAKE THE LIGHT LIGHTLY! REMEMBER LASERS?
YEAH! BESIDES: CONVINCE A WOOKIEE"?
OH, RIGHT.
PROFESSOR!

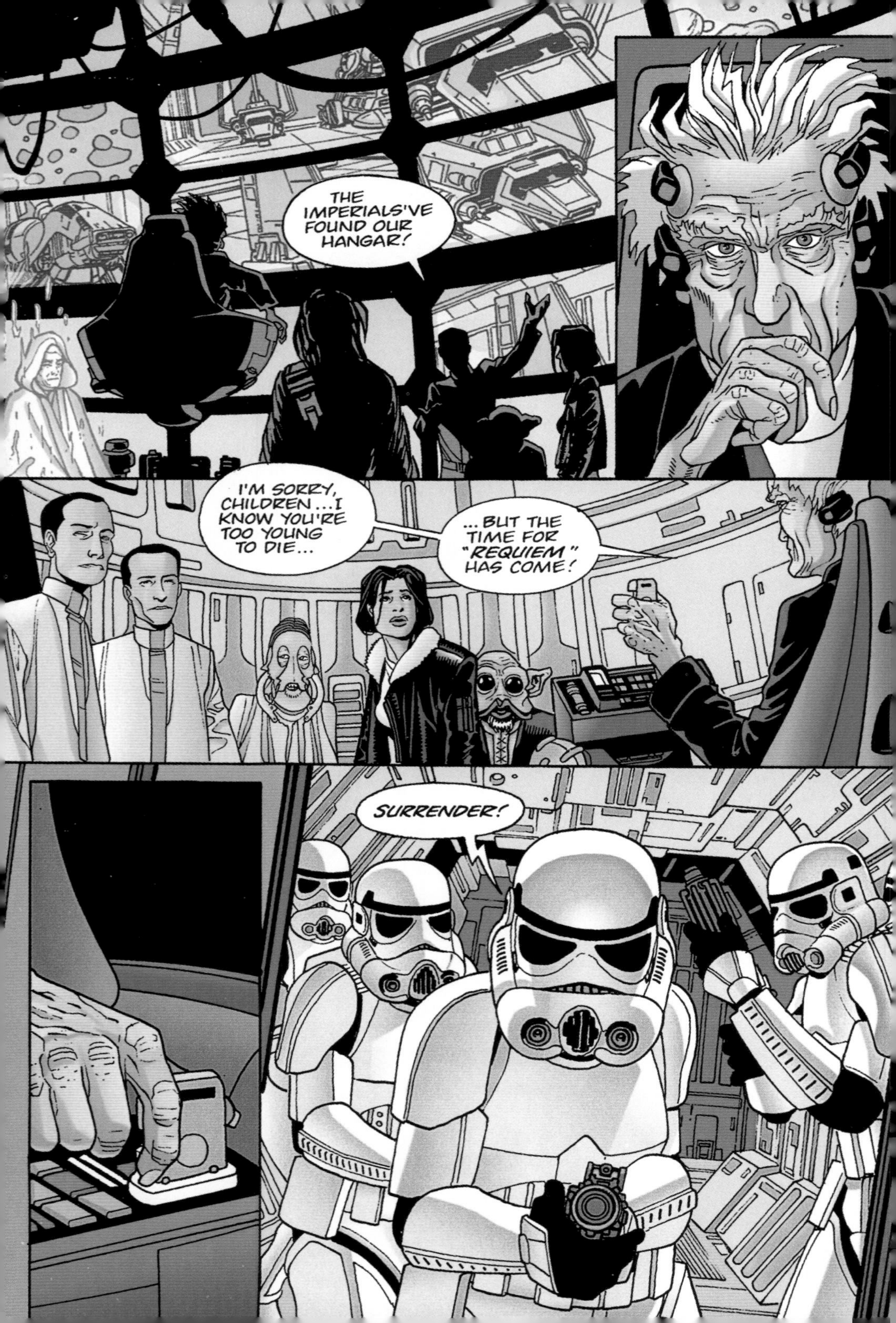
THE IMPERIALS'VE FOUND OUR HANGAR!
I'M SORRY, CHILDREN...I KNOW YOU'RE TOO YOUNG TO DIE...
...BUT THE TIME FOR "REQUIEM" HAS COME!
SURRENDER!

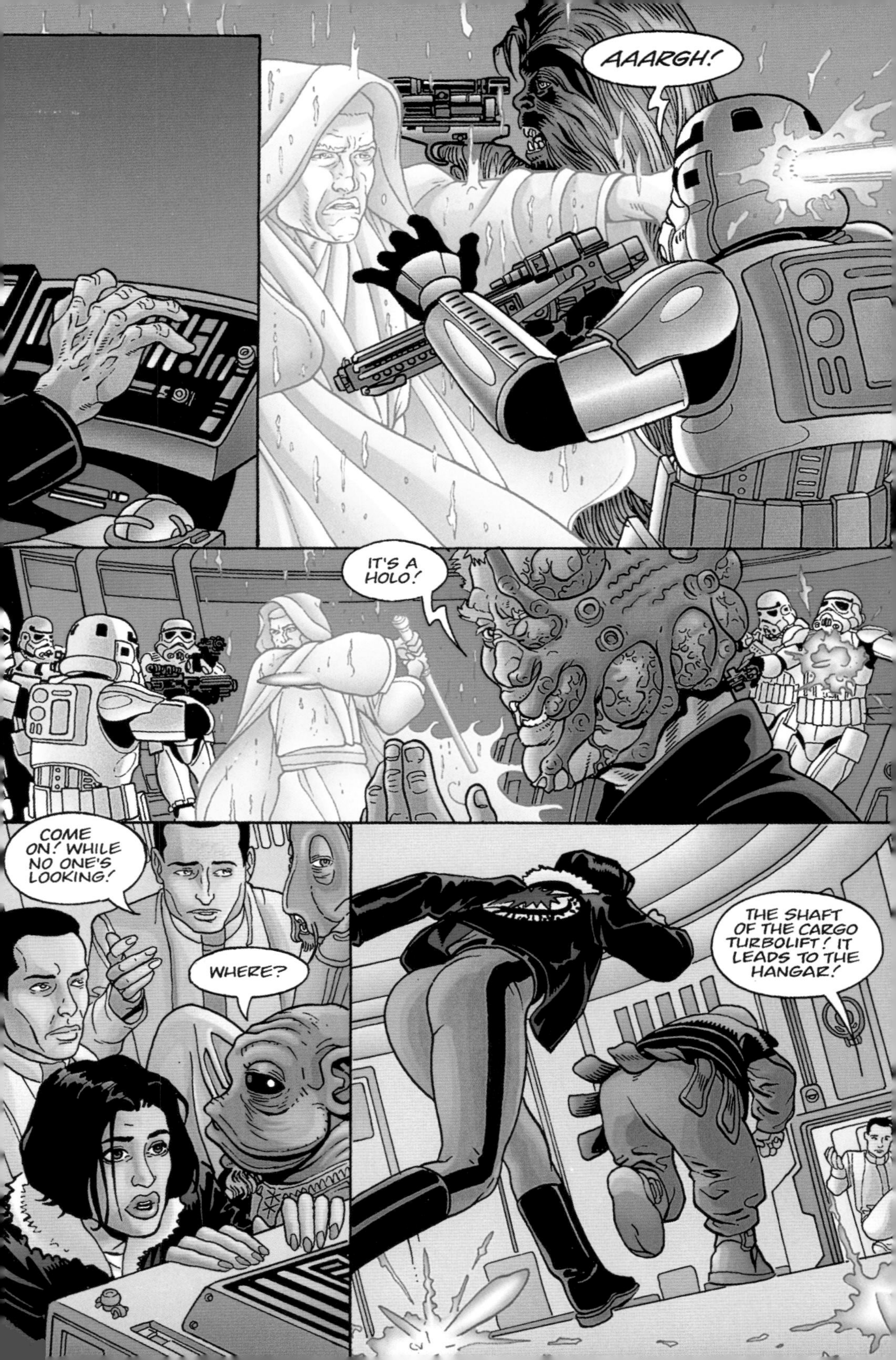
AAARGH!
IT'S A HOLO!
COME ON! WHILE NO ONE'S LOOKING!
WHERE?
THE SHAFT OF THE CARGO TURBOLIFT! IT LEADS TO THE HANGAR!

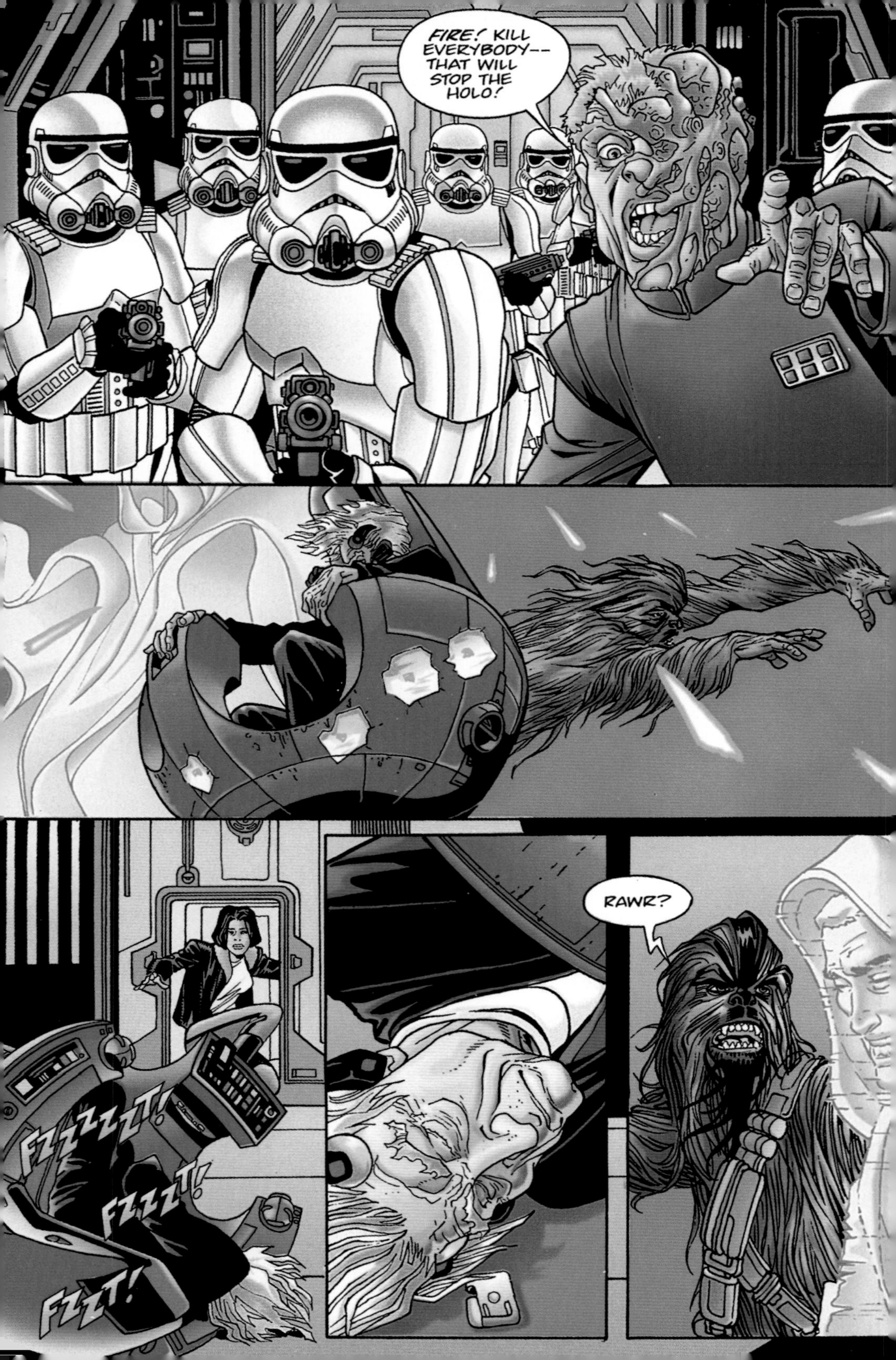
FIRE! KILL EVERYBODY-- THAT WILL STOP THE HOLO!
FZZZZZT!
FZZZT!
FZZT!
RAWR?

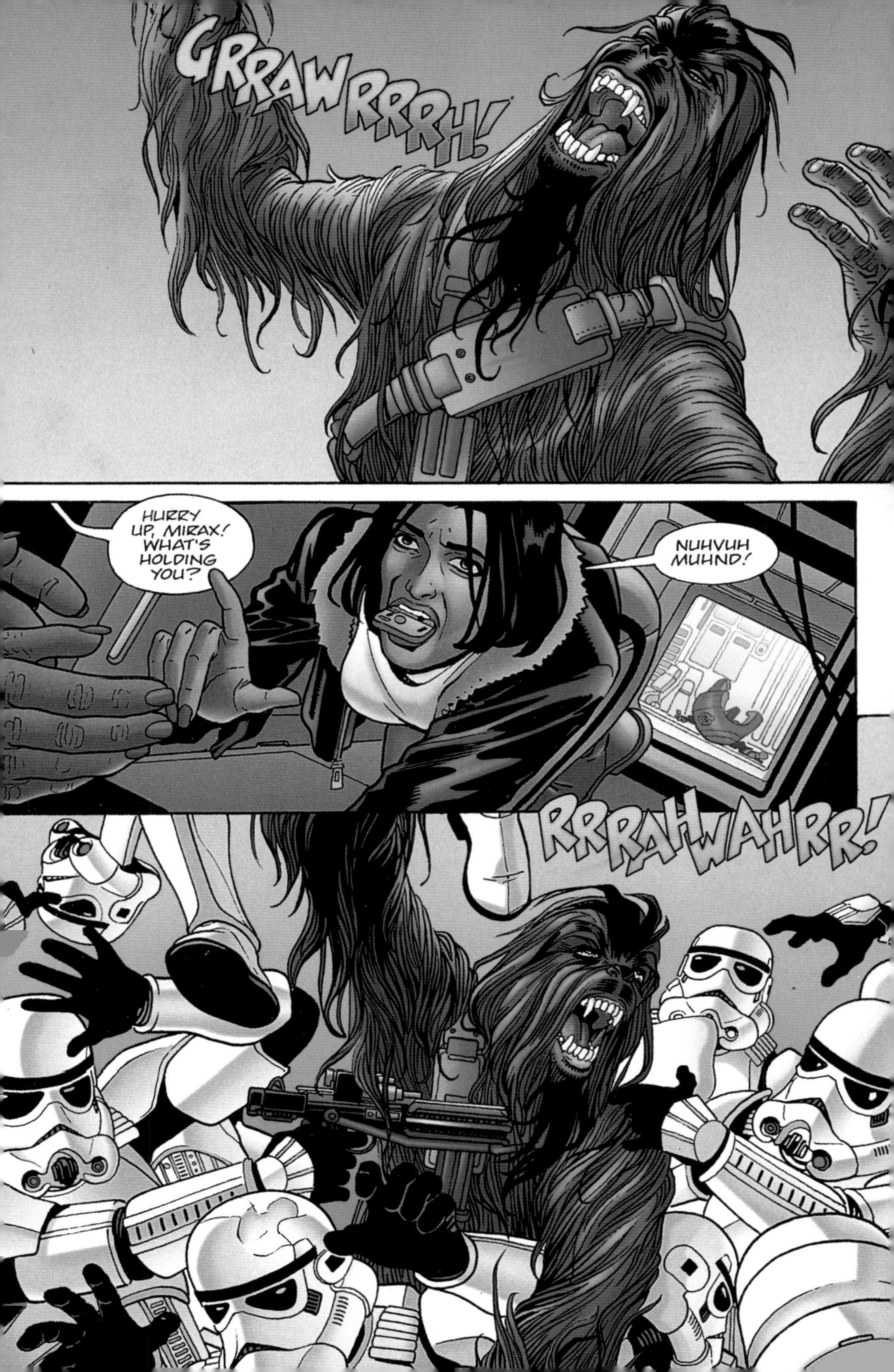
GRRAWRRRH!
HURRY UP, MIRAX! WHAT'S HOLDING YOU?
NUHVUH MUHND!
RRRAHWAHRR!

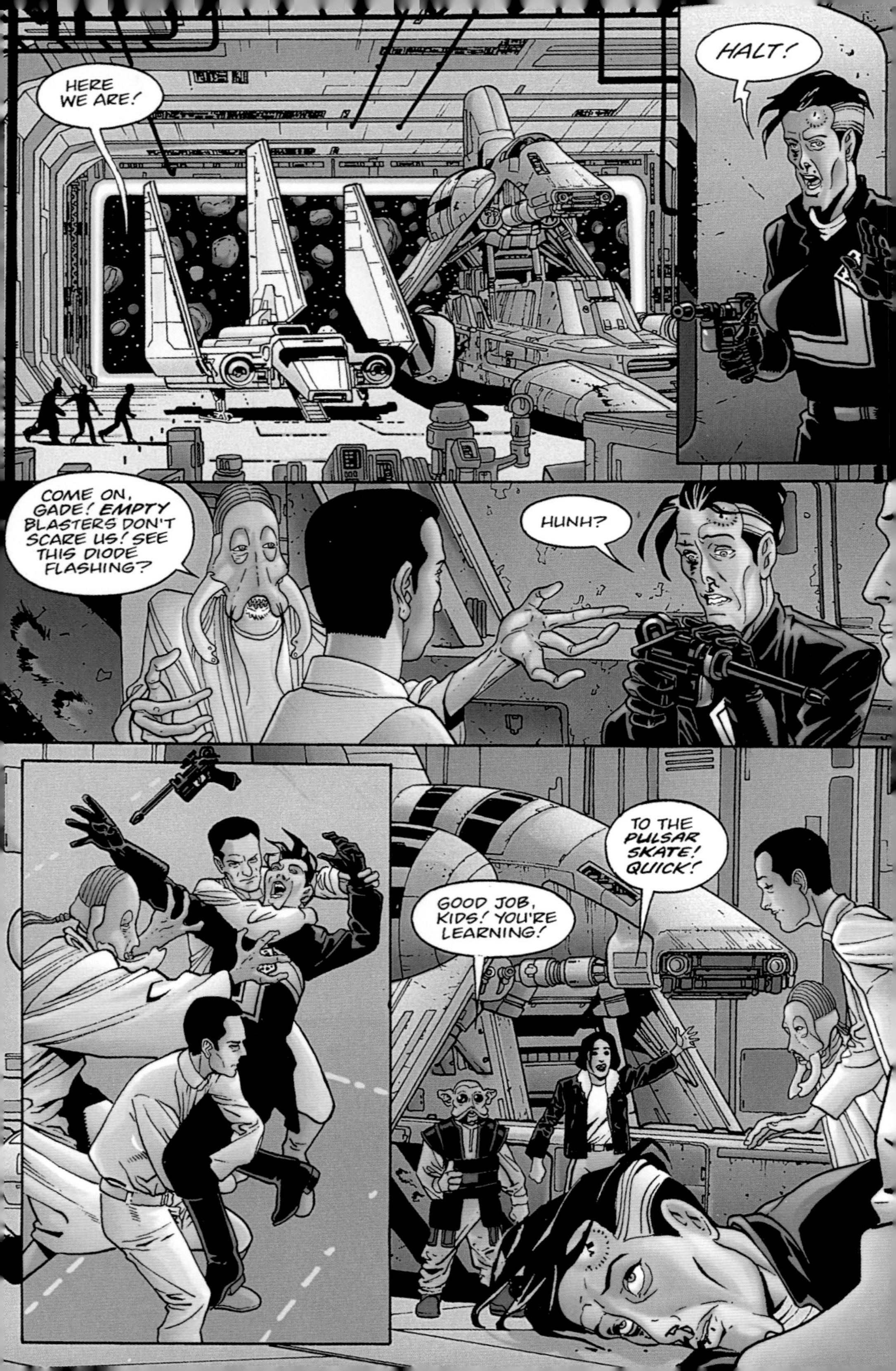
HERE WE ARE!
HALT!
COME ON, GADE! EMPTY BLASTERS DON'T SCARE US! SEE THIS DIODE FLASHING?
HUNH?
TO THE PULSAR SKATE! QUICK!
GOOD JOB, KIDS! YOU'RE LEARNING!

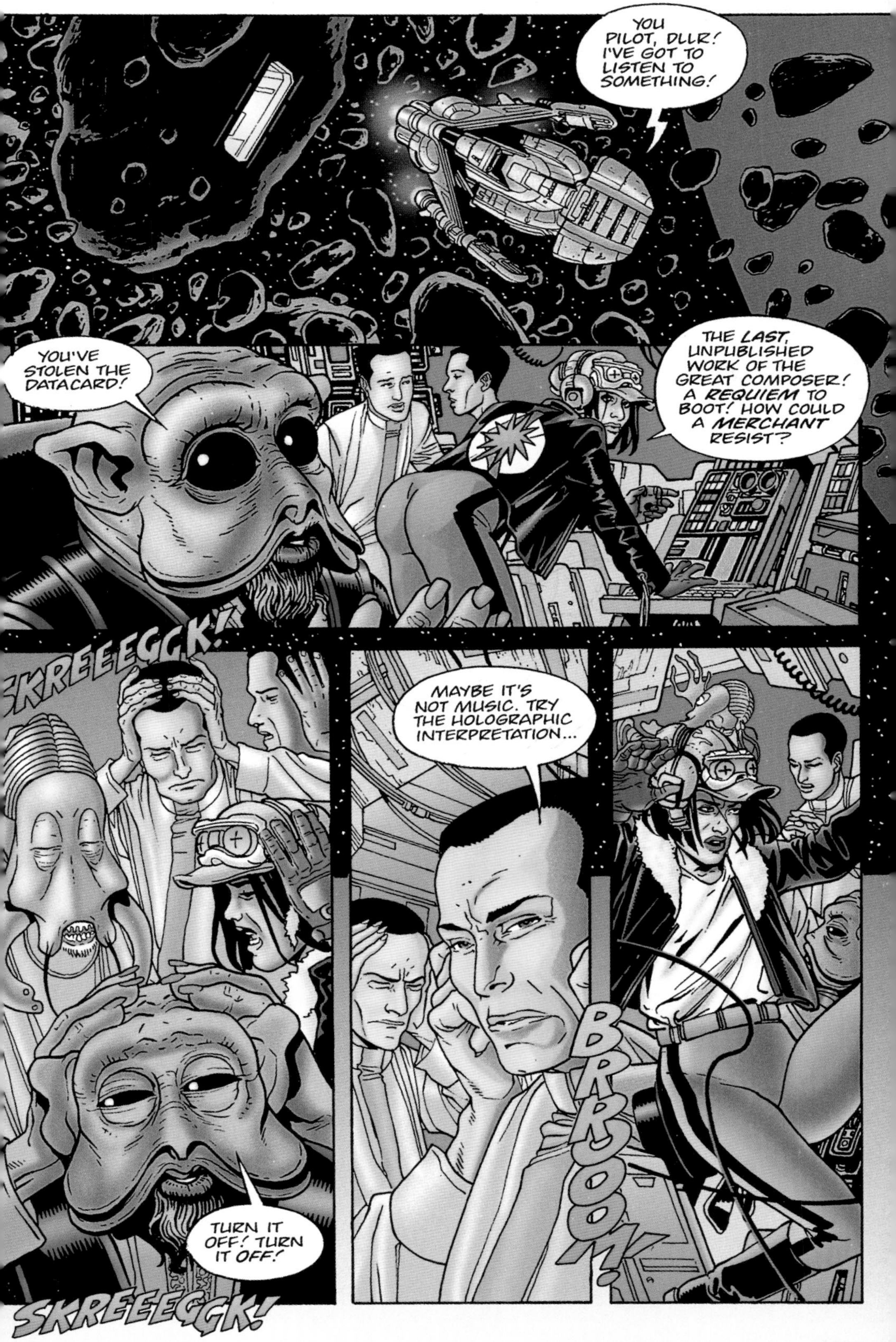
YOU PILOT, DLLR! I'VE GOT TO LISTEN TO SOMETHING!
YOU'VE STOLEN THE DATACARD!
THE LAST, UNPUBLISHED WORK OF THE GREAT COMPOSER! A REQUIEM TO BOOT! HOW COULD A MERCHANT RESIST?
SKREEEGGK!
TURN IT OFF! TURN IT OFF!
SKREEEGGK!
MAYBE IT'S NOT MUSIC. TRY THE HOLOGRAPHIC INTERPRETATION...
BRROOOM!

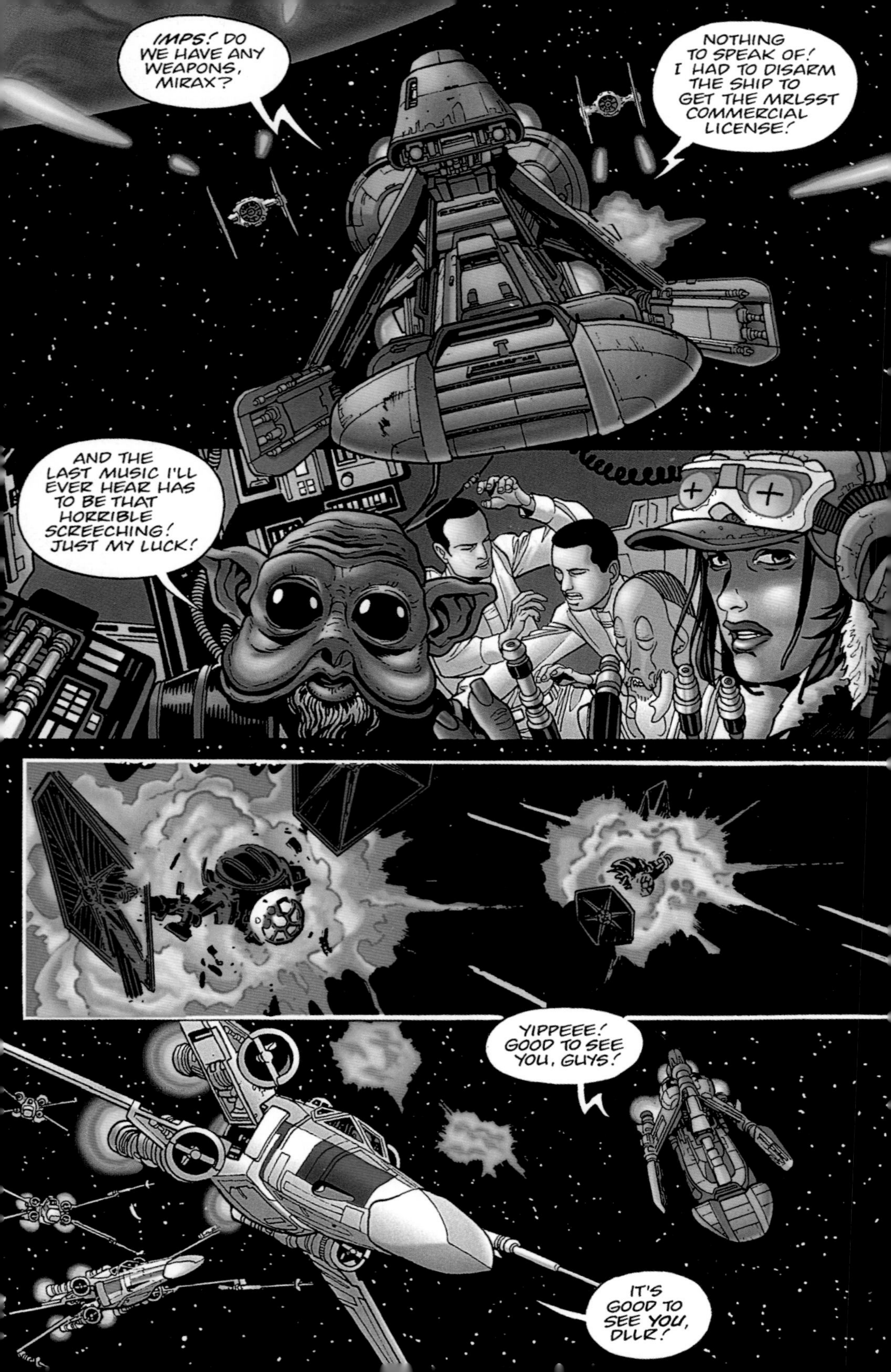
IMPS! DO WE HAVE ANY WEAPONS, MIRAX?
NOTHING TO SPEAK OF! I HAD TO DISARM THE SHIP TO GET THE MRLSST COMMERCIAL LICENSE!
AND THE LAST MUSIC I'LL EVER HEAR HAS TO BE THAT HORRIBLE SCREECHING! JUST MY LUCK!
YIPPEEE! GOOD TO SEE YOU, GUYS!
IT'S GOOD TO SEE YOU, DLLR!

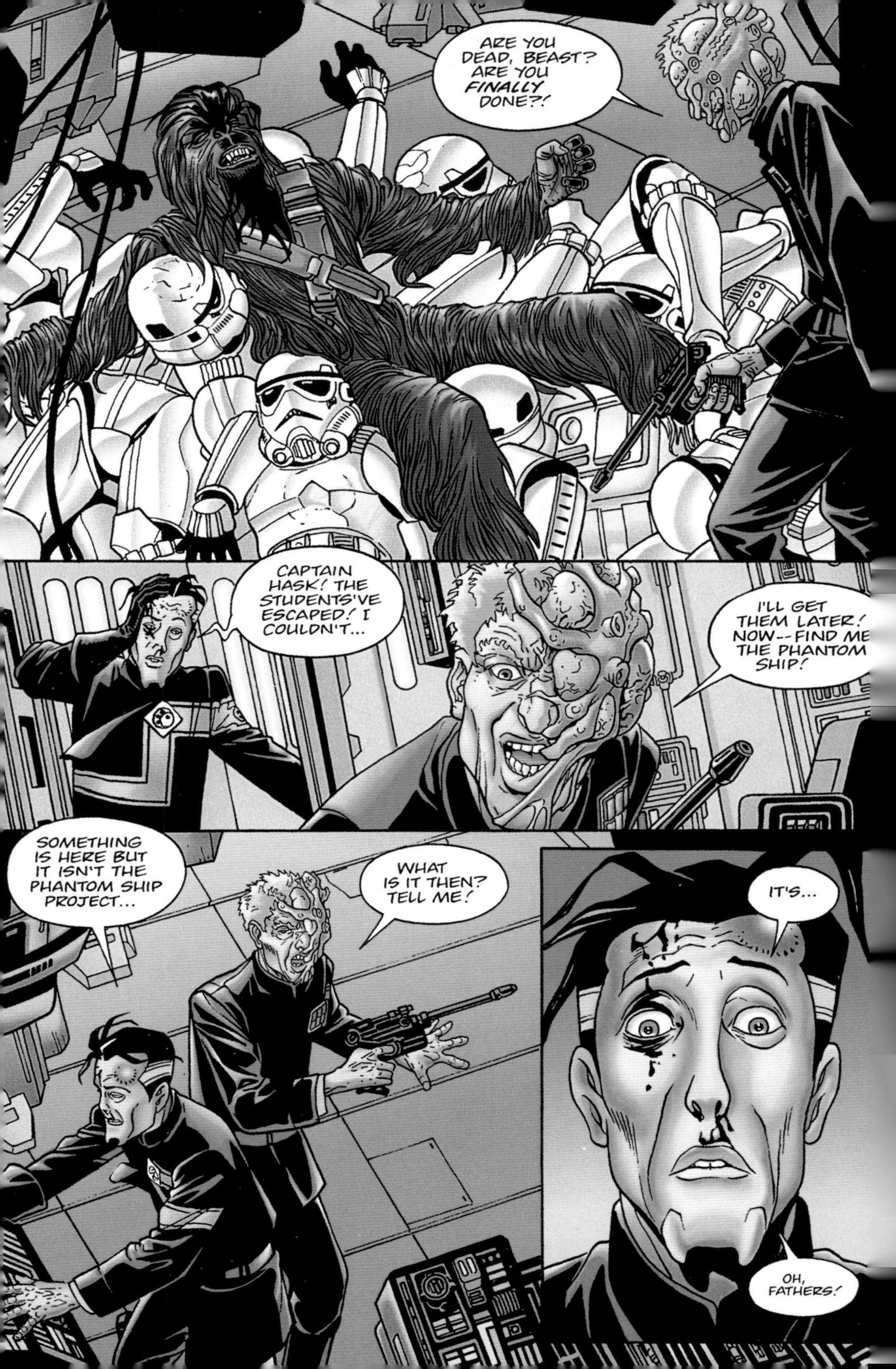
ARE YOU DEAD, BEAST? ARE YOU *FINALLY* DONE?!
CAPTAIN HASK! THE STUDENTS'VE ESCAPED! I COULDN'T...
I'LL GET THEM LATER! NOW--FIND ME THE PHANTOM SHIP!
SOMETHING IS HERE BUT IT ISN'T THE PHANTOM SHIP PROJECT...
WHAT IS IT THEN? TELL ME!
IT'S...
OH, FATHERS!

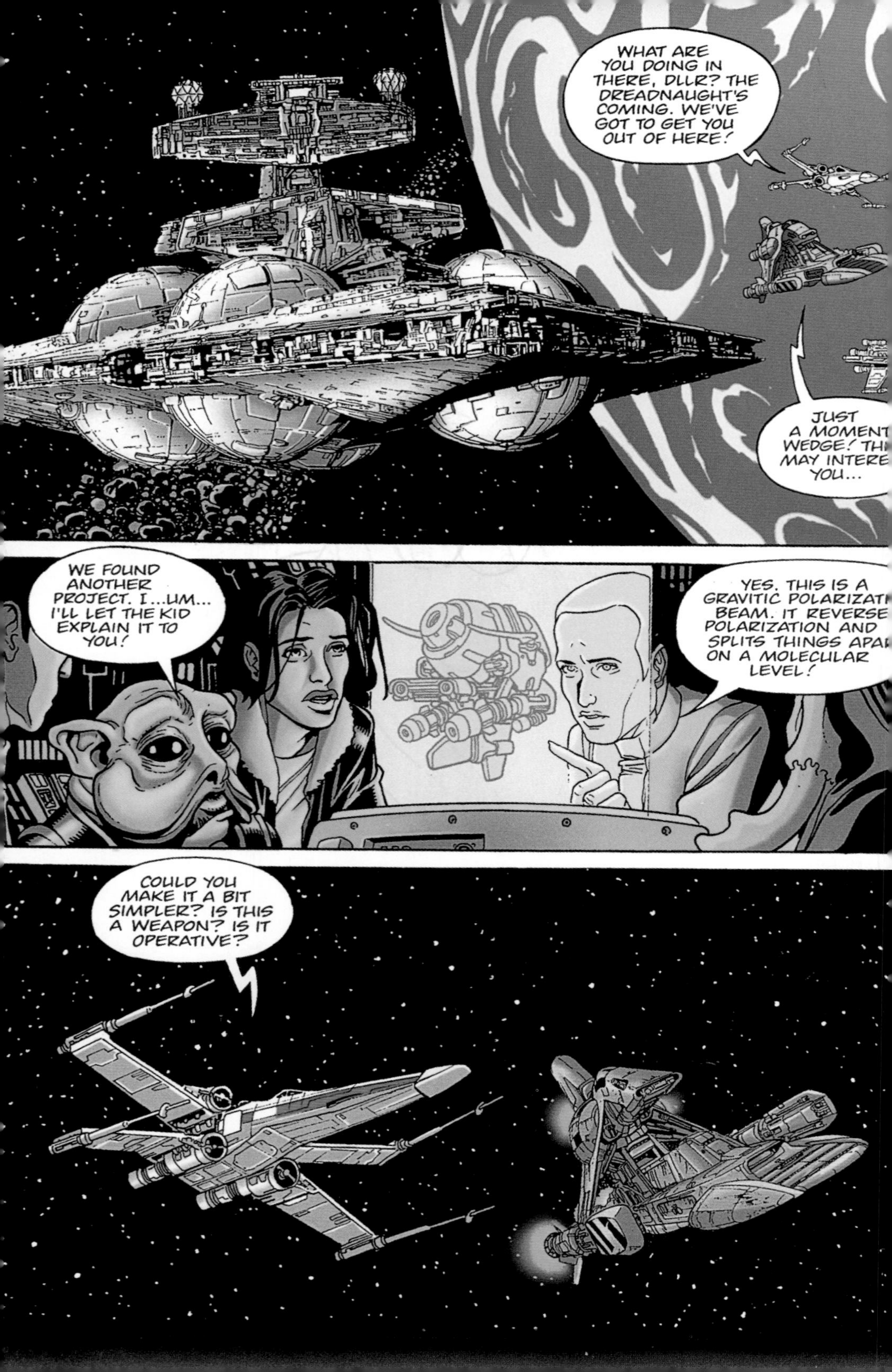
WHAT ARE YOU DOING IN THERE, DLLR? THE DREADNAUGHT'S COMING. WE'VE GOT TO GET YOU OUT OF HERE!
JUST A MOMENT WEDGE! THI MAY INTERE YOU...
WE FOUND ANOTHER PROJECT. I...UM... I'LL LET THE KID EXPLAIN IT TO YOU!
YES. THIS IS A GRAVITIC POLARIZATI BEAM. IT REVERSE POLARIZATION AND SPLITS THINGS APA ON A MOLECULAR LEVEL!
COULD YOU MAKE IT A BIT SIMPLER? IS THIS A WEAPON? IS IT OPERATIVE?

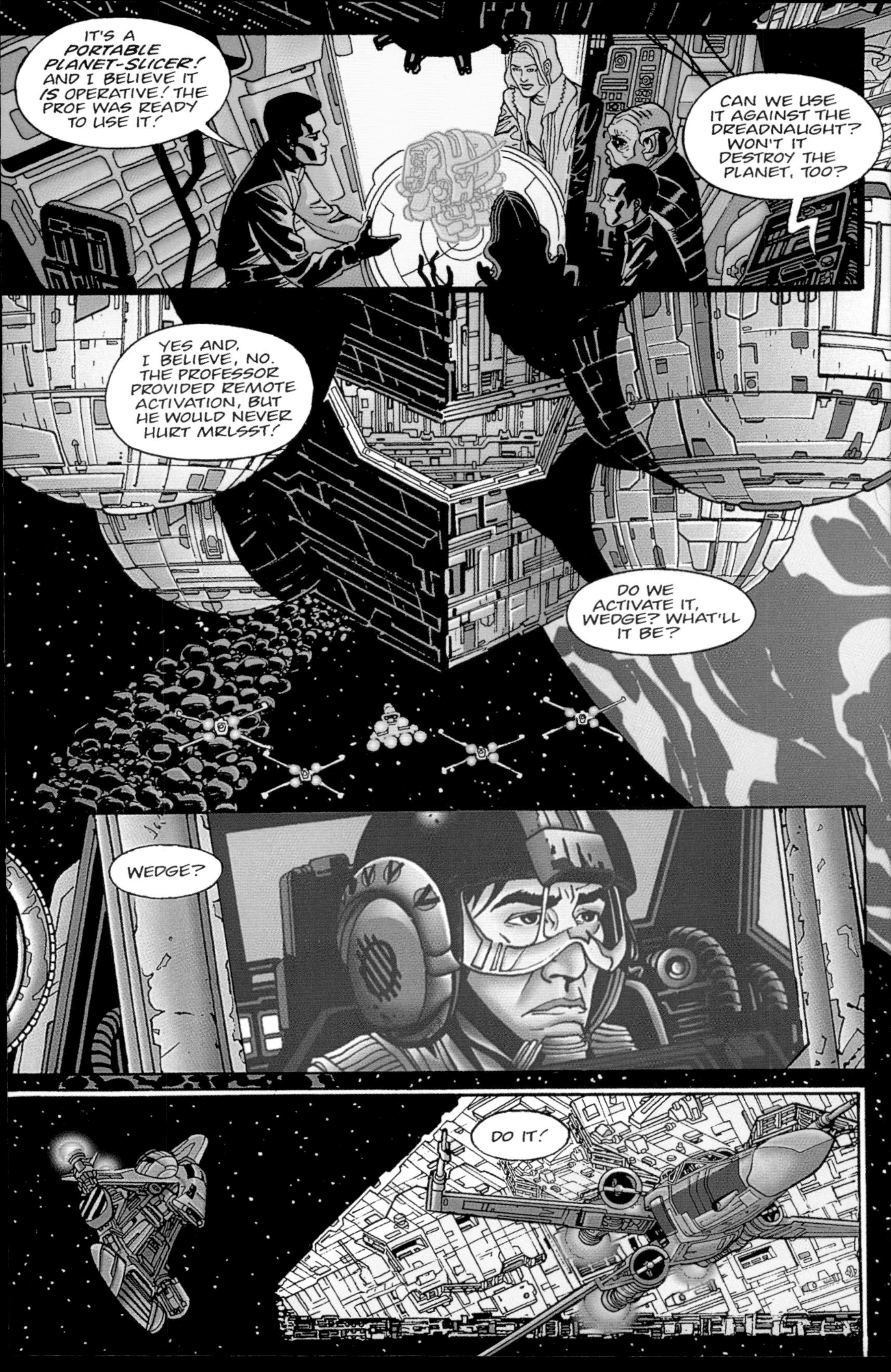
IT'S A PORTABLE PLANET-SLICER! AND I BELIEVE IT IS OPERATIVE! THE PROF WAS READY TO USE IT!
CAN WE USE IT AGAINST THE DREADNAUGHT? WON'T IT DESTROY THE PLANET, TOO?
YES AND, I BELIEVE, NO. THE PROFESSOR PROVIDED REMOTE ACTIVATION, BUT HE WOULD NEVER HURT MRLSST!
DO WE ACTIVATE IT, WEDGE? WHAT'LL IT BE?
WEDGE?
DO IT!

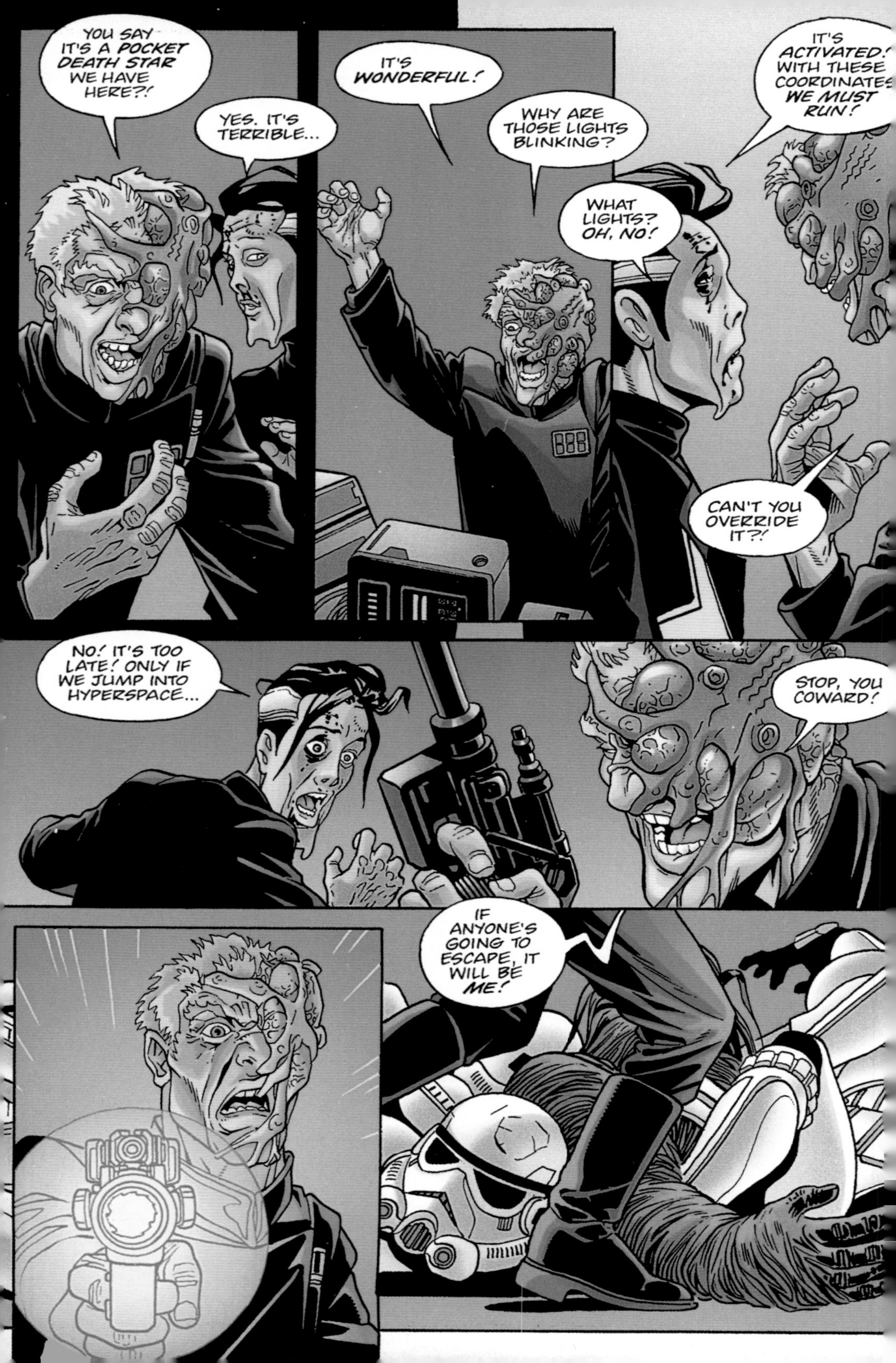

YOU SAY IT'S A POCKET DEATH STAR WE HAVE HERE?!
YES. IT'S TERRIBLE...
IT'S WONDERFUL!
WHY ARE THOSE LIGHTS BLINKING?
WHAT LIGHTS? OH, NO!
IT'S ACTIVATED! WITH THESE COORDINATES WE MUST RUN!
CAN'T YOU OVERRIDE IT?!
NO! IT'S TOO LATE! ONLY IF WE JUMP INTO HYPERSPACE...
STOP, YOU COWARD!
IF ANYONE'S GOING TO ESCAPE, IT WILL BE ME!

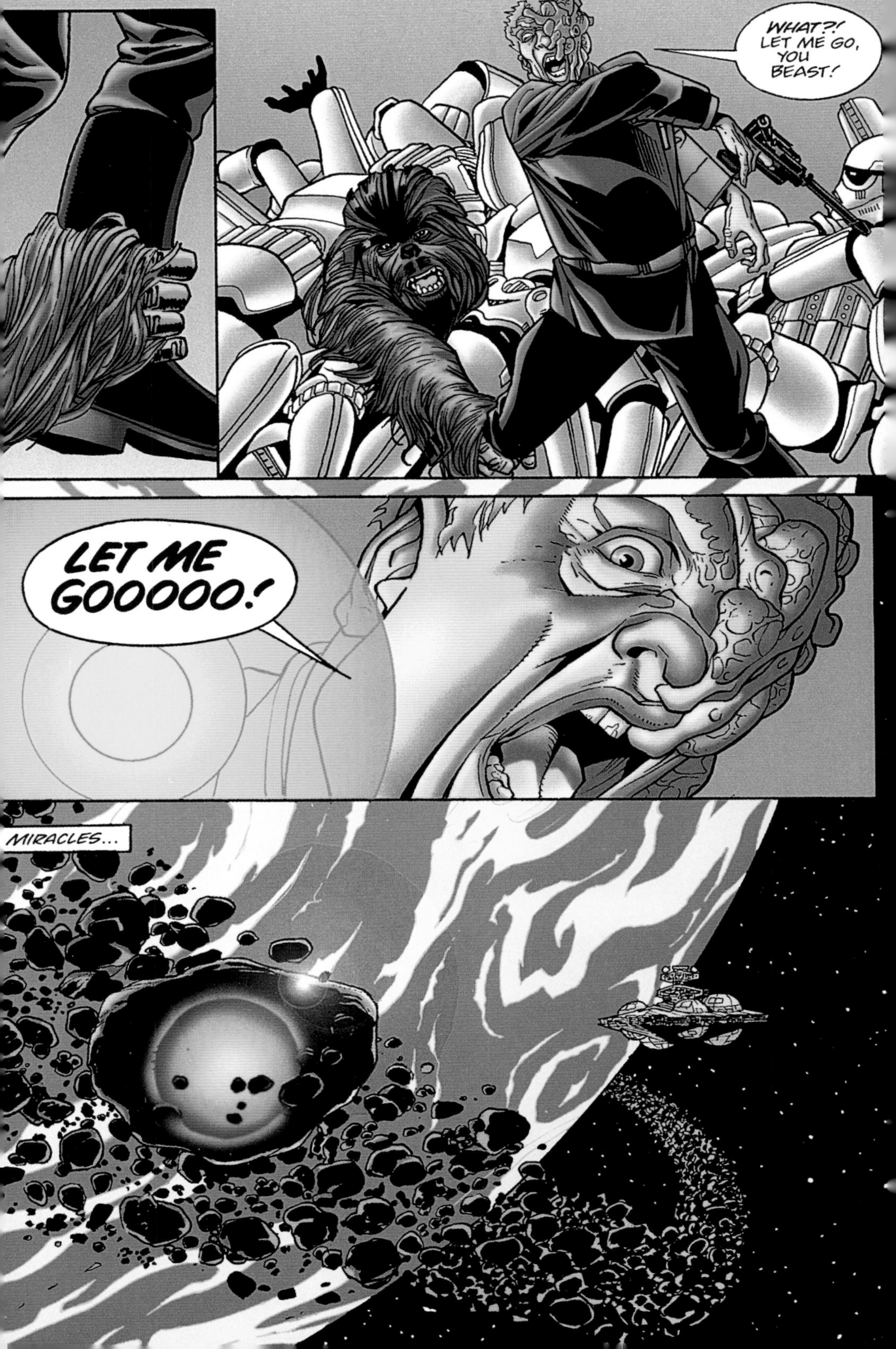
WHAT?! LET ME GO, YOU BEAST!
LET ME GOOOOO!
MIRACLES...

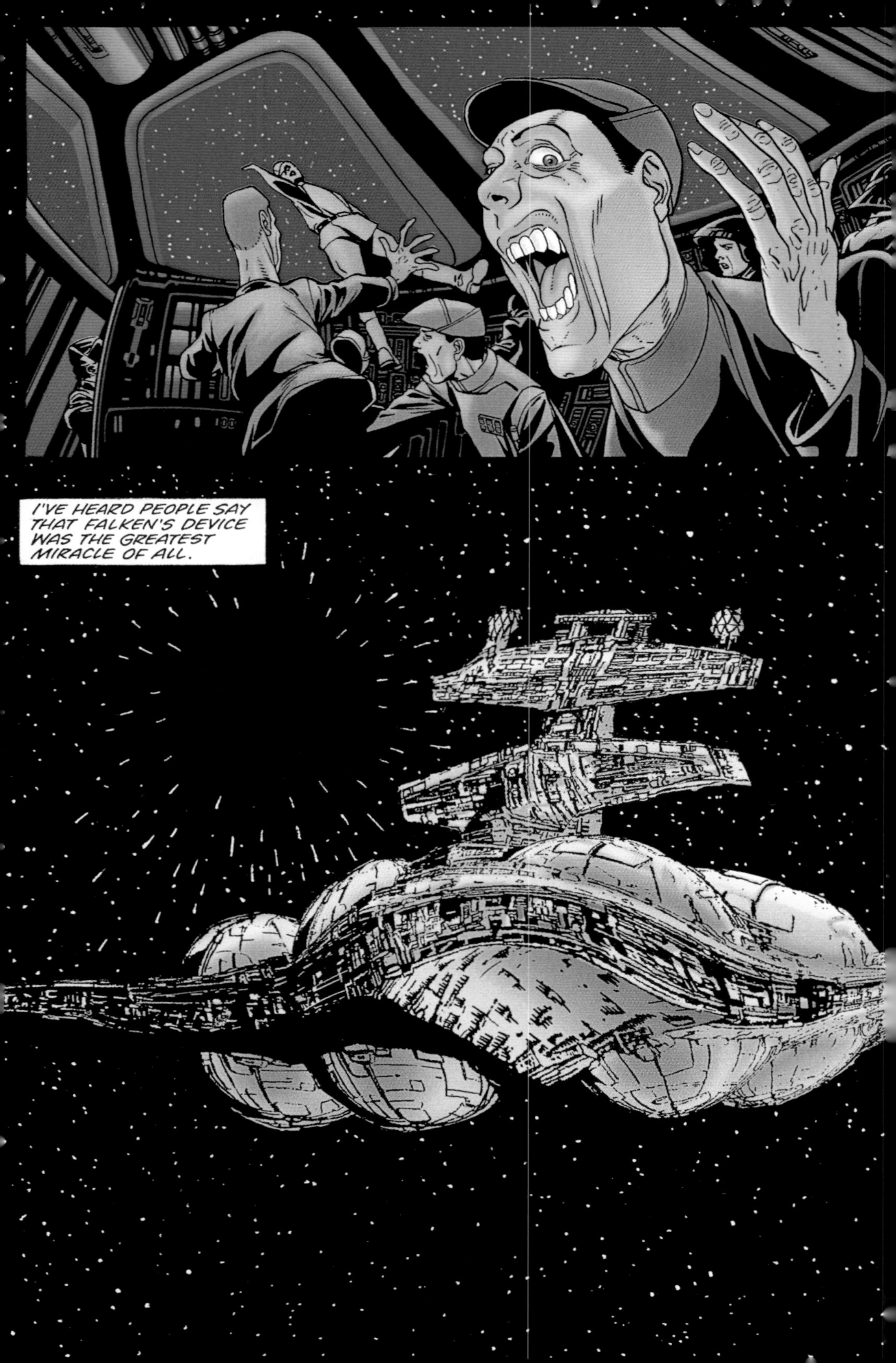
I'VE HEARD PEOPLE SAY THAT FALKEN'S DEVICE WAS THE GREATEST MIRACLE OF ALL.

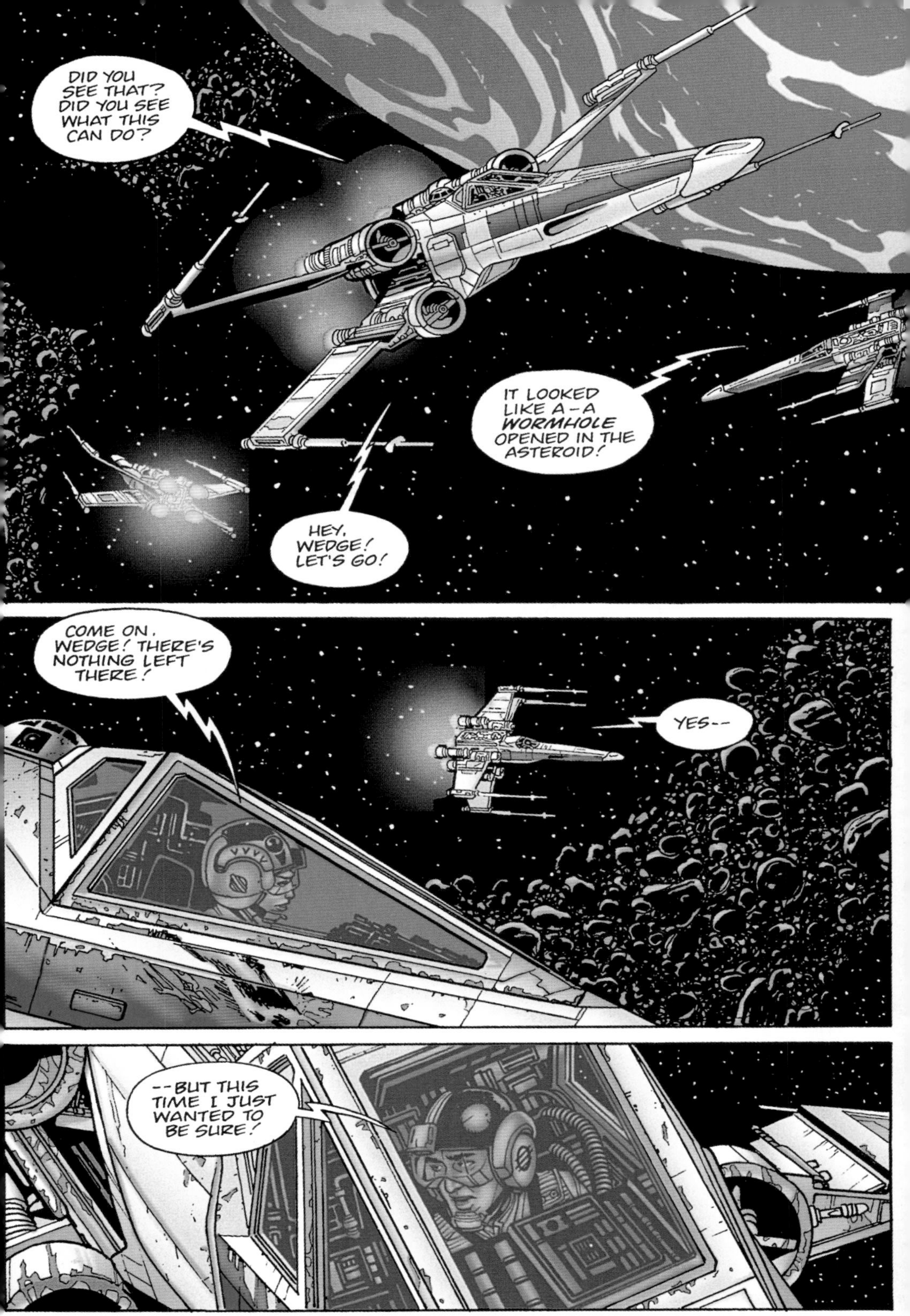
DID YOU SEE THAT? DID YOU SEE WHAT THIS CAN DO?
IT LOOKED LIKE A--A WORMHOLE OPENED IN THE ASTEROID!
HEY, WEDGE! LET'S GO!
COME ON, WEDGE! THERE'S NOTHING LEFT THERE!
YES--
--BUT THIS TIME I JUST WANTED TO BE SURE!

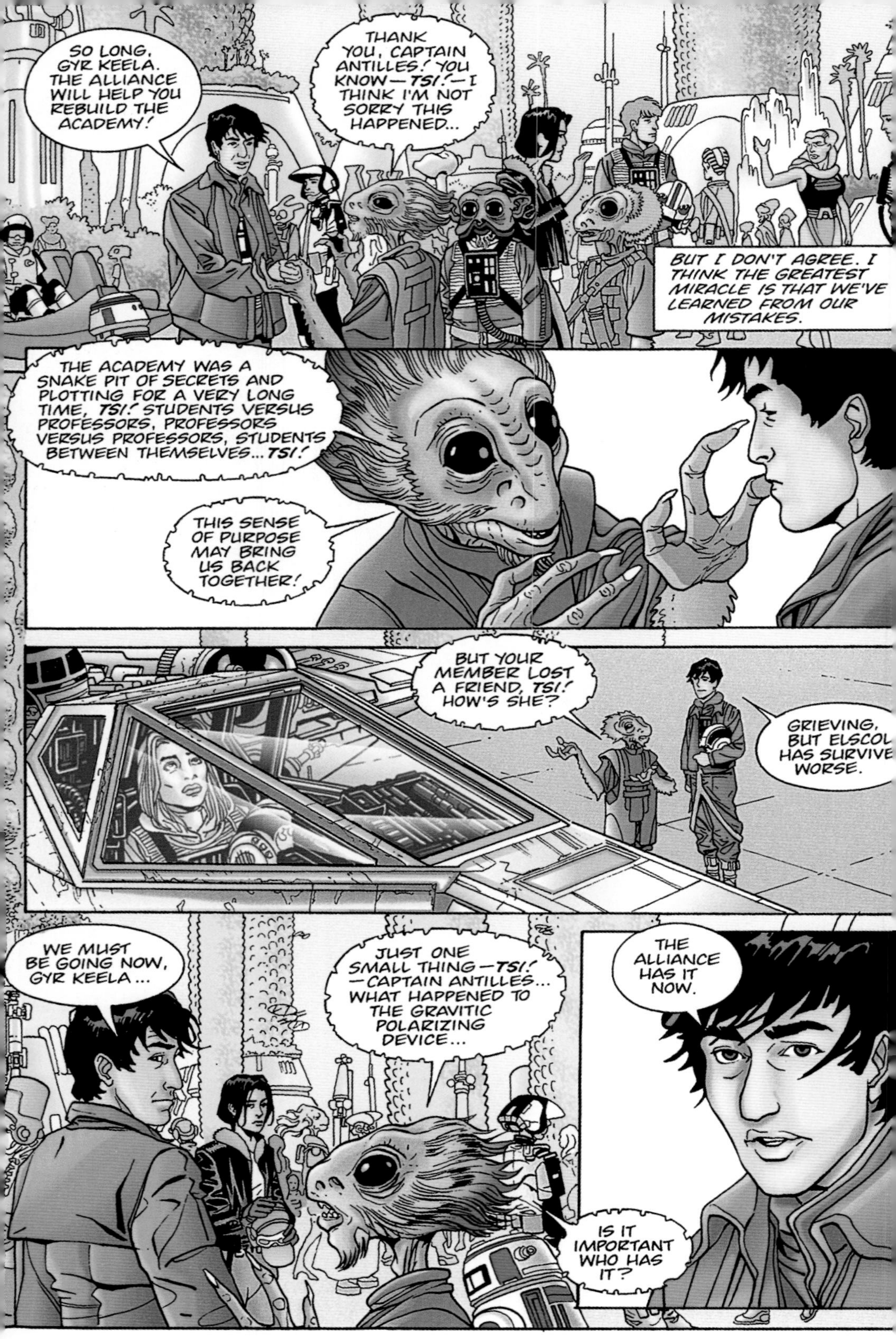
SO LONG, GYR KEELA. THE ALLIANCE WILL HELP YOU REBUILD THE ACADEMY!
THANK YOU, CAPTAIN ANTILLES! YOU KNOW—TSI!—I THINK I'M NOT SORRY THIS HAPPENED...
BUT I DON'T AGREE. I THINK THE GREATEST MIRACLE IS THAT WE'VE LEARNED FROM OUR MISTAKES.
THE ACADEMY WAS A SNAKE PIT OF SECRETS AND PLOTTING FOR A VERY LONG TIME, TSI! STUDENTS VERSUS PROFESSORS, PROFESSORS VERSUS PROFESSORS, STUDENTS BETWEEN THEMSELVES...TSI!
THIS SENSE OF PURPOSE MAY BRING US BACK TOGETHER!
BUT YOUR MEMBER LOST A FRIEND, TSI! HOW'S SHE?
GRIEVING, BUT ELSCOL HAS SURVIVE WORSE.
WE MUST BE GOING NOW, GYR KEELA...
JUST ONE SMALL THING—TSI! —CAPTAIN ANTILLES... WHAT HAPPENED TO THE GRAVITIC POLARIZING DEVICE...
THE ALLIANCE HAS IT NOW.
IS IT IMPORTANT WHO HAS IT?

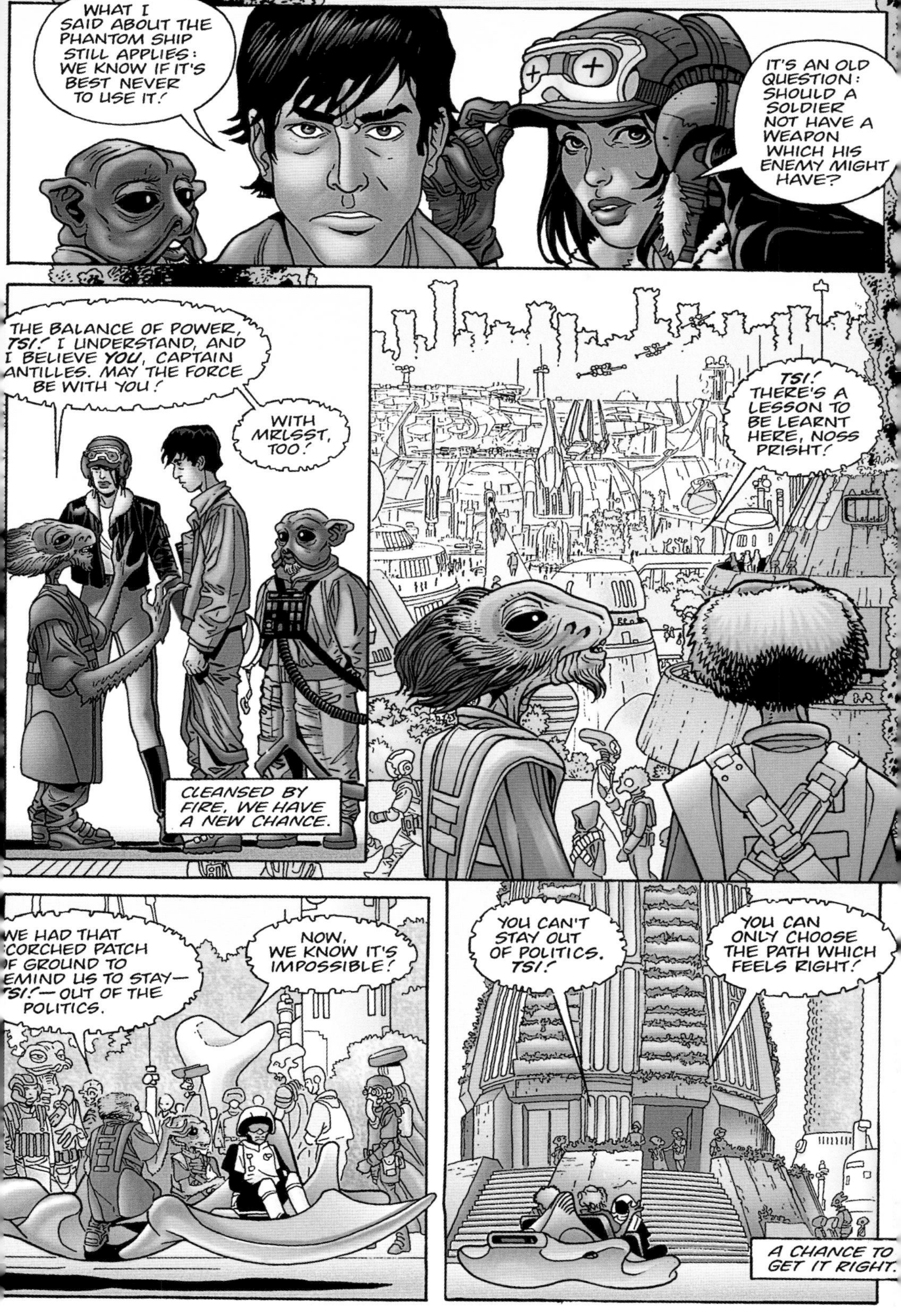
WHAT I SAID ABOUT THE PHANTOM SHIP STILL APPLIES: WE KNOW IF IT'S BEST NEVER TO USE IT!
IT'S AN OLD QUESTION: SHOULD A SOLDIER NOT HAVE A WEAPON WHICH HIS ENEMY MIGHT HAVE?
THE BALANCE OF POWER, TSI! I UNDERSTAND, AND I BELIEVE YOU, CAPTAIN ANTILLES. MAY THE FORCE BE WITH YOU!
WITH MRLSST, TOO!
CLEANSED BY FIRE, WE HAVE A NEW CHANCE.
TSI! THERE'S A LESSON TO BE LEARNT HERE, NOSS PRISHT!
WE HAD THAT SCORCHED PATCH OF GROUND TO REMIND US TO STAY— TSI!— OUT OF THE POLITICS.
NOW, WE KNOW IT'S IMPOSSIBLE!
YOU CAN'T STAY OUT OF POLITICS. TSI!
YOU CAN ONLY CHOOSE THE PATH WHICH FEELS RIGHT!
A CHANCE TO GET IT RIGHT.

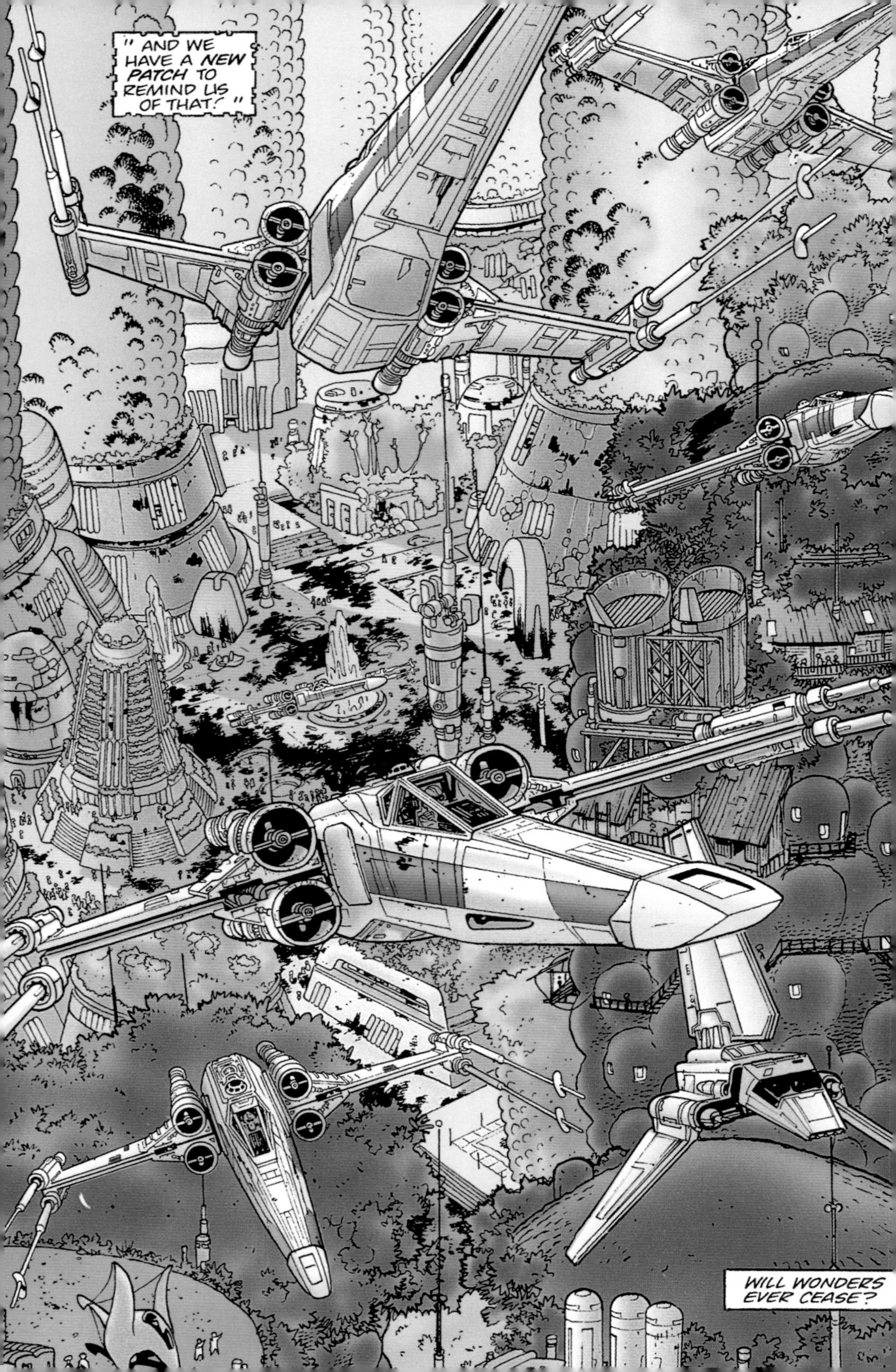
"AND WE HAVE A NEW PATCH TO REMIND US OF THAT!"
WILL WONDERS EVER CEASE?

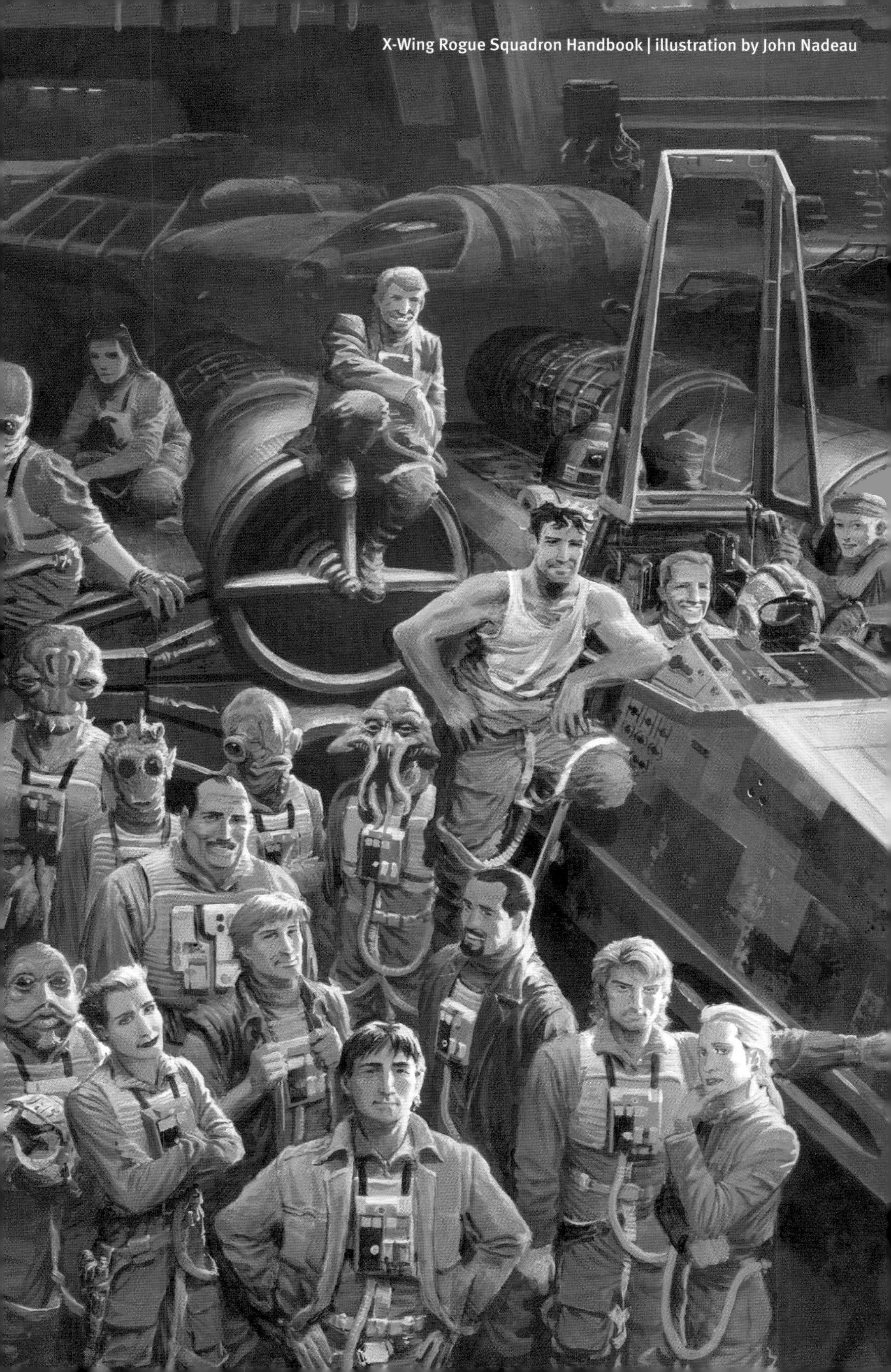

X-Wing Rogue Squadron Handbook | illustration by John Nadeau

On the next pages you'll find a helpful guide to some of the characters, important vessels, and situations that appear in this, and future volumes of the Rogue Squadron saga.

written by Peet Janes
art by Arthur Adams, Edvin Buikovic, Steve Crespo, Rodolfo Damaggio, Jordi Ensign, Dough Mahnke, John Nadeau, and Stan and Vince
colors by Dave Nestelle

ADMIRAL ACKBAR

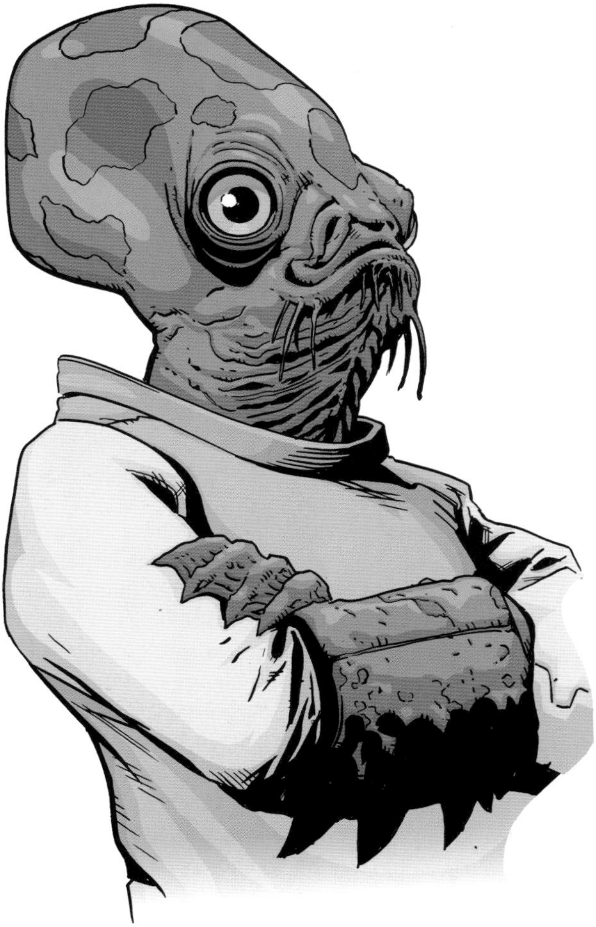

The Mon Calamari admiral of the Rebel Fleet is also a close personal friend of Wedge Antilles and often commands Rogue Squadron's various missions. After the wild success of the Battle of Endor, Ackbar became a popular figure in Alliance circles and joined the Rebel Provisional Council. The Mon Cal's refinement of the Alliance's snubfighter campaign, in which smaller ships were used to take out larger vessels, was a critically important element of Rebel victory.

After the Battle of Endor, the Rebel Fleet's main activities shifted from tide-turning, system-wide battles to planetary liberation and acquisition of strategic assets. Ackbar directed the many branches of the fleet in both open warfare and covert operations. His knowledge of many Imperial systems and tactics was a critical tool in the Rebel strategy. Rogue Squadron often figured prominently in Ackbar's plans; not only were they the best that the Alliance had to offer, but mere word of their presence on a battlefield was enough to send many less-organized Imperial units scrambling.

WEDGE ANTILLES

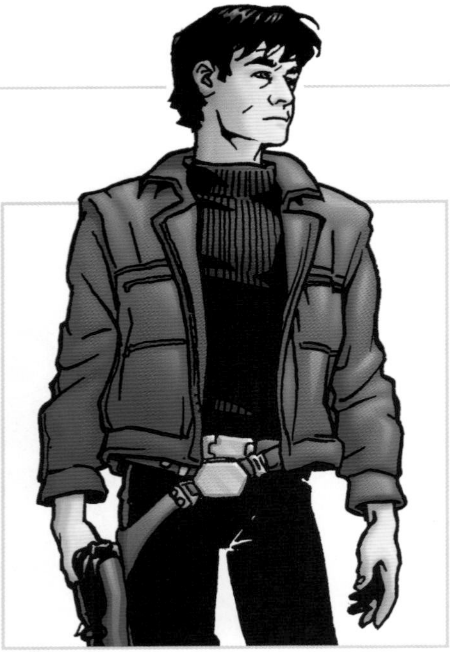

To many people, Wedge Antilles is one of the greatest heroes of the Galactic Civil War. Dedication to the Rebellion is evident in everything he does, and his long career stands as a powerful testament to his skill. To Princess Leia, Admiral Ackbar, and the other leaders of the Rebel Alliance, Wedge is one of their single greatest assets, yet he remains unassuming and approachable, a hero for the working person.

Raised in the neutral Corellian System, Wedge's youth was not disturbed by the growing unrest in the greater Empire. He spent half of each year on a farm school in Corellia's northern hemisphere and half on his parents' fueling station in high orbit. Both places taught him how to ride: on Corellia's rolling hills, he herded naugas and nerfs from the backs of thaks and slopewings; and in space, he piloted tugs and shuttles. His older sister Syal was estranged from the family, and he did not see her for many years.

At the age of seventeen, Wedge was looking forward to a career as an architect or a pilot, perhaps someday owning his own freighter. But a tragedy occurred that would change his life irrevocably and send him on the path of Rebellion: his parents' fueling station was set ablaze during an altercation with a pirate vessel. Jagged and Zena Antilles sacrificed their lives to save the thousands of other residents of the station, but Wedge was forced to watch helplessly as his parents' module spiraled away in flames.

Wedge took a modified Z-95 from a family friend and pursued the pirates, catching up to them near Jumus. In a blistering attack that foreshadowed his later years as an X-wing pilot, Wedge destroyed the pirate ship with a blast to its main weapons magazine.

With no family left to tie him to Corellia, Wedge purchased a freighter with insurance receipts and went into business. Since many of his connections were through famed smuggler Booster Terrik, more often than not he hauled items for the Rebel Alliance. When the Alliance made an open call for fighter pilots in their new campaign against the Empire, Wedge signed up.

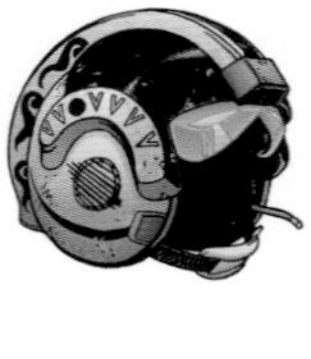

Having participated in many of the most significant battles of the Galactic Civil War, Wedge has become one of the most experienced pilots in the Rebel Alliance. His tactics are used as textbook examples to new generations of Rebel pilots, and his piloting of the Incom T-65 X-wing is considered definitive and is widely utilized in simulators throughout the galaxy. Even among Imperial squadrons, his name is spoken of with quiet reverence.

Wedge saved Luke Skywalker in the Battle of Yavin, allowing Luke to go on and destroy the Death Star. Since that time, he played crucial roles in the Battle of Hoth, the Battle of Endor, the Bakura Campaign, and dozens of sorties against other Imperial targets. Wedge shared the kill of the second Death Star with Lando Calrissian, but he characteristically remained more or less in the shadows.

BANTHA-CLASS TROOP CARRIER ASSAULT SHUTTLE

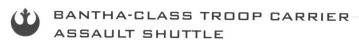

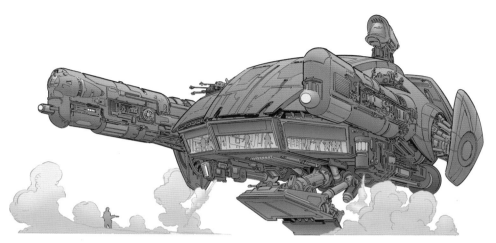

One of the most popular and long-anticipated additions to the Rebel Fleet took the form of a squat, slow vehicle with a hide as thick as its namesake. The Bantha-class assault shuttle, a joint creation of Mon Calamari and Sullustan engineers, was designed to fly behind a fighter screen into target areas—taking a beating while it disgorged or airlifted troops and small ground vehicles. With their large cargo capacity, just a few of these vehicles could land a strike force large enough to attack most any target.

The Bantha sports an unusually small footprint, extending a gimballed monopod, allowing it to land in the smallest of areas. The Bantha is powered by sturdy Sullustan sublight drives, and each shuttle carries a central processor equal to that of an advanced construction droid. The pilots of Banthas, many of whom happily refer to themselves as "bus drivers," often have bantering relationships with their ships, much as true bantha trainers share special bonds with their mounts.

The Bantha-class assault shuttle made its stunning debut during the assault on Oradin at the Battle for Brentaal.

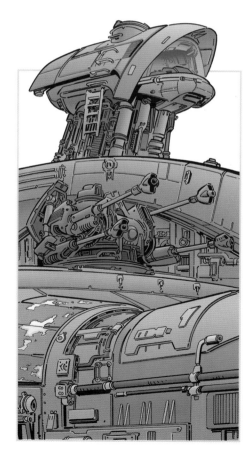

TYCHO CELCHU

The need for new pilots to fill the ranks of Rebel squadrons after the Battle of Yavin was acute. Many pilots volunteered, but only the best joined Wedge in what would become Rogue Squadron. Lt. Tycho Celchu was one of them.

Before joining the Rebellion, Tycho, a native of Alderaan, had been an Imperial pilot. When he learned that his homeworld, family, and life had been destroyed by the Death Star, Tycho deserted active service and disappeared into the hidden channels that the Rebel Alliance ran. Already a formidable TIE fighter pilot through his training with then-Captain Soontir Fel, Celchu quickly found his way into the ranks of the Rebel Fleet, being recruited by Luke Skywalker for his unit. During the Battle of Endor, as Commander Wedge Antilles and the *Millennium Falcon* attempted to destroy the second Death Star, Tycho flew an A-wing into the space station's unfinished superstructure, luring TIEs away from the critical operation.

When Wedge Antilles became leader of the squadron, Tycho became Antilles' second, a position he has held ever since.

Tycho has developed an ongoing relationship with the enigmatic Winter, although they have spent more time together dodging blaster bolts than they have counting stars in each other's eyes. Even in the most desperate of situations, though, the pair have found ways to enjoy each other's company.

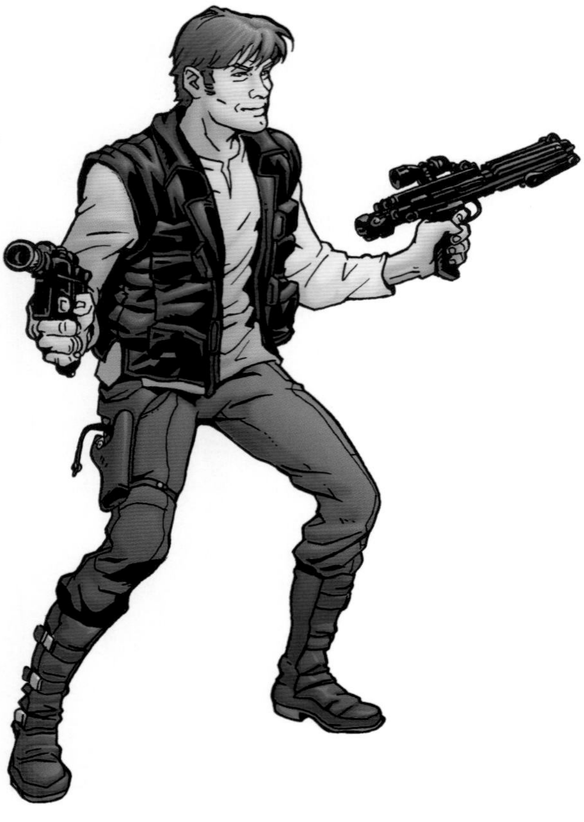

KAPP DENDO

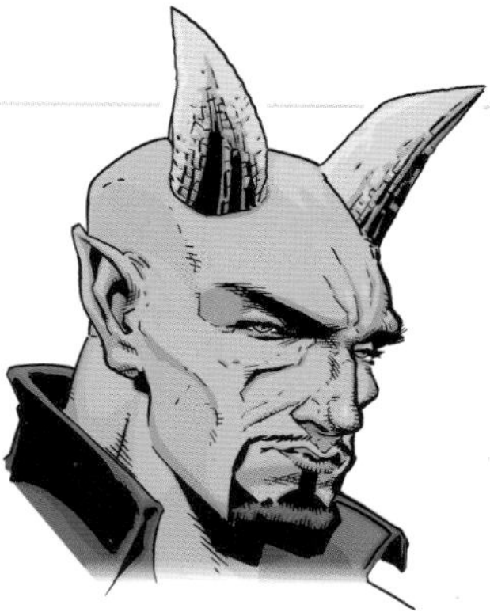

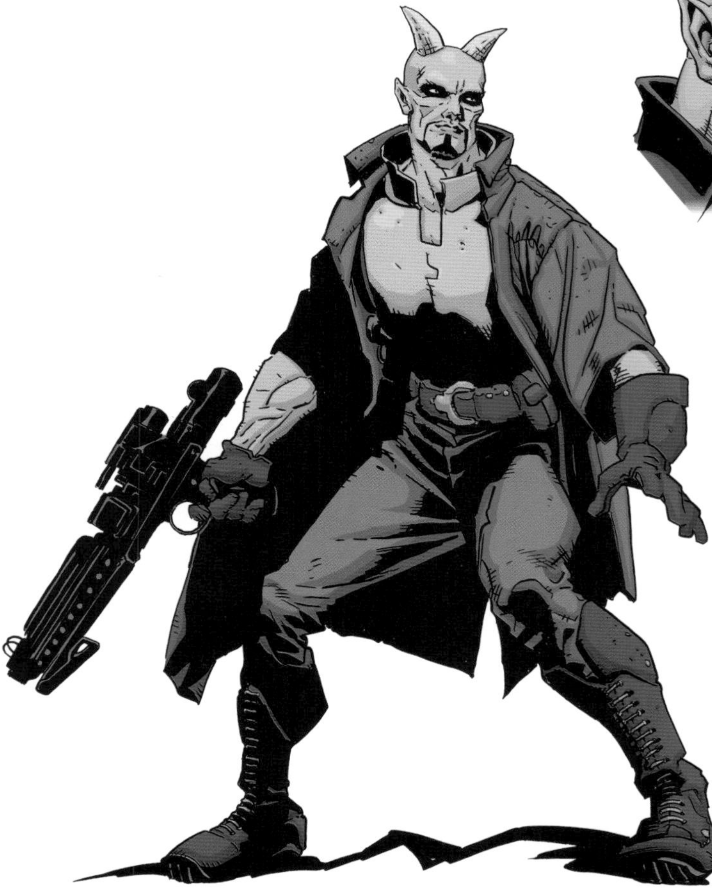

The Devaronian Kapp Dendo was among the best of the Rebel Alliance's special operatives, having a knack for recruiting talented individuals for the Alliance's many covert operations.

His first encounter with Rogue Squadron on Tatooine almost turned into a disaster when criminals under the command of Firith Olan interrupted the Alliance's operation to discern the whereabouts of an Imperial weapons cache. When Rogue Squadron attacked Dendo under the mistaken impression that he was a criminal ringleader, it took four Rogues to wrestle him to the ground. Later, all misunderstandings aside, Dendo began to cultivate a closer friendship with Plourr Ilo, whose strength and demeanor he admired (particularly after she knocked him out with her left hook). Toward the end of the operation, Dendo rescued Plourr from her crashed X-wing. While Plourr's later assumption of the throne of Eiattu—and the husband that came with it—prevented the pair from exploring their feelings further, they remain fast friends.

An ambitious redesign of a strike cruiser with TIE launch capability, the *Eidolon* was in fact a complex ruse created by Imperial vizier Sate Pestage to hide his secret efforts to establish storehouses in case Emperor Palpatine's government were ever to topple. Built under tremendous secrecy at the Kuat Drive Yards' satellite facility in the Seswanna Sector, the *Eidolon* was actually a mere shell of a craft.

Among the *Eidolon's* proposed advances was a dual TIE rack featuring a docking bay at the base of the command tower, which shunted racked TIEs back through maintenance and refueling areas and into launch corridors on either side of the ship, allowing a constant stream of short-mission fighter protection. The launch racks themselves were actually designed, built, and incorporated into Sate Pestage's base on Tatooine.

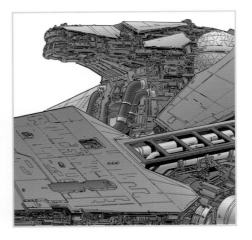

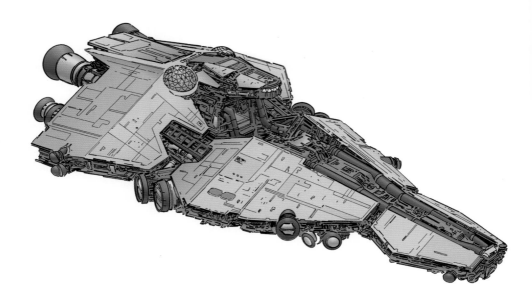

BARON SOONTIR FEL AND WYNSSA STARFLARE

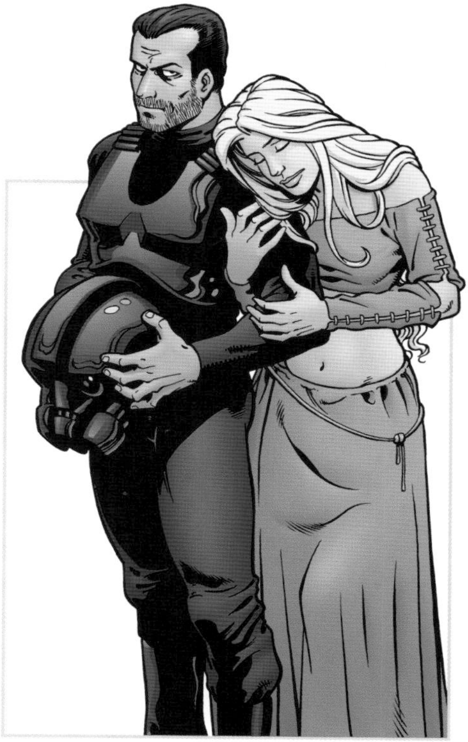

The man who was once the Empire's greatest TIE fighter pilot was ushered into the Rebel Alliance rather hastily by Wedge Antilles, who could see the integrity of the man behind the Imperial flight suit. Wedge was further motivated when he discovered that Fel was married to his estranged sister, Syal Antilles.

Already a hotshot pilot when he entered the Imperial Academy at Carida, Soontir adapted quickly to the TIE fighter. Even other talented cadets had difficulty keeping up with his level of performance. A new, higher level of trainee excellence followed Fel wherever he went, and Fel was eventually appointed as an instructor. Little did Fel know that he was training cadets who would someday be the greatest pilots of the Rebel Fleet, including Tycho Celchu, Biggs Darklighter, and Derek "Hobbie" Klivian. Darklighter and Klivian masterminded a daring mutiny, and delivered an entire Imperial ship and its cargo to the Rebel Alliance. Though he had no control over his former cadets' actions, Fel's career as an instructor was over.

Fel was then assigned to the 181st Imperial Fighter Wing, an unkempt TIE unit. Fel requested the opportunity to shape up the pilots of the "One-Eighty-Worst," and he turned the squadron into the Empire's top guns.

Duty sent Fel to Imperial Center, where he met holodrama star Wynssa Starflare, and their love blossomed. Fel proposed to Wynssa, and she was forced to divulge the secret that could destroy his life: her true name was Syal Antilles, and her brother Wedge was a Rebel hero. But Fel was in love, and the pair soon married.

As the 181st continued to build its reputation, Fel encountered another woman who would change his life. Imperial Intelligence officer Ysanne Isard attempted to seduce Fel. His rejection of her made her a lifelong enemy. Fel made secret plans with his wife to run from the Empire should Isard ever divine the truth about Wynssa Starflare.

Isard's duplicity also created doubt in his mind about the integrity of the Empire's mission. Ultimately, it was the hypocrisy of the Empire's reliance on the alien Grand Admiral Thrawn's plans that set Fel to thinking that the Empire was rotten to the core.

Fel and his squadron finally went up against Rogue Squadron during the Battle of Brentaal. Fel's TIE interceptor was disabled during a dogfight with Wedge Antilles. When Fel was captured by the Rebels, Wynssa fled Imperial Center. It was time for Fel to rethink his ties to the Empire. He had a better chance of finding Wynssa with the help of the Rebel Alliance. His Empire gone, if indeed it had ever existed, Fel thought that the ideals he upheld would be better served by this New Republic.

BIB FORTUNA AND FIRITH OLAN

The Twi'lek second to Jabba the Hutt fled his master's sailbarge to avoid the explosion of a thermal detonator he himself had placed on it. Fortuna had planned to take over the slimy crimelord's holdings, but the B'omarr Monks in their citadel beneath Jabba's palace had other ideas. The monks captured him instead and transferred his brain into a spider-droid body, the preferred vessel for those B'omarr High Priests who desired complete isolation for their meditation. By making him one of them, they hoped to purge him of criminal intent.

As Fortuna struggled to adjust to the shock of his new droid body and its unwieldy mechanical limbs, his distant cousin Firith Olan stepped in to take control of the palace's affairs—and a fortune in arms and other goods hidden in krayt dragon tunnels on Tatooine.

As Rogue Squadron and would-be warlord Captain Marl Semtin descended on the hidden weapons cache, and Firith himself became a casualty of the battle, Bib Fortuna stepped in, rescued the injured Twi'lek, and returned to the B'omarr Monks, who quickly and quietly transferred Fortuna's brain to Olan's body . . . and Firith Olan's brain to the spider droid.

The weapons caches were lost, but Bib Fortuna was once again whole, and filled with big plans for his former employer's criminal empire.

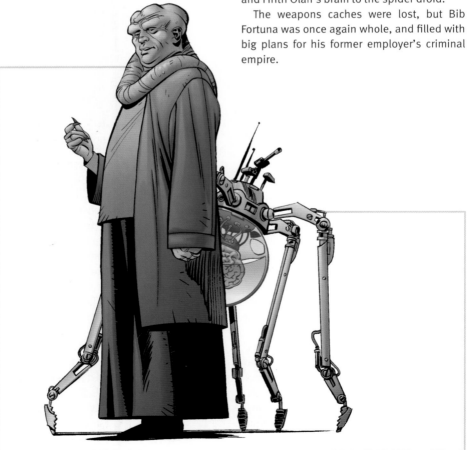

LOKA HASK

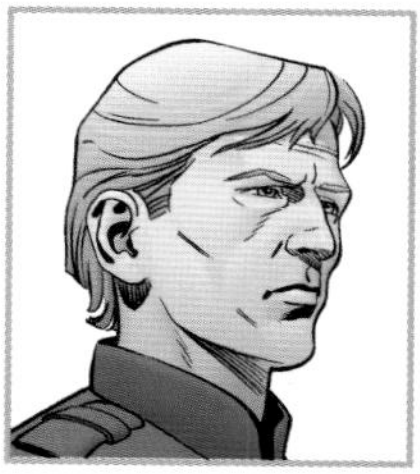

Loka Hask was a sociopathic firebrand whose skill at grifting his classmates at the Imperial Military Academy on Carida resulted in his expulsion. He returned to his homeworld in time to witness his estranged criminal father's public execution. Hask used his father's hidden stashes of credits to outfit a ship with a crew of glitbiters. Over the course of the next year, Hask and his pirate crew plundered more than a dozen vessels.

When Corellian Security Forces heard that Hask's ship was docked at a Corellian fueling station, they dispatched ships to intercept the pirates, with resulting tragedy. The pirates departed from the station before properly detaching, resulting in a fuel spill and firestorm across the busy station. Wedge Antilles was forced to watch as his parents' fueling platform spiralled into a solar trajectory. Wedge took a modified Z-95 headhunter, tracked the pirate ship, and destroyed it in a merciless barrage.

But Loka Hask had donned a vacsuit and left the ship moments before, and overhearing Wedge's name spoken over the comm, he had his target for revenge. It would change from mere revenge to vendetta seconds later, when a Corellian limpet that had slipped inside the suit attacked Hask and became a permanent part of his grim visage.

Years later, having somehow regained his commission, Imperial Captain Loka Hask once again encountered Wedge Antilles during negotiations for technology at the Mrlssti Academy. Hask framed Wedge and imprisoned the Rebel pilot, but Wedge escaped. Enraged, Hask ordered the campus bombed, and the asteroid lab ransacked. During the sacking of the lab, however, the Rogues stumbled across a device capable of splitting objects at a molecular level. Hask was near the device as it was remotely activated. Caught in a feedback loop, the device opened a wormhole that swallowed the asteroid, a star destroyer, and Loka Hask.

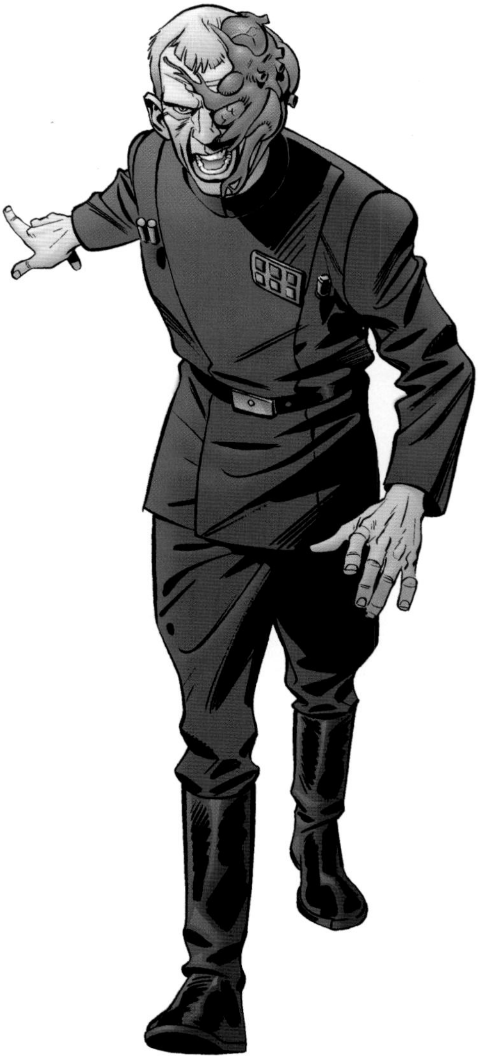

YSANNE ISARD

By its very nature, Imperial Intelligence attracted Emperor Palpatine's most loyal subjects. After his death, those same subjects were the most serious obstacle to the Rebel Alliance's quest for revolution. Ysanne Isard, also known as "Iceheart," held many of the strings of the puppet rulers who attempted to rule in Palpatine's absence, and over the course of her career, eventually came to desire the throne for herself.

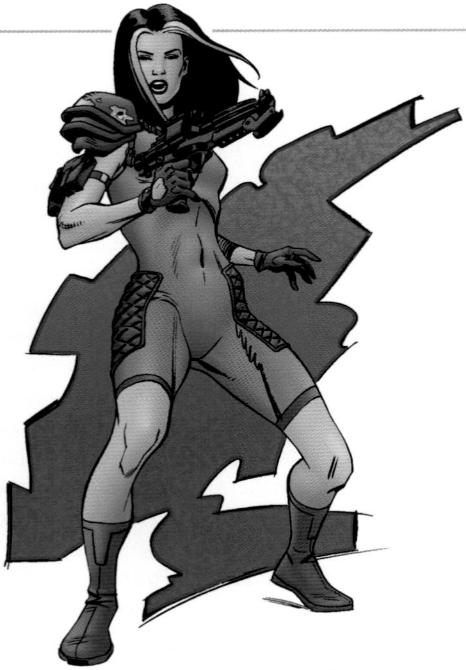

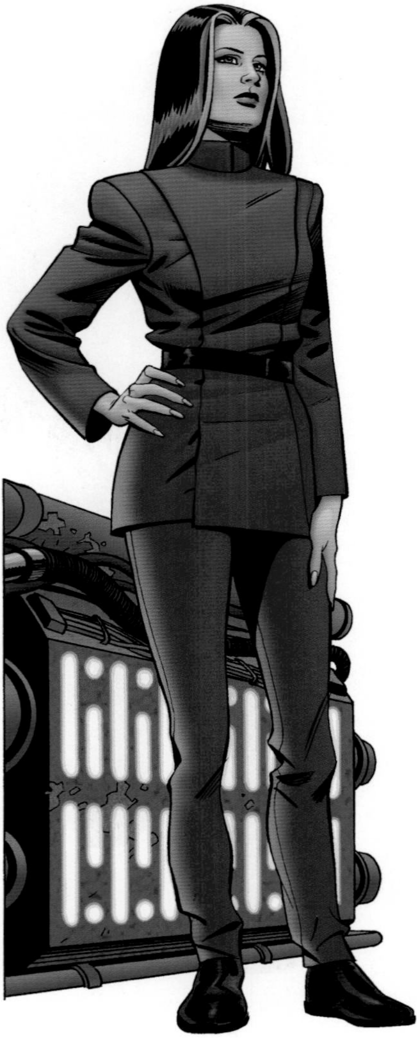

Rogue Squadron first came to Isard's attention during the siege of Brentaal, when she dispatched Baron Fel and the Imperial 181st to the strategic world to assist Admiral Lon Isoto in its defense. Isard knew that the Rebels would attempt to take the planet after she leaked word that "Isoto the Indecisive" was in charge. Isard had carefully set up Isoto as a pawn of both Emperor-proxy Sate Pestage and the Imperial Council, performing a delicate balancing act of lies between one and the other to destabilize both factions and allow her to step into a ruling position in the Empire.

The loss of Brentaal was a sharp blow near the heart of the Empire, but the payoff was worth it to Isard. Sate Pestage believed that the Council insisted on Isoto, and plotted their destruction. The Council saw Isoto as Pestage's man, and planted the seeds for a coup. All the while, Isard shuttled back and forth between them, playing the role of messenger, when in fact it was she who was in control of the Empire.

ELSCOL LORO AND GROZNIK

Along with her husband, Throm, and their Wookiee companion, Groznik, Elscol led the Cilpari Resistance against Imperial forces. Until Wedge Antilles and Rogue Squadron arrived on the strife-torn world, the Resistance had received little help from the Rebel Alliance, and were suspicious of the Rebels' motives. By that time, Elscol's husband had become a casualty of the war. In Elscol Loro, Wedge saw a powerful force against the Empire, if only her self-destructive behavior could be redirected.

After routing the Imperial presence on Cilpar, Wedge invited Elscol to join Rogue Squadron. While a capable pilot, and particularly effective against Imperial targets, Elscol remained morose, brooding over her husband's death and later, over the sacrifice of Groznik during the Phantom Affair on Mrlsst. She began to fly off the handle during critical flights, suicidally attacking capital ships and well-defended bases. While Wedge was happy that her unorthodox flying was racking up impressive wins on campaigns, her instability threatened the safety of the rest of the squadron. Wedge dismissed her from the squadron after the Tatooine Campaign, but managed to procure for her a quantity of confiscated Imperial weaponry with which she could create her own Rebel cell. Her last report to Rebel Command spoke of the cell's investigation of a possible hyperspace corridor from the Outer Regions to the galactic core, the control of which could alter the course of the war.

Groznik, the Wookiee companion of Elscol Loro, had a life-debt to Elscol's husband, Throm Loro. When Throm was struck down during the Cilpari Resistance, Groznik transferred the life-debt to Loro's grieving wife. An excellent mechanic, Groznik was an added bonus when Elscol joined Rogue Squadron. His devotion to the fiery-haired Elscol was only surpassed by his devotion to the memory of his good friend, Throm, and often Wookiee

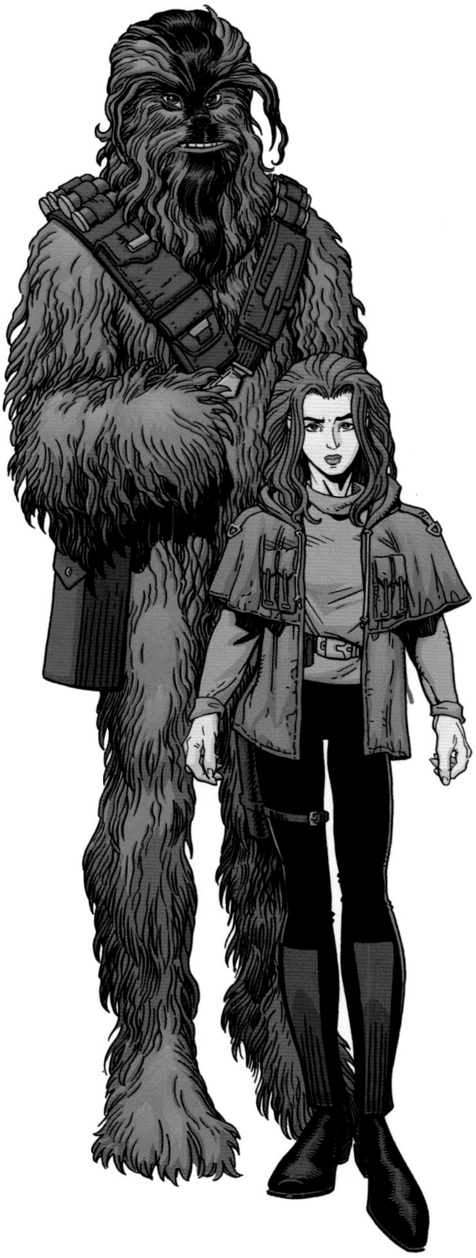

and human woman would share moments of melancholy and painful reminiscence.

FEYLIS ARDELE

Feylis Ardele, a cadet who had recently come from Commenor, a semi-neutral world with stronger ties to the Empire. She was a skilled TIE pilot, and Wedge pitted her against his Rogues in daily simulations. She distinguished herself on the T-65 as well, and participated with distinction in the Malrev incident and the Battle for Brentaal.

AVAN BERUSS

Trained with the best instructors available, Avan hailed from the Illodian Officers' Academy and a role as pilot in the system's acclaimed defense force. Avan is a competent pilot in the X-wing, and has worked closely with Feylis Ardele in order to learn TIE fighter systems.

XARRCE HUWLA

The Tunroth pilot joined Rogue Squadron just before the Battle of Brentaal, and subsequently asked to be transferred out of the unit. While she was no shirker of duty, she spoke quite logically of the high death rate in the squadron. But before long Xarrce had racked up impressive kills against Baron Fel's Imperial 181st. By the time the campaign was over,

Xarrce had found her place and made friends with the squadron, and there was no more talk of transfers.

HERIAN I'NGRE

A Rogue pilot of the Bith species, Herian was one of the few members of her species to pursue a career in the Rebellion. Herian sacrificed herself on the world of Malrev, flying her X-wing into a Sith temple and destroying it.

IBTISAM

Ibtisam joined Rogue Squadron shortly before the Eiattu Campaign and quickly proved herself not only an extremely capable pilot, but also an outstanding ground operative, with strength and resolve uncharacteristic of the female of her species.

Ibtisam shares an interesting friendship with her fellow Rogue, the Quarren Nrin Vakil. Mon Calamari and Quarren have shared the world of Mon Calamari as long as history has been recorded by either species. This deep-set acrimony was held in check by the two pilots, by order of Captain Wedge Antilles. Both Nrin and Ibtisam being relatively intelligent people, they were able to become close friends, even flirting with the idea of a closer relationship.

PLOURR ILO

Gruff, angry, and mean is how many people might describe Rogue pilot Plourr Ilo, but this tough, Eiattu-born woman is one of Rogue Squadron's most valued assets: a battle-hardened veteran—fearless, motivated, and talented. All of Plourr's bluster was an elaborate ruse to cover the fact that she was actually the sole surviving member of the planet Eiattu's ruling family. Despite her royal duties on Eiattu, Plourr continues to fly with Rogue Squadron.

WES JANSON

Janson back-seated Wedge Antilles in a snow-speeder during the Battle of Hoth, and later flew an X-wing defending Rebel transports during the evacuation of the frozen world. Wes proved his capability as a ground operative when he assisted Kapp Dendo in the sabotage of Imperial razers on Brentaal, and he would later trade in his pilot's helmet and become one of the New Republic's most sought-after flight instructors.

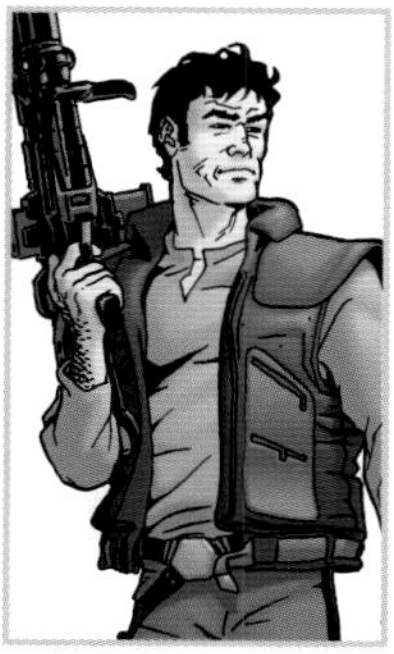

HOBBIE KLIVIAN

Derek "Hobbie" Klivian had participated in a daring mutiny and jump to the Alliance. While it is true that Hobbie's ships often seem to be magnetically attracted to the ground, his long experience flying the X-wing and his knack for surviving the worst crashes have made him a pillar of Rogue Squadron.

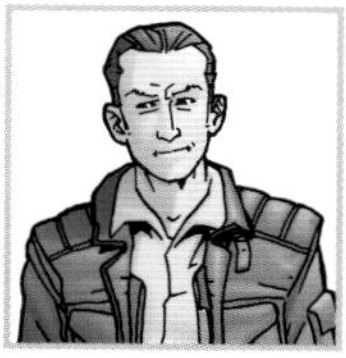

KOYI KOMAD

Koyi Komad left the Trade and Science Academy on Mrlsst to join Rogue Squadron as chief mechanic shortly before the Battle for Brentaal. She is a trusted friend and confidante to many Rogues and a mechanic of rare ability.

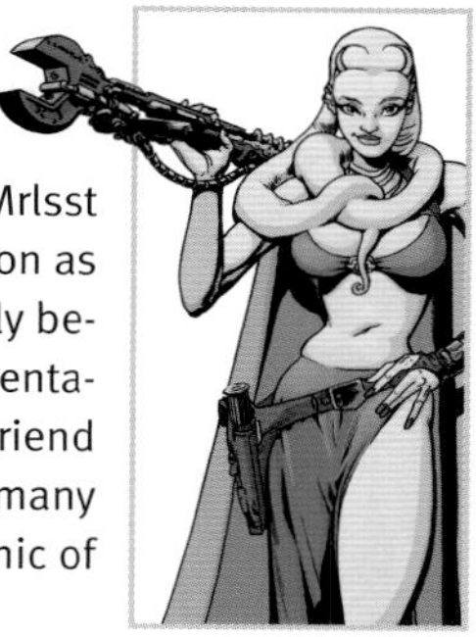

DLLR NEP

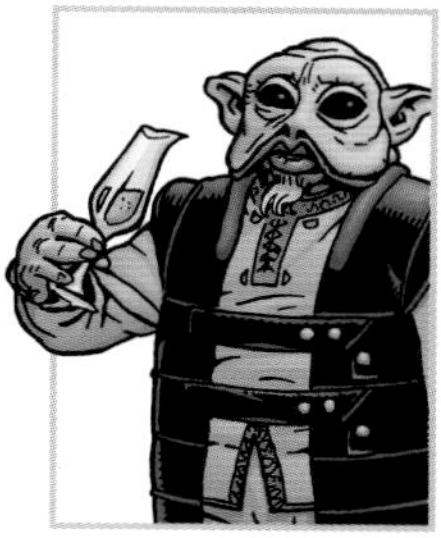

A Sullustan with a love of the exotic, Dllr distinguished himself during the Phantom Affair, and he made the ultimate sacrifice during the Malrev incident, absorbing Sith magic and leading fellow Rogue Herian I'ngre and her damaged X-wing into a temple to destroy it.

NRIN VAKIL

A native of Mon Calamari like his squadron-mate Ibtisam, Nrin fancied himself a knight, and the Rebel Alliance, his displaced and exiled lord.

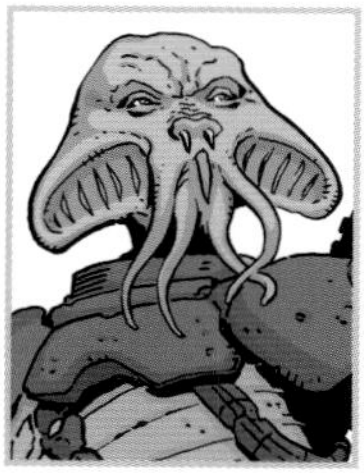

Nrin wore a custom flight suit which contained a coverall bladder of pressurized saltwater. The suit has the effect of reminding him of his homeworld's seas. Highly adaptable to new ships and situations, Nrin was often chosen to fly the unwieldy reconnaissance X-wings on scouting missions.

MARL SEMTIN

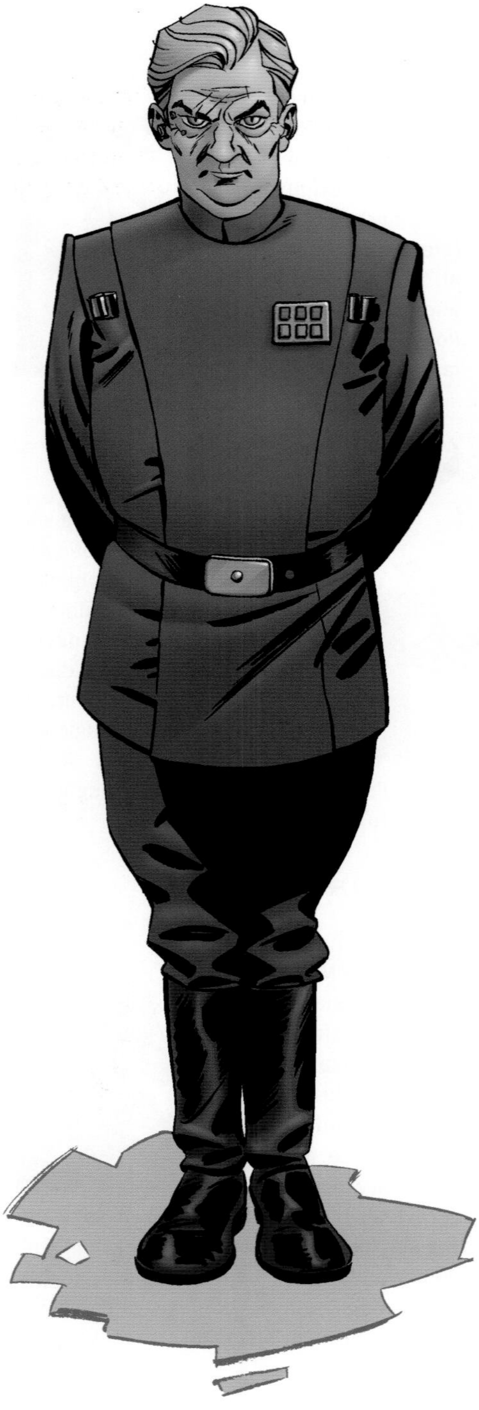

Marl Semtin was an Imperial officer who stumbled onto the secret that Sate Pestage, the Emperor's vizier, had orchestrated the stockpiling of weapons, currencies, and works of art. To pacify Captain Semtin, Pestage offered him a portion of the hidden wealth.

But Rogue Squadron arrived to aid the Rebel Special Operative Winter in her search for the cache. To further complicate matters, Semtin encountered Firith Olan, ostensibly the new boss of Jabba the Hutt's criminal empire, who wanted the materiel so he could rule Tatooine and the rest of the sector. Semtin offered Firith a deal: he could manage the cache for Sate Pestage in exchange for fair use. When Rogue Squadron attacked the hidden base too quickly, Semtin abandoned his plans in favor of escape. But he couldn't escape from Sixtus Quin, an Imperial Special Forces trooper angered by his Captain's dishonorable behavior. Marl Semtin was vaporized by his own troops.

MOFF LEONIA TAVIRA

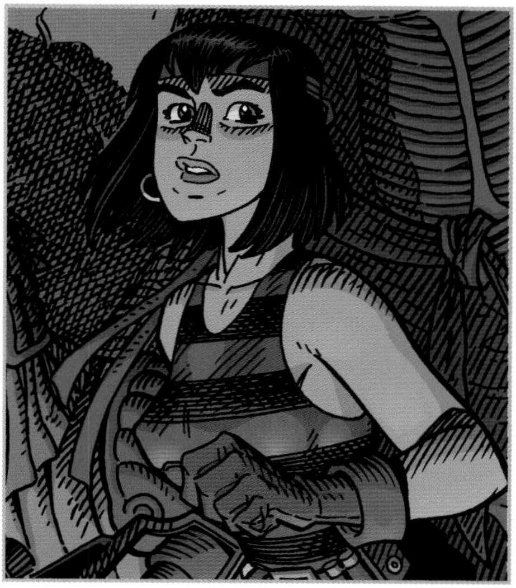

One of Rogue Squadron's most despicable foes was the vindictive, opportunistic teenager, Moff Leonia Tavira. When Moff Thavil Tavira took a wife from Eiattu's common population, he had no idea of the sort of duplicity of which the young girl was capable. When news came down that the Emperor had been killed during the destruction of the second Death Star, Tavira committed suicide. In the ensuing chaos, Leonia donned her husband's rank badges and cylinders, and named herself Moff of Eiattu. The transition garnered no notice on Imperial Center; Leonia simply failed to tell them that her husband had died. Leonia Tavira became the youngest Moff in the history of the Empire.

Leonia was determined to take control of the wealthy world and rule it like a queen. Her tool for this venture would be the impostor Prince Harran, leader of the People's Liberation Battalion and already a brainwashed dupe of Darth Vader.

Rogue Squadron, having accompanied Rogue Plourr Ilo to Eiattu to assist her in the assumption of the royal throne, thwarted Tavira's plans. The young Moff escaped Eiattu with a shuttle-full of Eiattu's riches, and later turned up among Kavil's Corsairs, a pirate group that wore the sign of the Blazing Claw.

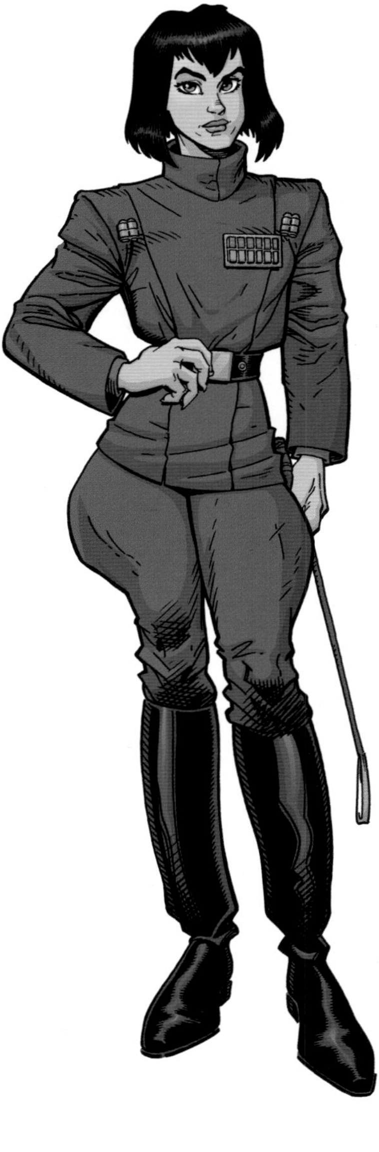

TIE FIGHTER ——————

The screaming emblem of the Imperial fleet, the Sienar TIE/ln Starfighter held sway over hundreds of systems during the Galactic Civil War. Modular and quick to build, the Empire dispatched vast numbers of TIEs throughout the galaxy. They served garrisons as air support; swarmed the ships of smugglers, Rebels, and pirates alike; fended off the Rebel penchant for snubfighters; and escorted thousands of dignitaries, including the Emperor.

Rogue pilots have flown so many missions against TIEs, that a sighting of incoming "eyes" is often met with the chatter, "Time for target practice!" The Empire's flooding of the galaxy with TIEs had the secondary effect of lots of surplus ships being made available to planetary militias and local defense forces. Consequently, thousands of citizens had the opportunity to become pilots, and many of them went to the Alliance.

TIE INTERCEPTOR ——————

The deadly blur of a "squint" was often the last thing that a Rebel pilot saw before his own ship became just another casualty in the ongoing Galactic Civil War. Sienar Flight System's TIE Interceptor was the Empire's response to the Rebellion's heavy reliance on a snubfighter campaign. With design elements incorporating the best aspects of Darth Vader's Advanced TIE prototype, the Interceptor could fly rings around its predecessor, the TIE/ln, and made short work of lumbering fighters like the Koensayr Y-wing. Even the venerable Incom X-wing suffered significant casualties against this new Imperial ship, and held its own only by way of stronger armor, shields, and talented pilots.

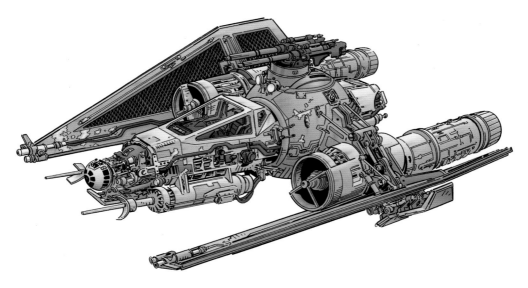

The hundreds of colloquial names for Uglies (Juicecans, Buzzzers, Z-wings) are a testament to the crafts' presence throughout the galaxy. Wherever scrapyards turn up the damaged or discarded modular components of the galaxy's various snubfighters and gunships, Ugly shops can be found churning out piecemeal fighter craft, most often for clients who prefer no questions asked.

Some of the most popular types of Uglies include Z-'ceptors, which utilize the main body of the Z-95 Headhunter and the bent solar arrays of the TIE Interceptors; and the TIE-wing, combining the pilot's pod of a TIE/ln with the nacelles of the Koensayr Y-wing. While dangerous to fly, some Ugly formats became so commonplace that, for all intents and purposes, they ceased to be mongrel ships and became their own craft.

Uglies could also be rapidly custom-built to mission specifications. Their modular design made it an easy matter of reformatting ships based on need. Nevertheless, there was never any denying that these were, in fact, second-hand vessels.

Kavil's Corsairs and other pirate groups under the Blazing Claw symbol used Uglies culled from the scrapyard moons of Axxila.

CARTARIUN

As a low-ranking Imperial technician at the Emperor's outpost on Malrev, he saw a chance to wield the limitless power of Sith magic, distilled from an ancient temple hidden deep within the planet's cloaking forests. After the death of Emperor Palpatine, the local Imperial garrison was decommissioned, but Cartariun stayed behind. Gaining a fundamental control over the magics of the temple, he set himself up as the overlord of the native Irrukiine. But the corrupting influence of Sith magic plunged him into insanity. By the time Rogue Squadron arrived in search of a lost Bothan passenger liner, Cartariun had plans of returning to the Empire and taking the throne for himself. Unfortunately, the Bothan agent Girov, able to temper the Sith magic via his skill in the Bothan martial art of Jeswandi, had also set his sights on the power of the temple, and Cartariun fell victim to the powers he once hoped to master.

PRINCE HARRAN

There were actually two Prince Harrans.

The first was the brother to Plourr Ilo, brainwashed by Darth Vader into assisting in the murder of his own family. Plourr was forced to kill him and escape their homeworld, Eiattu.

The second Prince Harran was an impostor—also brainwashed, but this time by Moff Leonia Tavira. When Plourr returned to Eiattu

to assume the throne, the impostor's hand was shot off during an altercation, and the brainwashing device was destroyed.

IRRUKIINE

The Irrukiine live in loose-knit aboriginal societies on their home planet of Malrev, an outpost world far off the galactic plane. The strange Sith temple hidden within Malrev's cloaking forests has influenced the Irrukiine dramatically for thousands of years, and the Irks will attack anything that comes near it. Only via manipulation of Sith magic can a being wield some degree of control over the species. Cartariun, a Devaronian Imperial technician, was able to telepathically control dozens of Irks in attacks against Rogue Squadron.

LON ISOTO

Admiral Lon Isoto, known in Alliance circles as "Isoto the Indecisive," managed to remain clear of the action between Imperial and Rebel forces until the Rebel Alliance noticed the

Admiral Lon Isoto, known in Alliance circles as "Isoto the Indecisive," managed to remain clear of the action between Imperial and Rebel forces until the Rebel Alliance noticed the Empire's plans to upgrade the defenses of Brentaal. The Empire used Isoto's incompetent reputation to lure the Rebels into a showdown,

KAVIL'S CORSAIRS

The chaos of the Galactic Civil War presented many opportunities for those individuals without scruples to make an easy living off of the vast, undefended spaceways. The pirates of the Blazing Claw were one such group. In the corridor of industrial worlds that contained Axxila, Vandyne, and Edusa, the Blazing Claw logo was seen more often than the Imperial crest or the Rebel banner.

Rogue Squadron flew against the Blazing Claw cadre known as Kavil's Corsairs during the undercover operation on Axxila. Kavil was another pawn of Leonia Tavira in her quest for power and wealth.

COUNT LAABANN

Representing everything that Plourr Ilo hated about the Eiattu aristocracy, Count Laabann fought to keep Eiattu's common people separate from the aristocracy that ruled them. Unfortunately for Count Laabann, and despite his efforts, the return of the Princess Isplourrdacartha would forever change Eiattu.

Later, Eiattu's induction into the New Republic was interrupted when Laabann helped Leonia Tavira kidnap the New Republic delegate. Laabann was captured and interrogated by Plourr, Han Solo, and Fel for the whereabouts of Princess Leia's stand-in, Winter, and Rogue pilot Tycho Celchu. The count only broke for Baron Fel, who compelled him to speak with an Imperial AT3 directive.

SATE PESTAGE

Sate Pestage had risen through the ranks of the Imperial elite not by ambition, but on the strength of his own quiet wisdom. Nevertheless, in the chaos following Palpatine's death, Pestage could do little but succumb to the machinations of those, like Ysanne Isard, who were ruled by ambition.

During the Battle for Brentaal, Pestage was able to finally understand the scale of Isard's scheming. Foreseeing his own administration's imminent demise, Pestage turned to the Alliance and offered them the keys to Coruscant, the world known as Imperial Center. The Rebels found themselves dealing with the man who had once orchestrated the massacres that had originally led to the formation of the Rebel Alliance.

ILIR POST

The wealthy, spoiled son of a Corellian agro-combine administrator, Ilir Post developed a hatred for Soontir Fel after the strapping young man rescued a friend from Post's unwanted advances. Through his father's management connections, Post was able to send Fel away from Corellia. Fel went on to become the Empire's greatest fighter ace. Post, meanwhile, continued to live the life of a wealthy dilettante, and became involved in many criminal ventures. But his hatred for Fel never diminished, and his schemes continued to trouble Fel even after he had defected to the Alliance.

 ## GADE YEDAN ───

The assistant to Gyr Keela of the Mrlsst Academy was also a staunch supporter of the Ante-Endor Association, which promoted the belief that the Emperor lived and that the destruction of Alderaan was caused by Rebel scientists testing their own superweapons. When Imperial Captain Loka Hask came to Mrlsst seeking new ship-cloaking technology, Gade Yedan became his primary agent. Yedan was shot by Loka Hask shortly before Dr. Falken's asteroid lab was consumed by a wormhole.

The enigmatic Rebel Special Forces operative and close friend to Princess Leia Organa
has crossed paths with Rogue Squadron
enough that she has formed a romantic relationship with Rogue pilot Tycho Celchu. But
one of the first things that the flyboy discovered about Winter was that when it was time
to work, she was all business and deserving of
her chilly name.

Winter's freighter—carefully disguised to
have the appearance of the sort of ship even the
most desperate thief would bypass—contains
an array of top-secret hardware, a bis.2 data-
storage module, and surveillance equipment
ranging from pin-sized transponders to specialized droids that can slice Imperial Holonet
transceiver satellites. Weaponry has mostly
been forsaken in favor of speed. The freighter's shields can be enormously powerful, and
the Corellian-built Aurum thrusters provide
dizzying speed. The vessel has undergone at
least as many name changes as the enigmatic
agent herself.

X-WING

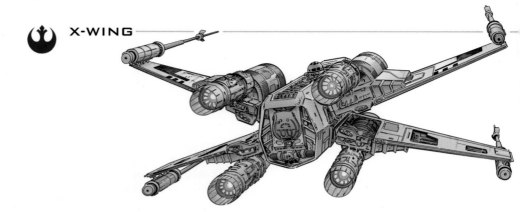

There are few superlatives left yet to describe the Incom T-65 X-wing. To many Rogue pilots, their personal X-wings are to them as a lightsaber is to a Jedi.

Following the destruction of the first Death Star, the Rebel Alliance rushed into the development of a formal navy. Admiral Ackbar was always a champion of snubfighting tactics, and many other Alliance strategists were hard-pressed to deny the facts: battles were often won by the fighter squadrons. Soon after, the A- and B-wings joined X-wings as some of the most visible of Alliance fighters. While the A-wing's blistering speed quickly became the standard tool on hit-and-fade missions, and the incredibly powerful B-wing could almost pull alongside a capital ship and take it on singlehandedly, the X-wing remained the soaring, knifing, cutting edge in fighter-to-fighter combat.

 ## RECONNAISSANCE X-WING

A complicated sensor packet and twin almond-shaped scanner pods mark the Recon T-65, also known as a "snoopscoot," as a surveillance and reconnaissance craft. Since the ship has neither room nor energy for weapons, Rebel engineers have boosted the power of the engines and incorporated prototype etheric-rudder technology, eliminating the need for attitude thrusters. The technology allows the ship to maneuver even more tightly than an X-wing, and it necessitates pilots of species that can withstand the increased stress.

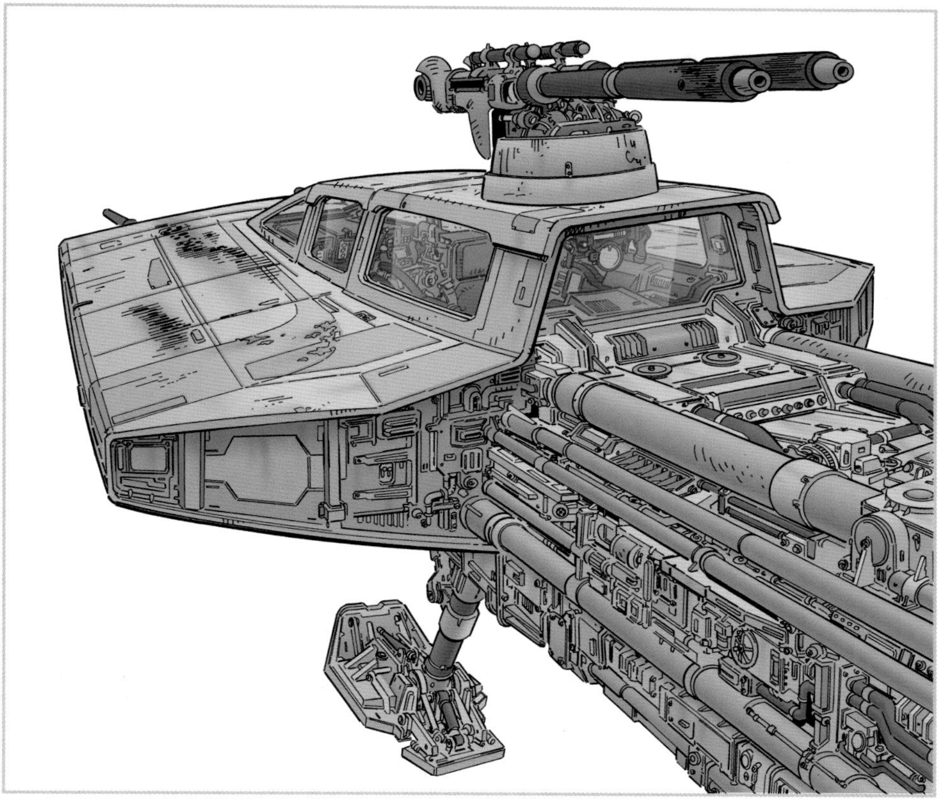

Built to take a beating, the Y-wing distinguished itself in early Rebel campaigns and became famous for its tenacity. Pilots of the unsightly craft would often leave carbon scoring and other cosmetic damage after action. The scars told tales of unrelenting battles and triumphant returns. It wasn't until the development of the Sienar TIE Interceptor that the Y-wing met its match. After the Battle for Brentaal, Y-wings were gradually relegated to missions where the chances of going up against the Interceptors were significantly reduced. Nevertheless, the Y-wing stays true to its tenacious nature and remains a frequently seen workhorse for the New Republic.

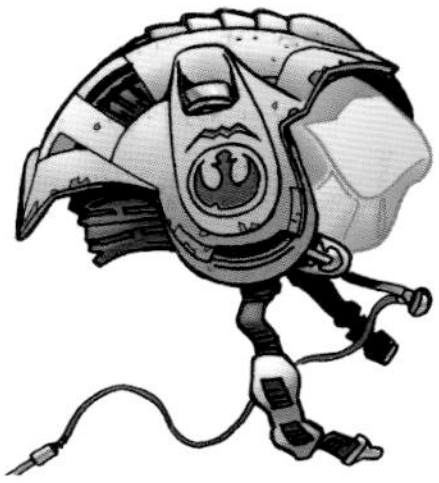

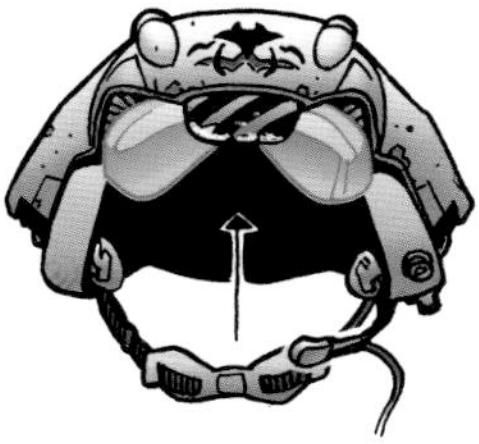

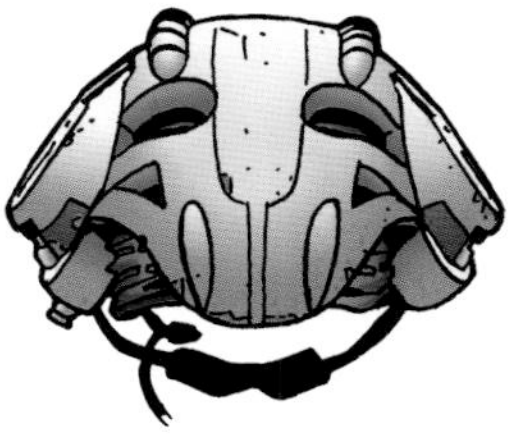

A Word About the Omnibus Collections

Dark Horse Comics' *Star Wars* Omnibus Collections were created as a way to showcase actual novel-length stories or series, and to provide homes for "orphaned" series, single-issue stories, and short stories which would otherwise never be collected, or which might fall out of print.